D0897872

# Ohio Guide to Genealogical Sources

# Guide • to
## Genealogical Sources

*Carol Willsey Bell, C.G.*

GENEALOGICAL PUBLISHING CO., INC.

# INTRODUCTION

This *Ohio Guide to Genealogical Sources* is an attempt to condense information about available records and sources. The guide makes no effort to instruct the reader in genealogical techniques, as there is a plethora of titles available on "how-to-do" genealogy. This writer has also compiled the *Ohio Genealogical Guide,* (4th edition, 1987) which treats subjects in more detail. New materials are being made available constantly, and it would be impossible to be aware of each new publication, although every effort has been made to include all current publications. The reader should be aware that there may be some duplication in entries, due to differences in cataloging methods used by various facilities. In many cases, incomplete information is given regarding a printed source since each item could not be personally examined. An effort has been made to include the abbreviation for at least one library which holds a particular source.

No attempt has been made to list each record group available in each courthouse. The listings include only those court records available on microfilm from the Ohio Historical Society and the Branch Libraries of the Family History Library of the Church of Jesus Christ of Latter-day Saints in Salt Lake City. The reader needs to be aware that additional records are available in the courthouses to include records up to the present (since microfilming dates), and that many record groups have never been microfilmed. Additionally, many records are also available in the Ohio Network of American History Research Centers indicated here as the Archival Districts. Many of these centers have published their own guides to their collections listing specific holdings.

There are also public libraries, historical societies, and genealogical societies in nearly every county in Ohio, all of which hold many special collections for their areas. Their current addresses have been included so that the researcher may contact them about their own collections.

Given these limitations, researchers should be able to expand their own particular needs in each Ohio county with the wealth of available materials and with those yet-to-be-discovered collections in each locality.


Carol Willsey Bell, C.G.

# ABBREVIATIONS:

LDS - Church of Jesus Christ of Latter-day Saints, Salt Lake City Utah, and branch libraries nationwide. The name of the library was changed in late 1987 to the Family History Library, and the genealogical department is known as the Family History Department.

LC - LIBRARY OF CONGRESS, Washington DC

OGS - OHIO GENEALOGICAL SOCIETY, Mansfield Ohio

OHS - OHIO HISTORICAL SOCIETY, Columbus Ohio

RPI - Research Publications Inc., 12 Lunar Dr., Drawer AB, Woodbridge CT 06525. Publishers of microfilm edition titled "COUNTY HISTORIES OF THE OLD NORTHWEST-OHIO." The initials RPI following an entry indicates the title is included in this microfilm collection.

SLO - STATE LIBRARY OF OHIO, Columbus Ohio

WRHS - WESTERN RESERVE HISTORICAL SOCIETY, Cleveland Ohio

Yo.Pub.Lib. - YOUNGSTOWN OHIO, PUBLIC LIBRARY

# EXPLANATION OF ENTRIES

**DATE CREATED:** The dates listed are those provided in the legislation creating each new county. In some cases, a county may have actually been *organized* at a somewhat later date, and records may not begin until the county was established for business purposes. The parent counties are listed with the creation date, and records prior to that date usually exist within the bounds of the parent counties.

**COUNTY SEAT:** Each county seat is listed with its zip code.

**COURT HOUSE:** The street address is given for most court houses. The hours vary from county to county, and a more extensive list of information may be found in the *Ohio County Courthouse Guide* by Thomas Stephen Neel, available from the Ashland County Chapter OGS, PO Box 681, Ashland OH 44805.

**LIBRARY:** In most cases, the library listed is the public library in the county seat, and other libraries with strong genealogical collections have also been given.

**HISTORICAL SOCIETIES:** The societies listed are taken from the most current *Directory of Historical Societies in Ohio* (1985/86). In most cases, the society is located in the county seat, and there are other societies listed for individual towns or townships. Some societies have a headquarters and a library, while others may not have genealogical collections.

**GENEALOGICAL SOCIETIES:** Nearly every county in Ohio has at least one genealogical society, most of them affiliated as Chapters of the Ohio Genealogical Society, with a few independent societies. The addresses listed are taken from the *Chapter Directory, Ohio Genealogical Society, May 1986* with corrections provided by OGS in February 1988. The majority of the societies have a permanent post office box address, while a few change addresses each time new officers are elected. It is advised that current addresses be checked with the Ohio Genealogical Society, PO Box 2625, Mansfield OH 44906.

**ARCHIVAL DISTRICTS:** There are currently seven archival districts in Ohio under the supervision of the Ohio Historical Society's Ohio Network of American History Research Centers. The network was established in 1970 "to provide cooperative statewide collecting, cataloging, and reference services for Ohio's historical source materials, with primary emphasis on local government records, manuscripts, newspapers, and audiovisual materials." Due to space limitations in many court houses, some records have been transferred to the network centers, and may no longer be available at the court houses. Each center maintains a current inventory of holdings, and some have published guides to their collections.

**HEALTH DEPARTMENTS:** The Ohio Department of Health, Division of Vital Statistics, 65 South Front St., Columbus OH 43266-0333 maintains records of birth and death for the state from 1908/09 to the present. The current price for certified copies is $7.00 each, although *uncertified* copies may be obtained from Columbus for $1.10 each. Each locality in Ohio also has LOCAL health departments which maintain records for their areas. The addresses included are taken from the *Roster of Registrars of Vital Statistics: Local, Deputy & Sub-registrars* dated October 1987. Each local health department is a separate entity which sets its own rules and prices for copies. The researcher may need to contact local health departments, although it is often more beneficial to contact the STATE office where uncertified copies can be obtained at a cheaper rate. The state office will also conduct a 10-year search of records for a fee.

**LAND SURVEYS:** Ohio had many different land surveys resulting in different types of records. It is important to know the type of survey in each county before attempting to do extensive land and deed research. An excellent publication, *Ohio Lands - A Short History*, by Thomas A. Burke, (1987) is available free of charge from the office of the Auditor of State, State Land Office, 88 East Broad St., Columbus OH 43266-0040. This work contains an extensive description of the laws passed for each land survey, as well as maps showing the area covered.

**BOUNDED BY:** Information has been included to show the counties which surround each Ohio county. It is frequently important to extend research into a neighboring county where additional records may be available.

**TOWNSHIPS:** The names of *current* townships have been included for each county since many records exist on the township level with Ohio's system of State, County, and Township government. Each township elects three Trustees and a township clerk, which are under the supervision of the County Commissioners. If it becomes necessary to contact the township officials, the name and address of the current clerk may be obtained from the Commissioners Office in each county court house. The researcher needs to be aware that some townships may have previously existed in a county, and were jurisdictionally moved when a new county was formed.

**SPECIAL NOTES:** Notes are included to inform the researcher about fires or floods which caused destruction of records. In most cases, not all records were destroyed, but some may be missing for this reason. "All the early records were burned" may not be a truthful statement, but rather, may be an excuse for lack of knowledge about record availability. Ohio has an open records law (Ohio Revised Code 149.43) which allows access to public records, with the exception of adoptions, mental cases, medical records, probation and parole proceedings. A separate law (Ohio Revised Code 3705.18, passed 3/19/1985) concerning adoptions prior to January 1, 1964 may be read in the OGS *Report* Volume 26 (1986) No.2 page 80.

**COURT RECORDS:** In this section, records are listed first by originating office, and then by record group and inclusive dates *only* for those records available on microfilm from the Ohio Historical Society and/or the Family History Library of the Church of Jesus Christ of Latter-day Saints and its branch libraries. Other records are available in the court house offices. A brief synopsis of record groups which may be of genealogical value is taken from the *Ohio County Records Manual, Revised Edition,* published by the Ohio Historical Society (1983).

> **AUDITOR:** Abstracts of tax, abstracts of delinquent tax, appraisals for inheritance tax, assessment lists, assessor's returns, relief records, Civil War bounties, commutation records, enumerations of deaf, dumb, blind, idiotic and insane, feebleminded, cripples, epileptics, enumerations of school aged youth, enumerations of soldiers and sailors, exemptions from military service, indigent soldier burials, justice of the peace reports, mothers' pension records, militia rolls, quadrennial enumerations, records of inmates in state benevolent institutions, road tax records, school land records, tax lists.

> **CLERK OF COURTS:** Records from Court of Common Pleas including probate records prior to 1851 when Probate Court was organized, Circuit Court, District Court, Superior Court, Supreme

Court and Justices of the Peace. Record groups include divorces, case files, criminal and civil records, appearance dockets, journals, record books, order books, trial dockets, witness records, complete records, execution dockets, chancery cases, jury records.

**COURT OF COMMON PLEAS:** Appearance dockets, appointments, case files, chancery records, complete records, insolvency, naturalizations, jury records, judgments, manumissions, partition records, poll books and tally sheets, quadrennial enumerations, records of justices and con stables, witness records, criminal arrest records, coroners inquests, grand jury reports, domestic relations records, divorces, juvenile court records (restricted), probation records (restricted).

**CHILDREN'S HOMES:** Law authorizing children's homes was passed in 1866, although many were not created that early. Previous to 1866, children were housed in county homes, infirmaries and poor houses with adults. Children's Home records, adoptions (restricted), case files, retarded children's files.

**CORONER:** Case files, death reports, inquests.

**COUNTY HOME:** (under supervision of County Commissioners), also known as poor house, county infirmary, and county home. Birth, death, burial, admission records, county home registers, indenture records, minutes, visitors' registers.

**COUNTY COMMISSIONERS:** Journals, county home records, road records, building plans, zoning records.

**PROBATE COURT:** Under the authority of Court of Common Pleas until 1851. Administration records, adoptions (restricted), birth & death records (1867-1908), boys and girls' industrial home records, case files, epilepsy records, feeble minded persons' records, guardianships, marriage records, journals, judgments, mentally ill persons' records, changes of name, nurses' certificates, record of ministers licensed, will records.

**RECORDER:** Land records, deeds, mortgages, cemetery deeds, corporation records, land entries, plat books, leases, military discharges, powers of attorney, soldiers' discharge records, soldiers' burials, and tract indexes.

**SHERIFF:** Complaints, criminal history files, jail registers and reports, probation records (restricted), sheriff's partition records.

**SOLDIERS' RELIEF COMMISSION:** Applications for headstones, burial applications, grave marker records, soldiers' relief records, service cards.

**TREASURER:** Estate tax records, forfeitures, sales tax records, tax duplicates, school land records, tax receipts.

**OHIO GENEALOGICAL SOCIETY:** PO Box 2625, Mansfield OH 44906. Phone: (419) 522-9077. The Society's new library building is located at 34 Sturges Ave., Mansfield. Hours are 9-5, Tuesday through Saturday. Membership dues are currently $19 single and $25 joint membership. Each member receives the monthly *Newsletter* and quarterly *The Report*. The Society is the "umbrella" organization for county chapters. There are currently 89 chapters, each of which is also a separate organization with separate membership fees. Many of the chapters are actively publishing records from their own counties, and some maintain their own research libraries with special collections. The state Society holds an annual convention, usually in April or May. The Society also sponsors First Families of Ohio, to honor pioneers who lived in Ohio prior to 1820. The application papers for FFO are maintained by the Society and provide a unique research tool. In addition, the library maintains an ancestor card file for members as well as published sources and microfilm.

**OHIO HISTORICAL SOCIETY:** 1982 Velma Avenue, Columbus OH 43211. Phone: (614) 297-2300. The building is located off Interstate 71 at 17th Avenue. Hours: 9-5, Tuesday through Saturday. Parking fee for non-members. Users must register and receive a researcher's pass. Security requires that purses, briefcases and bags be stored in provided lockers. The building houses the State Archives of Ohio, serves as the Network Center for central Ohio counties, as well as providing a genealogical and historical research library. Many special collections will be found, including the largest collection of Ohio newspapers (microfilm will be interlibrary loaned), original records from various state agencies and central Ohio counties. The library reading room contains many Ohio county publications on open shelves, but the majority of material is in closed stacks, requiring access by use of the card catalogs. Major collections include Ohio census microfilm and indices, an extensive name index to county histories, tax records to 1838 for most counties, some county records on microfilm, and manuscript collections of unique sources. The Society has published guides to newspapers and manuscript collections. A current policy limits written inquiries to Ohio residents only, and research will not be conducted by the staff.

**STATE LIBRARY OF OHIO:** 65 South Front St., Columbus OH 43266-0333. Phone: (614) 644-6966. Hours: 8-5, Monday through Thursday, 9-5, Friday. The Library is located on the 11th floor, and no fees are charged for its use. The genealogical section of the Library is strong in Ohio county and statewide publications, and Ohio censuses on microfilm. The Library serves as the depository library for copies of Daughters of the American Revolution compilations of Ohio county records, which were totally inventoried in *Master Index Ohio Society Daughters of the American Revolution Genealogical and Historical Records, Volume 1*, edited by Carol Willsey Bell, C.G. (1985), copies of which may be obtained from Mrs. Thomas B. Clark, Chairman, 24588 Framingham Drive, Westlake OH 44145. In addition, the Library has published *County by County in Ohio Genealogy* which lists the holdings of the Library. A brand new edition of this work is expected to be available by late 1988, and may be purchased from the Library. The Library also serves as the depository library for Ohio State Government documents which may also be useful in genealogical research. The Library staff will answer mail inquiries and will provide photocopies of specific sources after prepayment of the copying fee. The compiler acknowledges with gratitude the cooperation of the Library staff in providing material for this work.

**WESTERN RESERVE HISTORICAL SOCIETY:** 10825 East Blvd., Cleveland OH 44106. Phone: (216) 721-5722. Hours: 9-5, Tuesday through Saturday. Research fee charged on a per-day basis to non-members. Patrons are required to register with two pieces of identification, and to use lockers for purses, brief cases and coats. The Society's library focuses primarily upon Ohio, the Western Reserve, and the colonial states. There is an extensive collection of microfilm of federal censuses for Ohio and most states, through 1910, and the National Archives microfilm of Revolutionary War pension papers, as well as other record groups. Printed sources are available in open stacks. Extensive manuscript collections are available which have been outlined in two published guides, available from the Society. The library also serves as the Network Center for counties in northeastern Ohio, and many original court records are available.

**FAMILY HISTORY LIBRARY:** Church of Jesus Christ of Latter-day Saints, 35 North West Temple Street, Salt Lake City UT 84150. The Library is widely known for its extensive collections of worldwide records for genealogical research, with those on microfilm being available through the Branch Libraries located throughout the country. For purposes of this compilation, the microfiche of the Library's Locality Catalog, dated August 1987, has been used to list the Library's holdings for Ohio up to that date. The collections are constantly being expanded, and the Locality Catalog is updated periodically to include new accessions. The compiler acknowledges the Library's wonderful cooperation in providing data for this work.

**LIBRARY OF CONGRESS:** Washington DC. The extensive collections available at the Library of Congress have been culled from the LCCC and PREM data bases in the library, looking primarily for county and city histories and atlases without attempting to locate other types of genealogical data. The writer acknowledges with grateful appreciation all of the help provided by George W. Archer of McLean VA, in providing these entries due to his special interest in Ohio research.

**DAUGHTERS OF THE AMERICAN REVOLUTION LIBRARY:** 1776 D St.,NW, Washington DC 20006-5392. The Library of the National Society, DAR, contains many titles for Ohio, as well as the compilations created by DAR chapters throughout the country. These titles have been taken from the

Society's publication, *DAR LIBRARY CATALOG, VOLUME TWO, STATE AND LOCAL HISTORIES AND RECORDS* (1986).

**CENSUS RECORDS:** Microfilm of the federal census from the National Archives is available in many libraries across the United States, and may also be purchased from the National Archives or borrowed on inter-library loan. Census records listed here refer ONLY to federal census records, as state censuses were not taken in Ohio, with a few exceptions for some very early years. Additionally, the researcher needs to be aware that although the federal census was taken in 1810 in Ohio, having attained statehood in 1803, these 1810 schedules no longer exist. From 1820 through 1910, schedules exist for most counties in Ohio, one notable exception being the 1820 census of Franklin County, which is missing. The 1890 census was almost entirely destroyed by fire in 1921, with only a small portion of Hamilton County (Cincinnati) and Clinton County (Wayne Township) having survived. Instead, the special schedules enumerating Union Veterans and Widows of Union Veterans of the Civil War for 1890 are available for all counties on 16 rolls of microfilm. Soundex indices for 1880 and 1900 are available, as well as the Miracode index for the 1910 census of Ohio.

**TAX RECORDS:** Duplicates of the tax records for property owners were sent to the Auditor of State in Columbus, and a nearly complete collection exists for most counties through the year 1838. The originals are housed at the State Archives, Ohio Historical Society. They were microfilmed by the LDS Church, and the film is available at both OHS and the LDS Branch Libraries. It should be noted that most of the tax duplicates are for land owners *only*, and that schedules of personal property tax (horses, cattle and bank stock) exist in this collection for the years 1826 through 1834 *only*. In many cases, the original tax records are still available in each county, usually in the Auditor's or Treasurer's office, and many have collections going far beyond the 1838 date of the State Auditor's collection. Published indexes exist for 1800-1810 and 1825, with some compilations for various years for different counties.

**AGRICULTURAL CENSUS SCHEDULES:** These special schedules were taken in conjunction with the federal census, listing every farm with an annual produce worth $100 ($500 in 1880) or more, giving the name of the owner, agent or tenant, and the kind and value of acreage, machinery, livestock andproduce. The lists do not exist for each county for each year. The originals were transferred to the Ohio Historical Society, Columbus, and are also available on microfilm at the State Library of Ohio.

**PRODUCTS OF INDUSTRY SCHEDULES:** These special schedules were taken in conjunction with the federal census, listing information about manufacturing, mining, fisheries, and every mercantile, commercial and trading business with an annual gross product of $500 or more. The schedules show the name of the company or owner, kind of business, amount of capital invested, and quantity and value of materials, labor, machinery, and products. The lists do not exist for each county for each year. The originals were transferred to the Ohio Historical Society, Columbus, and are also available on microfilm at the State Library of Ohio. In addition, a special census of Manufactures was taken in 1820, listing information about the articles manufactured, market value, kind, quantity and costs, the number of persons employed, the kind of machinery, and the amount paid in wages, plus expenses and observations.

**MORTALITY SCHEDULES:** These special schedules were taken in conjunction with the federal census, recording information about people who died during the year preceding the census, ending on June 1st of each year. The information varies slightly from year to year. Lists exist for 1850: (Adams to Guernsey Co. only); 1860 (complete); 1870 (only for Seneca Co); and 1880: (Greene to Wyandot Co). Many of the lists have been published in periodicals, and can be located by checking *Ohio Genealogical Periodical Index: A County Guide,* by Carol Willsey Bell, C.G.

**DEFECTIVE, DEPENDENT AND DELINQUENT CLASSES SCHEDULES:** Special listings taken only in 1880 contain lists for idiots, insane, deaf-mutes, blind, homeless children, inhabitants in prison, and paupers. Lists exist only for Adams to Franklin Co., and Meigs to Wyandot Co., and are available on microfilm at the State Library of Ohio.

**GENEALOGICAL PERIODICALS:** There are well over 100 periodicals currently being published in Ohio by various genealogical and historical societies. The researcher is referred to *Ohio Genealogical*

*Periodical Index: A County Guide* (6th edition, 1987), by Carol Willsey Bell, C.G., 4649 Yarmouth Lane, Youngstown OH 44512, for a county-by-county listing of subject headings and exact citations to sources.

**NEWSPAPERS:** Newspaper collections were inventoried in *Guide to Ohio Newspapers, 1793-1973* (Columbus: Ohio Historical Society, 1975). The *Guide* is arranged by TOWN of publication, then by newspaper title, and lists comprehensive dates of extant papers. Included are the names of repositories holding the papers, and if available on microfilm. By far the largest collection of Ohio newspapers is found at the Ohio Historical Society, in both original paper and microfilm form. Those which have been microfilmed may be borrowed on inter-library loan. Many additional newspapers have been microfilmed since the *Guide* was published. Current prices and policies must be obtained from OHS. For purposes of this work, only the town of publication is given, and the reader is referred to the *Guide* for more complete information.

**PUBLISHED SOURCES:** Arranged by author, or title, if the author is unknown, complete bibliographical citations are included if available, and the abbreviation of at least one library which holds the publication, if known. In some cases, references are taken from lists of society publications, and a library location is not known. In other cases, titles have been included from sources created by various libraries, and may be more or less complete. If a work has been reprinted, both the original publisher and the reprint publisher are given, if known. In most cases, the reprinted work usually contains a newly created index not available in the original edition. The abbreviations "np" (for no place listed) and "nd" (for no date given) have been used when information is unavailable. This section sometimes includes unpublished items such as scrapbook collections or manuscript compilations which are available only as a typed manuscript.

# ACKNOWLEDGMENTS

The compiler wishes to thank the following persons for their assistance in obtaining material for this work:

George W. Archer, McLean VA.
Thomas A. Burke, State Land Office, Columbus OH.
Petta Khouw, and the Staff of the State Library of Ohio, Columbus OH.
David M. Mayfield, Director, Family History Library, Salt Lake City UT.
Carole C. Paprocki, Columbus OH.
Kip Sperry, C.G., Salt Lake City UT.

MAJOR LAND SURVEYS IN OHIO. SHOWING THE OLD DESIGNATIONS
(TOP) AND THE NEW NOMENCLATURE (BOTTOM).

(From *Ohio Lands: A Short History*, by Thomas A. Burke. Used with permission.)

OHIO SHOWING THE YEAR THE COUNTY WAS ESTABLISHED

(From *Ohio Lands: A Short History*, by Thomas A. Burke. Used with permission.)

# OHIO

## STATE AGENCIES:

**OHIO HISTORICAL SOCIETY: (MICROFILM)**
Adjutant General:
  Annual reports, 1896-1899.
  Civil War muster rolls, by regiment.
  Burials & Civil War prisoners records, 1861-1896. (OHS,LDS)
Auditor of State:
  1812 tax duplicate & name index.
  Tax duplicates of counties, to 1838. (see each county)
  Record of county claims of benevolent & educational institutions, 1917-1935.
  Chillicothe land office, 1801-1811.
  Cincinnati land office, 1801-1806.
  Marietta land office, 1800-1829.
  Steubenville land office, 1788-1812.
  Zanesville land office, 1800-1829.
  U.S.Surveys, field notes of reserves.
Bureau of Vital Statistics:
  Index of all births occurring in Ohio, 1908-1911. (OHS,LDS)
  Index of all deaths occurring in Ohio, 1908-1911. (OHS,LDS)
Board of Canal Commissioners:
  Correspondence, 1820-1842.
Canal Fund Commission:
  Letterbooks, 1825-1845.
County Histories:
  Name index to collected county histories. (card file at OHS)
County Records Inventory:
  County records inventory abstract, Ohio, 1803-1977.
General Assembly:
  Constitutions of the State of Ohio, 1802-1851 & 1874.
Legislative Reference Bureau:
  Ohio General Assembly, House & Senate bills, 1888-1942.
Mental Health & Retardation:
  Columbus Hospital for the Insane, admissions, 1838-1903.
  Columbus State Institute, admissions, 1881-1905,1912-1923.
Ohio Canals:
  Registration of boats on the canals, 1839-1857.
Public Works:
  Canal reservoir lands.
Rehabilitation and Correction:
  Pardon & parole commission minutes:
  Women's Reformatory, Mansfield, 1923-1950.
  Ohio State Reformatory, 1923-1955.
  London Prison Farm, 1925-1955.
  Ohio Penitentiary, register of prisoners (c1829-1919) (OHS,LDS)
  Fire in the Ohio Penitentiary, 1930.
  Girls Industrial School, Inmate case record, 1869-1911.
  Boys Industrial School, Inmate case record, 1858-1918.
Sinking Fund Commission:
  World War I bonus claims, disapproved, c1922-1923.
Soldiers' and Sailors' Home, Sandusky:
  Index to general records, 1888-1936.
  Death books, 1888-1963.
State Board of Pharmacy:
  Register of applicants for exam, 1914-1961.

Registered pharmacists index, A-Z.
Apprentice registration, 1915-1954.
Apprentice registrations index #2.
Pharmacists & asst. pharmacists, 1894-1913.
Works Progress Administration:
Slave narratives, 1937 interviews.
Miscellaneous:
Ohio institution for the deaf, register of pupils, 1829-1929. (OHS,LDS)
Miscellaneous Ohio bible records, by DAR.
Family & bible records of Ohio, by DAR.
Wills, bible & family records, by DAR.
Family records from 48 bibles, by DAR.
Miscellaneous Ohio cemeteries, by DAR.
Miscellaneous cemetery records, by DAR.

**United States records relating to Ohio:**
Adjutant General of U.S.:
Pay abstracts of 1st US Regt. & records, 1787-1801. (Mss.Div.)
Bureau of Indian Affairs:
Ratified treaties with Ohio indians, 1803-1854.
Indian trade, Fort Wayne Factory & indian agency, c1804-1818. (Mss.Div.)
Cemetery Relocation:
Relocations, 1973. Ohio River basin, Alum Creek Lake, burials, 1750's-1970's.
Centennial Homesteads Program:
Applications, 1977, for land held 100 years or more. (Mss.Div.)
Connecticut Land Company:
Western Reserve land draft, 1795-1809.
Draper Collection:
Lyman Draper papers relating to Ohio. (Mss.Div.)
General Land Office:
Letters, Registers of land offices, Marietta 1814-1829 & Bucyrus, 1838-1842; Lima, 1835-1843; Upper
Sandusky 1843-1848; & Defiance, 1848. (Mss.Div.)
Correspondence, Miami Canal Lands, 1828-1841 & Wabash & Erie Canal
Grant, 1829-1889. (Mss.Div.)
Land records:
Western Reserve & Connecticut Land Company papers. (Mss.Div.)
National Archives:
1900 census enumeration districts, Ohio.
Northwest Territory:
Transcript of executive journal of NWT govt. proceedings, 1789-1795. (Mss)
Postal Department, U.S.:
Appointments of Ohio postmasters, 1832-1930.
Welsh Settlements in Ohio:
Original papers in the National Library of Wales, 1847-1883. (Mss.Div.)

# PUBLISHED SOURCES:

**ATLASES & MAPS:**
Kilbourne, John. THE OHIO GAZETTEER, OR TOPOGRAPHICAL DICTIONARY. Columbus. 1833.
(Knightstown IN: Bookmark, 1978) 512p (OGS,LDS,OHS)
OHIO COUNTY MAPS & RECREATIONAL GUIDE (Thomas Publications, 1982) 136p
Walling, H.F. ATLAS OF THE STATE OF OHIO. 1868. (Reprint, Knightstown IN: Bookmark, 1976)
(OGS)

## BIOGRAPHY:

BIOGRAPHICAL ANNALS OF OHIO. 1905. 3v. (RPI)

BIOGRAPHICAL CYCLOPEDIA OF OHIO. 1883. 6v. (RPI)

Brennan, Fletcher. BIOGRAPHICAL CYCLOPEDIA & PORTRAIT GALLERY OF DISTINGUISHED MEN OF OHIO. 1876. (LDS) (RPI)

Coyle, William, ed. OHIO AUTHORS AND THEIR BOOKS...1796-1950. (Cleveland: World Pub.Co., 1962) 741p

Hissong, Clyde. OHIO LINES, THE BUCKEYE STATE BIOGRAPHICAL RECORD. (Hopkinsville KY: Histl Record Assn, 1968) 589p (OGS)

Mercer, James K. REPRESENTATIVE MEN OF OHIO. 1896. (LDS) (RPI) Ohio Newspaper Women's Association. WOMEN OF OHIO. (Chicago?: S.J. Clarke Pub.Co., nd) 4v

Taylor, William A. OHIO IN [U.S.] CONGRESS FROM 1803 TO 1901 WITH NOTES AND SKETCHES OF SENATORS AND REPRESENTATIVES. (Columbus: The XX Century Pub.Co., 1900) 318p

Van Tassel, Charles. FAMILIAR FACES OF OHIO. 1896. (RPI)

## BLACKS:

Fuller, Sara, ed. THE OHIO BLACK HISTORY GUIDE. (Columbus: Ohio Hist Soc., 1975) 221p. (OHS)

Nitchman, Paul E. BLACKS IN OHIO, 1880, IN THE COUNTIES OF ADAMS TO CARROLL, VOLUME 1. (Ft.Meade MD: author, 1986?) 178p

Nitchman, Paul E. BLACKS IN OHIO, 1880, IN THE COUNTIES OF CHAMPAIGN TO CLINTON, VOLUME 2 (Ft.Meade MD: author, 1986?) 193p

Nitchman, Paul E. BLACKS IN OHIO, 1880, IN THE COUNTIES OF COLUMBIANA TO FAYETTE, VOLUME 3 (Ft.Meade MD: author, 1986?) 168p

Nitchman, Paul E. BLACKS IN OHIO, 1880, IN THE COUNTIES OF FRANKLIN, FULTON, GALLIA & GEAUGA, VOLUME 4. (Ft.Meade MD: author, 1986) 163p

## CANALS:

Gieck, Jack. A PHOTO ALBUM OF OHIO'S CANAL ERA, 1825-1913. (Kent OH: Kent State University Press, 1988) c320p

## CEMETERIES:

Ohio Genealogical Society, State Cemetery Committee. GUIDE TO CEMETERY PRESERVATION. (Mansfield OH: author, 1987) 18p

Ohio Genealogical Society. OHIO CEMETERIES. (Mansfield OH: the society, 1978) 414p (OGS)

OHIO CEMETERY RECORDS EXTRACTED FROM OLD NORTHWEST GENEALOGICAL QUARTERLY. (Baltimore MD: Genealogical Pub.Co., 1984) 495p (OGS)

## CENSUS:

Harshman, Lida Flint. INDEX TO THE 1860 FEDERAL POPULATION CENSUS OF OHIO. (Ann Arbor MI: Edwards Bros., 1979) 2v, 1353p (OGS)

Ohio Family Historians. 1830 FEDERAL POPULATION CENSUS, OHIO, INDEX. (Columbus OH: Ohio Library Foundations, 1964) 2v, 1389p (OGS)

Ohio Family Historians. INDEX TO THE 1850 FEDERAL POPULATION CENSUS OF OHIO. (Ann Arbor MI: Edwards Bros.,1972) 1098p (OGS)

Ohio Library Foundation. 1820 FEDERAL POPULATION CENSUS OHIO. (Columbus OH: author, 1964) 831p (OGS)

Wilhelm, Hubert G.H. THE ORIGIN AND DISTRIBUTION OF SETTLEMENT GROUPS: OHIO 1850. (Athens OH: Ohio University, 1982)

Wilkins, Cleo G. INDEX TO 1840 FEDERAL POPULATION CENSUS OF OHIO. 1969, no pub, 4v (OGS)

## COURTHOUSES:

Neel, Thomas S. OHIO COUNTY COURTHOUSE GUIDE. (Ashland OH: Ashland Co Chapter OGS, 1985) 16p (OGS)

## EMIGRATION:

Kinton, Maxine. SOME OHIOANS TO LABETTE COUNTY KANSAS. (Mansfield OH: author, 1982) 44p. (OGS)

Sprague, Stuart S. KENTUCKIANS IN OHIO AND INDIANA. (Baltimore MD: Genealogical Pub.Co., 1986) 302p (OGS)

Wilhelm, Hubert G.H. THE ORIGIN AND DISTRIBUTION OF SETTLEMENT GROUPS: OHIO 1850. (Athens OH: Ohio University, 1982)

## FIRST FAMILIES OF OHIO:

Bell, Carol W., ed. FIRST FAMILIES OF OHIO, OFFICIAL ROSTER VOL.1. (Mansfield OH: Ohio Gen Soc., 1981) (OGS)

## GOVERNORS:

Hood, Marilyn G., ed. THE FIRST LADIES OF OHIO AND THE EXECUTIVE MANSIONS. (Columbus: Ohio Hist Soc., 1970) 32p (OHS)

THE GOVERNORS OF OHIO. (Columbus: Ohio Hist Soc., 1954,1969) 211p (OHS)

## HISTORY:

Curtis, J.R. THE GREAT STATE OHIO. (Greenville? OH: author, 1951) 28p (LC)

Ellis, William. THE ORDINANCE OF 1787: THE NATION BEGINS. (New York: Landfall Press, 1987)

Federal Writer's Project (WPA). OHIO IN THE NORTHWEST TERRITORY SESQUICENTENNIAL 1787-1788 (WPA, 1937-38)

Galbreath, Charles B. HISTORY OF OHIO. (Chicago, 1925) 5v

Hildreth, Samuel P. BIOGRAPHICAL & HISTORICAL MEMOIRS OF THE EARLY PIONEER SETTLERS OF OHIO. (Cincinnati: H.W.Derby & Co.,1852) 539p (LC)

Hochstetter, Nancy, ed. TRAVEL HISTORIC A GUIDE TO HISTORIC SITES & MARKERS. (Madison WI: Guide Press Co., 1986) 168p.

Howe, Henry. HISTORICAL COLLECTIONS OF OHIO (Cincinnati, 1907) 2v 992, 911pp

Howe, Henry. HOWE'S HISTORICAL COLLECTIONS OF OHIO. (Cincinnati: C.J. Krehbiel & Co., 1902) 2v, 992p, 2911p

Izant, Grace G. THIS IS OHIO: 88 COUNTIES IN WORDS AND PICTURES. 1953. 264p

Jordan, Philip. THE NATIONAL ROAD (U.S.40) (NY: Bobbs, 1948) 442p

Knepper, George. AN OHIO PORTRAIT. (Columbus: Ohio Hist Soc, 1976) 282p (OHS,OGS)

Knittle, Rhea. EARLY OHIO TAVERNS [OHIO FRONTIER SERIES 1767-1847] (Ashland OH, 1937) 46p

Morrison, Olin D. OHIO: THE GATEWAY STATE. (Athens OH: E.M.Morrison, 1960-62) 4v

OHIO, SPECIAL LIMITED SUPPLEMENT (New York: American Historical Society, 1925) 288p

Randall, Emilius O. & D.J.Ryan. HISTORY OF OHIO. (New York: Century History Co., 1912-1915) 6v.

Randall, Emilius O., ed. OHIO CENTENNIAL ANNIVERSARY CELEBRATION AT CHILLICOTHE 1903 (Columbus: Press of Fred Heer, 1903) 730p

Smith, Thomas H. AN OHIO READER, 1750 TO THE CIVIL WAR. (Grand Rapids MI: W.B.Eerdmans, 1975) 324p. (OHS)

Venable, W.H. FOOTPRINTS OF THE PIONEERS IN THE OHIO VALLEY. 1888. (Reprint, Bowie MD: Heritage Books,1987) 133p

## INDIANS:

Moorehead, Warren. THE INDIAN TRIBES OF OHIO. (Columbus: Ohio Arch & Hist Soc v7, 1899) 366p

## LAND:

Bell, Carol W. OHIO LANDS: STEUBENVILLE LAND OFFICE RECORDS, 1800-1820. (Youngstown OH: author, 1983) 181p (OGS)

Berry, Ellen & David. EARLY OHIO SETTLERS, PURCHASERS OF LAND IN SOUTH EASTERN OHIO 1800-1840. (Baltimore MD: Genealogical Pub.Co., 1985) 144p (OGS)

Berry, Ellen & David. EARLY OHIO SETTLERS, PURCHASERS OF LAND IN SOUTH WESTERN OHIO 1800-1840. (Baltimore MD: Genealogical Pub.Co., 1986) 372p (OGS)

Brumbaugh, Gaius M. REVOLUTIONARY WAR RECORDS, VOLUME 1, VIRGINIA. (Washington DC: author, 1936) (OHS,SLO)

Burke, Thomas A. OHIO LANDS - A SHORT HISTORY. (Columbus: Ohio Auditor of State, 1987) 54p

Clark, Marie T. OHIO LANDS: CHILLICOTHE LAND OFFICE, 1800-1829. (Chillicothe: author, 1984) 144p (OGS,SLO,OHS)

Clark, Marie T. OHIO LANDS: SOUTH OF THE INDIAN BOUNDARY LINE. (Chillicothe: author, 1984) (OGS)

Downs, Randolph C. EVOLUTION OF OHIO COUNTY BOUNDARIES. 1927. (Reprint, Columbus: Ohio Hist Soc., 1970) (OHS,OGS)

Dyer, Albion M. FIRST OWNERSHIP OF OHIO LANDS. 1911. 85p. (OGS,OHS,SLO)

McHenry, Chris. SYMMES PURCHASE RECORDS, 1787-1800. [BUTLER,HAMILTON & WARREN CO] (Lawrenceburg IN: author, 1979) 106p (OGS)

McMullin, Phillip, ed. GRASSROOTS OF AMERICA: A COMPUTERIZED INDEX TO THE AMERICAN STATE PAPERS: LAND GRANTS AND CLAIMS, 1789-1837. (Salt Lake City: Gendex Corp., 1972)

Page, Henry F. VIRGINIA MILITARY DISTRICT OF THE LAW OF WARRANTS, ENTRIES, SURVEYS AND PATENTS IN THE V.M.D. OF OHIO. (Columbus: J.H. Riley & Co., 1850) (OHS)

Peters, William E. OHIO LANDS AND THEIR SUBDIVISIONS, 3RD ed. (Athens OH: author, 1930) (OHS,SLO)

Riegel, Mayburt S. EARLY OHIOANS RESIDENCES FROM THE LAND GRANT RECORDS. (Mansfield OH: Ohio Gen Soc., 1976) 62p (OGS)

Rohrbaugh, Malcolm J. THE LAND OFFICE BUSINESS. (New York: Oxford University Press, 1968)

Sherman, Christopher E. ORIGINAL LAND SUBDIVISIONS, VOLUME III, FINAL REPORT-OHIO TOPOGRAPHIC SURVEY. 1925. (Reprint, Columbus: Ohio Dept Natural Resources, 1982) (OHS)

Smith, Clifford N. FEDERAL LAND SERIES: A CALENDAR OF ARCHIVAL MATERIAL ON THE LAND PATENTS ISSUED BY THE U.S.GOVERNMENT, VOL.1. (Chicago: American Library Assn., 1972) 369p (OHS,SLO,OGS)

Smith, Clifford N. FEDERAL LAND SERIES: A CALENDAR OF ARCHIVAL MATERIAL ON THE LAND PATENTS ISSUED BY THE U.S.GOVERNMENT, VOL.2: FEDERAL BOUNTY LAND WARRANTS OF THE AMERICAN REVOLUTION. (Chicago: American Library Assn., 1972) 416p (OHS,SLO,OGS)

Smith, Clifford N. FEDERAL LAND SERIES: A CALENDAR OF ARCHIVAL MATERIAL ON THE LAND PATENTS ISSUED BY THE U.S.GOVERNMENT, VOL.3. (Chicago: American Library Assn., 1980) 341p (OHS,SLO,OGS)

Smith, Clifford N. FEDERAL LAND SERIES: A CALENDAR OF ARCHIVAL MATERIAL ON THE LAND PATENTS ISSUED BY THE U.S.GOVERNMENT, VOL.4, PT 1 :GRANTS IN THE VIRGINIA MILITARY DISTRICT OF OHIO. (Chicago: American Library Assn., 1982) 395p (OHS,SLO,OGS)

Smith, Clifford N. FEDERAL LAND SERIES: A CALENDAR OF ARCHIVAL MATERIAL ON THE LAND PATENTS ISSUED BY THE U.S.GOVERNMENT, VOL.4, PT 2 :GRANTS IN THE VIRGINIA MILITARY DISTRICT OF OHIO. (Chicago: American Library Assn., 1986) 306p (OHS,SLO,OGS)

Wilson, Samuel M. CATALOGUE OF REVOLUTIONARY SOLDIERS AND SAILORS OF THE COMMONWEALTH OF VIRGINIA TO WHOM LAND BOUNTY WARRANTS WERE GRANT ED... (Reprint, Baltimore MD: Southern Book Co, 1953)

**LAW:**
Marshall, Carrington T. A HISTORY OF THE COURTS AND LAWYERS OF OHIO. 4v. 1934.

**LIBRARIES:**
DIRECTORY OF OHIO LIBRARIES, 1981. (Columbus: State Library of Ohio, 1981) 91p (SLO)

**MANUSCRIPT COLLECTIONS:**
Larson, David R., ed. GUIDE TO MANUSCRIPTS COLLECTIONS & INSTITUTIONAL RECORDS IN OHIO. (np: Society of Ohio Archivists, 1974) 315p. (OHS)

Lentz, Andrea, ed. A GUIDE TO MANUSCRIPTS AT THE OHIO HISTORICAL SOCIETY. (Columbus: Ohio Hist Soc., 1972) 281p (OHS)

Pike, Kermit J. A GUIDE TO THE MANUSCRIPTS AND ARCHIVES OF THE WESTERN RESERVE HISTORICAL SOCIETY. (Cleveland: WRHS, 1972) 425p. (WRHS,OHS, SLO)

Pike, Kermit J. A GUIDE TO MAJOR MANUSCRIPT COLLECTIONS ACCESSIONED AND PROCESSED BY THE LIBRARY OF THE WESTERN RESERVE HISTORICAL SOCIETY. (Cleveland: Western Reserve Hist.Soc., 1987) 91p (WRHS)

**MILITARY:**

Casey, James B. LIBBY PRISON AUTOGRAPH BOOK. JANUARY-FEBRUARY 1864. (Salt Lake City: Utah Genealogical Assn., 1984) 57p

Daughters of 1812, State of Ohio. INDEX TO THE GRAVE RECORDS OF SERVICEMEN OF THE WAR OF 1812 STATE OF OHIO. (Lima OH: the society, 1988) 300p

Erwin, James J. THE NAVAL RESERVES OF OHIO IN THE WAR WITH SPAIN 1898-99. 1899. 109p (OGS)

HISTORY OF FULLER'S OHIO BRIGADE 1861-1865: ITS GREAT MARCH. (Cleveland, 1909) 623p

INDEX TO ROSTER OF OHIO SOLDIERS WAR OF 1812. (Spokane WA: Eastern Washington Gen.Soc., 1974) 119p. (OHS,OGS,SLO,LDS)

OFFICIAL ROSTER OF THE SOLDIERS OF THE REVOLUTION BURIED IN OHIO, VOL.1 & 2, 1929,1938. (Reprint, Warren OH: Trumbull Co Chapter OGS, 1982) (OGS,SLO)

OFFICIAL ROSTER III: SOLDIERS OF THE AMERICAN REVOLUTION WHO LIVED IN THE STATE OF OHIO. (np: OHIO SOC. D.A.R., 1959) 448p (OHS,SLO,OGS,LDS)

OFFICIAL ROSTER OF THE SOLDIERS OF THE STATE OF OHIO IN THE WAR OF THE REBELLION, 1861-1866. (Columbus: Roster Commission, varies) 12v. (SLO,OHS,OGS,LDS)

OFFICIAL ROSTER OF THE SOLDIERS, SAILORS AND MARINES IN THE WORLD WAR 1917-1918. 23v. (SLO,OHS)

OHIO PENSIONERS OF 1883. [Index to] (Bowie MD: Heritage Books, 1987) 367p

OHIO STATE SOLDIERS' AND SAILORS' HOME, SANDUSKY, ADMISSION RECORDS OF VETERANS, 1888-1919. microfilm. (OHS,LDS)

OHIO VETERANS' HOME DEATH RECORDS, 1889-1983 [SOLDIERS' & SAILORS' HOME, SANDUSKY] (Sandusky OH: Erie Co Chapter OGS, 1985?) (OGS)

Petty, Gerald M. INDEX OF THE OHIO SQUIRREL HUNTERS ROSTER. (Columbus: Petty's Press, 1984) 108p. (OHS)

Regimental histories: see holdings at OHS.

Reid, Whitelaw. OHIO IN THE WAR: HER STATESMEN, HER GENERALS AND SOLDIERS. (Cincinnati: Moore, Wilstach & Baldwin, 1868) 2v (OHS)

ROSTER OF OHIO SOLDIERS IN THE WAR OF 1812. 1916. (Reprint, Baltimore MD: Genealogical Pub.Co., 1968) 157p. (OHS,SLO,OGS,LDS)

Stevens, A.Parsons. THE MILITARY HISTORY OF OHIO. (New York: Transcontinental Pub Co., 1885) 308p (LC)

U.S.Daughters of 1812. INDEX TO THE GRAVE RECORDS OF SERVICEMEN OF THE WAR OF 1812, STATE OF OHIO. (Lima OH: the society, 1988) 300p

Waldenmaier, Inez. REVOLUTIONARY WAR PENSIONERS LIVING IN OHIO BEFORE 1834. (Tulsa OK: author, nd) np (OGS?)

**NEWSPAPERS:**

Christian, Donna K. GUIDE TO NEWSPAPER HOLDINGS AT THE CENTER FOR ARCHIVAL COLLECTIONS. (Bowling Green OH: Bowling Green State Univ, 1980) 64p (OGS)

Green, Karen M. PIONEER OHIO NEWSPAPERS 1793-1810 (Galveston TX: Frontier Press, 1986) 383p (OGS)

Green, Karen M. PIONEER OHIO NEWSPAPERS 1802-1818 (Galveston TX: Frontier Press, 1988) 362p (OGS)

Gutgesell, Stephen. GUIDE TO OHIO NEWSPAPERS, 1793-1973. (Columbus: Ohio Hist.Soc., 1976) 412p. (OHS,OGS,SLO)

## OHIO HISTORICAL SOCIETY:
CITY AND COUNTY DIRECTORIES AT THE OHIO HISTORICAL SOCIETY. (Bowie MD: Heritage Books, 1985) 48p (OGS,OHS)
GENEALOGICAL RESEARCHER'S MANUAL: WITH SPECIAL REFERENCES FOR USING THE OHIO HISTORICAL SOCIETY LIBRARY. (Columbus: Franklin Co Chapter OGS, 1982?) 121p (OHS)

## OHIO GENEALOGICAL SOCIETY:
ANCESTOR CHARTS OF 1160 OGS MEMBERS (Mansfield OH: author, 1987) 1200pp
O.G.S.CHAPTER DIRECTORY, 1986. (Mansfield OH: author, 1986) 95p (OGS)

## PLACE NAMES:
Armstrong, J.R. A TABLE OF POST OFFICES IN OHIO. (Columbus: 1861) (OHS)
Fitak, Madge. PLACE NAMES DIRECTORY: NORTHEAST OHIO (Columbus: Ohio Dept Natural Resources, 1976) 41p
Fitak, Madge. PLACE NAMES DIRECTORY: SOUTHEAST OHIO (Columbus: Ohio Dept Natural Resources, 1980) 50p
Gallagher, John S. & A.Patera. THE POST OFFICES OF OHIO. (Burtonsville MD: The Depot, 1979) 318p (OHS)
OHIO GAZETTEER, OR TOPOGRAPHICAL DICTIONARY. 1833. (Knightstown IN: The Bookmark, 1978) 512p. (OHS,OGS,SLO)
Overman, William D. OHIO PLACE NAMES. (Akron OH: author, 1951) 86p.
Overman, William D. OHIO TOWN NAMES. (Akron OH: Atlantic Press, 1958) 155p. (OHS)

## PROBATE RECORDS:
Bell, Carol W. OHIO WILLS AND ESTATES TO 1850: AN INDEX. (Columbus: author, 1981) 400p. (OGS,OHS,SLO,LDS,LC)

## REGIONAL HISTORIES:
Brant & Fuller. HISTORY OF THE UPPER OHIO VALLEY. 1890. (Belmont & Jefferson Cos) 2v (RPI)
Brant & Fuller. HISTORY OF THE UPPER OHIO VALLEY. 1891. (Columbiana Co) 2v. (RPI)
Colket, Meredith. THE WIDELY KNOWN "WESTERN RESERVE" OF OHIO. (Cranbury NJ: Fairleigh Dickinson Univ Press, 1976) 12p. (WRHS,LDS)
COMMEMORATIVE BIOGRAPHICAL RECORD OF NORTHWESTERN OHIO. (Chicago: J.H. Beers & Co., 1899) 616p (LC)(RPI)
Hildreth, Samuel. BIOGRAPHICAL AND HISTORICAL MEMOIRS. 1852. (RPI)
HISTORY OF THE HOCKING VALLEY. (Chicago: Interstate Pub.Co., 1883) [Athens, Hocking, Vinton Cos] (OHS,SLO) (RPI)
MEMOIRS OF THE MIAMI VALLEY OHIO. [incl BUTLER, HAMILTON, LOGAN, MIAMI, MONTGOMERY, SHELBY & WARREN COS] (Chicago: Robert O.Law Co.,1919) 3v (OHS,SLO)
NORTHEASTERN OHIO BIOGRAPHICAL HISTORY OF ASHTABULA, LAKE, & GEAUGA COUNTIES OHIO. 1893. (RPI)
PROGRESSIVE MEN OF NORTHERN OHIO. (Cleveland: 1906) (RPI)
Shriver, Phillip R. A TOUR TO NEW CONNECTICUT IN 1811: THE NARRATIVE OF HENRY LEAVITT ELLSWORTH. (Cleveland: Western Reserve Hist.Soc., 1985) 141p
Summers, Ewing O. GENEALOGICAL AND FAMILY HISTORY OF EASTERN OHIO. 1903. (RPI)
Upton, Harriet T. HISTORY OF THE WESTERN RESERVE. 1910. 3v. (RPI)

## RELIGION:
Allbeck, Willard D. A CENTURY OF LUTHERANS IN OHIO. (Yellow Springs OH: The Antioch Press, 1966) 309p
Denlinger, Carolyn. EVERY NAME INDEX FOR HISTORY OF THE CHURCH OF THE BRETHREN OF THE SOUTHERN DISTRICT OF OHIO. (np: Brethren Histl. Committee, 1982) 42p. (OGS)
Gregg, Samuel. THE HISTORY OF METHODISM WITHIN THE BOUNDS OF THE ERIE ANNUAL CONFERENCE OF THE METHODIST-EPISCOPAL CHURCH. (New York: Carlton & Porter, 1865) 2v

Harter, Frances D. GUIDE TO THE MANUSCRIPT COLLECTION OF EARLY OHIO METHODISM. (Delaware OH: United Methodist Archives Center, 1981)

Hayden, A.S. EARLY HISTORY OF THE DISCIPLES IN THE WESTERN RESERVE, OHIO. 1875. (Reprint, Evansville IN: Unigraphic, 1979) 476p (OGS)

Heiss, Willard & L.S.Mote. EARLY SETTLEMENT OF FRIENDS IN THE MIAMI VALLEY. 1961 (OGS NL)

Hinshaw, William Wade. ENCYCLOPEDIA OF AMERICAN QUAKER GENEALOGY, VOL.IV, OHIO. (Reprint, Baltimore MD: Genealogical Pub.Co., 1973) 1424p (SLO,OHS,LDS)

Hinshaw, William Wade. ENCYCLOPEDIA OF AMERICAN QUAKER GENEALOGY, VOL.V, OHIO. (Reprint, Baltimore MD: Genealogical Pub.Co., 1973) (SLO, OHS,LDS)

Houck, George F. THE CHURCH [CATHOLIC] IN NORTHERN OHIO AND IN THE DIOCESE OF CLEVELAND FROM 1749 TO SEPTEMBER 1887. (Cleveland: Short & Forman, Printers, 1888) 2nd ed. 301p

LUTHERAN CHURCH CHURCH SURVEY FORMS, 1937-1940, BY W.P.A. (microfilm, 2 rolls, OHS)

METHODIST MINISTERS' CARD INDEX, OHIO CONFERENCES, 1797-1981. (micro film, 4 rolls, OHS)

Moherman, T.S. HISTORY OF THE CHURCH OF THE BRETHREN IN NORTHEASTERN OHIO. (Elgin IL: Brethren Pub.House, 1914)

Moore, L.H. THE HISTORY OF SOUTHERN BAPTISTS IN OHIO. (Columbus: State Convention of Baptists in Ohio, 1979) 310p

Sweet, William W. CIRCUIT-RIDER DAYS ALONG THE OHIO...BEING THE JOURNALS OF THE OHIO CONFERENCE...1812-1826. (New York: Methodist Book Concern, 1923) 299p

United Presbyterian Synod of Ohio. BUCKEYE PRESBYTERIANISM. 1968. 285p. (OGS)

Welsh, E.B., ed. BUCKEYE PRESBYTERIANISM. (np: United Presbyterian Synod of Ohio, 1968) 285p

**RIVER: (THE OHIO)**

Banta, R.E. THE OHIO. (Rivers of America Series) (New York: Rinehart & Co., 1949) 592p

Klein, Benjamin & Eleanor. THE OHIO RIVER HANDBOOK & PICTURE ALBUM. (Cincinnati: author, 1950) 376p

Roush, Herbert L. Sr. THE ADVENTURES OF T.C.COLLINS - BOATMAN: TWENTY-FOUR YEARS ON THE WESTERN WATERS, 1849-1873. (Baltimore MD: Gateway Press, 1985) 250p

**SOURCES:**

Adams, Marilyn. OHIO LOCAL AND FAMILY HISTORY SOURCES IN PRINT. (Jackson OH: author, 1984) 60p (OGS)

Bell, Carol W., ed. MASTER INDEX - OHIO SOCIETY DAUGHTERS OF THE AMERICAN REVOLU- TION GENEALOGICAL AND HISTORICAL RECORDS, VOL.I. (Westlake OH: Ohio Society DAR, 1985) 85p (OGS)

Bell, Carol W. OHIO WILLS AND ESTATES TO 1850: AN INDEX. (Columbus: author, 1981) 400p. (OGS,OHS,SLO,LDS)

Bell, Carol W. OHIO GENEALOGICAL GUIDE. (Youngstown OH: author, 1987, 4th ed) 117p (OGS,OHS,SLO)

Bell, Carol W. OHIO GENEALOGICAL PERIODICAL INDEX: A COUNTY GUIDE. (Youngstown OH: author, 1987, 6th ed) (OGS,LDS,OHS,SLO)

Biggs, Deb. GUIDE TO LOCAL GOVERNMENT RECORDS AT THE CENTER FOR ARCHIVAL COL- LECTIONS. (Bowling Green OH: Bowling Green State Univ, 1981) 104p (OGS)

Christian, Donna K. GUIDE TO NEWSPAPER HOLDINGS AT THE CENTER FOR ARCHIVAL COL- LECTIONS. (Bowling Green OH: Bowling Green State Univ, 1980) 64p (OGS)

Clark, Donna. OHIO STATE DIRECTORY OF GENEALOGICAL RECORDS BY TAD (Arvada CO: author, 1986) 142p (OGS)

DIRECTORY OF HISTORICAL ORGANIZATIONS IN OHIO, 1986/87. (Columbus: Ohio Hist Soc, 1986) 119p (OHS)

Folck, Linda. LOCAL GOVERNMENT RECORDS IN THE AMERICAN HISTORY RESEARCH CEN- TER AT THE UNIVERSITY OF AKRON. (Akron: U of Akron, 1982) 40p. (OGS)

Haller, Stephen E. & P.Nolan. FIRST STOP FOR LOCAL HISTORY RESEARCH. A GUIDE TO COUN-TY RECORDS PRESERVED AT WRIGHT STATE UNIVERSITY ARCHIVES AND SPECIAL COL-LECTIONS. 1976. 21p.

Hill, Rebecca B. GENEALOGICAL RESOURCES GUIDE, NORTHWEST OHIO LIBRARIES. (Bowling Green OH: Norweld, 1983) 86p. (OGS)

Levinson, Marilyn. GUIDE TO NEWSPAPER HOLDINGS AT THE CENTER FOR ARCHIVAL COL-LECTIONS. 2nd Edition. (Bowling Green OH: Bowling Green State Univ., 1987)

Levstik, Frank, et al. UNION BIBLIOGRAPHY OF OHIO PRINTED STATE DOCUMENTS, 1803-1970. (Columbus: Ohio Hist Soc., 1973) 750p (OHS)

Matusoff, Karen. CENTRAL OHIO LOCAL GOVERNMENT RECORDS AT THE OHIO HISTORICAL SOCIETY. (Columbus: Ohio Hist Soc., 1978) 38p. (OGS)

OHIO COUNTY RECORDS MANUAL, revised ed. (Columbus: Ohio Historical Society, 1983) 290p. (OHS)

OHIO, HER COUNTIES, HER TOWNSHIPS AND HER TOWNS. (Indianapolis: The Researchers, c1979) np

OHIO SOURCE RECORDS. FROM THE OHIO GENEALOGICAL QUARTERLY. 1937-1944. (Baltimore MD: Genealogical Pub.Co., 1986) 666p (OGS)

Ohio University. GUIDE TO LOCAL GOVERNMENT RECORDS AT OHIO UNIVERSITY. (Athens: OU Library, 1986) 61p.

Secretary of State. ANNUAL REPORT OF THE SECRETARY OF STATE TO THE GOVERNOR OF OHIO - APPENDIX B: RETURN OF THE NUMBER OF DEAF AND DUMB, BLIND, INSANE, AND IDIOTIC PERSONS, 1856. (Reprint, Bowie MD: Heritage Books, 1987) 231p (OGS)

Smith, Marjorie. OHIO MARRIAGES EXTRACTED FROM THE "OLD NORTHWEST" GENEALOGI-CAL QUARTERLY. 1977. (Reprint, Baltimore MD: Genealogical Pub.Co., 1986) 350p (OGS)

Thomson, Peter G. A BIBLIOGRAPHY OF THE STATE OF OHIO. (New York: Argonaut Press, 1966) 2v.

Trucksis, Theresa. A GUIDE TO LOCAL HISTORICAL MATERIALS IN THE LIBRARIES OF NORTH-EASTERN OHIO. (Youngstown OH: NE Oh Libr Assn, 1977) 72p (Yo Pub Lib)

Western Reserve Chapter D.A.R. BIBLE AND FAMILY RECORDS IN THE WESTERN RESERVE HIS-TORICAL SOCIETY VOLUMES I AND II. (Westlake OH: author, 1967) 325p,314p. (OGS)

**TAXES:**

OHIO TAX LISTS, 1800-1810. (Bountiful UT: Accelerated Indexing Systems, 1977) 458p. (OHS,OGS,SLO)

Petty, Gerald M. INDEX OF THE OHIO 1825 TAX DUPLICATE. (Columbus: Petty's Press, 1981) 189p. (OGS,OHS,SLO)

Petty, Gerald M. OHIO 1810 TAX DUPLICATE. (Columbus OH: author, 1976) 221p. (OHS)

Powell, Esther W. EARLY OHIO TAX RECORDS. WITH "INDEX TO EARLY OHIO RECORDS". 1971,1973. (Reprint, Baltimore MD: Genealogical Pub.Co., 1985) 632p (OGS)

# ADAMS COUNTY

| | |
|---|---|
| CREATED: | 1797 from Hamilton County |
| COUNTY SEAT: | WEST UNION 45693 |
| COURT HOUSE: | (no street address) WEST UNION 45693 |
| LIBRARY: | OHIO VALLEY DISTRICT FREE LIBRARY, 4th St., Manchester OH 45144 |
| HISTORICAL SOCIETY: | ADAMS CO. HISTORICAL SOCIETY, PO Box 306, West Union OH 45693 |
| GENEALOGICAL SOCIETY: | ADAMS CO. GENEALOGICAL SOCIETY, PO Box 231, West Union OH 45693 publication: OUR HERITAGE |
| ARCHIVAL DISTRICT: | UNIVERSITY OF CINCINNATI, CINCINNATI |
| HEALTH DEPARTMENT: | 508 EAST MAIN, WEST UNION 45693 |
| LAND SURVEYS: | VIRGINIA MILITARY DISTRICT |
| BOUNDED BY: | EAST:    SCIOTO CO. |
| | NORTH:  HIGHLAND & PIKE CO. |
| | WEST:    BROWN CO. |
| | SOUTH:   LEWIS & MASON CO., KENTUCKY |
| TOWNSHIPS: | Franklin, Green, Jefferson, Liberty, Manchester, Meigs, Monroe, Oliver, Scott, Sprigg, Tiffin, Wayne, Winchester. |
| | |
| SPECIAL NOTE: | A FIRE IN 1910 DESTROYED MANY COUNTY RECORDS |

## COURT RECORDS (LDS MICROFILM)
Assessor:
> Birth and death records, 1888-1893.

Auditor:
> Tax duplicates, 1816-1838.

Probate Court:
> Marriages, 1910-1967.
> Birth registration & corrections, 1941-1967.
> Index to births.
> Guardian records, 1955-1967.
> Guardian dockets, 1910-1967.
> Administration dockets, 1910-1967.
> Wills, 1910-1967.
> Record of journals, 1910-1967.

Recorder:
> Deeds, 1797-1900.

Miscellaneous:
> Mt.Leigh Presbyterian Church, West Union, records, 1838-1851.
> United Presbyterian church, Tranquility, records, 1829-1897.
> Presbyterian church records of Adams Co. Ohio, 1831-1861, by DAR
> Cemetery records, Manchester

## OHIO HISTORICAL SOCIETY: (MICROFILM)
Clerk of Courts:
> Common Pleas inventory of estates 1816-1826
> Marriages, by DAR, 1803-1902.

Miscellaneous:
> Bible records, by DAR. (SLO,OHS,LDS)
> Cemetery & tombstone inscriptions, by DAR.
> Cemeteries & 1860 mortality schedule.(OHS,LDS)

Daily School records of James Ebrite, 1866-1886. (SLO,OHS,LDS)

## STATE LIBRARY OF OHIO: (MICROFILM)
Bible records.
Cemetery records & cemeteries of southern Ohio.
Virginia Military Surveys.

## CENSUS RECORDS (OHS,SLO,OGS,LDS)
1820-1880, 1900-1910; 1890 VETERANS; 1880,1900 SOUNDEX; 1910 MIRACODE

## TAX RECORDS (OHS & LDS)
1801, 1806-1810, 1812-1814, 1816-1838.

## AGRICULTURAL CENSUS SCHEDULES (OHS,SLO-mic)
1850,1860,1870

## PRODUCTS OF INDUSTRY CENSUS SCHEDULE (OHS,SLO-mic)
1850,1870

## MORTALITY CENSUS SCHEDULES (OHS,SLO-mic)
1860,1880

## DAR COLLECTION, STATE LIBRARY OF OHIO
Church records, Bible records, cemeteries, school records
[for separate entries, see Ohio Society Daughters of the American Revolution, MASTER INDEX OSDAR GENEALOGICAL & HISTORICAL RECORDS VOLUME 1 (Decorah Iowa: Anundsen Publishers, 1985)]

## MANUSCRIPTS
John Hayslip Papers, West Union, 1801-1832 (WRHS)
Mt. Leigh Presbyterian Church, West Union, Records, 1838-1851 (WRHS,LDS)
Harvey Pemberton Collection, 1775-1949 (WRHS)
Strait Creek Baptist Assn., Seaman Ohio, Records, 1812-1850 (WRHS)
James M. Ebrite [school] Attendance Records, 1866-1883 (OHS)
Inventory of Estates, 1816-1826 (OHS)

## GENEALOGICAL PERIODICAL ARTICLES
Bell, Carol Willsey. OHIO GENEALOGICAL PERIODICAL INDEX: A COUNTY GUIDE (Youngstown OH: author, 6th ed., 1987)

## NEWSPAPERS: [GUIDE TO OHIO NEWSPAPERS, 1793-1973]
Manchester, Peebles, West Union, Winchester.

## PUBLISHED SOURCES:
Adams Co. Genealogical Society. ADAMS COUNTY, OHIO PROBATE COURT JOURNAL ABSTRACTS, GUARDIANSHIP AND ADMINISTRATOR'S BONDS, VOL.III, 1855-1859. (SLO)
Adams Co. Genealogical Society. ADAMS COUNTY OHIO PROBATE COURT JOURNAL ABSTRACTS, VOL.V, 1852-1879. (SLO)
Adams Co. Genealogical Society. WILL INDEX TO THE ONLY WILL BOOK SAVED FROM 1910 FIRE (1849-1860) (West Union OH: the society, nd)
Adams Co. Genealogical Society. MINI-TRAILS TO FINDING ADAMS COUNTY ANCESTORS (West Union OH: the society, nd) (SLO)
Adams Co. Genealogical Society. INDEX TO THE ADAMS CO. ESTATE INVENTORIES 1810-1849 (West Union OH: the society, nd)

Adams Co. Genealogical Society. ABSTRACTS OF SURVEYS OF PROPERTY OWNERS, EARLY AS
1812 (West Union OH: the society, nd)

Adams Co. Genealogical Society. ABSTRACTS OF SURVEYS OF PROPERTY OWNERS, EARLY AS
1814 (West Union OH: the society, nd)

Adams Co. Genealogical Society. ADAMS CO. BIRTH & DEATH RECORDS BOOK 1 (SCOTT, LIBER-
TY, JEFFERSON & FRANKLIN TOWNSHIPS) (West Union OH: the society, nd)

Adams Co. Genealogical Society. ADAMS CO. BIRTH & DEATH RECORDS BOOK 2 (MEIGS, MON-
ROE, OLIVER, SPRIGG, TIFFIN, WAYNE & WINCHESTER TOWNSHIPS) (West Union OH: the
society, nd)

Adams Co. Genealogical Society. ADAMS CO. CEMETERY BOOKS: SCOTT, JEFFERSON, OLIVER,
GREEN, MONROE, SPRIGG, MEIGS, WINCHESTER, FRANKLIN, LIBERTY, BRATTON,
BRUSHCREEK, TIFFIN, WAYNE [pub.by township in separate volumes] (West Union OH: the
society, nd.) (LDS,SLO)

Adams Co. Genealogical Society. ADAMS COUNTY FEDERAL CENSUS [published by townships]
1850: FRANKLIN, MEIGS, GREEN, MONROE, TIFFIN, SPRIGG & LIBERTY (West Union OH:
the society, nd) (SLO)

Adams Co. Genealogical Society. ADAMS COUNTY FEDERAL CENSUS [published by townships]
1870: SPRIGG, SCOTT, JEFFERSON, TIFFIN, MANCHESTER, WINCHESTER, LIBERTY (West
Union OH: the society, nd) (SLO)

Adams Co. Genealogical Society. INDEXES OF THE ADAMS COUNTY, OHIO COUNTY ARCHIVES,
VOL.1. (West Union OH: the society, 197?) 14p (LDS,SLO)

Adams Co. Genealogical Society. PROBATE COURT JOURNAL ABSTRACTS: GUARDIANSHIP
AND ADMINISTRATORS BONDS, V.3, 1855-1859. (West Union OH: the society, 197?) 14p (LDS)

Adams Co. Genealogical Society. PLACE NAMES, PAST AND PRESENT, IN ADAMS COUNTY,
OHIO. (West Union OH: the society, 1980) 25p (LDS,SLO)

Adams Co. Genealogical Society. RECORDS OF VIRGINIA MILITARY LAND SURVEYS, VOL.I. 1984.
(SLO)

Brien, Lindsay M. ABSTRACTS FROM HISTORY OF ADAMS COUNTY, OHIO [by Evans & Stiver,
1900] (np, author, nd) 47p (LDS)

Caldwell, John A. ILLUSTRATED HISTORICAL ATLAS OF ADAMS COUNTY, OHIO. (Newark OH:
J.A.Caldwell, 1880)(Reprint, Evansville IN: Unigraphic, 1974) 189p (LDS,SLO,OHS)(RPI)

CITY/COUNTY DIRECTORIES: check holdings of OHS & of local public library.

Colletta, Lillian. TOMBSTONE INSCRIPTIONS OF CHERRY FORK CEMETERY, ADAMS COUNTY,
OHIO & GENEALOGICAL GLEANINGS. (Denville NJ: author, 1964) (OHS,LDS,SLO,DAR)

Craig, Robert D. HISTORY, CEMETERIES & MARRIAGES OF ADAMS CO OHIO (Cincinnati: author,
1963) 2 v in 1. (Cincinnati: author, 1964) (OHS,SLO, DAR)

Craig, Robert D. ADAMS COUNTY OHIO MARRIAGE RECORDS 1803-1833.1976. 122p.
(OGS,LDS,SLO)

Craig, Robert D. ADAMS COUNTY OHIO RECORDS. (Cincinnati OH: author, c1963-64) 2v (LDS)

Daughters of the American Revolution. CEMETERIES OF SOUTHERN OHIO. [11 cemeteries in Adams
Co.] (SLO,LDS)

Daughters of the American Revolution. DAILY SCHOOL REGISTER OF JAMES M. EBRITE, 1866-
1886. 1952-53. 45p. (SLO,DAR)

Daughters of the American Revolution. PRESBYTERIAN CHURCH RECORDS OF ADAMS COUN-
TY OHIO (1831-1861); HILL PRAIRIE ILL. & A FEW BUTLER CO.PA.RECORDS, 1861-1884. 1951?
41p. (DAR,LDS)

Daughters of the American Revolution. TOMBSTONE INSCRIPTIONS: CEMETERIES IN ADAMS
COUNTY OHIO. 1958. 32p. (DAR)

Dole, C.Russell. NOTES ON FIVE PIONEER FAMILIES OF SPRIGG TOWNSHIP, ADAMS COUNTY
OHIO. (SLO)

Eckel, Edna W. BRUSH CREEK REFORMED PRESBYTERIAN COVENANTER CHURCH. 10p (SLO)

Evans, Nelson W. & Emmons B. Stivers. A HISTORY OF ADAMS COUNTY, OHIO FROM ITS EAR-
LIEST SETTLEMENT TO THE PRESENT TIME. 1900. (Reprint, Evansville IN: Unigraphic,1973)
946p (SLO,OHS,LDS,DAR) (RPI)

Historical Records Survey, Ohio. INVENTORY OF THE COUNTY ARCHIVES OF OHIO NO.1, ADAMS COUNTY (Columbus: author, 1938) 237p (OHS,LDS,DAR)

Hixson, W.W. PLAT BOOK OF ADAMS COUNTY, OHIO (Rockford IL: author,n.d.) (OHS)

Johnson, Harry W., Jr. ON TO ADAMS COUNTY, OHIO. (Peebles OH: author, 1986) 43p

Jones, David T. CONTRIBUTIONS TO ADAMS COUNTY (OHIO) GENEALOGY [VINTONIA VOL.8] (Ann Arbor MI: Edwards Bros., 1953) 20p (LDS,OHS,SLO)

Lazenby, H.N. TOMBSTONE INSCRIPTIONS: CEMETERIES IN ADAMS COUNTY OHIO. (SLO,LDS)

Nitchman, Paul E. BLACKS IN OHIO, 1880, IN THE COUNTIES OF ADAMS TO CARROLL, VOL.1. (Ft.Meade MD: author, 1986?) 178p

Palmer, Willis. A MANUAL OF METHODISM FOR THE WEST UNION M.E. CHURCH: WITH AN HISTORIC SUMMARY OF METHODISM IN THE BOUNDS OF THE OLD SCIOTO CIRCUIT. (Seaman OH: Kelley Pub., 1978) 98p (LDS)

Rayburn, Elsie. ADAMS COUNTY MARRIAGES VOL.I, 1803-1833 (Columbus: author, 1956) 209p (OHS)

Rayburn, Elsie. BIBLE RECORDS CONNECTED WITH ADAMS COUNTY OHIO AND LEWIS COUNTY KENTUCKY. (SLO,LDS)

Rayburn, Elsie. BIBLE RECORDS OF ADAMS COUNTY OHIO. 22p (SLO,LDS)

Rayburn, Elsie. CEMETERIES OF SOUTHERN OHIO. (SLO)

Rayburn, Elsie. EARLY MARRIAGE RECORDS OF ADAMS COUNTY OHIO 1799-1900. 3v. (SLO)

Rayburn, Elsie. EARLY MARRIAGE RECORDS OF ADAMS COUNTY OHIO, SUPPLEMENT TO VOLS 2 & 3. (SLO)

Rayburn, Elsie. EARLY MARRIAGES OF ADAMS COUNTY OHIO 1797-1803 AS RECORDED IN BOOKS I-II (np: author, nd) 6p (LDS,OHS)

Rayburn, Elsie. EARLY MARRIAGES FROM FAMILY RECORDS & HISTORIES OF ADAMS CO.FAMILY BIBLES & CEMETERIES (Columbus: author, 1949) 5p (OHS)

Rayburn, Elsie. SANDY SPRINGS PRESBYTERIAN CEMETERY, GREEN TWP., ADAMS COUNTY (np: author, nd) 22p (OHS)

SCHOOL MEMORIES OF ADAMS COUNTY RETIRED TEACHERS. 1976. 59p. (SLO)

Sellman, W.M. PIONEER HISTORY OF WINCHESTER, ADAMS COUNTY OHIO SESQUICENTENNIAL 1815-1965. 73p. (SLO)

Smith, Clifford N. FEDERAL LAND SERIES: A CALENDAR OF ARCHIVAL MATERIAL ON THE LAND PATENTS ISSUED BY THE U.S.GOVERNMENT, VOL.4, PT 1: GRANTS IN THE VIRGINIA MILITARY DISTRICT OF OHIO. (Chicago: Amer.Libr. Assn., 1982) 395p

Smith, Clifford N. FEDERAL LAND SERIES: A CALENDAR OF ARCHIVAL MATERIAL ON THE LAND PATENTS ISSUED BY THE U.S.GOVERNMENT, VOL.4, PT 2: GRANTS IN THE VIRGINIA MILITARY DISTRICT OF OHIO. (Chicago: Amer.Libr. Assn., 1986) 306p

Sproull, Grace & H.M.Crawford. TREBER CEMETERY, OLIVER TP., ADAMS CO OH (West Union OH: author, 1980)

THOMPSON'S HISTORICAL COLLECTION OF ADAMS CO., OHIO, VOLUME I (GENEALOGIES & OBITUARIES). (West Union OH: Adams Co. Hist. Soc.,1982?)

Thorson, Betty. INTRODUCTION TO THE REPRODUCTION OF CALDWELL'S ATLAS OF ADAMS CO., OHIO. [index to atlas] (Oakland CA: author, 1979) 79p (LDS)

Williams, Hazel B. STEAM FURNACE GRAVEYARD; LOWDER CEMETERY; TREBER CEMETERY. 4p (SLO,LDS)

## ALLEN COUNTY

CREATED: 1820, from Shelby County
COUNTY SEAT: LIMA 45801
COURT HOUSE: corner of NORTH MAIN & WEST NORTH, LIMA 45801
LIBRARY: LIMA PUBLIC LIBRARY
650 W. Market St., Lima 45801

| | |
|---|---|
| HISTORICAL SOCIETY: | ALLEN CO. HISTORICAL SOCIETY, |
| | 620 W. Market St., Lima 45801 |
| GENEALOGICAL SOCIETY: | ALLEN CO. CHAPTER, OGS |
| | 620 W. Market St., Lima 45801 |
| ARCHIVAL DISTRICT: | BOWLING GREEN STATE UNIVERSITY, BOWLING GREEN |
| | (see Biggs' Guide to records) |
| HEALTH DEPARTMENT: | 405 E.MARKET ST., LIMA 45802 |
| | (separate offices for Lima City & Delphos) |
| LAND SURVEYS: | CONGRESS LANDS, E & S OF 1ST PRIN.MERIDIAN |
| BOUNDED BY: | EAST:     HANCOCK & HARDIN CO. |
| | NORTH:  PUTNAM CO. |
| | WEST:     MERCER & VAN WERT CO. |
| | SOUTH:  AUGLAIZE CO. |
| TOWNSHIPS: | Amanda, Auglaize, Bath, German, Jackson, Lima City, Marion, |
| | Monroe, Ottawa, Perry, Richland, Shawnee, Spencer, Sugar Creek. |

## COURT RECORDS (LDS MICROFILM)
Assessor:
   Quadrennial enumeration, (males over 21), 1883,1887.
   Birth & death records, 1906-1907.
Auditor:
   Tax duplicates, 1832-33,1836,1839-1848,1850.
Soldiers' relief records, 1887-1916.
Board of Elections:
   Lists of electors and voters, 1904-1960.
Clerk of Courts:
   General index, civil, 1832-1857
   Appearance docket, vA, 1842-1849
   Journal, vA-D, 1831-1853.
   Chancery record, vA, 1833-1857.
   Supreme Court complete record, 1837-1851.
   Supreme Court journal, 1837-1851.
   District Court journal, 1852-1860.
   District Court Complete Records, 1852-1864.
   Witness docket, v1-15, 1859-1907.
   Record of justices' oaths, 1909-1947.
Commissioners:
   Soldiers' relief records, 1887-1916.
Coroner:
   Coroner's inquest record, 1886-1892,1911-1917.
Court of Common Pleas:
   Witness dockets, v1-11, v13-15,1859-1907.
   Record of justices' oaths, 1909-1947.
Probate Court:
   General index to estate & civil cases, v1-2, 1835-1926.
   Record of wills, vA-H, 1836-1905.
   Record of wills from Putnam & Van Wert Cos., 1837-1847.
   Marriage records, 1831-1917.
   General index to marriages, 1831-1919.
   Death records, v1-2, 1867-1909.
   Record of births, v1-3, 1867-1940.
   Guardians' docket, vD, 1881-1905.
   Guardians' bonds, vB-D,2, 1859-1899.
   Guardians' inventory, v1, 1883-1913.
   Administrators docket, vA-D, 1842-1899.

Administrators & executors bonds, 1831-1891.
Assignees bonds & letters, v1, 1876-1901.
Civil records, vA-I, 1852-1885.
Inventory & sale bills, vA-J, 1853-1886.
Inventories & sale bills transcribed from Putnam, Van Wert & Mercer Cos., 1838-1847.
Probate journal, vA-L, 1837-1887.
Final record of accounts, vA-P, 1837-1885.
Naturalization records, 1860-1929.
Index to naturalization records, 1851-1906.
Recorder:
Deed and mortgage records, vA-Y, 5-36, 1831-1882.
General index to deeds, 1831-1902.
Deeds from Van Wert, Putnam & Mercer Cos., 1832-1848.
Soldiers' discharge, v1-2, 1865-1923, 1946.
School examiners:
School examiners' record, 1865-1877.
Sheriff:
Jail register, 1870-1902,1907-1923.
Township Trustees:
Richland Township, v1-3, 1840-1879.
Miscellaneous:
Zion Mennonite church, Bluffton, records, 1840-1925.
Grace Mennonite Church minutes, Bluffton, 1893-1928.
First Mennonite Church of Bluffton, family records, 1915-1950.
Ebenezer Mennonite Church, Bluffton, v1-4, 1918-1961.
Emanuel Swiss German Reformed Church, Richland Tp, 1870-1904.
Misc. cemetery records by LDS Church.
Cemetery records, DAR collection, State Library of Ohio.

## OHIO HISTORICAL SOCIETY: (MICROFILM)
Clerk of Courts:
General index, civil, 1832-1857
Appearance docket, vA, 1842-1849
Journal, vA-D, 1831-1853.
Chancery record, vA, 1833-1857.
Supreme Court complete record, 1837-1851.
Supreme Court journal, 1837-1851.
District Court journal, 1852-1860.
District Court Complete Records, 1852-1864.
Probate Court:
Administrators bonds, v1, 1882-1887.
Will records, vI-J, 1904-1910.
Naturalization records, 1906-12, 1921-29.
Recorder:
Soldiers' discharge, v1-2, 1865-1923, 1946.
Miscellaneous:
Marriages, by DAR, 1831-1864.
Bible & Cemetery records, by DAR, v1-3.

## CENSUS RECORDS (OHS,SLO,OGS,LDS)
1830-1880, 1900-1910; 1890 VETERANS; 1880,1900 SOUNDEX; 1910 MIRACODE

## AGRICULTURAL CENSUS SCHEDULES (OHS,SLO-mic)
1850,1860,1870

**PRODUCTS OF INDUSTRY CENSUS SCHEDULE (OHS,SLO-mic)**
1850,1870

**MORTALITY CENSUS SCHEDULES (OHS,SLO-mic)**
1860,1880

**NEWSPAPERS: [GUIDE TO OHIO NEWSPAPERS, 1793-1973]**
Bluffton, Delphos, Kalida, Lima, Manhattan, Spencerville.

**TAX RECORDS (OHS & LDS)**
1831-1838; see parent counties

**GENEALOGICAL PERIODICAL ARTICLES**
Bell, Carol Willsey. OHIO GENEALOGICAL PERIODICAL INDEX: A COUNTY GUIDE (Youngstown
    OH:  author, 6th ed., 1987)

**PUBLISHED SOURCES:**
1836-1936 ST.MATTHEWS CENTENNIAL. 1936. (SLO)
Allen Co Chapter OGS.  CEMETERY RECORD OF THE CAMPBELL CEMETERY, MONROE
    TOWNSHIP. 1973. (LDS)
ATLAS OF ALLEN COUNTY OHIO (Chicago:  H.H.Hardesty, 1875) 87p (OHS)
ATLASES OF ALLEN COUNTY, OHIO. 1875,1880, repr 1974 (OGS)
Bell, Annie B.  RECORD OF MARRIAGES IN ALLEN COUNTY, OHIO...1831-1845. (Washington DC:
    author, 1934) 61p (LDS,DAR)
Biggs, Deb. GUIDE TO LOCAL GOVERNMENT RECORDS AT THE CENTER FOR ARCHIVAL COL-
    LECTIONS. (Bowling Green OH: Bowling Green State Univ, 1981) 104p (OGS)
Burkhardt, F.A.  ST.MATTHEW'S LUTHERAN CHURCH:  SHAWNEE TOWNSHIP, ALLEN COUN-
    TY OHIO.  (Lima OH:  News Gazette Printing, 1937?)  28p (DAR)
Carnes, John R., ed.  THE 1976 HISTORY OF ALLEN COUNTY OHIO.  (Evansville IN:  Unigraphic,
    1976) 831p (LDS)
Christian, Donna K. GUIDE TO NEWSPAPER HOLDINGS AT THE CENTER FOR ARCHIVAL COL-
    LECTIONS. (Bowling Green OH: Bowling Green State Univ, 1980) 64p (OGS)
Christy, Mae L.  MISCELLANEOUS RECORDS OF ALLEN COUNTY OHIO. 1973.  1v.  (DAR)
CITY/COUNTY DIRECTORIES:  check holdings of OHS & of local public library.
Daughters of the American Revolution. BIBLE & CEMETERY RECORDS OF ALLEN COUNTY OHIO,
    3v. 1944-1959. (LDS,SLO,DAR)
Daughters of the American Revolution.  CEMETERY RECORDS OF THE CAIRO WEST SIDE
    CEMETERY OR HARPSTER CEMETERY (SLO)
Daughters of the American Revolution.  CEMETERY RECORDS OF THE ROCKPORT METHODIST
    CHURCH [MONROE TP., ALLEN CO] 1971.  67p.  (DAR)
Daughters of the American Revolution.  BIBLE RECORDS OF FAYETTE, PICKAWAY AND ALLEN
    COUNTIES OHIO. (SLO)
Daughters of the American Revolution. MARRIAGE RECORDS, ALLEN COUNTY OHIO, 1831-1864.
    1v. (SLO,DAR,LDS)
FARM AND BUSINESS DIRECTORY OF ALLEN COUNTY OHIO 1948-50 (Bowling Green OH:  Rural
    Directories Inc, 1950?)  np (OHS)
Federal Writers Project, Ohio.  GUIDE TO LIMA AND ALLEN COUNTY.  (Lima:  WPA, 1938) 64p
    (OHS)
Grismore, Dale D. THE FIRST FAMILIES OF ALLEN COUNTY OHIO INDEX. (Estes Park CO: author,
    1983) 26p. (OGS,LDS)
Hardesty, H.H.  MILITARY HISTORY OF OHIO, 1886-1887:  ALLEN COUNTY.  (OHS)
Harrison, R.H. ATLAS OF ALLEN COUNTY OHIO.  (Philadelphia: author, 1880) (Reprint, Evansville
    IN:  Unigraphic, 1974) 141p (LDS,OHS,SLO,LC)(RPI)
Historical Records Survey, Ohio.  GUIDE TO COUNTY ARCHIVES OF OHIO, vol.II, ALLEN COUN-
    TY.  (Columbus: author, 1936) 114p (OHS,LDS,DAR)

HISTORY OF ALLEN COUNTY OHIO (Chicago: Warner Beers, 1885)(Reprint, Evansville IN: Unigraphic, 1972) 824p (SLO,OHS,LDS,DAR) (RPI)

Hixson, W.W. PLAT BOOK OF ALLEN COUNTY OHIO. (Rockford IL: author, nd) (OHS)

Howe, Henry. HISTORY OF ALLEN COUNTY OHIO 1820-1889: EXCERPTED FROM THE CENTEN-NIAL HISTORY OF OHIO [1898 edition of Howe's Historical Collections of Ohio] (Knightstown IN: Bookmark, 1977) 10p (LDS)

James, Peggie S. etal. INDEX TO HISTORY OF ALLEN COUNTY OHIO (Warner Beers, 1885)

James, Peggie S. ORIGINAL LAND ENTRIES OF ALLEN COUNTY OHIO, 1822-1860 (Ann Arbor MI: Edwards Bros., 1971) 152p (OGS,LDS,SLO,DAR)

Jennings, G. NAMES OF SOLDIERS WHO RESIDED IN ALLEN COUNTY AT THE TIME THEY VOLUNTEERED IN TO SERVICE OF US, 1861-65. nd 42p (OHS)

Jones, Charles H. HISTORICAL ATLAS OF ALLEN COUNTY OHIO. (Chicago: H.S. Hardesty & Co., 1875)(Reprint, Evansville IN: Unigraphic, 1974) 39,25p (LDS)

Knapp, Horace S. HISTORY OF THE MAUMEE VALLEY. (Toledo OH: author, 1872) 685p. (DAR,OHS,SLO)

Levinson, Marilyn. GUIDE TO NEWSPAPER HOLDINGS AT THE CENTER FOR ARCHIVAL COL-LECTIONS. 2nd Edition. (Bowling Green OH: Bowling Green State Univ., 1987)

Miller, Charles C. HISTORY OF ALLEN COUNTY OHIO & REPRESENTATIVE CITIZENS. (Chicago: Richmond & Arnold, 1906) 872p (LC,SLO,DAR,LDS)(RPI)

Nitchman, Paul E. BLACKS IN OHIO, 1880, IN THE COUNTIES OF ADAMS TO CARROLL, VOLUME 1. (Ft.Meade MD: author, 1986?) 178p

Parker, Sandra. CEMETERY RECORD OF THE CAMPBELL CEMETERY, MONROE TOWNSHIP, ALLEN COUNTY OHIO. (Lima OH: Allen Co Chapter OGS0, 1973) 23p (LDS)

PORTRAIT AND BIOGRAPHICAL RECORD OF ALLEN AND VAN WERT COUNTIES, OHIO (Chicago: A.W.Bowen & Co., 1896) 909p (OHS,LDS,DAR,SLO)(RPI)

PORTRAIT AND BIOGRAPHICAL RECORD OF ALLEN AND PUTNAM COUNTIES OHIO. (Chicago: A.W.Bowen & Co., 1896) 609p (OHS,LDS,DAR)

Raber, Nellie M. A DIGEST OF WILLS ALLEN COUNTY OHIO "A,B & 1" AND INDEX ONLY OF WILL RECORD C 1835-1882 (Lakewood OH: author, nd) 92p (LDS)

RURAL DIRECTORY OF ALLEN COUNTY OHIO, 1929-30 (Springfield OH: Southwestern Pub Co., 1930?) np (OHS)

Rusler, William. A STANDARD HISTORY OF ALLEN COUNTY OHIO. (Chicago: American Histori-cal Society, 1921) 2v (LC,SLO,LDS,DAR)

Stemen, Thomas F. THE SALEM MENNONITE CHURCH CEMETERY RECORDS, ROWS 1-19. (SLO)

Wagner, Charles W. MISCELLANEOUS CEMETERY RECORDS OF ALLEN, LICKING, HARDIN, MADISON, PICKAWAY AND VINTON COUNTIES. (SLO)

Winter, Nevin O. HISTORY OF NORTH WEST OHIO (Chicago: Lewis Pub., 1917) 3v (OHS,SLO)

Wood, Helen W. THE NAMING OF ALLEN COUNTY: THE STORY OF COLONEL JOHN ALLEN IN THE WAR OF 1812. (Lima OH: Longmeier Print., 1975) 22p. (SLO,DAR)

Yon, Paul D. GUIDE TO OHIO COUNTY AND MUNICIPAL GOVERNMENT RECORDS FOR URBAN RESEARCH. (Columbus: Ohio Hist Soc., 1973) (OHS)

# ASHLAND COUNTY

| | |
|---|---|
| CREATED: | 1846, FROM HURON, LORAIN, RICHLAND & WAYNE CO |
| COUNTY SEAT: | ASHLAND 44805 |
| COURT HOUSE: | WEST 2ND ST., ASHLAND 44805 |
| LIBRARY: | 224 CLAREMONT AVE., ASHLAND 44805 |
| HISTORICAL SOCIETY: | 602 CENTER ST., ASHLAND 44805 |
| GENEALOGICAL SOCIETY: | ASHLAND COUNTY CHAPTER OGS, |
| | PO BOX 681, ASHLAND 44805 |
| | publication: PASTFINDER |
| ARCHIVAL DISTRICT: | UNIVERSITY OF AKRON, AKRON, OHIO |
| | (see Folck's Guide to records) |

HEALTH DEPARTMENT:          CO.OFF.BLDG, 110 COTTAGE ST, ASHLAND 44805
                             (separate office for Ashland City)
PUBLIC LIBRARY:             224 CLAREMONT AVE., ASHLAND 44805
ARCHIVAL DISTRICT:          UNIVERSITY OF AKRON, AKRON, OHIO
LAND SURVEYS:               FIRE LANDS
                             CONNECTICUT WESTERN RESERVE
                             CONGRESS LANDS, OHIO RIVER SURVEY (NORTH)
BOUNDED BY:                 EAST:    WAYNE CO.
                             NORTH:   HURON & MEDINA CO.
                             WEST:    RICHLAND CO.
                             SOUTH:   HOLMES & KNOX CO.
TOWNSHIPS:                  Clear Creek, Green, Hanover, Jackson, Lake, Mifflin, Milton,
                             Mohican, Montgomery, Orange, Perry, Ruggles, Sullivan, Troy,
                             Vermilion.

## COURT RECORDS (LDS MICROFILM)
Common Pleas Court:
    General index, 1847-1852.
    Chancery records, v.1-2, 1846-1852.
    Civil journals, v1-4, 1846-1852.
    Appearance dockets, v1-5, 1846-1852.
    Supreme Court, complete record. 1847-1852.
Probate Court:
    (none listed)
Recorder:
    Deed records, 1846-1893.
    Grantor & Grantee index, 1847-1901.
Miscellaneous:
    Savannah Presbyterian Church, register, 1841-1882.
    Jeromesville Presbyterian Church, register, 1854-1884.
    Misc. Cemeteries, DAR collection, State Library of Ohio.

## OHIO HISTORICAL SOCIETY: (MICROFILM)
Clerk of Courts:
    Common Pleas general index, 1847-1867.
    Common Pleas Supreme Court complete record, 1847-1852.
    Common Pleas chancery record, 1846-1853.
    Common Pleas journal, v1-4, 1846-1852.
    Common Pleas appearance docket, v1-5, 1846-1852.
Miscellaneous:
    Marriages, by DAR, 1846-1865.
    Tombstone inscriptions, by DAR, v1-4.
    Connecticut Land Co. Western Reserve land draft, 1795-1809.

## CENSUS RECORDS (OHS,SLO,OGS,LDS)
1850-1880, 1900-1910; 1890 VETERANS; 1880,1900 SOUNDEX; 1910 MIRACODE

## AGRICULTURAL CENSUS SCHEDULES (OHS,SLO-mic)
1850,1860,1870

## PRODUCTS OF INDUSTRY CENSUS SCHEDULE (OHS,SLO-mic)
1850,1870

## MORTALITY CENSUS SCHEDULES (OHS,SLO-mic)
1860,1880

**NEWSPAPERS: [GUIDE TO OHIO NEWSPAPERS, 1793-1973]**
Ashland, Hayesville, Loudonville, Vermillion.

**TAX RECORDS (OHS & LDS)**
none listed; see parents counties.

**MANUSCRIPTS:**
Hayesville Baptist Church records, 1841-1859. (WRHS)

**GENEALOGICAL PERIODICAL ARTICLES**
Bell, Carol Willsey. OHIO GENEALOGICAL PERIODICAL INDEX: A COUNTY GUIDE (Youngstown OH: author, 6th ed., 1987)

**PUBLISHED SOURCES:**
1929 FARMERS' DIRECTORY OF ASHLAND COUNTY. (np: National Farm Directories Co., 1929) (OGS)
ASHLAND CITY DIRECTORY AND COUNTY GAZETEER 1927-1928. (Asheville NC: Piedmont Directory Co., 1928?) (OHS)
Ashland Co Chapter OGS. 1880 CENSUS INDEX ASHLAND COUNTY OHIO (Ashland OH: the society, 1982) 47p (OGS)
Ashland Co Chapter OGS. ASHLAND COUNTY OHIO, RESEARCH AID #1: HANOVER TOWNSHIP (Ashland OH: the society, 1984) 150p (OGS)
Ashland Co Chapter OGS. ASHLAND COUNTY OHIO, RESEARCH AID #2: GREEN TOWNSHIP. (Ashland OH: the society, 1985) 170p (OGS)
Ashland Co Chapter OGS. ASHLAND COUNTY OHIO, RESEARCH AID #3: LAKE TOWNSHIP. (Ashland Oh: the society, 1986) 96p (OGS)
Ashland Co Chapter OGS. ASHLAND COUNTY OHIO, RESEARCH AID #4: RUGGLES TOWNSHIP (Ashland OH: the society, 1986) 158p (OGS)
Ashland Co Chapter OGS. ASHLAND COUNTY OHIO, RESEARCH AID #5: PERRY TOWNSHIP (Ashland OH: the society, 1987) 200p (OGS)
Bailey, Rae. OLD KEYS: AN HISTORICAL SKETCH OF CLEAR CREEK TOWNSHIP, ASHLAND COUNTY OHIO, AND OF SAVANNAH, THE TOWNSHIP'S ONLY VILLAGE. (Washington DC: author, 1941) 454p (DAR,LDS)
Baughman, Abraham J. A CENTENNIAL BIOGRAPHICAL HISTORY OF RICHLAND & ASHLAND COUNTIES OHIO.(Chicago: Lewis Pub.Co., 1901) 831p (LDS,SLO, OGS,OHS,DAR)(RPI)
Baughman, Abraham J. HISTORY OF ASHLAND COUNTY, OHIO. (Chicago: S.J.Clarke Pub Co., 1909.) 864p (LDS, OHS, DAR, LC, SLO) (RPI)
Beem, Nelson C. LOUDONVILLE AND GREATER MOHICAN AREA SESQUICENTENNIAL, 1814-1964. 1964, 36p (LDS,SLO)
Boyd, Sidney R. ASHLAND, OHIO, PAST AND PRESENT IN WORD AND PICTURE. 1965. (Reprint, Fort Wayne IN: Allen Co.Pub.Lib., 1984) (LDS)
CALDWELL'S ATLAS OF ASHLAND COUNTY, OHIO. (Condit OH: J.A.Caldwell, 1874) (LDS,OHS,OGS,SLO,DAR)(RPI)
CITY/COUNTY DIRECTORIES: check holdings of OHS & of local public library.
Daughters of the American Revolution. ASHLAND COUNTY CEMETERY BOOK: REPRINT OF EARLY VITAL RECORDS OF ASHLAND COUNTY OHIO. (Ashland OH: author, 1979) 494p (LDS,OGS,DAR)
Daughters of the American Revolution. MARRIAGE RECORDS, ASHLAND COUNTY OHIO, v1-2, 1846-1865. 1936. (SLO,LDS,DAR)
Daughters of the American Revolution. TOMBSTONE INSCRIPTIONS, ASHLAND COUNTY, OHIO. (SLO,LDS)
Duff, William. ASHLAND: THE CITY OF PROGRESS AND PROSPERITY. (Ashland OH: Centennial Homecoming Assn., 1915) 187p (DAR,LDS)

Duff, William A. HISTORY OF NORTH CENTRAL OHIO EMBRACING RICHLAND, ASHLAND, WAYNE, MEDINA, LORAIN, HURON AND KNOX COUNTIES. (Topeka KS: Historical Pub Co., 1931) 3v (OHS,DAR)

FARM JOURNAL DIRECTORY, ASHLAND COUNTY OHIO (Philadelphia: W.Atkinson Co., 1915) (OHS)

Folck, Linda. LOCAL GOVERNMENT RECORDS IN THE AMERICAN HISTORY RESEARCH CENTER AT THE UNIVERSITY OF AKRON. (Akron: U of Akron, 1982) 40p. (OGS)

GENEALOGICAL DATA RELATING TO WOMEN IN THE WESTERN RESERVE BEFORE 1840 (1850) (Cleveland: Centennial Commission, 1943) (WRHS,LDS)

Hardesty, H.H. MILITARY HISTORY OF OHIO, 1886-1887, ASHLAND CO. (OHS)

Heyde, J.M. A BRIEF CENTENNIAL HISTORY OF LOUDONVILLE, OHIO, 1814-1914. 40p (LDS)

Hill, George W. HISTORY OF ASHLAND COUNTY, OHIO. (Cleveland OH: Williams Bros., 1880) 408p (LC,LDS,SLO,OHS,DAR)(RPI)

Historical Records Survey, Ohio. INVENTORY OF THE COUNTY ARCHIVES OF OHIO NO.3, ASHLAND COUNTY (Columbus: author, 1942) 396p (LDS,OHS,DAR)

Hixson, W.W. PLAT BOOK OF ASHLAND CO OHIO (Rockford IL: author, nd) (OHS)

Knapp, Horace S. A HISTORY OF THE PIONEER AND MODERN TIMES OF ASHLAND COUNTY. (Philadelphia: J.B.Lippincott & Co., 1863) 550p.(LDS,OHS, SLO,DAR)(RPI)

Lee, Sue & Rita Kopp. ASHLAND COUNTY OHIO MARRIAGES, 1860-1870, Vol.3. (Ashland OH: author,1980) 71p (SLO)

Lee, Sue & Rita Kopp. ASHLAND COUNTY OHIO MARRIAGES, 1846-1850. (Ashland OH: Ashland Co Chapter OGS, 1978) 41p (OGS,LDS)

LOUDONVILLE AND GREATER MOHICAN AREA SESQUICENTENNIAL COMMEMORATING OUR 150TH ANNIVERSARY. nd. 36p (LDS)

MINUTES OF THE SESSION OF THE FIRST PRESBYTERIAN CHURCH OF ASHLAND, OHIO, JULY 29, 1841-APRIL 8, 1855. (OGS)

Nitchman, Paul E. BLACKS IN OHIO, 1880, IN THE COUNTIES OF ADAMS TO CARROLL, VOLUME 1. (Ft.Meade MD: author, 1986?) 178p

Patterson, Virginia. EARLY HISTORY OF HAYESVILLE: HAYESVILLE ACADEMY AND VERMILLION TOWNSHIP. nd (LDS)

Raber, Nellie M. MARRIAGES, 1846-1865, ASHLAND COUNTY OHIO. (Lakewood OH: author, nd) 131p (LDS)

Riddle, Samuel. HISTORY OF THE ASHLAND COUNTY PIONEER HISTORICAL SOCIETY, 1875-1885. (OHS,LDS)

SCRAPBOOK - RICHLAND AND ASHLAND COUNTY OHIO. [OBITS, c1880-1900] 109p. (OGS)

Ungerer, Thelma S. GENEALOGICAL ABSTRACTS FROM LOUDONVILLE, ASHLAND CO.OHIO NEWSPAPERS, 1873-1892. (Wooster OH: author, 1979?) 95p (OGS,LDS)

Western Reserve Hist.Soc. INDEX TO THE MICROFILM EDITION OF GENEALOGICAL DATA RELATING TO WOMEN IN THE WESTERN RESERVE PRE 1840. (Cleveland: the society, 1976) 226p (OGS,WRHS)

Wickham, Gertrude V.W. MEMORIAL TO THE PIONEER WOMEN OF THE WESTERN RESERVE. (Cleveland: Cleveland Centennial Commission, 1896+) 2v (SLO)

Writers Program, Ohio. ASHLAND'S ETERNITY ACRES: A GUIDE TO COUNTY MEMORIALS. (Columbus: WPA, c1942) 95p (OHS)

# ASHTABULA COUNTY

CREATED: 1808, FROM GEAUGA & TRUMBULL COUNTIES
COUNTY SEAT: JEFFERSON 44047
COURT HOUSE: 25 W.JEFFERSON ST., JEFFERSON 44047
LIBRARIES: ASHTABULA COUNTY DISTRICT LIBRARY,
335 W. 44TH ST., ASHTABULA 44004
HENDERSON MEMORIAL LIBRARY,
54 E.JEFFERSON ST., JEFFERSON 44047

| | |
|---|---|
| HISTORICAL SOCIETY: | ASHTABULA COUNTY HISTORICAL SOCIETY, PO BOX 193, JEFFERSON 44047 |
| GENEALOGICAL SOCIETY: | ASHTABULA CO. CHAPTER OGS, c/o HENDERSON MEMORIAL LIBRARY, 54 E.JEFFERSON ST., JEFFERSON 44047 publication: ANCESTOR HUNT |
| HEALTH DEPARTMENT: | OLD COURT HOUSE, JEFFERSON 44047 (separate offices in Geneva, Ashtabula City, and Conneaut) |
| ARCHIVAL DISTRICT: | WESTERN RESERVE HIST.SOC., CLEVELAND |
| LAND SURVEYS: | CONNECTICUT WESTERN RESERVE |
| BOUNDED BY: | EAST: CRAWFORD & ERIE CO., PENNSYLVANIA |
| | NORTH: LAKE ERIE |
| | WEST: GEAUGA & LAKE CO. |
| | SOUTH: TRUMBULL CO. |
| TOWNSHIPS: | Andover, Ashtabula, Austinburg, Cherry Valley, Colebrook, Conneaut, Denmark, Dorset, Geneva, Harpersfield, Hartsgrove, Jefferson, Kingsville, Lenox, Monroe, Morgan, New Lyme, Orwell, Pierpont, Plymouth, Richmond, Rome, Saybrook, Sheffield, Trumbull, Wayne, Williamsfield, Windsor. |

## COURT RECORDS [LDS MICROFILM]
Auditor:
    Duplicate tax records, 1816-1838.
Probate Court:
    Probate record, vA-G, 1811-1854.
    Index to Probate docket and wills, 1833-1955.
    Probate docket, 1833-1889.
    Will record, 1853-1888.
    Probate journal, vA-J, 1852-1886.
    Marriage records, 1812-1915.
    Marriage licenses, 1864-1873.
    Naturalization records, 1858-1906.
    Birth records, 1867-1908.
    Death records, 1867-1908.
Recorder:
    Incorporation of religious societies & churches, 1818-1834,1844-1873.
    Deeds, 1811-1887.
    Index to deeds, 1798-1947.
Miscellaneous:
    Census, 1811-1835,1843; marriage licenses, 1832-1840. (WRHS)
    Jefferson First Baptist Church records, 1811-1921. (WRHS)
    Grand River Baptist Assn. church records, 1817-1842,1853-1871. (WRHS)
    Grand River Presbytery minutes, 1814-1818,1829-1870. (WRHS)
    Amboy Presbyterian Church records, 1840-1849.
    Bethel Union Baptist Church, Jefferson, records, 1829-1887. (WRHS)
    Record of Deaths 1869-1937 kept by Evert C.Holcomb. (SLO)

## OHIO HISTORICAL SOCIETY: (MICROFILM)
Probate Court:
    Naturalization record, 1875-1906.
Recorder:
    Certificates for religious societies, 1818-1834.
    Record of church corporations, 1845.
    Deed indexes, 1798-1947.
    Deeds, 1811-1887.

Miscellaneous:
    Marriages, by DAR, 1811-1868.
    Connecticut Land Company, Western Reserve land draft, 1795-1809.

**STATE LIBRARY OF OHIO: (MICROFILM)**
Death records, 1869-1937.
Original estate records, 2 reels.
Birth registrations & corrections, 9 reels.

**MANUSCRIPTS:**
George W. Stanley Docket Book, 1837-1841. (WRHS)
Quincy Case family diaries, 1864-71, 1903. (WRHS)
Alexander Harper family papers, 1814-1904. (WRHS)
Joel Blakeslee papers. (WRHS)
First Baptist Church, Jefferson, records, 1811-1921. (WRHS)
Wayne Congregational Church, records, 1826-1841. (WRHS)
Winchester Fitch papers. (WRHS)
Bethel Union Baptist Church, Jefferson, records 1829-1887. (WRHS)
Quintus Athens papers. (WRHS)
Edward Lampson papers, 1781-1948. (OHS)
Solomon Durkee papers, 1811-1880. (OHS)
Ashtabula Co. Female Anti-Slavery Society, records, 1835-1837. (WRHS)
George Tod, notebooks from Old Supreme Court, 1817,1820-21. (OHS)
Poll books & abstracts of votes returned, 1813. (OHS)
Historical & Philosophical Society of Ashtabula Co, records. (OHS)
Census records, 1847-1875. (WRHS)
Ashtabula Township records, c1840-1889. (WRHS)
Conneaut Township, JP records, 1830-1833. (WRHS)
Jefferson & Lenox Townships, school records, 1834-1888. (WRHS)
Trumbull Township school records, 1849-1898. (WRHS)
Windsor Township, board of education records, 1853-1879. (WRHS)
Windsor Township, school records, 1838-1886. (WRHS)
Windsor Township general records, 1811-1867. (WRHS)

**CENSUS RECORDS  (OHS,SLO,OGS,LDS)**
1820-1880, 1900-1910; 1890 VETERANS; 1880,1900 SOUNDEX; 1910 MIRACODE

**AGRICULTURAL CENSUS SCHEDULES  (OHS,SLO-mic)**
1850,1860,1870

**PRODUCTS OF INDUSTRY CENSUS SCHEDULE  (OHS,SLO-mic)**
1850,1870

**MORTALITY CENSUS SCHEDULES (OHS,SLO-mic)**
1860,1880

**NEWSPAPERS: [GUIDE TO OHIO NEWSPAPERS, 1793-1973]**
Andover, Ashtabula, Conneaut, Geneva, Jefferson, Kingsville, Orwell, Rock Creek, Salem, Wayne.

**TAX RECORDS (OHS & LDS)**
1812-1814, 1816-1838.

**GENEALOGICAL PERIODICAL ARTICLES**
Bell, Carol Willsey. OHIO GENEALOGICAL PERIODICAL INDEX: A COUNTY GUIDE (Youngstown
    OH: author, 6th ed., 1987)

**PUBLISHED SOURCES:**

ASHTABULA ANNUAL BUSINESS REVIEW (Canton OH: Review Pub Co, 1887) (OHS, LDS)

ASHTABULA CITY DIRECTORY, INCLUDING GENEVA (Pittsburgh PA: R.L.Polk & Co., 1931) (LDS)

ASHTABULA COUNTY ATLAS. (Ashtabula OH: Sill, Tucker & Co., 1905) 98p (LDS,OHS,SLO,LC)

ASHTABULA COUNTY ATLAS- INDEX (Ashtabula OH: Sill, Tucker & Co., 1905) (LDS)(RPI)

ASHTABULA COUNTY FARM JOURNAL ILLUSTRATED RURAL DIRECTORY (Wilmer Atkinson Co. 1918/23) (OHS)

Ashtabula Co. Genealogical Society. 1820 CENSUS INDEX, ASHTABULA COUNTY, OHIO. (Jefferson OH: the society, 1979) 13p (LDS)

Ashtabula Co. Genealogical Society. BIBLE RECORDS. (Jefferson OH: the society, 1978?) (LDS,SLO)

Ashtabula Co. Genealogical Society. BIRTH REGISTRATION AND CORRECTION INDEX OF ASHTABULA COUNTY OHIO. (Jefferson OH: the society, 1980) 107p (SLO,LDS)

Ashtabula Co. Genealogical Society. CEMETERY INSCRIPTIONS, ASHTABULA COUNTY OHIO. (Jefferson OH: the society, 1977-) (LDS)

Ashtabula Co. Genealogical Society. INDEX, ATLAS OF ASHTABULA COUNTY OHIO BY D.J.LAKE. (Jefferson OH: the society, 1981) 38p (LDS)

Ashtabula Co. Genealogical Society. INDEX OF THE NATURALIZATION RECORDS OF ASHTABULA COUNTY OHIO, 1875-1906. (Jefferson OH: the society, 1982) 110p (SLO,LDS)

Ashtabula County Teachers Institute. CATALOGS OF INSTRUCTORS & STUDENTS AT INSTITUTE, JEFFERSON, ASHTABULA CO [1846/47, 1849/50, 1848, 1851 OHS]

Bell, Carol W. ABSTRACTS FROM BIOGRAPHIES IN HISTORY OF NORTH EASTERN OHIO by John S. Stewart, 1935. (Indianapolis: Ye Olde Genealogie Shoppe, 1983)

BIOGRAPHICAL HISTORY OF NORTHEASTERN OHIO EMBRACING THE COUNTIES OF ASHTABULA, GEAUGA AND LAKE. (Chicago: Lewis Pub Co., 1893) 1028p (LDS,OHS,DAR)(RPI)

BIOGRAPHICAL HISTORY OF NORTHEASTERN OHIO EMBRACING THE COUNTIES OF ASHTABULA, TRUMBULL AND MAHONING. (Chicago: Lewis Pub.Co.,1893) 735p (SLO,DAR,LDS)

Bowman, Viola A. CEMETERIES OF GENEVA OHIO; AND LOT DEEDS FOR FAMILIES BURIED THERE. 1974. 200p (DAR)

CITY/COUNTY DIRECTORIES: check holdings of OHS & local public library)

Clark, Rufus. EARLY HISTORY OF THE SOUTH RIDGE. (Jefferson OH: Ashtabula Co.Gen.Soc., 197?) 8,55p (LDS)

Daughters of American Colonists. EARLY CHURCH LIFE IN CHERRY VALLEY: EXTRACTS FROM THE RECORD BOOK, REGULAR BAPTIST CHURCH IN CHERRY VALLEY, ASHTABULA COUNTY, OHIO, FEBRUARY 13, 1830--JANUARY 12, 1878. 198?. 18p (SLO,LDS)

Daughters of the American Revolution. MARRIAGES, ASHTABULA COUNTY OHIO, 1853-1869. (South Charleston OH: author, 1985) 109p (OGS)

Daughters of the American Revolution. ASHTABULA COUNTY OHIO CEMETERY INSCRIPTIONS, 1800-1970. (WRHS,LDS,OHS,DAR)

Daughters of the American Revolution. CENSUS OF PIONEER WOMEN OF ASHTABULA COUNTY OHIO...BEFORE 1850. (Warren OH: author, 1955) 1v (LDS,DAR)

Daughters of the American Revolution. OBITUARIES OF ASHTABULA COUNTY OHIO, 1831-1869. 1972. 213p. (WRHS,DAR,LDS)

DIRECTORY OF ALL BUSINESS AND PROFESSIONAL MEN, ASHTABULA COUNTY OHIO (Conneaut OH: Watson & Dorman, 1895) (OHS)

GENEALOGICAL DATA RELATING TO WOMEN IN THE WESTERN RESERVE BEFORE 1840 (1850) (Cleveland: Centennial Commission, 1943) (LDS,WRHS)

Hall, Mary E. READING CEMETERIES IN ASHTABULA COUNTY OHIO. (SLO)

HISTORY OF ASHTABULA COUNTY - THEN AND NOW. (Jefferson OH: Ashtabula Co Chapter OGS, 1985) 655p (OGS,LDS)

Hixson, W.W. PLAT BOOK OF ASHTABULA COUNTY OHIO. (Rockford IL: author, nd) (OHS)

Holcomb, Everet C. A RECORD OF DEATHS, 1869-1937, KEPT BY EVERET C. HOLCOMB OF ASHTABULA COUNTY OHIO. (SLO,LDS)

Howells, Joseph A. PIONEER LIFE IN ASHTABULA COUNTY. (Columbus OH: np, 1927) 562p (LC)

INDEX TO BIOGRAPHICAL HISTORY OF NORTHEASTERN OHIO EMBRACING THE COUNTIES OF ASHTABULA, GEAUGA AND LAKE. (Chicago: Lewis Pub Co., 1893) 162p (LDS)

Lake, D.J. ATLAS OF ASHTABULA COUNTY, OHIO. (Philadelphia, author, 1874) 93p (OGS,OHS,SLO,LC)(RPI)

Large, Moina W. HISTORY OF ASHTABULA COUNTY, OHIO. (Topeka Kan: Historical Pub Co., 1924) 2v (LC,LDS,OHS)

McGiffert, J.N. HISTORY OF THE PRESBYTERIAN CHURCH OF ASHTABULA OHIO. (Ashtabula: James Reed & Son, 1876) 15p (LDS)

MANUAL OF THE FIRST PRESBYTERIAN CHURCH OF ASHTABULA OHIO, JUNE 1, 1869. [includes communicants] (LDS)

Nitchman, Paul E. BLACKS IN OHIO, 1880, IN THE COUNTIES OF ADAMS TO CARROLL, VOLUME 1. (Ft.Meade MD: author, 1986?) 178p

North Eastern Ohio Library Assn. A GUIDE TO LOCAL HISTORICAL MATERIALS IN THE LIBRARIES OF NORTHEASTERN OHIO. (Youngstown OH: author, 1977) 72p (Yo Pub Lib)

Peet, Stephen D. THE ASHTABULA DISASTER. 1877. (Reprint, Evansville IN: Unigraphic, 1976) 1v. (DAR)

REPORT OF THE SEMI-CENTENNIAL, SEVENTY-FIFTH AND CENTENNIAL ANNIVERSARIES OF THE SETTLEMENT OF WAYNE TOWNSHIP, ASHTABULA COUNTY OHIO, 1853,1878,1903. (Conneaut OH: Post Herald Press, 1906) 202p (DAR,LDS)

Sargent, M.P. PIONEER SKETCHES: SCENES AND INCIDENTS OF FORMER DAYS (Erie PA: Herald Pub Co., 1891) (SLO)

Simon, Bernice H. NAME INDEX FOR GENEALOGICAL AND FAMILY HISTORY OF EASTERN OHIO by E.Summers, 1903. (Chagrin Falls OH: author, 1973) 28p (Yo Pub Lib)

Stewart, John S. HISTORY OF NORTHEASTERN OHIO. (Indianapolis: Historical Pub Co., 1935) 3v. (SLO)

Summers, Ewing. GENEALOGICAL AND FAMILY HISTORY OF EASTERN OHIO ILLUSTRATED. (New York: Lewis Pub Co., 1903) (Yo Pub Lib, OHS)

Talcott, Albert L. HISTORICAL NOTES OF ASHTABULA. (Cleveland: W.A.Robertson, 1906) 19p (OHS)

Trucksis, Theresa. A GUIDE TO LOCAL HISTORICAL MATERIALS IN THE LIBRARIES OF NORTH-EASTERN OHIO. (Youngstown OH: NE Oh Libr.Assn., 1977) 72p (Yo Pub Lib)

Udell, Cornelius. CONDENSED HISTORY OF JEFFERSON, ASHTABULA COUNTY OHIO. (Jefferson OH: J.A.Howells, 1878) 116p (OHS)

Upton, Harriet T. HISTORY OF THE WESTERN RESERVE (Chicago: Lewis Pub Co., 1910) 3v (SLO)

WATSON'S ASHTABULA COUNTY DIRECTORY. (Conneaut OH: D.R.Watson, 18__) (LC)

Western Reserve Hist.Soc. INDEX TO THE MICROFILM EDITION OF GENEALOGICAL DATA RELATING TO WOMEN IN THE WESTERN RESERVE PRE 1840. (Cleveland: the society, 1976) 226p (OGS,WRHS)

Wickham, Gertrude V.W. MEMORIAL TO THE PIONEER WOMEN OF THE WESTERN RESERVE. (Cleveland: Cleveland Centennial Commission, 1896+) 2v, repr 1981 (SLO)

Williams, William W. HISTORY OF ASHTABULA COUNTY, OHIO. (Philadelphia: Williams Bros., 1878)(Reprint, Ashtabula OH: Ashtabula Co.Gen.Soc., 1982) 256p (LC,LDS,OHS,SLO,DAR)(RPI)

# ATHENS COUNTY

| | |
|---|---|
| CREATED: | 1805, from WASHINGTON COUNTY |
| COUNTY SEAT: | ATHENS 45701 |
| COURT HOUSE: | (no street address) ATHENS 45701 |
| LIBRARIES: | NELSONVILLE P.L., 95 W.WASHINGTON, NELSONVILLE 45764 (NL FOR ATHENS) |
| HISTORICAL SOCIETY: | ATHENS CO.H.S., BOX 423, ATHENS 45701 |
| GENEALOGICAL SOCIETY: | ATHENS CO CHAPTER OGS, PO BOX 423, ATHENS 45701 publication: BULLETIN |

ALEXANDER LOCAL GEN. & HIST. SOCIETY,
c/o MARY BOWMAN, 2565 PLEASANT HILL RD.,
ATHENS 45701
publication: ALGHS NEWSLETTER

HEALTH DEPARTMENT: 278 WEST UNION, ATHENS 45701
   (separate offices for Athens City & Nelsonville)

ARCHIVAL DISTRICT: OHIO UNIVERSITY, ATHENS
   (see published Guide to records)

LAND SURVEYS: OHIO COMPANY
   OHIO UNIVERSITY GRANT

BOUNDED BY: EAST: WASHINGTON CO. & WOOD CO., W.VA.
   NORTH: HOCKING, MORGAN & PERRY CO.
   WEST: HOCKING & VINTON CO.
   SOUTH: MEIGS CO.

TOWNSHIPS: Alexander, Ames, Athens, Bern, Canaan, Carthage, Dover, Lee, Lodi,
   Rome, Trimble, Troy, Waterloo, York.

## COURT RECORDS (LDS MICROFILM)

Auditor:
 Tax duplicates, 1816-1838.
 Soldiers' burial record, 1898-1912.

Children's Home:
 Register of inmates, 1882-1911.

County Home:
 Register of inmates, 1857-1928.

Court of Common Pleas:
 Common Pleas minutes, v1,3-9, 1815-1822, 1825-1854.
 Common Pleas general index, 1815-1857.
 Supreme Court minutes, 1838-1851.
 Supreme Court record, 1809-1837,1846-1860.
 Chancery record, 1837-1855.
 Common Pleas appearance dockets, v1-5, 1842-1854.
 Common Pleas record, v1-3, 1807-1812, 1816, 1819-1839.
 District Court record, 1852-1860.

Probate Court:
 Marriage records, 1817-1911.
 Wills, v1-8, 1814-1879.
 Guardians' docket, 1875-1892.
 Administrators' docket, 1842-1876.
 Executors' bonds & letters, 1857-1897.
 Probate record, v1-4, 1852-1888.
 Probate journal, v1-5, 1852-1881.
 Probate court journal, 1858-1878.
 General index to estates, 1800-1945, 1956-1966.
 Death records, v1-3, 1867-1908.
 Birth records, v1-6, 1867-1941.
 Birth record registration & corrections, 1941-1960.
 Naturalizations, 1858-1878.

Recorder:
 Deed records, v1-44, 1792-1876.
 Soldiers' discharge records, 1861-1916.

## OHIO HISTORICAL SOCIETY: (MICROFILM)

Children's Home:
 Register of inmates, 1882-1911.

County Home:
    Register of inmates, 1857-1928.
Clerk of Courts:
    Common Pleas minutes, v1,3-9, 1815-1822, 1825-1854.
    Common Pleas general index, 1815-1857.
    Supreme Court minutes, 1838-1851.
    Supreme Court record, 1809-1837,1846-1860.
    Chancery record, 1837-1855.
    Common Pleas appearance dockets, v1-5, 1842-1854.
    Common Pleas record, v1-3, 1807-1812, 1816, 1819-1839.
    District Court record, 1852-1860.
Probate Court:
    Naturalization record, 1880-1906.
Recorder:
    Military discharges, v1-3, 1861-1902.
Sheriff:
    Jail register, 1881-1900.
Miscellaneous:
    Marriages, by DAR, 1805-1865.
    Wills, by DAR, 1795-1845.
    Genealogical material, Daughters of Founders & Patriots

**CENSUS RECORDS  (OHS,SLO,OGS,LDS)**
1820-1880, 1900-1910; 1890 VETERANS; 1880,1900 SOUNDEX; 1910 MIRACODE

**AGRICULTURAL CENSUS SCHEDULES  (OHS,SLO-mic)**
1850,1860,1870,1880

**PRODUCTS OF INDUSTRY CENSUS SCHEDULE  (OHS,SLO-mic)**
1850,1870

**MORTALITY CENSUS SCHEDULES (OHS,SLO-mic)**
1860,1880

**NEWSPAPERS: [GUIDE TO OHIO NEWSPAPERS, 1793-1973]**
Albany, Amesville, Athens, Glouster, Nelsonville.

**TAX RECORDS (OHS & LDS)**
1806,1808,1810,1812-1814,1816-1838.

**GENEALOGICAL PERIODICAL ARTICLES**
Bell, Carol Willsey. OHIO GENEALOGICAL PERIODICAL INDEX: A COUNTY GUIDE (Youngstown
    OH:  author, 6th ed., 1987)

**PUBLISHED SOURCES:**
Athens Co Oh Pioneer Assn. MEMORIAL & HISTORY OF THE WESTERN LIBRARY ASSN. OF
    ATHENS COUNTY OHIO ILLUSTRATED 1797-1897 CENTENNIAL. (Reprint, Athens OH: Athens
    Co.Hist.Soc.,1985) 102p (OGS)
ATLAS AND PLAT BOOK, ATHENS COUNTY OHIO 1975. (Rockford IL:  Rockford Map Pub., 1975)
    38p (OGS)
AMES TWP., ATHENS CO OH. (Cincinnati:  1882) 25p (LC)
Beatty, Elizabeth & M.Stone. GETTING TO KNOW ATHENS COUNTY. (Athens OH: author, 1984)
    298p (OGS,LDS)
Berry, Ellen T. & David. EARLY OHIO SETTLERS: PURCHASERS OF LAND IN SOUTHEASTERN
    OHIO, 1800-1840. (Baltimore: Genealogical Pub.Co., 1984) 129p (OHS,SLO,OGS,DAR)

Bleigh, Mildred A. & M.A.Davis. ATHENS COUNTY, OHIO OBITUARIES: JAN.1, 1980 THRU DEC.31, 1985. (Nelsonville OH: authors, 1987) 468p (OGS)

Blower, James G. ATHENS COUNTY, TRIMBLE TOWNSHIP, OHIO. 1974 (SLO)

Bowman, Mary L. SOME TOMBSTONE INSCRIPTIONS OF SOUTHWEST ATHENS COUNTY, OHIO. (Athens OH: Alexander Local Gen.& Hist.Soc., c1986) (LDS)

Bowman, Mary & B.Schumacher. GENEALOGICAL RESEARCHERS' ANCESTOR SURNAME FILE OF ATHENS COUNTY OHIO. (Athens OH: Athens Co.Hist.Soc., 1986) 32p (OGS,LDS)

Burdette, Elizabeth Y. ATHENS COUNTY OHIO, THREE TOWNSHIPS: CARTHAGE, ROME, TROY, INCLUDING THE 1850 U.S.CENSUS AND FAMILY NOTES. 1973. 1v. (DAR,LDS)

Burdette, Elizabeth & Clinton. SOME CEMETERY INSCRIPTIONS IN COOLVILLE, OHIO. (Akron OH: Daughters of American Colonists, 1981) 57p (LDS)

Bush, Fred W. THE CENTENNIAL ATLAS OF ATHENS COUNTY OHIO. (Athens OH: Centennial Atlas Assn.,1905)(Reprint, Athens OH: Ohio University Press, 1975). 146p. (LDS,SLO,OHS,DAR)

CITY/COUNTY DIRECTORIES: check holdings of OHS & local public library.

Cranmer, G.L. HISTORY OF THE UPPER OHIO VALLEY. (Madison WI: Brant & Fuller, 1891) 2v. (OHS)

Daughters of the American Revolution. ATHENS COUNTY MARRIAGE RECORDS, 1805-1865. 1936. 200p (DAR)

Daughters of the American Revolution. EARLY WILLS OF ATHENS COUNTY 1800-1847. 1942. 16p (SLO,LDS,DAR)

Harris, Charles H. HARRIS HISTORY - COLLECTION OF TALES OF SOUTHEASTERN OHIO. (Athens OH: Athens Messenger, 1957) 329p (OHS,SLO)

Hibbard, Mrs. Peter. HISTORY OF ATHENS. 1936. 125p (DAR)

Hildreth, Samuel P. BIOGRAPHICAL AND HISTORICAL MEMOIRS OF THE EARLY PIONEER SET-TLERS OF OHIO. (Cincinnati: H.W.Darby & Co.,1852) (OHS,LDS,SLO)

Hill, Agnes C. HISTORY OF COOLVILLE, OHIO 1818-1968. 1982. 138p (OGS,SLO,LDS)

Hinshaw, William Wade. ENCYCLOPEDIA OF AMERICAN QUAKER GENEALOGY, VOL.IV, OHIO. (Baltimore MD: Genealogical Pub.Co., 1973) 1424p (SLO,OHS,LDS)

Historical Records Survey. INVENTORY OF THE COUNTY ARCHIVES OF OHIO, NO.5, ATHENS COUNTY. (Columbus OH: author, 1939) 275p. (LDS,OHS,DAR)

HISTORIES OF ATHENS, GALLIA, MEIGS AND VINTON COUNTIES OHIO: NEWSPAPER CLIP-PINGS FROM THE DYE COLLECTION. (SLO,LDS)

HISTORY OF CHAUNCEY, OHIO. (SLO)

HISTORY OF HOCKING VALLEY, OHIO (Chicago: Interstate Pub.Co., 1883) 1392p (SLO,LDS,DAR)

Hixson, W.W. PLAT BOOK OF ATHENS COUNTY OHIO. (Rockford IL: author, nd) (OHS)

Hoover, Thomas N. THE HISTORY OF OHIO UNIVERSITY. (Athens OH: 1954) 274p

Howard, Scotty & Loraine. OBITUARIES OF ATHENS COUNTIANS, OHIO AND THEIR FAMILIES, VOL.I-V. (Athens OH: authors, 1984) (OGS)

Howard, Scotty & Loraine. PASTOR'S IDEAL VEST-POCKET RECORD & RITUAL AND FUNERAL BOOK, L.F.MILLER, AMESVILLE OHIO, 1916-1950. (Athens OH: authors, 1984) 38p (OGS,LDS)

Howard, Scotty & Loraine. TRIMBLE TOWNSHIP CEMETERIES, ATHENS COUNTY OHIO, VOLS.I & II. (Athens OH: authors, 1983) 40p,74p (OGS,LDS)

IMPORTANT EVENTS IN THE HISTORY OF ATHENS COUNTY, OHIO, ARRANGED IN CHRONOLOGICAL ORDER. 17p (LDS)

Lake, D.J. ATLAS OF ATHENS COUNTY, OHIO. (Philadelphia: Titus, Simmons & Titus, 1875) Reprint 1974. (LDS,OHS,OGS,SLO)(RPI)

Lewis, Thomas W. SOUTHEASTERN OHIO AND THE MUSKINGUM VALLEY, 1788-1928: COVER-ING ATHENS, BELMONT, COSHOCTON, GUERNSEY, LICKING, MEIGS, MONROE, MORGAN, MUSKINGUM, NOBLE, PERRY AND WASHINGTON COUNTIES. (Chicago: S.J.Clarke Co.,1928) 3v. (SLO,DAR,OHS)

Martzolff, Clement L. A BRIEF HISTORY OF ATHENS COUNTY, OHIO. (Athens OH: author, 1916) 40p (LC,SLO,OHS)

Mattox, A.H. THE ATHENS HOMECOMING REUNION. 1904. 103p (DAR)

Maxwell, Fay. ATHENS COUNTY, TRIMBLE TOWNSHIP HISTORY INDEX TO JAMES BLOWER'S HISTORY REPRINT. (Columbus OH: Ohio Genealogy Center, c1973) 1v (LDS)

Nitchman, Paul E. BLACKS IN OHIO, 1880, IN THE COUNTIES OF ADAMS TO CARROLL, VOLUME 1. (Ft.Meade MD: author, 1986?) 178p

Ohio University. GUIDE TO LOCAL GOVERNMENT RECORDS AT OHIO UNIVERSITY. (Athens OH: OU Library, 1986) 61p.

Peters, William E. ATHENS COUNTY AND WHERE AND HOW TO FIND. (Athens OH: Lawhead Press, 1942) (LC)

Peters, William E. ATHENS COUNTY OHIO. (Athens OH: 1947) 296p (LC,LDS)

Peters, William E. A RIDE AROUND ATHENS COUNTY AND WHERE AND HOW TO FIND IT. (Athens OH: author, 1938.) 24p (OHS)

Rose, Anna. YESTERDAYS OF THE PLAINS. (Athens OH: Athens Co.Hist.Soc., 1981) 138P (lds)

Sayre, Herman A. A CENTURY OF METHODISM IN NELSONVILLE, OHIO. (Nelsonville OH: author, 1933) 57p (DAR)

Schumacher, Beverly & M.Fletcher. ATHENS COUNTY OHIO 1870 CENSUS INDEX. (Athens OH: Athens Co.Hist.Soc., 1984) 87p (OGS,LDS,SLO)

Schumacher, Beverly & M.Fletcher. ATHENS COUNTY, OHIO INDEX TO THE 1880 FEDERAL CENSUS Marvin Fletcher. (Athens OH: Athens Co.Hist.Soc., 1984) 85pp. (OGS,LDS)

Schumacher, Beverly. CLARK'S CHAPEL CEMETERY INSCRIPTIONS, ATHENS COUNTY, OHIO: CLARKS CHAPEL UNITED METHODIST CHURCH. (Canaan Twp. OH: the church, c1984) 64p (LDS,SLO)

Schumacher, Beverly. DEATH RECORDS OF HUGHES FUNERAL HOME, ATHENS OHIO. (Athens OH: Athens Ancestree, 1986) 171p (LDS)

Schumacher, Beverly & M.Fletcher. INDEX TO BULLETIN, ATHENS COUNTY HISTORICAL SOCIETY, VOLUMES 1-3. (Athens OH: Athens Co.Hist.Soc., 1982) 48p (OGS,LDS)

Schumacher, Beverly & M.Fletcher. INDEX TO THE ATLASES OF ATHENS COUNTY OHIO, 1875 & 1905. (Athens OH: Athens Co.Hist.Soc.,1980) (OGS,LDS,SLO)

Schumacher, Beverly & M.Fletcher. MARRIAGE RECORDS, 1805-1866 ATHENS COUNTY OHIO. (Athens OH: Athens Co.Hist.Soc., 1985) 275p (OGS,LDS)

Schumacher, Beverly & M.Fletcher. MARRIAGE RECORDS, 1881-1895, ATHENS COUNTY OHIO. (Athens OH: Athens Co.Hist.Soc., 1982) 177p (OGS,LDS)

Schumacher, Beverly & M.Fletcher. MARRIAGE RECORDS, 1865-1905, ATHENS COUNTY OHIO. (Athens OH: Athens Co.Hist.Soc., 1981-83) 3v (OGS,LDS)

Schumacher, Beverly & M.Fletcher. MARRIAGE RECORDS, 1906-1913, ATHENS COUNTY OHIO. (Athens OH: Athens Co.Hist.Soc., 1986) 122p (OGS,LDS)

Schumacher, Beverly & M.Fletcher. MARSHFIELD/NEW MARSHFIELD CEMETERY INSCRIPTIONS, ATHENS CO OHIO (Athens OH: Athens Co.Hist.Soc., 1981) 85p (OGS,LDS,SLO)

Schumacher, Beverly. CLARKS CHAPEL CEMETERY INSCRIPTIONS, ATHENS COUNTY OHIO. (Athens OH: Clarks Chapel United Methodist Church, 1984) 64p (OGS)

Schumacher, Beverly. INDEX - 1830 CENSUS, ATHENS COUNTY OHIO. (Athens OH: Athens Co.Hist.Soc., 1983) np (OGS,OHS)

Super, Charles W. A PIONEER COLLEGE AND ITS BACKGROUND - THE OHIO UNIVERSITY. (Salem MA: Newcomb & Gauss, 1924) 133p. (LDS)

Tipton, J.C. ATHENS COUNTY ILLUSTRATED: PROGRAM OF 100 YEARS, 1797-1897. (Athens OH: Athens Messenger, 1897) 94p (OHS,LDS)

TOMBSTONE INSCRIPTIONS, SOUTHWESTERN ATHENS COUNTY. 5v. (SLO,OHS)

Walker, Charles M. HISTORY OF ATHENS COUNTY, OHIO. (Cincinnati: R.Clarke & Co., 1869) 600p (LC,OHS,LDS,SLO,DAR)(RPI)

WATERLOO TOWNSHIP, JUSTICE'S CIVIL DOCKET. (OHS)

WATERLOO TOWNSHIP, TREASURER'S ACCOUNT. (OHS)

Whiteman, Jane. 1850 ATHENS COUNTY OHIO CENSUS. (Dresden TN: author, 1978) 250p (DAR)

Whiteman, Jane. ATHENS COUNTY OHIO CEMETERY RECORDS. (Tulsa OK: author, 1983) 94p (OGS,SLO)

Whiteman, Jane. INDEX TO WIVES' MAIDEN NAMES IN THE 1850 ATHENS COUNTY OHIO CENSUS. (Tulsa OK: author, c1982) 50p (LDS)

Whiteman, Jane. SURNAME INDEX TO 1883 INTERSTATE PUB. HISTORY OF HOCKING VALLEY OHIO (Tulsa OK: author, nd) 27p (LDS)

Whiteman, Jane. SURNAME INDEX TO CHARLES H. HARRIS'S 1957 HARRIS HISTORY.
Whiteman, Jane. SURNAME INDEX TO HISTORY OF HOCKING VALLEY, OHIO, 1883.  (Dresden TN: author, 1980) 28p (LDS)
Whiteman, Jane. SURNAME INDEX TO HISTORY OF THE UPPER OHIO VALLEY, Brant & Fuller, 1891.

# AUGLAIZE COUNTY

| | |
|---|---|
| CREATED: | 1848, FROM ALLEN & MERCER COUNTIES |
| COUNTY SEAT: | WAPAKONETA 45895 |
| COURT HOUSE: | 200 WILLIPIE ST., WAPAKONETA 45895 |
| PUBLIC LIBRARY: | 203 PERRY ST., WAPAKONETA 45895 |
| HISTORICAL SOCIETY: | AUGLAIZE CO. HS, c/o MRS.J.HUDSON, RT.1, NEW BREMEN 45869 |
| GENEALOGICAL SOCIETY: | AUGLAIZE CO. CHAPTER OGS, PO BOX 2021, WAPAKONETA 45895 publication: FALLEN TIMBERS ANCES-TREE |
| HEALTH DEPARTMENT: | PO BOX 59, WAPAKONETA 45895 (separate offices in Wapakoneta City & St.Marys) |
| ARCHIVAL DISTRICT: | WRIGHT STATE UNIVERSITY, DAYTON (see Leggett's Guide to records) |
| LAND SURVEYS: | CONGRESS LANDS, E & S OF 1ST PRIN.MERIDIAN CONGRESS LANDS, MIAMI RIVER SURVEY |
| BOUNDED BY: | EAST: HARDIN & LOGAN CO. NORTH: ALLEN & VAN WERT CO. WEST: MERCER CO. SOUTH: SHELBY CO. |
| TOWNSHIPS: | Clay, Duchouquet, German, Goshen, Jackson, Logan, Moulton, Noble, Pusheta, St.Marys, Salem, Union, Washington, Wayne. |

## COURT RECORDS (LDS MICROFILM)
Clerk of Courts:
General index and appearance docket, 1850-1858.
Chancery records, v1-2, 1848-1858.
Civil appearance docket, 1848-1858.
Civil minutes journal, v1-2, 1848-1857.
General index, 1848-1858.
Supreme Court record, v1, 1850-1884.
District Court record, 1852-1884.
County Home:
Record of inmates, 1889-1935
Probate Court:
Marriage records, v1-13, 1848-1926.
Marriage consents, 1906-1926.
General index, v1-5, n.d.
Guardian docket, v1-2, 1861-1925.
Civil docket, v1-4, 1853-1890.
Administration docket, v2-3, 1861-1899.
Will records, v2-6, 1864-1903.
Record of bonds & letters, 1848-1902.
Guardians' bonds & letters, 1862-1883.
Journal appointments, 1875-1892.
Inventories & sale bills, 1857-1872.
Guardians' inventories, 1879-1896.

Record of settlements, 1852-1866.
Guardians' settlements, 1869-1875.
Administrators' settlements, 1874-1878.
Journal of settlements, 1875-1883.
Ledger fee book, 1852-1860.
Final record v2, 1852-1857.
Birth records, 1867-1908.
Death records, 1867-1938.
Naturalization records, 1854-1905.
Recorder:
Deed records, v1-42, 1835-1881.
General index to deeds, v1-11, 1835-1967.
Soldiers' discharge record, 1861-1927
Miscellaneous:
Wapakoneta Union school records, 1874-1883.
McDonald family probate records.

## OHIO HISTORICAL SOCIETY: (MICROFILM)
Clerk of Courts:
Chancery records, v1-2, 1848-1858.
Civil appearance docket, 1848-1858.
Civil minutes journal, v1-2, 1848-1857.
General index, 1848-1858.
Supreme Court record, v1, 1850-1884.
District Court record, 1852-1884.
County Home:
Record of inmates, 1889-1935
Recorder:
Soldiers' discharge record, 1861-1927
Miscellaneous:
Cemetery records, by DAR

## CENSUS RECORDS  (OHS,SLO,OGS,LDS)
1850-1880, 1900-1910; 1890 VETERANS; 1880,1900 SOUNDEX; 1910 MIRACODE

## AGRICULTURAL CENSUS SCHEDULES  (OHS,SLO-mic)
1850,1860,1870,1880

## PRODUCTS OF INDUSTRY CENSUS SCHEDULE  (OHS,SLO-mic)
1850,1870

## MORTALITY CENSUS SCHEDULES (OHS,SLO-mic)
1860,1880

## NEWSPAPERS: [GUIDE TO OHIO NEWSPAPERS, 1793-1973]
Minster, New Bremen, St.Mary's, Wapakoneta.

## TAX RECORDS (OHS & LDS)
none listed; see parent counties.

## GENEALOGICAL PERIODICAL ARTICLES
Bell, Carol Willsey. OHIO GENEALOGICAL PERIODICAL INDEX: A COUNTY GUIDE (Youngstown
OH: author, 6th ed., 1987)

**PUBLISHED SOURCES:**
ATLASES OF AUGLAIZE COUNTY, OHIO. 1880,1898,1917. (OGS,SLO)
ATLAS OF AUGLAIZE COUNTY, OHIO. (Wapakoneta OH: Atlas Pub.Co.,1898)(Reprint, Evansville IN: Unigraphic, 1975) (OHS,SLO,LDS)
Auglaize Co. Hist.Soc. A HISTORY OF AUGLAIZE COUNTY OHIO. (New Bremen OH: the society, 1980) 496p (OGS,SLO)
Block, Virginia. CHURCH RECORDS, ST.PETER'S AND ST.PAUL'S ROMAN CATHOLIC CONGREGATION OF PUSHETA TOWNSHIP, AUGLAIZE COUNTY, FREYBURG, OHIO, 1833-1954. 1976. 31p (LDS)
CITY/COUNTY DIRECTORIES: check holdings of OHS & local public library.
County Auditor. QUADRENNIAL APPRAISEMENT, 1910, CLAY TOWNSHIP, AUGLAIZE COUNTY OHIO. 16p. (OGS)
Dahlke, Vivian E. THE OHIO GENEALOGICAL CEMETERY INSCRIPTION COPYING FOR AUGLAIZE COUNTY OHIO. (Cridersville OH: author, 1975) 1v (LDS)
Daughters of the American Revolution. INDEX, HISTORY OF WESTERN OHIO AND AUGLAIZE COUNTY...BY C.W.WILLIAMSON. 54,9p (LDS)
Daughters of the American Revolution. OHIO CEMETERY RECORDS, COUNTIES OF AUGLAIZE, HIGHLAND AND MERCER OHIO. 1953. 68p (LDS,SLO,DAR)
Fecher, Con J. ANCESTRAL PORTRAITS OF OHIO SETTLERS. (Dayton OH: Univ. of Dayton Press, 1980) 321p (OGS,LDS)
Haller, Stephen E. & P.Nolan. FIRST STOP FOR LOCAL HISTORY RESEARCH. A GUIDE TO COUNTY RECORDS PRESERVED AT WRIGHT STATE UNIVERSITY ARCHIVES AND SPECIAL COLLECTIONS. 1976. 21p.
Hixson, H.H. PLAT BOOK OF AUGLAIZE COUNTY OHIO. (Rockford IL: author, nd) (OHS)
Howland, H.G. ATLAS OF AUGLAIZE COUNTY, OHIO. (Philadelphia: Robert Sutton, 1880)(Reprint, Evansville IN: Unigraphic, 1975) 138p (LDS,OHS,OGS,SLO)(RPI)
Knapp, Horace S. HISTORY OF THE MAUMEE VALLEY. (Toledo OH: author, 1872) 685p. (DAR,OHS,SLO)
Leggett, Nancy G. & D.E.Smith. A GUIDE TO LOCAL GOVERNMENT RECORDS AND NEWSPAPERS PRESERVED AT THE DEPARTMENT OF ARCHIVES AND SPECIAL COLLECTIONS WRIGHT STATE UNIVERSITY. (Dayton OH: Wright State U., 1987)
McMurray, William J., ed. HISTORY OF AUGLAIZE COUNTY OHIO. (Indianapolis: Historical Pub.Co., 1923) 2v. (OHS,DAR,LDS,SLO)
Meyer, J.H. ATLAS AND HISTORY OF AUGLAIZE COUNTY OHIO. (Piqua OH: Magee Bros., 1917) (Reprint, Evansville IN: Unigraphic, 1975) 166p. (LDS,OHS)
NEW BREMEN SESQUICENTENNIAL REFLECTIONS: NEW BREMEN, OHIO, 1833-1983. (Defiance OH: Hubbard Co., 1983) 220p (LDS,SLO)
Nitchman, Paul E. BLACKS IN OHIO, 1880, IN THE COUNTIES OF ADAMS TO CARROLL, VOLUME 1. (Ft.Meade MD: author, 1986?) 178p
PORTRAIT & BIOGRAPHICAL RECORD OF AUGLAIZE, LOGAN & SHELBY COUNTIES, OHIO. (Chicago: Chapman Bros., 1892) 593p (LDS,LC,OHS,SLO,DAR)(RPI)
Simkins, Joshua D. EARLY HISTORY OF AUGLAIZE COUNTY. (St.Marys OH: Argus Printing Co., 1901.) 119p (OHS,LDS,LC,SLO,DAR)(RPI)
Sutton, Robert. HISTORY OF AUGLAIZE COUNTY, OHIO. (Wapakoneta OH: R. Sutton, 1880.) 206p. (LC,SLO)(RPI)
Williamson, C.W. HISTORY OF WESTERN OHIO AND AUGLAIZE COUNTY. (Columbus OH: W.M.Linn & Sons, 1905.) 860p (OHS,LDS,LC,SLO,DAR)(RPI)
Winter, Nevin O. HISTORY OF NORTHWEST OHIO. (Chicago: Lewis Pub.Co., 1917) 3v (SLO,OHS)

# BELMONT COUNTY

CREATED:              1801, FROM JEFFERSON & WASHINGTON COUNTIES
COUNTY SEAT:         ST.CLAIRSVILLE 43950
COURT HOUSE:         MAIN ST., ST.CLAIRSVILLE 43950

PUBLIC LIBRARY:                 108 WEST MAIN ST., ST.CLAIRSVILLE 43950
HISTORICAL SOCIETY:             BELMONT COUNTY HISTORICAL SOCIETY,
                                532 N.CHESTNUT ST., BARNESVILLE 43713
GENEALOGICAL SOCIETY:           BELMONT COUNTY CHAPTER OGS,
                                361 S.CHESTNUT ST., BARNESVILLE 43713
                                publication:  BELMONT COUNTY GENEALOGY NEWS
HEALTH DEPARTMENT:              68501 BANNOCK RD., ST.CLAIRSVILLE 43950
                                (separate offices in MARTINS FERRY,
                                ST.CLAIRSVILLE CITY & BELLAIRE)
PUBLIC LIBRARY:                 108 W.  MAIN ST., ST.CLAIRSVILLE 43950
ARCHIVAL DISTRICT:              OHIO UNIVERSITY, ATHENS
                                (see published Guide to records)
LAND SURVEYS:                   CONGRESS LANDS, FIRST SEVEN RANGES
BOUNDED BY:                     EAST:     MARSHALL & OHIO CO.  WEST VIRGINIA
                                NORTH:   JEFFERSON CO.
                                WEST:     GUERNSEY & NOBLE CO.
                                SOUTH:   MONROE CO.
TOWNSHIPS:                      Colerain, Flushing, Goshen, Kirkwood, Mead, Pease, Pultney, Rich-
                                land, St. Clairsville, Smith, Somerset, Union, Warren, Washington,
                                Wayne, Wheeling, York.

SPECIAL NOTE:                   A COURTHOUSE FIRE IN 1980 DESTROYED SOME RECORDS.

## COURT RECORDS (LDS MICROFILM)
Auditor:
    Tax records, 1816-1838.  [OHS]
Childrens Home:
    Register of admittance & indentures, 1880-1947.
Clerk of Courts:
    Law index, v1-2, 1808-1855.
    Chancery law index, 1824-1858.
    Chancery records, v1-11, 1824-1854.
    Common Pleas journal, vA-N, 1808-1851.
    Common Pleas appearance dockets, 1825-1853.
    Supreme Court index, 1808-1854.
    Supreme Court appearance docket, v1, 1804-1846.
    Supreme Court record, v5, 1846-1852.
    District Court index, c1852-1854.
    District Court record, 1852.
County Home:
    Record of infirmary patients, 1883-1930.
Probate Court:
    Marriage records, vA-25, 1803-1917.
    Marriage records & licenses by justice of peace, 1803-1866.
    Birth records, v1-5, 1867-1908.
    Birth records, transcribed, v1-3, 1867-1893.
    Birth records index, v1-3, 1908-1940.
    Death records, v1-4, 1867-1908.
    General index to estates, 1801-1935.
    Will records, vA-O, 1804-1887.
    Wills & administrations, vA-I, 1804-1863.
    Executors' bonds, v1-2, 1849-1867.
    Administration docket, 1879-1889.
    Administrators' bonds, v1-3, 1849-1868.
    Inventory record, vA-Z, 1832-1887.

Probate Journal, v1-16, 1852-1887.
Naturalizations, 1860-1906.
Recorder:
Deed index, vA-Z, 1811-1942.
Deed records, vA-75, 1800-1881.
Soldiers' discharge record, 1865-1919.
Miscellaneous:
Wills, 1827-1835, copied by DAR.
Crabapple Presbyterian Church, records, 1821-1888.
McMahons Creek United Presbyterian Church, minutes, 1828-1888.
St.Clairsville United Presbyterian Church, register, 1833-1886.
St.Clairsville United Presbyterian Church, treasurer recs, 1857-1892.
Uniontown United Presbyterian Church minutes, 1843-1882.

## OHIO HISTORICAL SOCIETY: (MICROFILM)
Childrens' Home:
Register, 1880-1947.
Clerk of Courts.
Chancery records, v1-11, 1824-1854.
Chancery law index, 1824-1858.
Clerk of courts writs, 1808-1819.
Common Pleas journal, vA-N, 1805-1853.
Common Pleas record, 1808-1858.
Common Pleas record & minute book, 1801-1806.
Common Pleas appearance docket, v5-13, 1826-1853.
Common Pleas writs, 1808-1819.
Law index, v1-2, 1808-1855.
Supreme Court appearance docket, v1, 1804-1846.
Supreme Court journal, 1820-1851.
Supreme Court record, 1808-1851.
Supreme Court index, v1, 1808-1851.
Record of blacks & mulattoes, 1809-1854.
District Court record, 1852.
County Home:
Record of inmates, 1883-1930.
Infirmary record, 1877-1891.
Commissioners:
Journals, 1804-1815, 1817-1824, 1833-1902.
Index to journals, 1861-1875,1889-1902.
Record of fund commission, 1839-1846.
Recorder:
Military discharges, v1, 1865-1919.
Sheriff:
Jail register, 1866-1922.

## CENSUS RECORDS  (OHS,SLO,OGS,LDS)
1820-1880, 1900-1910; 1890 VETERANS; 1880,1900 SOUNDEX; 1910 MIRACODE

## AGRICULTURAL CENSUS SCHEDULES  (OHS,SLO-mic)
1850,1860,1870,1880

## PRODUCTS OF INDUSTRY CENSUS SCHEDULE  (OHS,SLO-mic)
1850,1870

**MORTALITY CENSUS SCHEDULES (OHS,SLO-mic)**
1860,1880

**NEWSPAPERS: [GUIDE TO OHIO NEWSPAPERS, 1793-1973]**
Barnesville, Bellaire, Bridgeport, Clarksburg, Martins Ferry, St.Clairsville.

**TAX RECORDS (OHS & LDS)**
1806-1810, 1812-1814, 1816-1838.

**GENEALOGICAL PERIODICAL ARTICLES**
Bell, Carol Willsey. OHIO GENEALOGICAL PERIODICAL INDEX: A COUNTY GUIDE (Youngstown
    OH: author, 6th ed., 1987)

**PUBLISHED SOURCES:**
Bell, Carol W. OHIO LANDS: STEUBENVILLE LAND OFFICE RECORDS, 1800-1820. (Youngstown
    OH: author, 1983) 181p (OGS)
BELMONT COUNTY OHIO HISTORY OF FACTS AND TRADITIONS. (St.Clairsville OH: Extension
    Homemakers Council, 1965,1967,1969,1971,1973,1975,1979,1981,1983) (OGS)
Berry, Ellen T. & David. EARLY OHIO SETTLERS: PURCHASERS OF LAND IN SOUTHEASTERN
    OHIO, 1800-1840. (Baltimore: Genealogical Pub.Co., 1984) 129p (OHS,SLO,OGS,DAR)
Caldwell, John A. HISTORY OF BELMONT AND JEFFERSON COUNTIES, OHIO. (Wheeling WV:
    Historical Pub.Co., 1880)(Reprint, Evansville IN: Whipporwill Pubs., 1983) 611p
    (OHS,LC,SLO,LDS,DAR)(RPI)
CENTENNIAL SOUVENIR BARNESVILLE, OHIO. nd. 45p (SLO)
CENTURY AND A QUARTER, 1830-1955: FIRST UNITED PRESBYTERIAN CHURCH,
    ST.CLAIRSVILLE, OHIO. 1956. 26p. (DAR)
CITY/COUNTY DIRECTORIES: check holdings of OHS & local public library.
Cochran, Fred. THE 100TH ANNIVERSARY HISTORY OF THE SCOTCH RIDGE PRESBYTERIAN
    CHURCH: 1869-1969. 1969-1971. 1v. (DAR)
Daughters of the American Revolution. WILLS, DEEDS AND LAND RECORDS FROM CUYAHOGA
    PORTAGE CHAPTER DAR. (SLO)
DiThomas, Mary E. EARLY MARRIAGES IN BELMONT COUNTY OHIO. (OGS) FIRST UNITED
    METHODIST CHURCH, MARTINS FERRY OHIO, 160TH ANNIVERSARY CELEBRATION. 1975.
    20p (OGS)
Gallaher, Thomas M. SOME THINGS I REMEMBER. [RECOLLECTIONS OF EARLY LIFE IN BEL-
    LAIRE OHIO] (Youngstown OH: author, 1974) 46p (OGS)
Hanna, Charles A. OHIO VALLEY GENEALOGIES, RELATING TO FAMILIES IN HARRISON, BEL-
    MONT & JEFFERSON COUNTIES OHIO, AND WASHINGTON, WESTMORELAND AND
    FAYETTE COUNTIES PENNSYLVANIA. (New York: J.J.Little, 1900) 128p (LC,OHS,DAR)
Harriss, Helen L. MARRIAGE RECORDS OF SQUIRES ISAAC AND JOSEPH F. MAYES, 1811-1844
    & 1862-1887. (Pittsburgh PA: author, 1978) 258p (LDS)
Hibbard, Francis C. ORIGIN OF SOME EARLY BELMONT COUNTY NEWSPAPERS. (Columbus
    OH, np, 1946) (LC,OHS)
Hinshaw, William Wade. ENCYCLOPEDIA OF AMERICAN QUAKER GENEALOGY, VOL.IV, OHIO.
    (Baltimore: Genealogical Pub.Co., 1973) 1424p (SLO,OHS,LDS)
Historical Records Survey. INVENTORY OF THE COUNTY ARCHIVES OF OHIO NO.7, BELMONT
    COUNTY. (Columbus: author, 1942) 326p (LDS,OHS)
HISTORY OF THE UPPER OHIO VALLEY. [edition includes Belmont & Jefferson Cos., & WVA Pan-
    handle] (Madison WI: Brant & Fuller, 1890). 2v.(OHS,SLO,LDS)
Hixson, H.H. PLAT BOOK OF BELMONT COUNTY OHIO. (Rockford IL: author, nd) (OHS)
Lathrop, J.M. ATLAS OF BELMONT COUNTY, OHIO. 1888. (Barnesville OH: Belmont Co Chapter
    OGS, 1981) 79p. (OHS,OGS,SLO)(RPI)
Laughlin, Emma E. PLACE NAMES OF BELMONT COUNTY, OHIO. 1941. 41p (SLO)
Lewis, Thomas W. SOUTHEASTERN OHIO AND THE MUSKINGUM VALLEY, 1788-1928: COVER-
    ING ATHENS, BELMONT, COSHOCTON, GUERNSEY, LICKING, MEIGS, MONROE, MORGAN,

MUSKINGUM, NOBLE, PERRY AND WASHINGTON COUNTIES. (Chicago: S.J.Clarke Co.,1928) 3v. (SLO,DAR,OHS)

McDonald, Robert D. & Beulah. THE LITTLE HOME HISTORIES IN OUR EARLY HOMES, BELMONT COUNTY OHIO. (Aldan PA:, author, nd) 154p. (OHS)

McKelvey, A.T. CENTENNIAL HISTORY OF BELMONT COUNTY, OHIO. (Chicago: Biographical Pub Co., 1903) 833p (LDS,LC,OHS,SLO,DAR)(RPI)

Main, Carl, Mr. & Mrs. BELMONT COUNTY MARRIAGES 1803-1816. 17p (SLO)

Main, Carl, Mr. & Mrs. BELMONT COUNTY INSCRIPTIONS, WEGEE CEMETERY, MEAD TOWNSHIP. (SLO)

Nitchman, Paul E. BLACKS IN OHIO, 1880, IN THE COUNTIES OF ADAMS TO CARROLL, VOLUME 1. (Ft.Meade MD: author, 1986?) 178p

Ohio University. GUIDE TO LOCAL GOVERNMENT RECORDS AT OHIO UNIVERSITY. (Athens OH: OU Library, 1986) 61p.

Ochsenbein, Irene & C.F.Fedorchak. BELMONT COUNTY BEFORE 1830. (Bridgeport OH: author, 1977) 235p (SLO,OHS,LDS)

Powell, Esther W. TOMBSTONE INSCRIPTIONS AND FAMILY RECORDS OF BELMONT COUNTY OHIO. (Akron OH: author, 1969) 326p (OGS,OHS,LDS,DAR,SLO)

Pruden, M.M. PRUDEN'S COMBINED BUSINESS DIRECTORY AND GAZETTEER. (Charleston WV: Pruden Pub.Co., 1900) 353p (LDS)

Schooley, George A., ed. THE JOURNAL OF DR. WILLIAM SCHOOLEY, PIONEER PHYSICIAN, QUAKER MINISTER...1794-1860, SOMERTON, BELMONT COUNTY OHIO. (Baltimore: Gateway Press, 1977) 261p (OHS)

Selby, Robert E. BELMONT COUNTY OHIO MARRIAGE RECORDS, 1801-1821. (Kokomo IN: Selby Pub., c1983) 53p (LDS)

Sheppard, Dempsey O. THE STORY OF BARNESVILLE OHIO 1808-1940. (Columbus: F.J.Heer Printing, 1942) 375p (LDS)

SUNSET HEIGHTS BICENTENNIAL HISTORY: 200th ANNIVERSARY OF INDEPENDENCE, 1776-1976.(Bridgeport OH: the committee, 1976) 149p (SLO,DAR)

THOSE WERE THE DAYS--SMITH TOWNSHIP 1819-1976. 1976. (SLO)

WIGGINS AND WEAVER'S OHIO RIVER DIRECTORY FOR 1871-1872. (Cleveland OH: authors, 1872) 419p (LDS)

Yarnell, Bruce A. SOMERTON AREA HERITAGE: HISTORY OF SOMERSET & WAYNE TWPS., BELMONT CO OH. (Somerton OH: author, 1986) 654p (OGS,SLO,OHS)

# BROWN COUNTY

CREATED:                    1818, FROM ADAMS & CLERMONT COUNTIES
COUNTY SEAT:                GEORGETOWN 45121
COURT HOUSE:               MAIN ST., GEORGETOWN 45121
LIBRARY:                    200 W. GRANT AVE., GEORGETOWN 45121
HISTORICAL SOCIETY:        PO BOX 238, GEORGETOWN 45121
GENEALOGICAL SOCIETY:      BROWN CO. CHAPTER OGS,
                           PO BOX 83, GEORGETOWN 45121
                           publication: ON THE TRAIL
HEALTH DEPARTMENT:         204-D E.CHERRY ST., GEORGETOWN 45121
ARCHIVAL DISTRICT:         UNIVERSITY OF CINCINNATI, CINCINNATI
LAND SURVEYS:              VIRGINIA MILITARY DISTRICT
BOUNDED BY:                EAST:    ADAMS & HIGHLAND CO.
                           NORTH:   CLINTON & HIGHLAND CO.
                           WEST:    CLERMONT CO.
                           SOUTH:   BRACKEN & MASON CO., KENTUCKY
TOWNSHIPS:                 Byrd, Clark, Eagle, Franklin, Green, Huntington, Jackson, Jefferson,
                           Lewis, Perry, Pike, Pleasant, Scott, Sterling, Union, Washington.

**SPECIAL NOTE:**              A COURTHOUSE FIRE IN 1977 DESTROYED SOME RECORDS.

**COURT RECORDS (LDS MICROFILM)**
Auditor:
   Tax records, 1819-1838. [OHS]
Childrens Home:
   Record of indentures, 1886-1921.
Clerk of Courts:
   Common Pleas partition records, division of land, 1914-1916.
   Appearance dockets, v1-4, 1821-1854.
   Chancery records, v1-11, 1820-1854.
   Civil minutes journals, v1,3-11,14, 1818-1850.
   Supreme Court chancery records, vA,1-3, 1821-1856.
   Naturalization records, v1, 1833-1834.
   Law records, v1-3, 1818-1826.
Probate Court:
   Marriage records, vA-31, 1818-1939.
   Marriage index, v1-3, 1818-1939.
   Will records & index, v1-12, 1817-1902.
   Death records & index, 1867-1909.
   Birth records, v1-3, 1867-1909.
   Birth records, delayed registration, v1-5, dates vary.
   Administrators' bonds, 1852-1886.
   Naturalization records, 1856-1906.
   Administrators record, v1, 1852-1853.
   Record of bonds, 1852-1857.
   Bonds & letters, 1862-1871.
   General index to files, 1820-1952.
   Administration docket v1, 1882-1887.
   Civil docket, v1-5, 1853-1888.
   Guardians' docket, v1, 1882-1896.
   Index to probate journals, v1-6, 1852-1867.
   Probate journals, v1-18, 1858-1885.
Recorder:
   General index to deeds, v1-8, 1818-1902.
   Deed records, 1818-1916.
   Soldiers' discharge, 1864-1899.
Miscellaneous:
   New Hope Second Creek Baptist Church, records, 1836-1881.
   Cemetery records, by LDS Church.
   Misc. Cemeteries, DAR collection, State Library of Ohio.

**OHIO HISTORICAL SOCIETY: (MICROFILM)**
Auditor:
   Enumeration of school-aged youth, 1829-1887, scattered.
Childrens' Home:
   Record of indentures, v1, 1886-1921.
   Inmates, 1885-1924.
   Journal, 1885-1935.
Clerk of Courts:
   Common Pleas appearance docket, 1821-1854.
   Chancery records, v1-3,5-11, 1820-1831, 1837-1854.
   Civil minutes journal, v1,3-4,6-11,14, 1818-1820,1823-1827,1830-1842,1846-1850.
   Naturalization record, 1833-1834.
   Supreme Court Chancery record, 1821-1856.

Supreme Court journal, 1819-1841.
District Court record, 1852-1856.
Index to law record, 1838-1839.
Law record, 1818-1854.
Abstract of votes, 1881-1887.
Quadrennial enumeration, 1887,1891,1903.
Commissioners:
Journal, 1843-1904
Index to journals, 1884-1887.
Recorder:
Soldiers' discharge record, 1864-1899.
Sheriff:
Jail register, 1909-1927.
Miscellaneous:
Marriages, 1818-1865, by DAR.
Cemeteries, by DAR.

**CENSUS RECORDS (OHS,SLO,OGS,LDS)**
1820-1880, 1900-1910; 1890 VETERANS; 1880,1900 SOUNDEX; 1910 MIRACODE

**AGRICULTURAL CENSUS SCHEDULES (OHS,SLO-mic)**
1850,1860,1870,1880

**PRODUCTS OF INDUSTRY CENSUS SCHEDULE (OHS,SLO-mic)**
1850

**MORTALITY CENSUS SCHEDULES (OHS,SLO-mic)**
1860,1880

**NEWSPAPERS: [GUIDE TO OHIO NEWSPAPERS, 1793-1973]**
Aberdeen, Feesburg, Georgetown, Higginsport, Levanna, Ripley.

**TAX RECORDS (OHS & LDS)**
1819-1838.

**GENEALOGICAL PERIODICAL ARTICLES**
Bell, Carol Willsey. OHIO GENEALOGICAL PERIODICAL INDEX: A COUNTY GUIDE (Youngstown
OH: author, 6th ed., 1987)

**PUBLISHED SOURCES:**
Brown Co. Chapter OGS. ABSTRACTS OF NATURALIZATIONS RECORDED IN BROWN COUN-
TY OHIO 1818-1926. (Georgetown: the society, 1984) 98p (OGS,LDS)
Brown Co. Chapter OGS. CEMETERY INSCRIPTIONS OF BROWN CO OHIO, BOOK I. (Georgetown
OH: the society, 1981) 187p (OGS)
Brown Co. Chapter OGS. NATURALIZATION CHRONOLOGICAL INDEX, BROWN COUNTY
OHIO, 1818-1906. (Georgetown OH: the society, nd) 27p (LDS)
Brown Co. Chapter OGS. REFERENCE GUIDE TO RESEARCH SOURCES OF BROWN CO OHIO
(Georgetown OH: the society, 1981) 48p (OGS,LDS,SLO)
Brown County Historical Society.HISTORY OF BROWN COUNTY. (Ripley OH: the society, 1968) 80p.
(OHS)
BROWN COUNTY OHIO HISTORICAL HIGHLIGHTS. (SLO)
CEMETERIES IN BROWN COUNTY OHIO. 1941. 22p (OHS,DAR)
CITY/COUNTY DIRECTORIES: check holdings of OHS & local public library.
Colletta, Lillian. INDEX TO WILLS OF BROWN COUNTY OHIO, 1818-1910. (Greencastle PA: author,
1965) 28p (SLO,LDS,OHS,DAR)

Colletta, Lillian & L.Puckett. TOMBSTONE INSCRIPTIONS OF BROWN COUNTY OHIO. (Greencastle PA: author, 1969) 2v. (SLO,OHS,LDS,DAR)

Craig, Robert D. BROWN COUNTY OHIO CEMETERIES, 2v in 1 (SLO,LDS,OHS)

Daughters of the American Revolution. EARLY MARRIAGE RECORDS, 1818-1865, BROWN COUNTY OHIO. 3v in 2. (SLO,LDS,DAR)

Daughters of the American Revolution. GENEALOGICAL RECORDS, GEORGETOWN, BROWN COUNTY OHIO. 1954. 27p. (DAR)

Daughters of the American Revolution. SHORT HISTORY OF NEW HARMONY CHURCH AND VICINITY. (SLO)

Daughters of the American Revolution. TOMBSTONE INSCRIPTIONS BROWN COUNTY OHIO. 1964. 112p. (DAR,LDS,SLO)

Donaldson, Patricia. BROWN COUNTY OHIO MARRIAGE RECORDS 1818-1850. (Georgetown OH: author, 1986) 203p (OGS,LDS)

Donaldson, Patricia. BROWN COUNTY COURT RECORDS, SERIES I, 1818-1850. (Georgetown OH: author, 1980) 79p (OGS,SLO)

Helton, Mrs. Walter. BROWN COUNTY OHIO CEMETERY RECORDS. (Corbin KY: author, 197?) 108p (LDS)

Historical Records Survey. INVENTORY OF THE COUNTY ARCHIVES OF OHIO NO.8, BROWN COUNTY. (Columbus: author, 1938) 204p. (OHS,LDS,DAR)

HISTORY OF BROWN COUNTY, OHIO. (Chicago: W.H.Beers & Co., 1883) 703p (LDS,OHS,LC,SLO,DAR)(RPI)

HISTORY OF FAMILIAR SURNAMES (NEWS CLIPPINGS). (McKeesport PA: Fact Bureau, 1971) (LDS)

Hixson, W.W. PLAT BOOK OF BROWN COUNTY OHIO. (Rockford IL: author, nd) (OHS)

Lake, D.J. ATLAS OF BROWN COUNTY OHIO. (Philadelphia: Lake, Griffing & Stevenson, 1876) 80p.(OHS,SLO,LC) (RPI)

MARRIAGES PERFORMED BY SQUIRE THOMAS SHELDON, ABERDEEN, OHIO, 1822-1955 (SLO)

News Democrat, Georgetown. BROWN COUNTY TO DATE: HISTORICAL, BIOGRAPHICAL SOUVENIR. (Georgetown OH: author, 1912) 28p (OHS)

Nitchman, Paul E. BLACKS IN OHIO, 1880, IN THE COUNTIES OF ADAMS TO CARROLL, VOLUME 1. (Ft.Meade MD: author, 1986?) 178p

RIPLEY, OHIO: ITS HISTORY AND FAMILIES. 1965. 235p (SLO,LDS)

Stivers, Eliese. RIPLEY, OHIO: ITS HISTORY AND FAMILIES. 1965. 235p. (DAR) Thompson, Carl N. HISTORICAL COLLECTIONS OF BROWN COUNTY OHIO. (Ripley OH: author, 1969) 1340p (SLO,LDS,OHS,DAR)

Thompson, Carl N. TREASURES OF PISGAH & LEVANNA OHIO. (Greencastle PA: L.F.Colletta, 1966) 398p (DAR,OGS,LDS)

U.S.Grant Memorial Centenary Assn. CENTENARY CELEBRATION COMMEMORATING THE BIRTH OF GENERAL U.S.GRANT, OFFICIAL PROGRAM AND SOUVENIR BOOK, 1822-1922 (Cincinnati: Court Index, 1922) 66p (LDS)

WIGGINS AND WEAVER'S OHIO RIVER DIRECTORY FOR 1871-1872. (Cleveland OH: authors, 1872) 419p (LDS)

Williams, Byron. HISTORY OF CLERMONT & BROWN COUNTIES OHIO (Milford OH: Hobart Pub Co., 1913) 2v (LC,LDS,OHS,DAR)

Wilson, Linda. CEMETERY INSCRIPTIONS OF BROWN COUNTY OHIO. BOOK I. (Georgetown OH: author, c1977) (LDS,SLO)

# BUTLER COUNTY

| | |
|---|---|
| CREATED: | 1803 FROM HAMILTON COUNTY |
| COUNTY SEAT: | HAMILTON 45011 |
| COURT HOUSE: | 2ND & HIGH ST., HAMILTON 45011 |
| LIBRARY: | 300 N. 3RD ST., HAMILTON 45011 |
| HISTORICAL SOCIETY: | 327 N.2ND ST., HAMILTON 45011 |

| | |
|---|---|
| GENEALOGICAL SOCIETY: | BUTLER CO. CHAPTER OGS,<br>PO BOX 2011, MIDDLETOWN 45044<br>publication: PATHWAYS |
| HEALTH DEPARTMENT: | ADM.CENTER, 130 HIGH ST., HAMILTON 45011<br>(separate offices in Hamilton City, Fairfield, Oxford,<br>Trenton, Middletown) |
| ARCHIVAL DISTRICT: | UNIVERSITY OF CINCINNATI, CINCINNATI |
| LAND SURVEYS: | CONGRESS LANDS, MIAMI RIVER SURVEY<br>CONGRESS LANDS, BETWEEN THE MIAMI RIVER SURVEY<br>SYMMES PURCHASE<br>MIAMI UNIVERSITY GRANT |
| BOUNDED BY: | EAST:      WARREN CO.<br>NORTH:   MONTGOMERY & PREBLE CO.<br>WEST:     FRANKLIN & UNION CO.  INDIANA<br>SOUTH:   HAMILTON CO. |
| TOWNSHIPS: | Fairfield, Hanover, Lemon, Liberty, Madison, Milford, Morgan,<br>Oxford, Reily, Ross, St.Clair, Union, Wayne |

## COURT RECORDS (LDS MICROFILM)
Assessor:
Returns of births & deaths, 1856-1857.
Auditor:
Tax duplicates, 1816-1838.
Clerk of Courts:
Common Pleas miscellaneous court records, v1-28, 1836-1939.
Court journals, v1-35, 1852-1916.
Common Pleas record, v1-23, 1803-1848.
Judgments & proceedings, criminal cases, v3, 1824-1835.
Probate Court:
General index to decedents & estates, v1-2, 1851-1929.
Probate record, v1-21, 1876-1939.
Probate minutes, v1-5, 1852-1883.
Probate journal, v6-30, 1883-1916.
Marriage records, v1-30, 1803-1930.
Index to marriage records, v1-4, 1803-1937.
Will records, v1-12, 1851-1912.
Death records, 1856-1857, 1867-1908.
Birth records, 1856-1857, 1867-1908.
Registered births, v5-11, 1950-1961.
Guardian inventory, 1867-1951.
Guardianship, 1951-1960.
Testamentary records, 1852-1884.
Recorder:
Deed index, v1-3, 1803-1863.
Deeds, vA-Z,1-66, 1803-1876.
Miscellaneous:
Fairfield Meeting, Society of Friends, records, 1807-1941.
Oxford First Presby. Church, session records, 1850-1869.
Oxford United Presby. Church, minutes, 1851-1917.
Misc. cemetery records, DAR collection, State Library of Ohio.

## OHIO HISTORICAL SOCIETY: (MICROFILM)
Commissioners:
Index to journals, 1804-1900.
Journals, 1804-1901.

County Home:
  Infirmary record, 1880-1913.
Recorder:
  Deed records, vA-Z,1-66, 1803-1876.
  Index to deeds, v1-3, 1803-1876.
Miscellaneous:
  Old records & surveys, 1803-1855.
  Cemetery records, wills & marriages, 1803-1813.
  Marriage records, 1835-1847, by DAR.
  Cemetery & church records, by DAR.

**MANUSCRIPTS:**
Collection of account books, 1838-1841. (WRHS)

**CENSUS RECORDS (OHS,SLO,OGS,LDS)**
1820-1880, 1900-1910; 1890 VETERANS; 1880,1900 SOUNDEX; 1910 MIRACODE

**AGRICULTURAL CENSUS SCHEDULES (OHS,SLO-mic)**
1850,1860,1870,1880

**PRODUCTS OF INDUSTRY CENSUS SCHEDULE (OHS,SLO-mic)**
1850,1870

**MORTALITY CENSUS SCHEDULES (OHS,SLO-mic)**
1860,1880

**NEWSPAPERS: (GUIDE TO OHIO NEWSPAPERS, 1793-1973)**
Fairfield, Hamilton, Middletown, Oxford, Rossford.

**TAX RECORDS (OHS & LDS)**
1806-1807,1809-1810,1812-1813,1816-1838.

**GENEALOGICAL PERIODICAL ARTICLES**
Bell, Carol Willsey. OHIO GENEALOGICAL PERIODICAL INDEX: A COUNTY GUIDE (Youngstown
  OH: author, 6th ed., 1987)

**PUBLISHED SOURCES:**
1875 BICENTENNIAL ATLAS, BUTLER COUNTY [OHIO]. (Hamilton OH: Journal News, 1875)
  (LDS,SLO)
Bartlow, Bert S. CENTENNIAL HISTORY OF BUTLER COUNTY, OHIO. (np: B.F.BOWEN & Co.,
  1905) 989p (OHS,LC,SLO,DAR,LDS)(RPI)
Bartlow, Bert S. HISTORY OF PIONEER ASSOCIATION. (SLO)
Berry, Ellen T. & David A. EARLY OHIO SETTLERS: PURCHASERS OF LAND IN SOUTHWESTERN
  OHIO, 1800-1840. (Baltimore: Genealogical Pub.Co., 1986) 372p (OGS,SLO,OHS)
Blount, James. THE MILITARY HISTORY OF BUTLER COUNTY. (Hamilton OH: author, 1971) 44p.
  (OHS)
Brien, Lindsay D. CEMETERY RECORDS, PARTS OF BUTLER, GREEN & PREBLE COUNTY. [MIAMI
  VALLEY RECORDS, VOL.6] nd, 155p. (LDS)
Brien, Lindsay D. MIAMI VALLEY CEMETERY RECORDS (MIAMI VALLEY RECORDS VOL.7)
  (Hamilton OH: author, nd) (LDS)
Brien, Lindsay D. MARRIAGES: BUTLER, GREENE, MIAMI, PREBLE & WARREN COUNTIES OHIO
  [MIAMI VALLEY RECORDS, VOL.8] nd, 227p. (LDS)
BUTLER COUNTY ATLAS AND PICTORIAL REVIEW. (Hamilton OH: Republican Pub Co.,1914)
  112p (LC)

Butler Co.Chapter OGS. 1807 CENSUS BUTLER COUNTY. (Middletown OH: the society, 1988?) (OGS)

Butler Co.Chapter OGS. BUTLER COUNTY 1880 CENSUS (INDEX) (Middletown OH: the society, 1988?) 220p (OGS)

Butler Co.Chapter OGS. AMANDA CEMETERY, LEMON TOWNSHIP, BUTLER COUNTY OHIO. (Middletown OH: the society, 1985) 6p (OGS)

Butler Co.Chapter OGS. CALVARY CEMETERY GRAVE INSCRIPTIONS. (Middletown OH: the society, 1988?) 50p (OGS)

Butler Co.Chapter OGS. INDEX OF THE 1880 CENSUS OF BUTLER COUNTY. (Middletown OH: the society, 1988?) (OGS)

Campbell, James E. BUTLER COUNTY IN THE CIVIL WAR. 1915. 15p (LC,SLO,OHS)

Chidlaw, B.W. AN HISTORICAL SKETCH OF PADDY'S RUN, BUTLER COUNTY, OHIO, DELIVERED JULY 30, 1876. (LDS)

CITY/COUNTY DIRECTORIES: check holdings of OHS & local public library.

Cone, Stephen D. BIOGRAPHICAL AND HISTORICAL SKETCHES: A NARRATIVE OF HAMILTON AND ITS RESIDENTS, FROM 1792 TO 1896. (Hamilton OH: Republican Pub.Co., 1896-1901) 2v (SLO,DAR)(RPI)

Craig, Robert D. BUTLER COUNTY MARRIAGES, 1803-1823.(Cincinnati: author, 1964) 2v in 1. (SLO,LDS,OHS)

Craig, Robert D. BUTLER COUNTY OHIO BIBLE RECORDS. c1967. 18p. (LDS,OHS)

Crout, George C. MIDDLETOWN, U.S.A.: ALL-AMERICA CITY. (Middletown OH: Perry Printing, 1960) 160p (LDS)

Cullen, Avis W. 150-YEAR HISTORY OF OXFORD GOVERNMENT 1830-1980: THE PRESIDENTS, THE MAYORS AND THOSE WHO SERVED WITH THEM [and] HISTORY OF OXFORD VOLUNTEER FIRE DEPARTMENT. (Oxford OH: Smith Library of Regional History, 1984) 154p

Daughters of the American Revolution. BUTLER COUNTY OHIO CEMETERY RECORDS, WILLS AND MARRIAGE RECORDS. (SLO)

Daughters of the American Revolution. BUTLER COUNTY EARLY MARRIAGE RECORDS: 1803-1817. 1938. 200p. (DAR,LDS,SLO)

Daughters of the American Revolution. BUTLER COUNTY MARRIAGE RECORDS, 1808-1847. 3v (DAR)

Daughters of the American Revolution. EARLY MARRIAGE RECORDS OF BUTLER COUNTY OHIO, VOLUME 3, 1835-1847. (SLO,LDS)

Daughters of the American Revolution. EARLY VITAL RECORDS OF OHIO [WILLS OF BUTLER, FULTON & LAKE COUNTIES OHIO]. 1948. 38p. (DAR,LDS)

Everts, L.H. COMINATION ATLAS MAP OF BUTLER COUNTY, OHIO. (Philadelphia: author, 1875) 147p (OHS,OGS)

Gilbert, Audrey & Rose Shilt. BUTLER COUNTY OHIO 1850 CENSUS. (West Alexander OH: author, c1982) (OGS)

Havighurst, Walter. THE MIAMI YEARS 1809-1969. (Oxford OH: Miami University, 1968) 332p. (OGS)

Heiser, Alta H. HAMILTON IN THE MAKING. (Oxford OH: Mississippi Valley Press, 1941) 402p (LDS)

Heiss, Willard. CENSUS OF 1807, BUTLER COUNTY OHIO. (Knightstown IN: Eastern Pub Co., nd) 23p (OGS,LDS,OHS,SLO)

HISTORY & BIOGRAPHICAL CYCLOPEDIA OF BUTLER COUNTY, OHIO. (Cincinnati OH: Western Biographical Pub.Co., 1882) 666p (OHS,LDS,LC,DAR,SLO)(RPI)

Hudson, Thelma. INDEX TO THE 1882 HISTORY OF BUTLER COUNTY OHIO. (Lebanon OH: author, 1984) 39p (OGS)

Jenkins, Perry W. JENKINS' OHIO AND INDIANA CEMETERY RECORDS. 1940. 39p. (LDS)

Lewis, Lester L. LOST CEMETERY IN THE WOODS, ROSS, OHIO. 1963? (LDS)

Lyons, Margaret & Richard. AMANDA CEMETERY RECORD, LEMON TOWNSHIP, BUTLER COUNTY OHIO. nd (OGS)

MacClean, J.P. THE MOUND BUILDERS...OF BUTLER COUNTY OHIO. (Cincinnati: R.Clarke & Co., 1885) 233p (LDS)

McBride, James. PIONEER BIOGRAPHY: SKETCHES OF SOME OF THE EARLY SETTLERS IN BUT-
LER COUNTY OHIO. (Cincinnati: R.Clarke, 1869-1871) 2v  (LDS,SLO,DAR) (RPI)

McClung, David W. THE CENTENNIAL ANNIVERSARY OF THE CITY OF HAMILTON OHIO: SEP-
TEMBER 17-19,1891. (Hamilton OH: the committee, 1892) 322p (DAR,LDS)

McHenry, Chris. SYMMES PURCHASE RECORDS, 1787-1800. [BUTLER,HAMILTON & WARREN
CO] (Lawrenceburg IN: author, 1979) 106p (OGS,LDS)

Mallory, Henry. GEMS OF THOUGHT AND CHARACTER SKETCHES: A COLLECTION OF PER-
SONAL REMINISCENCES. (Hamilton OH: Republican Pub., 1893) 256p (LDS)

MEMOIRS OF THE MIAMI VALLEY OHIO. (Chicago: Robert O.Law Co.,1919) 3v (OHS)

MEMORIAL RECORD OF BUTLER COUNTY, OHIO. (Chicago, Record Pub.Co., 1894) 447p
(LDS,LC,SLO,DAR)(RPI)

MIDDLETOWN DIRECTORY OF HOUSEHOLDERS 1930-31. (Cincinnati: Williams Directory Co.,
1930-31) (LDS)

Naegele, H.W. HISTORY OF THE LIFE AND WORK OF THE METHODIST PROTESTANT CHURCH
OF MIDDLETOWN OHIO: COMMEMORATING ITS DIAMOND JUBILEE, 1855-1925. (Middletown OH: the church, 1925) 174p (LDS)

Nitchman, Paul E. BLACKS IN OHIO, 1880, IN THE COUNTIES OF ADAMS TO CARROLL, VOLUME
1. (Ft.Meade MD: author, 1986?) 178p

Porter, Thomas. HISTORY OF THE PRESBYTERIAN CHURCH OF OXFORD, 1818-1825. 1900. (Oxford OH: author, 1902) 212p. (LDS)

Republican Publishing Co. BUTLER COUNTY ATLAS AND PICTORIAL REVIEW. (Hamilton OH:
author, 1914) 112p. (OHS)

Rerick Bros. COUNTY OF BUTLER, OHIO: AN IMPERIAL ATLAS AND ART FOLIO. (Reprint,
Knightstown IN: Bookmark, 1979) 96p (LDS)

Ridlen, Colleen. BUTLER COUNTY OHIO MARRIAGES, 1803-1812. (Indianapolis IN: The Researchers, 198?) 25p (LDS)

SESQUICENTENNIAL--MONROE, OHIO, 1817-1967. (Monroe OH: History Committee, 1967) 53p
(LDS)

Shewalter, Virginia. A HISTORY OF UNION TOWNSHIP, BUTLER COUNTY OHIO. (Bicentennial
Committee, 1979) 148p (DAR)

Skinner, Jane K. CEMETERY RECORDS OF BUTLER COUNTY OHIO. 1949. 37p. (DAR)

Skinner, Jane K. MARRIAGE RECORDS OF BUTLER COUNTY OHIO, 1803-1839. (Oxford OH: Miami
University, 1950) 80p. (LDS)

Skinner, Jane K. OLD GRAVEYARD RECORDS, BUTLER COUNTY OHIO. (Cincinnati: author, 1945)
87p. (LDS)

Smith, Ophia D. OLD OXFORD HOUSES AND THE PEOPLE WHO LIVED IN THEM. (Oxford OH:
Oxford Historical Press, 1941) 149p (LDS)

Smith, William E. HISTORY OF SOUTHWESTERN OHIO, THE MIAMI VALLEYS, 1964, 3v (SLO,OHS)

Stander, Thomas F. THE UNIVERSALIST SAGA OF BUNKER HILL. (Baltimore: Gateway Press,
1974) 35p (LDS)

Stroup, Hazel. BUTLER COUNTY OHIO CHURCH RECORDS. 1980. (SLO)

Stroup, Hazel. BUTLER COUNTY CEMETERY AND CHURCH RECORDS. (Cincinnati: R.D.Craig,
1962?-1968) 11v in 2 (SLO,LDS,OHS,DAR)

Stroup, Hazel. BUTLER COUNTY OHIO CEMETERY RECORDS SUPPLEMENT, VOLUMES I-VII.
(SLO)

Thompson, Carl N. TREASURES OF PISGAH AND LEVANNA, OHIO. (Greencastle PA: L.F.Colet-
ta, 1966) 398p (SLO,LDS)

Williams, Stephen R. THE SAGA OF THE PADDY'S RUN. 1945. (SLO)

Yon, Paul D. GUIDE TO OHIO COUNTY & MUNICIPAL GOVERNMENT RECORDS. (Columbus:
Ohio Hist Soc., 1973) 216p (OHS)

# CARROLL COUNTY

| | |
|---|---|
| CREATED: | 1833 FROM COLUMBIANA, HARRISON, JEFFERSON, STARK & TUSCARAWAS COUNTIES. |
| COUNTY SEAT: | CARROLLTON 44615 |
| COURT HOUSE: | PUBLIC SQUARE, CARROLLTON 44615 |
| HISTORICAL SOCIETY: | PO BOX 176, CARROLLTON 44615 |
| LIBRARY: | 70 N.LISBON ST., CARROLLTON 44615 |
| GENEALOGICAL SOCIETY: | CARROLL COUNTY CHAPTER OGS, 59 3RD ST.NE, CARROLLTON 44615 publication: CARROLL COUSINS |
| HEALTH DEPARTMENT: | 24 2ND ST., NE, CARROLLTON 44615 |
| ARCHIVAL DISTRICT: | UNIVERSITY OF AKRON, AKRON, OHIO (see Folck's Guide to records) |
| LAND SURVEYS: | CONGRESS LANDS, FIRST SEVEN RANGES CONGRESS LANDS, OHIO RIVER (NORTH) |
| BOUNDED BY: | EAST:    COLUMBIANA & JEFFERSON CO. NORTH:  COLUMBIANA & STARK CO. WEST:    STARK & TUSCARAWAS CO. SOUTH:  HARRISON CO. |
| TOWNSHIPS: | Augusta, Brown, Center, East, Fox, Harrison, Lee, Loudon, Monroe, Orange, Perry, Rose, Union, Washington. |

## COURT RECORDS (LDS MICROFILM)
Auditor:
Tax duplicates, 1833-1838.
Clerk of Courts:
Common Pleas Naturalization records, 1860-1903.
Common Pleas appearance docket, vA-E, 1833-1871.
Chancery records, vA-C, 1834-1854.
Supreme Court record, 1833-1851.
Probate Court:
Wills & probate records, vA-F, 1833-1879.
Marriage records, 1833-1910.
Probate journal, 1852-1876.
Probate docket, vA-D, 1833-1910.
Guardians' dockets, 1900-1926.
Birth records, 1867-1909.
Birth records, delayed, 1941-1964.
Death records, 1867-1908.
Omitted birth and death records, 1932-1940.
Naturalization records, v1-4, 1860-1903.
Recorder:
General index to deeds, 1826-1893.
Deeds, 1833-1876.
Land patent index, 1833-1850.
Miscellaneous:
New Harrisburg Presbyterian church, records, 1843-1863.
Kilgore Presbyterian Church, records, 1828-1892.

## OHIO HISTORICAL SOCIETY (Microfilm):
Clerk of Courts:
Chancery record, 1834-1854.
Supreme Court record, 1833-1851.

**MANUSCRIPTS:**
Peter M. Herold Papers, 1901-1911. (WRHS)
General county records, 1834-1869. (WRHS)
Washington Township school records, 1857-1887. (WRHS)
Benjamin Kepner Daybook, 1817-1819, Perrysville. (OHS)

**CENSUS RECORDS  (OHS,SLO,OGS,LDS)**
1840-1880, 1900-1910; 1890 VETERANS; 1880,1900 SOUNDEX; 1910 MIRACODE

**AGRICULTURAL CENSUS SCHEDULES  (OHS,SLO-mic)**
1870,1880

**PRODUCTS OF INDUSTRY CENSUS SCHEDULE  (OHS,SLO-mic)**
1850,1870

**MORTALITY CENSUS SCHEDULES (OHS,SLO-mic)**
1860,1880

**NEWSPAPERS: [GUIDE TO OHIO NEWSPAPERS, 1793-1973]**
Carrollton, Harlem Springs, Leesville, Malvern, Sherrodsville.

**TAX RECORDS (OHS & LDS)**
1833-1838.

**GENEALOGICAL PERIODICAL ARTICLES**
Bell, Carol Willsey. OHIO GENEALOGICAL PERIODICAL INDEX: A COUNTY GUIDE (Youngstown
    OH:  author, 6th ed., 1987)

**PUBLISHED SOURCES:**
Bell, Carol W. CARROLL COUNTY OHIO 1833 TAX LIST. (Columbus OH: author, 1980) 50p (OGS,LDS)
Bell, Carol W. OHIO LANDS: STEUBENVILLE LAND OFFICE RECORDS, 1800-1820. (Youngstown
    OH: author, 1983) 181p (OGS,SLO)
Carroll Co Chapter OGS.  1880 CENSUS INDEX FOR CARROLL COUNTY OHIO.(Carrollton OH:  the
    society, 1986) 46pp. (OGS,LDS)
Carroll Co Chapter OGS. CARROLL COUNTY OHIO EARLY MARRIAGES 1833-1849, VOL.I.  (Car-
    rollton OH:  the society, 1984) 136p (OGS,DAR,LDS,SLO)
CARROLLTON CENTENNIAL, SOUVENIR EDITION, FREE PRESS STANDARD, 1815-1915.  (Car-
    rollton OH:  Carroll Co Chapter OGS, 1985) 64p (OGS,LDS)
CITY/COUNTY DIRECTORIES:  check holdings of OHS & local public library.
COMMEMORATIVE BIOGRAPHICAL RECORD OF HARRISON AND CARROLL COUNTIES OHIO.
    1891.  (Reprint, Evansville IN:  Unigraphic, 1977) 1150p. (SLO,LDS,OGS,OHS,DAR)(RPI)
Daughters of the American Revolution.   BICENTENNIAL HISTORY OF THE MINERVA AREA
    FAMILIES. 2v. (SLO)
Daughters of the American Revolution.  OHIO CEMETERY AND BIBLE RECORDS. (SLO)
Daughters of the American Revolution.  TWELVE OHIO COUNTIES CHURCH AND CEMETERY
    RECORDS. 124p. (SLO)
Dolle, Genevieve M.  RECORDS TRANSCRIBED FROM CHURCH RECORD BOOKS FOR THE
    PERIOD 1835-1877, REV.JOSEPH A. ROOF. 1v (OHS)
Eberhardt, G.A. ILLUSTRATED HISTORICAL ATLAS OF CARROLL COUNTY OHIO.  1874.  (Reprint,
    Evansville IN:  Unigraphic, 1979) 89p (DAR,OGS,LDS,SLO)
Eckley, Harvey J. HISTORY OF CARROLL AND HARRISON COUNTIES OHIO (Chicago: Lewis Pub
    Co., 1921) 2v (OGS,OHS,LC,SLO,DAR,LDS)
Folck, Linda. LOCAL GOVERNMENT RECORDS IN THE AMERICAN HISTORY RESEARCH CEN-
    TER AT THE UNIVERSITY OF AKRON. (Akron: U of Akron, 1982) 40p. (OGS)

Griffin, Velma & L.Fox.  EARLY HISTORY OF CARROLL COUNTY.  (Carrollton OH:  Carroll Co Hist.Soc., 1968)  20p (OHS,SLO)

Griffin, Velma & L.Fox.  SESQUICENTENNIAL HISTORY OF THE CARROLLTON AREA, 1815-1965.  (Carrollton OH:  Carrollton Standard Printing Co., 1965) 97p (OHS)

Hardesty, H.H.  ILLUSTRATED HISTORICAL ATLAS OF CARROLL COUNTY OHIO.  (Chicago: author,  1874) 89p (LC,OGS,SLO,OHS,LDS) (RPI)

Harrison, Joseph T.  THE STORY OF THE DINING FORK.  (Cincinnati:  C.J.Krehbiel Co., 1927)  370p (SLO,OHS)

Hemming, Lois J.  CENSUS ABSTRACTS TAKEN FROM 1850 FEDERAL POPULATION CENSUS FOR UNION TWP., CARROLL CO. OHIO.  (Carrollton OH:  Carroll Co Chapter OGS, 1981) 10p (OGS,LDS)

Hixson, W.W.  PLAT BOOK OF CARROLL COUNTY OHIO.  (Rockford IL:  author, nd) (OHS)

Nitchman, Paul E.  BLACKS IN OHIO, 1880, IN THE COUNTIES OF ADAMS TO CARROLL, VOLUME 1.  (Ft.Meade MD:  author, 1986?) 178p

Powell, Esther W.  TOMBSTONE INSCRIPTIONS & FAMILY RECORDS OF CARROLL COUNTY OHIO.  (Akron OH: author,1973) 168p  (SLO,OGS,LDS)

Roof, Joseph A.  BIRTHS, MARRIAGES AND DEATHS TRANSCRIBED FROM CHURCH RECORD BOOKS OF REV.JOSEPH A.ROOF OF PICKAWAY COUNTY OHIO (1834-1855) WITH RECORDS FROM TUSCARAWAS, HARRISON AND CARROLL COUNTIES OHIO.  1958.  95p (DAR)

Scarlott, Jean.  COURT APPOINTED & CHOSEN GUARDIANS, CARROLL COUNTY OHIO, FROM WILL BOOK A, 1833-1843.  (Carrollton OH:  Carroll Co Chapter OGS, 1981) 15p (OGS,LDS,SLO)

Scarlott, Jean.  WILL ABSTRACTS FROM WILL BOOK A, 1833-1843, CARROLL COUNTY OHIO.  (Carrollton OH:  Carroll Co Chapter OGS, 1981) 19p (OGS,SLO)

Scott, Beulah M.  INDEX OF ILLUSTRATED HISTORICAL ATLAS OF CARROLL COUNTY, OHIO, BY EBERHART.  31p (LDS)

SESQUICENTENNIAL HISTORY OF THE CARROLLTON AREA, 1815-1965.  OFFICIAL SOUVENIR PROGRAM.  (Carrollton OH:  Standard Printing Co., 1965) 97p (OGS)

# CHAMPAIGN COUNTY

| | |
|---|---|
| CREATED: | 1805 FROM FRANKLIN & GREENE COUNTIES |
| COUNTY SEAT: | URBANA 43078 |
| COURT HOUSE: | 200 N.MAIN ST., URBANA 43078 |
| LIBRARY: | 160 W.  MARKET ST., URBANA 43078 |
| HISTORICAL SOCIETY: | 208 E.CHURCH ST., URBANA 43078 |
| GENEALOGICAL SOCIETY: | CHAMPAIGN CO.  CHAPTER OGS, |
| | PO BOX 680, URBANA 43078 |
| | publication:  MAD RIVER COURANT |
| HEALTH DEPARTMENT: | 319 COURT HOUSE, URBANA 43078 |
| | (separate office for Urbana City) |
| ARCHIVAL DISTRICT: | WRIGHT STATE UNIVERSITY, DAYTON |
| | (see Leggett's Guide to records) |
| LAND SURVEYS: | VIRGINIA MILITARY DISTRICT |
| | CONGRESS LANDS:  BETWEEN THE MIAMI RIVER SURVEY |
| BOUNDED BY: | EAST:      MADISON & UNION CO. |
| | NORTH:  LOGAN CO. |
| | WEST:      MIAMI & SHELBY CO. |
| | SOUTH:   CLARK CO. |
| TOWNSHIPS: | Adams, Concord, Goshen, Harrison, Jackson,  Johnson, Mad River, Rush, Salem, Union, Urbana, Wayne. |
| | |
| SPECIAL NOTE: | A COURTHOUSE FIRE IN 1948 DESTROYED SOME RECORDS. |

## COURT RECORDS (LDS MICROFILM)
Auditor:
   Tax records, 1816-1838.
Childrens Home:
   Record of inmates, 1892-1910.
Clerk of Courts:
   Common Pleas naturalization records, 1860-1898.
   Minutes, v1-22, 1805-1855.
   Chancery record, v16-24, 1833-1854.
   Supreme Court record, v1-6, 1805-1851.
County Home:
   Record of inmates, 1838-1963.
Probate Court:
   General index to estates, 1905-1967.
   Will records, vA-Z,1-22, 1808-1967.
   Administration docket, v1-22, 1861-1967.
   Marriage records, vA-Y, 1805-1967.
   Index to marriages, 1805-1967.
   Birth records, v1-3, 1867-1908.
   Record of births, corrections & registrations, 1941-1967.
   Death records, 1867-1909.
   Probate journal, v1-79, 1852-1967.
   Administrators' bonds, v37-49, 1954-1962.
   Final record, v1-18, v35-59, 1804-1941, 1952-1968.
   Final record, vI-AC, 1885-1947.
   Final record, v50-59, 1962-1968.
   Final record of estate, v1-9, 1852-1891.
   Executors' bonds, v19-34, 1941-1952.
   Final record of guardians, v1-8, 1857-1893.
   Guardians' records, v1-15, 1808-1967.
   Guardians' letters, 1879-1891.
   Guardians' docket, v1-7, 1861-1967.
   Guardians' inventory, 1952-1967.
   Guardians' appointments for idiots, 1908-1931.
   Miscellaneous record, vK-Z,1-10, 1901-1967.
   Real estate record, v1-21, 1946-1967.
   Transfer of real estate, v1-9, 1941-1967.
   Land record, vA-H, 1852-1891.
Recorder:
   General index to deeds, v1-22, 1806-1968.
   Deeds, v1-5, A-Z, 29-49, 1805-1877.
   Deeds, v50-83, 1876-1901.
   Soldiers' discharge, v1-8, 1865-1968.
Miscellaneous:
   Nettle Creek Baptist Church, records, 1822-1905. [WRHS]
   Urbana United Presbyterian Church, minutes, 1844-1882.
   Adams Twp., quadrennial appraisement, 1910.
   Misc. Cemeteries, DAR collection, State Library of Ohio.

## OHIO HISTORICAL SOCIETY: (MICROFILM)
Childrens' Home:
   Record of inmates, 1892-1910.
Clerk of Courts:
   Chancery records, v16-24, 1833-1854.
   General index, 1805-1878.

Common Pleas minutes, v1-22, 1805-1855.
Supreme Court record, v1-6, 1805-1851.
County Home:
Record of inmates, 1838-1963.
Miscellaneous:
Marriages, 1805-1864, by DAR.
Deaths, Champaign & Union Cos., by DAR.
Tombstone & Cemetery records, by DAR.

**MANUSCRIPTS:**
Urbana Township Clerk records, 1855-1892. (WRHS)

**CENSUS RECORDS (OHS,SLO,OGS,SLC)**
1820-1880, 1900-1910; 1890 VETERANS; 1880,1900 SOUNDEX; 1910 MIRACODE

**AGRICULTURAL CENSUS SCHEDULES (OHS,SLO-mic)**
1870,1880

**PRODUCTS OF INDUSTRY CENSUS SCHEDULE (OHS,SLO-mic)**
1850,1870

**MORTALITY CENSUS SCHEDULES (OHS,SLO-mic)**
1860,1880

**NEWSPAPERS: [GUIDE TO OHIO NEWSPAPERS, 1793-1973]**
Mechanicsburg, North Lewisburg, Saint Paris, Urbana.

**TAX RECORDS (OHS & LDS)**
1806-1807,1809-1810,1813-1814,1816-1838.

**MANUSCRIPTS:**
Urbana Township Clerk Records, 1855-1892. (WRHS)

**GENEALOGICAL PERIODICAL ARTICLES**
Bell, Carol Willsey. OHIO GENEALOGICAL PERIODICAL INDEX: A COUNTY GUIDE (Youngstown OH: author, 6th ed., 1987)

**PUBLISHED SOURCES:**
Antrim, Joshua. HISTORY OF CHAMPAIGN AND LOGAN COUNTIES. (Bellefontaine OH: Press Printing Co.,1872) 460p (SLO,LDS,OHS,DAR) (RPI)
Berry, Ellen T. & David A. EARLY OHIO SETTLERS: PURCHASERS OF LAND IN SOUTHWESTERN OHIO, 1800-1840. (Baltimore: Genealogical Pub.Co., 1986) 372p (OGS,SLO,OHS)
Birt, Susan M. MARRIAGE AND DEATH NOTICES TAKEN FROM CHAMPAIGN COUNTY OHIO NEWSPAPERS 1825-1855. (Urbana OH: author, 1987?) 106p (OGS)
Brand, William A. ROLL OF HONOR. THE SOLDIERS OF CHAMPAIGN COUNTY WHO DIED FOR THE UNION. (Urbana OH: Saxton & Brand, 1876) 68p (OHS,LDS)
Burnham, Maria D. MISCELLANEOUS DEATHS OCCURRING IN UNION AND CHAMPAIGN COUNTIES. (SLO,LDS)
CENTENNIAL BIOGRAPHICAL HISTORY OF CHAMPAIGN COUNTY. (New York: Lewis Pub.Co., 1902.) 724p (OHS,LC,SLO,DAR,LDS)(RPI)
Champaign Co Chapter OGS. AN ATLAS OF CHAMPAIGN CO OHIO LANDMARKS. (Urbana OH: the society, 1987) 78p (OGS)
Champaign Co Chapter OGS. CHAMPAIGN DEMOCRAT, URBANA OHIO HISTORICAL REPRINT JUNE 15, 1905. (Urbana OH: the society, 1987) 40p (OGS)
CHAMPAIGN COUNTY'S CENTENNIAL CELEBRATION. Urbana OH: 1905. 132p (LC)

CITY/COUNTY DIRECTORIES: check holdings of OHS & local public library.

Daughters of the American Revolution. CEMETERY RECORDS, TOMBSTONES PRIOR TO 1900, CHAMPAIGN COUNTY OHIO. (Urbana OH: 1959) (SLO,OHS,LDS)

Daughters of the American Revolution. CEMETERY RECORDS: CHAMPAIGN COUNTY OHIO. 1955-1960. 6v. (DAR,SLO)

Daughters of the American Revolution. FAMILY AND BIBLE RECORDS: CHAMPAIGN COUNTY, URBANA, OHIO. 1968-1977. 2v. (DAR,SLO)

Daughters of the American Revolution. FIRST BAPTIST CHURCH RECORDS, URBANA, OHIO, BY REV.SAMUEL FURROW FROM 1928 UNTIL 1952. 1979. 177p (DAR,SLO)

Daughters of the American Revolution. HUMPHREYS AND SON CO., FUNERAL HOME RECORDS FROM 1873 TO 1909. 1969. 2v (LDS,SLO)

Daughters of the American Revolution. MARRIAGE RECORDS, PROBATE COURT, URBANA, CHAMPAIGN COUNTY OHIO. 1934-1935. 2v. (DAR,LDS,SLO)

Daughters of the American Revolution. METHODIST CHURCH RECORDS, URBANA, CHAMPAIGN COUNTY OHIO: 1859-1876. 1982. 130p (DAR,SLO)

Daughters of the American Revolution. METHODIST CHURCH RECORDS, URBANA, CHAMPAIGN COUNTY OHIO: 1896-1914. 1982. 108p (DAR)

Daughters of the American Revolution. METHODIST CHURCH RECORDS, URBANA, CHAMPAIGN COUNTY OHIO: 1913-1923. 1982. 139p (DAR)

Daughters of the American Revolution. MISCELLANEOUS RECORDS, CHAMPAIGN COUNTY, OHIO. 1981. (SLO)

Enoch, Cecil R. A HISTORY OF CHAMPAIGN COUNTY OHIO TO 1860. 1930. 95p. (OHS)

Everhart, Warren G. CLIPPINGS FROM THE URBANA OHIO NEWSPAPER, CHAMPAIGN CO OHIO (SLO)

GENERAL BUSINESS REVIEW OF CHAMPAIGN COUNTY OHIO. (Newark OH: American Pub House, 1889) (OHS)

Haller, Stephen E. & P.Nolan. FIRST STOP FOR LOCAL HISTORY RESEARCH. A GUIDE TO COUNTY RECORDS PRESERVED AT WRIGHT STATE UNIVERSITY ARCHIVES AND SPECIAL COLLECTIONS. 1976. 21p.

HISTORY OF CHAMPAIGN COUNTY, OHIO. (Chicago: W.H.Beers & Co., 1881)(Reprint, Evansville IN: Unigraphic, 1982) 921p (LC,LDS,OHS,SLO,DAR)(RPI)

HISTORY OF NORTH LEWISBURG, OHIO: ITS PEOPLE, BUSINESSES AND INSTITUTIONS, 1826-1976. (North Lewisburg OH: NLSC, c1976) 76p (LDS)

Hixson, W.W. PLAT BOOK OF CHAMPAIGN COUNTY OHIO. nd (OHS)

Hooker, Malcolm D. HISTORY OF PRESBYTERIANISM IN CHAMPAIGN COUNTY. (Urbana OH: author, 1953) 88p (OHS,SLO)

Kite, Marjorie J. EARLY MARRIAGE RECORDS, CHAMPAIGN COUNTY OHIO [1805-1865] 1981. 245p (DAR)

Knight, W.J. HISTORY OF PRETTY PRAIRIE. nd. 37p. (LDS)

Leggett, Nancy G. & D.E.Smith. A GUIDE TO LOCAL GOVERNMENT RECORDS AND NEWSPAPERS PRESERVED AT THE DEPARTMENT OF ARCHIVES AND SPECIAL COLLECTIONS WRIGHT STATE UNIVERSITY. (Dayton OH: Wright State U., 1987)

Manington, H.D. CHAMPAIGN COUNTY'S CENTENNIAL CELEBRATION. (OHS)

Middleton, Evan P. HISTORY OF CHAMPAIGN COUNTY, OHIO. (Indianapolis: B.F. Bowen & Co., 1917) 2v (SLO,LDS,OHS,DAR)

MISCELLANEOUS DEATHS OCCURRING IN UNION AND CHAMPAIGN COUNTIES, OHIO FROM 1880s TO 1930s, KEPT BY MARIA DAVIS BURNHAM. (DAR collection, State Library of Ohio) (LDS,OHS)

Moore, Denise M. CHAMPAIGN COUNTY RECORDS, PART 1: CEMETERY RECORDS OF ADAMS & JOHNSON TOWNSHIP. (Gautier MS: author, 1982) (LDS,SLO)

Moore, Denise M. CHAMPAIGN COUNTY RECORDS, PART 2: CEMETERY AND CHURCH RECORDS OF MAD RIVER AND JACKSON TOWNSHIP. (Gautier MS: author, 1984) (SLO,LDS,OGS)

Moore, Denise M. CHAMPAIGN COUNTY, OHIO RECORDS, PART 3: CEMETERY RECORDS OF CONCORD TOWNSHIP AND JACKSON TOWNSHIP. (Gautier MS: author, 1984) (OGS,SLO,LDS)

Nitchman, Paul E. BLACKS IN OHIO, 1880, IN THE COUNTIES OF CHAMPAIGN TO CLINTON, VOLUME 2 (Ft.Meade MD: author, 1986?) 193p

Pooler, Marjorie R. FAMILY AND BIBLE RECORDS FROM CHAMPAIGN CO., OHIO. (DAR,LDS)

Probate Court: CHAMPAIGN COUNTY WILLS. 2 reels. (SLO)

Recorder's Office: CHAMPAIGN COUNTY OHIO DEEDS & INDEX, 1806-1877. (SLO)

Saxbe, William B. Jr. & A.Short. INDEX TO CHAMPAIGN COUNTY OHIO WILLS & ADMINISTRA-TIONS, 1806-1850. (Mechanicsburg OH: authors, 1979) (SLO)

Saxbe, William B. LANDOWNERS IN CHAMPAIGN COUNTY OHIO, 1874 [INDEX TO STARR & HEADINGTON'S ATLAS] (Mechanicsburg OH: author, 1981) 58p (OGS,LDS,SLO)

Sibley, Warren D. EARLY HISTORY OF WOODSTOCK OHIO. 1907. 50p. (OHS,DAR)

Smith, Clifford N. FEDERAL LAND SERIES: A CALENDAR OF ARCHIVAL MATERIAL ON THE LAND PATENTS ISSUED BY THE U.S.GOVERNMENT, VOL.4, PT 1: GRANTS IN THE VIR-GINIA MILITARY DISTRICT OF OHIO. (Chicago: Amer.Libr.Assn., 1982) 395p

Smith, Clifford N. FEDERAL LAND SERIES: A CALENDAR OF ARCHIVAL MATERIAL ON THE LAND PATENTS ISSUED BY THE U.S.GOVERNMENT, VOL.4, PT 2: GRANTS IN THE VIR-GINIA MILITARY DISTRICT OF OHIO. (Chicago: Amer.Libr.Assn., 1986) 306p

Starr, J.W. ATLAS OF CHAMPAIGN COUNTY OHIO. (Urbana OH: Starr & Headington, 1874) (LDS,LC,OHS,OGS,SLO)(RPI)

Stewart, Maryruth C. DAY-BOOK RECORD OF SOME OF THE PIONEERS OF WESTVILLE, CHAM-PAIGN COUNTY OHIO, 1827-1830, KEPT BY JOHN ARROWSMITH. (Washington IA: author, 1937) 6p. (OHS)

URBANA AND CHAMPAIGN COUNTY. 1942. 147p (SLO)

Vicory, Jacqueline. MILO UNION LIST OF GENEALOGIES IN THE LIBRARIES OF CHAMPAIGN, CLARK, DARKE, GREENE, MIAMI, MONTGOMERY, AND PREBLE COUNTIES, OHIO. (Dayton OH: Miami Valley Library Organization, 1977) 122p (LDS)

Ware, Joseph. HISTORY OF MECHANICSBURG OHIO. nd. 89p (LDS)

Watts, Ralph M. HISTORY OF THE UNDERGROUND RAILROAD IN MECHANICSBURG. (Urbana OH: Champaign Co Hist Soc., nd)

WIGGINS AND MCKILLOP'S DIRECTORY OF CHAMPAIGN COUNTY FOR 1878-79. (Wellsville OH: author, 1878) 1v (DAR)

Works Projects Administration. URBANA AND CHAMPAIGN COUNTY. (Urbana OH: Gaumer Pub Co, c1942) 147p (LDS,OHS)

WORLD WAR NEWS OF OHIO: CHAMPAIGN COUNTY, 1917-1919. (OHS)

# CLARK COUNTY

| | |
|---|---|
| CREATED: | 1818 FROM CHAMPAIGN, GREENE & MADISON COUNTIES |
| COUNTY SEAT: | SPRINGFIELD 45502 |
| COURT HOUSE: | 31 N.LIMESTONE ST., SPRINGFIELD 45502 |
| LIBRARY: | 137 E. HIGH ST., SPRINGFIELD 45501 |
| HISTORICAL SOCIETY: | 818 NORTH FOUNTAIN AVE., SPRINGFIELD OH 45504. |
| GENEALOGICAL SOCIETY: | CLARK CO. CHAPTER OGS, |
| | PO BOX 1571, SPRINGFIELD 45501-1571 |
| | publication: CLARK COUNTY KIN |
| HEALTH DEPARTMENT: | 301 S.FOUNTAIN AVE., SPRINGFIELD 45506 |
| | (separate offices for Springfield City & New Carlisle) |
| ARCHIVAL DISTRICT: | WRIGHT STATE UNIVERSITY, DAYTON |
| | (see Leggett's Guide to records) |
| LAND SURVEYS: | VIRGINIA MILITARY DISTRICT |
| | CONGRESS LANDS: BETWEEN THE MIAMI RIVER SURVEY |
| BOUNDED BY: | EAST: MADISON CO. |

NORTH:    CHAMPAIGN CO.
WEST:     MIAMI & MONTGOMERY CO.
SOUTH:    GREENE CO.
TOWNSHIPS:            Bethel, German, Greene, Harmony, Madison, Mad River, Moorefield,
                     Pike, Pleasant, Springfield.

**COURT RECORDS (LDS MICROFILM)**
Auditor:
    Tax duplicates, 1818-1838.
    Enumeration of Soldiers & Sailors, 1865-1900.
    Blind Relief records, 1906-1936.
    Enumeration for school & deaf & dumb, 1822-1833.
Childrens' Home:
    Record of inmates, 1878-1891,1902-1920.
    Trustees minutes, 1878-1920.
Clerk of Courts:
    Index to complete record, 1818-1906.
    Naturalizations, 1856-1877.
    Common Pleas Minutes, v4-14, 1820-1854.
    Common Pleas civil docket, v1-3, 1821-1852.
    Common Pleas chancery record, v1-9,, 1820-1855.
    Supreme Court chancery records, 1821-1851.
    Supreme Court law records, 1819-1850.
County Home:
    Record of inmates, 1836-1922.
    Directors minutes, 1893-1904.
    Indenture records, 1878-1913.
Probate Court:
    Marriage records, v1-61, 1818-1968.
    General Index, Probate Court, 1818-1964.
    Wills, vA1-15, 1819-1902.
    Birth records, v1-12, 1867-1968.
    Death records, v1-3, 1867-1908.
    Naturalization record, v1-7, 1861-1906.
    Appointment journal, vA-E, 1879-1900.
    Record of bonds, vA-5, 1824-1897.
    Bonds & letters, 1828-1902.
    Executors' bonds, 1860-1904.
    Guardians' bonds, 1860-1904.
    Administration docket, v1-60, 1873-1965.
    General journal, v1-16, 1852-1902.
    Settlement record, 1827-1901.
    Account & settlement journal, 1873-1903.
Recorder:
    Grantor index to deeds, 1818-1968.
    Grantee index to deeds, 1818-1968.
    Deed records, 1818-1968.
    Index to mortgagor & mortgagee, 1818-1968.
    Mortgages, 1837-1851.
    Record of soldiers' discharge, 1864-1964.
Soldiers' Relief:
    Burial record, 1884-1918.
    Minutes, 1887-1951.
Miscellaneous:
    Springfield First Presbyterian Church, minutes, 1853-1893.

Springfield Second Presbyterian Church, treas. recs., 1861-1872.
New Carlisle First Presbyterian Church, minutes, 1810-1884.
Green Plain Monthly Meeting, records, 1826-1921.
Green Plain Monthly Meeting (Hicksite), 1815-1896.
Misc. cemetery records, LDS Church.

## OHIO HISTORICAL SOCIETY: (MICROFILM)
Auditor:
  Enumeration of Soldiers & Sailors, 1865-1900.
  Blind Relief records, 1906-1936.
  Enumeration for school & deaf & dumb, 1822-1833.
Childrens' Home:
  Record of inmates, 1878-1891,1902-1920.
  Trustees minutes, 1878-1920.
Clerk of Courts:
  Chancery records, v1-9, 1820-1855.
  Civil docket, 1821-1852.
  Index to complete record, 1818-1906.
  Common Pleas court minutes, v4-14, 1820-1854.
  Supreme Court chancery record, v1-9,1821-1851.
  Supreme Court law Record, 1819-1850.
  Naturalizations, 1856-1877.
County Home:
  Record of inmates, 1836-1922.
  Directors minutes, 1893-1904.
  Indenture records, 1878-1913.
Soldiers' Relief:
  Burial record, 1884-1918.
  Minutes, 1887-1951.
Springfield City Council:
  Council minutes, 1827-1913.
  City Commission minutes, 1914-1926.
  City ordinances, 1851-1915.
  Minutes of the park board, 1898-1924.
T.B. Hospital:
  Patient register, 1910-1929.
  Trustees minutes, 1935-1965.
Miscellaneous:
  Tax records, 1818-1819, by DAR.
  Marriages, 1818-1865, by DAR.

## CENSUS RECORDS  (OHS,SLO,OGS,LDS)
1820-1880, 1900-1910; 1890 VETERANS; 1880,1900 SOUNDEX; 1910 MIRACODE

## AGRICULTURAL CENSUS SCHEDULES  (OHS,SLO-mic)
1880

## PRODUCTS OF INDUSTRY CENSUS SCHEDULE  (OHS,SLO-mic)
1850,1870

## MORTALITY CENSUS SCHEDULES (OHS,SLO-mic)
1860,1880

## NEWSPAPERS: [GUIDE TO OHIO NEWSPAPERS, 1793-1973]
New Carlisle, South Charleston, Springfield.

**TAX RECORDS (OHS & LDS)**
1818-1838.

**MANUSCRIPTS:**
Snyder family records, 1839-1867, incl daybooks & ledgers of general store, 1839-1912, Springfield OH. (OHS)

**GENEALOGICAL PERIODICAL ARTICLES**
Bell, Carol Willsey. OHIO GENEALOGICAL PERIODICAL INDEX: A COUNTY GUIDE (Youngstown OH: author, 6th ed., 1987)

**PUBLISHED SOURCES:**
Allbeck, W.D. CLARK COUNTY BOYS IN BLUE. (Springfield OH: Clark Co Hist Soc, 1961?) 16p.(OHS)
ASBURY CEMETERY RECORDS, PLEASANT TOWNSHIP, CLARK COUNTY OHIO. (Salt Lake City: LDS Church, 1956) 33p (LDS)
Berry, Ellen T. & David A. EARLY OHIO SETTLERS: PURCHASERS OF LAND IN SOUTHWESTERN OHIO, 1800-1840. (Baltimore: Genealogical Pub.Co., 1986) 372p (OGS,SLO,OHS)
BIOGRAPHICAL RECORD OF CLARK COUNTY, OHIO. (New York: S.J.Clarke Pub.Co., 1902) 824p (LDS,OHS,LC,SLO,DAR)(RPI)
Brien, Lindsay M. ABSTRACTS FROM HISTORY OF CLARK COUNTY (BEERS 1881) OHIO. (Dayton Pub.Lib., LDS)
CENTENNIAL CELEBRATION OF SPRINGFIELD, OHIO. 1901. 296p (SLO)
CHANCERY SUITS OF CLARK COUNTY: 1818-1844. typescript. (LDS)
CITY/COUNTY DIRECTORIES: check holdings of OHS & local public library. Clark County Agricultural Society. Premium list of the 27th annual fair, 1879. (OHS)
Clark County Children's Home. ANNUAL REPORT, 5th, 1883. (OHS)
Clark Co Historical Society. SOLDIERS OF THE REVOLUTION IN CLARK COUNTY OHIO. (Springfield OH: the society, 1976) 38p (DAR,LDS)
Clark Co Historical Society. SOLDIERS OF THE REVOLUTION IN CLARK COUNTY OHIO, PART II. (Springfield OH: the society, 1982) 34p (OGS,LDS)
Clark Co Historical Society. YESTER YEAR IN CLARK COUNTY, VOL.1 (Springfield OH: the society, 1947) (LDS)
CLARK COUNTY, OHIO, TERRITORY BOOK. (Saginaw MI: Appleby, 1905) (LDS) COUNTY OF CLARK, OHIO, AN IMPERIAL ATLAS. (Richmond IN: Rerick Bros., 1894) 118p (LC,OHS)
Croft, Grace. INDEX OF NAMES TO HISTORY OF CLARK CO OHIO BY BEERS, 1881. (Evansville IN: Unigraphic, 1972) 93p. (LDS)
Daughters of the American Revolution. BETHEL BAPTIST CHURCH HISTORY, 1822-1972. (SLO)
Daughters of the American Revolution. CEMETERY INSCRIPTIONS OF GREENE COUNTY OHIO AND GREEN PLAINS, CLARK COUNTY OHIO. 1969. 336p (DAR)
Daughters of the American Revolution. CEMETERY RECORDS & BIOGRAPHICAL INFORMATION ON REVOLUTIONARY SOLDIERS BURIED IN CLARK COUNTY. (SLO)
Daughters of the American Revolution. COPY OF TAX DUPLICATE, 1818 AND 1819, CLARK COUNTY OHIO. 1959. 57p (SLO,OHS,LDS)
Daughters of the American Revolution. MARRIAGE RECORDS, BOOKS 1-6, CLARK COUNTY OHIO, 1818-1865. (LDS,SLO,DAR)
Daughters of the American Revolution. RECORD OF WILLS, PROBATE COURT, CLARK CO: BOOKS NO.1-2, 1819-1855. 1966. 18,47p (DAR,SLO)
Daughters of the American Revolution. ROSTER AND BURIAL PLACE OF THE DECEASED VETERANS OF ALL WARS FROM CLARK COUNTY OHIO. (SLO)Daughters of the American Revolution. TAX DUPLICATES CLARK AND MUSKINGUM COUNTY. 1974. 1v (DAR)
Daughters of the American Revolution. SOME AMERICAN REVOLUTIONARY SOLDIERS AND THEIR DESCENDANTS. (Springfield OH: the chapter, c1976) 41p (LDS)
DIALTON-BALLENTINE ROAD CEMETERY RECORDS, PIKE TOWNSHIP, CLARK COUNTY OHIO. (Salt Lake City: LDS Church, 1956) 1p (LDS)

EARLY CLARK COUNTY, OHIO FAMILIES, VITAL STATISTICS – SPRINGVILLE, OHIO. (Springfield OH: Friends of the library, 1985-1986) 2v (LDS)

Evans, Walter B. CEDAR BOG. 1944. (Reprint, Springfield OH: Clark Co. Hist.Soc., 1974)

Everts, L.H. & Co. ILLUSTRATED HISTORICAL ATLAS OF CLARK COUNTY, OHIO. (Philadelphia: author, 1875)(Reprint, Knightstown IN: Bookmark, 1974) 94p (OHS,OGS,SLO,LDS)(RPI)

FLETCHER CHAPEL CEMETERY RECORDS, HARMONY TOWNSHIP, CLARK COUNTY, OHIO. (Salt Lake City: LDS Church, 1956) 20p (LDS)

Friends of the Library. EARLY CLARK COUNTY OHIO FAMILIES - VITAL STATISTICS, VOL.I. (Springfield OH: Warder Public Library, 1985) 208p (OGS)

GREENMOUNT CEMETERY RECORDS, SPRINGFIELD, CLARK COUNTY, OHIO. (Salt Lake City: LDS Church, 1956) 7p (LDS)

Haller, Stephen E. & P.Nolan. FIRST STOP FOR LOCAL HISTORY RESEARCH. A GUIDE TO COUNTY RECORDS PRESERVED AT WRIGHT STATE UNIVERSITY ARCHIVES AND SPECIAL COLLECTIONS. 1976. 21p.

Hardesty, H.H. MILITARY HISTORY OF OHIO: CLARK COUNTY EDITION, 1886-87. (OHS)

Hinshaw, William Wade. ENCYCLOPEDIA OF AMERICAN QUAKER GENEALOGY, VOL.V, OHIO. (Baltimore: Genealogical Pub.Co., 1973) (SLO,OHS,LDS)

HISTORY OF CLARK COUNTY, OHIO CONTAINING A HISTORY OF THE COUNTY. (Chicago, W.H.Beers & Co., 1881)(Reprint, Evansville IN: Unigraphic, 1972) 1085p (LDS,OHS,LC,SLO)(RPI)

HISTORY OF SOUTHWESTERN OHIO, THE MIAMI VALLEYS. 1964. 3v (SLO)

Hixson, W.W. PLAT BOOK OF CLARK COUNTY OHIO. (Rockford IL: author, nd) (OHS)

Johnson, P.R. CLASSIFIED BUSINESS AND PROFESSIONAL DIRECTORY OF PROMINENT TOWNS AND CITIES OF OHIO AND EASTERN INDIANA. (Columbus OH: Berlin Printing, 1899) 303p (LDS)

Kiefer, Joseph W. SPRINGFIELD AND CLARK COUNTY OHIO, HISTORICALLY CONSIDERED. (OHS)

Kinnison, William A. SPRINGFIELD AND CLARK COUNTY: AN ILLUSTRATED HISTORY. (Springfield OH: Clark Co.Hist.Soc., 1985) 152p

Kinnison, William A. WITTENBERG IN CLARK COUNTY. (Springfield OH: Clark Co.Hist.Soc., 1970)

Lake, D.J. ATLAS OF CLARK COUNTY, OHIO. (Philadelphia: B.N.Griffing, 1870)(Reprint, Clark Co.Hist.Soc.,1977) (LDS,OGS,OHS,SLO)(RPI)

Leggett, Nancy G. & D.E.Smith. A GUIDE TO LOCAL GOVERNMENT RECORDS AND NEWSPAPERS PRESERVED AT THE DEPARTMENT OF ARCHIVES AND SPECIAL COLLECTIONS WRIGHT STATE UNIVERSITY. (Dayton OH: Wright State U., 1987)

Ludlow, John. EARLY SETTLEMENT OF SPRINGFIELD, OHIO (LUDLOW PAPERS). (Springfield OH: Clark Co.Hist.Soc., 1963)

McMillen, Emilia A. RECORD OF WILLS. (DAR,LDS)

MAD RIVER VALLEY PIONEER. (Springfield: Clark Co Hist Soc.,1870) (OHS)

Miller, Guy G. NEW BOSTON: CLARK COUNTY'S VANISHED TOWN. (Springfield OH: Clark Co.Hist.Soc., 1955)

Miller, Mary M. A BRIEF HISTORY OF CLARK COUNTY OHIO. (Springfield OH: author, 1961) 7p (OHS)

Miller, Mary M. DAUGHTERS OF SPRINGFIELD: A DIRECTORY; SOME DESCENDANTS OF CERTAIN REPRESENTATIVICE CITIZENS OF EARLY SPRINGFIELD OHIO. (Springfield OH: Chantry Music Press, 1969) 16p (LDS)

Miller, Samuel S. EARLY SETTLERS AND EARLY TIMES ON DONNELS CREEK AND VICINITY, CLARK COUNTY OHIO. (Springfield OH: H.S.Limbocker, 1887) 44p (OHS)

Mills, Dorothy B. FRIENDSHIP QUILT, BACKGROUND OF HISTORY. (Springfield OH: Clark Co Hist Soc., 1960) 50p (OHS,SLO,DAR)

Mills, Dorothy B. OLD PENNSYLVANIA HOUSE. 14p (SLO)

MYERS CEMETERY RECORDS, PIKE TOWNSHIP, CLARK COUNTY OHIO. (Salt Lake City: LDS Church, 1956) 14p (LDS)

Neer, S.Mahlon. PLEASANT TOWNSHIP OF CLARK COUNTY, OHIO. (np: author, 197?) 95p (LDS)

Nitchman, Paul E. BLACKS IN OHIO, 1880, IN THE COUNTIES OF CHAMPAIGN TO CLINTON, VOLUME 2 (Ft.Meade MD: author, 1986?) 193p

PLEASANT HILL CEMETERY RECORDS, CLARK COUNTY, OHIO. (Salt Lake City: LDS Church, 1956) 23p (LDS)

Pooler, Marjorie R. FAMILY AND BIBLE RECORDS FROM CHAMPAIGN CO., OHIO. 1971? (DAR,LDS)

PORTRAIT & BIOGRAPHICAL ALBUM OF GREENE & CLARK COUNTIES OHIO. (Chicago: Chapman Bros., 1890) 924p (LDS,OHS,LC,SLO,DAR)(RPI)

Prince, Benjamin F. A STANDARD HISTORY OF SPRINGFIELD AND CLARK COUNTY OHIO. (Chicago: American Historical Soc., 1922) 2v (LC,LDS,OHS,DAR)

Prince, Benjamin F. THE CENTENNIAL CELEBRATION OF SPRINGFIELD OHIO, HELD AUGUST 4TH TO 10TH 1901. (Springfield OH: Springfield Pub.Co., 1901) 296p (DAR,LDS)

Reeder, Albert. SKETCHES OF SOUTH CHARLESTON, OHIO. 1910. 39p. (SLO)

REVOLUTIONARY ANCESTORS LISTS ALPHABETIZED CHAPTERS AND MEMBERS. (SLO)

Rinkliff, George L. THE FIRST EVANGELICAL LUTHERAN CHURCH OF SPRINGFIELD: A CENTENNIAL HISTORY. (Philadelphia: Muhlenberg Press, c1941) 202p (LDS)

Rockel, William M. 20TH CENTURY HISTORY OF SPRINGFIELD & CLARK CO.OHIO & REPRESENTATIVE CITIZENS. (Chicago: Biographical Pub Co, 1903.) 1054p (LDS,LC,SLO,OHS,DAR)

Schmalenberger, Carol A. BOARD OF EDUCATION, MAD RIVER SPECIAL SCHOOL DISTRICT, POLL BOOK, ELECTION, NOVEMBER 4, 1919, CLARK COUNTY OHIO. (Des Moines IA: author, 1988) (OGS)

Shoup, Lela M. A BRIEF HISTORY OF THE DONNELS CREEK OLD GERMAN BAPTIST CHURCH. (np: author, 1976) 44p (LDS)

Skardon, Mary K. BATTLE OF PIQUA, AUGUST 8, 1780. (Springfield OH: Clark Co.Hist.Soc., 1964)

Skardon, Mary K. BY HORSEBACK TO OHIO: JOSEPH KEIFER'S JOURNAL. (Springfield OH: Clark Co.Hist.Soc., 1965)

Skardon, Mary K. DIARY OF CAPT. SAMUEL BLACK-WAR OF 1812. (Springfield OH: Clark Co.Hist.Soc., 1962)

Skinner, Herbert K. SCRAPBOOK OF NEWSPAPER ARTICLES ON SPRINGFIELD HISTORY. 1967. (SLO)

Slager, Albert L. REVOLUTIONARY WAR SOLDIERS BURIED IN CLARK COUNTY OHIO. (OHS)

Smith, Clifford N. FEDERAL LAND SERIES: A CALENDAR OF ARCHIVAL MATERIAL ON THE LAND PATENTS ISSUED BY THE U.S.GOVERNMENT, VOL.4, PT 1: GRANTS IN THE VIRGINIA MILITARY DISTRICT OF OHIO. (Chicago: Amer.Library Assn., 1982) 395p

Smith, Clifford N. FEDERAL LAND SERIES: A CALENDAR OF ARCHIVAL MATERIAL ON THE LAND PATENTS ISSUED BY THE U.S.GOVERNMENT, VOL.4, PT 2: GRANTS IN THE VIRGINIA MILITARY DISTRICT OF OHIO. (Chicago: Amer.Library Assn., 1986) 306p

Snodgrass, Ann B. CLARK COUNTY OHIO NEWSPAPER ABSTRACTS, 1829-1832. 1984. (SLO)

SPRINGFIELD AND CLARK COUNTY, OHIO. (Springfield OH: Springfield Tribune Printing Co., c1941) 136p (LC,SLO)

VERNON CEMETERY RECORDS, PLEASANT TOWNSHIP, CLARK COUNTY OHIO. (Salt Lake City: LDS Church, 1956) 7p (LDS)

Vicory, Jacqueline. MILO UNION LIST OF GENEALOGIES IN THE LIBRARIES OF CHAMPAIGN, CLARK, DARKE, GREENE, MIAMI, MONTGOMERY, AND PREBLE COUNTIES, OHIO. (Dayton OH: Miami Valley Library Organization, 1977) 122p (LDS)

Woodward, R.G. SKETCHES OF SPRINGFIELD. 1852. (Reprint, Springfield OH: Clark Co.Hist.Soc., 1958)

WORLD WAR NEWS OF OHIO: CLARK COUNTY. 1914-1918. (OHS)

Wright State University Library. AN INDEX TO NATURALIZATION RECORDS FROM GREENE COUNTY OHIO, 1831-1958 AND CLARK COUNTY OHIO 1820-1906. (Dayton: author, 1987?)

YESTERYEAR IN CLARK COUNTY OHIO, v1-6, 1947-1972. (Springfield OH: Clark Co Hist Soc) (LDS,OHS)

Yon, Paul D. GUIDE TO OHIO COUNTY AND MUNICIPAL GOVERNMENT RECORDS FOR URBAN RESEARCH. (Columbus: Ohio Hist Soc., 1973) 216p.(OHS)

# CLERMONT COUNTY

CREATED:                    1800 FROM HAMILTON COUNTY
COUNTY SEAT:                BATAVIA 45103
COURT HOUSE:                270 MAIN ST., BATAVIA 45103
LIBRARY:                    180 S. 3RD ST., BATAVIA 45103
HISTORICAL SOCIETY:         PO BOX 14, BATAVIA 45103
GENEALOGICAL SOCIETY:       CLERMONT CO. CHAPTER OGS,
                            PO BOX 394, BATAVIA 45103
                            publication: NEWSLETTER
HEALTH DEPARTMENT:          BOX 365, BATAVIA 45103
                            (separate offices for Milford & Loveland)
ARCHIVAL DISTRICT:          UNIVERSITY OF CINCINNATI, CINCINNATI
LAND SURVEYS:               VIRGINIA MILITARY DISTRICT
BOUNDED BY:                 EAST:   BROWN CO.
                            NORTH:  WARREN CO.
                            WEST:   HAMILTON CO.
                            SOUTH:  BRACKEN, CAMPBELL & PENDLETON CO KY
TOWNSHIPS:                  Batavia, Franklin, Goshen, Jackson, Miami, Monroe, Ohio, Pierce,
                            Stonelick, Tate, Union, Washington, Wayne, Williamsburg.

## COURT RECORDS (LDS MICROFILM)
Assessor:
    Returns of birth and death, 1856-1857.
    Returns of marriages, 1856-1858.
Auditor:
    Tax records, 1816-1838. (OHS)
Clerk of Courts:
    Chancery records, v1-7, 1824-1858.
    Civil record, v1 & 3, 1846-49, 1851-53.
    Civil minutes journal, vC-U, 1817-1852.
    Supreme Court record, vA-G, 1801-51.
Probate Court:
    Marriage records & returns, v1-29, 1801-1910.
    Will records, v1-2, A-V, 1810-1900.
    Birth records, v1-5, 1856-1857, 1867-1908.
    Birth registrations & corrections, v1-13, 1941-1963.
    Death records, 1856-1857, 1867-1908.
    Probate journal, v1-15, 1852-1876.
    Minutes, v1-23, 1852-1885.
    Probate record, 1854-1889.
    Naturalization records, v1-2, 1880-1905.
    Guardian docket, A-6, 1849-1900.
    Settlements, v12-30, 1865-1912.
    Guardians' letters, 1873-1910.
    Dockets & appointments, 1871-1910.
    Bonds, v1-3, 1860-1916.
    Settlements notices, 1867-1899.
    General index to petition record, v1, 1896-1974.
    Civil docket, v3-4, 1873-1889.
Recorder:
    Deed index, 1800-1879.
    Deeds, 1800-1877.
    Soldiers' discharge records, v1-3, 1863-1893.

Miscellaneous:
> General county records: census 1801,1802,1819; tax 1801-1802, births, deaths & marriages, 1856-1857. (WRHS)
> Misc. cemetery records, DAR Collection, State Library of Ohio.
> Misc. cemetery records, LDS Church.

## OHIO HISTORICAL SOCIETY: (MICROFILM)
Clerk of Courts:
> Chancery records, v1-7, 1824-1858.
> Civil record, v1 & 3, 1846-49, 1851-53.
> Civil minutes journal, vC-U, 1817-1852.
> Supreme Court record, vA-G, 1801-51.

Recorder:
> Soldiers' discharge record, 1863-1893.

Miscellaneous:
> Marriage records, 1800-1854, by DAR.
> Bible records, v1, by DAR.
> Cemetery records pre 1900, v1-9, by DAR.

## CENSUS RECORDS (OHS,SLO,OGS,LDS)
1820-1880, 1900-1910; 1890 VETERANS; 1880,1900 SOUNDEX; 1910 MIRACODE

## AGRICULTURAL CENSUS SCHEDULES (OHS,SLO-mic)
1880

## PRODUCTS OF INDUSTRY CENSUS SCHEDULE (OHS,SLO-mic)
1850,1870

## MORTALITY CENSUS SCHEDULES (OHS,SLO-mic)
1860,1880

## NEWSPAPERS: [GUIDE TO OHIO NEWSPAPERS, 1793-1973]
Batavia, Bethel, Felicity, Milford, New Richmond, Williamsburg.

## TAX RECORDS (OHS & LDS)
1806-1807,1809-1810,1812-1814,1816-1838.

## GENEALOGICAL PERIODICAL ARTICLES
Bell, Carol Willsey. OHIO GENEALOGICAL PERIODICAL INDEX: A COUNTY GUIDE (Youngstown OH: author, 6th ed., 1987)

## PUBLISHED SOURCES:
Bancroft, Arthur P. GAZETTEER AND DIRECTORY OF CLERMONT COUNTY. 1882. (OHS,SLO)(RPI)

Barringer, Betty J. RECORDS OF REV. HEZEKIAH HILL (1833-1914), SUPPLY MINISTER FOR MT. ZION METHODIST EPISCOPAL CHURCH, STONELICK TOWNSHIP, CLERMONT COUNTY, OHIO. (SLO)

BETHEL TATE CEMETERY AND BETHEL & BANTOM CEMETERY RECORDS. (Salt Lake City: LDS Church, 1959) 279p (LDS)

Brien, Lindsay M. ABSTRACTS FROM HISTORY OF CLERMONT COUNTY OHIO, BY L.H. EVERTS, 1880. nd. 50p (LDS)

Brown Co Chapter OGS. 1802 CENSUS CLERMONT COUNTY OHIO. (Georgetown OH: the society, nd) np (OGS)

CEMETERY RECORDS, CLERMONT COUNTY OHIO. (Salt Lake City: LDS Church, 1960) 238p (LDS)

CITY/COUNTY DIRECTORIES: check holdings of OHS & local public library.

Clermont Co. Gen.Soc. CLERMONT COUNTY OHIO, 1980: A COLLECTION OF GENEALOGICAL AND HISTORICAL WRITINGS, VOL.1 (New Richmond OH: the society, 1984) 315p (DAR,LDS,SLO)

Clermont Co.Gen.Soc. INDEX TO 1795 HISTORY OF CLERMONT COUNTY OHIO, 1880. (Batavia OH: the society, 198?) 128p (LDS)

Clermont Co.Gen.Soc. MAPS OF HISTORIC CLERMONT COUNTY, OHIO: A MAP HISTORY OF CLERMONT COUNTY OHIO FROM ITS EARLIEST LOCATION IN THE NORTHWEST TERRITORY, 1787, SHOWING ITS DEVELOPMENT TO PRESENT DAY, 1979. (Batavia OH: the society, 1979) 14p (LDS)

Clermont Co.Gen.Soc. MARRIAGE RECORDS OF CLERMONT COUNTY, OHIO 1800-1850. (Batavia OH: the society, 1979) 243p (SLO)

Clermont Co.Gen.Soc. T.P.WHITE FUNERAL HOME, NEW RICHMOND, OHIO, BURIAL RECORDS, 1889-1925. (Batavia OH: the society, 1988) 127p (OGS)

CLERMONT COUNTY INFIRMARY, ANNUAL REPORT. 1884/85. (OHS)

CLERMONT COUNTY, OHIO 1980 (Batavia OH: Clermont Co Gen Soc., 1980) (OGS)

Craig, Robert D. BIBLE RECORDS OF CLERMONT COUNTY OHIO, VOL.VI. c1967. (LDS)

Craig, Robert D. CLERMONT COUNTY OHIO MARRIAGES, 1800-1821. (Cincinnati: author, c1964) 25p. (OHS,LDS)

Craig, Robert D. CLERMONT COUNTY OHIO CEMETERY RECORDS. (Cincinnati: author, 1964-73) 7v (OHS,LDS)

Craig, Robert D. CLERMONT COUNTY OHIO, 1820-1830 CENSUS, ALPHABETICALLY ARRANGED, WITH 1880 CENSUS OF TATE TP, WILLIAMSBURG TP., AND BETHEL VILLAGE. nd. (LDS)

Daughters of the American Revolution. BIBLE, MARRIAGE AND CEMETERY RECORDS, CLERMONT COUNTY OHIO. 9v (SLO,LDS)

Daughters of the American Revolution. MARRIAGE RECORDS [1810-1865] OF CLERMONT COUNTY OHIO. 1950-1966. 8v (DAR,LDS,SLO)

Daughters of the American Revolution. MONUMENT INSCRIPTIONS PRIOR TO 1900 FROM CEMETERIES IN CLERMONT COUNTY OHIO. 1948-1962. (Evansville IN: Unigraphic, 1974) 1152p (SLO,OHS,DAR,LDS)

Everts, L.H. HISTORY OF CLERMONT CO. OHIO, WITH ILLUSTRATIONS AND BIOGRAPHICAL SKETCHES, 1795-1880. (Philadelphia: author, 1880) (Reprint, Utica KY: McDowell Pubs., 198?) 557p (SLO,OHS,LDS,DAR)(RPI)

Hirschauer, Grace M. INDEX TO WILLS, 1800-1915, CLERMONT CO OHIO.(Cincinnati: Ralph Printing Co., c1966) 34p (LDS,SLO,OHS)

HISTORICAL SOUVENIRS OF CLERMONT COUNTY OHIO. [reprint of (1) Ency.Directory of Clermont Co 1903; (2) Atlas, 1891; (3) Early Days by Slade & (4) Down Memory Lane) (Batavia OH: Little Miami & East Fork Rivers Citizens Hist Soc., 1977] (SLO)

HISTORY OF SOUTHWESTERN OHIO, THE MIAMI VALLEYS. 1964. 3v (SLO)

Hixson, W.W. PLAT BOOK OF CLERMONT COUNTY OHIO. nd. (OHS)

Hoberg, Rosanna. HISTORY OF BATAVIA, OHIO: IN WORDS AND PICTURES. (Batavia OH: Clermont Sun, 1964) 47p (LDS)

Lake, D.J. ATLAS OF CLERMONT COUNTY OHIO. (Philadelphia: C.O.Titus, 1870) 59p (LC,SLO,OHS) (RPI)

Lake, D.J. ATLAS OF CLERMONT COUNTY OHIO. (Philadelphia: Lake & Gordon, 1891) 86p.(OHS,SLO)(RPI)

Lipps, Virginia & G.Hirschauer. INDEX TO WILLS (1800-1915) OF CLERMONT COUNTY OHIO. (Cincinnati: Ralph Printing Co., 1966) 34p (DAR)

McPHERSON'S RURAL MAIL DIRECTORY OF CLERMONT COUNTY, OHIO 1932-1933-1934. (Batavia OH: Clermont Co Hist Soc., 1985) 112p (OGS)

MOUNT MORIAH CEMETERY RECORDS BATAVIA TOWNSHIP, CLERMONT COUNTY OHIO. (Salt Lake City: LDS Church, 1960) 269p (LDS)

Nitchman, Paul E. BLACKS IN OHIO, 1880, IN THE COUNTIES OF CHAMPAIGN TO CLINTON, VOLUME 2 (Ft.Meade MD: author, 1986?) 193p

Robinson, George. CENSUS OF WHITE MALES ABOVE 21, 1847, BATAVIA TOWNSHIP. (Washington Court House OH: author, 1944) 8p (OHS)

Sewanie Lodge No.95 IOOF. APPLICATIONS FOR BURIAL PERMITS. (SLO)

Slade, Robert K. EARLY DAYS IN CLERMONT COUNTY. (Manchester OH: Manchester Signal, 1964) 84p. (OHS,LDS)

Smith, Alma. MT.CARMEL & SUMMERSIDE OHIO FROM 1788 TO MODERN TIMES. (Cincinnati: author, 1983) 101p (OGS,DAR,LDS,SLO)

Smith, Alma. THE VIRGINIA MILITARY SURVEYS OF CLERMONT AND HAMILTON COUNTIES OHIO 1787-1849. (Cincinnati: author, 1985) 253p (OGS,LDS)

Smith, Clifford N. FEDERAL LAND SERIES: A CALENDAR OF ARCHIVAL MATERIAL ON THE LAND PATENTS ISSUED BY THE U.S.GOVERNMENT, VOL.4, PT 2: GRANTS IN THE VIRGINIA MILITARY DISTRICT OF OHIO. (Chicago: Amer.Libr.Assn., 1986) 306p

Smith, Clifford N. FEDERAL LAND SERIES: A CALENDAR OF ARCHIVAL MATERIAL ON THE LAND PATENTS ISSUED BY THE U.S.GOVERNMENT, VOL.4, PT 1: GRANTS IN THE VIRGINIA MILITARY DISTRICT OF OHIO. (Chicago: Amer.Libr.Assn., 1982) 395p

THIREY & MITCHELL'S ENCYCLOPEDIC DIRECTORY & HISTORY OF CLERMONT CO OHIO. (Cincinnati: S.Rosenthal, (1896?) c1902) 208p (LC,OHS)

Vogt, Paul L. A RURAL LIFE SURVEY OF GREENE AND CLERMONT COUNTIES OHIO. (Oxford OH: author, 1914) 82p (LC,OHS)

Whitt, Aileen. CLERMONT COUNTY OHIO -1870: ATLAS & HISTORY. (New Richmond OH: author, 1985) 88p (OGS,LDS)

Whitt, Aileen. CLERMONT COUNTY GENEALOGICAL GUIDE: A LIST OF AIDS TO CLERMONT COUNTY OHIO GENERALOGICAL (sic) RESEARCH. (New Richmond OH: author, 1981) 43p (DAR,LDS,SLO)

Whitt, Aileen. CLERMONT COUNTY OHIO DEATHS 1856-1908: AN INDEX. (New Richmond OH: author, 1988) 232p

Whitt, Aileen. CLERMONT COUNTY OHIO PIONEERS 1798-1812: A SUBSTITUTE CENSUS FOR 1800-1810. (New Richmond OH: author, 1983) 163p (OGS,LDS)

Whitt, Aileen. CLERMONT COUNTY OHIO WILLS, ESTATES & GUARDIANSHIPS 1800-1851 AN INDEX. (New Richmond OH: author, 1986) 217p (OGS,LDS)

Whitt, Aileen. CLERMONT COUNTY OHIO WILLS, ESTATES, GUARDIANSHIPS 1851-1900: AN INDEX. (New Richmond OH: author, 1987) 184p (OGS)

Williams, Byron. HISTORY OF CLERMONT & BROWN COUNTIES OHIO (Milford OH: Hobart Pub Co., 1913) 2v (LC,OHS,LDS,DAR)

# CLINTON COUNTY

CREATED: 1810 FROM HIGHLAND & WARREN COUNTIES.
COUNTY SEAT: WILMINGTON 45177
COURT HOUSE: 46 S. MAIN ST., WILMINGTON 45177
LIBRARY: WILMINGTON PUBLIC LIBRARY
268 N.SOUTH ST., WILMINGTON 45177
HISTORICAL SOCIETY: CLINTON CO. HISTORICAL SOCIETY
140 E.LOCUST ST., WILMINGTON 45177
GENEALOGICAL SOCIETY: NONE KNOWN.
HEALTH DEPARTMENT: COURTHOUSE, WILMINGTON 45177
(separate office for Wilmington City)
ARCHIVAL DISTRICT: UNIVERSITY OF CINCINNATI, CINCINNATI
LAND SURVEYS: VIRGINIA MILITARY DISTRICT
BOUNDED BY: EAST: FAYETTE & HIGHLAND CO.
NORTH: FAYETTE & GREENE CO.
WEST: WARREN CO.
SOUTH: BROWN & HIGHLAND CO.
TOWNSHIPS: Adams, Chester, Clark, Green, Jefferson, Liberty, Marion, Richland, Union, Vernon, Washington,Wayne, Wilson.

**COURT RECORDS: (LDS MICROFILM)**
Auditor:
    Tax records, 1816-1838. [OHS]
Board of elections:
    Abstracts of votes, 1880-1890.
Childrens' Home:
    Record of admittance & indenture, 1884-1926.
Clerk of Courts:
    Register of Blacks in Ohio counties, 1838-1861.
    Chancery records, vB-6, 1817-1855.
    Chancery & law record, v2-12, 1812-1853.
    Civil docket, vA-1, 1810-1857.
    Civil journal/minutes, v1-4, 1812-1834.
    General index, v1A-2, 1812-1906.
    Supreme Court docket, v1-2, 1810-1844.
    Supreme Court journal/minutes, v1,1812-1814.
    Supreme Court record, v1-3, 1812-1850.
    Quadrennial enumeration, 1907.
    Abstract of votes, 1880-90.
County Home:
    Directors' minutes, 1836-1909.
    Indentures & apprenticeships, 1824-1831.
Probate Court:
    Marriage records, v1-9, 1817-1904.
    Marriage index, 1817-1886.
    Record of wills, vA-7, 1810-1901.
    Index to wills, 1826-1931.
    Birth records, v1-4, 1868-1908.
    Birth register, v1-10, 1941-1967.
    Death records, v1-3, 1867-1900.
    Testamentary record, v1-21, 1852-1902.
    Guardian docket & bonds, v1-6, 1858-1904.
    Naturalization records, 1872-1895.
    Journal of settlement, 1874-1897.
    Final record, v1-19, 1825-1902.
    Administrator bonds & letters, v1-5, 1853-1901.
    Appointment journal, 1880-1897.
    Journal, v1-17, 1852-1901.
Recorder:
    Index to deeds, v1-11, 1811-1963.
    Deeds, vA-Z, v1-63, 1806-1923.
    Mortgages, v1-2, 1836-1853.
    Index to mortgages, v1-4, 1850-1913.
    Soldiers' discharge record, v1-2, 1865-1919.
    Indenture record, 1824-1831.
Sheriff:
    Jail register, 1917-1927.
Miscellaneous:
    WILMINGTON COLLEGE LIBRARY QUAKER COLLECTIONS:
    Bloomington Monthly Meeting, records, 1920-1932.
    Caesar's Creek Monthly Meeting, records, 1754-1952.
    Center Monthly Meeting, records, 1807-1921.
    Center Quarterly Meeting, records, 1884-1893.
    Chester Monthly Meeting, minutes, 1921-1966.
    Cuba Monthly Meeting, minutes, 1923-1948.

Dover Monthly Meeting, records, 1808-1965.
Fairview Monthly Meeting, records, 1891-1951.
Grassy Run Monthly Meeting, records, 1835-1932.
Lees Creek Monthly Meeting, records, 1817-1831.
Newberry Monthly Meeting, records, 1816-1926.
New Burlington Monthly Meeting, records, 1871-1928.
New Vienna Monthly Meeting, records, 1862-1929.
Ogden Monthly Meeting, minutes, 1897-1941.
Sabina Monthly Meeting, records, 1881-1948.
Springfield Monthly Meeting, records, 1813-1974.
Westfork Monthly Meeting, minutes, 1891-1955.
Wilmington Monthly Meeting, records, 1862-1949.
Misc. Cemetery records, DAR Collection, State Library of Ohio.

## OHIO HISTORICAL SOCIETY: (MICROFILM)
Childrens' Home:
    Record of admittance & indenture, 1884-1926.
Clerk of Courts:
    Register of Blacks in Ohio counties, 1838-1861.
    Chancery records, vB-6, 1817-1855.
    Chancery & law record, v2-12, 1812-1853.
    Civil docket, vA-1, 1810-1857.
    Civil journal/minutes, v1-4, 1812-1834.
    General index, v1A-2, 1812-1906.
    Supreme Court docket, v1-2, 1810-1844.
    Supreme Court journal/minutes, v1,1812-1814.
    Supreme Court record, v1-3, 1812-1850.
    Quadrennial enumeration, 1907.
    Abstract of votes, 1880-90.
Commissioners:
    Journal, 1875-1902.
    Index to journal, 1901-1907.
County Home:
    Directors' minutes, 1836-1909.
Recorder:
    Soldiers' discharge record, v1-2, 1865-1919.
    Indenture record, 1824-1831.
Sheriff:
    Jail register, 1917-1927.
Miscellaneous:
    Marriage records, 1810-64, 1888-93, by DAR.
    Tax lists, Wilmington, 1822-1826, by DAR.

## CENSUS RECORDS (OHS,SLO,OGS,LDS)
1820-1880, 1900-1910; 1890 VETERANS; 1880,1900 SOUNDEX; 1910 MIRACODE

## AGRICULTURAL CENSUS SCHEDULES (OHS,SLO-mic)
1880

## PRODUCTS OF INDUSTRY CENSUS SCHEDULE (OHS,SLO-mic)
1850,1870

## MORTALITY CENSUS SCHEDULES (OHS,SLO-mic)
1860,1880

**NEWSPAPERS: [GUIDE TO OHIO NEWSPAPERS, 1793-1973]**
Blanchester, Clarksville, New Vienna, Sabina, Wilmington.

**TAX RECORDS (OHS & LDS)**
1810,1812-1814,1816-1838.

**GENEALOGICAL PERIODICAL ARTICLES**
Bell, Carol Willsey. OHIO GENEALOGICAL PERIODICAL INDEX: A COUNTY GUIDE (Youngstown OH: author, 6th ed., 1987)

**PUBLISHED SOURCES:**
ATLAS OF CLINTON COUNTY OHIO. 1903. (SLO)
Brown, Albert J. HISTORY OF CLINTON COUNTY OHIO: ITS PEOPLE, INDUSTRIES AND INSTITUTIONS. 1915. (Reprint, Evansville IN: Unigraphic, 1980) 967p (SLO,OGS,DAR,LDS)
Carnahan, James E. HISTORY OF BLANCHESTER OHIO. 1978. (Reprint, Evansville IN: Unigraphic, 1979) (DAR)
CITY/COUNTY DIRECTORIES: check holdings of OHS & local public library.
Clinton Co. Historical Society. CEMETERY RECORDS OF CLINTON COUNTY OHIO 1798-1978. (Wilmington OH: genealogical committee, 1980) 375p (OGS,SLO,DAR,LDS)
Clinton Co. Historical Society. CLINTON COUNTY, OHIO, 1982: A COLLECTION OF HISTORICAL SKETCHES AND FAMILY HISTORIES. (Wilmington OH: the society, c1982) (LDS,SLO)
Daughters of the American Revolution. CEMETERY INSCRIPTIONS MISCELLANEOUS VOLUME OHIO, 1957-1958. (SLO)
Daughters of the American Revolution. EARLY MARRIAGES OF CLINTON COUNTY OHIO 1810-1864 & MARRIAGES OF FIRST BAPTIST CHURCH OF WILMINGTON, 1888-1933. 1943. (SLO,LDS,DAR)
Daughters of the American Revolution. HISTORY OF THE CHURCHES OF BLANCHESTER, OHIO. 1940. 8p (SLO)
Daughters of the American Revolution. NOTES OF POSSIBLE GENEALOGICAL INTEREST FROM THE JOURNAL REPUBLICAN, WILMINGTON, OHIO, 1866-1871. 1972. 1v (DAR,LDS,SLO)
Daughters of the American Revolution. ORIGINAL (FIRST) TAX RECORD, CLINTON COUNTY OHIO, 1822-1826; AND TAX LIST CLARK TOWNSHIP, CLINTON COUNTY 1826. 1959-1961. (SLO,LDS)
Daughters of the American Revolution. SKETCH OF REV. NOBLE EDGAR BENNETT: MARRIAGE RECORDS, FIRST BAPTIST CHURCH, WILMINGTON. 1957. (DAR,LDS,SLO)
GENEALOGICAL MISCELLANY, NUMBER ONE, CLINTON COUNTY OHIO. nd. 1v. (LDS)
Hadley, Lucile F. QUAKER HISTORICAL COLLECTIONS: SPRINGFIELD FRIENDS' MEETING, 1809-1959, NEAR WILMINGTON, CLINTON COUNTY, OHIO. (Wilmington OH: Ames Print.Ship, c1959) 108p (LDS)
Hardesty, H.H. MILITARY HISTORY OF OHIO - CLINTON COUNTY EDITION. 1886/87. (OHS)
Hinshaw, William Wade. ENCYCLOPEDIA OF AMERICAN QUAKER GENEALOGY, VOL.V, OHIO. (Baltimore: Genealogical Pub.Co., 1973) (SLO,OHS,LDS)
HISTORY OF CLINTON COUNTY, OHIO. (Chicago: W.H.Beers & Co., 1882) 1180p (LC,SLO,LDS,DAR)(RPI)
HISTORY OF SOUTHWESTERN OHIO, THE MIAMI VALLEYS. 3v. (SLO)
ILLUSTRATED HISTORICAL ATLAS OF CLINTON COUNTY, OHIO. (Philadelphia: Lake, Griffing & Stevenson, 1876)(OGS,DAR)(RPI)
Kier, N.Kenneth. 1919 SOUVENIR EDITION CLINTON COUNTY OHIO. (Wilmington OH: author, 1919) 48p
Mart, Larry D. CLINTON COUNTY OHIO NEWSPAPERS DEATH AND OBITUARY ABSTRACTS 1838-1867. (Lima OH: author, 1973) (OHS,DAR,LDS,SLO)
Mart, Larry D. CLINTON COUNTY OHIO NEWSPAPERS DEATH AND OBITUARY ABSTRACTS 1867-1875. (Lima OH: author, 1976) (OHS,DAR,LDS)
Mitchell, Thirey & Hahn. HISTORICAL-DIRECTORY AND ATLAS, CLINTON COUNTY OHIO. (Cincinnati: S.Rosenthal, 1903) 95p. (LC,DAR)

Nitchman, Paul E. BLACKS IN OHIO, 1880, IN THE COUNTIES OF CHAMPAIGN TO CLINTON, VOLUME 2 (Ft.Meade MD: author, 1986?) 193p

QUAKER HISTORICAL COLLECTIONS [SPRINGFIELD MM, WILMINGTON, 1809-1981]. (np: Springfield Friends Meeting Book Committee, 1981) 171p (OGS,LDS)

Slaughter, Raymond D. INDEX 1900 CENSUS, CLINTON COUNTY OHIO. (SLO)

Smith, Clifford N. FEDERAL LAND SERIES: A CALENDAR OF ARCHIVAL MATERIAL ON THE LAND PATENTS ISSUED BY THE U.S.GOVERNMENT, VOL.4, PT 1: GRANTS IN THE VIRGINIA MILITARY DISTRICT OF OHIO. (Chicago: Amer.Library Assn., 1982) 395p

Smith, Clifford N. FEDERAL LAND SERIES: A CALENDAR OF ARCHIVAL MATERIAL ON THE LAND PATENTS ISSUED BY THE U.S.GOVERNMENT, VOL.4, PT 2: GRANTS IN THE VIRGINIA MILITARY DISTRICT OF OHIO. (Chicago: Amer.Library Assn., 1986) 306p

Turpin, Joan. REGISTER OF BLACK, MULATTO & POOR PERSONS IN FOUR OHIO COUNTIES, [CLINTON,HIGHLAND,LOGAN & ROSS] 1791-1861. (Bowie MD: Heritage Books, 1985) 44p (OHS,LDS)

Wadsworth, Mary F. INSCRIPTIONS TAKEN FROM TOMBSTONES AT SHARON METHODIST CHURCH, KINGMAN, CHESTER TOWNSHIP, WILMINGTON, OHIO. (Wilmington OH: author, c1973) 17p (LDS)

Williams, Kathryn E. ABSTRACTS OF GENEALOGICAL INTEREST FROM CLINTON REPUBLICAN, WILMINGTON, OHIO: JULY 19, 1866 THROUGH DECEMBER 31, 1868. 1967. 48p (DAR)

WILMINGTON DIRECTORY. (Binghamton NY: Calkin-Kelly Directory Co., 1930) (LDS)

# COLUMBIANA COUNTY

| | |
|---|---|
| CREATED: | 1803 FROM JEFFERSON & WASHINGTON COUNTIES |
| COUNTY SEAT: | LISBON 44432 |
| COURT HOUSE: | 105 S.MARKET ST., LISBON 44432 |
| LIBRARY: | LEPPER LIBRARY, 303 E.LINCOLN WAY, LISBON 44432 |
| | SALEM PUBLIC LIBRARY, |
| | 821 E.STATE ST., SALEM 44460 |
| HISTORICAL SOCIETIES: | COLUMBIANA CO. HISTL.ASSN., BOX 131, LISBON 44432 |
| | COLUMBIANA (VILLAGE) HIST.SOC., |
| | 18 1/2 S.MAIN ST., COLUMBIANA 44408 |
| | SALEM HIST.SOC., 208 S.BROADWAY, SALEM 44460 |
| | E. LIVERPOOL H.S., PO BOX 60, E.LIVERPOOL 43920 |
| | WELLSVILLE H.S., 711 RIVERSIDE, WELLSVILLE 43968 |
| GENEALOGICAL SOCIETY: | COLUMBIANA CO. CHAPTER OGS, |
| | PO BOX 861, SALEM 44460 |
| | publication: COLUMBIANA CONNECTIONS |
| HEALTH DEPARTMENT: | corner BROADWAY & FRANKLIN, SALEM 44460 |
| | (separate offices for East Liverpool, Salem, Wellsville & East Palestine) |
| ARCHIVAL DISTRICT: | UNIVERSITY OF AKRON, AKRON, OHIO |
| | (see Folck's Guide to records) |
| LAND SURVEYS: | CONGRESS LANDS, FIRST SEVEN RANGES |
| | CONGRESS LANDS, OHIO RIVER (NORTH) |
| BOUNDED BY: | EAST:    BEAVER CO. PENNSYLVANIA |
| | NORTH:  MAHONING CO. |
| | WEST:   STARK CO. |
| | SOUTH:  CARROLL & JEFFERSON CO.; HANCOCK W.VA. |
| TOWNSHIPS: | Butler, Center, Elkrun, Fairfield, Franklin, Hanover, Knox, Liverpool, Madison, Middleton, Perry, Saint Clair, Salem, Unity, Washington, Wayne, West, Yellow Creek. |
| SPECIAL NOTE: | A FIRE IN ANNEX BLDG. IN 1976 DESTROYED SOME RECORDS. |

**COURT RECORDS: (LDS MICROFILM)**
Auditor:
    Tax records, 1816-1838.
    Assessment of lots, 1859.
    Returns of delinquent lands & lots, 1837-1848.
Clerk of Courts:
    Quadrennial enumeration, 1899-1903.
    Common Pleas Issue docket, 1831-1836.
    Commissioners:
    Journal, 1803-1829, 1859-1905.
    Index to journals, 1859-1903.
County Home:
    Infirmary records, 1856-1885.
    County Home register, 1834-1911.
Probate Court:
    Index to files, 1803-1940.
    Will records, v1-8, 1853-1887.
    Marriage records, 1803-1918.
    Index to marriages, 1803-1957.
    Birth records, v1-6, 1867-1908.
    Death records, v1-4, 1867-1908.
    Appearance docket, v1-6, 1852-1886.
    Guardians' bonds & letters, v1-5, 1852-1890.
    Administrators' bonds & letters, v3-6, 1861-1888.
    Executors' bonds & letters, v2-5, 1857-1888.
    Journal, v1-13, 1852-1886.
    Inventory, v1,14-29, 1834-36, 1856-1887.
    Probate records, v1-38, 1803-1886.
Recorder:
    Grantor & grantee indexes, 1798-1969.
    Deed records, v1-133, 1803-1881.
    Mortgage records, v30-130, 1846-1880.
    Church record (incorporation of) 1845-1879.
    Township records, 1837-1839.
Treasurer:
    Township records, 1837-1839.
Miscellaneous:
    Elkton M.E.Church records, 1864-1940. (WRHS)
    Centre Twp. estray record, 1805-1813.
    Centre Twp. records, 1844-1860.
    Hanoverton, New Lebanon United Presby. Ch, minutes, 1865-1889.
    Mahoning Baptist Assn., minutes, 1820-1827.
    New Garden Monthly meeting, records, 1762-1868.
    New Garden Quarterly meeting, women's minutes, 1824-1850.
    Salem Baptist Church, records, 1823-1902. (WRHS)
    Salem First Presbyterian Church, records, 1832-1876.
    Wellsville, United Presbyterian Church, records, 1847-1900.

**OHIO HISTORICAL SOCIETY: (MICROFILM)**
Commissioners:
    Journal, 1803-1829, 1859-1905.
    Index to journals, 1859-1903.
County Home:
    Infirmary records, 1856-1885.

County Home register, 1834-1911.
Common Pleas:
Quadrennial enumeration, 1899-1903.
Miscellaneous:
Abstracts of Wills & administrations, 1805-1825
Marriage records, by DAR, 1804-1835.
Will abstracts, by DAR, 1803-1850.
Civil War veterans cemetery records, by DAR.
Early records of places & people, by DAR.

## CENSUS RECORDS  (OHS,SLO,OGS,LDS)
1820-1880, 1900-1910; 1890 VETERANS; 1880,1900 SOUNDEX; 1910 MIRACODE

## AGRICULTURAL CENSUS SCHEDULES  (OHS,SLO-mic)
1880

## PRODUCTS OF INDUSTRY CENSUS SCHEDULE  (OHS,SLO-mic)
1850,1870

## MORTALITY CENSUS SCHEDULES (OHS,SLO-mic)
1860,1880 [PUBLISHED IN CEMETERY INSCRIPTIONS SERIES]

## NEWSPAPERS: [GUIDE TO OHIO NEWSPAPERS, 1793-1973]
Alliance, Columbiana, E.Liverpool, E.Palestine, Leetonia, Lisbon, New Waterford, Rogers, Salem, Salineville, Wellsville.

## TAX RECORDS (OHS & LDS)
1806-1814,1816-1838.

## MANUSCRIPTS:
Perry Twp. School District 5, records, 1838-1852. (WRHS)
Butler Twp. School District 5, records, 1846-1861. (WRHS)
New Lisbon Records, 1844-1851. (WRHS)
Centre Twp. Justice of Peace Records, 1818-1821. (WRHS)
General county records, 1803-1854. (WRHS)
Charles E. Rice collection, 1735-1930. (OHS)
Gen. Ephraim Holloway Papers, 1863-1865. (OHS)
Elkton M.E.Church, records, 1864-1940. (WRHS,LDS)
Baptist Church of Salem, records, 1823-1902. (WRHS)
Vallandigham & Laird family papers, 1797-1866. (WRHS)
New Lisbon M.E. Church, records, 1836-1865. (WRHS)
Ohio Militia, 4th Division, records, 1809-1867. (WRHS)
19th Regiment, OVI, 1861-1864, roll book of Capt.Firestone (WRHS)
GAR, Trescott Post #10, Salem, records, 1868-1874. (WRHS)
Freemason's Masonic Lodge #65, New Lisbon, records, 1822-1833. (WRHS)
Young Women's Christian Temperance Union, Salem, records, 1889-1891.(WRHS)

## GENEALOGICAL PERIODICAL ARTICLES
Bell, Carol Willsey. OHIO GENEALOGICAL PERIODICAL INDEX: A COUNTY GUIDE (Youngstown OH: author, 6th ed., 1987)

## PUBLISHED SOURCES:
150TH ANNIVERSARY OF GRACE UNITED CHURCH OF CHRIST, COLUMBIANA OHIO. 1814-1964. 34p (Col'ana Pub Lib)
A PROUD HERITAGE: A HISTORY OF LISBON OHIO. (Lisbon: Hist.Soc., 1976) 23p

Aley, Howard C. INTERESTING PEOPLE OF OUR COMMUNITY...EMBRACING MAHONING, TRUMBULL & COLUMBIANA COUNTIES OHIO (Youngstown OH: author, 1948) 173p

Aley, Howard C. THE BEGINNINGS OF OUR COMMUNITY...EMBRACING MAHONING, TRUMBULL & COLUMBIANA COUNTIES OHIO (Youngstown OH: author, 1950) 247p

Aley, Howard C. THE STORY OF OUR COMMUNITY...EMBRACING MAHONING, TRUMBULL & COLUMBIANA COUNTIES OHIO (Youngstown OH: author, 1954) 263p

Aley, Howard C. UNDERSTANDING THE RESOURCES OF OUR COMMUNITY...EMBRACING MAHONING, TRUMBULL & COLUMBIANA COUNTIES OHIO. (Youngstown OH: author, 1951) 193p

ATLAS OF COLUMBIANA COUNTY OHIO 1870 & 1902. (Evansville IN: Unigraphic, 1975) (SLO)

Audretsch, Robert. THE SALEM OHIO 1850 WOMAN'S RIGHTS CONVENTION PROCEEDINGS. (Salem OH: Moore Printing, 1976) 72p

Baldwin, Henry R. OLDEST INSCRIPTIONS, WITH REVOLUTIONARY AND WAR OF 1812 RECORDS, OF THE CEMETERIES OF OHIO & PENNSYLVANIA. (SLO,LDS)

Baldwin, Henry R. WILLS OF COLUMBIANA, MAHONING AND TRUMBULL COUNTIES OHIO. (SLO,LDS)

Barth, Harold B. HISTORY OF COLUMBIANA COUNTY OHIO. (Topeka: Historical Pub.Co., 1926) 2v (LC,SLO,LDS,DAR)

Beard, Leila F. HISTORY OF METHODISM IN COLUMBIANA OHIO. (Columbiana OH: Fisher Printing, 1950) 73p (YSU)

Bell, Carol W. ABSTRACTS FROM BIOGRAPHIES IN HISTORY OF NORTH EASTERN OHIO by John S. Stewart, 1935. (Indianapolis: Ye Olde Genealogie Shoppe, 1983)

Bell, Carol W. COLUMBIANA COUNTY OHIO AREA KEY. (Kiowa CO: Area Keys, 1977.) 95p. (SLO)

Bell, Carol W. COLUMBIANA COUNTY OHIO DEED ABSTRACTS, VOLUME I, 1803-1808. (Youngstown OH:author,1983) 54p (SLO,OHS,OGS,DAR,LDS)

Bell, Carol W. COLUMBIANA COUNTY, OHIO: RECORD OF WILLS, 1880-1883, Volume 6. (Youngstown OH: author,1984) 49p (OGS,LDS)

Bell, Carol W. COLUMBIANA COUNTY OHIO NEWSPAPER ABSTRACTS VOL.1 (Youngstown, OH: author, 1986) 70p (OGS,LDS)

Bell, Carol W. COLUMBIANA COUNTY OHIO NEWSPAPER ABSTRACTS VOL.2 (Bowie MD: Heritage Books, 1987) 150p (OGS)

Bell, Carol W. COLUMBIANA COUNTY OHIO 1820 CENSUS (Youngstown OH: author, 1986) 33p (OGS,LDS)

Bell, Carol W. COLUMBIANA COUNTY, OHIO, 1850 CENSUS. (Mansfield OH: Ohio Gen Soc,1973) 285p (OGS,OHS,SLO,LDS,DAR)

Bell, Carol W. COLUMBIANA COUNTY OHIO 1860 CENSUS INDEX.(Youngstown OH: author,1972) (SLO,OHS,OGS,LDS)

Bell, Carol W. COLUMBIANA COUNTY OHIO 1870 CENSUS INDEX. (Columbus OH: author,1980) 89p (OHS)

Bell, Carol W. COLUMBIANA COUNTY OHIO 1880 CENSUS INDEX. (Youngstown OH: author, 1987) 48p (OGS)

Bell, Carol W. COLUMBIANA COUNTY OHIO CEMETERY LOCATION MAPS. (Salem OH: Columbiana Co Chapter OGS, 1986) 24p (OGS)

Bell, Carol W. COLUMBIANA CO OHIO: PENSIONERS OF 1883. (Youngstown OH: author, 1983) 7p

Bell, Carol W. OHIO LANDS: STEUBENVILLE LAND OFFICE RECORDS, 1800-1820. (Youngstown OH: author, 1983) 181p (OGS)

Bonar, Elaine. HISTORY OF READING CHURCH OF THE BRETHREN, INCLUDING SANDY DISTRICT. (author, 1976) 113p

Butler, Jean T. DEATHS AND MARRIAGES FROM THE EAST LIVERPOOL TRIBUNE AND THE WELLSVILLE PATRIOT. (East Liverpool OH: author, 1977) 1v (LDS)

CITY/COUNTY DIRECTORIES: check holdings of OHS & local public library.

Columbiana Co Chapter OGS. COLUMBIANA CO OHIO CEMETERY INSCRIPTIONS, vol.1-13, (Salem, OH: the society,1977-1986) (OGS,LDS)

Columbiana Co Chapter OGS. COMBINED ATLAS OF COLUMBIANA COUNTY OHIO, 1841-1860. (Salem: the society, 1984) 78p (LDS)

Columbiana Co Chapter OGS. SOUVENIR HISTORY OF OLD VILLAGE OF NEW LISBON (1903) & THE OLD TOWN OF SALEM OHIO (1906) (Salem: the society, 1987) 174p (OGS)

COLUMBIANA CO OHIO 1874-1875 DIRECTORY. (Cleveland: J.Wiggins & Co., 1875) (Salem PL)

COLUMBIANA COUNTY FARM & BUSINESS DIRECTORY, 1948-49-50 (Bowling Green OH: Rural Directories Inc., 1948) 828p.

Columbiana County Map and Atlas Company. ATLAS OF SURVEYS OF COLUMBIANA COUNTY OHIO. (Lisbon OH: author, 1902)(Reprint, Evansville IN: Unigraphic, 1975) (LC,LDS,DAR)

COLUMBIANA SESQUICENTENNIAL, 1805-1955: OFFICIAL HISTORICAL PROGRAM (Columbiana OH: the committee, 1955) 56p (LDS)

Covington, Mary H. RECOLLECTIONS OF NEW LISBON: A STOREBOAT TRIP ON THE OHIO RIVER IN 1838-9; LISBON REVISITED. (St.Charles IL: J.C.Williams, 1960) 39p (LDS)

DAMASCUS THROUGH THE YEARS, 1808-1983 (175TH ANNIVERSARY). 80p

Daughters of the American Revolution. ABSTRACTS OF ALL THE WILLS, LETTERS OF ADMINISTRATION AND GUARDIAN RECORDS IN PROBATE RECORD BOOKS 1-4, COLUMBIANA CO OHIO. 1958. (SLO,LDS,DAR)

Daughters of the American Revolution. CIVIL WAR VETERANS BURIED IN COLUMBIANA COUNTY OHIO. 1963. (SLO,LDS)

Daughters of the American Revolution. COLUMBIANA COUNTY OHIO FAMILY, CHURCH AND TOWNSHIP RECORDS. 1973. 1v (DAR)

Daughters of the American Revolution. COURT, CHURCH, AND FAMILY RECORDS OF MAHONING AND COLUMBIANA COUNTIES OHIO OHIO. 1943. 119,20p (DAR,LDS)

Daughters of the American Revolution. EARLY RECORDS OF PLACES AND PEOPLES IN COLUMBIANA, MAHONING, PORTAGE & STARK COUNTIES OHIO. 1963. (SLO,LDS)

Daughters of the American Revolution. MARRIAGE RECORDS, COLUMBIANA COUNTY OHIO 1804-1835. 1963. (SLO,LDS,DAR)

Daughters of the American Revolution. MARRIAGE RECORDS OF COLUMBIANA COUNTY OHIO: JANUARY 1, 1835 THROUGH DECEMBER 31, 1848. 1969. 253p (DAR)

Daughters of the American Revolution. MISCELLANEOUS RECORDS FROM THE FIRST PRESBYTERIAN CHURCH OF LISBON, OHIO, CENTER TOWNSHIP, COLUMBIANA CO, AND ST.JACOB'S CHURCH OF SALEM TOWNSHIP, COLUMBIANA COUNTY OHIO. 1962. 75,56p (DAR,LDS)

Daughters of the American Revolution. QUAKER BOOK OF RECORDS: WOMEN'S QUARTERLY MEETING FOR NEWGARDEN. 1953. 81p (DAR,LDS)

Daughters of the American Revolution. SOME TRANSCRIBED RECORDS FROM THE UNITED REFORMED AND LUTHERAN CONGREGATION CHURCH BOOK OF SPRINGFIELD TOWNSHIP, COLUMBIANA COUNTY, NOW MAHONING COUNTY OHIO: CALLED OLD SPRINGFIELD CHURCH. 1959? 85p (DAR)

Durr, Marilyn, ed. HISTORICAL COLLECTIONS FROM COLUMBIANA AND FAIRFIELD TOWNSHIP, 1805-1975. 1976. 120p (SLO)

EAST PALESTINE CENTENNIAL 1875-1975. (East Palestine: The Association, 1975) 193p

EAST PALESTINE OHIO. CON SURVEY CITY DIRECTORY. (Hebron, Neb: Mullin-Kille Co., 1941) 164p

EAST PALESTINE OHIO. CON SURVEY CITY DIRECTORY. (East Palestine: Chamber of Commerce, 1947) 278p

EAST LIVERPOOL CITY DIRECTORY. (Pittsburgh PA: R.L.Polk & Co, 1921-22) (LDS)

Firestone, Mrs. Ross. HISTORICAL SKETCH COMPILED FOR THE SESQUICENTENNIAL CELEBRATION OF LISBON, 1953. (Lisbon OH: author,1953) 202p (LDS)

FIRST CHRISTIAN CHURCH, LISBON OHIO, 150 YEARS, 1827-1977. 1977. 9p

Folck, Linda. LOCAL GOVERNMENT RECORDS IN THE AMERICAN HISTORY RESEARCH CENTER AT THE UNIVERSITY OF AKRON. (Akron: U of Akron, 1982) 40p. (OGS)

Gard, R.Max & W.Vodrey. SANDY AND BEAVER CANAL. (East Liverpool OH: East Liverpool Hist Soc., 1952) repr 1972. 210p

Gard, R.Max. THE END OF THE MORGAN RAID. (Lisbon OH: Buckeye Pub Co., 1963) 22p

Gates, William C. Jr. & Dana Ormerod. THE EAST LIVERPOOL POTTERY DISTRICT: IDENTIFICATION OF MANUFACTURERS AND MARKS (Society for Historical Archaelogy, 1982) 358p

Gates, William C. Jr. THE CITY OF HILLS & KILNS: LIFE & WORK IN EAST LIVERPOOL OHIO. (East Liverpool: East Liverpool Hist Soc., 1984) 500p

Hanover Township Hist.Soc. HISTORY OF HANOVER (HANOVERTON) COLUMBIANA COUNTY OHIO 1914-1976. (Hanoverton OH: author, 1976) 93p (OGS)

Hardesty, H.H. MILITARY HISTORY OF OHIO - COLUMBIANA COUNTY EDITION. 1886/87. (OHS)

Harris, Elizabeth W. A BRIEF HISTORY OF SALEM. (Salem: Salem Hist Soc., 1949) 24p

Hinshaw, William Wade. ENCYCLOPEDIA OF AMERICAN QUAKER GENEALOGY, VOL.IV, OHIO. (Baltimore: Genealogical Pub.Co., 1973) 1424p (SLO,OHS,LDS)

Hise, Nora. PAP'S DIARY [DIARY OF DANIEL HISE, SALEM OHIO] (Springfield OH: Weingart Printing, 1967) 56p

Historical Record Survey. INVENTORY OF THE COUNTY ARCHIVES OF OHIO: COLUMBIANA COUNTY OHIO. 1942. (OHS,DAR)

HISTORICAL SKETCH OF THE OLD VILLAGE OF NEW LISBON OHIO: WITH BIOGRAPHICAL NOTES OF ITS CITIZENS PROMINENT IN THE AFFAIRS OF THE VILLAGE, STATE AND NATION. (Lisbon OH: J.J.Bennett, 19??) 203p (LDS)

HISTORY OF THE UPPER OHIO VALLEY: WITH HISTORICAL ACCOUNT OF COLUMBIANA COUNTY OHIO. (Chicago: Brant & Fuller, 1891) 2v (SLO,LDS,DAR)

Howell, Thomas S. THE SALEM STORY, 1806-1956. (Salem OH: Salem Historical Soc., 1956) 153p (LDS)

Hunt, George D. HISTORY OF SALEM AND THE IMMEDIATE VICINITY, COLUMBIANA COUNTY OHIO. (Salem OH: author, 1898)(Reprint, Evansville IN: Unigraphic, 1976) 241p (LDS,SLO,DAR)(RPI)

Index committee. INDEX TO PAP'S DIARY. [PAP HISE] (Salem OH: 1974) 27p.

Jones, Hazel J. HISTORY OF MIDDLE SANDY PRESBYTERIAN CHURCH FORMED AS MIDDLE SANDY CREEK CONGREGATION 1816 AT HOMEWORTH OHIO. (Alliance OH: Jarman Printing, 1971) 200p

Kensington Boosters Club. HISTORY OF KENSINGTON OHIO 1876-1976. (Kensington: the committee, 1976) 50p

Kunkle, George W. HISTORY OF HANOVER, COLUMBIANA COUNTY, OHIO. (Alliance OH: Review Pub.Co.1913) 191p (SLO,DAR)

Lafferty, George L. ONE SQUARE MILE OF AMERICA: A HISTORY OF LISBON OHIO. (Lisbon OH: Print Shop, 1970) 12p

Lake, D.J. ATLAS OF COLUMBIANA COUNTY, OHIO. (Philadelphia: Titus Co., 1870)(Reprint, Evansville IN: Unigraphic, 1975) (OGS,LDS)(RPI)

Leedy, Roy. EVANGELICAL CHURCH IN OHIO, 1816-1951.

McCord, William B. HISTORY OF COLUMBIANA COUNTY OHIO. (Chicago: Biographical Pub.Co.,1905) (Reprint, Evansville IN: Whipporwill, 1984) 848p (SLO,OGS,LDS,DAR)(RPI)

McCord, William B. A SOUVENIR HISTORY OF YE OLD TOWN OF SALEM OHIO. (Salem OH: author, 1906) 126p (LDS)

Mack, Horace. HISTORY OF COLUMBIANA COUNTY OHIO. (Philadelphia: D.W.Ensign, 1879)(Reprint, Evanville IN: Unigraphic, 1976) 334p (SLO,LDS,OHS,DAR)(RPI)

Mansfield, Ira F. OHIO AND PENNSYLVANIA REMINISCENCES. [Mahoning & Columbiana Co] (Beaver Falls PA: Tribune Printing Co., 1916) 204p (OHS)

MARRIAGE RECORDS KEPT BY JUSTICES OF THE PEACE, BEAVER COUNTY, PENNA., 1850-1869. [incl. Columbiana Co. residents] 8p (LDS)

Murphy, James L. MILLS ALONG THE LITTLE BEAVER. (East Liverpool: East Liverpool Hist Soc., 1975) 26p (OHS)

Murray, Rev.Carl. NEW GARDEN UNITED METHODIST CHURCH, 135TH ANNIVERSARY. 1975. 17p

Nitchman, Paul E. BLACKS IN OHIO, 1880, IN THE COUNTIES OF COLUMBIANA TO FAYETTE, VOLUME 3 (Ft.Meade MD: author, 1986?) 168p

PLAT BOOK OF COLUMBIANA COUNTY OHIO AND INDEX OF OWNERS. (LaPorte IN: Town & County Pubs., 1973) 48p

Pruden, M.M. PRUDEN'S COMBINED BUSINESS DIRECTORY AND GAZETTEER: EMBRACING...EAST LIVERPOOL.... (Charleston WV: Pruden Pub.Co., 1900) 353p (LDS)

Raber, Nellie M. A COLLECTION OF DATA PERTAINING TO THE FOUNDING OF NEW LISBON, OHIO BY LEWIS KINNEY JR., OHIO STATESMAN AND SOLDIER. 1984. 100p (LDS)

SALEM CITY DIRECTORY (Pittsburgh PA: R.L.Polk & Co., 1902-03,1930) (LDS)

Salem Historical Society: FIFTH ANNUAL FOUNDERS WEEK: SALEM'S PAST IN PEN-PIC-TURES. (Salem: author, 1975) 32p

Salem Historical Society:SIXTH ANNUAL FOUNDERS WEEK: SALEM FOLKS IN FOCUS. (Salem: author,1976) 81p

Salem Historical Society:EIGHTH ANNUAL FOUNDERS WEEK: SALEM SETTLERS BEFRIENDED SLAVES. (Salem: author, 1978) 31p

Salem Historical Society:TWELFTH ANNUAL FOUNDERS WEEK: A LITTLE BIT OF SALEM AND HER NEIGHBORS. (Salem: author, 1982) 26p

Salem Historical Society:THIRTEENTH ANNUAL FOUNDERS WEEK: SESQUICENTENNIAL OF PERRY TOWNSHIP. (Salem: author,1983) 19p

Shaffer, Dale E. REFLECTIONS OF SALEM'S PAST. (Salem OH: author, 1984) 80p

Shaffer, Dale E. SOME REMEMBRANCES OF SALEM'S PAST. (Salem OH: author, 1983) 52p (LDS)

Smith, Clifford N. FEDERAL LAND SERIES: A CALENDAR OF ARCHIVAL MATERIAL ON THE LAND PATENTS ISSUED BY THE U.S.GOVERNMENT, VOL.1. (Chicago: American Library Assn., 1972) 369p (OHS,SLO,OGS)

Smith, Margaret. THE CENTENNIAL YELLOW CREEK PRESBYTERIAN CHURCH, 1827-1927, WELLSVILLE OHIO. (np, author, 1927)

Smith, William W. HISTORY OF THE OAK RIDGE UNITED PRESBYTERIAN CHURCH OF YELLOW CREEK TOWNSHIP, COLUMBIANA COUNTY OHIO. (Steubenville OH: Braceland Bros., 1979) 273p

Society of Friends. OBSERVING OUR 150TH YEARLY MEETING: OHIO QUAKER SESQUI-CENTEN-NIAL, 1812-1962. (Damascus OH: author,1962) 111p (LDS)

SOUVENIR HISTORY, 1806-1906, SALEM OHIO. (Salem: the committee, 1906) 128p

SOUVENIR PROGRAM TO COMMEMORATE THE 155TH ANNIVERSARY OF THE SETTLEMENT OF WELLSVILLE OHIO: 1950. (Wellsville OH: committee,1950) 60p (LDS)

Speaker, C.S. AN HISTORICAL SKETCH OF THE OLD VILLAGE OF NEW LISBON OHIO. 1903. 202p (LDS,DAR)

Stewart, John S. HISTORY OF NORTHEASTERN OHIO. (Indianapolis: Historical Pub Co., 1935) 3v. (SLO)

THE SALEM STORY: 1806-1956, WITH ILLUSTRATED VINTAGE PHOTOS. (Salem: Salem Hist Soc, 1956) 180p (SLO,LDS)

Trucksis, Theresa. A GUIDE TO LOCAL HISTORICAL MATERIALS IN THE LIBRARIES OF NORTH-EASTERN OHIO. (Youngstown OH: NE Oh Libr.Assn., 1977) 72p (YPL)

Van Fossan, Jean. FIRST PRESBYTERIAN CHURCH OF LISBON, BAPTISMS 1807-1879; MEMBERS 1807-1879; PASTORS, ELDERS AND DEATHS, 1812-1895. nd. 54p.(LDS)

Van Fossan, Jean. ST.JACOB'S CHURCH, SALEM TWP., BAPTISMS 1813-1899, AND MEMBERS AND GRAVE RECORDS. nd. 56p (LDS)

Walker, Pearl. MEMORIES OF EARLY SALEM. (Salem: Salem Hist Soc, 1974) 17p

Walker, Pearl. ZADOCK STREET AND JOHN STRAWN. (Salem: Salem Hist Soc, 1973) 15p

Westover, Beatrice O. ELKTON & ELKRUN T.W.P.HISTORY. (no place: author, 1980) 323p (Warren PL)

Wiggins & McKillop. INDUSTRIES & RESOURCES OF OHIO: COLUMBIANA & JEFFERSON COUN-TIES. c1881. (OHS)

WINONA CENTENNIAL, 1869-1959. LOOKING BACK OVER THE YEARS, WINONA, BUTLER TWP., COLUMBIANA COUNTY OHIO. (the committee, 1969) 160p (OGS)

Wolfgang, Chauncey S. HISTORY OF COLUMBIANA OHIO. (Columbiana OH: author, 1912?) 85p (Yo.Pub.Lib)

Woodall, Rev.William. LEETONIA CENTENNIAL, 1866-1966. (Leetonia, author, 1966) 29p+.

Woods, Wessie Voglesong. HISTORY OF HANOVER, 1804-1908. (Alliance OH: Review Pub Co., 1908) 191p (OHS,LDS)

Worman, John. SALEM TOWNSHIP HISTORY AND THE STORY OF LEETONIA, 1776-1976. (Leetonia OH: author, 1976) 93p

# COSHOCTON COUNTY

CREATED: 1810 FROM MUSKINGUM & TUSCARAWAS COUNTIES
COUNTY SEAT: COSHOCTON 43812
COURT HOUSE: MAIN ST., COSHOCTON 43812
LIBRARY: 655 MAIN ST., COSHOCTON 43812
HISTORICAL SOCIETY: COSHOCTON CO.H.S., JOHNSON-HUMRICKHOUSE MUSEUM, COSHOCTON 43812
GENEALOGICAL SOCIETY: COSHOCTON CO. CHAPTER OGS, PO BOX 117, COSHOCTON 43812
publication: KINSMAN COURIER
HEALTH DEPARTMENT: COUNTY: 724 S.7th ST., COSHOCTON 43812
CITY: 760 CHESTNUT ST., COSHOCTON 43812
ARCHIVAL DISTRICT: UNIVERSITY OF AKRON, AKRON, OHIO
(see Folck's Guide to records)
LAND SURVEYS: UNITED STATES MILITARY DISTRICT
BOUNDED BY: EAST: GUERNSEY & TUSCARAWAS CO.
NORTH: HOLMES CO.
WEST: KNOX & LICKING CO.
SOUTH: MUSKINGUM CO.
TOWNSHIPS: Adams, Bedford, Bethlehem, Clark, Crawford, Franklin, Jackson, Jefferson, Keene, Lafayette, Linton, Mill Creek, Monroe, New Castle, Oxford, Perry, Pike, Tiverton, Tuscarawas, Virginia, Washington, White Eyes.

## COURT RECORDS: (LDS MICROFILM)
Auditor:
Enrollment of militia, 1857-1858.
Tax records, 1816-1838. (OHS)
Clerk of Courts:
Record, general index, 1811-1852.
Common Pleas record, 1811-1852.
Minutes, 1811-1817.
Appearance docket, v1-10, 1811-1855.
Chancery record, & index, vA-F, 1814-1857.
General index, 1811-1859.
Journal, v2-10, 1817-1855.
Supreme Court record, 1814-1846.
Supreme Court record index, 1814-1852.
Supreme & District court record, 1849-1863.
Quadrennial enumeration, 1883 & 1891.
County Commissioners:
Index to journal, 1879-1902.
Journal, 1812-1902.
Probate Court:
Will records, v1-4, 1811-1888, 1888-1912.
Marriage records, vA-12, 1811-1917.
Marriage licenses issued, 1837-1854.
Birth records, v1-3, 1867-1908.
Index of births, v1-3, 1867-1908.
Death records, v1-2, 1867-1908.
Index to estates, 1853-1944.
Probate journal, v1-7, 1852-1885.
Sales & inventories of estates, v1-9, 1855-1887.

Sales & inventory, 1837-1855, 1887-1918.
Administration docket, vA-3, 1811-1897.
Administration bonds & letters, v1-2, 1863-1883.
Administrators bonds, 1839-1843, 1850-1863.
Administrators bonds & letters, 1883-1921.
Letters of administration, 1839-1852.
Executors' bonds & letters, v1-2, 1863-1896.
Executors bonds & letters, 1839-40,1850-62,1898-1923.
Guardian docket, 1837-1864, 1869-1893,1893-1925.
Administration of estates, 1858-1866.
Guardians' bonds & letters, v1-2, 1869-1888.
Guardians' bonds & letters, 1839-1870,1891-1925.
Civil docket, 1883.
Naturalization records, 1839-1880, 1889-1906.
Declaration of intent to naturalize, 1917-1929,1932.
Naturalization, 1866,1880-1904.
Naturalization petition & record, 1904-1917,1926-1929.
Recorder:
Grantor & Grantee index, v1-5, 1800-1907.
Deed records, vA-55, 1800-1881.
Sheriff:
Jail register, 1870-1927.
Miscellaneous:
Coshocton Presbyterian Church, records, 1836-1879.
Keene Presbyterian Church, records, 1827-1888.
New Bedford, St.John's Lutheran Church, records, 1876-1910.

## OHIO HISTORICAL SOCIETY: (MICROFILM)
Auditor:
Enrollment of militia, 1857-1858.
Clerk of Courts:
Record, general index, 1811-1852.
Common Pleas record, 1811-1852.
Minutes, 1811-1817.
Appearance docket, v1-10, 1811-1855.
Chancery record, & index, vA-F, 1814-1857.
General index, 1811-1859.
Journal, v2-10, 1817-1855.
Supreme Court record, 1814-1846.
Supreme Court record index, 1814-1852.
Supreme & District court record, 1849-1863.
Quadrennial enumeration, 1883 & 1891.
County Commissioners:
Index to journal, 1879-1902.
Journal, 1812-1902.
Probate Court:
Administration dockets, 1849-1897.
Administrators bonds, 1839-1843, 1850-1863.
Administrators bonds & letters, 1883-1921.
Declaration of intent to naturalize, 1917-1929,1932.
Naturalization, 1866,1880-1904.
Naturalization petition & record, 1904-1917,1926-1929.
Sales & inventory, 1837-1855, 1887-1918.
Executors bonds & letters, 1839-40,1850-62,1898-1923.
Guardian docket, 1893-1925.

Guardians bonds & letters, 1839-1870,1891-1925.
Letters of administration, 1839-1852.
Wills, v5-9, 1888-1912.
Sheriff:
Jail register, 1870-1927.

## CENSUS RECORDS (OHS,SLO,OGS,LDS)
1820-1880, 1900-1910; 1890 VETERANS; 1880,1900 SOUNDEX; 1910 MIRACODE

## AGRICULTURAL CENSUS SCHEDULES (OHS,SLO-mic)
1880

## PRODUCTS OF INDUSTRY CENSUS SCHEDULE (OHS,SLO-mic)
1850,1870

## MORTALITY CENSUS SCHEDULES (OHS,SLO-mic)
1860,1880

## NEWSPAPERS: [GUIDE TO OHIO NEWSPAPERS, 1793-1973]
Coshocton.

## TAX RECORDS (OHS & LDS)
1812-1814,1816-1838.

## MANUSCRIPTS:
Ohio Militia, 2nd Regiment, records, 1809-1819. (WRHS)
Johnson & Humrickhouse family papers [incl Presby.Ch.records] (WRHS)
Misc. cemetery records, DAR Collection, State Library of Ohio.

## GENEALOGICAL PERIODICAL ARTICLES
Bell, Carol Willsey. OHIO GENEALOGICAL PERIODICAL INDEX: A COUNTY GUIDE (Youngstown, OH: author, 6th ed., 1987)

## PUBLISHED SOURCES:
1985 HISTORY OF COSHOCTON COUNTY, OHIO. (Coshocton OH: Coshocton Co Chapter OGS) (OGS)

Bahmer, William J. CENTENNIAL HISTORY OF COSHOCTON COUNTY, OHIO. (Chicago: S.J.Clarke Pub.Co.,1909)(Reprint, Coshocton OH: Coshocton Co Chapter OGS, 1983) (LDS,OGS,SLO)(RPI)

Beachy, Leroy. CEMETERY DIRECTORY OF THE AMISH COMMUNITY IN EASTERN HOLMES AND ADJOINING COUNTIES IN OHIO. (np: author, c1975) 200p (LDS)

Bock, George J. ATLAS OF COSHOCTON COUNTY OHIO. (Coshocton OH: 1910) (LC)

Bucklew, William H. HISTORICAL COLLECTIONS II, WARSAW AND THE WALHONDING VALLEY. (Warsaw OH: Business Assn., 1984) 198p (LDS)

CITY/COUNTY DIRECTORIES: check holdings of OHS & local public library.

Cordray, Mrs. Fred. BROOMSTICK CEMETERY, PIKE TOWNSHIP, COSHOCTON COUNTY, OHIO. 1979? 19p (LDS,SLO)

COSHOCTON COUNTY OHIO: ROBINSON CEMETERY, BLOOMING GROVE CEMETERY. typescript. (LDS)

COSHOCTON COUNTY OHIO CEMETERIES, MARRIAGES, WILLS. (SLO)

COSHOCTON OHIO DIRECTORY. (Binghamton NY: Calkin-Kelley Directory Co., 1930) (LDS)

Coshocton Co Chapter OGS. 1830 CENSUS INDEX, COSHOCTON COUNTY OHIO. (Coshocton OH: the society, 1985) 18p (OGS)

Coshocton Co Chapter OGS. COSHOCTON COUNTY OHIO CEMETERIES VOL.1 - MILL CREEK TOWNSHIP. (Coshocton OH: the society, 1985) 42p (OGS)

Coshocton Co Chapter OGS. COSHOCTON COUNTY OHIO CEMETERIES VOL. II -ADAMS TOWNSHIP. (Coshocton OH: the society, 1985) 91p (OGS)

Coshocton Co Chapter OGS. COSHOCTON COUNTY OHIO HISTORY BOOK. (Coshocton OH: the society, 1988?) 2v (OGS)

COSHOCTON COUNTY OHIO BIRTHS 1867-1875. (SLO)

Coshocton Public Library. INDEX TO NEWSPAPER OBITUARIES, COSHOCTON COUNTY OHIO, 1826-1908 IN THE LIBRARY'S MICROFILM NEWSPAPER FILES. (Coshocton OH: the library,1964) 206p (LDS,SLO)

Darr, Betty & C.Erman. ONE HUNDRED YEARS OF METHODISM IN CANAL LEWISVILLE: 1870-1970. 1970. 48p. (DAR)

Daughters of the American Revolution. BIRTH RECORDS, COSHOCTON COUNTY OHIO: 1867-1875. 1975. 148p (DAR)

Daughters of the American Revolution. CEMETERIES, MARRIAGES, WILLS. (SLO)

Daughters of the American Revolution. DEATHS, COSHOCTON COUNTY OHIO: 1867-1909. 1975. 118p (OGS,DAR,SLO)

Daughters of the American Revolution. MARRIAGES COSHOCTON COUNTY OHIO, 1811-1930. 1967. 2v (DAR)

Daughters of the American Revolution. PRESBYTERIAN CHURCH OF COSHOCTON, OHIO: HISTORY AND RECORDS (1818-1909). 1974. 228p (DAR)

Daughters of the American Revolution. TWELVE OHIO COUNTIES. (SLO)

Eberle, Maxine. A BRIEF HISTORY OF CHURCHES AND MINISTERS IN AREA E. (COSHOCTON, HOLMES AND TUSCARAWAS COUNTIES) EASTERN OHIO ASSOCIATION OF THE OHIO CONFERENCE, UNITED CHURCH OF CHRIST. (Strasburg OH: Gordon Printing, 1976) 29p (DAR)

Eberle, Maxine. CHILI, COSHOCTON CO.OHIO ST.JOHN'S EVANGELICAL 1879-1941. (Ragersville OH: The Hist.Soc., 1982) 30p (LDS,SLO)

Eberle, Maxine. CHURCH RECORDS BOOK FOR FIAT ST.PETERS CONGREGATION, BUCKS TP., TUSC. CO OHIO, 1849-1936 AND FOR SALEM'S REFORMED CONGREGATION, BAKERSVILLE, COSHOCTON CO OHIO, 1892-1946. (Ragersville OH: The Hist.Soc., 1981,1984) 182p (SLO)

Eberle, Maxine. HALIFAX, COSHOCTON CO.OHIO ZION'S EVANGELICAL 1889-1942. (Ragersville OH: The Hist.Soc., 1983) 31p (LDS,SLO)

Folck, Linda. LOCAL GOVERNMENT RECORDS IN THE AMERICAN HISTORY RESEARCH CENTER AT THE UNIVERSITY OF AKRON. (Akron: U of Akron, 1982) 40p. (OGS)

GEOLOGY OF COSHOCTON COUNTY. (Columbus, np, 1954) 245p (LC)

Hershman, Robert R. THE STORY OF COSHOCTON, OHIO. (Coshocton OH: 1958)42p (LC)

Hill, Norman N. HISTORY OF COSHOCTON COUNTY, OHIO. (Newark OH: A.A.Graham & Co., 1881) 833p (SLO,LDS,OGS,DAR,OHS)(RPI)

Hunt, William E. HISTORICAL COLLECTIONS OF COSHOCTON COUNTY, OHIO. (Cincinnati: R.Clarke & Co., 1876) 264p (LC,LDS,DAR,SLO)(RPI)

Hunter, Miriam C. INDEX TO NEWSPAPER OBITUARIES: COSHOCTON COUNTY OHIO, 1826-1908, IN THE LIBRARY'S MICROFILM NEWSPAPER FILES. (Coshocton OH: Public Library, 1964) 206p (DAR)

Hunter, Miriam C. MARRIAGES, COSHOCTON COUNTY OHIO 1811-1930. 2v (SLO)

Hunter, Miriam C. THE ONE-ROOM SCHOOLS OF COSHOCTON COUNTY OHIO. (Ann Arbor MI: Braun-Brumfield, 1974) 932p (DAR,SLO)

Hunter, Miriam C. POSTAL HISTORY OF COSHOCTON COUNTY, 1805-1961. (Fresno OH: Hunter, 1961) 284p (SLO,LDS,DAR)

Lake, D.J. ATLAS OF COSHOCTON COUNTY OHIO. (Philadelphia: C.O.Titus, 1872) (Reprint, Coshocton OH: Coshocton Co.Gen.Soc., 1981) 36,26p (SLO,OGS,LDS)(RPI)

Lawrence, Jay. A HISTORY OF THE KEENE CHURCHES. 1968. 26p (DAR)

Lewis, Thomas W. SOUTHEASTERN OHIO AND THE MUSKINGUM VALLEY, 1788-1928: COVERING ATHENS, BELMONT, COSHOCTON, GUERNSEY, LICKING, MEIGS, MONROE, MORGAN, MUSKINGUM, NOBLE, PERRY AND WASHINGTON COUNTIES. (Chicago: S.J.Clarke Co.,1928) 3v. (SLO,DAR,OHS)

Meredith, Helen. MARRIAGES 1811-1837, WILLS 1811-1852. 78p (SLO,LDS)

Meredith, Helen. CEMETERY RECORDS OF COSHOCTON COUNTY, OHIO. 6v. (LDS)

Nicholas, Samuel H. COSHOCTON COUNTY CENTENNIAL HISTORY 1811-1911. Coshocton Co
    Chapter OGS, repr 1984. 84p (OGS)
Nitchman, Paul E. BLACKS IN OHIO, 1880, IN THE COUNTIES OF COLUMBIANA TO FAYETTE,
    VOLUME 3 (Ft.Meade Md: author, 1986?) 168p
ONE ROOM SCHOOLS OF COSHOCTON COUNTY OHIO. (Coshocton OH: Johnson-Humrickhouse
    Museum, nd) 932p.
PICTORIAL HISTORY OF COSHOCTON COUNTY OHIO. (Coshocton OH: Coshocton Co Chapter
    OGS) (OGS)
Schneider, Norris F. THE MUSKINGUM RIVER: A HISTORY AND GUIDE. (Columbus: Ohio Hist.Soc.,
    c1968) 48p (LDS)
Shaw, L.C. HISTORICAL COLLECTIONS OF WARSAW, OHIO AND THE WALHONDING VALLEY.
    (Warsaw OH: Business Assn., 1984) 1v. (LDS,SLO)
Smith, Clifford N. FEDERAL LAND SERIES: A CALENDAR OF ARCHIVAL MATERIAL ON THE
    LAND PATENTS ISSUED BY THE U.S.GOVERNMENT, VOL.2: FEDERAL BOUNTY LAND WAR-
    RANTS OF THE AMERICAN REVOLUTION. (Chicago: Amer.Libr.Assn., 1972) 416p
White, Wava R. ST.JOHN'S LUTHERAN CHURCH, NEW BEDFORD, OHIO. 1973. 80p (DAR,SLO)

# CRAWFORD COUNTY

| | |
|---|---|
| CREATED: | 1820 FROM DELAWARE COUNTY |
| COUNTY SEAT: | BUCYRUS 44820 |
| COURT HOUSE: | 112 E.MANSFIELD ST., BUCYRUS 44820 |
| LIBRARY: | 200 MANSFIELD ST., BUCYRUS 44820 |
| HISTORICAL SOCIETY: | BUCYRUS H.S., PO BOX 493, BUCYRUS 44820 |
| GENEALOGICAL SOCIETY: | CRAWFORD CO. CHAPTER, OGS |
| | PO BOX 92, GALION OH 44833 |
| | publication: TRACKING IN CRAWFORD COUNTY |
| HEALTH DEPARTMENT: | COURT HOUSE, BUCYRUS 44820 |
| | (separate offices for Bucyrus City, Crestline & Galion) |
| ARCHIVAL DISTRICT: | BOWLING GREEN STATE UNIVERSITY, BOWLING GREEN |
| | (see Biggs' Guide to records) |
| LAND SURVEYS: | CONGRESS LANDS, E & S OF 1ST PRIN.MERIDIAN |
| | CONGRESS LANDS, OHIO RIVER SURVEY (NORTH) |
| BOUNDED BY: | EAST:    RICHLAND CO. |
| | NORTH:  HURON & SENECA CO. |
| | WEST:    WYANDOT CO. |
| | SOUTH:   MARION & MORROW CO. |
| TOWNSHIPS: | Auburn, Bucyrus, Chatfield, Cranberry, Dallas, Holmes, Jackson, Jefferson, Liberty, Lykens, Polk, Sandusky, Texas, Todd, Vernon, Whetstone. |

**SPECIAL NOTE:**      A COURTHOUSE FIRE IN 1831 DESTROYED SOME RECORDS.

**COURT RECORDS: (LDS MICROFILM)**
Auditor:
    Tax records, 1826-1838. (OHS)
Commissioners:
    Journal, v1-10, 1831-1910, & index.
Common Pleas Court:
    Chancery record, 1851-1854.
    Common Pleas journal, 1839-1853.
    Judgment index, 1831-1873.
    Supreme/District court, appearance docket, 1833-1884.
    Supreme/District court, complete record, 1832-1857.

Supreme/District court, journal, 1832-1884.
Probate Court:
Marriage records, v1-21, 1831-1929.
Marriage index, v1-3.
Will records, v1-9, 1831-1901.
Death records, 1868-1909.
Birth records, 1866-1908.
Birth registration & corrections, v1-13.
Probate Journals, v1-33, 1852-1913.
Index to estates, v1-3, 1834-1969.
Index to guardians & trustees, 1826-1940.
Appearance dockets, v1-3, 1852-1894.
Administration docket, v1, 1826-1840.
Administrators & guardians docket, v1-5, 1834-1888.
Record of bonds, v1-4, 1834-1889.
Executors bonds, v5, 1883-1899.
Naturalization records, 1847-1905.
Recorder:
Soldiers' discharges, v1-12, 1861-1965.
General index to deeds, v1-28, 1824-1967.
Deeds, v1A-82, 1816-1902.
Deeds, v296-311, 1961-1967.
Record of church incorporation, 1875-1933.
Miscellaneous:
Bucyrus Township clerk records, 1833-1847.
Bucyrus Journal, 1853-1900.
The People's Forum, Bucyrus, 1850-1851.
Crawford County Forum, 1851-1899.
Crawford County News, 1897-1900.
Tiro First Presbyterian Church, minutes, 1853-79, 1891-1910.
Crestline First Presbyterian Church, records, 1870-1896.
Chatfield, Evangelical Luth. Nazareth Church, records, 1840-1972.
Chatfield, Evangelical Luth. Peace Church, records, 1842-1914.
Chatfield, Windfall Reformed Church, records, 1853-1942.
Bucyrus, St.John's United Church of Christ, records, 1837-1961.
Crestline, First English Ev.-Luth.Church, records, 1854-1935.
Crestline, First Presby.Church, minutes, 1870-1897.
Galion, First United Methodist Church, records, 1850-1945.
New Washington, St.John's Lutheran Church, records, 1829-1970.
Oceola, United Brethren Church, records, 1850-1927.
Olentangy, Emmanuel Lutheran Church, records, 1902-1936.
Sulphur Springs, St.Paul's Lutheran Church, records, 1838-1927.
Tiro, Oakland Lutheran Church, records, 1842-1945.
Vernon Twp., St.Paul's Lutheran Church, records, 1854-1951.
Whetstone Twp., St.John's German Ev.-Ref.Church, records, 1859-1876.
Misc. Cemetery Records, DAR collection.

## OHIO HISTORICAL SOCIETY: (MICROFILM)
Common Pleas Court:
Chancery record, 1851-1854.
Common Pleas journal, 1839-1853.
Judgment index, 1831-1873.
Supreme/District court, appearance docket, 1833-1884.
Supreme/District court, complete record, 1832-1857.
Supreme/District court, journal, 1832-1884.

Miscellaneous:
  Cemetery records, by DAR.

**MANUSCRIPTS:**
Bucyrus M.E.Church, records, 1871-1888 (WRHS)
Chatfield Windfall Church Records, 1853-1921 (OHS/Hayes Lib)
Bucyrus Mayor's Court records, 1868-1876. (WRHS)
Bucyrus Township Trustees Records, 1858-1877. (WRHS)
Holmes Township General records, 1829-1849. (WRHS)
Receipt book, 1864, of draftees in Erie, Crawford, Huron, Ottawa, Sandusky & Seneca Counties Ohio
  who purchased substitutes. (OHS)

**CENSUS RECORDS (OHS,SLO,OGS,LDS)**
1830-1880, 1900-1910; 1890 VETERANS; 1880,1900 SOUNDEX; 1910 MIRACODE

**AGRICULTURAL CENSUS SCHEDULES (OHS,SLO-mic)**
1880

**PRODUCTS OF INDUSTRY CENSUS SCHEDULE (OHS,SLO-mic)**
1850,1870,1880

**MORTALITY CENSUS SCHEDULES (OHS,SLO-mic)**
1860,1880

**NEWSPAPERS: [GUIDE TO OHIO NEWSPAPERS, 1793-1973]**
Bucyrus, Crestline, Degraff, Galion, New Washington.

**TAX RECORDS (OHS & LDS)**
1826-1838.

**GENEALOGICAL PERIODICAL ARTICLES**
Bell, Carol Willsey. OHIO GENEALOGICAL PERIODICAL INDEX: A COUNTY GUIDE (Youngstown,
  OH: author, 6th ed., 1987)

**PUBLISHED SOURCES:**
Arnold, Daniel G. ABOUT BUCYRUS. (SLO)
ATLAS OF CRAWFORD COUNTY OHIO, CA.1855 [reprint of wall map] (Galion OH: Crawford Co
  Chapter OGS, 1983) (LDS,SLO)
ATLAS OF CRAWFORD COUNTY, OHIO. 1907. (SLO)
BEAUTIFUL BUCYRUS, HEALTHIEST CITY IN OHIO. (Bucyrus OH: Bucyrus Industrial Assn., 1911)
  52p
Biggs, Deb. GUIDE TO LOCAL GOVERNMENT RECORDS AT THE CENTER FOR ARCHIVAL COL-
  LECTIONS. (Bowling Green OH: Bowling Green State Univ, 1981) 104p (OGS)
Black, Ross B. etal. HISTORY OF THE FIRST PRESBYTERIAN CHURCH, BUCYRUS, OHIO, 1828-
  1933: REV.DAVID N. ROLLER, PASTOR. 1933. 122p (DAR)
BUCYRUS, GALION AND CRESTLINE DIRECTORY FOR 1875/76. (Bucyrus OH: Forum Steam Job
  Print, 1875) (LDS)
CENTENNIAL BIOGRAPHICAL HISTORY OF CRAWFORD COUNTY OHIO. (Chicago: Lewis Co.,
  1902) 868p (LC,OGS,SLO,OHS,LDS,DAR)(RPI)
Christian, Donna K. GUIDE TO NEWSPAPER HOLDINGS AT THE CENTER FOR ARCHIVAL COL-
  LECTIONS. (Bowling Green OH: Bowling Green State Univ, 1980) 64p (OGS)
CITY/COUNTY DIRECTORIES: check holdings of OHS & local public library.
CRAWFORD COUNTY OHIO SCRAPBOOK - CLIPPINGS FROM AUBURN TWP., 1880's. (OGS)
Crawford Co Chapter OGS. CEMETERIES OF CRAWFORD COUNTY OHIO VOL.1. (Galion OH: the
  society, 1987) 315p (OGS,LDS)

Crawford Co Chapter OGS. FAMILIES OF CRAWFORD COUNTY OHIO 1978-1979. (Galion OH: the society, 1979) 470p (OGS,LDS,SLO)

Dapper, Paul. GERMAN LUTHERAN CHURCH MEMBERSHIP. 1980. (SLO)

Daughters of the American Revolution. CEMETERY RECORDS OF CRAWFORD COUNTY OHIO FRIENDS CHURCH, MONNETT CHAPEL, 1953. (SLO,LDS)

Daughters of the American Revolution. CRAWFORD COUNTY OHIO CEMETERY RECORDS. 1952. 51p (SLO,DAR,LDS)

Daughters of the American Revolution. CRAWFORD COUNTY OHIO MARRIAGES, 1831-1864 (SLO,LDS)

Daughters of the American Revolution. MARRIAGE RECORDS OF CRAWFORD COUNTY OHIO: 1831-1865. 1934. 250p (DAR)

Daughters of the American Revolution. MISCELLANEOUS OHIO CEMETERIES VOLUME 1. (SLO,LDS)

Daughters of the American Revolution. OHIO BIBLE RECORDS CONCERNING FAMILIES OF CRAW-FORD,DARKE,FAIRFIELD,MIAMI,MONTGOMERY,PICKAWAY,PREBLE AND SHELBY COUN-TIES. 1970. 126p (DAR)

FIRST UNITED CHURCH OF CHRIST, GALION OHIO, 1876-1976. 1976. 36p (OGS)

FIRST UNITED METHODIST CHURCH, GALION-CRAWFORD COUNTY OHIO. (Galion OH: the Church, 1986) 93p (OGS)

Fisher, David G. RECORDS OF FIRST ENGLISH EVANGELICAL LUTHERAN CHURCH, CRESTLINE OHIO 1854-1935. [CRAWFORD & RICHLAND COS.] (Columbus OH: author, 1979) 95p (OGS,SLO)

Fisher, Jane & C.Ratz. CRAWFORD COUNTY OHIO PROBATE COURT RECORDS. (Galion OH: authors, 1980) 210p (OGS,DAR,SLO)

Gould, Hueston T. ILLUSTRATED ATLAS OF CRAWFORD COUNTY. 1873. Reprint 1974. (OGS,SLO)(RPI)

Hardesty, H.H. MILITARY HISTORY OF OHIO - CRAWFORD COUNTY EDITION. 1886/87. (OHS)

HISTORY AND CALENDAR OF GOOD HOPE EVANGELICAL LUTHERAN CHURCH, BUCYRUS, OHIO. (Toledo OH: Camp Printery, 19??) 29p (LDS)

HISTORY OF CRAWFORD COUNTY AND OHIO. (Chicago: Baskin & Battey, 1881) 1047p (LDS,LC,SLO,DAR)(RPI)

Hopley, John E. HISTORY OF CRAWFORD COUNTY, OHIO. (Chicago: Richmond-Arnold Pub Co., 1912) 2v (LC,SLO,LDS,DAR)

Hopley Printing Co. CRAWFORD COUNTY, 1912, ATLAS. (Bucyrus OH: author, 1912) 28p. (LC)

Houyouse, Linda. PEACE EVANGELICAL LUTHERAN CONGREGATION AT WINDFALL CRAW-FORD COUNTY OHIO, 1833-1915. (Carrollton OH: author, 1984) 53p (OGS)

Hughes, Robert. HISTORY OF THE FIRST BAPTIST CHURCH: BUCYRUS, OHIO; REV.ROY H. LON-GENECKER, PASTOR. (Bucyrus OH: 1938) 40p (DAR)

Johnson, P.R. CLASSIFIED BUSINESS AND PROFESSIONAL DIRECTORY OF PROMINENT TOWNS AND CITIES OF OHIO AND EASTERN INDIANA. (Columbus OH: Berling Printing Co., 1899) 303p (LDS)

Knapp, Horace S. HISTORY OF THE MAUMEE VALLEY. (Toledo OH: author, 1872) 685p. (DAR,OHS,SLO)

Langjahr, Bertha. ST.JOHN'S EVANGELICAL LUTHERAN CHURCH HISTORY: 150 YEARS, 1834-1984, NEW WASHINGTON OHIO. (New Washington OH: Herald Printing Co., 1984) 292p (LDS)

Levinson, Marilyn. GUIDE TO NEWSPAPER HOLDINGS AT THE CENTER FOR ARCHIVAL COL-LECTIONS. 2nd Edition. (Bowling Green OH: B.G.State Univ.,1987)

MOMENTS OF MEMORY: CHATFIELD COMMUNITY BICENTENNIAL CELEBRATION. 1976. (SLO)

Nitchman, Paul E. BLACKS IN OHIO, 1880, IN THE COUNTIES OF COLUMBIANA TO FAYETTE, VOLUME 3 (Ft.Meade Md: author, 1986?) 168p

Perrin, William H. HISTORY OF CRAWFORD COUNTY AND OHIO. (Chicago: Baskin & Battey, 1881) 1047p (LDS)

Riedesel, Gerhard A. BLOSSOMS ON THE THISTLE: AN ACCOUNT OF THE LIVES AND CHRIS-TIAN MINISTRY OF THE REV. & MRS. CHARLES H. RIEDESEL, 1871 TO 1960. (includes bap-tisms, marriages & funerals in Ohio) (Pullman WA: author, c1975) 122p (LDS)

Scott, Beulah M. INDEX OF ILLUSTRATED ATLAS OF CRAWFORD COUNTY OHIO by Gould & Sarr. 1983. (LDS)

Short, Anita. OHIO BIBLE RECORDS CRAWFORD, DARKE, FAIRFIELD, MIAMI, MONTGOMERY, PICKAWAY, PREBLE AND SHELBY COUNTIES. (SLO)

Shumaker, Carl E. INDEX OF BURIALS IN FAIRVIEW CEMETERY. (SLO)

Weber, H.L. THE 1894 ATLAS OF CRAWFORD COUNTY OHIO. (Bucyrus OH: Weber & Swingley, 1894) (LC)

Winter, Nevin O. HISTORY OF NORTHWEST OHIO. (Chicago: Lewis Pub Co, 1917) 3v (SLO,OHS)

## CUYAHOGA COUNTY

| | |
|---|---|
| CREATED: | 1808 FROM GEAUGA COUNTY |
| COUNTY SEAT: | CLEVELAND 44113 |
| COURT HOUSE: | 1 LAKESIDE AVE., CLEVELAND 44113 |
| LIBRARIES: | CLEVELAND PUBLIC LIBRARY, |
| | 325 SUPERIOR AVE., CLEVELAND 44114 |
| | CUYAHOGA COUNTY PUBLIC LIBRARY, |
| | 4510 MEMPHIS AVE., CLEVELAND 44144 |
| | WESTERN RESERVE HISTORICAL SOCIETY & LIBRARY, |
| | 10825 EAST BLVD., CLEVELAND 44106. |
| HISTORICAL SOCIETY: | WESTERN RESERVE HISTORICAL SOCIETY & LIBRARY, |
| | 10825 EAST BLVD., CLEVELAND 44106. |
| GENEALOGICAL SOCIETIES: | BRECKSVILLE CHAPTER OGS, |
| | PO BOX 41114, BRECKSVILLE 44141 |
| | publication: FOOTSTEPS TO THE PAST |
| | EAST CUYAHOGA CHAPTER OGS, |
| | PO BOX 24182, LYNDHURST 44124 |
| | publication: SPEAKING RELATIVELY |
| | GREATER CLEVELAND CHAPTER OGS, |
| | PO BOX 40254, CLEVELAND 44140-0254 |
| | publication: CERTIFIED COPY |
| | PARMA CHAPTER OGS, |
| | 6428 NELWOOD RD., CLEVELAND OH 44130 |
| | SOUTHWEST CUYAHOGA CHAPTER OGS, |
| | 18631 HOWE RD., STRONGSVILLE 44136 |
| | publication: NEWSLETTER |
| | WEST CUYAHOGA CHAPTER OGS, |
| | PO BOX 26196, FAIRVIEW PARK 44126-0196 |
| | publication: TRACER |
| HEALTH DEPARTMENT: | CITY BLDG., 601 LAKESIDE AVE., CLEVELAND 44114 |
| | (separate offices in Bedford, Berea, Cleveland Hts., |
| | East Cleveland, Euclid, Garfield Hts., Lakewood, Maple Hts., |
| | Parma, Rocky River, Shaker Hts., South Euclid, University Hts.) |
| ARCHIVAL DISTRICT: | WESTERN RESERVE HIST.SOC., CLEVELAND |
| LAND SURVEYS: | CONNECTICUT WESTERN RESERVE |
| BOUNDED BY: | EAST: GEAUGA & LAKE CO. |
| | NORTH: LAKE ERIE |
| | WEST: LORAIN CO. |
| | SOUTH: MEDINA & SUMMIT CO. |
| TOWNSHIPS: | Bedford, Brecksville, Brooklyn, Cleveland, Dover, Euclid, Independence, Mayfield, Middleburgh, Newburgh, Olmstead, Orange, Parma, Rockport,Royalton, Solon, Strongsville, Warrensville. |
| | [NOTE: many of these townships have disappeared due to the expansion of Cleveland city.] |

**COURT RECORDS: (LDS MICROFILM)**
Auditor:
    Tax records, 1816-1836,1838 [OHS]
Clerk of Courts:
    Common Pleas journals, 1823-1852.
    Supreme Court records, 1831-1851.
    Supreme Court journals, 1839-1842.
    Naturalizations petitions, 1888-1889, 1902-1906.
    Alien docket, 1818-1856,1859.
    Declaration of intention, 1902-1906.
Probate Court:
    Birth records, v1-10, 1867-1908.
    Death records, v1-17, 1868-1908.
    Marriage records, v1-95, 1810-1916.
    Marriage index, v1-9, 1810-1929.
    Marriage license applications, 1831-1875.
    Will records, vA-Z, 1852-1893.
    Index to administration & guardians dockets, 1888-1904.
    Index to administration dockets, 1811-1896.
    Probate record, 1811-1833.
    Probate journal, vA-Z, 1852-1886.
    Naturalizations, v1-26, 1859-1901.
    Probate docket, 1811-1888.
    Declaration of intent of minors, v1-8, 1858-1888.
Recorder:
    Index to deeds & mortgages, 1810-1900.
Miscellaneous:
    Brecksville, First Congregational Church, records, 1816-1947 (WRHS)
    Cleveland, Case Ave. Presbyterian Church, records, 1867-1889
    Cleveland, Westminster Presbyterian Church, records, 1853-1880
    Cleveland, Bethany Presbyterian Church, records, 1889-1917 (WRHS)
    Cleveland, Eells Memorial Presby.Church, register, 1882-1911.
    Cleveland, Third Baptist Church, records, 1852-1867, 1880-1900 (WRHS)
    Cleveland, Woodland Ave. M-E Church, records, 1874-1886 (WRHS)
    Cleveland, St.John's Episcopal Church, records, 1835-1871 (WRHS)
    Cleveland, St.John's Prot.-Episc. Church, register, 1835-1844 (WRHS)
    Dover, Baptist Church, records, 1836-1856 (WRHS)
    East Cleveland, First Presbyterian Church, records, 1807-1911 (WRHS)
    Euclid,First Regular Baptist Church, records,1820-1892,1901-1916 (WRHS)
    Parma, First Congregational Church, records, 1835-1874 (WRHS)
    Maps of Cleveland, 1855 & 1876.
    Cleveland Light Artillery Assn., records, 1856-1914 (WRHS)
    Amos Townsend Papers, c1880 (WRHS)
    Alfred Mewett Papers, 1736-1955 (incl.church records) (WRHS)
    Misc. cemeteries, DAR Collection, State Library of Ohio

**OHIO HISTORICAL SOCIETY: (MICROFILM)**
Clerk of Courts:
    Common Pleas journals, 1823-1852.
    Supreme Court records, 1831-1841.
    Supreme Court journals, 1839-1842.
    Naturalizations petitions, 1888-1889, 1902-1906.
    Alien docket, 1818-1856,1859.
    Declaration of intention, 1902-1906.

Miscellaneous:
  Western Reserve land draft, 1795-1809
  Marriages, 1810-1857, by DAR
  Bible records, by DAR
  Cemeteries, by DAR
  Church records, by DAR
  Annals of Cleveland, Cleveland Leader Index, 1872-1876.

## CENSUS RECORDS (OHS,SLO,OGS,SLC)
1820-1880, 1900-1910; 1890 VETERANS; 1880,1900 SOUNDEX; 1910 MIRACODE

## AGRICULTURAL CENSUS SCHEDULES (OHS,SLO-mic)
1880

## PRODUCTS OF INDUSTRY CENSUS SCHEDULE (OHS,SLO-mic)
1850,1870,1880

## MORTALITY CENSUS SCHEDULES (OHS,SLO-mic)
1860,1880

## NEWSPAPERS: [GUIDE TO OHIO NEWSPAPERS, 1793-1973]
Bedford, Berea, Bratenahl, Brecksville, Brooklyn, Chagrin Falls, Cleveland, Cuyahoga Hts., Collinwood, E.Cleveland, Euclid, Fairview Park, Garfield Hts., Gates Mills, Lakewood, Maple Hts, Newburg Hts., Nottingham, Ohio City, Olmsted Falls, Parma, Rocky River, Shaker Hts., Westlake.

## TAX RECORDS (OHS & LDS)
1810,1812-1814,1816-1838.

## MANUSCRIPTS:
(see also those listed under LDS microfilm)
Early Settlers Assn. of Western Reserve, genealogical data (WRHS)
WPA: Historic sites of Cleveland. (WRHS)
Brooklyn Congregational Church, Women's Missionary Society, 1875-83 (WRHS)
Cleveland, St.Paul's Episcopal Church, records, 1846-1862 (WRHS)
Cleveland, First M-E Church, records, 1900-1942 (WRHS)
Cleveland, First Regular Baptist Church, records, 1820-1916 (WRHS)
Pepper Pike, Trinity Congregational Church, records, 1894-1954 (WRHS)
W.Bingham Co. records, 1841-1849, 1854-1857 (WRHS)
George C. Entrican account books, Brecksville, 1824-1842 (WRHS)
Hattie Cowing papers [Rev.War & War 1812 soldiers] (WRHS)
George W. Stanley docket book, 1837-1841 (WRHS)
Rudolphus Edwards papers & JP docket, 1815-1818 (WRHS)
Luther R.Prentiss papers & JP dockets, 1841-1853 (WRHS)
Samuel S. Baldwin papers & J.P.docket, 1809-1810 (WRHS)
Cleveland Central High School, literary society, records 1855-56 (WRHS)
Elyria, Anchor Lodge No.119, Knights of Honor, records, 1875-1884 (WRHS)
Auditor: tax duplicates, 1819,1823-1869; records, 1899-1901 (WRHS)
Common Pleas Court: records, 1810-1912, 51v (WRHS)
General county records, 1809-1896 (WRHS)
Treasurer: records, 1810-1828 (WRHS)
Brooklyn Twp. records, 1855-1924, 48v (WRHS)
Cleveland, Board of Elections, records, 1896,1907-08 (WRHS)
Cleveland Fire Dept. Engine Co. No.5, records, 1885-1886 (WRHS)
Cleveland Common Schools, district No.1, records, 1836-1867 (WRHS)
Mayfield Twp. common schools, records, 1842-1864 (WRHS)

Newburgh Twp. general records, 1815-1915 (WRHS)
Newburgh Twp. school records, 1827-1879 (WRHS)
Ohio City general records, 1836-1851 (WRHS)
Olmsted Twp. clerk records, 1827-1886 (WRHS)
Parma Twp. Justice of the Peace records, 1835-1841 (WRHS)
Rockport Twp. Justice of the Peace records, 1843-1854 (WRHS)
Royalton Twp. Justice of the Peace records, 1858-1876, 1899 (WRHS)
Warrensville Twp. common school records, 1884-1890 (WRHS)
Willeyville general records, 1835-1846 (WRHS)

## GENEALOGICAL PERIODICAL ARTICLES
Bell, Carol Willsey. OHIO GENEALOGICAL PERIODICAL INDEX: A COUNTY GUIDE (Youngstown, OH: author, 6th ed., 1987)

## PUBLISHED SOURCES:
Andrica, Theodore. ROMANIAN AMERICANS AND THEIR COMMUNITIES OF CLEVELAND.(Cleveland: Cleveland State University, 1977) 216p (LDS)
ANNALS OF CLEVELAND [newspaper abstracts, 1818-1935] (Cleveland: Block, 197?) (LDS)(OHS)
ANNALS OF THE EARLY SETTLERS ASSN. OF CUYAHOGA COUNTY. (Committee, 1880) (SLO)
ANNALS OF THE EARLY SETTLERS ASSN. OF CUYAHOGA COUNTY, v1-3. (Committee, 1882-1897) (SLO,LDS)
ANNALS OF THE EARLY SETTLERS ASSN. OF CUYAHOGA COUNTY. (Committee, 1908-1912) 3v (DAR)
Avery, Elroy M. A HISTORY OF CLEVELAND AND ITS ENVIRONS: THE HEART OF NEW CON-NECTICUT. (Chicago: Lewis Pub.Co., 1918) 3v (LDS,DAR)
Bard, Nelson P. PIONEERS WITH WEB FEET. (Solon OH: Solon Sesquicentennial Committee, 1970) 80p (OGS)
Basalt & Hatch. ATLAS OF CUYAHOGA COUNTY OUTSIDE CLEVELAND. 1903. (SLO)(RPI)
Baldwin, Henry R. OLDEST INSCRIPTIONS, WITH REVOLUTIONARY AND WAR OF 1812 RECORDS OF THE CEMETERIES OF OHIO AND PENNSYLVANIA (SLO)
Benton, Elbert J. CULTURAL HISTORY OF AN AMERICAN CITY: CLEVELAND. (Cleveland: Western Reserve Hist.Soc., 1943)
BOOK OF CLEVELANDERS; A BIOGRAPHICAL DICTIONARY OF LIVING MEN OF THE CITY OF CLEVELAND. (Cleveland OH: Burrows Bros., 1914) 1v (LDS)
Butler, Margaret M. THE LAKEWOOD STORY. (New York: Stratford House, 1949) 271p (LDS)
Cadzow, John F. LITHUANIAN AMERICANS AND THEIR COMMUNITIES OF CLEVELAND (Cleveland: Cleveland State University, 1978) 187p (LDS)
Callahan, Nelson J. & W.Hickey. IRISH AMERICANS AND THEIR COMMUNITIES OF CLEVELAND OHIO. (Cleveland: Cleveland State University, 1978) 254p (OGS,LDS)
CITY/COUNTY DIRECTORIES: check holdings of OHS & local public library.
CLEVELAND. [SPECIAL LIMITED EDITION]. (Chicago: Lewis Pub.Co., 1918) 2v (DAR)
CLEVELAND, PAST AND PRESENT; ITS REPRESENTATIVE MEN. (Cleveland: Fairbanks, Benedict & Co., 1869) 500p (DAR)
Coates, William R. HISTORY OF CUYAHOGA COUNTY AND THE CITY OF CLEVELAND. (Chicago: American Hist.Soc.,1924) 3v (SLO,LDS,DAR)
Corlett, William T. THE PEOPLE OF ORRISDALE AND OTHERS: FAMILY SKETCHES, 1918. (Cleveland: Lakeside, 1918) (LDS)
CUYAHOGA COUNTY 1852 LANDOWNERSHIP MAP INDEX. (Cleveland: Greater Cleveland Gen.Soc., 1975) 104p (LDS)
Cuyahoga County Commissioners. JOURNAL OF THE CUYAHOGA COUNTY ARCHIVES. VOL.1. 1981. (LDS)
Cuyahoga West Chapter OGS. INDEX TO CUYAHOGA COUNTY OHIO CORONER FILES 1833-1900. (Fairview Park OH: the society, 1983) 108p (OGS,LDS,SLO)
Cuyahoga West Chapter OGS. INDEX TO MARRIAGE LICENSE APPLICATIONS, CUYAHOGA COUNTY OHIO, 1829-1851, VOLS. 1-6. (Fairview Park OH: the society, 1985) 288p (OGS,LDS)

Cuyahoga West Chapter OGS. TOMBSTONE INSCRIPTIONS AND OTHER RECORDS OF ST.ADEL-BERTS CEMETERY. (Fairview Park OH: the society, 1982?) 58p (OGS)

Davidson, Kenneth. CLEVELAND DURING THE CIVIL WAR. (Columbus: OSU Press, 1962)

Daughters of the American Revolution. BIBLE & FAMILY RECORDS. 1967-1981. 6v (SLO,DAR,LDS)

Daughters of the American Revolution. BIBLE RECORDS, CUYAHOGA COUNTY OHIO. 1951. 22p (DAR,LDS,SLO)

Daughters of the American Revolution. CEMETERY & TOMBSTONE RECORDS (SLO,LDS)

Daughters of the American Revolution. CUYAHOGA COUNTY OHIO CEMETERY INSCRIPTIONS. 1978. 276p (DAR,SLO)

Daughters of the American Revolution. CUYAHOGA COUNTY OHIO MARRIAGE RECORDS, 1857-1861. 1976. 208p (DAR)

Daughters of the American Revolution. CUYAHOGA COUNTY OHIO TAX LISTS, LAND AND PER-SONAL, 1819-1825. 1974. 215p (DAR)

Daughters of the American Revolution. EARLY DAYS OF LAKEWOOD. 1936. 107p (DAR,SLO)

Daughters of the American Revolution. DATA COPIED FROM THE RECORDS OF THREE LAKEWOOD CHURCHES. (SLO)

Daughters of the American Revolution. INDEX ST. JOHN'S EPISCOPAL CHURCH RECORDS: 1835-1871. 1976?. 42,8p (DAR,SLO)

Daughters of the American Revolution. MARRIAGE RECORDS, CUYAHOGA COUNTY OHIO: BOOK XI, 1860-1864. 1943. 75p (DAR)

Daughters of the American Revolution. MARRIAGE RECORDS OF CUYAHOGA COUNTY OHIO. 5v (SLO,DAR)

Daughters of the American Revolution. ST.MALACHI CHURCH, CLEVELAND, OHIO: BIRTH AND MARRIAGE RECORDS. 1976. 1v (DAR)

Daughters of the American Revolution. SOME CEMETERY RECORDS OF CUYAHOGA,FUL-TON,MEDINA,LORAIN, & WAYNE COUNTIES. 1938. 175p (DAR)

Daughters of the American Revolution. TOMBSTONE INSCRIPTIONS OF DENISON STREET CEMETERY AND OF THE BROADVIEW CEMETERY, CLEVELAND, CUYAHOGA CO., OHIO. 1971. 1v (DAR)

Davis, Russell H. MEMORABLE NEGROES IN CLEVELAND'S PAST. (Cleveland: Western Reserve Hist.Soc., 1969) 58p (LDS,WRHS)

Ellis, William D. A HISTORY OF WESTLAKE, OHIO: 1811-1961, BOOK I, 1810-1901. 1961? (LDS)

Ellis, William D. CUYAHOGA RIVER [RIVERS OF AMERICA SERIES], c1966.

Fuessner, Henry. RECORD BOOK FOR THE MARRIAGES, BAPTISMS, BURIALS FROM THE YEAR 1884 TO 1928, WHICH I PERFORMED. [Evangelical minister] (LDS)

Gartner, Lloyd P. HISTORY OF THE JEWS OF CLEVELAND. 1978. (Reprint, Cleveland OH: Western Reserve Hist.Soc., 1987) (WRHS)

GENEALOGICAL DATA RELATING TO WOMEN IN THE WESTERN RESERVE BEFORE 1840 (1850). (Cleveland: Centennial Commission, 1943) (LDS,WRHS)

Gleason, William J. HISTORY OF THE CUYAHOGA COUNTY SOLDIERS' AND SAILORS' MONU-MENT. (Cleveland OH: The Monument Commissioners, 1894) 770p (LC)

Goebelt, Margaret S. FAIRVIEW PARK IN HISTORICAL REVIEW. (Fairview Park OH: the Hist.Soc., c1978) 364p (DAR,OGS)

Greater Cleveland Chapter OGS. CUYAHOGA COUNTY 1852 LAND OWNERSHIP INDEX & MAPS. (Cleveland: the society, nd) (OGS)

Greater Cleveland Chapter OGS. ST.MALACHI BAPTISMAL INDEX, 1883-1886. (Cleveland: the society, nd) (OGS)

Greater Cleveland Chapter OGS. ST.MALACHI CATHOLIC CHURCH, CLEVELAND, OHIO, RECORDS OF MARRIAGES, VOL.I, 1865-1899. (Cleveland: the society, 1978) 37p (OGS,SLO)

Harris, Mary. PROUD HERITAGE OF CLEVELAND HEIGHTS OHIO. 1966. 160p (SLO)

Hinshaw, William Wade. ENCYCLOPEDIA OF AMERICAN QUAKER GENEALOGY, VOL.IV, OHIO. (Baltimore: Genealogical Pub.Co., 1973) 1424p (SLO,OHS,LDS)

HISTORIC SITES OF CLEVELAND OHIO. 1942. 739p (SLO)

Historical Records Survey. INVENTORY OF BUSINESS RECORDS. (Cleveland OH: author, 1941) 104p (LDS)

Historical Records Survey. INVENTORY OF THE COUNTY ARCHIVES OF OHIO NO.18, CUYAHOGA
    COUNTY. (Cleveland OH: author, 1937) 346p (OHS,LDS,DAR)
Historical Records Survey. INVENTORY OF THE MUNICIPAL ARCHIVES OF OHIO, CUYAHOGA
    COUNTY (CLEVELAND). (Columbus: author, 1939-1941) 3v (DAR)
HISTORICAL SKETCHES OF THE VILLAGE OF GATES MILLS. (Gates Mills OH: Community Club,
    1943) 132p (LDS)
HISTORY OF STRONGSVILLE, CUYAHOGA COUNTY OHIO, 1903 BICENTENNIAL EDITION.
    (Strongsville OH: Strongsville Hist.Soc., 1976) 170p (OGS)
HISTORY OF STRONGSVILLE, CUYAHOGA COUNTY, OHIO: WITH PHOTOGRAPHS. (Strongsville
    OH: Historical Soc., 1967-1968) 2v (LDS)
HISTORY OF THE UNITARIAN CHURCH, CLEVELAND, 1836-1930. (Cleveland OH: the church,
    1930?) 31p (LDS)
Holzworth, Walter F. STORY OF CEDAR POINT VALLEY. 1980. 34p. (OGS)
Hopkins, G.M. Co. PLAT BOOK OF CUYAHOGA COUNTY OHIO. (Philadelphia: author, 1914,1920,
    1920-22,1941) (LC)
Houck, George F. THE CHURCH IN NORTHERN OHIO AND IN THE DIOCESE OF CLEVELAND
    FROM 1749 TO 1890. (Cleveland: Short & Forman, 1890, 4th ed., c1887) 324p (DAR)
Houck, George F. HISTORY OF CATHOLICITY IN NORTHERN OHIO AND IN THE DIOCESE OF
    CLEVELAND from 1749 to 1900. (Cleveland, 1903) 2v (LDS)
Hynes, Michael J. HISTORY OF THE DIOCESE OF CLEVELAND. (Cleveland: The Diocese, 1953)
INDEXES OF ST. JOHN'S EPISCOPAL CHURCH RECORDS (SLO)
Ingham, Mary B. WOMEN OF CLEVELAND & THEIR WORK, PHILSOPHICAL, EDUCATIONAL,
    LITERARY, MEDICAL & ARTISTIC. (Cleveland: author, 1893) 362p (DAR)
Joblin, Maurice, pub. CLEVELAND, PAST AND PRESENT. (Cleveland OH: Fairbanks, Benedict & Co.,
    1869) 500p (LDS)
Johnson, Crisfield. HISTORY OF CUYAHOGA COUNTY OHIO. (Philadelphia: D.W. Ensign & Co.,
    1879)(Reprint, Evansville IN: Whipporwill, 1984) 534,110p (LC,SLO,LDS,DAR)(RPI)
Kennedy, James H. HISTORY OF THE CITY OF CLEVELAND: ITS SETTLEMENT, RISE, AND
    PROGRESS, 1796-1896. (Cleveland: Imperial Press, 1896) 585p (SLO,LDS,DAR)(RPI)
Lake, D.J. ATLAS OF CUYAHOGA COUNTY, OHIO. (Philadelphia: Titus, Simmons & Titus, 1874)
    205p (OGS,SLO,LDS)(RPI)
Lampson, Edward C. A REAL CUYAHOGA PIONEER: SOME LITTLE KNOWN HISTORY OF
    CLEVELAND AND THE WESTERN RESERVE. (Jefferson OH: np,1927) 35p (LC)
Lindstrom, E.George. STORY OF LAKEWOOD, OHIO. (Lakewood: author, 190?)
    (LDS)
MacCabe, Julius P. DIRECTORY OF THE CITIES OF CLEVELAND AND OHIO. (Cleveland OH: San-
    ford & Lott, 1837-1838) (LDS,DAR)
MacLean, J.P. SHAKERS OF OHIO: FUGITIVE PAPERS CONCERNING THE SHAKERS OF OHIO,
    WITH UNPUBLISHED MANUSCRIPTS. (Columbus: F.J.Heer, 1907) 415p (DAR)
McIntyre, Mrs. M.D. SERIES OF HISTORICAL SKETCHES OF EARLY LAKEWOOD. 1938. 13p (SLO)
MEMORIAL RECORD OF THE COUNTY OF CUYAHOGA AND CITY OF CLEVELAND OHIO
    (Chicago: Lewis Pub.Co., 1894)(Reprint, Cleveland OH: Genealogical Committee, Western Reserve
    Hist.Soc., 1988,index) 924p (WRHS,LC,SLO,LDS,DAR)(RPI)
Meyer, Mrs.C.C. MARRIAGES PERFORMED BY REV.STEVENS IN TOMPKINS AND GENESSEE
    COUNTIES, NEW YORK, HURON, TRUMBULL AND CUYAHOGA COUNTIES OHIO, 1825-
    1859. (Severna Park MD: author, 1959) 9p (LDS)
Mueller, Nina. CHURCH RECORDS, CHURCH OF THE ASCENSION (EPISCOPAL) 1881-1901. (LDS)
Mueller, Nina. CUYAHOGA COUNTY OHIO DATA COPIED FROM THE RECORDS OF THREE
    LAKEWOOD CHURCHES. (DAR,LDS)
Musselman, Barbara. SURNAME INDEX: 1975. (Cleveland OH: Greater Cleveland Gen.Soc., 1975) 37p
    (LDS)
Nitchman, Paul E. BLACKS IN OHIO, 1880, IN THE COUNTIES OF COLUMBIANA TO FAYETTE,
    VOLUME 3 (Ft.Meade MD: author, 1986?) 168p
Offenberg, Bernice W. OVER THE YEARS IN OLMSTED, TOWNSHIP 6, RANGE 15. nd 153p (LDS)

OFFICIAL PROGRAMME OF THE CENTENNIAL CELEBRATION OF THE FOUNDING OF THE CITY OF CLEVELAND: AND THE SETTLEMENT OF THE WESTERN RESERVE, 1796-1896. 45p (LDS)

Orth, Samuel P. HISTORY OF CLEVELAND OHIO. (Chicago: S.J.Clarke Co.,1910) 3v (SLO,LDS,DAR,OHS)(RPI)

OUR FAITH AND HERITAGE, 100 YEARS, ST.ADALBERT PARISH, BEREA OHIO 1981. 1981. 80p (OGS,LDS)

Papp, Susan M. HUNGARIAN AMERICANS AND THEIR COMMUNITIES OF CLEVELAND. (Cleveland: Cleveland State University, 1981) 324p (LDS)

Pike, Kermit J. A GUIDE TO THE MANUSCRIPTS AND ARCHIVES OF THE WESTERN RESERVE HISTORICAL SOCIETY. (Cleveland: WRHS, 1972) 425p. (WRHS,OHS,SLO)

Pike, Kermit J. A GUIDE TO MAJOR MANUSCRIPT COLLECTIONS ACCESSIONED AND PROCESSED BY THE LIBRARY OF THE WESTERN RESERVE HISTORICAL SOCIETY. (Cleveland: Western Reserve Hist.Soc., 1987) 91p (WRHS)

REPRESENTATIVE CLEVELANDERS. (Cleveland OH: Cleveland Topics Co., 1927) 416p (DAR)

Robishaw, William M. WESTLAKE, LOOKING BACK TO DOVER. (Westlake OH: Hist. Soc., 1980) 1v (LDS)

Robison, W.Scott. HISTORY OF THE CITY OF CLEVELAND. (Cleveland OH: Robison & Crockett, 1887) 510p (SLO,LDS,DAR)(RPI)

Rose, William G. CLEVELAND: THE MAKING OF A CITY. (Cleveland: World Pub.Co., 1950) 1272p (SLO,LDS)

Rutherford, Roy. BOYS GROWN TALL: A STORY OF AMERICAN INITIATIVE, A REPRINT OF 51 BIOGRAPHICAL SKETCHES OF CLEVELAND INDUSTRIALISTS. (Cleveland: Plain Dealer, 1944) 119p (LDS)

Shaw, Willard H. HISTORICAL FACTS CONCERNING BEREA AND MIDDLEBURGH TOWNSHIP: BEREA CENTENNIAL, 1836-1936. (Berea OH: Mohler Printing Co., 1936) 50p (DAR)

Simpson, Helen M. MAKERS OF HISTORY. (Evansville IN: L.B.Warren, c1981) 112p (LDS)

Smith, Clifford N. EARLY NINETEENTH CENTURY GERMAN SETTLERS IN OHIO (MAINLY CIN-CINNATI AND ENVIRONS), KENTUCKY AND OTHER STATES. [records of Der Deutsche Pioniereverien] (McNeal AZ: author, 1984) (LDS)

Snow, Dorcas. BRECKSVILLE SCHOOL DAYS: AROUND THE TOWN, VOLS. 1 & 2. (Brecksville OH: author, 1985) 404p (OGS)

Southwest Cuyahoga Chapter OGS. INDEX TO HISTORY OF STRONGSVILLE 1903. (Strongsville OH: the society, 1983) 27p (OGS)

Squire, Dick. THE BOOK OF BEDFORD, IN COMMEMORATION OF THE 125TH ANNIVERSARY. (Bedford OH: committee, 1962) 52p (LDS)

Storer, Winifred A. HISTORY OF THE UNITARIAN CHURCH, CLEVELAND: 1836-1930. (Cleveland: Cain & Oliver, 1930) 31p (LDS)

Strongsville Historical Society. HISTORY OF STRONGSVILLE, CUYAHOGA CO OHIO, 1900-1967 BOOK I & II. 1967-8. (Strongsville OH: the society, 1967-8) 293p (OGS)

Strongsville Historical Society. HISTORY OF STRONGSVILLE, CUYAHOGA CO OHIO, BICENTEN-NIAL EDITION. 1903. (Reprint, Strongsville OH: the society, 1976) 170p (DAR)

Turner, James. THE HERITAGE OF PARMA HEIGHTS, OHIO. 1969. (SLO)

Upton, Harriet T. HISTORY OF THE WESTERN RESERVE (Chicago: Lewis Pub.Co., 1910) 3v (SLO)

Van Tassel, David D. & J.J.Grabowski. THE ENCYCLOPEDIA OF CLEVELAND HISTORY. (Bloomington IN: Indiana University, 1987?) 1200p (WRHS,OGS)

Veronesi, Gene P. ITALIAN AMERICANS AND THEIR COMMUNITIES OF CLEVELAND. (Cleveland: Cleveland State University, 1977) 358p (LDS)

Waite, Frederick C. WESTERN RESERVE UNIVERSITY: THE HUDSON ERA. (Cleveland: Western Reserve Univ.Press, 1943)

Wallen, James. CLEVELAND'S GOLDEN STORY: A CHRONICLE OF... (Cleveland?: W.Taylor Son & Co, 1920) 93p (DAR)

Western Reserve Hist.Soc. INDEX TO THE MICROFILM EDITION OF GENEALOGICAL DATA RELATING TO WOMEN IN THE WESTERN RESERVE PRE 1840. (Cleveland: the society, 1976) 226p (OGS,WRHS)

Whittlesey, Charles. EARLY HISTORY OF CLEVELAND OHIO. (Cleveland OH: Fairbanks, Benedict & Co., 1867) 487p (SLO,LDS,DAR,RPI)

Wickham, Gertrude V.W. MEMORIAL TO THE PIONEER WOMEN OF THE WESTERN RESERVE. (Cleveland: Cleveland Centennial Commission, 1896+) 2v (SLO,DAR)

Wickham, Gertrude V.W. PIONEER FAMILIES OF CLEVELAND: 1796-1840. (Evangelical Pub.House, 1914) 2v (DAR,WRHS,LDS)

Wilson, Ella. FAMOUS OLD EUCLID AVENUE OF CLEVELAND. 1937. (SLO)

Works Projects Administration. ANNALS OF CLEVELAND. [Newspaper abstracts, 1818-1935] (Cleveland: WPA, dates vary) 200v. (LDS)

Wynar, Lubomyr R. ETHNIC GROUPS IN OHIO, WITH SPECIAL EMPHASIS ON CLEVELAND: AN ANNOTATED BIBLIOGRAPHICAL GUIDE. (Cleveland: Cleveland State University, 1975) 254p (LDS)

Yon, Paul D. GUIDE TO OHIO COUNTY AND MUNICIPAL GOVERNMENT RECORDS FOR URBAN RESEARCH. (Columbus: Ohio Hist.Soc., 1973) 216p.(OHS)

# DARKE COUNTY

| | |
|---|---|
| CREATED: | 1809 FROM MIAMI COUNTY |
| COUNTY SEAT: | GREENVILLE 45331 |
| COURT HOUSE: | BROADWAY & 4TH, GREENVILLE 45331 |
| LIBRARY: | 520 SYCAMORE ST., GREENVILLE 45331 |
| HISTORICAL SOCIETY: | 205 N.BROADWAY, GREENVILLE 45331 |
| GENEALOGICAL SOCIETY: | DARKE CO. CHAPTER OGS, |
| | 205 BROADWAY, GREENVILLE 45331 |
| | publication: DARKE COUNTY KINDLING |
| HEALTH DEPARTMENT: | 111 DELAWARE, GREENVILLE 45331 |
| | (separate office for Greenville City) |
| ARCHIVAL DISTRICT: | WRIGHT STATE UNIVERSITY, DAYTON |
| | (see Leggett's Guide to records) |
| LAND SURVEYS: | CONGRESS LANDS, MIAMI RIVER SURVEY |
| BOUNDED BY: | EAST:    MIAMI & SHELBY CO. |
| | NORTH:  MERCER CO. |
| | WEST:    JAY, RANDOLPH & WAYNE CO., INDIANA |
| | SOUTH:  MONTGOMERY & PREBLE CO. |
| TOWNSHIPS: | Adams, Allen, Brown, Butler, Franklin, Greenville, Harrison, Jackson, Liberty, Mississinawa, Monroe, Neave, Patterson, Richland, Twin, Van Buren, Wabash, Washington, Wayne, York. |

**COURT RECORDS: (LDS MICROFILM)**

Auditor:
    Tax records, 1818-1838 (OHS)
Children's Home:
    Record of admittance/indenture, 1889-1915.
    Record of inmates, 1889-1915.
Clerk of Courts:
    Appearance docket, v1-2, 1837-1856.
    Civil & Chancery records, v1-8, 1818-1853.
    Civil minutes, v1-11, 1817-1853.
    General index, 1818-1853.
    Judgment index, 1818-1853.
    Naturalizations, 1856-1873.
    Reverse index, 1818-1853.
    Supreme Court minutes, 1820-1851.
    Supreme Court record, 1817-1850.

County Home:
>   Record of inmates, 1856-1951.

Probate Court:
>   Marriage records, vA-N, 1817-1911.
>   Birth records, v1-4, 1867-1908.
>   Death records, v1-4, 1867-1905.
>   Will record, vA1-L, 1818-1910.
>   Naturalizations, 1876-1906.
>   Civil journal, vA-R, 1852-1887.
>   Civil record, vA-K, 1852-1887.
>   General index to estates, 1818-1925.

Recorder:
>   Deeds, 1822-1838

Miscellaneous:
>   Marriage, bible & cemetery records, by DAR
>   Misc. cemeteries, DAR collection, State Library of Ohio


## OHIO HISTORICAL SOCIETY: (MICROFILM)

Children's Home:
>   Record of admittance/indenture, 1889-1915.
>   Record of inmates, 1889-1915.

Clerk of Courts:
>   Appearance docket, v1-2, 1837-1856.
>   Civil & Chancery records, v1-8, 1818-1853.
>   Civil minutes, v1-11, 1817-1853.
>   General index, 1818-1853.
>   Judgment index, 1818-1853.
>   Naturalizations, 1856-1873.
>   Reverse index, 1818-1853.
>   Supreme Court minutes, 1820-1851.
>   Supreme Court record, 1817-1850.

County Home:
>   Record of inmates, 1856-1951.

Probate Court:
>   Marriage records, vA-N, 1817-1911.
>   Birth records, v1-4, 1867-1908.
>   Death records, v1-4, 1867-1905.
>   Will record, vA1-L, 1818-1910.
>   Naturalizations, 1876-1906.
>   Civil journal, vA-R, 1852-1887.
>   Civil record, vA-K, 1852-1887.
>   General index to estates, 1818-1925.

City of Greenville, City Council:
>   Cemetery deeds, 1878-1948.
>   Cemetery trustee minutes, 1914-1917.
>   Planning commission minutes, 1960-1976.
>   Zoning board minutes, 1968-1976.
>   City council minutes, 1863-1877, 1887-1967.
>   Ordinance & resolutions, 1857-1976.

Miscellaneous:
>   Marriages, 1817-1865, by DAR.
>   Cemetery records, by DAR.


## CENSUS RECORDS  (OHS,SLO,OGS,LDS)

1820-1880, 1900-1910; 1890 VETERANS; 1880,1900 SOUNDEX; 1910 MIRACODE

AGRICULTURAL CENSUS SCHEDULES  (OHS,SLO-mic)
1850,1860,1880

PRODUCTS OF INDUSTRY CENSUS SCHEDULE  (OHS,SLO-mic)
1850,1870,1880

MORTALITY CENSUS SCHEDULES (OHS,SLO-mic)
1860,1880

NEWSPAPERS: [GUIDE TO OHIO NEWSPAPERS, 1793-1973]
Ansonia, Arcanum, Greenville, New Madison, Versailles.

TAX RECORDS (OHS & LDS)
1818-1838.

MANUSCRIPTS:
Frazer Wilson Collection, 1796-1944. (J.P. records) (OHS)

GENEALOGICAL PERIODICAL ARTICLES
Bell, Carol Willsey. OHIO GENEALOGICAL PERIODICAL INDEX: A COUNTY GUIDE (Youngstown,
    OH: author, 6th ed., 1987)

PUBLISHED SOURCES:
ATLAS OF DARKE COUNTY OHIO. 1875. (Reprint, Evansville IN: Unigraphic, 1973) (SLO,DAR)
ATLAS OF DARKE COUNTY OHIO 1875 AND 1888 COMBINED. (Versailles OH: Darke Co.Chapter
    OGS, 1988) (OGS,SLO)
Berkheimer, Mrs. B.F. CEMETERY RECORDS OF DARKE COUNTY OHIO. (SLO)
Berry, Ellen T. & David A. EARLY OHIO SETTLERS: PURCHASERS OF LAND IN SOUTHWESTERN
    OHIO, 1800-1840. (Baltimore: Genealogical Pub.Co., 1986) 372p (OGS,SLO,OHS)
BIOGRAPHICAL HISTORY OF DARKE CO OHIO AND COMPENDIUM OF NATIONAL BIOG-
    RAPHY. (Chicago: Lewis Pub.Co., 1900) 758pp (LC,SLO,LDS,DAR)(RPI)
Bowers, Ruth. DARKE COUNTY CEMETERIES VOL.6 (Union City OH: author, nd) np
Bowers, Ruth. DARKE COUNTY, OHIO GERMAN REFORMED CHURCH, UNITED BRETHREN IN
    CHRIST, HILLGROVE FEDERATED, HILLGROVE, OHIO, 1865-1979. 1984. 12p (LDS)
Brien, Lindsay M. ABSTRACTS FROM HISTORY OF DARKE COUNTY, OHIO, BEERS 1880. (Fort
    Wayne IN: Allen Co.Pub.Lib., 1966) 48p (LDS)
Burns, Norman. JACOB C. CARLOCK, FOUNDER OF WEBSTER, AND OTHER EARLY SETTLERS
    THERE. (Arlington VA: author, 1976) 36p (LDS)
Chase, J.Jr. MAP OF DARKE COUNTY OHIO, FROM SURVEYS AND COUNTY RECORDS. (Philadel-
    phia: S.H.Matthews, 1857) (Reprint, Evansville IN: Unigraphic, 1973) 69p (LDS,SLO)
CITY/COUNTY DIRECTORIES: check holdings of OHS & local public library.
Darke Co.Chapter OGS. DARKE COUNTY, OHIO, MARRIAGES, 1851-1898. (Greenville: the society,
    1986) 430p (LDS)
Daughters of the American Revolution. ADDITIONAL RECORDS OF TOMBSTONE INSCRIPTIONS
    OF CEMETERIES IN DARKE COUNTY OHIO. (SLO)
Daughters of the American Revolution. BIBLE RECORDS OF DARKE, MIAMI AND MONTGOMERY
    COUNTIES OHIO. (SLO)
Daughters of the American Revolution. CEMETERY INSCRIPTIONS, DARKE COUNTY OHIO. 1968-
    1978. 4v (DAR)
Daughters of the American Revolution. CEMETERY RECORDS OF DARKE COUNTY OHIO. (Green-
    ville OH: Fort Greeneville Chapter, 1962) (OHS)
Daughters of the American Revolution. CHURCH RECORDS [DARKE CO OHIO]. 1974. 133p (DAR)
Daughters of the American Revolution. CHURCH RECORDS FOR THE FIRST PRESBYTERIAN
    CHURCH AT GREENVILLE, DARKE CO., OHIO. 1972. 103p (DAR)

Daughters of the American Revolution. CHURCH RECORDS, DARKE COUNTY, OHIO: ST.MATTHEW'S EVANGELICAL LUTHERAN CHURCH AND ST.PAUL'S LUTHERAN CHURCH. 1975. 1v (DAR)

Daughters of the American Revolution. CHURCH RECORDS OF THE UNITED BRETHREN IN CHRIST CHURCH: GREENVILLE, OHIO, THE UNITED BRETHREN IN CHRIST CHURCH, HILLGROVE, OHIO, ALSO THE UNION PRESBYTERIAN CHURCH, HILLGROVE, OHIO. 1977. 180p (DAR)

Daughters of the American Revolution. DARKE COUNTY OHIO BIBLE RECORDS. 1971- . -v (DAR,LDS)

Daughters of the American Revolution. DARKE COUNTY OHIO RECORDS FORM THE FAMILY BIBLE OF ALANSON BROWN, FAMILY RECORDS OF GARST, STOLTZ AND MENKE. (SLO)

Daughters of the American Revolution. DARKE COUNTY OHIO DEED RECORDS 1817-1834: DEED BOOKS A THROUGH D. 1977. 133,36p (DAR)

Daughters of the American Revolution. EARLY MARRIAGES OF DARKE COUNTY OHIO, 1817-1865. 1936. 3v (SLO,DAR)

Daughters of the American Revolution. MARRIAGES-BIRTHS-DEATHS, 1852-1900: ST.JOHN LUTHERAN CHURCH, GREENVILLE OHIO. 1972. 101p (DAR)

Daughters of the American Revolution. MORE RECORDS OF OLD CEMETERIES OF DARKE COUNTY OHIO. 1962. 29p (DAR)

Daughters of the American Revolution. MORE TOMBSTONE INSCRIPTIONS, ADAMS, BROWN ETC. (SLO)

Daughters of the American Revolution. NEWSPAPER DEATH NOTICES, DARKE COUNTY OHIO: VOLUMES II,III,VI. 1976. 100p (DAR)

Daughters of the American Revolution. OHIO BIBLE RECORDS: CONCERNING FAMILIES OF CRAWFORD,DARKE,FAIRFIELD,MIAMI,MONTGOMERY,PICKAWAY,PREBLE AND SHELBY COUNTIES. 1970. 126p (SLO,DAR)

Daughters of the American Revolution. OHIO CHURCH RECORDS: THE EVANGELICAL LUTHERAN TRINITY CONGREGATION NOW TRINITY LUTHERAN CHURCH RECORDS, VERSAILLES, OHIO, DARKE COUNTY, WAYNE TOWNSHIP. 1974-5. 2v (DAR,SLO)

Daughters of the American Revolution. OHIO CHURCH RECORDS: TRINITY LUTHERAN CHURCH, VERSAILLES, OHIO, DARKE COUNTY, WAYNE TOWNSHIP. 1979. 138p (DAR)

Daughters of the American Revolution. RECORDS OF ST.VALBERT, ST.DENIS & HOLY FAMILY PARISHES. (SLO)

Daughters of the American Revolution. TWELVE OHIO COUNTIES (CEMETERIES) (SLO)

Eby, Lela. EVERY NAME INDEX: HISTORY OF THE MISSISSINEWA, CHURCH OF THE BRETHREN BY RALPH G. RARICK, 1917. 6p (LDS)

Eller, Mrs. Denver. CHURCH RECORD FOR THE FIRST PRESBYTERIAN CHURCH AT GREENVILLE, DARKE CO., OHIO. 1984. 103p (LDS)

Eller, Mrs. Denver. CHURCH RECORD FOR ST.PAUL'S LUTHERAN CHURCH AT GREENVILLE, DARKE COUNTY, OHIO. 1984. 39p (LDS)

Eller, Mrs. Denver. EVANGELICAL LUTHERAN TRINITY CHURCH, NOW TRINITY LUTHERAN CHURCH RECORDS BOOK II, GREENVILLE OHIO. 1984. 49p (LDS)

Eller, Mrs. Denver. ST.JOHN LUTHERAN CHURCH RECORDS, 1852-1900. 1973. (LDS)

Fecher, Con J. ANCESTRAL PORTRAITS OF OHIO SETTLERS. (Dayton OH: Univ. of Dayton Press, 1980) 321p (OGS,LDS)

Finton, Ken. MORE RECORDS OF OLD CEMETERIES OF DARKE COUNTY OHIO. 1959-1961. 47p (LDS,SLO)

Finton, Ken. RECORDS OF SOME OLD CEMETERIES OF DARKE COUNTY, OHIO. 1958. 41p (SLO,LDS)

FIRST CHRISTIAN CHURCH, GREENVILLE, OHIO: CHURCH RECORDS. 1852-1900. 1984. 133p (LDS)

Fisher, Joanne. NEWSPAPER DEATH RECORDS, DARKE COUNTY OHIO, VOL.2, 1880-1885. (Union City IN: author, nd) 45p

Fisher, Joanne. NEWSPAPER DEATH RECORDS, DARKE COUNTY OHIO, VOL.3, 1886-1891. (Union City IN: author, nd) 55p

Fisher, Joanne. NEWSPAPER DEATH RECORDS, DARKE COUNTY OHIO, VOL.4, 1892-1898. (Union City IN: author, nd) 100p

Fox, John H. GRAVESTONE INSCRIPTIONS, OHIO. 197? (LDS)

Gerling, Juanita. VIEWS OF VERSAILLES AND SURROUNDING AREA. (Versailles OH: Policy Pub.Co., c1976) 160p (DAR)

Gilbert, Audrey. DARKE COUNTY OHIO 1900 CENSUS. 425p (SLO)

Griffing, B.N. ATLAS OF DARKE COUNTY, OHIO. (Philadelphia: Griffing, Gordon, 1888)(Reprint, Evansville IN: Unigraphic, 1973) 76p (SLO,OGS,LDS)(RPI)

Haller, Stephen E. & P.Nolan. FIRST STOP FOR LOCAL HISTORY RESEARCH. A GUIDE TO COUNTY RECORDS PRESERVED AT WRIGHT STATE UNIVERSITY ARCHIVES AND SPECIAL COLLECTIONS. 1976. 21p.

Hardesty, H.H. MILITARY HISTORY OF OHIO - DARKE COUNTY EDITION. 1886/87. (OHS)

HISTORY OF ANSONIA AND BROWN TOWNSHIP. 1976? 112p (DAR)

Lake, D.J. ATLAS OF DARKE COUNTY OHIO. (Philadelphia: Lake, Griffing & Stevenson, 1875)(Reprint, Evansville IN: Unigraphic, 1973) 79p (LC,SLO,LDS) (RPI)

Leggett, Nancy G. & D.E.Smith. A GUIDE TO LOCAL GOVERNMENT RECORDS AND NEWSPAPERS PRESERVED AT THE DEPARTMENT OF ARCHIVES AND SPECIAL COLLECTIONS WRIGHT STATE UNIVERSITY. (Dayton OH: Wright State U., 1987)

Long, Samuel. A PIONEER HISTORY OF WAYNE TOWNSHIP, DARKE COUNTY, OHIO. 1901. Reprint 1978. (SLO)

McIntosh, W.H. THE HISTORY OF DARKE COUNTY, OHIO. (Chicago: W.H.Beers, 1880) 772p (LC,SLO,LDS,DAR)(RPI)

Miller, Stephen J. THE PALESTINE BOOK: HISTORY OF LIBERTY (GERMAN) TOWNSHIP, DARKE COUNTY, OHIO. (Defiance OH: Hubbard Co., 1983) 280p (LDS,SLO)

Montgomery Co. Chapter OGS. INDEX TO DARKE COUNTY NATURALIZATION RECORDS, COMMON PLEAS COURT MINUTES, 1812-1857. (Dayton OH: the society, 1985) 3p (LDS)

Nitchman, Paul E. BLACKS IN OHIO, 1880, IN THE COUNTIES OF COLUMBIANA TO FAYETTE, VOLUME 3 (Ft.Meade MD: author, 1986?) 168p

Perry, Robert E. HISTORY OF BRADFORD THROUGH THE YEARS. 1966. 310p (SLO)

Pouget, Luella R. CEMETERY INSCRIPTIONS FROM MONTGOMERY, MIAMI, PREBLE AND DARKE COUNTIES OHIO. 1960. (LDS)

Seiler, Toni. GREENVILLE'S OLD HOMES - PAST AND PRESENT. (Greenville OH: Darke Co Hist.Soc., 1976) 44p (SLO)

Shilt, Rose. DARKE COUNTY OHIO 1850 CENSUS. (Mansfield OH: Ohio Gen.Soc.,1978) 185p (OGS,LDS)

Short, Anita & R.Bowers. DARKE COUNTY OHIO COMMON PLEAS COURT RECORDS 1817-1860. c1972. 140p (SLO,LDS,DAR)

Short, Anita. INDEX OF WILL RECORDS 1818-1900 DARKE COUNTY OHIO. (SLO)

Short, Anita. OHIO BIBLE RECORDS CONCERNING THE FAMILIES OF CRAWFORD, DARKE, ETC. COUNTIES (SLO)

Short, Anita & R.Bowers. DARKE COUNTY OHIO DEED RECORDS 1817-1834.(Arcanum OH: authors, c1977) 169p (SLO,LDS)

Short, Mrs. Don & Mrs.D.Bowers. CEMETERY INSCRIPTIONS OF DARKE COUNTY OHIO, c1968. 5v (SLO,LDS)

Short, Mrs. Don & Mrs.D.Bowers. DARKE COUNTY OHIO MARRIAGE RECORDS, 1817-1840 INCLUSIVE. (Greenville OH: authors, 1966) 46p (LDS)

Short, Mrs. Don & Mrs.D.Bowers. DARKE COUNTY OHIO MARRIAGE RECORDS, 1841-1850 VOL.2. (Greenville OH: authors, c1972) (LDS,DAR)

Short, Mrs. Don & Mrs.D.Bowers. DARKE COUNTY OHIO WILL ABSTRACTS, 1818-1857 INCLUSIVE. nd. 49p (SLO,LDS,DAR)

Short, Anita. WATER STREET CEMETERY, GREENVILLE, OHIO. (Greenville OH: DAR, 1972) 21p (DAR)

Smith, William E. HISTORY OF SOUTHWESTERN OHIO. 1964. 3v. (SLO)

Straker, Robert L. SOME EARLY FAMILIES OF WAYNE AND PATTERSON TOWNSHIPS, DARKE COUNTY OHIO. (Troy OH: author, 1930) 1v (LDS)

THE TREATY CITY, GREENVILLE, OHIO: HISTORY, BUILDINGS, ORGANIZATIONS, AND INDUSTRY. (Greenville OH: Rotary Club, 1933) 22p (DAR)

Trostel, Scott D. BRADFORD, THE RAILROAD TOWN: A RAILROAD TOWN HISTORY OF BRADFORD, OHIO. (Fletcher OH: Cam-Tech Pub., c1987) 152p (LDS)

Vicory, Jacqueline. MILO UNION LIST OF GENEALOGIES IN THE LIBRARIES OF CHAMPAIGN, CLARK, DARKE, GREENE, MIAMI, MONTGOMERY, AND PREBLE COUNTIES, OHIO. (Dayton OH: Miami Valley Library Organization, 1977) 122p (LDS)

VIEWS OF VERSAILLES AND SURROUNDING AREAS. 1976. 160p (SLO)

Wilke, Katherine. NEWSPAPER: DEATH RECORDS, DARKE COUNTY, OHIO 1850-1891 INCLUSIVE. (Union City IN: author, c1968) 3v (LDS,SLO)

Wilson, Fraser E. HISTORY OF DARKE COUNTY OHIO: FROM ITS EARLIEST SETTLEMENT TO THE PRESENT TIME. (Milford OH: Hobart Pub.Co., 1914) 2v (DAR,LC,SLO,LDS)

Wolfe, George W. A PICTORIAL OUTLINE HISTORY OF DARKE COUNTY OHIO. (Newark OH: Lyon & Ickes, Pubs., nd) 393p (LDS)

# DEFIANCE COUNTY

| | |
|---|---|
| CREATED: | 1845 FROM HENRY, PAULDING & WILLIAMS COUNTIES |
| COUNTY SEAT: | DEFIANCE 43512 |
| COURT HOUSE: | 221 CLINTON ST., DEFIANCE 43512 |
| LIBRARY: | 320 FORT ST., DEFIANCE 43512 |
| HISTORICAL SOCIETY: | PO BOX 801, DEFIANCE 43512 |
| GENEALOGICAL SOCIETY: | DEFIANCE CO. CHAPTER OGS, PO BOX 675, DEFIANCE 43512 publication: YESTERYEARS TRAIL |
| HEALTH DEPARTMENT: | 113 BIEDE AVE., DEFIANCE 43512 (separate office for Defiance City) |
| ARCHIVAL DISTRICT: | BOWLING GREEN STATE UNIVERSITY, BOWLING GREEN (see Biggs' Guide to records) |
| LAND SURVEYS: | CONGRESS LANDS, E & N OF 1ST PRIN.MERIDIAN |
| BOUNDED BY: | EAST: HENRY CO. |
| | NORTH: WILLIAMS CO. |
| | WEST: DE KALB CO., INDIANA |
| | SOUTH: PAULDING & PUTNAM CO. |
| TOWNSHIPS: | Adams, Defiance, Delaware, Farmer, Hicksville, Highland, Mark, Milford, Noble, Richland, Tiffin, Washington. |

## COURT RECORDS: (LDS MICROFILM)

Children's Home:
    Admittance records, 1884-1925.
Clerk of Courts:
    Appearance docket, 1845-1853.
    Journal, v1-2, 1845-1854.
    Chancery record, 1845-1865.
    Judgment index, direct & reverse, 1845-1878.
    Supreme Court complete record, 1846-1859.
    Supreme Court journal, 1846-1884.
County Home:
    Death record, 1886-1980.
    Register, 1880-1980.
Probate Court:
    Administration record, 1845-1853.
    General index to files, 1845-1972.
    Wills, v1, 1845-1852, v1-8, 1853-1910.

Marriages, v1-6, 1845-1912,1912-1918.
Death records, v1-2, 1867-1908.
Birth records, v1-3, 1867-1908.
Index to births, 1867-1908.
Naturalizations, 1870-1906.
Naturalization intentions, 1848-1894.
Record of accounts, 1851-1885.
Inventories & sale bills, 1853-1886.
Journal, v1-5, 1852-1889.
Administrators & guardians bonds, 1860-1905.
Civil docket, v1, 1853-1879; v3, 1883-1908.
Final record, v1-5, 1853-1889.
Recorder:
Record of veterans' graves, 1869-1972.
Deed records, v1-31, 1824-1881.
Deeds, v31-39, 1880-1886.
Deed index, v1-16, 1823-1969.
Deeds transcribed from Williams Co, 1824-1845.
Miscellaneous:
Marriages, 1845-1865, by DAR.
Defiance Presbyterian Church, records, 1836-1865.
Bryan, Trinity Lutheran Church, records, 1862-1961.
Union Presbyterian Church, Farmer Tp., records, 1848-1858.

**OHIO HISTORICAL SOCIETY: (MICROFILM)**
Children's Home:
Admittance records, 1884-1925.
Clerk of Courts:
Appearance docket, 1845-1853.
Journal, v1-2, 1845-1854.
Chancery record, 1845-1865.
Judgment index, direct & reverse, 1845-1878.
Supreme Court complete record, 1846-1859.
Supreme Court journal, 1846-1884.
County Home:
Death record, 1886-1980.
Register, 1880-1980.
Probate Court:
Administration record, 1845-1853.
Naturalization intentions, 1848-1894.
Index to births, 1867-1908.
Marriages, 1912-1918.
Final record, v1-5, 1853-1889.
Will record, v7-8, 1902-1910.
Recorder:
Deeds, v31-39, 1880-1886.
Miscellaneous:
Marriages, 1840-1864, by DAR.

**CENSUS RECORDS (OHS,SLO,OGS,LDS)**
1850-1880, 1900-1910; 1890 VETERANS; 1880,1900 SOUNDEX; 1910 MIRACODE

**AGRICULTURAL CENSUS SCHEDULES (OHS,SLO-mic)**
1850,1860,1880

**PRODUCTS OF INDUSTRY CENSUS SCHEDULE (OHS,SLO-mic)**
1850,1870,1880

**MORTALITY CENSUS SCHEDULES (OHS,SLO-mic)**
1860,1880

**NEWSPAPERS: [GUIDE TO OHIO NEWSPAPERS, 1793-1973]**
Defiance, Hicksville.

**TAX RECORDS (OHS & LDS)**
none listed; see parent counties.

**GENEALOGICAL PERIODICAL ARTICLES**
Bell, Carol Willsey. OHIO GENEALOGICAL PERIODICAL INDEX: A COUNTY GUIDE (Youngstown,
    OH: author, 6th ed., 1987)

**PUBLISHED SOURCES:**
Andrews, Joseph G. SURGEON'S MATE AT FORT DEFIANCE. 1957. 91p (SLO)
Battershell, James. HISTORY OF HICKSVILLE. (SLO)
Biggs, Deb. GUIDE TO LOCAL GOVERNMENT RECORDS AT THE CENTER FOR ARCHIVAL COL-
    LECTIONS. (Bowling Green OH: Bowling Green State Univ, 1981) 104p (OGS)
Carter, William. FORT DEFIANCE CENTENNIAL. (Defiance OH: Daily Crescent Printing, 1894) 50p
    (LC)
CENTENARY HISTORY OF THE FIRST PRESBYTERIAN CHURCH, HICKSVILLE, OHIO, 1855-1955.
    (SLO)
Christian, Donna K. GUIDE TO NEWSPAPER HOLDINGS AT THE CENTER FOR ARCHIVAL COL-
    LECTIONS. (Bowling Green OH: Bowling Green State Univ, 1980) 64p (OGS)
CITY/COUNTY DIRECTORIES: check holdings of OHS & local public library.
Clegg, Michael, ed. DEFIANCE, FULTON, HENRY, PAULDING, PUTNAM, WILLIAMS & WOOD
    COUNTIES OHIO NEWSPAPER OBITUARY ABSTRACTS, 1838-1870 (OHIO NEWSPAPER SERIES
    VOL.5) (Ft.Wayne IN: author, 1987) 75p (OGS)
COMMEMORATIVE BIOGRAPHICAL RECORD OF NORTHWESTERN OHIO INCLUDING THE
    COUNTIES OF DEFIANCE, HENRY, WILLIAMS & FULTON. (Chicago: J.H.Beers & Co., 1899)
    616p (LDS,OGS,SLO,DAR)(RPI)
Daughters of the American Revolution. BIBLE RECORDS OF CUYAHOGA COUNTY AND PICK-
    AWAY COUNTY, OHIO, ALSO WILLS OF DEFIANCE COUNTY OHIO. (SLO,LDS)
Daughters of the American Revolution. RELATING TO MARRIAGES OF DEFIANCE COUNTY OHIO.
    1940. 75p (SLO,DAR,LDS)
Daughters of the American Revolution. WILLS DEFIANCE,RICHLAND,MAHONING COUNTIES.
    1936? 200p (DAR)
Defiance Co.Hist.Soc. DEFIANCE COUNTY OHIO: A COLLECTION OF HISTORICAL SKETCHES
    AND FAMILY HISTORIES COMPILED BY MEMBERS AND FRIENDS OF THE DEFIANCE COUN-
    TY HISTORICAL SOCIETY. (Defiance OH: the society, 1976) 632p (LDS)
Griffing, B.N. ATLAS OF DEFIANCE COUNTY, OHIO. (Philadelphia: Griffing, Gordon, 1890)
    (SLO)(RPI)
Hardesty, H.H. HISTORICAL ATLAS OF DEFIANCE COUNTY OHIO. 1876. Reprint 1979.
    (SLO,OGS,OHS)
Harter, Fayne E. EARLY DEATH RECORDS OF DEFIANCE COUNTY OHIO, 1867-1884. 1970. 174p
    (LDS)
Harter, Fayne E. RECORDS OF THE PERKINS & REEB FUNERAL HOME, HICKSVILLE, DEFIANCE
    COUNTY OHIO. 1966. 521p. (LDS)
HISTORY OF DEFIANCE COUNTY OHIO: CONTAINING A HISTORY OF THE COUNTY. (Chicago:
    Warner Beers, 1883) 374p (SLO,DAR,LDS)(RPI)
HISTORY OF DEFIANCE COUNTY OHIO. (Defiance OH: Defiance Co.Hist.Soc., 1976)
Hixson, W.W. PLAT BOOK OF DEFIANCE COUNTY. (Rockford IL: author, nd) (OHS)

Knapp, Horace S. HISTORY OF THE MAUMEE VALLEY. (Toledo OH: author, 1872) 685p. (DAR,OHS,SLO)

Levinson, Marilyn. GUIDE TO NEWSPAPER HOLDINGS AT THE CENTER FOR ARCHIVAL COLLECTIONS. 2nd Edition. (Bowling Green OH: Bowling Green State Univ., 1987)

Maumee Valley Pioneer Assn. ADDRESSES, MEMORIALS, AND SKETCHES. 1900, 1901. (SLO)

Nitchman, Paul E. BLACKS IN OHIO, 1880, IN THE COUNTIES OF COLUMBIANA TO FAYETTE, VOLUME 3 (Ft.Meade Md: author, 1986?) 168p

OGS CEMETERIES OF DEFIANCE, OTTAWA AND WOOD COUNTIES OHIO. (SLO)

PANORAMIC SOUVENIR OF THE 1913 FLOOD IN DEFIANCE, OHIO. (Cleveland: Corday & Gross Co., c1913) 24p (LC)

SAINT MARY CATHOLIC CHURCH, DEFIANCE OHIO. (Chicago: CPD Corp, 1979) 54p (OGS)

Simonis, Louis A. MAUMEE RIVER 1835 - WITH THE WILLIAM C. HOLGATE JOURNAL. (Defiance: Defiance Co Hist Soc, 1979) 302p. (OGS,SLO)

Van Tassel, Charles S. STORY OF THE MAUMEE VALLEY, TOLEDO AND THE SANDUSKY REGION. (Chicago: S.V.Clarke, 1929) 4v (OHS)

Winter, Nevin O. HISTORY OF NORTHWEST OHIO. (Chicago: Lewis Pub Co, 1917) 3v (SLO)

# DELAWARE COUNTY

| | |
|---|---|
| CREATED: | 1808 FROM FRANKLIN COUNTY |
| COUNTY SEAT: | DELAWARE 43015 |
| COURT HOUSE: | 91 N.SANDUSKY ST., DELAWARE 43015 |
| LIBRARY: | 101 N.SANDUSKY ST., DELAWARE 43015 |
| HISTORICAL SOCIETY: | PO BOX 317, DELAWARE 43015 |
| GENEALOGICAL SOCIETY: | DELAWARE CO. CHAPTER OGS, PO BOX 1126, DELAWARE 43015 publication: DELAWARE GENEALOGIST |
| HEALTH DEPARTMENT: | 115 NORTH SANDUSKY ST., DELAWARE 43015 (separate offices for Delaware City & Westerville) |
| ARCHIVAL DISTRICT: | OHIO HISTORICAL SOCIETY, COLUMBUS |
| LAND SURVEYS: | UNITED STATES MILITARY DISTRICT VIRGINIA MILITARY DISTRICT |
| BOUNDED BY: | EAST:     KNOX & LICKING CO. NORTH:   MARION & MORROW CO. WEST:     UNION CO. SOUTH:   FRANKLIN CO. |
| TOWNSHIPS: | Berkshire, Berlin, Brown, Concord, Delaware, Genoa, Harlem, Kingston, Liberty, Marlboro, Montgomery, Orange, Oxford, Porter, Radnor, Thompson, Trenton, Troy. |
| SPECIAL NOTE: | A COURTHOUSE FIRE IN 1835 DESTROYED MANY EARLY RECORDS. |

## COURT RECORDS: (LDS MICROFILM)
Auditor:
    Tax records, 1816-1838 (OHS).
Clerk of Courts:
    Supreme Court record, v3-4, 1834-1851.
    Supreme Court journal, 1833-1851.
    Common Pleas record, v3, 1818-1827.
    Common Pleas journal, v9, 1835-1838.
    Record of estates, v2, 1835-1849.
    Appearance docket, 1835-1851.
    Chancery record, 1825-1854.

Estates, 1835-1849.
Journal, 1821-1831,1835-1855.
Journal index, 1835-1855.
Commissioners:
    Burial of ex-Union soldiers, 1884-1898.
Probate Court:
    Marriage records, v1-15, 1835-1927.
    Death records, 1867-1899.
    Birth records, 1867-1909.
    Will records, v1-33, 1812-1952.
    Guardianship bonds, 1858-1879.
    Civil dockets, 1859-1877.
    Administrators bonds, 1860-1884.
    Executors bonds, 1853-1879.
    Probate records, v1-27, 1852-1908.
    Probate journals, v1-27, 1852-1908.
    Probate & juvenile records, 1959-1960.
    Probate case files, 1959-1960.
Miscellaneous:
    Delaware, First Presby.Church, records, 1836-1969.
    Delaware, Second Presby.Church, records, 1841-1853.
    Ostrander, Little Millcreek Presby.Church, records, 1814-1886.
    Scioto Village, State of Ohio, Girls industrial school, inmate case record, 1869-1911.
    Ostrander, Little Mill Creek Presb.Church, records, 1814-1886.
    Misc. cemeteries, DAR Collection, State Library of Ohio.

## OHIO HISTORICAL SOCIETY: (MICROFILM)

Clerk of Courts:
    Supreme Court record, v3-4, 1834-1851.
    Supreme Court journal, 1833-1851.
    Common Pleas record, v3, 1818-1827.
    Common Pleas journal, v9, 1835-1838.
    Record of estates, v2, 1835-1849.
    Appearance docket, 1835-1851.
    Chancery record, 1825-1854.
    Estates, 1835-1849.
    Journal, 1821-1831,1835-1855.
    Journal index, 1835-1855.
Commissioners:
    Burial of ex-Union soldiers, 1884-1898.
Miscellaneous:
    1826 tax list, by DAR.
    Marriages, 1832-1865, by DAR.
    Probate index, letters A-C, by DAR.
    Cemetery records, by DAR.
    Revolutionary soldiers, by DAR.

## CENSUS RECORDS  (OHS,SLO,OGS,LDS)
1820-1880, 1900-1910; 1890 VETERANS; 1880,1900 SOUNDEX; 1910 MIRACODE

## AGRICULTURAL CENSUS SCHEDULES  (OHS,SLO-mic)
1850,1860,1880

## PRODUCTS OF INDUSTRY CENSUS SCHEDULE  (OHS,SLO-mic)
1850,1870,1880

**MORTALITY CENSUS SCHEDULES (OHS,SLO-mic)**
1860,1880

**NEWSPAPERS: [GUIDE TO OHIO NEWSPAPERS, 1793-1973]**
Ashley, Delaware, Sunbury, Westerville.

**TAX RECORDS (OHS & LDS)**
1808-1810,1812-1814,1816-1838.

**MANUSCRIPTS:**
Michael Jacoby papers, Justice of the Peace, 1809-1955 (OHS)
Oxford Twp., records, 1828-1843 (WRHS)

**GENEALOGICAL PERIODICAL ARTICLES**
Bell, Carol Willsey. OHIO GENEALOGICAL PERIODICAL INDEX: A COUNTY GUIDE (Youngstown,
    OH: author, 6th ed., 1987)

**PUBLISHED SOURCES:**
Arnold, Randall R. HISTORICAL HISTORY OF TOWNSHIPS IN CENTRAL OHIO, AND OF THE
    EARLY SETTLERS NORTH OF COLUMBUS: IN CONNECTION WITH OTHER REMINISCEN-
    CES. (Westerville OH: author, 1891) (LDS)
Beers, Frederick W. ATLAS OF DELAWARE COUNTY OHIO. 1866. (SLO)(RPI)
Bell, Carol W. DELAWARE COUNTY, OHIO, GENEALOGICAL ABSTRACTS. (Columbus, OH: author,
    1980) 72p (SLO,OGS,OHS)
Bouic, Margaret Main. GENEALOGICAL INDEX OF DELAWARE, UNION AND MORROW COUN-
    TIES. (SLO,OGS,DAR,LDS)
Bouic, Margaret. HISTORY OF SCIOTO TOWNSHIP DELAWARE COUNTY OHIO. 1965? 255p
    (SLO,DAR,LDS)
Bouic, Margaret. OSTRANDER PRESBYTERIAN CHURCH AND ITS MEMBERS. 1960? 58p (DAR,LDS)
Bricker, John W. CEMETERY RECORDS OF DELAWARE COUNTY OHIO. 1970-71. 2v (SLO,DAR,LDS)
BROWN TOWNSHIP, DELAWARE COUNTY OHIO. 1937? 25p (DAR)
Buckingham, Ray E. DELAWARE COUNTY THEN & NOW. 1976. 407p. (OGS,SLO)
Buckingham, Ray E. HISTORICAL HIGHLIGHTS 1810-1985, FIRST PRESBYTERIAN CHURCH,
    DELAWARE, OHIO. (Delaware OH: Delaware Co Chapter OGS, 1985) 61p (OGS)
Buckingham, Ray E. MOSES BYXBE, HIS IMPACT AND IMAGE. 1979. 83p. (OGS)
CITY/COUNTY DIRECTORIES: check holdings of OHS & local public library.
Crist, A.C. THE HISTORY OF MARION PRESBYTERY: ITS CHURCHES, ELDERS, MINISTERS, MIS-
    SIONARY SOCIETIES, ETC. 1908. 352p (DAR)
Cryder, Marilyn & George. DELAWARE COUNTY OHIO WILL BOOK NO.4 1859-1869. ABSTRACT
    AND INDEX. (Delaware OH: author, 1986) 64p (OGS,lds)
Daughters of the American Revolution. ABSTRACTS OF WILLS, V.1-3, DELAWARE CO., OHIO, 1811-
    1859. 3v (DAR,LDS)
Daughters of the American Revolution. CEMETERY INSCRIPTIONS IN THE FILES OF DELAWARE
    COUNTY HISTORICAL SOCIETY. 1969. 151p (DAR)
Daughters of the American Revolution. DELAWARE COUNTY OHIO, OAK GROVE CEMETERY -
    LUCIUS C. STRONG BIBLE. 1952. 23p (DAR,LDS)
Daughters of the American Revolution. DELAWARE, OHIO, RECORDS. 1970? 101p (DAR)
Daughters of the American Revolution. EARLY MARRIAGE BONDS OF DELAWARE COUNTY OHIO,
    1832-1865. 3v (SLO,LDS,OHS,DAR)
Daughters of the American Revolution. FAMILY RECORDS OF DELAWARE COUNTY OHIO. 1969.
    102p (SLO,DAR)
Daughters of the American Revolution. INDEX OF REVOLUTIONARY SOLDIERS BURIED IN
    DELAWARE COUNTY OHIO. (SLO,LDS)

Daughters of the American Revolution. MARRIAGES, PROBATE COURT INDEX, CEMETERY AND AUDITORS TAX RECORDS, DELAWARE COUNTY OHIO. (SLO,LDS)

Daughters of the American Revolution. REVOLUTIONARY SOLDIER AND FAMILY RECORDS, DELAWARE COUNTY OHIO. 1972. 77p (DAR)

Delaware Co Chapter OGS. MALE INHABITANTS OVER THE AGE OF 21 IN DELAWARE COUNTY OHIO IN 1835. (Delaware OH: the society, 1988) 102p (OGS)

Delaware Co Chapter OGS. 1987 GUIDE TO THE CEMETERIES OF DELAWARE COUNTY OHIO & INDEX TO THE WPA VETERANS GRAVE REGISTRATION. (Delaware OH: the society, 1987) 175p (OGS)

Delaware Co Chapter OGS. DELAWARE COUNTY OHIO GRANTOR AND GRANTEE INDEX TO THE 1800-1820 LAND RECORDS IN THE COUNTY RECORDER'S OFFICE. (Delaware OH: the society, 1988) (OGS)

Delaware Co Chapter OGS. 1988 EVERY MEMBER SURNAME INDEX, PART 1. (Delaware OH: the society, 1987?) (OGS)

Diem, W.Roy. THE PRESBYTERIAN CHURCH OF DELAWARE, OHIO: 1810-1960. (Delaware OH: Independent Print Shop, 1960) 114p (DAR)

Drake, Paul. THE DAY BOOK OF DR. WILLIAM K. DRAKE FOR THE PERIOD 1841-1856 [PICKAWAY, DELAWARE & HANCOCK COS]. (Crab Orchard TN: author, 1984) 105p (OGS)

Edelblute, Clara. EVERSOLE CEMETERY, HILL CEMETERY, CONCORD TWP., DELAWARE COUNTY OHIO. (SLO)

Everts, L.H. ILLUSTRATED HISTORICAL ATLAS OF DELAWARE COUNTY. 1875. (SLO, OGS)(RPI)

Fry, Harriet. LIBERTY PRESBYTERIAN CHURCH AND THE LIBERTY COMMUNITY.(SLO)

Girl Scouts Troop 484, Delaware. THE GENEALOGICAL INFORMATION AS RELATED TO THOSE BURIED IN THE HOUK ROAD CEMETERY, DELAWARE, OHIO, AND THEIR DESCENDANTS. (Delaware OH: the Troop, 1979) 72p (DAR,LDS)

Graham, Thomas D. HISTORICAL SKETCH OF THE WILLIAM STREET METHODIST CHURCH, DELAWARE OHIO 1818-1958. 1958? (SLO)

Hancock, Harold. THE HISTORY OF WESTERVILLE OHIO. (Westerville OH: Otterbein College, 1979) 309p (OGS)

Hancock, Harold. NINETEENTH CENTURY WESTERVILLE. (Westerville OH: Otterbein College, 1980) 194p (OGS)

Hardesty, H.H. MILITARY HISTORY OF OHIO - DELAWARE COUNTY EDITION. 1886/87. (OHS)

Hinshaw, William Wade. ENCYCLOPEDIA OF AMERICAN QUAKER GENEALOGY, VOL.IV, OHIO. (Baltimore: Genealogical Pub.Co., 1973) 1424p (SLO,OHS,LDS)

HISTORY OF DELAWARE COUNTY AND OHIO. (Chicago: O.L.Baskin & Co., 1880) (Reprint, Evansville IN: Unigraphic, 1973) 855p (LC,SLO,LDS,DAR,OHS) (RPI)

Kuhns, Charlotte S. SYNOPSIS OF WILLS DELAWARE COUNTY OHIO. 1966. 1v (DAR)

Lytle, James R. 20TH CENTURY HISTORY OF DELAWARE COUNTY OHIO AND REPRESENTATIVE CITIZENS. (Chicago: Biographical Pub Co., 1908) 896p (LC, SLO,LDS,DAR)(RPI)

McCormick, Esther. SUNBURY'S PART IN OHIO HISTORY. 1966. 158p (SLO)

Main, Florence. 1826 AUDITOR'S TAX LIST. 1955. 99p (SLO,LDS,DAR)

Main, Florence & Carl. DELAWARE COUNTY OHIO INSCRIPTIONS. 1956. 296p (DAR) Matusoff, Karen. CENTRAL OHIO LOCAL GOVERNMENT RECORDS AT THE OHIO HISTORICAL SOCIETY. (Columbus: Ohio Hist Soc., 1978) 38p. (OGS)

MEMORIAL RECORD OF THE COUNTIES OF DELAWARE, UNION AND MORROW. (Chicago: Lewis Pub.Co., 1895) 501p (SLO,LDS,DAR)(RPI)

Modie. ATLAS OF DELAWARE COUNTY OHIO. 1908. (SLO)(RPI)

Nitchman, Paul E. BLACKS IN OHIO, 1880, IN THE COUNTIES OF COLUMBIANA TO FAYETTE, VOLUME 3 (Ft.Meade Md: author, 1986?) 168p

Obetz, Genevieve M. THE FIRST REGULAR BAPTIST CHURCH AND OTHER BAPTIST CHURCHES OF COLUMBUS AND CENTRAL OHIO, 1825-1884. (Columbus: Franklin Co.Gen.Soc., 1984) 69p (LDS)

Ohio Genealogical Society. BIBLIOGRAPHY AND GUIDE TO RESEARCH IN MARION, MORROW AND DELAWARE COUNTIES OHIO. (Columbus OH: the society, 1975) 10p (LDS)

Pabst, Anna S. BERLIN TOWNSHIP & DELAWARE COUNTY OHIO HISTORY. (Delaware OH: author, c1955-) 6v (LC,LDS,DAR,OGS,SLO)

Pabst, Anna S. CLEVELAND, CINCINNATI, CHICAGO AND ST.LOUIS RAILWAY COMPANY. 1963. 82p (SLO,DAR)

Pabst, Anna S. DELAWARE COUNTY BURIALS, REVOLUTIONARY WAR SOLDIERS. (SLO,LDS)

Pabst, Anna S. HISTORICAL ATLAS OF DELAWARE COUNTY OHIO. (Delaware OH: author, 1963) 128p (LC,LDS,DAR)

Pabst, Anna S. RECORDS OF DELAWARE COUNTY OHIO FOUND IN THE OFFICE OF PROBATE JUDGE, A-C. 1952. 22p (SLO,DAR)

Pabst, Anna S. REVOLUTIONARY WAR RECORDS, NATIONAL AND LOCAL FROM ORIGINAL MANUSCRIPTS. (Delaware OH: author, 1966) 75p (OGS,DAR,LDS)

Pabst, Anna S. SOME RECORDS OF PIONEERS OF DELAWARE COUNTY OHIO. VOLS.1 & 2. (Delaware OH: author, 1966-) 261p (LC,OGS,LDS,DAR)

Pabst, Anna S. THE BIRTHPLACE OF RUTHERFORD B. HAYES, DELAWARE, OHIO. (author, 1972) 128p. (OGS)

Pierce, Doris W. HISTORY OF THE BERLIN PRESBYTERIAN CHURCH: FOUNDED 1829, BERLIN TOWNSHIP, DELAWARE COUNTY OHIO. c1964. 51p (SLO,DAR)

PLAT BOOK: DELAWARE COUNTY. (Columbus: Diversity Shop, 1964) 73p (LC)

PORTRAIT GALLERY OF PROMINENT PERSONS OF DELAWARE COUNTY OHIO: WITH BIOGRAPHICAL NARRATIVES. (Mansfield OH: Biographical Pub.Co., 1891) 150p (DAR)

Powell, Esther W. TOMBSTONE INSCRIPTIONS & OTHER RECORDS OF DELAWARE CO OHIO, INCLUDING PORTIONS OF MORROW AND MARION COUNTIES. (Akron OH: author, 1972) 448p (OGS,SLO,LDS,DAR)

RECORD BOOK OF BERKSHIRE TOWNSHIP, DELAWARE COUNTY OHIO. 1823. 159p (SLO)

Scott, Beulah M. INDEX OF ATLAS, DELAWARE COUNTY OHIO, BY F.W.BEERS. (LDS)

Scott, Beulah M. INDEX OF ILLUSTRATED HISTORICAL ATLAS OF DELAWARE COUNTY OHIO BY L.H.EVERTS, 1875. (LDS)

Smith, Clifford N. FEDERAL LAND SERIES: A CALENDAR OF ARCHIVAL MATERIAL ON THE LAND PATENTS ISSUED BY THE U.S.GOVERNMENT, VOL.2: FEDERAL BOUNTY LAND WAR-RANTS OF THE AMERICAN REVOLUTION. (Chicago: Amer.Libr.Assn., 1972) 416p

Smith, Clifford N. FEDERAL LAND SERIES: A CALENDAR OF ARCHIVAL MATERIAL ON THE LAND PATENTS ISSUED BY THE U.S.GOVERNMENT, VOL.4, PT 1: GRANTS IN THE VIRGINIA MILITARY DISTRICT OF OHIO. (Chicago: Amer.Libr.Assn., 1982) 395p

Smith, Clifford N. FEDERAL LAND SERIES: A CALENDAR OF ARCHIVAL MATERIAL ON THE LAND PATENTS ISSUED BY THE U.S.GOVERNMENT, VOL.4, PT 2: GRANTS IN THE VIRGINIA MILITARY DISTRICT OF OHIO. (Chicago: Amer.Libr.Assn., 1986) 306p

Steyle, Fr.Philip & Dr.CG Gray. MEMORIAL RECORD OF ST.MARY'S PARISH, DELAWARE OHIO 1911-1986. (Delaware OH: St.Mary's Church, 1986) 100p

Swickheimer, Mary R. EARLY HISTORY OF RADNOR TOWNSHIP, DELAWARE COUNTY OHIO. (Delaware OH: author, 1971) 225p (DAR,SLO)

Treasurer: DELAWARE COUNTY OHIO TREASURER'S BOOK, 1813-1819. (SLO)

Truxall, Harry F. THESE MANY YEARS, 1821-1971: HISTORY OF ST.MARK'S EVANGELICAL LUTHERAN CHURCH, DELAWARE, OHIO. (Sunbury OH: author, 1971) 62p (DAR)

Truxall, Ruth D. FROM THEN TILL NOW; METHODISM IN SUNBURY, OHIO. (Sunbury OH: author, 1964) 171p (SLO,LDS,DAR)

# ERIE COUNTY

| | |
|---|---|
| CREATED: | 1838 FROM HURON & SANDUSKY COUNTIES |
| COUNTY SEAT: | SANDUSKY 44870 |
| COURT HOUSE: | 323 COLUMBUS AVE., SANDUSKY 44870 |
| LIBRARY: | COLUMBUS AVE. & W.ADAMS ST., SANDUSKY 44870 |
| HISTORICAL SOCIETY: | 629 S.MARKET ST., SANDUSKY 44870 |

| | |
|---|---|
| GENEALOGICAL SOCIETY: | ERIE CO. CHAPTER OGS, |
| | PO BOX 1301, SANDUSKY 44870 |
| HEALTH DEPARTMENT: | 420 SUPERIOR ST., PO BOX 375, SANDUSKY 44870 |
| | (separate offices for Sandusky City, Huron & Vermilion) |
| ARCHIVAL DISTRICT: | BOWLING GREEN STATE UNIVERSITY, BOWLING GREEN |
| | (see Biggs' Guide to records) |
| LAND SURVEYS: | FIRE LANDS |
| | CONNECTICUT WESTERN RESERVE |
| BOUNDED BY: | EAST: LORAIN CO. |
| | NORTH: LAKE ERIE |
| | WEST: SANDUSKY CO. |
| | SOUTH: HURON CO. |
| TOWNSHIPS: | Berlin, Florence, Groton, Huron, Kelley's Island, Margaretta, Milan, |
| | Oxford, Perkins, Vermilion. |

## COURT RECORDS: (LDS MICROFILM)

Assessor:
Birth & death returns, 1870-1909.
Auditor:
Tax records, 1838-1851.
Clerk of Courts:
Appearance dockets & index, 1838-1853.
Supreme Court journal, vA, 1839-1852.
Supreme Court chancery record, 1840-1850.
Supreme Court complete record & index, 1839-1851.
District Court complete record & index, 1852-1857.
Common Pleas journal & index, 1838-1854.
Common Pleas chancery record, v1-4, 1839-1853.
Commissions, oaths & JP certificates, 1838-1919.
Commissioners:
Record of civil bonds, 1860-1904.
Probate Court:
Marriage records, v1-15, 1838-1919.
Marriage record index, 1838-1920.
Will records, 1853-1911.
Birth, marriage & death record, 1856-1865.
Birth & death returns, 1870-1909.
Birth records, 1867-1908.
Report of births & deaths, 1896-1913.
Civil records, 1852-1902.
Naturalization records, 1838-1844, 1852-1929.
Probate journal, v1-23, 1852-1902.
Probate record, vA-X, 1838-1902.
Bonds & letters, 1838-1907.
Administrators, executors & guardian dockets, 1866-1907.
Administration docket, vA-2, 1838-1888.
General index to probate records, 1852-1961.
Inventories & sale bills, v1-15, 1855-1902.
Recorder:
Deeds, 1881-1886.
Deed index, v1-8, 1837-1905.
Soldiers discharge, 1865-1919,1944-1945.
Soldiers Relief:
Records, 1890-1930.

Miscellaneous:
>   Diary of 1st Lt.W.M.Brown, Confederate prisoners at Johnson's Island.
>   Cemetery & marriage records, 1838-1865, by DAR.
>   Misc. cemeteries, DAR Collection, State Library of Ohio.

## OHIO HISTORICAL SOCIETY: (MICROFILM)
Clerk of Courts:
>   Appearance dockets & index, 1838-1853.
>   Supreme Court journal, vA, 1839-1852.
>   Supreme Court chancery record, 1840-1850.
>   Supreme Court complete record & index, 1839-1851.
>   District Court complete record & index, 1852-1857.
>   Common Pleas journal & index, 1838-1854.
>   Common Pleas chancery record, v1-4, 1839-1853.
Probate Court:
>   Will records, v13-16, 1901-1911.
>   Administration docket, vA-2, 1838-1888.
Recorder:
>   Deeds, 1881-1886.
>   Soldiers discharge, 1865-1919,1944-1945.

## CENSUS RECORDS  (OHS,SLO,OGS,LDS)
1840-1880, 1900-1910; 1890 VETERANS; 1880,1900 SOUNDEX; 1910 MIRACODE

## AGRICULTURAL CENSUS SCHEDULES  (OHS,SLO-mic)
1850,1860,1880

## PRODUCTS OF INDUSTRY CENSUS SCHEDULE  (OHS,SLO-mic)
1850,1870,1880

## MORTALITY CENSUS SCHEDULES (OHS,SLO-mic)
1860,1880

## NEWSPAPERS: [GUIDE TO OHIO NEWSPAPERS, 1793-1973]
Berlin Heights, Birmingham, Castalia, Florence, Huron, Milan, Sandusky, Vermilion.

## TAX RECORDS (OHS & LDS)
1838.

## MANUSCRIPTS:
Kelley family papers & JP docket, 1865-1877 (WRHS)
Johnson's Island papers, 1862-1865 (WRHS)
Birmingham Twp cemetery records, 1839-1890 (WRHS)
Florence Twp. general records, 1866-1880 (WRHS)
Kelley's Island Twp. Trustees records, 1840-1872 (WRHS)
Receipt book, 1864, of draftees in Erie, Crawford, Huron, Ottawa, Sandusky & Seneca Counties Ohio
>   who purchased substitutes. (OHS)

## GENEALOGICAL PERIODICAL ARTICLES
Bell, Carol Willsey. OHIO GENEALOGICAL PERIODICAL INDEX: A COUNTY GUIDE (Youngstown,
>   OH: author, 6th ed., 1987)

## PUBLISHED SOURCES:
Aldrich, Lewis C. HISTORY OF ERIE COUNTY OHIO. (Syracuse NY: D.Mason & Co., 1889) 653p
>   (SLO,LDS,DAR)(RPI)

Biggs, Deb. GUIDE TO LOCAL GOVERNMENT RECORDS AT THE CENTER FOR ARCHIVAL COL-LECTIONS. (Bowling Green OH: Bowling Green State Univ, 1981) 104p (OGS)

CEMETERY INSCRIPTIONS FROM THE JEWISH CEMETERY, SANDUSKY, OHIO. (Cincinnati: American Jewish Archives, 1977) (LDS)

Cherry, Marjorie L. BLOCKHOUSES AND MILITARY POSTS OF THE FIRELANDS. (Shippensburg PA: author, 1934) 94p (LDS)

Cherry, Marjorie L. [COUNTY HISTORIES OF OHIO] ERIE COUNTY. 1932-1939. 32p (DAR)

Cherry, Marjorie L. INDEX OF THE FIRE LANDS, COMPRISING HURON AND ERIE COUNTIES OHIO, WILLIAMS, 1879. (Evansville IN: Unigraphic, 1973) 94p (LDS)

Cherry, Marjorie L. MOTHERS OF ERIE COUNTY. (Sandusky? OH, author, 1932) 23p (LC,SLO,LDS)

Christian, Donna K. GUIDE TO NEWSPAPER HOLDINGS AT THE CENTER FOR ARCHIVAL COL-LECTIONS. (Bowling Green OH: Bowling Green State Univ, 1980) 64p (OGS)

CITY/COUNTY DIRECTORIES: check holdings of OHS & local public library.

Collier, Mrs. S.E. ERIE COUNTY MISCELLANEA: MARRIAGES FROM SANDUSKY CLARION, MAY 1824-OCTOBER 1827. 4p (SLO,LDS)

COMBINATION ATLAS MAP OF ERIE COUNTY OHIO. 1874. (Reprint, Evansville IN: Unigraphic, 1980) 72,27p (DAR,SLO)

Daughters of the American Revolution. CEMETERY RECORDS OF ERIE COUNTY OHIO. 1938. 175p (DAR)

Daughters of the American Revolution. ERIE COUNTY OHIO CEMETERY INSCRIPTIONS. 1950? 2v (SLO,DAR,LDS)

Daughters of the American Revolution. INDEX TO ERIE COUNTY OHIO WILLS, 1838-1851. (SLO)

Daughters of the American Revolution. MARRIAGE RECORDS ERIE COUNTY 1838-1864. 1936-7. 3v (SLO,DAR,LDS)

Daughters of the American Revolution. REVOLUTIONARY SOLDIERS, ALPHABETIZED AN-CESTRAL LISTS OF CHAPTERS, DAR OF OHIO. (SLO)

Daughters of the American Revolution. TOMBSTONE INSCRIPTIONS, OAKLAND CEMETERY, SAN-DUSKY, ERIE COUNTY OHIO: 1777-1938. 1941. 65p (DAR,LDS)

Daughters of the American Revolution. TOMBSTONE INSCRIPTIONS ERIE COUNTY OHIO. (SLO)

Fire Lands Historical Society. FIRELANDS PIONEER, VOL.1, JUNE 1858-VOL.13, JULY 1878. (Nor-walk OH: the society, 1858-1878) (LDS,SLO)

Fire Lands Historical Society. FIRELANDS PIONEER, Series 2, v.1-14, 1882-1937. (Norwalk OH: the society, 1882-1937) (LDS)

Fire Lands Historical Society. FIRELANDS PIONEER, THIRD SERIES, VOL.1, 1980--. (LDS)

Franklin Co.Chapter OGS. CONFEDERATE CEMETERIES IN OHIO: CAMP CHASE & JOHNSON IS-LAND. (Columbus: the society, 1980) 55p (LDS)

Frohman, Charles E. A HISTORY OF SANDUSKY AND ERIE COUNTY. (Columbus: Ohio Hist.Soc., 1965) 61p (OGS,LDS)

Frohman, Charles E. PUT-IN-BAY, ITS HISTORY. (Columbus: Ohio Hist.Soc., 1971) 156p (OGS)

Frohman, Charles E. REBELS ON LAKE ERIE. 1965. (OGS)

Frohman, Charles E. SANDUSKY POTPOURRI. (Columbus: Ohio Hist.Soc., 1974) 88p (OGS)

Frohman, Charles E. SANDUSKY'S YESTERDAYS. 1968. (OGS)

GENEALOGICAL DATA RELATING TO WOMEN IN THE WESTERN RESERVE BEFORE 1840 (1850) (Cleveland: Centennial Commission, 1943) (WRHS,LDS)

Hankamer, Anna W. INDEX TO ERIE COUNTY WILLS 1838-1851 (Sandusky: Martha Pitkin Chapter DAR,nd) (SLO)

Hankamer, Anna W. INDEX TO ERIE COUNTY INTESTATES 1838-1851, PART 2 (Sandusky: Martha Pitkin Chapter DAR,nd) (SLO)

Hansen, Helen M. AT HOME IN EARLY SANDUSKY. 1975. (LDS)

HONOR ROLL OF OHIO: AN ILLUSTRATED BIOGRAPHICAL HISTORY COMPILED FROM PUBLIC AND PRIVATE RECORDS OF THE WORLD WAR, 1917-1918, ERIE COUNTY EDITION. (Canton OH: Liberty Pub.Co., c1919) 295p (DAR)

ILLUSTRATED ATLAS AND DIRECTORY OF ERIE COUNTY OHIO. (Battle Creek MI: Atlas Pub.Co., 1896) (LC,SLO) (RPI)

Johnson, P.R. CLASSIFIED BUSINESS AND PROFESSIONAL DIRECTORY OF PROMINENT TOWNS AND CITIES OF OHIO AND EASTERN INDIANA. (Columbus OH: Berlin Printing Co., 1899) 303p (LDS)

Levinson, Marilyn. GUIDE TO NEWSPAPER HOLDINGS AT THE CENTER FOR ARCHIVAL COL-LECTIONS. 2nd Edition. (Bowling Green OH: Bowling Green State Univ., 1987)

McKELVEY'S SANDUSKY DIRECTORY, CITY GUIDE, AND BUSINESS MIRROR FOR 1867-8. (Sandusky OH: Kinney Bros., 1867) 190p (DAR)

Marshall, Emogene N. EARLY METHODISM IN SANDUSKY: A BRIEF HISTORY OF THE ACTIVITIES OF THE METHODIST EPISCOPAL CHURCH IN SANDUSKY AND VICINITY. 1930? 28p (DAR)

Nitchman, Paul E. BLACKS IN OHIO, 1880, IN THE COUNTIES OF COLUMBIANA TO FAYETTE, VOLUME 3 (Ft.Meade Md: author, 1986?) 168p

OLD FIRST CHURCH DIRECTORY, 1929-1930. 1929. 64p (DAR)

Pascoe, Patty D. ERIE COUNTY BIRTHS VOLUMES II,III & IV. [1878-1908] (Sandusky OH: author, 1982) 70-120p (OGS,LDS)

Pascoe, Patty D. ERIE COUNTY DEATHS VOLS.I,II,III. (Sandusky: author, 1982) (OGS,LDS)

Peeke, Hewson L. THE CENTENNIAL HISTORY OF ERIE COUNTY, OHIO. (Cleveland: Penton Press Co., 1925) 2v (LC,SLO)

Peeke, Hewson L. A STANDARD HISTORY OF ERIE COUNTY OHIO. (Chicago: Lewis Pub.Co., 1916) 2v (LDS,DAR)

Ross, Harry H. ENCHANTING ISLES OF ERIE. c1949. 80p (LDS)

Ryan, James A. THE TOWN OF MILAN. (Sandusky OH: author, 1928) 96p (LDS)

SANDUSKY OF TODAY (HISTORICALLY REVIEWED). (Sandusky OH: G.G.Nichols, 1888) 93p (DAR)

Stewart & Page. COMBINATION ATLAS MAP OF ERIE COUNTY OHIO. (Philadelphia: author, 1874) 72p (LC,DAR)

Upton, Harriet T. HISTORY OF THE WESTERN RESERVE (Chicago: Lewis Pub.Co., 1910) 3v (SLO)

Von Schulenburg, Ernst. SANDUSKY THEN AND NOW. (Cleveland OH: Western Reserve Hist.Soc., 1959) 325p (SLO,LDS,DAR)

Ways, Ed L. HISTORICAL SKETCH AND OFFICIAL SOUVENIR PROGRAM OF THE 100TH AN-NIVERSARY OF THE INCORPORATION OF THE CITY OF SANDUSKY, OHIO. (Sandusky OH?: the committee, 1924) 135p (DAR)

Western Reserve Hist.Soc. INDEX TO THE MICROFILM EDITION OF GENEALOGICAL DATA RELATING TO WOMEN IN THE WESTERN RESERVE PRE 1840. (Cleveland: the society, 1976) 226p (OGS,WRHS)

White, Wallace B. MILAN TOWNSHIP AND VILLAGE, ONE HUNDRED AND FIFTY YEARS. (Milan OH: Ledger Pub., 1959) 64p (LDS)

Wickham, Gertrude V.W. MEMORIAL TO THE PIONEER WOMEN OF THE WESTERN RESERVE. (Cleveland: Cleveland Centennial Commission, 1896+) 2v (SLO)

Williams, William W. HISTORY OF THE FIRE LANDS, COMPRISING HURON AND ERIE COUN-TIES, OHIO. (Cleveland: Press of Leader Printing Co., 1879) 524p (LC,SLO,LDS,DAR)(RPI)

# FAIRFIELD COUNTY

| | |
|---|---|
| CREATED: | 1800 FROM ROSS & WASHINGTON COUNTIES |
| COUNTY SEAT: | LANCASTER 43130 |
| COURT HOUSE: | 224 E. MAIN ST., LANCASTER 43130 |
| LIBRARY: | 219 N.BROAD ST., LANCASTER 43130 |
| HISTORICAL SOCIETY: | 105 E.WHEELING ST., LANCASTER 43130 |
| GENEALOGICAL SOCIETY: | FAIRFIELD CO.CHAPTER OGS, |
| | PO BOX 203, LANCASTER 43130-0203 |
| | publication: FAIRFIELD TRACE |
| HEALTH DEPARTMENT: | 1587 GRANVILLE PIKE, LANCASTER 43130 |
| | (separate office for Lancaster City & Reynoldsburg) |
| ARCHIVAL DISTRICT: | OHIO HISTORICAL SOCIETY, COLUMBUS |

LAND SURVEYS:            CONGRESS LANDS, OHIO RIVER SURVEY (SOUTH)
                        REFUGEE TRACT
                        ZANE'S TRACTS
BOUNDED BY:             EAST:    PERRY CO.
                        NORTH:   LICKING CO.
                        WEST:    FRANKLIN & PICKAWAY CO.
                        SOUTH:   HOCKING CO.
TOWNSHIPS:              Amanda, Berne, Bloom, Clear Creek, Greenfield, Hocking, Liberty,
                        Madison, Pleasant, Richland, Rush Creek, Violet, Walnut.

## COURT RECORDS: (LDS MICROFILM)
Auditor:
   Tax duplicates, 1816-1838.
Clerk of Courts:
   Common Pleas journal, 1838-1854.
   Naturalization index, c1820-1900.
   Quadrennial enumeration, 1831,1839,1847-1851,1859.
   Quarter sessions & minute book, 1801-1803,1803-1838.
   Supreme Court docket, 1833-1879.
   Supreme court minute book, 1803-1822.
Commissioners:
   Journals, 1812-1942.
   Index to journals, 1909-1962.
   General index, 1835-1962.
Probate Court:
   Court journal, v1-14, 1852-1886.
   Wills, v1-6, 1803-1877.
   General index to probate records, 1802-1969.
   Marriages, 1803-1880.
   Births, v1-4, 1867-1909.
   Deaths, v1-3, 1867-1909.
   Guardianship records, v1-2, 1842-1913.
   Guardians bonds, 1835-1879.
   Administrators bonds, 1835-1847.
   Letters of administration, 1852-1859.
   Naturalizations, 1879-1904.
Recorder:
   Deeds, vA-Z, 1-84, 1801-1898.
   Index to deeds, 1801-1899.
Miscellaneous:
   Church of Jesus Christ of Latter-day Saints, members, 1931-1941.
   Fairfield School for Boys, Lancaster, State of Ohio boys industrial school inmate case records,
      1858-1918.
   Lancaster, First Presbyterian Church, records, 1806-1917.
   Bible, family, cemetery & marriage records, by DAR.
   Misc. cemetery records, DAR collection, State Library of Ohio.

## OHIO HISTORICAL SOCIETY: (MICROFILM)
Clerk of Courts:
   Common Pleas journal, 1838-1854.
   Naturalization index, c1820-1900.
   Quadrennial enumeration, 1831,1839,1847-1851,1859.
   Quarter sessions & minute book, 1801-1803,1803-1838.
   Supreme Court docket, 1833-1879.
   Supreme court minute book, 1803-1822.

Commissioners:
    Journals, 1812-1942.
    Index to journals, 1909-1962.
    General index, 1835-1962.
Probate Court:
    Naturalization, 1879-1904.
Miscellaneous:
    Marriage records, 1803-1865, by DAR.
    Bible & family records, by DAR.
    Tombstone & cemetery records, by DAR.
    Tombstone inscriptions of Fairfield,Knox,Lake & Perry Cos., by DAR.

**CENSUS RECORDS  (OHS,SLO,OGS,LDS)**
1820-1880, 1900-1910; 1890 VETERANS; 1880,1900 SOUNDEX; 1910 MIRACODE

**AGRICULTURAL CENSUS SCHEDULES  (OHS,SLO-mic)**
1850,1860,1880

**PRODUCTS OF INDUSTRY CENSUS SCHEDULE  (OHS,SLO-mic)**
1850,1870,1880

**MORTALITY CENSUS SCHEDULES (OHS,SLO-mic)**
1860,1880

**NEWSPAPERS: [GUIDE TO OHIO NEWSPAPERS, 1793-1973]**
Baltimore, Bremen, Lancaster, Pleasantville.

**TAX RECORDS (OHS & LDS)**
1806-1808,1810,1812-1814,1816-1838.

**GENEALOGICAL PERIODICAL ARTICLES**
Bell, Carol Willsey. OHIO GENEALOGICAL PERIODICAL INDEX: A COUNTY GUIDE (Youngstown,
    OH: author, 6th ed., 1987)

**PUBLISHED SOURCES:**
Ashbaugh, Lewis E. THE FAIRFIELD COUNTY OHIO FAMILIES. (Washington DC: author, 1945) 31p
    (LC)
BIOGRAPHICAL RECORD OF FAIRFIELD AND PERRY COUNTIES, OHIO. (New York:  S.J.Clarke
    Pub Co., 1902) 483p (LC,SLO,OHS,OGS,DAR,LDS)(RPI)
BREMEN, 1834-1934. (Bremen OH: Chamber of Commerce, 1934) 168p (DAR)
Brill, Harry E. METHODISM IN PICKERINGTON, OHIO, 1812-1905. (SLO)
CITY/COUNTY DIRECTORIES: check holdings of OHS & local public library.
Clark, Marie T. OHIO LANDS: CHILLICOTHE LAND OFFICE, 1800-1829. (Chillicothe: author, 1984)
    144p (OGS,SLO,OHS)
Collier, Jean S. FAIRFIELD COUNTY OHIO CEMETERY INSCRIPTIONS. (Columbus: author, 1979)
    (OGS,SLO)
Collier, Jean S. GRANDVIEW CEMETERY, BREMEN, OHIO, FAIRFIELD COUNTY, OHIO. 1981. (SLO)
Collier, Jean S. COMMON PLEAS COURT, FAIRFIELD COUNTY OHIO, PARTITION RECORDS #7,
    1851-1855. (OGS)
Daughters of the American Revolution. BIBLE AND FAMILY RECORDS FOR FAIRFIELD, HANCOCK,
    HURON, LORAIN, MAHONING AND WARREN COUNTIES OHIO. (SLO)
Daughters of the American Revolution. BIBLE AND FAMILY RECORDS: LANCASTER, FAIRFIELD
    COUNTY OHIO. 1939. 147p (DAR)
Daughters of the American Revolution. CEMETERY INSCRIPTIONS, FAIRFIELD COUNTY OHIO
    WITH 2 PAGES ON PICKAWAY COUNTY OHIO. (SLO)

Daughters of the American Revolution. CEMETERY RECORDS BY D.W.DENTON BETWEEN APRIL 20 AND DECEMBER 6, 1963. (SLO)

Daughters of the American Revolution. CEMETERY RECORDS: FAIRFIELD, PICKAWAY, ROSS & FRANKLIN COUNTIES OHIO. 1953. 33p (SLO,DAR,LDS)

Daughters of the American Revolution. CEMETERY RECORDS PERRY, FAIRFIELD, PICKAWAY & LICKING COUNTIES OHIO. 1967? 54p (SLO,DAR,LDS)

Daughters of the American Revolution. CEMETERY RECORDS RECORDED BY D.W.DENTON. 1963-66. 45p (DAR)

Daughters of the American Revolution. COPIES OF TOMBSTONES IN CEMETERIES OF FAIRFIELD COUNTY OHIO. (SLO,LDS)

Daughters of the American Revolution. EARLY MARRIAGE RECORDS OF FAIRFIELD COUNTY OHIO 1803-1865. 1940-49. 2v. (SLO,DAR,LDS)

Daughters of the American Revolution. FAIRFIELD COUNTY OHIO MARRIAGE RECORDS 1803-1865, INDEX OF BRIDES. 1977. 81p (DAR)

Daughters of the American Revolution. GRAVESTONE INSCRIPTIONS IN COUNTIES SURROUND-ING PICKAWAY COUNTY OHIO. (SLO)

Daughters of the American Revolution. MISCELLANEOUS GROUP TOMBSTONE INSCRIPTIONS KNOX, FAIRFIELD AND PERRY COUNTIES OHIO, VOL.1. (SLO)

Daughters of the American Revolution. OHIO BIBLE RECORDS: CONCERNING FAMILIES OF CRAW-FORD,DARKE,FAIRFIELD,MIAMI,MONTGOMERY,PICKAWAY,PREBLE AND SHELBY COUN-TIES. 1970. 126p (DAR)

Daughters of the American Revolution. PERRY AND FAIRFIELD COUNTIES OHIO CEMETERY RECORDS. 1959. 1v (DAR)

Daughters of the American Revolution. RECORDS FROM ELIZABETH SHERMAN REESE CHAPTER, FAIRFIELD COUNTY OHIO. (SLO)

Daughters of the American Revolution. TOMBSTONE INSCRIPTIONS, FIVE CEMETERIES IN PERRY COUNTY, ONE CEMETERY IN FAIRFIELD COUNTY OHIO. (SLO)

Everts, Louis H. COMBINATION ATLAS MAP OF FAIRFIELD COUNTY OHIO. (Chicago: author, 1875) 110p. (SLO,LC,LDS)

Fairfield Co. Chapter OGS. 1880 FAIRFIELD COUNTY CENSUS INDEX. (Lancaster OH: the society, nd) (OGS)

Fairfield Co. Chapter OGS. CEMETERIES OF BERNE TOWNSHIP,FAIRFIELD COUNTY OHIO (Lan-caster OH: the society, 1983) 385p (OGS,LDS)

Fairfield Co. Chapter OGS. CEMETERIES OF MADISON TOWNSHIP. (Lancaster OH: the society, nd)

Fairfield Co. Chapter OGS. CHURCH RECORDS OF THE EVANGELICAL LUTHERAN CHURCHES, AMANDA PARISH, 1811-21, 1864-1916. (Lancaster OH: the society, 1982) 39p (LDS,OGS)

Fairfield Co. Chapter OGS. EARLY FAIRFIELD COUNTY MARRIAGES, FROM DEED BOOKS. (Lan-caster OH: the society, nd) (OGS)

Fairfield Co. Chapter OGS. EVERY NAME INDEX TO EVERT'S 1875 COMBINATION ATLAS MAP OF FAIRFIELD COUNTY OHIO. (Lancaster OH: the society, 1982) (OGS,SLO)

Fairfield Co. Chapter OGS. GENEALOGIES IN THE HISTORICAL COLLECTION OF THE FAIRFIELD COUNTY DISTRICT LIBRARY, LANCASTER OHIO. (Lancaster OH: the society, 1983) 18p (LDS,OGS)

Fairfield Co. Chapter OGS. INDEX TO FAMILY HISTORIES OF FAIRFIELD CO OHIO, AT THE FAIR-FIELD CO DISTRICT LIBRARY. (Lancaster OH: the society, 1982) 10p (OGS,SLO)

Fairfield Co. Chapter OGS. INDEX TO 1870 CENSUS, FAIRFIELD CO OHIO (Lancaster OH: the society, 1982) 81p (OGS,LDS,SLO)

Fairfield Co. Chapter OGS. INDEX TO NATURALIZATIONS OF FAIRFIELD COUNTY OHIO. (Lan-caster OH: the society, 1983) 48p (OGS,LDS,SLO)

Fairfield Co. Chapter OGS. INDEX TO COMBINATION ATLAS MAP OF FAIRFIELD CO OHIO by L.H.Everts 1875. (Lancaster OH: the society,1982) 64p.(OGS)

Fairfield Co. Chapter OGS. LIBERTY TOWNSHIP TRUSTEE RECORDS, FAIRFIELD COUNTY, OHIO, 1835-1866. (Lancaster OH: the society, nd)

Fairfield Co. Chapter OGS. MEMBERSHIP ANCESTOR INDEX. (Lancaster OH: the society, 1985) 45p (LDS,OGS)

Fairfield Co. Chapter OGS. PARTITION RECORD ABSTRACTS, FAIRFIELD COUNTY, OHIO, 1812-1851, BOOKS 1,1A,2,3,4,5,6. (Lancaster OH: the society, nd)

Fairfield Co. Chapter OGS. RICHLAND TOWNSHIP CEMETERIES. (Lancaster OH: the society, 1984) 132p (LDS,OGS)

Fairfield Co. Chapter OGS. ST.MATTHEW LUTHERAN CHURCH RECORDS, SUGAR GROVE OHIO, 1854-1891. (Lancaster OH: the society, 1985) 51p (OGS)

Fairfield Co. Chapter OGS. ST.MICHAEL'S (BICKEL) GERMAN REFORMED CHURCH BAPTISMAL RECORDS, 1805-1841, LIBERTY TOWNSHIP, FAIRFIELD COUNTY, OHIO. (Lancaster OH: the society, 1986) 12p (LDS)

Fairfield Co. Chapter OGS. TRINITY (SPONOGLE) LUTHERAN CHURCH DEATH RECORDS, 1842-1892, BERNE TOWNSHIP, FAIRIFLED CO OHIO. (Lancaster OH: the society, 1985) 39p (OGS,LDS)

FARMERS DIRECTORY OF FAIRFIELD COUNTY OHIO. (n.p.: Wilmer Atkinson Co., 1915) 384p

Fischer, Della R. FIRST LUTHERAN CHURCH OF GREENSBURG, WESTERMORELAND COUNTY PA. 1965. 281p. (contains Fairfield Co marriages 1816-1830)

Fosnaugh, Sally & V.Robinson. CHURCH RECORDS, AMANDA PARISH OF EVANGELICAL LUTHERAN CHURCH (ISRAEL CHURCH, ST.PETER'S CHURCH, TRINITY CHURCH). 1982.(SLO)

Gobel, Irma B. INDEX, NAMES OF MEN AND WOMEN, HISTORY OF FAIRFIELD COUNTY. 39p (LDS)

Goslin, Charles R. CROSSROADS AND FENCE CORNERS: HISTORICAL LORE OF FAIRFIELD COUNTY. 1976. 303p. (SLO)

Goslin, Charles R. FAIRFIELD COUNTY COURTHOUSE STORY. (Lancaster OH: Fairfield Co.Commissioners, 1975)

Goslin, Charles R. HISTORICAL SKETCH & PROGRAM FOR THE SESQUICENTENNIAL CELEBRATION, THE FIRST METHODIST CHURCH, LANCASTER OHIO 1812-1962. 1962. np (OHS)

Graham, Albert A. HISTORY OF FAIRFIELD AND PERRY COUNTIES, OHIO. (Chicago: W.H.Beers & Co., 1883) 1186p (LDS,LC,SLO,DAR,OHS)(RPI)

Hannum, E.S. ATLAS OF FAIRFIELD COUNTY OHIO. (Lancaster OH: author, 1866) (LC,SLO) (RPI)

HISTORICAL SKETCH AND PROGRAM FOR THE SESQUICENTENNIAL CELEBRATION, THE FIRST METHODIST CHURCH, LANCASTER, OHIO, 1812-1962. (Lancaster OH: the church, 1962) 54p (LDS,SLO)

HISTORICAL SOUVENIR OF THE TRINITY REFORMED CONGREGATION, BASIL, OHIO, JANUARY 1, 1900. (SLO)

HISTORY OF ISRAEL'S CHURCH CLEAR CREEK TOWNSHIP, FAIRFIELD COUNTY OHIO. (SLO)

LANCASTER AND FAIRFIELD COUNTY, OHIO. (Cincinnati: Kraemer, 1901) 221p (LDS)

LANCASTER CITY DIRECTORY, ALSO A BUYERS' GUIDE AND A COMPLETE CLASSIFIED BUSINESS DIRECTORY. (Columbus: R.L.Polk & Co., 1931-) (LDS)

Martin, Lois F. ST.MATTHEW LUTHERAN CHURCH RECORDS, SUGAR GROVE, BERNE TOWNSHIP, FAIRFIELD COUNTY, OHIO, 1854-1891. (Lancaster OH: Fairfield Co.Chapter OGS, 1985) 43p (OGS,LDS)

Matusoff, Karen. CENTRAL OHIO LOCAL GOVERNMENT RECORDS AT THE OHIO HISTORICAL SOCIETY. (Columbus: Ohio Hist Soc., 1978) 38p. (OGS)

Mercy, Dorothy H. INDEX TO NEW HISTORICAL ATLAS OF FAIRFIELD COUNTY OHIO: 1875. 197?. 29p (DAR)

Miller, Charles C. HISTORY OF FAIRFIELD COUNTY OHIO AND REPRESENTATIVE CITIZENS. (Chicago: Richmond-Arnold Pub.Co., 1912) 820p (LC,SLO,LDS)

Nitchman, Paul E. BLACKS IN OHIO, 1880, IN THE COUNTIES OF COLUMBIANA TO FAYETTE, VOLUME 3 (Ft.Meade Md: author, 1986?) 168p

Raber, Nellie M. INDEX OF WILLS, FAIRFIELD COUNTY (BOOKS 1-3, 1803-1855), KNOX COUNTY (BOOKS A-C, 1808-1855) AND TUSCARAWAS COUNTY OHIO (BOOKS 1-9, 1809-1894). (Lakewood OH: author, 1955). 77p (LDS)

Rankin, Maude P. PERRY AND FAIRFIELD COS. OHIO CEMETERY RECORDS. (DAR,LDS)

Sanderson, George. A BRIEF HISTORY OF THE EARLY SETTLEMENT OF FAIRFIELD COUNTY. (Lancaster OH: T.Wetzler, 1851) 32p (LC)

Scott, Hervey. A COMPLETE HISTORY OF FAIRFIELD COUNTY, OHIO, 1795-1876. (Columbus: Siebert & Lilley, 1877)(Reprint, Marceline MO: Walsworth, 1983) 304p (LDS,LC,SLO,DAR)(RPI)
Short, Anita. OHIO BIBLE RECORDS FOR CRAWFORD, DARKE, FAIRFIELD, ETC., COUNTIES. (SLO)
Slaughter, Raymond D. INDEX 1900 CENSUS OF FAIRFIELD COUNTY OHIO. (SLO)
Swinehart, Carol F. GRAVESTONE ART: THE TOMBSTONE CUTTERS OF EARLY FAIRFIELD COUNTY OHIO AND THEIR ART. (Lancaster OH: Fairfield Co.Chapter OGS, 1984) 93p (OGS,LDS)
Wagner, Charles W. CEMETERY RECORDS OF FAIRFIELD COUNTY OHIO. 2v. (SLO)
WILLIAMS' CIRCLEVILLE AND LANCASTER DIRECTORY, CITY GUIDE AND BUSINESS MIRROR, VOLUME 1, 1859-1860. (Circleville OH: L.N.Olds, 1859) 124,72p (LDS)
Wiseman, Charles M. CENTENNIAL HISTORY OF LANCASTER OHIO AND LANCASTER PEOPLE. (Lancaster OH: author, 1898) 407p (SLO,LDS)(RPI)
Wiseman, Charles M.L. PIONEER PERIOD AND PIONEER PEOPLE OF FAIRFIELD COUNTY OHIO. (Columbus: F.J.Heer Co., 1901)(Reprint, Lancaster OH: Fairfield Co Chapter OGS, 1984) 430p (LDS,LC,SLO,DAR)(RPI)

# FAYETTE COUNTY

| | |
|---|---|
| CREATED: | 1810 FROM HIGHLAND & ROSS COUNTIES |
| COUNTY SEAT: | WASHINGTON COURT HOUSE 43160 |
| COURT HOUSE: | 110 E.COURT ST., WASHINGTON C.H.43160 |
| LIBRARY: | 127 S.NORTH ST., WASHINGTON C.H.43160 |
| HISTORICAL SOCIETY: | 517 COLUMBUS AVE., WASHINGOTN C.H.43160 |
| GENEALOGICAL SOCIETY: | FAYETTE CO. CHAPTER, OGS |
| | PO BOX 342, WASHINGTON C.H.43130-0203 |
| | publication: FAYETTE CONNECTION |
| HEALTH DEPARTMENT: | 317 S.FAYETTE ST., WASHINGTON C.H.43160 |
| | (separate office for Washington C.H.) |
| ARCHIVAL DISTRICT: | OHIO HISTORICAL SOCIETY, COLUMBUS |
| LAND SURVEYS: | VIRGINIA MILITARY DISTRICT |
| BOUNDED BY: | EAST:      PICKAWAY & ROSS CO. |
| | NORTH:   MADISON CO. |
| | WEST:     CLINTON & GREENE CO. |
| | SOUTH:   HIGHLAND CO. |
| TOWNSHIPS: | Concord, Green, Jasper, Jefferson, Madison, Marion, Paint, Perry, Union, Wayne. |

**SPECIAL NOTE:**            A COURTHOUSE FIRE IN 1828 DESTROYED SOME RECORDS.

**COURT RECORDS: (LDS MICROFILM)**
Auditor:
    Militia roll, 1865.
    Tax duplicates, 1816-1838.
Commissioners:
    Journal, 1828-1902, scattered.
Common Pleas Court:
    Quadrennial enumeration, 1887-1891,1899.
County Home:
    Infirmary record, v1, 1885-1913.
Probate Court:
    Marriage records, vA-C, 1-8, 1810-1909.
    Marriage index, 1810-1937.
    Birth records, v1-3, 1867-1908.
    Birth registrations & corrections, dates vary.

Death records, 1868-1907.
Wills, vA-C, 1-2, 1828-1888.
General index to wills, v.1, 1810-1957.
General index to probate records, v1-3, 1853-1887.
Index to probate files (estates), n.d.
Index to probate files (criminal), n.d.
Civil docket v.1, 1882-1889.
Administrators bonds & letters, 1868-1878.
Official bonds, vA, 1859-1875.
Administrators, executors & guardian bonds 1828-1859.
Guardians bonds & letters, v2-3, 1867-1890.
Letters of guardianship, v1-2, 1867-1881.
Probate minutes, vA-G, 1852-1886.
Probate record, vA-G, 1852-1899.
Naturalization records, 1880-1900.
Recorder:
　　Deeds, vA-Z,1, 1810-1877.
　　Index to deeds, 1810-1913.
Miscellaneous:
　　New Martinsburg, Friends, Monthly meeting, minutes, 1827-1930.
　　Presbyterian church records, 1834-1882, by DAR.
　　Marriages, cemeteries, bibles, Common Pleas records, wills by DAR.
　　Misc. cemeteries, DAR collection, State Library of Ohio.

## OHIO HISTORICAL SOCIETY: (MICROFILM)
Auditor:
　　Militia roll, 1865.
Commissioners:
　　Journal, 1828-1902, scattered.
Common Pleas Court:
　　Quadrennial enumeration, 1887-1891,1899.
County Home:
　　Infirmary record, v1, 1885-1913.
Miscellaneous:
　　Deed records, vA, 1810-1815, by DAR.
　　Abstracts of wills, 1883-1900, by DAR.
　　Abstracts of Common Pleas records, 1870-1905, by DAR.
　　Marriage records, c1843-1855, by DAR.
　　Wills, c1825-c1880, by DAR.
　　Bible & obituary clippins, v.2, by DAR.
　　Cemetery & tombstone records, by DAR.
　　Index to 1850 census, by DAR.
　　Jeffersonville, 100 years, by DAR.
　　200 Pioneer families, by DAR.

## MANUSCRIPTS:
Election records, 1836-1873. (WRHS)
Hegler family papers, 1809-1919. (Ohio militia papers & military poll books 1813-1832; daybook 1830)
　　(OHS)

## CENSUS RECORDS  (OHS,SLO,OGS,LDS)
1820-1880, 1900-1910; 1890 VETERANS; 1880,1900 SOUNDEX; 1910 MIRACODE

## AGRICULTURAL CENSUS SCHEDULES  (OHS,SLO-mic)
1850,1860,1870,1880

**PRODUCTS OF INDUSTRY CENSUS SCHEDULE (OHS,SLO-mic)**
1850,1870,1880

**MORTALITY CENSUS SCHEDULES (OHS,SLO-mic)**
1860,1880

**NEWSPAPERS: [GUIDE TO OHIO NEWSPAPERS, 1793-1973]**
Washington Court House.

**TAX RECORDS (OHS & LDS)**
1810,1812-1814,1816-1838.

**GENEALOGICAL PERIODICAL ARTICLES**
Bell, Carol Willsey. OHIO GENEALOGICAL PERIODICAL INDEX: A COUNTY GUIDE (Youngstown, OH: author, 6th ed., 1987)

**PUBLISHED SOURCES:**
Allen, Frank M. HISTORY OF FAYETTE COUNTY, OHIO, HER PEOPLE, INDUSTRIES AND INSTITUTIONS. (Indianapolis: B.F.Bowen & Co., 1914) 756p (LC,LDS,SLO,DAR)
Beam, Virginia H. OBITUARY CLIPPINGS FROM THE SCRAPBOOK OF ETTA AND EMMA WAIN, FAYETTE COUNTY, OHIO, 1888-1949. (SLO)
CITY/COUNTY DIRECTORIES: check holdings of OHS & local public library.
Daughters of the American Revolution. ABSTRACT OF COMMON PLEAS COURT RECORDS, FAYETTE COUNTY OHIO. 1958. VOL.II. (SLO)
Daughters of the American Revolution. ABSTRACT OF WILLS FAYETTE COUNTY OHIO. 1942? 34p (SLO,DAR,LDS)
Daughters of the American Revolution. BIBLE RECORDS KILPATRICK, BUSH, SLAGLE AND BRYAND FAMILIES, ASBURY CHAPEL SUNDAY SCHOOL. (SLO)
Daughters of the American Revolution. CHANCERY AND COMMON PLEAS COURT RECORDS, FAYETTE COUNTY OHIO, 1828-1879. 1952-58. 2v (SLO,DAR)
Daughters of the American Revolution. CHURCH RECORDS, GUARDIANSHIPS AND WILLS OF FAYETTE COUNTY OHIO. (SLO,LDS)
Daughters of the American Revolution. CEMETERIES OF FAYETTE COUNTY OHIO. 1972. 302p (DAR)
Daughters of the American Revolution. CEMETERY RECORDS FAYETTE COUNTY OHIO: WASHINGTON COURT HOUSE CITY CEMETERY WITH A FEW FROM SURROUNDING COUNTIES. 1950-51. 2v. (SLO,DAR)
Daughters of the American Revolution. DEED BOOK "A" 1810-1815 FAYETTE COUNTY OHIO. 1947. 94p (SLO,DAR,LDS)
Daughters of the American Revolution. EARLY MINUTE BOOKS A.E.F.G. OF THE CHANCERY COURT OF FAYETTE COUNTY OHIO. 1962. 105p (SLO,DAR)
Daughters of the American Revolution. FAYETTE COUNTY: EARLY MARRIAGE RECORDS (1811-1855). 1938? 137p (SLO,DAR,LDS)
Daughters of the American Revolution. FAYETTE COUNTY OHIO PRESBYTERIAN CHURCHES. 1957. 47,67p (DAR)
Daughters of the American Revolution. GRAVESTONE INSCRIPTIONS IN COUNTIES SURROUNDING PICKAWAY COUNTY OHIO. (SLO,LDS)
Daughters of the American Revolution. JASPER TOWNSHIP, FAYETTE COUNTY OHIO. 1958. 45p. (SLO)
Daughters of the American Revolution. JEFFERSONVILLE-ONE HUNDRED YEARS AGO. 1937. 22p. (SLO,DAR,LDS)
Daughters of the American Revolution. LIST OF THE REVOLUTIONARY SOLDIERS BURIED IN FAYETTE COUNTY, OHIO. (DAR,LDS)
Daughters of the American Revolution. PIONEER FAMILIES OF FAYETTE COUNTY OHIO. 1951-62. 2v (DAR)

Daughters of the American Revolution. PRESBYTERIAN CHURCH OF BLOOMINGBURG, FAYETTE COUNTY OHIO. (SLO,LDS)

Daughters of the American Revolution. RECORDS FROM 78 BIBLES FOR FAYETTE, PICKAWAY AND ALLEN COUNTIES OHIO. (SLO)

Daughters of the American Revolution. RECORDS FROM FAYETTE COUNTY OHIO: CONSISTING OF GUARDIANSHIPS AND WILLS, BLOOMINGBURG CHURCH RECORDS, 29 CEMETERY IN-SCRIPTIONS. 1936? 160p (DAR)

Daughters of the American Revolution. TOMBSTONE INSCRIPTIONS OF FAYETTE COUNTY OHIO. 1943. 137p (SLO,DAR)

Daughters of the American Revolution. VOLUME ONE, 200 PIONEER FAMILIES OF FAYETTE COUN-TY OHIO. (SLO,LDS)

Daughters of the American Revolution. VOLUME TWO, BIBLE RECORDS AND NEWSPAPER CLIP-PINGS OF OBITUARIES. (LDS,SLO)

Daughters of the American Revolution. WASHINGTON CEMETERY, WASHINGTON COURT HOUSE, FAYETTE COUNTY OHIO. 1966. 209p (SLO,DAR)

Dills, R.S. HISTORY OF FAYETTE COUNTY OHIO. (Dayton OH: Odell & Mayer, 1881) 1039p. (LDS,SLO,OHS,DAR)(RPI)

Everts, L.H. ILLUSTRATED HISTORICAL ATLAS OF FAYETTE COUNTY. 1875. (SLO)(RPI)

Fackler, Sandy. THE FAYETTE COUNTY CHRONICLE: A COLLECTION OF GENEALOGICAL & HIS-TORICAL RECORDS, Vol.2. (Washington CH OH: author, 1987?) 70p

Fackler, Sandy. THE FAYETTE COUNTY CHRONICLE: A COLLECTION OF GENEALOGICAL & HIS-TORICAL RECORDS, Vol.1. (Washington CH OH: author, 1987?) 87p

Fayette Co Chapter OGS. HISTORY OF FAYETTE COUNTY OHIO 1984. (Washington CH: the society, 1984) 327p (OGS,SLO)

Freeman, B.F. DAY BOOK, 1847-1852, FROM WATERLOO, FAYETTE COUNTY, OHIO. (LDS)

Haines, Marion T. & Mary E. WHITE OAK GROVE CEMETERY TOMBSTONE INSCRIPTIONS & IN-TERMENTS, 1836-1974. 1981. (SLO)

Historical Records Survey. INVENTORY OF THE COUNTY ARCHIVES OF OHIO NO.24, FAYETTE COUNTY OHIO. (Columbus: author, 1940) 297p. (OHS,LDS,DAR)

Matusoff, Karen. CENTRAL OHIO LOCAL GOVERNMENT RECORDS AT THE OHIO HISTORICAL SOCIETY. (Columbus: Ohio Hist Soc., 1978) 38p. (OGS)

Mathews, Mirian P. RECORD OF BIRTHS IN MADISON, FAYETTE AND PICKAWAY COUNTIES OHIO. (SLO)

Nitchman, Paul E. BLACKS IN OHIO, 1880, IN THE COUNTIES OF COLUMBIANA TO FAYETTE, VOLUME 3 (Ft.Meade Md: author, 1986?) 168p

PORTRAIT AND BIOGRAPHICAL RECORD OF FAYETTE, PICKAWAY AND MADISON COUNTIES, OHIO. (Chicago: Chapman Bros., 1892) 877p (LDS,LC,SLO,DAR)(RPI)

Putnam, Rufus. PIONEER RECORD & REMINISCENCES OF EARLY SETTLERS OF FAYETTE COUN-TY OHIO. (Cincinnati: Applegate, Poundsford & Co.,1872) 120p (LDS,SLO,DAR)(RPI)

Rankin, Maude P. & G.A.Robinson. CHANCERY AND COMMON PLEAS COURT RECORDS OF FAYETTE COUNTY OHIO 1828-1878. (Indiana PA: Heffelfingers, 1957) 186p (LDS,SLO,OHS)

Rankin, Mrs. Harry M. INDEX TO FAYETTE COUNTY OHIO 1850 CENSUS. (SLO,LDS)

Robinson, George Jr. EARLY MINUTE BOOKS A,E,F,G CHANCERY COURT FAYETTE COUNTY OHIO. [1817-1841] (Washington CH: author, 1981) 105p. (OGS,LDS)

Smith, Clifford N. FEDERAL LAND SERIES: A CALENDAR OF ARCHIVAL MATERIAL ON THE LAND PATENTS ISSUED BY THE U.S.GOVERNMENT, VOL.4, PT 1 : GRANTS IN THE VIR-GINIA MILITARY DISTRICT OF OHIO. (Chicago: American Library Assn., 1982) 395p

Smith, Clifford N. FEDERAL LAND SERIES: A CALENDAR OF ARCHIVAL MATERIAL ON THE LAND PATENTS ISSUED BY THE U.S.GOVERNMENT, VOL.4, PT 2 : GRANTS IN THE VIR-GINIA MILITARY DISTRICT OF OHIO. (Chicago: American Library Assn., 1986) 306p

WASHINGTON COURT HOUSE DIRECTORY. (Binghamton NY: Calkin-Kelly Directory Co., 1930?) 187p (LDS)

Wheeler, Jack. INDEX TO PIONEER RECORD AND REMINISCENCES OF THE EARLY SETTLERS...BY RUFUS PUTNAM. (Washington C.H. OH: author, 1973) 22p (LDS)

# FRANKLIN COUNTY

| | |
|---|---|
| CREATED: | 1803 FROM ROSS & WAYNE CO. MICH. |
| COUNTY SEAT: | COLUMBUS 43215 |
| COURT HOUSE: | 369 S. HIGH ST., COLUMBUS 43215 |
| LIBRARIES: | COLUMBUS PUBLIC LIBRARY |
| | 96 S.GRANT ST., COLUMBUS 43215 |
| | STATE LIBRARY OF OHIO |
| | 65 S.FRONT ST., COLUMBUS 43266-0333 |
| | OHIO HISTORICAL SOCIETY LIBRARY |
| | 1985 VELMA AVE., COLUMBUS 43211 |
| | FRANKLIN CO. CHAPTER OGS LIBRARY |
| | 570 W.BROAD ST., COLUMBUS 43216 |
| HISTORICAL SOCIETY: | OHIO HISTORICAL SOCIETY & STATE ARCHIVES |
| | 1985 VELMA AVE., COLUMBUS 43211 |
| | NORTHWEST FRANKLIN CO.H.S., |
| | PO BOX 413, HILLIARD 43026 |
| GENEALOGICAL SOCIETY: | FRANKLIN CO. CHAPTER, OGS, |
| | PO BOX 2503, COLUMBUS 43216 |
| | publication: THE FRANKLINTONIAN |
| HEALTH DEPARTMENT: | 181 WASHINGTON BLVD., COLUMBUS 43215 |
| | (separate offices for Columbus City, Bexley, Grandview Hts., Upper Arlington, Whitehall, Worthington, Grove City, Hilliard, Reynoldsburg, Westerville & Gahanna.) |
| STATE HEALTH DEPARTMENT: | 65 S.FRONT STREET, COLUMBUS 43266-0333 |
| ARCHIVAL DISTRICT: | OHIO HISTORICAL SOCIETY, COLUMBUS |
| LAND SURVEYS: | UNITED STATES MILITARY DISTRICT |
| | VIRGINIA MILITARY DISTRICT |
| | REFUGEE TRACT |
| | CONGRESS LANDS, OHIO RIVER SURVEY (SOUTH) |
| BOUNDED BY: | EAST:    FAIRFIELD & LICKING CO. |
| | NORTH:  DELAWARE & UNION CO. |
| | WEST:   MADISON CO. |
| | SOUTH:  PICKAWAY CO. |
| TOWNSHIPS: | Blendon, Brown, Clinton, Franklin, Hamilton, Jackson, Jefferson, Madison, Marion, Mifflin, Norwich, Perry, Plain, Pleasant, Prairie, Sharon, Truro, Washington. [Some townships have been absorbed by the city of Columbus] |

**SPECIAL NOTE:**                    A COURTHOUSE FIRE IN 1879 DESTROYED SOME RECORDS.

**COURT RECORDS: (LDS MICROFILM)**
Auditor:
  Tax duplicates, 1816-1838.
Clerk of Courts:
  Common Pleas minute book, v1, 1809-1813.
  Appraisement of personal property, 1803-1818.
  Common Pleas order books, 1816-1841, 1838-1839, 1842-1844, 1846-1853.
  Common Pleas record, 1803-1804,1838-1839,1843-1848.
  Record of incorporations, 1821-1822.
  Complete record index, 1810-1872.
  Complete record, 1803-1807,1811-1820.
  Naturalization intentions, 1846-1850.
  Chancery record, v1-11, 1823-1852.

Supreme Court order book, v3-4, 1836-1851.
Supreme Court record, v1-8, 1810-1824, 1840-1851.
Supreme Court complete record, 1824-1839.
Probate Court:
Death records, v1-9, 1867-1908.
Birth records, v1-10, 1867-1907.
Marriage records, 1803-1908.
Marriage records index, 1803-1918.
Marriage affidavits, 1844-1857.
Will records, vA-Z, 1805-1905.
Index to will records, v1-2, 1805-1932.
Complete record, v1-18, 1852-1886.
Court journal, v1-26, 1852-1886.
Administrators records, 1831-1886.
Index to estates, assignments & trusts, 1801-1919.
Guardian bonds, 1849-1895.
Index to guardians & wards, v1-2, 1806-1919.
Administrators & executors bonds & letters, 1849-1901.
Executors bonds, 1855-1886.
Naturalization records, 1850-1906.
Index to naturalizations, 1850-1906.
Declaration of intent, 1850-1906.
Recorder:
Deed books, vA-H, 1-131, 1804-1877. (also SLO)
Index to deed books, 1804-1877.
Deed books (early 1800) incl. Ross & Fairfield Cos.
Miscellaneous:
Columbus First Presbyterian Church, records, 1831-1887.
Grove City First Presbyterian Church, minutes, 1858-1894.
Columbus, Tifereth Israel Congregation, cemetery records, 1906-1974.
Columbus Branch, LDS, record of members, 1931-1941.
Misc. cemetery records, by LDS.
Misc. cemetery records, DAR Collection, State Library of Ohio.
Bible, cemetery & wills of Franklin Co., by DAR.
Marriages, 1803-1864, by DAR.
Death records from newspapers, 1811-1832, by DAR.
Biographical sketches of Revolutionary soldiers, by DAR.
Eastlawn cemetery inscriptions.
Data on Franklin Co. families, diaries of Martha Merion, 1867-1921.

## OHIO HISTORICAL SOCIETY: (MICROFILM)
Clerk of Courts:
Common Pleas minute book, v1, 1809-1813.
Appraisement of personal property, 1803-1818.
Common Pleas order books, 1816-1841, 1838-1839, 1842-1844, 1846-1853.
Common Pleas record, 1803-1804,1838-1839,1843-1848.
Record of incorporations, 1821-1822.
Complete record index, 1810-1872.
Complete record, 1803-1807,1811-1820.
Naturalization intentions, 1846-1850.
Chancery record, v1-11, 1823-1852.
Supreme Court order book, v3-4, 1836-1851.
Supreme Court record, v1-8, 1810-1824, 1840-1851.
Supreme Court complete record, 1824-1839.

Commissioners:
  Bridges & culverts, 1908-1956.
  Board of assessors, dept. of probation, 1914.
  Childrens' Home repairs, 1910.
  Memorial Hall, misc., 1919-1944.
  Miscellaneous, 1906-1957.
  Ohio Bell Telephone Co. permits, 1939-1952.
  Old county cars, 1917.
  Old paroles by commissioners, 1922-1943.
  Old soldiers & undertakers expenses, 1909.
  Pay insurance to Co.Treasurer, 1906-1920,1929-1948.
  Poor relief reports, 1945-1957.
  Private water & sewer lines, 1923-1954.
  Purchase of infirmary land deeds, 1910.
  Railway electric pole lines, 1910.
  Records on county home, 1917-1927.
  Sewer district records, c1917-c1929.
  Treasurer's receipts, 1949.
County Home/Infirmary:
  Register of inmates, 1867-1883.
  Paupers & criminals, 1859-1885.
  Board of directors' minutes, v1-7, 1860-1899.
  Payment ledgers, 1879-1883.
Probate Court:
  Administration record, 1831-1886, 1853-1919.
  Administration bonds & letters, 1855-1901.
  Administrators' bonds, v1-121, 1849-1951.
  Applications for blind relief, 1904.
  Birth records, 1897-1907.
  Birth index, 1867-1899.
  Blind relief applications, 1904.
  Blood tests, 1941-1957.
  Civil docket index, 1860-1932.
  Complete record, 1852-1921.
  Coroner's inquest inventory, 1904-1920.
  Death records, 1867-1908.
  Death records index, 1867-1908.
  Estate accounts, 1803-1879.
  Estates & trust index, 1801-1970.
  Executors' bonds & letters, 1849-1900.
  Guardians' bonds, 1849-1895.
  Guardians & wards index, 1806-1919.
  Marriage affidavits, 1844-1857.
  Marriage applications, 1845-1857.
  Marriage index, males, 1803-1969.
  Marriage index, females, 1803-1969.
  Marriage records, v1-330, 1803-1968.
  Marriage consents, 1882-1931, 1940-1957.
  Marriage certified abstract, 1969-1976.
  Marriage ministers' returns, 1803-1956.
  Naturalization index, 1850-1906.
  Naturalization declarations of intent, 1850-1906.
  Naturalization intention index, 1859-1905.
  Naturalization papers, 1856-1876.
  Naturalization records, 1880-1905.

Naturalization declarations, minors & soldiers, 1895-1904.
Probate case files, n.d.
Probate journal, 1852-1922.
State tax liens, c1957-c1958.
Will index, 1805-1932.
Will records, 1805-1906.
Miscellaneous:
Bible & family records, by DAR.
Bible records, by DAR.
Index to cemetery records, by DAR.
Marion Tp. poor relief, 1920-1929,1932-1937.
Military District cemetery records, by DAR.
Marriages, 1803-1865, by DAR.
Abstracts of wills, 1803-1865, by DAR.
Temple Israel records, Columbus, 1868-1955. (in Mss.Div.)
Columbus city directories, 1843-1862.

**CENSUS RECORDS (OHS,SLO,OGS,LDS) [1820 MISSING]**
1830-1880, 1900-1910; 1890 VETERANS; 1880,1900 SOUNDEX; 1910 MIRACODE

**AGRICULTURAL CENSUS SCHEDULES (OHS,SLO-mic)**
1850,1860,1870,1880

**PRODUCTS OF INDUSTRY CENSUS SCHEDULE (OHS,SLO-mic)**
1850,1870,1880

**MORTALITY CENSUS SCHEDULES (OHS,SLO-mic)**
1860,1880

**NEWSPAPERS: [GUIDE TO OHIO NEWSPAPERS, 1793-1973]**
Bexley, Canal Winchester, Columbus, Franklinton, Gahanna, Grandview Hts., Grove City, Hilliard, Reynoldsburg, Upper Arlington, Westerville, Whitehall, Worthington.

**TAX RECORDS (OHS & LDS)**
1806-1810,1812-1814,1816-1838.

**GENEALOGICAL PERIODICAL ARTICLES**
Bell, Carol Willsey. OHIO GENEALOGICAL PERIODICAL INDEX: A COUNTY GUIDE (Youngstown, OH: author, 6th ed., 1987)

**PUBLISHED SOURCES:**
Arnold, Randall R. HISTORICAL HISTORY OF TOWNSHIPS IN CENTRAL OHIO, AND OF THE EARLY SETTLERS NORTH OF COLUMBUS. (Westerville OH: author, 1891) 218p (LDS)
Bareis, G.F. HISTORY OF MADISON TOWNSHIP, INCLUDING GROVEPORT AND CANAL WINCHESTER, FRANKLIN COUNTY OHIO. (Canal Winchester OH: author, 1902) 515p. (LDS,SLO,OHS,DAR)(RPI)
Bell, Carol W. FRANKLIN COUNTY OHIO NATURALIZATION INTENTIONS, 1846-1850. (Columbus: author, 1981) 11p (OHS)
Bell, Carol W. FRANKLIN COUNTY OHIO: 1821 TAX LIST FOR THE YEAR 1820. (Columbus: author, 1980) 12p. (OHS,SLO,OGS)
Bell, Carol W. etal. FRANKLIN CO OHIO: INDEX TO PROBATE COURT COMPLETE RECORDS 1852-1900 (Youngstown OH: author, 1986) 45p (OGS,LDS)
Bodie & Kilmer. FRANKLIN COUNTY [atlas] (Columbus OH: author, 1910) (LC)
Brill, Harry E. METHODISM IN PICKERINGTON, OHIO, 1812-1905. (SLO)

Caldwell, Joseph A. CALDWELL'S ATLAS OF FRANKLIN COUNTY AND OF THE CITY OF COLUM-BUS OHIO. (Columbus: Caldwell & Gould, 1872) (Reprint, Evansville IN: Unigraphic, 1973) (LC,OGS,SLO,LDS)(RPI)

Carter, James G. UPPER ARLINGTON HISTORY: NOTES ON THE EARLY OWNERS OF LAND WHICH LATER BECAME UPPER ARLINGTON OHIO. 1974. 11p. (SLO,LDS)

Catholic Record Society. BULLETIN OF THE CATHOLIC RECORD SOCIETY, DIOCESE OF COLUM-BUS., VOL.I-IX, 1975-1983. (SLO)

CENTENARY, 1824-1924, THE FIRST BAPTIST CHURCH, COLUMBUS, OHIO, PROGRAM, MAY 16-18, 1924. (Columbus OH: the church, 1924) 20p (LDS)

CENTENNIAL BIOGRAPHICAL HISTORY OF THE CITY OF COLUMBUS AND FRANKLIN COUN-TY, OHIO. (Chicago: Lewis Pub.Co., 1901) 1012p (LC,SLO,LDS,DAR)(RPI)

CITY/COUNTY DIRECTORIES: check holdings of OHS & local public library.

Clark, Marie T. OHIO LANDS: CHILLICOTHE LAND OFFICE, 1800-1829. (Chillicothe: author, 1984) 144p (OGS,SLO,OHS)

Columbus Research bureau. FIRST EVENTS IN COLUMBUS OHIO: A HISTORY. 1946. 95p. (SLO)

Cummings, Abbott L. ALFRED KELLY HOUSE OF COLUMBUS OHIO. 1953. 52p. (SLO)

DATA ON FRANKLIN COUNTY FAMILIES ABSTRACTED FROM THE DIARIES OF MRS. MARTHA (WALTON) MERION, 1867-1921. Typescript. (LDS)

Daughters of the American Revolution. ABSTRACTS OF WILLS OF FRANKLIN CO., OHIO: 1803-1865. 1939? 133p (DAR)

Daughters of the American Revolution. BIBLE AND CEMETERY RECORDS COPIED BY MEMBERS OF OHIO DAR CHAPTERS, 1966-1967. (SLO)

Daughters of the American Revolution. CEMETERY INSCRIPTIONS IN THE UNITED STATES MILITARY DISTRICT. (SLO,LDS)

Daughters of the American Revolution. CEMETERY INSCRIPTIONS MISCELLANEOUS VOLUME OHIO 1957-1958, V.2. (SLO,LDS)

Daughters of the American Revolution. CEMETERY RECORDS: FAIRFIELD, PICKAWAY, ROSS & FRANKLIN COUNTY OHIO. 1953. 33p (DAR,LDS)

Daughters of the American Revolution. EARLY BIBLE AND FAMILY RECORDS OF FRANKLIN COUN-TY OHIO. 1940? 216p (SLO,DAR,LDS)

Daughters of the American Revolution. FRANKLIN COUNTY OHIO DEATHS 1811-1832. (SLO)

Daughters of the American Revolution. FRANKLIN COUNTY OHIO EARLY MARRIAGE RECORDS 1803-1864. 1938. 6v. (SLO,DAR)

Daughters of the American Revolution. REVOLUTIONARY SOLDIERS OF FRANKLIN COUNTY OHIO. 1915? 33p (DAR,LDS)

Daughters of the American Revolution. TWELVE OHIO COUNTIES, OHIO CHURCH AND CEMETERY RECORDS. (SLO)

Davis, Mrs. J.B. ROSTER OF GRAVES IN KEMPTON CEMETERY, CLINTON TWP., FRANKLIN COUN-TY OHIO. (SLO)

DEATHS AND MARRIAGES FROM THE ARK, AND ODD FELLOWS' WESTERN MONTHLY MAGAZINE, 1845-1846. (Columbus OH: 198?) 26p (LDS)

Federal Writers' Project. WESTERVILLE IN THE AMERICAN TRADITION. c1940. 119p (DAR)

First Baptist Church, Columbus. DEDICATION PROGRAM: THE FIRST BAPTIST CHURCH, COLUM-BUS, OHIO, JANUARY 6-9, 1927. (Columbus OH: the church, 1927) 13p (LDS)

FIRST PRESBYTERIAN CHURCH OF WORTHINGTON OHIO. (SLO)

Fitzpatrick, Stephen A. HISTORY OF COLUMBUS CELEBRATION, FRANKLINTON CENTENNIAL. (Columbus: New Franklin Printing Co.,1897) 258p. (SLO,LDS)

Franklin Co. Chapter OGS. ABSTRACTED WILLS, 1805-1831, FROM FRANKLIN COUNTY OHIO COURT RECORDS. (Columbus: the society, 1982.) 81p (OHS,OGS,LDS)

Franklin Co. Chapter OGS. ANCESTRAL SURNAME INDEX, VOL.1. (Columbus OH: the society, 1980?) (OGS,LDS,SLO)

Franklin Co. Chapter OGS. ANCESTRAL SURNAME INDEX, VOL.2. (Columbus OH: the society, 1981) (OGS,SLO)

Franklin Co. Chapter OGS. ANCESTRAL SURNAME INDEX, VOL.3. (Columbus OH: the society, 1982) 103p (OGS,SLO)

Franklin Co. Chapter OGS. ANCESTRAL SURNAME INDEX, VOL.4. (Columbus OH: the society, nd) (OGS)

Franklin Co. Chapter OGS. ANCESTRAL SURNAME INDEX, VOL.5. (Columbus OH: the society, 1986) 131p (OGS)

Franklin Co. Chapter OGS. CONFEDERATE CEMETERIES IN OHIO: CAMP CHASE & JOHNSON ISLAND NEAR SANDUSKY. (Columbus: the society, 1980) 55p (OHS,LDS)

Franklin Co. Chapter OGS. FRANKLIN COUNTY OHIO CEMETERIES: MIFFLIN & MARION TWPS. VOL.1. (Columbus: the society, 1980) 136p (OHS,OGS,LDS)

Franklin Co. Chapter OGS. FRANKLIN COUNTY OHIO CEMETERIES: MADISON TWP. VOL.2. (Columbus: the society, 1981) 148p (OHS,OGS,LDS)

Franklin Co. Chapter OGS. FRANKLIN COUNTY OHIO CEMETERIES: JEFFERSON & TRURO TWPS. VOL.3. (Columbus: the society, 1981) 151p (OHS,OGS,LDS)

Franklin Co. Chapter OGS. FRANKLIN COUNTY OHIO CEMETERIES: BLENDON & PLAIN TWPS. VOL.4. (Columbus: the society, 1981) 176p (OHS,OGS,LDS)

Franklin Co. Chapter OGS. FRANKLIN COUNTY OHIO CEMETERIES: SHARON & PERRY TWPS. VOL.5. (Columbus: the society, 1983) 142p (OHS,OGS,LDS)

Franklin Co. Chapter OGS. FRANKLIN COUNTY OHIO CEMETERIES: WASHINGTON, CLINTON, MONTGOMERY & BROWN TWPS, VOL.6. (Columbus: the society, 1983) 103p (OHS,OGS,LDS)

Franklin Co. Chapter OGS. FRANKLIN COUNTY OHIO CEMETERIES: NORWICH TOWNSHIP, VOLUME 7. (Columbus OH: the society, nd) (OGS,LDS)

Franklin Co. Chapter OGS. FRANKLIN COUNTY OHIO CEMETERIES: PRAIRIE AND FRANKLIN TOWNSHIPS, VOLUME 8. (Columbus OH: the society, 1984) 157p (OGS,LDS)

Franklin Co. Chapter OGS. FRANKLIN COUNTY OHIO CEMETERIES: HAMILTON TOWNSHIP, VOL.9. (Columbus OH: the society, 1987) 183p (OGS,LDS)

Franklin Co. Chapter OGS. GENEALOGICAL NAME INDEX TO THE OHIO SUPREME COURT RECORDS, FRANKLIN COUNTY, VOLS.1-4, 1783-1839. (Columbus: the society, 1983) 88p (OHS,OGS,LDS)

Franklin Co. Chapter OGS. GENEALOGICAL INDEX TO CHANCERY BOOK VOLUMES 1-4, 1823-1840, FRANKLIN COUNTY OHIO COURT OF COMMON PLEAS. (Columbus: the society, 1987) 174p (OGS)

Franklin Co. Chapter OGS. GREENLAWN CEMETERY RECORDS, COLUMBUS. (Columbus: the society, 1982) 20 rolls mic. (Fra Co Chapter OGS)

Franklin Co. Chapter OGS. INDEX TO FRANKLIN CO OHIO HISTORY by Martin.

Franklin Co. Chapter OGS. NAME INDEX TO THE FRANKLIN CO OHIO PLAT MAPS, 1842,1856,1883. (Columbus: the society, 1982) 174p (OHS,OGS,LDS,SLO)

Franklin Co. Chapter OGS. THE STUDER INDEX, for Jacob Studer's 1873 Franklin County History. (Columbus OH: the society, nd)

FRANKLIN COUNTY AT THE BEGINNING OF THE TWENTIETH CENTURY. (Columbus OH: Historical Pub.Co., 1901) 459p (OHS,DAR,LDS)

FRANKLIN COUNTY HISTORICAL SOCIETY BULLETIN. (SLO)

Franklin Co. Pioneer Assn. IN MEMORY OF SOLDIERS OF THE WAR OF 1812 FROM FRANKLIN COUNTY. 1924. (SLO)

Gahanna Historical Society. HISTORY OF GAHANNA: INCLUDING MIFFLIN AND JEFFERSON TOWNSHIPS. 1976. 200p (SLO)

GOLDEN JUBILEE OF THE FIRST CONGREGATIONAL CHURCH, COLUMBUS OHIO: SEPTEMBER 28 TO OCTOBER 1, 1902. 1902. 126p (DAR)

Gossett, Lillian B. BY ONE SPIRIT: HISTORY OF THE CENTRAL COLLEGE UNITED PRESBYTERIAN CHURCH, THE CENTRAL COLLEGE OF OHIO, THE BLENDON CENTRAL CEMETERY. (Greenfield OH: Greenfield Print.& Pub., 1976) 249p (LDS)

Haddox, Rosalie R. FROM OLD NEWSPAPERS FRANKLIN COUNTY DEATH RECORDS: FROM JULY 17, 1811 TO OCTOBER 18, 1832. 1971? 77p (DAR,LDS)

Hancock, Harold. MINUTES OF THE TRUSTEES OF HARRISON AND BLENDON TOWNSHIPS, FRANKLIN COUNTY OHIO. (Westerville OH: Westerville Hist Soc, 1987) 118p (OGS)

Hancock, Harold. OUR ANCESTORS OF THE WESTERVILLE AREA: A GENEALOGICAL HISTORY. 1981. 329p. (OGS,LDS)

Hancock, Harold. NINETEENTH CENTURY WESTERVILLE. (Westerville OH: Otterbein College, 1980) 194p (OGS)

Hancock, Harold. THE HISTORY OF WESTERVILLE OHIO. (Westerville OH: Otterbein College, 1979) 309p (OGS,LDS)

Hardesty, H.H. MILITARY HISTORY OF OHIO - FRANKLIN COUNTY EDITION. 1886/87. (OHS)

Heer, Stephen M. ALPHABETICAL LIST OF THE ORIGINAL SURVEYS IN THE VIRGINIA MILITARY DISTRICT IN FRANKLIN COUNTY OHIO. (SLO)

Herrel, Edith & L. Hogg. BEXLEY IMAGES. 1978. (SLO)

Hinshaw, William Wade. ENCYCLOPEDIA OF AMERICAN QUAKER GENEALOGY, VOL.IV, OHIO. (Baltimore: Genealogical Pub.Co., 1973) 1424p (SLO,OHS,LDS)

Historical Publishing Co., Columbus. FRANKLIN COUNTY AT THE BEGINNING OF THE TWEN- TIETH CENTURY. (Columbus: Sheppard & Co., 1901) 460p (LC,LDS)

Historical Records Survey. INVENTORY OF THE COUNTY ARCHIVES OF OHIO NO.25, FRANKLIN COUNTY. (Columbus: author, 1942) 528p. (OHS,LDS,DAR)

HISTORY OF FRANKLIN AND PICKAWAY COUNTIES, OHIO. (Cleveland: Williams Bros., 1880) 593p (LC,SLO,OHS,LDS,DAR)(RPI)

HISTORY OF GAHANNA: INCLUDING MIFFLIN AND JEFFERSON TOWNSHIPS. (Gahanna OH: Rocky Fork Printing, 1976) 200p (DAR)

HISTORY OF ONE-HUNDRED YEARS, 1839-1939, CENTRAL PRESBYTERIAN CHURCH. (SLO)

HISTORY OF UPPER ARLINGTON, A SUBURB OF COLUMBUS OHIO. (Upper Arlington OH: Bicen- tennial Commission History Committee, 1977-78). 337p. (SLO,OGS)

Hooper, Osman C. HISTORY OF THE CITY OF COLUMBUS OHIO. (Columbus: Memorial Pub.Co.,1920) 485p. (LDS,SLO,DAR,OHS)

Hunker, H.L. INDUSTRIAL EVOLUTION OF COLUMBUS OHIO. 1958. 260p. (SLO) INDEX TO ES- TATE RECORDS OF FRANKLIN CO 1803-1850. (Columbus: 1984) 79p. (OHS)

Huntington, Webster. THE MEN BEHIND THE GUNS IN THE MAKING OF GREATER COLUMBUS OHIO. 1906. (SLO)

INDEX TO GUARDIANSHIP RECORDS OF FRANKLIN CO. OHIO, 1803-1850. (Columbus: 1983) 75p (OHS)

Johnson, P.R. CLASSIFIED BUSINESS AND PROFESSIONAL DIRECTORY OF PROMINENT TOWNS AND CITIES OF OHIO AND EASTERN INDIANA. (Columbus OH: Berlin Printing, 1899) 303p (LDS)

Katzenbach, Mary B. MULTIPLY AND DIVIDE: A HISTORY OF THE CHURCH OF JESUS CHRIST OF LATTER-DAY SAINTS IN CENTRAL OHIO. (Columbus: Columbus Ohio Stake, 1981) 276p (LDS)

Lee, Alfred E. HISTORY OF THE CITY OF COLUMBUS, CAPITOL OF OHIO. (NY: Munsell & Co., 1892) 1799p. (OHS,SLO,LDS,DAR)(RPI)

Lee, Charles R. HISTORY OF WALNUT GROVE CEMETERY. (Naples FL: Neapolitan Pubs., c1970) 124p (DAR)

MacLeod, D.W. HISTORY OF THE MIFFLIN PRESBYTERIAN CHURCH. (SLO) McKENDREE STORY, 125 YEARS OF HISTORY OF THE McKENDREE METHODIST CHURCH. (SLO)

Mark, Clara G. FRANKLIN COUNTY OHIO, CEMETERY INSCRIPTIONS IN THE UNITED STATES MILITARY DISTRICT. 1948. 36p (DAR)

Marsten, Francis E. AFTER EIGHTY YEARS [history of the First Presbyterian Church in Columbus Ohio] (Columbus OH: A.H.Smythe, 1886) 127p (LDS)

Martin, William T. HISTORY OF FRANKLIN COUNTY OHIO: A COLLECTION OF REMINISCEN- CES. (Columbus: Follett, Foster & Co., 1858)(Reprint, Columbus: Linden Heights Kiwanis Club, 1969) 449p (LC,SLO,LDS,OHS,DAR)(RPI)

Matusoff, Karen. CENTRAL OHIO LOCAL GOVERNMENT RECORDS AT THE OHIO HISTORICAL SOCIETY. (Columbus: Ohio Hist Soc., 1978) 38p. (OGS)

Maxwell, Fay. EARLY GERMAN VILLAGE HISTORY: SOUTH COLUMBUS, OHIO. (Columbus: Elic Press, 1971)42p. (SLO,LDS,DAR)

Maxwell, Fay. IRISH REFUGEE TRACT ABSTRACT DATA. (Columbus: Maxwell Pub., 1974) 128p. (SLO,LDS)

Mettle, Suzanne W. FRANKLIN COUNTY OHIO GENEALOGICAL RESOURCE GUIDE. (Columbus OH: Franklin Co.Chapter OGS, 1983) 11p (LDS)

Miller, Mary W. HILLIARD UNITED METHODIST CHURCH, 1855-1980. (np: author, 1980) 23p (LDS,SLO)

Miller, Mary W. SURNAME LISTING, MEMBERS OF THE METHODIST CHURCH, 1852-1977, HILLIARD, OHIO. 12p (LDS)

Miller, Mary W. THE QUARTOQUECENTENNIAL OF A PRIDE COMMUNITY, 1978, HILLIARD, OHIO. (np: author, 1978) 50p (LDS)

Mollenkamp, Medrith & M.Scott. INDEX AND GENEALOGICAL NOTES TO "SELLSVILLE, CA.1900" THE HEADQUARTERS OF THE SELLS BROS. CIRCUS COLUMBUS OHIO. (Columbus: Franklin Co Chapter OGS, 1986) 64p (OGS)

Moore, Orpha. HISTORY OF FRANKLIN COUNTY, OHIO. (Topeka: Historical Pub.Co.,1930) 3v (LC,SLO,LDS,OHS,DAR)

NINETY YEARS IN HIS SERVICE, TRINITY UNITED METHODIST CHURCH, COLUMBUS, OHIO. (SLO)

Nitchman, Paul E. BLACKS IN OHIO, 1880, IN THE COUNTIES OF FRANKLIN, FULTON,GALLIA & GEAUGA, VOLUME 4. (Ft.Meade Md: author, 1986) 163p

Obetz, Genevieve M. FIRST REGULAR BAPTIST CHURCH AND OTHER BAPTIST CHURCHES OF COLUMBUS AND CENTRAL OHIO, 1825-1884. (Columbus OH: Franklin Co.Chapter OGS, 1984) 69p (LDS)

Otterbein College. ALUMNI DIRECTORY, 1980. (Westerville OH: author, 1980) 387p (OGS)

Parkinson, Cornelia M. HISTORY OF REYNOLDSBURG & TRURO TWP., OHIO. (Reynoldsburg OH: author, 1981) 219p (LDS,SLO)

PICTORIAL AND BIOGRAPHICAL HISTORY OF COLUMBUS, FRANKLIN COUNTY, OHIO. 1909. 293p. (SLO)

Postle, Herman R. A BRIEF GEOGRAPHY AND CIVIL GOVERNMENT OF FRANKLIN COUNTY, OHIO. (Columbus: J.L.Trauger, 1897) 131p (LC)

Prugh, Daniel F. THE COLUMBUS FEMALE BENEVOLENT SOCIETY: 150 YEARS OF HUMANITARIAN SERVICE, 1835-1985. (Columbus: Franklin Co. Hist.Soc., 1985) 28p

Raphael, Marc L. JEWS AND JUDAISM IN A MIDWESTERN COMMUNITY: COLUMBUS, OHIO, 1840-1975. (Columbus OH: Ohio Hist.Soc., 1979) 483p (OHS,LDS)

RECORD OF THE FORMER NORTH M.E.CHURCH (OR ARMBRUSTER) CEMETERY, COLUMBUS, FRANKLIN COUNTY, OHIO. 1962. (SLO)

REYNOLDSBURG AND A HISTORY OF GAHANNA. 7p. (SLO)

Rings, Blanche T. FRANKLIN COUNTY OHIO MATERIAL. 185p (LDS)

Rippley, LaVern J. THE COLUMBUS GERMANS. 1968. 42p. (OGS)

RIVERSIDE CHURCH HISTORY, 1842-1978. (SLO)

Schlegel, Donald M. COLUMBUS CATHOLIC CEMETERY, HISTORY & RECORDS, 1846-1874. (Columbus: Columbus History Service, 1983) 66p (OHS,OGS,LDS)

Schlegel, Donald M. COLUMBUS CITY GRAVEYARDS. (Columbus: Columbus History Service, 1985) 216p (LDS)

Schlegel, Donald M. FRANKLIN COUNTY OHIO DIVORCES BEFORE 1870. (Columbus: Columbus History Service, 1983) 107p (OHS,LDS,SLO)

Schlegel, Donald M. LAGER AND LIBERTY: GERMAN BREWERS OF NINETEENTH CENTURY COLUMBUS. (Columbus OH: author, 1982) 82p (LDS)

Selby, Robert E. FRANKLIN COUNTY OHIO MARRIAGE RECORDS, 1803-1815. (Kokomo IN: Selby Pub.Co., 1983) 14p (LDS)

SEVENTY-FIVE YEARS OF THE HANNAH NEIL MISSION AND HOME OF THE FRIENDLESS: 1858-1933. 1933. 48p (DAR)

Shedd, C.B. TALES OF OLD COLUMBUS. 1951. 48p. (SLO)

SHEDDING LIGHT ON WORTHINGTON: THE WOODROW GUILD OF THE FIRST PRESBYTERIAN CHURCH OF WORTHINGTON, OHIO. (Worthington OH: the Guild, 1931) 79p (SLO,DAR)

SHELTERING A HERITAGE, OLD HOMES OF GRANDVIEW HEIGHTS AND MARBLE CLIFF, OHIO. 1976. 32p. (SLO)

Smith, Clifford N. FEDERAL LAND SERIES: A CALENDAR OF ARCHIVAL MATERIAL ON THE LAND PATENTS ISSUED BY THE U.S.GOVERNMENT, VOL.2: FEDERAL BOUNTY LAND WARRANTS OF THE AMERICAN REVOLUTION. (Chicago: American Library Assn., 1972) 416p

Smith, Clifford N. FEDERAL LAND SERIES: A CALENDAR OF ARCHIVAL MATERIAL ON THE LAND PATENTS ISSUED BY THE U.S.GOVERNMENT, VOL.4, PT 1 : GRANTS IN THE VIRGINIA MILITARY DISTRICT OF OHIO. (Chicago: American Library Assn., 1982) 395p

Smith, Clifford N. FEDERAL LAND SERIES: A CALENDAR OF ARCHIVAL MATERIAL ON THE LAND PATENTS ISSUED BY THE U.S.GOVERNMENT, VOL.4, PT 2 : GRANTS IN THE VIRGINIA MILITARY DISTRICT OF OHIO. (Chicago: American Library Assn., 1986) 306p

Studer, Jacob H. COLUMBUS OHIO: ITS HISTORY, RESOURCES AND PROGRESS. (Columbus: author, 1873) 584p (SLO,LDS,OHS,DAR)

Sullivant, Joseph. HISTORICAL SKETCH RELATING TO THE ORIGINAL BOUNDARIES AND EARLY TIMES OF FRANKLIN COUNTY. (Columbus: Ohio State Journal Print, 1871) 10p (LC)

SURNAME LISTING, MEMBERS OF THE METHODIST CHURCH, HILLIARD OHIO 1852-1977. (SLO)

Taylor, Edward L. IN MEMORY OF SOLDIERS OF THE WAR OF 1812 FROM FRANKLIN COUNTY. (Columbus OH: Franklin Co.Pioneer Assn., 1924) 26p (DAR)

Taylor, William A. CENTENNIAL HISTORY OF COLUMBUS AND FRANKLIN COUNTY OHIO. (Chicago: S.J.Clarke Pub Co., 1909) 2v (LC,SLO,LDS,DAR)

Turpin, Joan. TURPIN INDEX: A LIST OF MARRIAGE LICENSES ISSUED BY THE FRANKLIN COUNTY PROBATE COURT AS PUBLISHED IN THE DAILY DISPATCH. [1871-1875] (Dublin OH: Genealogical Indexing Services, 1978) (LDS,SLO)

Tyler, J.I. ONE HUNDRED YEARS OF METHODISM ON GROVEPORT CIRCUIT, OHIO CONFERENCE. (Canal Winchester OH: Gayman Pub.Co., 1905) 104p (DAR)

Upper Arlington History Committee. HISTORY OF UPPER ARLINGTON, A SUBURB OF COLUMBUS OHIO. (Upper Arlington OH: author, 1977-78) 337p (OGS)

Vesey, S.A. FRANKLIN COUNTY AT THE BEGINNING OF THE TWENTIETH CENTURY. 1901. 459p. (SLO)(RPI)

Wagner, Charles W. CEMETERY RECORDS OF FRANKLIN COUNTY OHIO. (SLO,LDS)

Watkins, Raymond W. CONFEDERATE BURIALS IN SANDUSKY AND COLUMBUS OHIO CEMETERIES. (LDS)

Watkins, Raymond W. A LIST OF CONFEDERATE SOLDIERS WHO, WHILE PRISONERS OF WAR, DIED AT CAMP CHASE, NEAR COLUMBUS, OHIO OR CAMP DENNISON, NEAR CINCINNATI, OHIO AND ARE NOW BURIED IN CAMP SHASE CONFEDERATE CEMETERY, COLUMBUS, OHIO. 1978. 74p (LDS)

Weaver, Don E. A SESQUICENTENNIAL HISTORY: THE FIRST BAPTIST CHURCH, 583 E.BROAD ST., COLUMBUS OHIO, 1824-1974. 1974. 45p (SLO,LDS,DAR)

Weisenburger, Francis P. COLUMBUS DURING THE CIVIL WAR. (Columbus: OSU Press, 1963)

WESTERVILLE OHIO CHURCH OF THE MESSIAH UNITED METHODIST. (SLO)

White, Ruth Y. WE TOO BUILT COLUMBUS. (Columbus OH: Stoneman Press, 1936) 480p. (SLO,DAR)

WHO'S WHO IN COLUMBUS: WITH BLUE BOOK APPENDIX, A BIOGRAPHICAL COMPENDIUM OF THE NOTABLE MEN AND WOMEN OF THE CAPITAL CITY. (Columbus OH: Neman Pub.Co., 1915) 177p (DAR)

Writer's Program. WESTERVILLE IN THE AMERICAN TRADITION. 1940. 119p. (SLO)

Yantis, Richard P. & Jane. WESTERVILLE OHIO 1910 CENSUS AND GENEALOGICAL DATA. (Westerville: the Hist.Soc., 1985) 100p (OGS)

Yon, Paul D. GUIDE TO OHIO COUNTY AND MUNICIPAL GOVERNMENT RECORDS. (Columbus: Ohio Hist.Soc., 1973) 216p (OHS)

# FULTON COUNTY

| | |
|---|---|
| CREATED: | 1850 FROM HENRY, LUCAS & WILLIAMS COUNTIES |
| COUNTY SEAT: | WAUSEON 43567 |
| COURT HOUSE: | S. FULTON ST., WAUSEON 43567 |
| LIBRARY: | 117 E.ELM ST., WAUSEON 43567 |

HISTORICAL SOCIETY:          229 MONROE ST., WAUSEON 43567
GENEALOGICAL SOCIETY:        FULTON CO. CHAPTER OGS
                             305 CHESTNUT ST., SWANTON 43558
                             publication: FULTON FOOTPRINTS
HEALTH DEPARTMENT:           734 S.SHOOP AVE., WAUSEON 43567
                             (separate office for Wauseon City)
ARCHIVAL DISTRICT:           BOWLING GREEN STATE UNIVERSITY, BOWLING GREEN
                             (see Biggs' Guide to records)
LAND SURVEYS:                CONGRESS LANDS, E & N OF 1ST PRIN.MERIDIAN
                             MICHIGAN SURVEY
BOUNDED BY:                  EAST:      LUCAS CO.
                             NORTH:   LENAWEE CO., MICHIGAN
                             WEST:      WILLIAMS CO.
                             SOUTH:   HENRY CO.
TOWNSHIPS:                   Amboy, Clinton, Dover, Franklin, Fulton, German, Gorham, Jeffer-
                             son, Pike, Royalton, Swan Creek, York.

**SPECIAL NOTE:**                A COURTHOUSE FIRE ABOUT 1860 DESTROYED SOME
                             RECORDS.

## COURT RECORDS: (LDS MICROFILM)
Auditor:
   Burial record of indigent soldiers, v.1, 1885-1892.
   Militia records, 1864.
   Soldiers' relief, v.1, 1886-1913.
Board of Education:
   School examiners' record, 1861-1879.
   Teachers' examination record, 1892-1902.
Commissioners:
   Infirmary records, 1874-1926.
   Record of minutes, v1, 1874-1896.
   Directors' record of minutes, v2, 1897-1912.
   Commissioners record, v2-3, 1863-1885.
   General index to records, 1883-1894.
Coroner:
   Record of inquests, 1888-1948.
Probate Court:
   Index to files, v1-3, 1865-1972.
   Will records, 1853-1899.
   General index to wills, 1853-1972.
   Marriage records, v3-13, 1864-1930.
   Birth records, 1867-1951.
   Delayed birth records, dates vary.
   Death records, 1867-1951.
   Administrators & executors bonds & letters, 1868-1893.
   Administrators & executors docket, v1, 1870-1893.
   Guardians docket, v1, 1864-1889.
   Journal of probate cases, 1864-1887.
   Naturalizations, 1872-1906.
   Bonds of county officials, 1852-1887.
Recorder:
   Index to deeds, 1835-1850.
   Deed index, 1881-1887.
   Soldiers discharge, 1865-1952.
   Deed records, v1-4, 1835-1850.

General index to deeds v10-41,67-81.
Deed records, v10-61, 1859-1893.
Abstract title, v0-5, n.d.
Transfer deeds, 1850-1854, 1877-1910.
Record of bridge building & poor orders, 1858-1870.
Sheriff:
Jail register, 1869-1922.
Miscellaneous:
Church records, by DAR.
Marriage records, 1863-1866, by DAR.
Delta Presbyterian Church, register, 1848-1898.
Misc. cemetery records, DAR collection, State Library of Ohio.

## OHIO HISTORICAL SOCIETY: (MICROFILM)
Recorder:
Deed index, 1881-1887.
Soldiers discharge, 1865-1952.
Miscellaneous:
Marriages of Fulton, Lawrence & Mercer Cos., 1863-1866, by DAR.
Cemetery records, by DAR.
Church & family tombstone inscriptions, by DAR.
Tombstone inscriptions, v1-3, by DAR.

## CENSUS RECORDS (OHS,SLO,OGS,LDS)
1850-1880, 1900-1910; 1890 VETERANS; 1880,1900 SOUNDEX; 1910 MIRACODE

## AGRICULTURAL CENSUS SCHEDULES (OHS,SLO-mic)
1850,1860,1870,1880

## PRODUCTS OF INDUSTRY CENSUS SCHEDULE (OHS,SLO-mic)
1850,1870,1880

## MORTALITY CENSUS SCHEDULES (OHS,SLO-mic)
1860,1880

## DEFECTIVE & DEPENDENT CENSUS SCHEDULES (OHS,SLO-mic)
1880

## NEWSPAPERS: [GUIDE TO OHIO NEWSPAPERS, 1793-1973]
Archbold, Delta, Elmira, Fayette, Lyons, Metamora, Pettisville, Swanton, Wauseon.

## TAX RECORDS (OHS & LDS)
none listed; see parent counties.

## GENEALOGICAL PERIODICAL ARTICLES
Bell, Carol Willsey. OHIO GENEALOGICAL PERIODICAL INDEX: A COUNTY GUIDE (Youngstown,
OH: author, 6th ed., 1987)

## PUBLISHED SOURCES:
Aldrich, Lewis C. HISTORY OF HENRY AND FULTON COUNTIES OHIO. (Syracuse NY: D.Mason
& Co., 1888) (Reprint, Swanton OH: Fulton Co.Chapter OGS, 1985) 713p (OGS,LDS,LC,SLO,DAR)
(RPI)
Biggs, Deb. GUIDE TO LOCAL GOVERNMENT RECORDS AT THE CENTER FOR ARCHIVAL COL-
LECTIONS. (Bowling Green OH: Bowling Green State Univ, 1981) 104p (OGS)

Broglin, Jana. OBITUARIES APPEARING IN THE "SWANTON ENTERPRISE" SWANTON OHIO 1922-1978. (Swanton OH: author, nd) 150p (OGS,LDS)

Broglin, Jana. PATENT DEEDS OF FULTON COUNTY OHIO. (Swanton OH: author, 1985) 140p (OGS,LDS)

Burgoon, L.D. HISTORY OF THE FIRST METHODIST EPISCOPAL CHURCH, WAUSEON, OHIO. 1935. 40p (SLO,DAR)

Christian, Donna K. GUIDE TO NEWSPAPER HOLDINGS AT THE CENTER FOR ARCHIVAL COLLECTIONS. (Bowling Green OH: Bowling Green State Univ, 1980) 64p (OGS)

CITY/COUNTY DIRECTORIES: check holdings of OHS & local public library.

Clegg, Michael, ed. DEFIANCE, FULTON, HENRY, PAULDING, PUTNAM, WILLIAMS & WOOD COUNTIES OHIO NEWSPAPER OBITUARY ABSTRACTS, 1838-1870 (Ohio Newspaper Abstracts Series, Vol.5) (Ft.Wayne IN: author, 1987) 75p (OGS)

COMBINED ATLASES AND MAP OF FULTON COUNTY OHIO, 1858,1875,1888,1903. (Evansville IN: Unigraphic, 1980) 280p (OGS,LDS,SLO)

COMMEMORATIVE BIOGRAPHICAL RECORD OF NORTHWESTERN OHIO: INCLUDING THE COUNTIES OF DEFIANCE, HENRY, WILLIAMS & FULTON. (Chicago: J.H.Beers & Co., 1899) (LDS,OGS,SLO,DAR,OHS)(RPI)

Daughters of the American Revolution. ABSTRACTS FROM WILLS (VOL.1,2,3) FULTON COUNTY OHIO COURT HOUSE AT WAUSEON, OHIO. 1969. 96p (DAR)

Daughters of the American Revolution. BIBLE RECORDS AND WILLS OF FULTON COUNTY OHIO. (SLO)

Daughters of the American Revolution. CEMETERY INSCRIPTIONS OF FULTON COUNTY OHIO. (SLO,LDS)

Daughters of the American Revolution. CEMETERY RECORDS FULTON COUNTY OHIO. 1952-56. 2v. (LDS,SLO,DAR)

Daughters of the American Revolution. CHURCH RECORDS, FAMILY RECORDS, AND TOMBSTONE INSCRIPTIONS OF FULTON COUNTY OHIO. 1943. 161p (SLO,DAR,LDS)

Daughters of the American Revolution. EARLY VITAL RECORDS OF OHIO [WILLS OF BUTLER, FULTON AND LAKE COUNTIES OHIO]. 1948. 38p (DAR,LDS)

Daughters of the American Revolution. FULTON COUNTY OHIO MARRIAGES, 1864-1925. 1982. (SLO)

Daughters of the American Revolution. GRAVESTONE RECORDS OF LUCAS AND FULTON COUNTIES: SITUATED SOUTH OF LENAWEE COUNTY MICHIGAN TO OLD STATE LINE. 1944-1951. 278p (DAR,LDS)

Daughters of the American Revolution. MARRIAGE RECORDS MERCER, LAWRENCE AND FULTON COUNTIES OHIO. 1947? 54p (LDS,SLO,DAR)

Daughters of the American Revolution. PIONEER FAMILIES OF FULTON COUNTY OHIO. 1972-73. 5v (DAR)

Daughters of the American Revolution. PIONEERS AROUND DELTA, OHIO. 1979. 180p (DAR)

Daughters of the American Revolution. SOME CEMETERY RECORDS OF CUYAHOGA, FULTON, MEDINA, LORAIN & WAYNE COUNTIES. 1938. 175p (DAR,LDS)

Daughters of the American Revolution. SOME RECORDS FROM FULTON COUNTY, WAUSEON, OHIO: AS FOUND IN THE COURT HOUSE. 1971. 96p (DAR)

Daughters of the American Revolution. TOMBSTONE INSCRIPTIONS FULTON COUNTY OHIO. 1955. 3v. (SLO,DAR)

Daughters of the American Revolution. WILLS AND PIONEERS FULTON COUNTY OHIO. (SLO)

Fulton Co Chapter OGS. ANCESTOR SURNAME INDEX. 1981. (SLO)

Fulton Co Chapter OGS. TOMBSTONE INSCRIPTIONS, FULTON CO.OHIO. (Swanton OH: the society, 1986) 234p (OGS,LDS)

Fulton Co Chapter OGS. TOMBSTONE INSCRIPTIONS, FULTON COUNTY, OHIO, VOL.II. (Swanton OH: the society, 1986) 196pp (OGS,LDS)

FULTON COUNTY, OHIO: A COLLECTION OF HISTORICAL SKETCHES AND FAMILY HISTORIES. (Wauseon OH: Fulton Co.Hist.Soc., 1977) 632p (DAR)

Geitgey, Frances. INDEX TO 1860 CENSUS, FULTON CO. OHIO. c1973.

Grieser, Orland R. & E.Beck. OUT OF THE WILDERNESS; HISTORY OF THE CENTRAL MENNONITE CHURCH, 1835-1960. (Grand Rapids MI: Dean-Hicks Co., 1960) 243p (LDS)

Griffing, B.N. ATLAS OF FULTON COUNTY OHIO. (Philadelphia: Griffing, Gordon & Co., 1888) (Reprint, Evansville IN: Unigraphic, 1980) 64,51p (SLO,LDS)

Griffing, B.N. ATLAS OF FULTON COUNTY OHIO. 1880. (SLO)(RPI)

Guilford, Russell H. OFFICIAL SOUVENIR BOOKLET IN CELEBRATION OF 200 YEARS OF NATIONAL FREEDOM 1776-1976 EMPHASIZING FULTON COUNTY, OHIO 1850-1976. 1976. 96p (DAR,SLO)

Hardesty, H.H. MILITARY HISTORY OF OHIO - FULTON COUNTY EDITION. 1886/87. (OHS)

Hardesty, H.H. HISTORICAL ATLAS OF THE WORLD, ILLUSTRATED: FULTON COUNTY REFERENCES. (Chicago: author, 1875) (LDS)

HISTORY OF SPRING HILL METHODIST EPISCOPAL CHURCH, CENTENNIAL EDITION, 1842-1942. (Tedrow OH: the church, 1942?) 1v. (LDS)

Jewell, Mrs. Walter T. INSCRIPTIONS FROM ...BLAKE BURYING GROUND, NEAR SWAN CREEK OHIO. n.d. 13p. (LDS)

Knapp, Horace S. HISTORY OF THE MAUMEE VALLEY. (Toledo OH: author, 1872) 685p. (DAR,OHS,SLO)

Levinson, Marilyn. GUIDE TO NEWSPAPER HOLDINGS AT THE CENTER FOR ARCHIVAL COLLECTIONS. 2nd Edition. (Bowling Green OH: Bowling Green State Univ., 1987)

Maddox, Mrs. W.H. HISTORY OF SPRING HILL METHODIST EPISCOPAL CHURCH: 1842-1942. 1942? 21p (SLO,DAR)

Mikesell, Thomas, ed. THE COUNTY OF FULTON: A HISTORY OF FULTON COUNTY OHIO. (Madison WI: Northwestern Histl. Assn., 1905) (Reprint, Evansville IN: Whipporwill Pub., 1983) 661,41p (OGS,LDS,SLO)

Monagon, George P. HISTORY OF FULTON COUNTY OHIO. 1877. 14p. (SLO,DAR)

NEW ATLAS OF FULTON COUNTY. (Wauseon OH: Wauseon Republican, 1903) (LDS)

Nitchman, Paul E. BLACKS IN OHIO, 1880, IN THE COUNTIES OF FRANKLIN, FULTON, GALLIA & GEAUGA, VOLUME 4. (Ft.Meade Md: author, 1986) 163p Reighard, Frank H. A STANDARD HISTORY OF FULTON COUNTY OHIO. (Chicago: Lewis Pub Co, 1920) 2v (LC,SLO,DAR,LDS)

Seaman, Vashti. BIBLE RECORDS & WILLS OF FULTON COUNTY, 1850-1875. 74p (SLO)

Seaman, Vashti. FAMILY RECORDS OF EARLY PIONEERS OF GORHAM TOWNSHIP, FULTON COUNTY OHIO: 1835-50. 1968. 27p (DAR,LDS,SLO)

Seaman, Vashti. FULTON COUNTY WILLS AND PIONEERS. VOL.4. 1874-1882. (SLO)

Seaman, Vashti. PIONEERS AROUND DELTA OHIO. [news clippings] (LDS,SLO)

Seaman, Vashti. PIONEERS OF FULTON COUNTY OHIO: MARRIAGES, WILLS & LAND RECORDS VOL.5. (SLO)

Seaman, Vashti. RECORDS OF RELATED FAMILIES WHO COME TO THE SIX MILES WOODS. 1967. 108p (SLO,DAR,LDS)

Seaman, Vashti. SOME RECORDS FROM FULTON COUNTY, WAUSEON, AS FOUND IN THE COURT HOUSE. 1971. (SLO,LDS)

Seaman, Vashti. ORIGINAL FULTON COUNTY LAND RECORDS. (Swanton OH: J.Broglin, 1985) 50p (OGS)

Spring, Mrs. Everett E. INSCRIPTIONS AND PHOTOGRAPHS, SOCIETY OF FRIENDS MEETING HOUSE AND BURYING GROUND, FRANKLIN TWP., FULTON CO., OHIO. (Wauseon OH: author, 1951-52) (LDS)

Winter, Nevin O. HISTORY OF NORTHWEST OHIO. (Chicago: Lewis Pub.Co.,1917) 3v. (SLO)

# GALLIA COUNTY

| | |
|---|---|
| CREATED: | 1803 FROM ADAMS & WASHINGTON COUNTIES |
| COUNTY SEAT: | GALLIPOLIS 45631 |
| COURT HOUSE: | LOCUST ST., GALLIPOLIS 45631 |
| LIBRARY: | 641 SECOND AVE., GALLIPOLIS 45631 |
| HISTORICAL SOCIETY: | 16 STATE ST., GALLIPOLIS 45631 |

GENEALOGICAL SOCIETY:      GALLIA CO. CHAPTER, OGS,
                                            PO BOX 295, GALLIPOLIS 45631
                                            publication: NEWSLETTER
HEALTH DEPARTMENT:          COURTHOUSE, LOCUST ST., GALLIPOLIS 45631
                                            (separate office for Gallipolis City)
ARCHIVAL DISTRICT:           OHIO UNIVERSITY, ATHENS
                                            (see published Guide to records)
LAND SURVEYS:                 OHIO COMPANY
                                            OHIO RIVER SURVEY (SOUTH)
BOUNDED BY:                   EAST:      MASON & CABELL CO., W.VA.
                                            NORTH:   MEIGS & VINTON CO.
                                            WEST:     JACKSON CO.
                                            SOUTH:   LAWRENCE CO.
TOWNSHIPS:                     Addison, Cheshire, Clay, Gallipolis, Green, Greenfield, Guyan,
                                            Harrison, Huntington, Morgan, Ohio, Perry, Raccoon, Springfield,
                                            Walnut.

SPECIAL NOTE:                  A COURTHOUSE FIRE IN 1981 DESTROYED SOME RECORDS.

## COURT RECORDS: (LDS MICROFILM)
Auditor:
    Enumeration of school-aged youth, 1867-1899.
    Tax duplicates, 1816-1838.
Childrens' Home:
    Register, 1885-1942.
    Trustees' minutes, 1885-1918.
Clerk of Courts:
    Chancery record, v1-3, 1835-1852.
    Common Pleas journal, v4-5, 1846-1853.
    Common Pleas record, 1811-1849.
    Supreme Court Record, vE-F, 1829-1851.
    Quadrennial enumeration, 1899.
    Complete record, 1849-1852.
Commissioners:
    Journal, 1860-1891,1897-1904.
County Home:
    Register, 1877-1974.
    Director's minutes, 1896-1912.
Probate Court:
    Marriage records, 1803-1911.
    Index to marriages, 1803-1941.
    Wills, 1803-1883.
    Index to wills, 1803-1963.
    Death records, 1867-1916.
    Birth records, 1864-1921.
    Naturalization records, 1880-1906.
    Civil journal, vA-3, 1852-1881.
Recorder:
    Deeds, 1803-1876.
    Index to deeds, 1789-1892.
    Military Discharges, 1862-1903,1918.
Sheriff:
    Jail register, 1869-1893,1896-1928.
Treasurer:
    Commutations, military fund record, 1864.

Miscellaneous:
> Huntington Tp. First Presbyterian Church, minutes, 1829-1839.
> History of Meigs,Vinton,Gallia & Athens, from Dye Collection.
> Abel Larkin family papers, inc.court record book, 1818-1822.
> Marriages, 1805-1865, by DAR.
> War dead records, Gallia Co.Ohio. 1963.

## OHIO HISTORICAL SOCIETY: (MICROFILM)
Auditor:
> Enumeration of school-aged youth, 1867-1899.

Childrens' Home:
> Register, 1885-1942.
> Trustees' minutes, 1885-1918.

Clerk of Courts:
> Chancery record, v1-3, 1835-1852.
> Common Pleas journal, v4-5, 1846-1853.
> Common Pleas record, 1811-1849.
> Supreme Court Record, vE-F, 1829-1851.
> Quadrennial enumeration, 1899.
> Complete record, 1849-1852.

Commissioners:
> Journal, 1860-1891,1897-1904.

County Home:
> Register, 1877-1974.
> Director's minutes, 1896-1912.

Recorder:
> Military Discharges, 1862-1903,1918.

Sheriff:
> Jail register, 1869-1893,1896-1928.

Treasurer:
> Commutations, military fund record, 1864.

Miscellaneous:
> Marriage records, 1805-1865, by DAR.

## CENSUS RECORDS  (OHS,SLO,OGS,LDS)
1820-1880, 1900-1910; 1890 VETERANS; 1880,1900 SOUNDEX; 1910 MIRACODE

## AGRICULTURAL CENSUS SCHEDULES  (OHS,SLO-mic)
1850,1860,1870

## PRODUCTS OF INDUSTRY CENSUS SCHEDULE  (OHS,SLO-mic)
1850,1870,1880

## MORTALITY CENSUS SCHEDULES (OHS,SLO-mic)
1860,1880

## DEFECTIVE & DEPENDENT CENSUS SCHEDULES (OHS,SLO-mic)
1880

## NEWSPAPERS: [GUIDE TO OHIO NEWSPAPERS, 1793-1973]
Gallipolis, Rio Grande, Vinton.

## TAX RECORDS (OHS & LDS)
1806,1808,1810,1812-1814,1816-1838.

**MANUSCRIPTS:**
Abel Larkin family papers, inc.court record book, 1818-1822. (WRHS)
Free Will Baptist records, Sandfork, 1819-1916. (OHS)
Free Will Baptist records, Cheshire, 1819-1916. (OHS)
Gallipolis Township trustee records, 1828-1839. (WRHS)

**GENEALOGICAL PERIODICAL ARTICLES**
Bell, Carol Willsey. OHIO GENEALOGICAL PERIODICAL INDEX: A COUNTY GUIDE (Youngstown,
    OH: author, 6th ed., 1987)

**PUBLISHED SOURCES:**
Adams, Marilyn. SOUTHERN OHIO TAXPAYERS IN THE 1820'S: GALLIA & JACKSON COS.OHIO.
    (Atlanta GA: Heritage Research, 1979) 53p (LDS,SLO)
Adams, Marilyn. INDEX TO CIVIL WAR VETERANS & WIDOWS IN SOUTHERN OHIO, 1890
    FEDERAL CENSUS (Cols,OH: Franklin Co Chapter OGS,1986) 84p
Belote, Theodore T. THE SCIOTO SPECULATION AND THE FRENCH SETTLEMENT AT GAL-
    LIPOLIS. (Cincinnati: University of Cincinnati, 1907) 82p (LDS)
Berry, Ellen T. & David. EARLY OHIO SETTLERS: PURCHASERS OF LAND IN SOUTHEASTERN
    OHIO, 1800-1840. (Baltimore: Genealogical Pub.Co., 1984) 129p (OHS,SLO,OGS,DAR)
Bradbury, Anne etal. ABOUT GALLIPOLIS OHIO. (Gallipolis: Gallia Co Chapter OGS, nd)
Cherrington, Susan M. GALLIA COUNTY (OUTSIDE OF GALLIPOLIS) RECORDS OF WAR DEAD.
    (SLO,LDS)
CITY/COUNTY DIRECTORIES: check holdings of OHS & local public library.
Clark, Marie T. OHIO LANDS: CHILLICOTHE LAND OFFICE, 1800-1829. (Chillicothe: author, 1984)
    144p (OGS,SLO,OHS)
Cranmer, G.L. HISTORY OF THE UPPER OHIO VALLEY. (Madison WI: Brant & Fuller, 1891) 2v. (OHS)
Daughters of the American Revolution. EARLY MARRIAGE RECORDS GALLIA COUNTY OHIO
    1805-1865. 1937-38. 2v. (SLO,DAR,LDS)
Daughters of the American Revolution. TAX RECORDS OF GALLIA COUNTY OHIO: FOR THE YEAR
    1828. 1972. 58p (DAR)
Evans, Henrietta & Mary James. GALLIA COUNTY OHIO 1819 TAX DUPLICATE. (Gallipolis: author,
    1984) 8p (OGS,LDS,SLO)
Evans, Henrietta & Mary P. Wood. EARLY GALLIA COUNTY COURT RECORDS, 1846-1900. (Gal-
    lipolis: author, 1984) 24p. (OGS,LDS,SLO)
Evans, Henrietta & Mary P. Wood. DEATH NOTICES, OBITUARIES AND MARRIAGES NOTICES
    TAKEN FROM THE GALLIA COUNTY OHIO NEWSPAPERS FROM 1825 TO 1875. (Gallipolis
    OH: author, 1986) 280p (LDS,OHS)
Evans, Henrietta & Mary P. Wood. INDEX OF GALLIA COUNTY OHIO 1900 CENSUS. (Gallipolis:
    author, 1981) 42p. (OGS)
Evans, Henrietta & Mary P. Wood. ABSTRACTS OF GALLIA CO OHIO CHANCERY RECORDS 1835-
    1852. (Gallipolis: author, 1984) 75p (OGS,LDS)
Evans, Henrietta & Mary P. Wood. INDEX OF GALLIA COUNTY OHIO 1900 CENSUS. (Gallipolis:
    author, 1981) np (OGS)
Evans, Henrietta & Mary P. Wood. REVOLUTIONARY SOLDIERS WHO LIVED IN GALLIA COUN-
    TY OHIO. (Gallipolis OH: Gallia Co.Chapter OGS,1985) 82p (OGS,SLO,LDS)
Federal Writers' Program. GALLIPOLIS: BEING AN ACCOUNT OF THE FRENCH FIVE HUNDRED
    AND OF THE TOWN THEY ESTABLISHED ON LA BELLE RIVIERE. 1940. 47p (DAR)
Foureselter, Helene. SURNAME INDEX TO GALLIPOLIS OHIO HISTORY OF THE ESTABLISHMENT
    OF FIVE-HUNDRED FRENCH IN THE OHIO VALLEY AT THE END OF THE 18TH CENTURY.
    (SLO)
Gallia Co Chapter OGS. ABSTRACTS OF THE JOURNAL OF WILLS, INVENTORY & SALE BILLS,
    GALLIA CO OHIO, 1803-1824. (Gallipolis: the society, 1985) 52p (OGS,LDS)
Gallia Co Chapter OGS. CEMETERIES OF ADDISON TOWNSHIP. (Gallipolis: the society, nd)
    (OGS,SLO)

Gallia Co Chapter OGS. CEMETERIES OF CHESHIRE TOWNSHIP. (Gallipolis: the society, 1980) 91p (LDS,OGS,SLO)

Gallia Co Chapter OGS. CEMETERIES OF CLAY TOWNSHIP. (Gallipolis: the society, 1976) 44p (OGS,LDS,SLO)

Gallia Co Chapter OGS. CEMETERIES OF GALLIPOLIS TOWNSHIP. (Gallipolis: the society, 1977) 156p (LDS,OGS,SLO)

Gallia Co Chapter OGS. CEMETERIES OF GREEN TOWNSHIP. (Gallipolis: the society, 1981) 59p (LDS,OGS,SLO)

Gallia Co Chapter OGS. CEMETERIES OF GREENFIELD TOWNSHIP. (Gallipolis: the society, 1981) 32p (LDS,OGS,SLO)

Gallia Co Chapter OGS. CEMETERIES OF GUYAN TOWNSHIP. (Gallipolis: the society, 1981) 70p (LDS,OGS,SLO)

Gallia Co Chapter OGS. CEMETERIES OF HARRISON TOWNSHIP. (Gallipolis: the society, 1980) 22p (LDS,OGS,SLO)

Gallia Co Chapter OGS. CEMETERIES OF HUNTINGTON TOWNSHIP. (Gallipolis: the society, 1979) 65p (LDS,OGS,SLO)

Gallia Co Chapter OGS. CEMETERIES OF MORGAN TOWNSHIP. (Gallipolis: the society, 1978) 32p (OGS,SLO)

Gallia Co Chapter OGS. CEMETERIES OF OHIO TOWNSHIP. (Gallipolis: the society, 197?) 32p (OGS,SLO)

Gallia Co Chapter OGS. CEMETERIES OF PERRY TOWNSHIP. (Gallipolis: the society, 1982) 37p (LDS,OGS,SLO)

Gallia Co Chapter OGS. CEMETERIES OF RACCOON TOWNSHIP. (Gallipolis: the society, 1979) 58p (LDS,OGS,SLO)

Gallia Co Chapter OGS. CEMETERIES OF SPRINGFIELD TOWNSHIP. (Gallipolis: the society, 1979) 34p (LDS,OGS,SLO)

Gallia Co Chapter OGS. CEMETERIES OF WALNUT TOWNSHIP. (Gallipolis: the society, 1981) 49p (LDS,OGS,SLO)

Gallia Co Chapter OGS. DEATH NOTICES, OBITUARIES, AND MARRIAGE NOTICES, TAKEN FROM THE GALLIA COUNTY NEWSPAPERS, 1825-1875. (Gallipolis: the society, nd) (OGS)

Gallia Co Chapter OGS. EVERYNAME INDEX TO HARDESTY'S 1882 HISTORY OF GALLIA COUNTY. (Gallipolis: the society, 1988) (OGS)

Gallia Co Chapter OGS. INDEX TO THE 1870 GALLIA COUNTY OHIO CENSUS. (Gallipolis: the society, nd)

Gallia Co Chapter OGS. MARRIAGE RECORDS 1803-1850, BOOK 2, GALLIA CO OHIO. (Gallipolis: the society, 1983) 116p (OGS)

Gallia Co Chapter OGS. GALLIA COUNTY OHIO SOLDIER DISCHARGE BOOK VOL. 1 (Gallipolis: the society, nd)

Gallia Co Chapter OGS. REVOLUTIONARY WAR SOLDIERS WHO LIVED IN GALLIA COUNTY OHIO. (Gallipolis: the society, nd)

Gallia Co. Historical Society. GALLIA COUNTY, OHIO, PEOPLE IN HISTORY TO 1980. 1980. 383p (SLO)

Griffith, William. ILLUSTRATED ATLAS OF GALLIA CO. OHIO. (Cincinnati: Strobridge & Co., 1874) (OHS)

Hardesty, H.H. HISTORICAL HAND-ATLAS OF LAWRENCE AND GALLIA COUNTIES OHIO. (Chicago: author, 1882)(Reprint, Gallipolis OH: St.Peter's Episcopal Church, 1976) 45p (LDS,OHS,SLO) (RPI)

Hardesty, H.H. HISTORICAL HAND ATLAS OF GALLIA CO OHIO, 1882. (Gallipolis: St.Peter's Episcopal Church, 1976) 45p (OGS)

Harris, Charles H. THE HARRIS STORY. 1957. 329p (SLO)

Hill, Frank. HISTORY OF GALLIA COUNTY COURTHOUSES, 1806-1981. (Gallipolis: Gallia Co Chapter OGS, 1981) 8p (LDS)

HISTORIES OF ATHENS, GALLIA, MEIGS AND VINTON COUNTIES, OHIO: NEWSPAPER CLIPPINGS FROM THE DYE COLLECTION. (LDS,SLO)

Hixson, W.W. PLAT BOOK OF GALLIA COUNTY OHIO. (Rockford IL: author, nd) (OHS)

ILLUSTRATED HISTORICAL & BUSINESS REVIEW OF MEIGS & GALLIA COUNTIES OHIO. (Coshocton: Union Pub Co., 1891) (OHS)

Ingles, Wayne B. SYMMES CREEK: HISTORICAL EVENTS & STORIES OF THE SYMMES VALLEY., INCLUDING JACKSON, GALLIA & LAWRENCE COUNTIES. (Zanesville: author, 1976) (OHS,SLO)

Jewell, Mrs. Walter T. INSCRIPTIONS FROM...NORTHUP OR ROSE CEMETERY & McCALL GRAVEYARD, NEAR NORTHUP. (Arlington VA: author, nd) (LDS)

Naret, Edward & J.P.R.Bureau. HISTORY OF THE EARLY FRENCH SETTLERS. (Gallipolis: Gallia Co Chapter OGS, 1977) 17p (LDS)

Nitchman, Paul E. BLACKS IN OHIO, 1880, IN THE COUNTIES OF FRANKLIN, FULTON, GALLIA & GEAUGA, VOLUME 4. (Ft.Meade Md: author, 1986) 163p

Ohio University. GUIDE TO LOCAL GOVERNMENT RECORDS AT OHIO UNIVERSITY. (Athens: OU Library, 1986) 61p.

Pierce, Homer. 1820 CENSUS, GALLIA COUNTY OHIO. (Orangeburg SC: author, nd) (OHS)

Pierce, Homer. 1830 CENSUS, GALLIA COUNTY OHIO. (Orangeburg SC: author, nd) (OHS)

Pierce, Homer. 1840 CENSUS, GALLIA COUNTY OHIO. (Orangeburg SC: author, nd) (OHS)

Potts, Genevieve. ABSTRACTS OF WILLS & ADMINISTRATIONS OF WASHINGTON CO., 1788-1855 AND GALLIA COUNTY, 1788-1806. (Columbus: author, 1939) (OHS)

SECOND ANNUAL CATALOGUE OF RIO GRANDE COLLEGE 1878-1879. (Rio Grande OH: Rio Grande College, 1878) 13p (OHS)

Sibley, William G. THE FRENCH FIVE HUNDRED. (Gallipolis: Gallia Co Hist Soc., 1933) (OHS,LDS)

Sibley, William G. THE FRENCH FIVE-HUNDRED. (Gallipolis: Tribune Press, 1901) 303p (SLO,DAR)

STANDARD HISTORY OF THE HANGING ROCK IRON REGION OF OHIO. 1916. (SLO)

Trowbridge, Michael. GALLIA COUNTY OHIO SOLDIER DISCHARGE BOOK, VOL.1. (Gallipolis OH: Gallia Co.Chapter OGS, 1986)(LDS,OHS)

Trowbridge, Michael. MARRIAGE RECORDS 1803-1850 GALLIA COUNTY OHIO. (Gallipolis: Gallia Co Hist Soc, 1983) 116p (OGS,LDS)

Trowbridge, Michael. MARRIAGE RECORDS OF GALLIA COUNTY BOOK 2, 1851-1900. (OHS,LDS)

Trowbridge, Michael. MARRIAGE RECORDS OF GALLIA COUNTY BOOK 3, 1901-1925. (Gallipolis: Gallia Co Hist Soc., 1987) (WRHS)

Whiteman, Jane. SURNAME INDEX TO THE HARRIS HISTORY BY CHARLES H. HARRIS, 1957. (Tulsa OK: author, 1978)

Whiteman, Jane. SURNAME INDEX TO HISTORY OF THE UPPER OHIO VALLEY, Brant & Fuller, 1891. (Tulsa OK: author, nd)

WIGGINS & WEAVER'S OHIO RIVER DIRECTORY FOR 1871-1872: EMBRACING...GALLIPOLIS. (Cleveland OH: authors, 1872) 419p (LDS)

Work Projects Administration. GALLIPOLIS: BEING AN ACCOUNT OF THE FRENCH FIVE HUNDRED AND OF THE TOWN THEY ESTABLISHED ON LA BELLE RIVIERE. (Columbus: Ohio Hist.Soc., 1940) 47p. (SLO,LDS)

# GEAUGA COUNTY

| | |
|---|---|
| CREATED: | 1806 FROM TRUMBULL COUNTY |
| COUNTY SEAT: | CHARDON 44024 |
| COURT HOUSE: | PUBLIC SQUARE, CHARDON 44024 |
| LIBRARY: | 110 E.PARK ST., CHARDON 44024 |
| HISTORICAL SOCIETY: | 14653 E.PARK ST., BURTON 44021 |
| GENEALOGICAL SOCIETY: | GEAUGA CO. CHAPTER OGS, |
| | PO BOX 497, MIDDLEFIELD 44062 |
| | publication: RACONTEUR |
| HEALTH DEPARTMENT: | 219 MAIN ST., CHARDON 44024-1296 |
| ARCHIVAL DISTRICT: | WESTERN RESERVE HIST.SOC., CLEVELAND |
| LAND SURVEYS: | CONNECTICUT WESTERN RESERVE |

BOUNDED BY:

TOWNSHIPS:

EAST: ASHTABULA & TRUMBULL CO.
NORTH: LAKE CO.
WEST: CUYAHOGA CO.
SOUTH: PORTAGE CO.
Auburn, Bainbridge, Burton, Chardon, Chester, Claridon, Hampden, Huntsburg, Middlefield, Montville, Munson, Newbury, Parkman, Russell, Thompson, Troy.

## COURT RECORDS: (LDS MICROFILM)
Auditor:
Tax maps, 1880.
Tax records, 1820-1850.
Delinquent tax list, 1820-1825,1854-1868.
Assessors returns, 1846-1852.
List of personal property, 1833-1835,1838-1839,1843-1845.
Clerk of Courts:
Common Pleas general index, 1807-1890.
Common Pleas direct index, 1808-1895.
Common Pleas docket, 1833-1839.
Common Pleas execution docket, 1828-1837.
Common Pleas journal, vA-P, 1806-1851.
Common Pleas record, vA-Y, 1806-1842,1841-1850.
Chancery records, vAA-EE, 1839-1852.
Execution docket, 1811-1852.
Final record, 1806-1852.
Court record book, 1806-1831.
Supreme Court execution docket & bonds, 1828-1884.
Supreme Court journal, 1806-1814,1844-1849.
Supreme Court records, 1806-1852.
Supreme Court docket, 1828-1862.
Trial list, 1859-1862.
District Court records, 1853-1857.
Appearance docket, 1866-1874.
Witness record, 1848-1857,1864-1870.
Commissioners:
Road records, 1806-1884.
Probate Court:
Marriage records, 1803-1853.
Marriage records and licenses, 1806-1919.
Index to marriages, v1, 1806-1886.
Death and birth records, 1867-1908.
Will records, 1853-1910.
Final record, vA-E, 1852-1889.
Probate record, vA-I, 1806-1853.
Probate journal, vA-G, 1852-1887.
Letters of administration, 1871-1898.
Guardian docket, v1, 1876-1910.
Guardian record, v1, 1867-1886.
Administrators & executors docket, v2, 1870-1897.
Appointments, bonds & letters, 1858-1870.
Administrators & executors bonds & letters, vA-B, 1871-1887.
Inventory & sale bills, vA-G, 1853-1886.
Naturalization record, 1860-1906.
Recorder:
Deed and mortgage records, vA-43, 1800-1851.

Deeds, 1835-1886.
General index to deeds, 1795-1875.
Mortgage index, 1795-1880.
Index of leases, 1830-1921.
County record book of land, 1806-1808.
Record of incorportations, 1845-1906.
Indentures of apprenticeship, 1825-1858.
Record of mechanics' liens, 1848-1880.
Surveyors' records, 1834-1874.
School Board:
School accounts, 1839-1866.
Treasurer:
Book of accounts, 1819-1865.
Order books, 1831-1868.
Witness record, 1848-1872.
Miscellaneous:
Manuscript survey map of Burton.
Chester Township Free Will Baptist Church, records, 1863-1904.
Chardon Regular Baptist Church, records, 1831-1905.
Geauga Baptist Assn. minutes, 1835-1861.
Francis M. Leonard, journal, 1831-1836.
Grand River Baptist Assn. records, 1817-1842,1853-1871.
Grand River Presbytery minutes, 1814-1818,1829-1870.
Russell Twp. Trustee records, 1827-1850.
Bainbridge Twp. Trustee records, 1822-1894.
Lake & Geauga Co. Marriages, Vol.II, 1817-1825.
Marriage records, 1805-1865, by DAR.
Record of Revolutionary soldiers buried in Lake & Geauga Cos., by DAR.
Docket Book of Benj.Morse, JP in Geauga & Trumbull Cos.,1805-1809.

## OHIO HISTORICAL SOCIETY: (MICROFILM)
Clerk of Courts:
Common Pleas general index, 1807-1890.
Common Pleas direct index, 1808-1895.
Chancery record, 1839-1852.
Common Pleas docket, 1833-1839.
Common Pleas record, 1841-1850.
Common Pleas execution docket, 1828-1837.
Supreme Court docket, 1828-1862.
Supreme Court record, 1806-1852.
Probate Court:
Letters of administration, 1871-1898.
Wills, 1891-1910.
Recorder:
Deeds, 1835-1886.
Miscellaneous:
Connecticut Land Co., Western Reserve land draft, 1795-1809.
Marriage records, 1805-1865, by DAR.

## CENSUS RECORDS  (OHS,SLO,OGS,LDS)
1820-1880, 1900-1910; 1890 VETERANS; 1880,1900 SOUNDEX; 1910 MIRACODE

## AGRICULTURAL CENSUS SCHEDULES  (OHS,SLO-mic)
1850,1860,1870

**PRODUCTS OF INDUSTRY CENSUS SCHEDULE (OHS,SLO-mic)**
1850,1870,1880

**MORTALITY CENSUS SCHEDULES (OHS,SLO-mic)**
1860,1880

**DEFECTIVE & DEPENDENT CENSUS SCHEDULES (OHS,SLO-mic)**
1880

**NEWSPAPERS: [GUIDE TO OHIO NEWSPAPERS, 1793-1973]**
Burton, Chardon, Middlefield.

**TAX RECORDS (OHS & LDS)**
1807-1808,1810,1812-1814,1816-1838.

**MANUSCRIPTS:**
Bainbridge Township general records, 1822-1931. (WRHS)
Russell Township trustees records, 1827-1850. (WRHS)
Chardon, Regular Baptist church, records, 1831-1905. (WRHS)
Boanergean Lodge, Burton, account book, 1855-1857. (WRHS)
Geauga Baptist Assn., minutes, 1835-1861. (WRHS)
Chester Township, Free Will Baptist Church, records, 1863-1904. (WRHS)
Francis Leonard journal, 1831-1836. (WRHS)

**GENEALOGICAL PERIODICAL ARTICLES**
Bell, Carol Willsey. OHIO GENEALOGICAL PERIODICAL INDEX: A COUNTY GUIDE (Youngstown, OH: author, 6th ed., 1987)

**PUBLISHED SOURCES:**
1857 LANDOWNERS' MAPS: GEAUGA AND LAKE COUNTIES OHIO. (Painesville OH: Lake & Geauga Chapters OGS, 1985) 66p (OGS,LDS)
Backman, Milton V. PROFILE OF LATTER-DAY SAINTS OF KIRTLAND, OHIO AND MEMBERS OF ZION'S CAMP, 1830-1839, VITAL STATISTICS AND SOURCES. 1983. (SLO)
Baldwin, Henry R. OLDEST INSCRIPTIONS WITH REVOLUTIONARY WAR AND WAR OF 1812 RECORDS OF OHIO AND PENNSYLVANIA. (SLO)
Bell, Carol W. ABSTRACTS FROM BIOGRAPHIES IN HISTORY OF NORTH EASTERN OHIO by John S. Stewart, 1935. (Indianapolis: Ye Olde Genealogie Shoppe, 1983)
BIOGRAPHICAL HISTORY OF NORTHEASTERN OHIO EMBRACING THE COUNTIES OF ASHTABULA, GEAUGA AND LAKE. (Chicago: Lewis Pub Co., 1893) 1028p (LDS,OHS,DAR)(RPI)
BONDSTOWN BICENTENNIAL GAZETTE: HAMBDEN, OHIO, 1801-1976. (Chardon OH: Hambden Bicentennial Committee, 1976) 12p (LDS)
CITY/COUNTY DIRECTORIES: check holdings of OHS & local public library.
Clark, Pliny O. OUR HUNTSBURG HERITAGE: HISTORICAL SKETCHES OF HUNTSBURG, GEAUGA COUNTY, OHIO FAMILIES DURING THE YEARS 1850-1910. 1963. 373p (SLO ,DAR,LDS)
Collacott, Margaret O. INDEX FOR HISTORY OF GEAUGA AND LAKE COUNTIES OHIO. (Mentor OH: Lake Co.Hist.Soc., 1964) 100p (LDS)
Daughters of the American Revolution. FAMILY AND BIBLE RECORDS, CHILDS TAYLOR CHAPTER. (SLO)
Daughters of the American Revolution. MISCELLANEOUS RECORDS OF LAKE COUNTY OHIO [AND GEAUGA COUNTY]. 1974. 1v (DAR)
Daughters of the American Revolution. RECORD OF MARRIAGE LICENSES IN GEAUGA COUNTY OHIO 1805-1865. 1928-38. 200p (SLO,DAR,LDS)

Daughters of the American Revolution. A RECORD OF THE REVOLUTIONARY SOLDIERS BURIED IN LAKE COUNTY OHIO, WITH A PARTIAL LIST OF THOSE IN GEAUGA COUNTY. 1902. 94p (DAR,LDS,SLO)

Daughters of the American Revolution. RECORDS OF THOMPSON TOWNSHIP, GEAUGA COUNTY OHIO. 1975. c300p (DAR)

Daughters of the American Revolution. RECORDS OF TWO CEMETERIES: EVERGREEN AND MAPLE GROVE, THOMPSON TWP., GEAUGA COUNTY, OHIO. 1975. 209p (DAR)

Daughters of the American Revolution. TOMBSTONE INSCRIPTIONS AND INTERMENT RECORDS OF HAMBDEN TOWNSHIP CEMETERY, GEAUGA COUNTY, OHIO, 1818-1979. (SLO)

Daughters of the American Revolution. WILLS: GEAUGA AND TUSCARAWAS COUNTIES, OHIO, ETC. 1977. c100p (DAR)

Davis, Mrs. Howard. EARLY MARRIAGES IN GEAUGA COUNTY OHIO, ARRANGED BY TOWNSHIP. (WRHS,LDS)

Ford, Margaret O. EARLY MARRIAGES IN GEAUGA COUNTY. (Burton OH: author, nd) 261p (LDS)

Geauga County Historical Society. EARLY PIONEERS OF THE WESTERN RESERVE. 1973.

Geauga County Historical Society. PIONEER AND GENERAL HISTORY OF GEAUGA COUNTY WITH SKETCHES OF SOME OF THE PIONEERS AND PROMINENT MEN. 1880. 822p. (LDS)

GEAUGA COUNTY ATLAS AND DIRECTORY. (Warren OH: Atlas Pub.Co., nd) (LC)

GENEALOGICAL DATA RELATING TO WOMEN IN THE WESTERN RESERVE BEFORE 1840 (1850) (Cleveland: Centennial Commission, 1943) (WRHS,LDS)

Hardesty, H.H. MILITARY HISTORY OF OHIO, GEAUGA COUNTY EDITION. (New York: author, 1887) 313p (OHS,LDS)

Hawley, Emma N. WESTERN RESERVE MARRIAGES, GEAUGA COUNTY OHIO, 1805-1824. (Cleveland OH: author, n.d.) (LDS)

Held, Frances H. LETTERS BY NABBY L. HICKOX, BURTON OHIO, 1854-1868. (Hudson OH: author, 1983) 110p (OGS)

Historical Records Survey. INVENTORY OF THE COUNTY ARCHIVES OF OHIO, NO.28, GEAUGA COUNTY. (Columbus: author, 1942) 323p (OHS,LDS,DAR)

Historical Society of Geauga Co.Ohio. PIONEER AND GENERAL HISTORY OF GEAUGA COUNTY. (Burton? OH: 1880) 822p (LC,SLO) (RPI)

HISTORY OF GEAUGA AND LAKE COUNTIES OHIO. (Philadelphia: Williams Bros., 1878) (Reprint, Evansville IN: Unigraphic, 1973) 259p (LC,SLO,LDS,OHS,DAR) (RPI)

INDEX TO THE MICROFILM EDITION OF GENEALOGICAL DATA RELATING TO WOMEN IN THE WESTERN RESERVE BEFORE 1840 (1850). 1940. (Cleveland: Western Reserve Hist Soc., 1976) 226p (OGS)

Kent State University. PATRIOTS AND PIONEERS OF GEAUGA COUNTY OHIO. (Chardon OH: Academic Center, 1969) 3p, map. (LDS)

LAKE COUNTY AND GEAUGA COUNTY OHIO MARRIAGES, VOL.II, 1817-1825, 550 MARRIAGES. [from New Haven CT Hist.Soc.] 22p (LDS)

Lake, D.J. ATLAS OF LAKE AND GEAUGA COUNTIES. (Philadelphia: Titus, Simmons & Titus, 1874) (Reprint, Evansville IN: Unigraphic, 1973) 95p (SLO,OHS,LDS,DAR)(RPI)

Mathews, S.H. MAP OF GEAUGA AND LAKE COUNTIES OHIO. (Philadelphia: author, 1857) (LDS)

Nitchman, Paul E. BLACKS IN OHIO, 1880, IN THE COUNTIES OF FRANKLIN, FULTON, GALLIA & GEAUGA, VOLUME 4. (Ft.Meade Md: author, 1986) 163p

PATRIOTS AND PIONEERS OF GEAUGA COUNTY OHIO. (Kent OH: Geauga Co.Academic Center, 1974?) (LDS)

Phillips, Vernon S. LAKE COUNTY AND GEAUGA COUNTY OHIO MARRIAGES. (Akron OH: author, 1934?) (LC,LDS,DAR)

PIONEER AND GENERAL HISTORY OF GEAUGA COUNTY: WITH SKETCHES OF SOME OF THE PIONEERS AND PROMINENT MEN. (Hist.Soc.of Geauga Co.,1880) (Reprint, Evansville IN: Unigraphic, 1973) 822p (DAR,LDS,SLO)

PIONEER AND GENERAL HISTORY OF GEAUGA COUNTY OHIO. (Geauga Co.Hist.& Mem. Soc., 1953) 783p. (SLO,DAR)

Selby, Robert E. GEAUGA COUNTY OHIO MARRIAGE RECORDS, 1806-1821. (Kokomo IN: Selby Pub., 1983) 20p (LDS)

Sherman, Edith. CEMETERY INSCRIPTIONS, GEAUGA OHIO. 1925-27. 359p (DAR,SLO)

Sherman, Mrs. E.H. REVOLUTIONARY SOLDIERS BURIED IN GEAUGA COUNTY OHIO. (LDS, WRHS)

Stebbins, Judy J. GUIDE TO THE PAINSVILLE (OHIO) TELEGRAPH, 1822-1829.: NEWSPAPER ABSTRACTS WITH INDEXES. (Willoughby OH: Genealogical Research, 1982) 375 p (LDS,SLO)

Stewart, John S. HISTORY OF NORTHEASTERN OHIO. (Indianapolis: Historical Pub. Co., 1935) 3v. (SLO)

Stranahan, H.B. & Co. ATLAS OF GEAUGA COUNTY OHIO. (Cleveland: author, 1900) (LC,OGS)

Trucksis, Theresa. A GUIDE TO LOCAL HISTORICAL MATERIALS IN THE LIBRARIES OF NORTH-EASTERN OHIO. (Youngstown OH: NE Oh Libr.Assn., 1977) 72p (Yo PL)

Upton, Harriet T. HISTORY OF THE WESTERN RESERVE (Chicago: Lewis Pub Co., 1910) 3v (SLO,OHS)

Warren, Violet & J. Grosvenor. A MONUMENTAL WORK INSCRIPTIONS AND INTERMENTS IN GEAUGA COUNTY OHIO THROUGH 1983. (Chardon OH: Geauga Co Chapter OGS, 1985) 770p (OGS,LDS)

Western Reserve Hist.Soc. INDEX TO THE MICROFILM EDITION OF GENEALOGICAL DATA RELATING TO WOMEN IN THE WESTERN RESERVE PRE 1840. (Cleveland: the society, 1976) 226p (OGS,WRHS)

Wickham, Gertrude V.W. MEMORIAL TO THE PIONEER WOMEN OF THE WESTERN RESERVE. (Cleveland: Cleveland Centennial Commission, 1896+) 2v, repr 1981 (SLO)

Zethmayr, Frank R. GEAUGA COUNTY OHIO. (Chardon OH: author, c1928) (LC)

# GREENE COUNTY

CREATED: 1803 FROM HAMILTON & ROSS COUNTIES
COUNTY SEAT: XENIA 45385
COURT HOUSE: 45 N. DETROIT ST., XENIA 45385
LIBRARY: 76 E. MARKET ST., XENIA 45385
HISTORICAL SOCIETY: 74 W. CHURCH ST., XENIA 45385
GENEALOGICAL SOCIETY: GREENE CO. CHAPTER OGS,
   PO BOX 706, XENIA 45385
   publication: LEAVES OF GREENE
HEALTH DEPARTMENT: 360 WILSON DR., XENIA 45385
   (separate offices for Xenia City, Beavercreek, Bellbrook, & Fairborn)
ARCHIVAL DISTRICT: WRIGHT STATE UNIVERSITY, DAYTON
   (see Leggett's Guide to records)
LAND SURVEYS: VIRGINIA MILITARY DISTRICT
   CONGRESS LANDS: BETWEEN THE MIAMI RIVER SURVEY
BOUNDED BY: EAST: FAYETTE & MADISON CO.
   NORTH: CLARK CO.
   WEST: MONTGOMERY CO.
   SOUTH: CLINTON & WARREN CO.
TOWNSHIPS: Bath, Beaver Creek, Caesar Creek, Cedarville, Jefferson, Miami, New Jasper, Ross, Silver Creek, Spring Valley, Sugar Creek, Xenia.

**COURT RECORDS: (LDS MICROFILM)**
Auditor:
   Tax duplicates, 1816-1838.
   Real estate tax list, v1-12, 1839-1850.
   Enumeration of school-aged youth, 1831-1833.
Board of Elections:
   Minute book, 1891-1940.
Childrens' Home:
   Indenture record, 1896-1910,1912-1919.

Inmates record, v1-2, 1904-1924.
Trustees' minutes, 1911-1926.

Clerk of Courts:
Common Pleas civil docket, v1-35, 1853-1902.
Chancery record, vA-G, 1821-1854.
Civil minutes journal, 1804-1813, 1853-1901.
Civil record, 1809-1826,1831-1909.
General index, direct & reverse, 1802-1878.
Judgment index, direct & reverse, 1879-1910.
Index to pending suits, 1871-1902.
Superior Court appearance docket, 1870-1875.
Superior Court execution docket, 1877-1882.
Superior Court record, v1-3, 1871-1875.
Superior Court general index, 1871-1882.
Superior Court minutes, v1-2, 1871-1875.
Supreme Court chancery record, vA-B, 1824-1851.
Supreme Court minutes, 1810-1818.
Supreme Court record, vA-D, 1803-1860.
Appearance docket, v36-50, 1902-1930.
District Court minute book, 1852-1885.
Circuit court journal, 1885-1913.
Record of black and mulatto persons, 1805-1844.
Emancipation record, 1805-1844.

Commissioners:
Journal, v1-7, 1804-1859.
Record, 1859-1902.
Record of blind beneficiaries, 1917-1919.

County Home:
Record of inmates, v1-3, 1829-1907.
Indenture record, 1884-1886,1899.
Director's minutes, 1861-1908.
Relief & indenture record, 1881-1891.

Probate Court:
Record of deaths, 1870-1903.
Record of births, 1869-1909.
Registration & correction of births, 1941-1962.
Marriage records, vA-31, 1803-1968.
Will records, vA-16, 1803-1959.
General index to wills, 1807-1949.
General index to probate court, n.d.
General index to estates, n.d.
General index to miscellaneous, n.d.
Final record, vA-41, 1852-1957.
Settlement journal, v1-15, 1880-1960.
Administrators & executors docket, vC-1, 1814-1884.
Administrators & executors docket, v1-23, 1885-1967.
Administrators bonds & letters, v1-38, 1852-1958.
Guardians docket, v3-5, 1885-1962.
Guardians bonds & letters, vA-H, 4-5, 1868-1955.
Minutes, vA-K, 1852-1876.
Minutes & journal books, vA-74, 1852-1967.
Journals, vL-74, 1876-1967.
Naturalization record, 1880-1906.

Recorder:
Deed records, v1A-91, 1798-1901.

General index to deeds, 1803-1965.
Mortgage record, v1-3C, 1839-1853.
Mortgage index, 1839-1967.
Real estate docket, 1885-1966.
Record of soldiers' discharges, v1-15, 1863-1965.
Miscellaneous:
Jamestown Monthly Meeting of Friends, minutes, 1910-1945.
Xenia Monthly Meeting of Friends, minutes, 1925-1943.
Cedarville Reformed Presbyterian Church, minutes, 1853-1872.
Cedarville United Presbyterian Church, minutes, 1858-1900.
Cedarville, Massie's Creek United Presb.Church, records, 1859-1882.
Cedarville, Massie's Creek Reformed Presb.Ch., minutes, 1829-1859.
Cedarville, Associate Reformed Church, minutes, 1844-1858.
Misc. cemetery records, by LDS.
Misc. cemetery records, by DAR.
Marriage records, v1-2, 1803-1861, by DAR.

## OHIO HISTORICAL SOCIETY: (MICROFILM)
Auditor:
Real estate tax list, v1-12, 1839-1850.
Enumeration of school-aged youth, 1831-1833.
Board of Elections:
Minute book, 1891-1940.
Childrens' Home:
Indenture record, 1896-1910,1912-1919.
Inmates record, v1-2, 1904-1924.
Trustees' minutes, 1911-1926.
Clerk of Courts:
Common Pleas civil docket, v1-35, 1853-1902.
Chancery record, vA-G, 1821-1854.
Civil minutes journal, 1804-1813, 1853-1901.
Civil record, 1809-1826,1831-1909.
Emancipation record, 1805-1844.
General index, direct & reverse, 1802-1878.
Judgment index, direct & reverse, 1879-1910.
Index to pending suits, 1871-1902.
Superior Court appearance docket, 1870-1875.
Superior Court execution docket, 1877-1882.
Superior Court record, v1-3, 1871-1875.
Superior Court general index, 1871-1882.
Superior Court minutes, v1-2, 1871-1875.
Supreme Court chancery record, vA-B, 1824-1851.
Supreme Court minutes, 1810-1818.
Supreme Court record, vA-D, 1803-1860.
Appearance docket, v36-50, 1902-1930.
District Court minute book, 1852-1885.
Circuit court journal, 1885-1913.
Commissioners:
Journal, v1-7, 1804-1859.
Record, 1859-1902.
Record of blind beneficiaries, 1917-1919.
County Home:
Record of inmates, v1-3, 1829-1907.
Indenture record, 1884-1886,1899.
Director's minutes, 1861-1908.

Relief & indenture record, 1881-1891.
Probate Court:
    Marriages, 1803-1870.
    Naturalizations, minors & soldiers, 1892
    Naturalization record, v1-3, 1880-1906.
Recorder:
    Soldiers' discharge records, v1-2, 1862-1900.
Veterans' service:
    Soldiers' relief commission, 1892-1900.
    Minutes & relief records, 1909-1949.
Works Progress Administration:
    Church survey forms.
Xenia City Council:
    Minutes & ordinances, 1834-1841,1857-1868.
    Minutes, v1-17, 1868-1977.
    Ordinance record, vA-N, 1867-1977.
Yellow Springs Village Council:
    Minutes, v1-11, 1861-1977.
    Ordinance record, 1886-1977.
    Resolution record, 1953-1977.
    Planning Commission minutes, 1950-1977.
Miscellaneous:
    Marriages, v1-2, 1803-1861, by DAR.
    Index to marriages, by DAR.
    History of Greene County, by DAR.

**CENSUS RECORDS  (OHS,SLO,OGS,LDS)**
1820-1880, 1900-1910; 1890 VETERANS; 1880,1900 SOUNDEX; 1910 MIRACODE

**AGRICULTURAL CENSUS SCHEDULES  (OHS,SLO-mic)**
1850,1860,1870

**PRODUCTS OF INDUSTRY CENSUS SCHEDULE  (OHS,SLO-mic)**
1850,1870,1880

**MORTALITY CENSUS SCHEDULES (OHS,SLO-mic)**
1860

**DEFECTIVE & DEPENDENT CENSUS SCHEDULES (OHS,SLO-mic)**
1880

**NEWSPAPERS: [GUIDE TO OHIO NEWSPAPERS, 1793-1973]**
Bellbrook, Cedarville, Fairborn, Hustead, Jamestown, Osborn, Spring Valley, Xenia, Yellow Springs.

**TAX RECORDS (OHS & LDS)**
1806-1810,1812-1814,1816-1838.

**MANUSCRIPTS:**
Reformed Presbyterian Church, Xenia, records, 1859-1882. (WRHS)
Daybook of William Crowl?, Spring Valley O., 1849-1850. (OHS)
Mennonite church records,1864-1907,of John Mouk, Osborn OH (OHS)
Ohio Soldiers & Sailors Home Orphanage School, papers, 1932-1933.(OHS)

## GENEALOGICAL PERIODICAL ARTICLES
Bell, Carol Willsey. OHIO GENEALOGICAL PERIODICAL INDEX: A COUNTY GUIDE (Youngstown, OH: author, 6th ed., 1987)

## PUBLISHED SOURCES:
1855 ATLAS FROM THE MAP OF GREENE COUNTY OHIO. (SLO)

Barron, William P. THE FLOOD OF MARCH 1913, THE MIAMI CONSERVANCY DISTRICT, AND THE EFFECT ON THE VILLAGE OF OSBORN, OHIO. (Willard OH: Family Heritage Pubs. 1983) 64p

Bell, Carol W. (Flavell). GREENE COUNTY OHIO AREA KEY. (Kiowa CO: Area Keys 1977). 82p (SLO)

Berry, Ellen T. & David A. EARLY OHIO SETTLERS: PURCHASERS OF LAND IN SOUTHWESTERN OHIO, 1800-1840. (Baltimore: Genealogical Pub.Co., 1986) 372p (OGS,SLO,OHS)

BOWERSVILLE CEMETERY RECORDS, 1820-1940. (LDS)

Brien, Lindsay M. CEMETERY RECORDS, PARTS OF BUTLER COUNTY, GREENE COUNTY, PREBLE COUNTY [MIAMI VALLEY RECORDS v6]. 155p (LDS)

Brien, Lindsay M. MIAMI VALLEY CEMETERY RECORDS. [MIAMI VALLEY RECORDS v7] (LDS)

Brien, Lindsay M. MARRIAGES: BUTLER CO., GREENE CO., MIAMI CO., PREBLE CO & WARREN CO OHIO [MIAMI VALLEY RECORDS v8]. 227p (LDS)

BROEKHOVEN'S XENIA AND GREENE COUNTY DIRECTORY. (Columbus OH: L.O.Broekhoven, 1898-1899, 1904-1905) (OHS)

Broadstone, M.A. HISTORY OF GREENE COUNTY OHIO: ITS PEOPLE, INDUSTRIES, AND INSTITU-TIONS. (Indianapolis IN: B.F.Bowen & Co., 1918) (OHS,DAR)

Brown, Hallie Q. PEN PICTURES OF PIONEERS OF WILBERFORCE. (Xenia OH: Aldine Pub.Co., 1937) 96p (DAR)

CATALOGUE OF THE UNION FEMALE SEMINARY. (Xenia OH: Union Female Seminary, 1857-1858) (OHS)

CITY/COUNTY DIRECTORIES: check holdings of OHS & local public library.

COMBINATION ATLAS MAP OF GREENE COUNTY, OHIO. 1874. (Reprint, Knightstown IN: Book-mark, 1974) 100p (OGS,DAR,SLO)

Cox, Mrs. S.V. THE STORY OF WHITEHALL FARM. 1963? 17p (DAR)

Daughters of the American Revolution. CEMETERY INSCRIPTIONS MISCELLANEOUS VOLUME OHIO 1957-1958, VOL.2. (SLO)

Daughters of the American Revolution. CEMETERY INSCRIPTIONS OF GREENE COUNTY, OHIO: AND GREEN PLAINS, CLARK COUNTY, OHIO. 1969. 336p (DAR,LDS)

Daughters of the American Revolution. INDEX TO "HISTORY OF GREENE COUNTY OHIO" BY R.S.DILLS, 1881. (SLO,LDS)

Daughters of the American Revolution. GREENE COUNTY EARLY MARRIAGE RECORDS 1803-1860. 1938. 3v (SLO,DAR,LDS)

Dills, R.S. HISTORY OF GREENE COUNTY OHIO. (Dayton OH: Odell & Mayer, 1881) (Reprint, Xenia OH: Greene Co.Hist.Soc., 1974) 1018p (SLO,OGS,OHS,DAR)(RPI)

EDMONDSON'S XENIA CITY DIRECTORY. (Xenia OH: Edmondson Bros & Gray, 1875-1876) (OHS)

Elam, Harvey W. UNION NEIGHBORHOOD, GREENE COUNTY OHIO, HISTORICAL NOTES. (Xenia OH: author, 1940) 492p (OHS)

Everts, L.H. COMBINATION ATLAS OF GREENE COUNTY OHIO. (Chicago: author, 1874) 100p (LDS,LC,SLO,OHS) (RPI)

Galloway, William A. HISTORY OF GLEN HELEN, NEAR YELLOW SPRINGS, GREENE COUNTY OHIO. (Columbus OH: F.J.Heer, 1932) 83p (SLO,OHS,LDS)

Greene Co.Chapter OGS. GREENE COUNTY OHIO CEMETERY INSCRIPTIONS VOL.I -MIAMI TP. (Xenia OH: the society, 1982) 143p (OGS,LDS,SLO)

Greene Co.Chapter OGS. GREENE COUNTY OHIO CEMETERY INSCRIPTIONS VOL.II -SILVER CREEK TWP. (Xenia OH: the society, 1984) 185p (OGS,LDS,SLO)

Greene Co.Chapter OGS. GREENE COUNTY OHIO CEMETERY INSCRIPTIONS VOL.III (Xenia OH: the society, 1985) 135p (OGS,LDS)

Greene Co.Chapter OGS. GREENE COUNTY OHIO CEMETERY INSCRIPTIONS VOL.IV -SPRING VALLEY & SUGARCREEK TOWNSHIPS. (Xenia OH: the society, 1985) 109p (OGS)

Greene Co.Chapter OGS. GREENE COUNTY OHIO CEMETERY INSCRIPTIONS, VOL.V -CEDAR-
VILLE TOWNSHIP AND ROSS TOWNSHIP. (Xenia OH: the society, 1986) 106p (OGS)

Greene Co.Chapter OGS. GREENE COUNTY SURNAME LIST, VOLUME 3, 1986. (Xenia OH: the
society, 1986) 58p (LDS)

Greene Co.Chapter OGS. HEADS OF HOUSEHOLD - 1820 FEDERAL CENSUS, GREENE COUNTY
OHIO. (Xenia OH: the society, 1987) 18p (OGS)

Greene County Home Coming Assn. GREENE COUNTY, 1803-1908. (Xenia OH: Aldine Pub.House,
1908) 226p (OHS)

GREENE COUNTY IN THE WAR. (Xenia OH: Torchlight Job Rooms, 1872) 196p (LC)

GREENE COUNTY 1803-1908. (Xenia OH: Aldine Pub house, 1908) 226p (SLO,LDS)

Greene Co. Sesquicentennial Organization. OUT OF THE WILDERNESS; AN ACCOUNT OF EVENTS
IN GREENE COUNTY OHIO. (Ann Arbor: Edwards Bros., 1953) 306p (LC,OHS,SLO)

Haller, Stephen E. & P.Nolan. FIRST STOP FOR LOCAL HISTORY RESEARCH. A GUIDE TO COUN-
TY RECORDS PRESERVED AT WRIGHT STATE UNIVERSITY ARCHIVES AND SPECIAL COL-
LECTIONS. 1976.21p.

Hixson, W.W. PLAT BOOK OF GREENE COUNTY OHIO. (Rockford IL: author, n.d.) (OHS)

Hodge, Robert & Lois. MARRIAGE & DEATH NOTICES FROM THE XENIA TORCHLIGHT 1844-
1870. (SLO)

JAMESTOWN AREA SESQUICENTENNIAL, 1816-1966. 72p. (OGS,OHS,LDS)

Johnson, P.R. CLASSIFIED BUSINESS AND PROFESSIONAL DIRECTORY OF PROMINENT TOWNS
AND CITIES OF OHIO AND EASTERN INDIANA. (Columbus OH: Berlin Printing, 1899) 303p
(LDS)

Kilner, Arthur. CEMETERY TOMBSTONE INSCRIPTIONS AND PHOTOGRAPHS OF SELECTED
GREENE COUNTY OHIO PIONEERS FROM THE 1700'S AND 1800'S. (Xenia OH: author, 1983)
102p. (OGS,LDS,SLO)

Kilner, Arthur. HISTORY OF 1 & 2 ROOM SCHOOLHOUSES-GREENE COUNTY OHIO. (Xenia OH:
author, 1983) 93p. (OGS)

Leggett, Nancy G. & D.E.Smith. A GUIDE TO LOCAL GOVERNMENT RECORDS AND NEWSPAPERS
PRESERVED AT THE DEPARTMENT OF ARCHIVES AND SPECIAL COLLECTIONS WRIGHT
STATE UNIVERSITY. (Dayton OH: Wright State U., 1987)

McDonald, Cleveland. THE HISTORY OF CEDARVILLE COLLEGE. (Cedarville OH: Cedarville College, 1966) 170p (OHS)

MIDDLERUN CEMETERY RECORDS, SUGAR CREEK TOWNSHIP, GREENE COUNTY, OHIO. 1956?
5p (LDS)

Miller, Mrs. Wallace. BIBLE RECORDS, FAIRBORN, OHIO, 1733-1967. (SLO)

Mills, William. CENTENNIAL HISTORICAL ADDRESS. (Xenia OH: Gazette Steam Print, 1876) 56p
(LC,SLO,OHS)

OUT OF THE WILDERNESS: AN ACCOUNT OF EVENTS IN GREENE COUNTY, OHIO. 1953.306p
(SLO)

Overton, Julie M. THE TOWNS AND TOWNSHIPS OF GREENE COUNTY OHIO. (Xenia OH: Greene
Co.Hist.Soc., 1975) 11p (LDS)

Owens, Ira S. GREENE COUNTY IN THE WAR. BEING A HISTORY OF THE 74th REGIMENT... (Xenia
OH: Torchlight job rooms, 1872) (OHS)

Owens, Ira S. GREENE COUNTY SOLDIERS IN THE LATE WAR. (Dayton OH: Christian Pub House,
1894) 294p (LC)

Patterson, Austin M. GREENE COUNTY, 1803-1908. (Xenia OH: Aldine Pub.Co., 1908) 215p (DAR)

PORTRAIT AND BIOGRAPHICAL ALBUM OF GREENE AND CLARK COUNTIES OHIO. (Chicago:
Chapman Bros, 1890) 924p (LC,SLO,LDS,OHS,DAR) (RPI)

Riddell, Levi. RIDELLS ATLAS OF GREENE COUNTY, OHIO. (Xenia OH: author, 1896) (Reprint, Xenia
OH: Greene Co Chapter OGS, 1981) 49p (OGS,SLO,OHS) (RPI)

Robinson, George F. AFTER THIRTY YEARS. A COMPLETE ROSTER BY TOWNSHIPS OF GREENE
COUNTY OHIO SOLDIERS IN THE LATE CIVIL WAR. (Xenia OH: W.B.Chew, printer, 1895)
(LDS,LC,OHS,SLO)

Robinson, George F. HISTORY OF GREENE COUNTY OHIO. (Chicago: S.J.Clarke Pub., 1902) (Reprint,
Xenia OH: Greene Co.Hist.Soc., 1973) 927p (LC,SLO,OHS,OGS,DAR) (RPI)

Roe, Carleene O. CHURCH RECORDS OF BEAVER UNITED CHURCH OF CHRIST, BEAVᴱRCREEK TWP., GREENE COUNTY, OHIO: IN 1824 THE GERMAN EVANGELICAL LUTHᴸRAN AND GERMAN UNION CHURCH. 1984. 44p (LDS)

Sale, Walter. THE BONNER GRAVEYARD, GREENE COUNTY OHIO: HISTORY... (Fairborn OH: Cincinnati Branch Library, 1973) (LDS)

Santmyer, Helen H. OHIO TOWN. (Columbus: Ohio State Univ.Press, 1962) 309p (OHS)

Smith, Clifford N. FEDERAL LAND SERIES: A CALENDAR OF ARCHIVAL MATERIAL ON THE LAND PATENTS ISSUED BY THE U.S.GOVERNMENT, VOL.4, PT 1 : GRANTS IN THE VIRGINIA MILITARY DISTRICT OF OHIO. (Chicago: American Library Assn., 1982) 395p

Smith, Clifford N. FEDERAL LAND SERIES: A CALENDAR OF ARCHIVAL MATERIAL ON THE LAND PATENTS ISSUED BY THE U.S.GOVERNMENT, VOL.4, PT 2 : GRANTS IN THE VIRGINIA MILITARY DISTRICT OF OHIO. (Chicago: American Library Assn., 1986) 306p

Smith, William E. HISTORY OF SOUTHWESTERN OHIO, THE MIAMI VALLEYS. 1964. 3v. (SLO)

TWIN RUN CEMETERY RECORDS, SUGAR CREEK TOWNSHIP, GREENE COUNTY OHIO. 1956? 6p (LDS)

Vicory, Jacqueline. MILO UNION LIST OF GENEALOGIES IN THE LIBRARIES OF CHAMPAIGN, CLARK, DARKE, GREENE, MIAMI, MONTGOMERY, AND PREBLE COUNTIES, OHIO. (Dayton OH: Miami Valley Libr.Org., 1977) 122p (LDS)

Vogt, Paul L. A RURAL LIFE SURVEY OF GREENE AND CLERMONT COUNTIES OHIO. (Oxford OH: author, 1914) 82p (LC,OHS)

WIGGINS & McKILLOP'S DIRECTORY OF GREENE COUNTY. (Columbus: Wiggins & McKillop, 1878) (OHS)

WILLIAMS' XENIA DIRECTORY, TO WHICH IS ADDED A BUSINESS DIRECTORY OF GREENE COUNTY. (Xenia OH: Williams & Co., 1870-1871) (OHS)

WORLD'S WAR NEWS OF OHIO, GREENE COUNTY. 1918-1919. (OHS)

Wright State University Library. AN INDEX TO NATURALIZATION RECORDS FROM GREENE COUNTY OHIO, 1831-1958 AND CLARK COUNTY OHIO 1820-1906. (Dayton: author, 1987?)

XENIA COLLEGE, ANNUAL CATALOGUE. (Xenia OH: the college, 1863-64,1873-74,1874-75,1884-85) (OHS)

Yellow Springs Community Council. WHY THEY CAME; THE STORY OF YELLOW SPRINGS OHIO COMMEMORATING ITS CENTENNIAL. (Yellow Springs OH: centennial committee, c1956) 64p (OHS)

# GUERNSEY COUNTY

| | |
|---|---|
| CREATED: | 1810 FROM BELMONT & MUSKINGUM COUNTIES |
| COUNTY SEAT: | CAMBRIDGE 43725 |
| COURT HOUSE: | WHEELING AVE & 8TH ST., CAMBRIDGE 43725 |
| LIBRARY: | 800 STEUBENVILLE AVE., CAMBRIDGE 43725 |
| HISTORICAL SOCIETY: | P.O.BOX 741, CAMBRIDGE 43725 |
| GENEALOGICAL SOCIETY: | GUERNSEY CO. CHAPTER OGS, |
| | P.O.BOX 472, CAMBRIDGE 43725 |
| | publication: ROOTS & BRANCHES |
| HEALTH DEPARTMENT: | 326 HIGHLAND AVE., CAMBRIDGE 43725 |
| | (separate office for Cambridge City) |
| ARCHIVAL DISTRICT: | OHIO UNIVERSITY, ATHENS |
| | (see published Guide to records) |
| LAND SURVEYS: | CONGRESS LANDS, SEVEN RANGES |
| | CONGRESS LANDS, OHIO RIVER SURVEY (SOUTH) |
| | UNITED STATES MILITARY DISTRICT |
| BOUNDED BY: | EAST:  BELMONT CO. |
| | NORTH: HARRISON & TUSCARAWAS CO. |
| | WEST:  COSHOCTON & MUSKINGUM CO. |
| | SOUTH: NOBLE CO. |

TOWNSHIPS:                    Adams, Cambridge, Center, Jackson, Jefferson, Knox, Liberty,
                              Londonderry, Madison, Millwood, Monroe, Oxford, Richland,
                              Spencer, Valley, Washington, Westland, Wheeling, Wills.

## COURT RECORDS: (LDS MICROFILM)
Auditor:
   Fee book & peddlers licenses, 1833-1861.
   Tax duplicates, 1816-1832.
Childrens' Home:
   Director's minutes, 1884-1929.
Clerk of Courts:
   Common Pleas journal, vA-P, 1810-1853.
   Common Pleas appearance docket, 1810-1822,1829-1834.
   Common Pleas record, 1810-1840,1842,1844-1852.
   Chancery record, vA-E, 1836-1853.
   Index to chancery records, 1837-1862.
   Common Pleas record, vA-G, 1810-1836.
   General law index, 1838-1861.
   Supreme Court appearance docket, 1811-1852.
   Supreme Court record, vB-C, 1838-1851.
   District Court record, 1852-1856.
Commissioners:
   Journal, 1810-1901.
   Index to journals, 1810-1899.
County Home:
   Inmates, 1880-1945.
   Directors minutes, 1868-1885,1910-1912.
Probate Court:
   Marriage records, 1810-1916.
   Index to marriage records, 1810-1930.
   Marriage certificates, 1810-1863.
   Death record, v1-3, 1867-1908.
   Birth record, v1-3, 1867-1909.
   Record of wills, 1812-1891.
   Index to wills, 1812-1972.
   Probate journal, v1-6, 1852-1887.
   Inventories & bills of sale, 1826-1887.
   Index to files, 1812-1942.
   Administration dockets, 1829-1886.
   Naturalization record, 1864-1906.
Recorder:
   Deed records, 1810-1881.
   Index to deeds, 1802-1968.
   Military discharges, v1, 1861-1865.
Sheriff:
   Jail register, 1893-1902.
Miscellaneous:
   Old Washington First Presbyterian Church, records, 1840-1884.
   Misc. cemetery records, by DAR.
   Misc. cemetery records, by LDS.

## OHIO HISTORICAL SOCIETY: (MICROFILM)
Auditor:
   Fee book & peddlers licenses, 1833-1861.

Childrens' Home:
  Director's minutes, 1884-1929.
Clerk of Courts:
  Common Pleas journal, vA-P, 1810-1853.
  Common Pleas appearance docket, 1810-1822,1829-1834.
  Common Pleas record, 1810-1840,1842,1844-1852.
  Chancery record, vA-E, 1836-1853.
  Index to chancery records, 1837-1862.
  Common Pleas record, vA-G, 1810-1836.
  General law index, 1838-1861.
  Supreme Court appearance docket, 1811-1852.
  Supreme Court record, vB-C, 1838-1851.
  District Court record, 1852-1856.
Commissioners:
  Journal, 1810-1901.
  Index to journals, 1810-1899.
County Home:
  Inmates, 1880-1945.
  Directors minutes, 1868-1885,1910-1912.
Recorder:
  Military discharges, v1, 1861-1865.
Sheriff:
  Jail register, 1893-1902.
Miscellaneous:
  Cemetery records, by DAR.
  Cemeteries of Guernsey,Knox,Morrow & Richland Cos., by DAR.

**CENSUS RECORDS (OHS,SLO,OGS,LDS)**
1820-1880, 1900-1910; 1890 VETERANS; 1880,1900 SOUNDEX; 1910 MIRACODE

**AGRICULTURAL CENSUS SCHEDULES (OHS,SLO-mic)**
1850,1860,1870

**PRODUCTS OF INDUSTRY CENSUS SCHEDULE (OHS,SLO-mic)**
1850,1870,1880

**MORTALITY CENSUS SCHEDULES (OHS,SLO-mic)**
1860

**DEFECTIVE & DEPENDENT CENSUS SCHEDULES (OHS,SLO-mic)**
1880

**NEWSPAPERS: [GUIDE TO OHIO NEWSPAPERS, 1793-1973]**
Cambridge, Cumberland, Old Washington, Quaker City, Washington.

**TAX RECORDS (OHS & LDS)**
1810,1812,1814,1816-1832,1834.

**MANUSCRIPTS:**
Cambridge Township Trustee records & poll books, 1815-1845. (WRHS)
Ryan Gowdy & Co., daybook, 1836-1837. (WRHS)

**GENEALOGICAL PERIODICAL ARTICLES**
Bell, Carol Willsey. OHIO GENEALOGICAL PERIODICAL INDEX: A COUNTY GUIDE (Youngstown, OH: author, 6th ed., 1987)

**PUBLISHED SOURCES:**

Beach, Doris P. GUERNSEY COUNTY OHIO LIBERTY TOWNSHIP CEMETERIES. (Columbus OH: author, 1986) 83p (OGS,OHS)

Bell, Carol W. OHIO LANDS: STEUBENVILLE LAND OFFICE RECORDS, 1800-1820. (Youngstown OH: author, 1983) 181p (OGS)

Berry, Ellen T. & David. EARLY OHIO SETTLERS: PURCHASERS OF LAND IN SOUTHEASTERN OHIO, 1800-1840. (Baltimore: Genealogical Pub.Co., 1984) 129p (OHS,SLO,OGS,DAR)

CEMETERIES, MILLWOOD TOWNSHIP. (SLO)

CEMETERY INSCRIPTIONS KNOX, MORROW, RICHLAND AND GUERNSEY COUNTIES OHIO. (SLO)

CENTENNIAL HISTORY [Guernsey Co OH]. (Cambridge OH: Jeffersonian Power Press, 1876) (LC)

CITY/COUNTY DIRECTORIES: check holdings of OHS & local public library.

Conner, E.M. FOUNDERS' CEMETERY & OLD CITY CEMETERY OF CAMBRIDGE OHIO, 1806 TO 1851.

Conner, E.M. PIONEER CEMETERIES OF GUERNSEY COUNTY OHIO. 1963. 225,190p (SLO,LDS,DAR)

Conner, E.M. PIONEER FAMILIES OF GUERNSEY COUNTY OHIO. 1963. (LDS)

Conner, E.M. PIONEER LAND GRANTS OF GUERNSEY COUNTY OHIO. (Cambridge OH: author, 1964) 16p. (SLO,LDS,DAR)

Conner, E.M. PIONEER MARRIAGES OF GUERNSEY COUNTY OHIO, 1810-1830. (Cambridge OH: author, 1964) 16p (SLO,LDS,DAR)

Conner, E.M. PIONEER SOLDIERS OF GUERNSEY COUNTY OHIO. 1964. 15p.(LDS,DAR)

Conner, E.M. PIONEER WILLS INDEX OF GUERNSEY COUNTY OHIO 1810 TO 1900. (LDS)

Conner, E.M. SALT FORK BAPTIST CHURCH, OXFORD TWP. GUERNSEY COUNTY. 1960.

Davis, Carson B. ATLAS OF GUERNSEY COUNTY, OHIO. 1914. (OGS)

Dudley, Kenneth O. GUERNSEY COUNTY OHIO, MT.ZION CEMETERY, NORTH OF CLAYSVILLE, WESTLAND TWP; BETHEL CEMETERY, VALLEY TWP. 1963. 6,12p (LDS)

ENON CEMETERY DIRECTORY, BYESVILLE, OHIO. (SLO)

Fedorchak, Catharine F. SOME REVOLUTIONARY SOLDIERS OF GUERNSEY COUNTY OHIO. (Gary IN: author, 1959) 1v. (LDS,DAR)

Fedorchak, Mrs. John. GUERNSEY CO., OHIO, RECORDS. (Crown Point IN: author, 1970) 162p (DAR,LDS)

FIRST PRESBYTERIAN CHURCH, CAMBRIDGE, OHIO. (SLO)

FOR THE BOYS AND GIRLS OF CAMBRIDGE, OHIO. (SLO)

Guernsey Co Chapter OGS. DO YOU REMEMBER MAIN STREET, CAMBRIDGE OHIO? (Cambridge: the society, nd) (OGS)

Guernsey Co Chapter OGS. 1863 CIVIL WAR DRAFT LIST, GUERNSEY COUNTY OHIO. (Cambridge: the society, 1985) 22p (OGS)

Guernsey Co.Chapter OGS. MARRIAGES OF GUERNSEY COUNTY OHIO, VOL.A, 1810-1832. (Cambridge OH: the society, 1987) 27p (OGS)

Guernsey Co Chapter OGS. INDIANS OF GUERNSEY COUNTY. (Cambridge: the society, nd)

Guernsey Co Chapter OGS. 175th ANNIVERSARY OF GUERNSEY COUNTY. (Cambridge: the society, nd) (OGS)

Guernsey Co Chapter OGS. CAMBRIDGE M.E.CHURCH, 1878 MEMBERSHIP (Cambridge: the society, nd) (OGS)

Guernsey Co Chapter OGS. CEMETERIES OF GUERNSEY COUNTY OHIO. VOL.1: KNOX TWP.(Cambridge: the society, 1983) 33p (OGS)

Guernsey Co Chapter OGS. CEMETERIES OF GUERNSEY COUNTY OHIO, MILLWOOD TOWNSHIP, VOL.II. (Cambridge OH: the society, 1986) 150p (OGS)

Guernsey Co Chapter OGS. CEMETERIES OF GUERNSEY CO OHIO, LIBERTY TWP., VOL.3 (Cambridge OH: the society, 1986) 58p (OGS)

Guernsey Co Chapter OGS. CORONERS' INQUEST OF GUERNSEY COUNTY OHIO. (Cambridge OH: the society, 1987) 30p (OGS)

Guernsey Co Chapter OGS. FIVE GENERATIONS IN GUERNSEY COUNTY. (Cambridge:the society, 1986) 400p (OGS)

Guernsey Co Chapter OGS. FIVE GENERATIONS IN GUERNSEY COUNTY OHIO, VOLUME II. (Cambridge OH: the society, 1987) 208p (OGS)

Guernsey Co Chapter OGS. HISTORICAL VIEWS & MAPS OF GUERNSEY COUNTY [OHIO]. (Cambridge: the society, 1982) 98p (OGS,LDS,SLO)

Guernsey Co Chapter OGS. 1880 CENSUS OF GUERNSEY COUNTY OHIO. (Cambridge OH: the society, 1986) 84p (OGS)

Guernsey Co Chapter OGS. YESTERDAY AND TODAY IN GUERNSEY COUNTY OHIO. (Cambridge OH: the society, 1979) 347p (OGS,SLO)

GUERNSEY MILESTONES: SOUVENIR PROGRAM OF THE SESQUICENTENNIAL CELEBRATION OF THE FIRST PERMANENT SETTLEMENT IN GUERNSEY COUNTY, OHIO. (SLO)

Hastings, William B. COPY OF A RECORD BOOK OF THE PLEASANT HILL METHODIST CHURCH, WASHINGTON TWP., GUERNSEY CO OHIO. (SLO,LDS)

ILLUSTRATED ATLAS OF GUERNSEY COUNTY OHIO. (Atlas Pub Co.,1902) (SLO)(RPI)

Klaiber, Teresa L.M. GUERNSEY COUNTY OHIO WILLS & ESTATES 1850-1900 INDEX. (Cambridge OH: Guernsey Co.Chapter OGS, 1987) 110p (OGS)

Lake, D.J. ATLAS OF GUERNSEY COUNTY OHIO. (Philadelphia: C.O.Titus, 1870) (LC,OGS,SLO) (RPI)

Lewis, Thomas W. SOUTHEASTERN OHIO AND THE MUSKINGUM VALLEY, 1788-1928: COVERING ATHENS, BELMONT, COSHOCTON, GUERNSEY, LICKING, MEIGS, MONROE, MORGAN, MUSKINGUM, NOBLE, PERRY AND WASHINGTON COUNTIES. (Chicago: S.J.Clarke Co.,1928) 3v. (SLO,DAR,OHS)

Longsworth, Ferne M. RECORDS OF THE PLEASANT HILL METHODIST CHURCH IN WASHINGTON TOWNSHIP, GUERNSEY COUNTY, OHIO. (Lima OH: author, 1953) 58p (DAR,LDS)

McMahan, Fulton J. THE FIRST PRESBYTERIAN CHURCH, CAMBRIDGE OHIO. (Cambridge OH: Callihan & Stottlemire Co., 1927) 48p (DAR)

MARRIAGES AND DEATHS AS FOUND IN THE CAMBRIDGE JEFFERSONIAN, 1844-1873. 1982. 8,3p (LDS)

Miskimens, Dorothea. INDEX FOR PIONEER CEMETERIES OF GUERNSEY COUNTY OHIO. (Sylmar CA: author, 1982) 19p. (OGS,LDS)

Miskimens, Dorothea. ISAAC MISKIMENS ACCOUNT BOOK, 1833-1847. (Sylmar CA: author, 1983) 237p (LDS)

MT. ZION CEMETERY, NORTH OF CLAYSVILLE, WESTLAND TWP., GUERNSEY CO OHIO. (SLO)

OFFICIAL PROGRAM OF HISTORICAL PAGEANT "CAMBRIDGE OLD AND NEW" DURING OLD HOME WEEK AT THE CITY PARK, CAMBRIDGE, OHIO, FRIDAY, OCTOBER 7, 1921. (SLO)

Ohio University. GUIDE TO LOCAL GOVERNMENT RECORDS AT OHIO UNIVERSITY. (Athens: OU Library, 1986) 61p.

PORTRAIT AND BIOGRAPHICAL RECORD OF GUERNSEY COUNTY OHIO. (Chicago: C.O.Owen & Co., 1895) (Reprint, Evansville IN: Unigraphic, 1974) 545p (SLO,LDS)

Sarchet, Cyrus P.B. HISTORY OF GUERNSEY COUNTY OHIO. (Indianapolis IN: B.F.Bowen & Co., 1911) 2v (LC,SLO,LDS,DAR)

Smith, Clifford N. FEDERAL LAND SERIES: A CALENDAR OF ARCHIVAL MATERIAL ON THE LAND PATENTS ISSUED BY THE U.S.GOVERNMENT, VOL.2: FEDERAL BOUNTY LAND WARRANTS OF THE AMERICAN REVOLUTION. (Chicago: American Library Assn., 1972) 416p

Snider, Wayne L. GUERNSEY COUNTY'S BLACK PIONEERS, PATRIOTS AND PERSONS. (Columbus: Ohio Hist.Soc., 1979).144p (OGS,OHS,DAR,LDS,SLO)

Williams, T.F. HOUSEHOLD GUIDE AND INSTRUCTOR. 1882. 197p. (SLO)

Wolfe, William G. STORIES OF GUERNSEY COUNTY OHIO: HISTORY OF AN AVERAGE OHIO COUNTY. (Cambridge OH: author, 1943) 1093p (LC,SLO,LDS,DAR)

# HAMILTON COUNTY

| | |
|---|---|
| CREATED: | 1790, ORIGINAL COUNTY |
| COUNTY SEAT: | CINCINNATI 45202 |
| COURT HOUSE: | 1000 MAIN ST., CINCINNATI 45202 |

| | |
|---|---|
| LIBRARY: | PUBLIC LIBRARY OF CINCINNATI |
| | 800 VINE ST., CINCINNATI 45202 |
| HISTORICAL SOCIETY: | HAMILTON COUNTY CO. HISTORICAL SOCIETY, |
| | EDEN PARK, CINCINNATI 45202 |
| GENEALOGICAL SOCIETY: | HAMILTON CO. CHAPTER OGS |
| | PO BOX 15815, CINCINNATI 45215 |
| | publication: THE TRACER |
| HEALTH DEPARTMENT: | COURT HOUSE, 138 E.COURT ST., CINCINNATI 45202 |
| | (separate offices for Cincinnati City, Norwood, Cheviot, Read- |
| | ing, St.Bernard, North College Hill, Deer Park, Lincoln Hts., |
| | Wyoming, Mt.Healthy, Blue Ash, Madeira, Silverton, Loveland, |
| | Sharonville, Forest Park, Indian Hill, Montgomery, Springdale, |
| | Harrison & Milford) |
| ARCHIVAL DISTRICT: | UNIVERSITY OF CINCINNATI, CINCINNATI |
| LAND SURVEYS: | CONGRESS LANDS, MIAMI RIVER SURVEY |
| | CONGRESS LANDS, BETWEEN THE MIAMI RIVER SURVEY |
| | VIRGINIA MILITARY DISTRICT |
| | SYMMES PURCHASE |
| BOUNDED BY: | EAST:     CLERMONT CO. |
| | NORTH:   BUTLER & WARREN CO. |
| | WEST:    DEARBORN CO., INDIANA |
| | SOUTH:   BOONE, CAMPBELL & KENTON CO., KENTUCKY |
| TOWNSHIPS: | Anderson, Colerain, Columbia, Crosby, Delhi, Green, Harrison, |
| | Miami, Mill Creek, Springfield, Sycamore, Symmes, Whitewater. |

| | |
|---|---|
| **SPECIAL NOTE:** | COURTHOUSE FIRES IN 1814, 1849 & 1884 DESTROYED MANY |
| | RECORDS. |

**COURT RECORDS: (LDS MICROFILM)**
Auditor:
    Tax duplicates, 1816-1838.
Clerk of Courts:
    Aliens index, c1880-1890.
    Declaration of intention, restored, 1845-1895.
    Declarations of intention, 1848-c1890.
    Naturalization index, n.d.
    Naturalizations, restored, c1830-1880.
    Circuit court records, 1844-1847.
Probate Court:
    Death records, 1881-1908.
    Birth records & index, 1863-1908.
    Marriage records, 1852-1928; restored records, 1808-1873.
    Marriage licenses, 1822-1832.
    Probate court minutes, 1790-1852.
    Probate journals, 1879,1884-1891; restored 1858,1860,1864-1891.
    Guardianship dockets, 1852-1901.
    Guardianship applications, v11-36, 1884-1900.
    Administration dockets, 1852-1887.
    Will records, 1792-1901.
    Declarations of intent, naturalizations, 1850-1902.
    Naturalizations & index, 1850-1902.
    Societies & church records of incorporation, 1847-1919.
Recorder:
    Deed records, & index, 1787-1877
    Butler Co. deeds transcribed from Hamilton Co., 1803-1811.

Church records:
    Cincinnati, First United Presby.Church, minutes, 1841-1881.
    Cincinnati, First Presby.Church, misc.records, 1795-1845.
    Cincinnati, Third Presby.Church, baptisms, 1836-1860.
    Cincinnati Monthly Meeting of Friends, misc.records, 1815-1896.
    Cincinnati Monthly Meeting of Friends, records, 1762-1961.
    Cincinnati, United Jewish Cem.Assn., cemetery records, 1850-1959.
    Cincinnati Branch, LDS Church, records, 1856-1861.
    Cincinnati, LDS Church, record of members, 1856-1861.
    Cincinnati, Pleasant Ridge Presby.Church, session book, 1812-1847.
Miscellaneous:
    Cincinnati City Directories, 1819-1910, scattered.
    Centinel of the North-Western Territory (newspaper) 1793-1796.
    Cincinnati Enquirer, 1818-1859.
    Der Wahrheits-Freund: ein Blatt fur katholisches Leben, 1847-1848.
    Amanda Cemetery records, near Middletown.
    Pioneer Assn. of Whitewater, records, 1866-1869.
    Hebrew Union College Library, American Jewish archives, cards.
    Chestnut St. Cemetery inscriptions.
    Congregation Bene Israel, mortuary records, 1895-1942.
    United Jewish cemetery Assn., cemetery records, 1850-1959.

## OHIO HISTORICAL SOCIETY: (MICROFILM)
Clerk of Courts:
    Aliens index, c1880-1890.
    Declaration of intention, restored, 1845-1895.
    Declarations of intention, 1848-c1890.
    Naturalization index, n.d.
    Naturalizations, restored, c1830-1880.
Probate Court:
    Declarations of intent, naturalizations, 1850-1902.
    Naturalizations & index, 1850-1902.
Miscellaneous:
    Marriages, 1817-1846, by DAR.
    Spring Grove Cemetery records, by DAR.
    Madisonville M-E Church marriage & family records, 1861-1937, by DAR.

## MANUSCRIPTS:
Cincinnati, Western Bapt.Educ.Soc., records, 1834-42; 1848-55 (WRHS)
John Stevens papers, incl. Cinc.Baptist Missionary Soc. 1824- (WRHS)
Pioneer Assn. of Whitewater, residents pre 1825. (WRHS)

## CENSUS RECORDS (OHS,SLO,OGS,LDS)
1820-1880, 1900-1910; 1890 VETERANS; 1880,1900 SOUNDEX; 1910 MIRACODE

## AGRICULTURAL CENSUS SCHEDULES (OHS,SLO-mic)
1850,1860,1870

## PRODUCTS OF INDUSTRY CENSUS SCHEDULE (OHS,SLO-mic)
1850,1870,1880

## MORTALITY CENSUS SCHEDULES (OHS,SLO-mic)
1850,1860

**DEFECTIVE & DEPENDENT CENSUS SCHEDULES (OHS,SLO-mic)**
1880

**NEWSPAPERS: [GUIDE TO OHIO NEWSPAPERS, 1793-1973]**
Cheviot, Cincinnati, Cleves, Cumminsville, Elmwood Place, Evanston, Harrison, Indian Hill, Lockland, Loveland, Madisonville, Milford, Montgomery, Mt.Healthy, Norwood, Plainville, St.Bernard, Sharonville, Wyoming.

**TAX RECORDS (OHS & LDS)**
1801,1806-1814,1816-1838.

**GENEALOGICAL PERIODICAL ARTICLES**
Bell, Carol Willsey. OHIO GENEALOGICAL PERIODICAL INDEX: A COUNTY GUIDE (Youngstown, OH: author, 6th ed., 1987)

**PUBLISHED SOURCES:**
125TH ANNIVERSARY, 1851-1976, STS.PETER & PAUL CHURCH, READING, OHIO. 1976. 56p (LDS)
135TH ANNIVERSARY FOUNDING OF THE TOWN OF COLUMBIA BY MAJOR BENJAMIN STITES. 1923. 12p (SLO)
150TH ANNIVERSARY OF THE NEWTOWN METHODIST CHURCH, 1813-1963, NEWTOWN, OHIO. (SLO)
Berry, Ellen T. & David A. EARLY OHIO SETTLERS: PURCHASERS OF LAND IN SOUTHWESTERN OHIO, 1800-1840. (Baltimore: Genealogical Pub.Co., 1986) 372p (OGS,SLO,OHS)
Black, Robert L. THE CINCINNATI ORPHAN ASYLUM (Cincinnati, 1952) 236p
Brien, Lindsay M. ABSTRACTS FROM HISTORY OF HAMILTON CO. OHIO BY FORD AND FORD, 1881: APPENDED EARLY SETTLERS AND 1808 TAX LIST. nd (LDS)
Burress, Marjorie. CINCINNATI AND HAMILTON COUNTY OHIO POST OFFICE LETTER LISTS, 1794-1814: FROM NEWSPAPER FILES OF THE CINCINNATI HISTORICAL SOCIETY AND THE PUBLIC LIBRARY OF CINCINNATI AND HAMILTON COUNTY. (North Bend OH: author, 1982) 95p (LDS)
Burress, Marjorie. EARLY ROSTERS OF CINCINNATI & HAMILTON COUNTY. (North Bend OH: author, 1984) 207p (OGS,LDS)
Burress, Marjorie. IT HAPPENED ROUND NORTH BEND: A HISTORY OF MIAMI TOWNSHIP. 1970. (Reprint, North Bend OH: author, 1987) 128p (DAR)
Burress, Marjorie. A COLLECTION OF PIONEER MARRIAGE RECORDS, HAMILTON COUNTY OHIO, 1789-1817, VOL.I (Cincinnati: author, 1978) 84p (SLO,LDS)
Burress, Marjorie. WHITEWATER OHIO: VILLAGE OF SHAKERS 1824-1916. (Cincinnati: author, 1979) 97p (SLO,LDS)
Chambrun, Clara. CINCINNATI: STORY OF THE QUEEN CITY. 1939. 342p (SLO)
Cincinnati Land Office. LAND SALES, 1801-1810. (SLO)
CINCINNATI: A GUIDE TO THE QUEEN CITY AND ITS NEIGHBORS, 1943. 570p (SLO)
CINCINNATI, PAST AND PRESENT. (Cincinnati: M.Joblin & Co., 1872) 447p (DAR)
Cincinnati Pioneer Assn. THE CINCINNATI PIONEER. (Cincinnati: J.D.Caldwell, 1885) 1v (LDS)
CINCINNATI SOCIETY BLUE BOOK AND FAMILY DIRECTORY. (Cincinnati: Thomson, 1879) 838p (LDS)
Cist, Charles. CINCINNATI MISCELLANY. 1846. 346p (SLO)
CITY/COUNTY DIRECTORIES: check holdings of OHS & local public library.
Cist, Charles. CINCINNATI IN 1841. (Cincinnati: Morgan & Co., 1841) 300p (DAR,LDS)
Cist, Charles. SKETCHES AND STATISTICS OF CINCINNATI IN 1851. (Cincinnati: W.H.Moore & Co., 1851) 363p (DAR,LDS)
Cist, Charles. SKETCHES AND STATISTICS OF CINCINNATI IN 1859. (Cincinnati: Wm.H.Moore & Co., 1859) 363p (DAR,LDS)
CITY/COUNTY DIRECTORIES: check holdings of OHS & local public library.
Clarke, Robert. EARLY DISTRIBUTION AND SALE OF LOTS IN LOSANTIVILLE, 1789-1790. 1870. 11p. (Cinci PL,SLO)

Cline, R.A. PROFILES OF CINCINNATI. 1967. 96p (SLO)

Cone, Stephen D. BIOGRAPHICAL AND HISTORICAL SKETCHES: A NARRATIVE OF HAMILTON AND ITS RESIDENTS FROM 1792... (Hamilton OH: Republican Pub.Co., 1896) 2v (SLO,LDS)

Cone, Stephen D. A CONCISE HISTORY OF HAMILTON, OHIO. (Middletown OH: Press of Geo.Mitchell, 1901) 1v (LDS)

Coombs, Elizabeth L. REFORM CRUSADE IN CINCINNATI, OHIO. 1894. (SLO)

Craig, Robert D. COLUMBIA TOWNSHIP, HAMILTON COUNTY, OHIO, TAX LIST, 1796. (Cincinnati: author, 1963) 7p (LDS)

Craig, Robert D. HAMILTON COUNTY OHIO RECORDS: PIONEERS, MARRIAGES, DEATHS n.d., 27p (SLO,LDS)

Craig, Robert D. HAMILTON COUNTY OHIO CEMETERY INSCRIPTIONS VOL.2 1970? (SLO,LDS)

Craig, Robert D. MARRIAGES, 1844-1847, AND DEATHS, 1844-1845 AND 1847-1848 FOR THE CITY OF CINCINNATI, HAMILTON COUNTY OHIO, THAT WERE EXTRACTED OUT OF NEWSPAPERS. nd (LDS)

Craig, Robert D. REVOLUTIONARY SOLDIERS IN HAMILTON COUNTY OHIO. (Salt Lake City: author, c1965) 40p (LDS,SLO)

Cummins, Virginia R. HAMILTON COUNTY OHIO: COURT AND OTHER RECORDS. (Cincinnati: General Printing Co., 1966-69) 3v (SLO,DAR,LDS)

Dabney, Wendell P. CINCINNATI'S COLORED CITIZENS: HISTORICAL, SOCIOLOGICAL AND BIOGRAPHICAL. (Cincinnati: Dabney Pub.Co., 1926) 440p (LDS)

Daughters of the American Revolution. BIBLE AND FAMILY RECORDS, CEMETERY INSCRIPTIONS, FAMILY HISTORY, CINCINNATI, OHIO. 1972. 139p (DAR,LDS)

Daughters of the American Revolution. EARLIEST RECORDS OF SPRING GROVE CEMETERY, CINCINNATI, OHIO, 1826-51. 1963. 149p (DAR)

Daughters of the American Revolution. EARLIEST MARRIAGE AND FAMILY RECORDS OF HAMILTON COUNTY OHIO. 1941. 186p (DAR,LDS)

Daughters of the American Revolution. HAMILTON COUNTY MARRIAGES, EARLY TO 1846. 1936. 5v (DAR,LDS)

Daughters of the American Revolution. HAMILTON COUNTY OHIO MARRIAGE RECORDS, 1820-1825. 1967. 147p (DAR)

Daughters of the American Revolution. LAUREL CEMETERY, HAMILTON COUNTY OHIO, BURIALS, MARCH 19, 1863–1909. 1969. 169p (DAR,LDS)

Daughters of the American Revolution. LAUREL CEMETERY, HAMILTON COUNTY, OHIO, DEEDS. 1970. 91p (DAR,LDS)

Daughters of the American Revolution. LIST OF CEMETERIES AND THEIR LOCATION IN THE CITY OF CINCINNATI AND HAMILTON COUNTY OHIO. 1943. 21p (DAR)

Daughters of the American Revolution. MARRIAGE RECORDS OF MADISONVILLE METHODIST EPISCOPAL CHURCH, 1861-1937. 186p. (SLO,LDS)

Daughters of the American Revolution. MISCELLANEOUS BIBLE RECORDS. 1964-1972. 4v (DAR,LDS)

Daughters of the American Revolution. SESSION BOOK OF DUCK CREEK CHURCH OF THE PRESBYTERIAN, MIAMI, STATE OF OHIO 1814-1847. 1968. 120p (DAR)

Dickore, Marie. CENSUS FOR CINCINNATI, OHIO 1817 AND HAMILTON COUNTY OHIO VOTERS' LISTS 1798 AND 1799. (Cincinnati: author, 1960) 98p (SLO,DAR)

Dickore, Marie. HAMILTON COUNTY OHIO CEMETERY INSCRIPTIONS. (Cincinnati: R.Craig, 1963) 96p (SLO,DAR,LDS)

Dickore, Marie. HAMILTON COUNTY OHIO MARRIAGE RECORDS (1808-1820) AND WILLS (1790-1810). (Cincinnati: author, 1959) 68p (SLO,DAR,LDS)

Dickore, Marie. THE MOUND BUILDERS OF CINCINNATI. (Reprint, Columbus: Ohio Arch.& Hist.Soc., 1909) 27p (LDS)

Drake, B. & E.D.Mansfield. CINCINNATI IN 1826. (Cincinnati: Morgan, Lodge & Fisher, 1827) 100p (LDS)

Drake, Benjamin. TALES AND SKETCHES FROM THE QUEEN CITY. 1838. 180p (SLO)

Eling, Carl P. STORY OF READING ROAD: ONCE A FAMOUS STAGE AND MAIL ROUTE. (np: Mill Creek Valley History, 198?) 29p (LDS)

Feck, Luke. YESTERDAY'S CINCINNATI. (Miami FL: E.A.Seemann Pub., 1975) 142p.

Federal Writer's Project. THEY BUILT A CITY: 150 YEARS OF INDUSTRIAL CINCINNATI. (Cincinnati: Cin.Post, 1938) 402p (SLO,DAR)

Ford, Henry A. & Kate. HISTORY OF CINCINNATI OHIO: WITH ILLUSTRATIONS AND HISTORICAL SKETCHES. (Cleveland: H.A.Williams & Co.,1881) 534p (SLO,DAR,LDS)(RPI)

Ford, Henry A. & Kate. HISTORY OF HAMILTON COUNTY OHIO: WITH ILLUSTRATIONS AND BIOGRAPHICAL SKETCHES. (Cleveland: L.A.Williams, 1881) (Reprint, Evansville IN: Unigraphic, 1974) 208p (SLO,OHS,DAR,LDS)

Fox, John H. GRAVESTONE INSCRIPTIONS, OHIO. 197? 10p (LDS)

Goss, Charles F. CINCINNATI, THE QUEEN CITY, 1788-1912. (Chicago: S.J.Clarke Pub.Co., 1912) 4v (SLO,DAR,LDS)

Green, Karen M. PIONEER OHIO NEWSPAPERS, 1793-1810: GENEALOGICAL & HISTORICAL ABSTRACTS. (Galveston TX: Frontier Press, 1986) 383p (OGS)

Green, Karen M. PIONEER OHIO NEWSPAPERS, 1802-1818: GENEALOGICAL & HISTORICAL ABSTRACTS. (Galveston TX: Frontier Press, 1988) 362p (OGS)

Greve, Charles T. CENTENNIAL HISTORY OF CINCINNATI AND REPRESENTATIVE CITIZENS. (Chicago: Biographical Pub.Co., 1904) 2v. (SLO,DAR,LDS)

Hamilton Co Chapter OGS. ABSTRACT OF BOOK 1 & BOOK A PROBATE RECORD 1791-1826 HAMILTON COUNTY OHIO. (Cincinnati: the society, 1977) 290p (OGS,SLO)

Hamilton Co Chapter OGS. ABSTRACT OF BOOK 3 PROBATE RECORD 1829-1834 (Cincinnati: the society, 1981) (OHS,OGS,SLO,DAR,LDS)

Hamilton Co Chapter OGS. ABSTRACT OF BOOK 4, PROBATE RECORD 1834-1837, HAMILTON COUNTY OHIO. (Cincinnati: the society, 1985) 216p (OGS,LDS)

Hamilton Co Chapter OGS. HAMILTON COUNTY CEMETERY RECORDS, VOL.I. (Cincinnati: the society, 1982?)

Hamilton Co Chapter OGS. HAMILTON COUNTY OHIO BURIAL RECORDS, VOLUME ONE, WESLEYAN CEMETERY, 1842-1971. (Cincinnati: the society, 1984) 254p (OGS,DAR,LDS,SLO)

Hamilton Co Chapter OGS. HAMILTON COUNTY OHIO NATURALIZATION AND MARRIAGE RECORDS IN THE UNIVERSITY OF CINCINNATI ARCHIVES, VOL.1, MARRIAGE RECORDS. (Cincinnati: the society, 1988) 16p (OGS)

Hamilton Co Chapter OGS. WILL INDEX OF HAMILTON COUNTY, OHIO, 1792-1850. (Cincinnati: the society, 1975) 75p (LDS)

Harrison, R.H. TITUS'S ATLAS OF HAMILTON COUNTY, 1869 (SLO)(RPI)

HARRISON OHIO CENTENNIAL CELEBRATION, 1850-1950. (Harrison OH: Centennial Committee, 1950) 60p (LDS)

Harlow, Alvin. SERENE CINCINNATIANS. (New York: 1950) 442p

Hickenlooper, A. MAP OF THE CITY OF CINCINNATI AS RE-DISTRICTED. 1872. (LDS)

Hinshaw, William Wade. ENCYCLOPEDIA OF AMERICAN QUAKER GENEALOGY, VOL.V, OHIO. (Baltimore MD: Genealogical Pub.Co., 1973) (SLO,OHS,LDS)

Historical Records Survey. INVENTORY OF THE COUNTY ARCHIVES OF OHIO: HAMILTON COUNTY (CINCINNATI). (Columbus: author, 1937) 311p (DAR,OHS,LDS)

HISTORY OF CINCINNATI AND HAMILTON COUNTY OHIO. (Cincinnati: S.B.Nelson Pub., 1894) 1056p (SLO,LDS,DAR)(RPI)

Huston, Alexander B. HISTORICAL SKETCH OF FARMERS' COLLEGE. (Cincinnati: Students' Assn., 190?) 175p (LDS)

Jones, Adolphus E. EXTRACTS FROM THE HISTORY OF CINCINNATI AND THE TERRITORY OF OHIO. (Cincinnati: Cohen & Co., 1888) 133p (LDS)

Kaiser, Ramona. GLIMPSES INTO THE PAST: TALES OF PEOPLE, SETTLEMENTS, AND EVENTS WITHIN COLUMBIA, SYMMES AND SYCAMORE TOWNSHIPS, HAMILTON COUNTY, OHIO. (Madeira OH: Madeira Press, 1940) 44p (DAR)

Kaiser, Ramona. HAMILTON COUNTY OHIO REVOLUTIONARY SOLDIERS. 1941. 140p (DAR,LDS)

Kenney, D.J. ILLUSTRATED CINCINNATI: A PICTORIAL HANDBOOK OF THE QUEEN CITY. (Cincinnati: Geo.E.Stevens & Co., 1875) 368p (DAR)

Kenney, D.J. ILLUSTRATED GUIDE TO CINCINNATI AND THE WORLD'S COLUMBIAN EXPOSITION. (Cincinnati: R.Clarke & Co., 1893) 432p (DAR)

Kirtley, J.A. HISTORY OF BULLITTSBURG CHURCH: WITH BIOGRAPHIES OF ELDERS.(Covington KY: Davis, 1872) 64p (LDS)

Leonard, Lewis A. GREATER CINCINNATI AND ITS PEOPLE; A HISTORY. (Chicago:Lewis Histl.Pub. Co., 1927) 4v (LDS)

Lewis, Margaret P. READING-LOCKLAND PRESBYTERAN CHURCH HISTORY (LOCKLAND, HAMILTON CO., OHIO) 1980? 25,9p (LDS)

McHenry, Chris. SYMMES PURCHASE RECORDS, 1787-1800. [BUTLER,HAMILTON & WARREN CO] (Lawrenceburg IN: author, 1979) 106p (OGS,LDS)

Mansfield, Edward D. PERSONAL MEMORIES: SOCIAL, POLITICAL AND LITERARY: WITH SKETCHES OF MANY NOTED PEOPLE, 1803-1843. (Cincinnati OH: Robert Clarke & Co., 1879) 348p (LDS)

Means, Mrs. Russell. BIBLE RECORDS, HAMILTON COUNTY, OHIO. (SLO)

MEMOIRS OF THE MIAMI VALLEY OHIO. (Chicago: R.O.Law Co.,1919) 3v (OHS,SLO)

Miller, F.W. CINCINNATI'S BEGINNINGS. 1880. 235p (SLO)

Miller, L.B. SESSION BOOK OF DUCK CREEK CHURCH OF THE PRESBYTERIANS. (SLO)RECORD OF THE DISTRIBUTION AND SALE OF LOTS IN THE TOWN OF LOSANTIVILLE. 1870. 11p (SLO)

Morrow, Josiah. HISTORY OF THE SYCAMORE ASSOCIATE REFORMED CHURCH, NOW UNITED PRESBYTERIAN. (Cincinnati: author, 1930) 52p (LDS)

Myers, Julia S. RECORDS OF ANDERSON TOWNSHIP, HAMILTON COUNTY OHIO: CEMETERY AND BIBLE. (Terrace Park OH: DAR, 1967) 121p (DAR)

Phillips, R.C. MAP OF CINCINNATI. (Cincinnati: Ehrgott Forbriger & Co., 1868) (LDS)

READING CENTENNIAL SOUVENIR: CITY OF READING, OHIO, FOUNDED 1797, INCOR-PORATED IN 1851. (Reading OH: np, 1951) 88p (LDS)

Reemelin, Charles. HISTORICAL SKETCH OF GREENE TOWNSHIP, HAMILTON COUNTY, OHIO. 1882. 33p (SLO)

Rudig, Robert W. CINCINNATI TURNER VEREIN. (Cincinnati?: author, 1985) 12p (LDS)

Schulze, M.E. ELM TREE DAYS. 1946. 132p (SLO)

SHAFFER'S ADVERTISING DIRECTORY. 1840. (SLO)

Shotwell, John B. A HISTORY OF THE SCHOOLS OF CINCINNATI. (Cincinnati, 1902) 608p

Sikes, Jane. THE FURNITURE MAKERS OF CINCINNATI, 1790-1849. (Cincinnati, author, 1976) 264p (OHS)

Simons, C.S. CINCINNATI HISTORY WITH SPECIAL REFERENCE TO THE FIRST CENTURY OF THE CITY'S GROWTH. 1936. 45p (SLO)

Sloan, Mary R. HISTORY OF CAMP DENNISON: 1796-1956. (Camp Dennison OH: the committee, c1956) 175p (DAR)

SMALL PART OF THE HISTORY OF THE VILLAGE OF CLEVES AND SURROUNDING AREA. 1958. 62p (DAR)

Smith, Alma. THE VIRGINIA MILITARY SURVEYS OF CLERMONT AND HAMILTON COUNTIES OHIO 1787-1849. (Cincinnati: author, 1985) 253p (OGS,LDS)

Smith, Clifford N. FEDERAL LAND SERIES: A CALENDAR OF ARCHIVAL MATERIAL ON THE LAND PATENTS ISSUED BY THE U.S.GOVERNMENT, VOL.4, PT 1: GRANTS IN THE VIRGINIA MILITARY DISTRICT OF OHIO. (Chicago: Amer.Libr.Assn.,1982) 395p

Smith, Clifford N. FEDERAL LAND SERIES: A CALENDAR OF ARCHIVAL MATERIAL ON THE LAND PATENTS ISSUED BY THE U.S.GOVERNMENT, VOL.4, PT 2: GRANTS IN THE VIRGINIA MILITARY DISTRICT OF OHIO. (Chicago: Amer.Libr.Assn., 1986) 306p

Smith, William C. QUEEN CITY YESTERDAYS: SKETCHES OF CINCINNATI IN THE EIGHTIES. (Crawfordsville IN: R.E.Banta, 1959) 66p (LDS)

Smith, William E. HISTORY OF SOUTHWESTERN OHIO, THE MIAMI VALLEYS. 1511p, 3v (SLO)

Sons of the American Revolution, Ohio Society. THE 1958 LINEAGE BOOK OF THE CINCINNATI CHAPTER, OHIO. (Cincinnati: the society, c1958) 540p (LDS)

SOUVENIR HISTORY OF CUMMINSVILLE. 1914. 142p (SLO)

SPRING GROVE CEMETERY: ITS HISTORY & IMPROVEMENTS [with LOT OWNERS] (Cincinnati: Robert Clarke & Co., 1869) (SLO,LDS)

SPRING GROVE CEMETERY, REPORT FOR 1857. (Cincinnati: C.F.Bradley & Co., 1857) 130p (LDS)

Stevens, George E. THE CITY OF CINCINNATI. (Cincinnati: George S. Blanchard & Co., 1869) 186p (LDS)

Stewart, J. MAP OF THE CITY OF CINCINNATI & VICINITY. (Cincinnati: E.Mendenhall, 1855) (LDS)

Teetor, Henry B. THE PAST AND PRESENT OF MILL CREEK VALLEY, HAMILTON COUNTY OHIO. (Cincinnati: Cogen & Co., 1882) 328p (SLO,DAR,LDS)

TITUS' ATLAS OF HAMILTON COUNTY, OHIO. (Philadelphia: C.O.Titus, 1869) 114p (OGS,LDS)

Tolzmann, Don H. CATALOG OF THE GERMAN-AMERICANA COLLECTION, UNIVERSITY OF CINCINNATI. (New York: K.G.Saur Inc., 1987?) 800p

Tolzmann, Don H. THE CINCINNATI GERMANS AFTER THE GREAT WAR. (New York: Peter Lang Pub., 1987?) 232p

Tunison, J.S. CINCINNATI RIOT: ITS CAUSES AND RESULTS. 1886. 93p (SLO)

Venable, William H. A CENTENNIAL HISTORY OF CHRIST CHURCH, CINCINNATI, 1817-1917. (Cincinnati: Stewart & Kidd, 1918) 172p (DAR,LDS)

Work Projects Administration. TALES OF OLD CINCINNATI. (Cincinnati: Good Government League, c1940) 48p (DAR)

Workman, Beth B. DEED RECORDS OF HAMILTON CO., OHIO, 1787-1877, REGISTER.(Salt Lake City: Genealogical Society, LDS, 1964) 11p (LDS)

Wulsin, Lucien. THE STORY OF THE FOURTH REGIMENT OHIO VETERAN VOLUNTEER CAVALRY: FROM THE ORGANIZATION OF THE REGIMENT, AUGUST 1861, TO ITS 50TH ANNIVERSARY, AUGUST 1911. (Cincinnati: author, 1912) 216p (LDS)

Yon, Paul D. GUIDE TO OHIO COUNTY & MUNICIPAL GOVERNMENT RECORDS. (Columbus: Ohio Hist Soc, 1973) 216p (OHS)

# HANCOCK COUNTY

CREATED:                          1820 FROM LOGAN COUNTY
COUNTY SEAT:                      FINDLAY 45840
COURT HOUSE:                      300 S.MAIN ST., FINDLAY 45840
LIBRARY:                          206 BROADWAY, FINDLAY 45840
HISTORICAL SOCIETY:               422 W. SANDUSKY ST., FINDLAY 45845
GENEALOGICAL SOCIETY:             HANCOCK CO. CHAPTER, OGS
                                      PO BOX 672, FINDLAY 45839-0672
                                      publication: HANCOCK COUNTY HERITAGE
HEALTH DEPARTMENT:                222 BROADWAY, FINDLAY 45840
                                      (separate offices for Findlay City & Fostoria)
ARCHIVAL DISTRICT:                BOWLING GREEN STATE UNIVERSITY, BOWLING GREEN
                                      (see Biggs' Guide to records)
LAND SURVEYS:                     CONGRESS LANDS, E & N OF 1ST PRIN.MERIDIAN
                                  CONGRESS LANDS, E & S OF 1ST PRIN.MERIDIAN
BOUNDED BY:                       EAST:     SENECA & WYANDOT CO.
                                  NORTH:    WOOD CO.
                                  WEST:     ALLEN & PUTNAM CO.
                                  SOUTH:    HARDIN CO.
TOWNSHIPS:                        Allen, Amanda, Big Lick, Blanchard, Cass, Delaware, Eagle, Jackson,
                                  Liberty, Madison, Marion, Orange, Pleasant, Portage, Union,
                                  Van Buren, Washington.

**COURT RECORDS: (LDS MICROFILM)**
Auditor:
    Tax duplicates, 1828-1838.
Clerk of Courts:
    Chancery record, v2-3, 1847-1856.
    Common Pleas journal, v1-4, 1828-1857.
    Index to Common Pleas journal, 1847-1857.

Supreme Court complete record, 1833-1843.
Supreme Court journal, 1833-1851.
District Court journal, 1852-1867.
Judgment index, 1833-1874.
County Home:
Register, 1868-1947.
Probate Court:
Death records, 1867-1880.
Birth records, v1-3A, 1867-1909.
Probate index to files, 1828-1970.
Original probate papers, case #1-6223, 1829-1907.
Civil docket, 1852-1889.
Administration dockets, vA-E, 1847-1916.
Record of wills, v1-8, 1829-1903.
Inventories, sale bills, vA-J, 1850-1889.
Final records, v2-13, 1857-1889.
Marriage records, v1-15, 1828-1918.
Administration record, 1845-1850.
Recorder:
Grantor & grantee index, vA-3, 1830-1936.
Deeds, v1-56, 1820-1887.
Soldiers' discharge record, v1-2, 1865-1946.
Miscellaneous:
Arcadia, Presbyterian Church, session record, 1859-1887.
Findlay, First Presby.Church, session records, 1830-1913.
Cemetery inscriptions, State Library of Ohio collection.

**OHIO HISTORICAL SOCIETY: (MICROFILM)**
Clerk of Courts:
Chancery record, v2-3, 1847-1856.
Common Pleas journal, v1-4, 1828-1857.
Index to Common Pleas journal, 1847-1857.
Supreme Court complete record, 1833-1843.
Supreme Court journal, 1833-1851.
District Court journal, 1852-1867.
Judgment index, 1833-1874.
County Home:
Register, 1868-1947.
Probate Court:
Marriage records, v1-15, 1828-1918.
Administration record, 1845-1850.
Recorder:
Deed records, v46-56, 1881-1887.
Soldiers' discharge record, v1-2, 1865-1946.
Miscellaneous:
Marriage records, 1828-1864, by DAR.
Tombstone inscriptions, v1-7, by DAR.

**CENSUS RECORDS (OHS,SLO,OGS,LDS)**
1830-1880, 1900-1910; 1890 VETERANS; 1880,1900 SOUNDEX; 1910 MIRACODE

**AGRICULTURAL CENSUS SCHEDULES (OHS,SLO-mic)**
1850,1860,1870,1880

**PRODUCTS OF INDUSTRY CENSUS SCHEDULE (OHS,SLO-mic)**
1850,1870

**MORTALITY CENSUS SCHEDULES (OHS,SLO-mic)**
1850,1860

**DEFECTIVE & DEPENDENT CENSUS SCHEDULES (OHS,SLO-mic)**
1880

**NEWSPAPERS: [GUIDE TO OHIO NEWSPAPERS, 1793-1973]**
Arcadia, Arlington, Findlay, McComb, Mt.Blanchard, Rawson.

**TAX RECORDS (OHS & LDS)**
1828-1838.

**GENEALOGICAL PERIODICAL ARTICLES**
Bell, Carol Willsey. OHIO GENEALOGICAL PERIODICAL INDEX: A COUNTY GUIDE (Youngstown,
    OH: author, 6th ed., 1987)

**PUBLISHED SOURCES:**
Beardsley, Daniel B. HISTORY OF HANCOCK COUNTY OHIO FROM ITS EARLIEST SETTLEMENT
    TO THE PRESENT TIME. (Springfield OH: Republic Printing Co., 1881) 472p (SLO,LDS,DAR)(RPI)
Biggs, Deb. GUIDE TO LOCAL GOVERNMENT RECORDS AT THE CENTER FOR ARCHIVAL COL-
    LECTIONS. (Bowling Green OH: Bowling Green State Univ, 1981) 104p (OGS)
CENTENNIAL BIOGRAPHICAL HISTORY OF HANCOCK COUNTY OHIO. (Chicago: Lewis Pub.Co.,
    1903) 595p (SLO,LDS)(RPI)
Christian, Donna K. GUIDE TO NEWSPAPER HOLDINGS AT THE CENTER FOR ARCHIVAL COL-
    LECTIONS. (Bowling Green OH: Bowling Green State Univ, 1980) 64p (OGS)
CITY/COUNTY DIRECTORIES: check holdings of OHS & local public library.
Daughters of the American Revolution. BIBLE RECORDS CONTRIBUTED BY PEOPLE OF HANCOCK
    COUNTY OHIO FOR THE BICENTENNIAL PROJECT OF FORT FINDLAY CHAPTER DAR. 1976.
    102p (DAR,SLO)
Daughters of the American Revolution. INDEX TO MARRIAGES OF HANCOCK COUNTY OHIO
    1828-1864. 1972. 139p (DAR)
Daughters of the American Revolution. MARRIAGE RECORDS OF HANCOCK COUNTY OHIO 1828-
    1864. 268p (SLO,DAR,LDS)
Daughters of the American Revolution. TOMBSTONE INSCRIPTIONS FROM CEMETERIES IN HAN-
    COCK COUNTY OHIO. 1952-1958. 7v (LDS,DAR,SLO)
Drake, Paul. THE DAY BOOK OF DR. WILLIAM K. DRAKE FOR THE PERIOD 1841-1856 [PICK-
    AWAY, DELAWARE & HANCOCK COS]. (Crab Orchard TN: author, 1984)105p (OGS)
Eberhart, G.A. ILLUSTRATED HISTORICAL ATLAS OF HANCOCK COUNTY, OHIO. 1875.
    (OGS,SLO,LDS)(RPI)
Emerine, Andrew. FOSTORIA HIGHLIGHTS: OF SOME OF THE OCCURRENCES IN FOSTORIA
    DURING THE PAST 120 YEARS, IN CONJUNCTION WITH FOSTORIA'S 100 YEARS ANNIVER-
    SARY CELEBRATION, 1954. (Fostoria OH: First National Bank, 1954) 32p (LDS)
Hancock Co Chapter OGS. 1860 HANCOCK COUNTY OHIO CENSUS INDEX. (Findlay: the society,
    nd)
Hancock Co Chapter OGS. 1870 HANCOCK COUNTY OHIO CENSUS INDEX. (Findlay OH: the
    society, nd) (SLO)
Hancock Co Chapter OGS. 1880 HANCOCK COUNTY OHIO CENSUS INDEX. (Findlay OH: the
    society, 1986?) 94p (OGS)
Hancock Co Chapter OGS. EARLY LAND RECORDS OF HANCOCK COUNTY OHIO. (Findlay OH:
    the society, 1986) 107p (OGS,LDS)
Hancock Co Chapter OGS. GEORGE VANEMAN–HANCOCK COUNTY PRESBYTERIAN MINISTER
    (DAYBOOK & GENEALOGY). (Findlay OH: the society, 1988) (OGS)

Hancock Co Chapter OGS. HANCOCK COUNTY OHIO ANCESTRAL CHARTS. 1984. (SLO)

Hancock Co Chapter OGS. HANCOCK COUNTY OHIO CEMETERY INSCRIPTIONS--ALLEN TOWNSHIP. (Findlay OH: the society, 1987) 210p (OGS)

Hancock Co Chapter OGS. HANCOCK COUNTY OHIO CHAPTER SURNAME LIST. (Findlay OH: the society, 1986) 25p (OGS)

Hancock Co Chapter OGS. HANCOCK COUNTY OHIO FEDERAL CENSUS 1830-1840. (Findlay OH: the society, nd)

Hancock Co Chapter OGS. HANCOCK COUNTY OHIO, INDEX TO EARLY WILLS 1850-1900. (Findlay OH: the society, nd)

Hancock Co Chapter OGS. HANCOCK COUNTY FIVE GENERATION CHART BOOK. (Findlay OH: the society, 1984) 213p (LDS,OGS)

Hancock Co Chapter OGS. INDEX TO BEER'S HISTORY OF HANCOCK COUNTY OHIO, 1883. (Mc-Comb OH: the society, 1982.) 76p (OGS)

Hancock Co Chapter OGS. INDEX TO BROWN'S HISTORY OF HANCOCK COUNTY, 1886. (Findlay OH: the society, nd) (SLO)

Hancock Co Chapter OGS. INDEX TO MAPLE GROVE CEMETERY, FINDLAY OHIO, HANCOCK COUNTY, VOL.9, 1854-1912. (Findlay OH: the society, 1985) 145p (OGS,LDS)

Hancock Co Chapter OGS. INDEX TO NATURALIZATION PAPERS FOUND IN HANCOCK COUNTY OHIO COURT RECORDS. (Findlay,OH: the society, 1985) 75p (OGS,LDS)

Hancock Co Chapter OGS. MARRIAGE RECORDS OF HANCOCK COUNTY OHIO, 1828-1864 (Findlay OH: the society, 1986) 170p (OGS)

Hancock Co Chapter OGS. MARRIAGE RECORDS OF HANCOCK COUNTY OHIO VOL.II, 1865-1884. (Findlay OH: the society, 1987) 215p (OGS)

Hancock Co Chapter OGS. ORIGINAL LAND ENTRIES, HANCOCK COUNTY. (Findlay OH: the society, nd)

Hancock Co Chapter OGS. POWELL MEMORIAL HISTORY BY REV.JOHN POWELL, 1880 (Findlay OH: the society, nd)

Hancock Co Chapter OGS. SESQUI-CENTENNIAL CELEBRATION, VAN BUREN, ALLEN TOWNSHIP, HANCOCK COUNTY OHIO. (Findlay OH: the society, nd)

Hancock Co Chapter OGS. SURNAME LIST OF MEMBERS (Findlay OH: the society, nd)

HANCOCK COUNTY OHIO IN THE WORLD WAR. 117p. (OHS)

Heminger, R.L. ACROSS THE YEARS IN FINDLAY AND HANCOCK COUNTY. (Findlay OH: Republican-Courier, 1965) 205p (DAR)

Historical Records Survey. INVENTORY OF THE COUNTY ARCHIVES OF OHIO NO.32, HANCOCK COUNTY. (Columbus: author, 1941) 356p (OHS,LDS,DAR)

HISTORY OF HANCOCK COUNTY OHIO. (Chicago: Warner Beers, 1886)(Reprint, Evansville IN: Unigraphic, 1978) 867p (DAR,LDS,SLO)(RPI)

Hronek, Richard E. VAN BUREN, OHIO, 1833-1983: A HISTORY COMPILED FOR THE SESQUICEN-TENNIAL YEAR, 1983. (Van Buren OH: Sesquicentennial Committee, 1983) 143p (LDS,SLO)

Humphrey, W.D. FINDLAY: THE STORY OF A COMMUNITY. 1961. 223p (SLO)

Kimmell, J.A. 20TH CENTURY HISTORY OF FINDLAY & HANCOCK CO OHIO. (Chicago: Rich-mond, Arnold Pub Co, 1910) 656p (SLO,LDS,DAR)(RPI)

King, A.E. EVANGELICAL UNITED BRETHREN CHURCH OF MT.CORY, HANCOCK CO OHIO 1800-1929. 1972. (LDS)

Knapp, Horace S. HISTORY OF THE MAUMEE VALLEY. (Toledo OH: author, 1872) 685p. (DAR,OHS,SLO)

Levinson, Marilyn. GUIDE TO NEWSPAPER HOLDINGS AT THE CENTER FOR ARCHIVAL COL-LECTIONS. 2nd Edition. (Bowling Green OH: Bowling Green State Univ., 1987)

Moorhead, Rex K. INDEX TO THE 1870 FEDERAL POPULATION CENSUS OF HANCOCK COUN-TY OHIO. 1976. (Reprint, Findlay OH: Hancock Co Chapter OGS 1985) 60p (LDS,SLO,OHS)

Moorhead, Rex K. INDEX TO THE 1860 FEDERAL POPULATION CENSUS OF HANCOCK COUN-TY OHIO. 1976. (Reprint, Findlay OH: Hancock Co Chapter OGS 1985) 35p (SLO,LDS,OHS)

Murray, Melvin L. HISTORY OF THE METHODIST CHURCH IN FOSTORIA, OHIO, 1833-1900: THE RETURN OF RISDON. (Fostoria OH: Gray Printing, 1968) 39p (LDS)

PLAT BOOK OF HANCOCK COUNTY [OHIO]. (np: Midwest Map Pub., 1964) (OGS)

Slocum, C.E. HISTORY OF THE MAUMEE RIVER BASIN FROM THE EARLIEST ACCOUNT TO ITS
    ORGANIZATION INTO COUNTIES. 1905. 638p (SLO)
Spaythe, Jacob A. HISTORY OF HANCOCK COUNTY OHIO. (Toledo OH: B.F.Wade Co.,1903) 312p.
    (SLO,LDS)(RPI)
Winter, Nevin O. HISTORY OF NORTHWEST OHIO. (Chicago: Lewis Pub.Co.,1917) 3v. (SLO,OHS)

# HARDIN COUNTY

CREATED:                    1820 FROM LOGAN COUNTY
COUNTY SEAT:                KENTON 43326
COURT HOUSE:                PUBLIC SQUARE, KENTON 43326
LIBRARY:                    325 E. COLUMBUS ST., KENTON 43326
HISTORICAL SOCIETY:         121 N. DETROIT ST., KENTON 43326
GENEALOGICAL SOCIETY:       HARDIN CO. CHAPTER, OGS
                            PO BOX 520, KENTON 43326
                            publication: TRACK AND TRACE
HEALTH DEPARTMENT:          921 E.FRANKLIN ST., PO BOX 550, KENTON 43326
ARCHIVAL DISTRICT:          BOWLING GREEN STATE UNIVERSITY, BOWLING GREEN
                            (see Biggs' Guide to records)
LAND SURVEYS:               CONGRESS LANDS, E & S OF 1ST PRIN.MERIDIAN
                            VIRGINIA MILITARY DISTRICT
BOUNDED BY:                 EAST:     MARION & WYANDOT CO.
                            NORTH:    HANCOCK CO.
                            WEST:     ALLEN & AUGLAIZE CO.
                            SOUTH:    LOGAN & UNION CO.
TOWNSHIPS:                  Blanchard, Buck, Cessna, Dudley, Goshen, Hale,  Jackson, Liberty,
                            Lynn, McDonald, Marion, Pleasant, Roundhead, Taylor Creek,
                            Washington.

SPECIAL NOTE:               COURTHOUSE FIRE IN 1853 DESTROYED MANY RECORDS.

**COURT RECORDS: (LDS MICROFILM)**
Assessor:
    Quadrennial enumeration, 1887-1907.
Auditor:
    Tax duplicates, 1821,1833,1838-1847,1850.
Clerk of Courts:
    Bond records, 1833-1859.
    Common Pleas journals, vA-C, 1833-1850.
    Chancery record, vB, 1842-1846.
    Judgment index, 1833-1867.
    Supreme Court complete record, 1837-1851.
    Supreme Court journal, 1836-1852.
    District Court journal, 1852-1857.
    Jury list, 1885-1890.
    Witness book, 1853-1859.
Commissioners:
    Journals & index, 1853-1903.
Coroner:
    Record of inquests, 1885-1921.
Infirmary:
    Infirmary record, 1871-1957.
    Death record, 1872-1913.
    Directors' journal, v1-2, 1871-1905.

Probate Court:
    Administration docket, v1, 1879-1888.
    Administration docket, 1848.
    Admrs. bonds vB-C, 1866-1893.
    Admin., exec., grdn. 2nd bonds, 1871-1895.
    Admrs. & execs. accounts, vF-J, 1875-1890.
    Birth records, & index, v1-5, 1867-1908.
    Civil docket, v1-2, 1853-1872.
    Death records & index, v1-4, 1867-1908.
    Executors, administrators & guardians docket, 1873-1882.
    Final record, 1834-1848; 1853-1898.
    Final records of cases, vA-8, 1853-1888.
    General index to estates, v1-2, 1850-1960.
    Guardians' bonds, vB-C, 1866-1893.
    Guardians' letter record, vA, 1873-1893.
    Guardians' accounts, v1-3, 1878-1887.
    Guardians' docket, v1-2, 1865-1889.
    Inventories & sale bills, vA-G, 1849-1887.
    Journal of appointments, v1, 1875-1882.
    Marriage records, v1-17, 1833-1918.
    Marriage general index, v1-5, 1833-1960.
    Marriage records, v16-17, 1910-1918.
    Ministers' licenses, 1846-1880.
    Naturalization records, 1875-1900.
    Probate record, v1, 1834-1848.
    Probate journal, v1-G, 1852-1885.
    Record of letters, v1, 1871-1885.
    Record of bonds, vA, 1846-1877.
    Will record, vA-F, 1830-1912.
    Wills, general index, 1830-1963.
Recorder:
    Deed records, v52-61, 1881-1886.
    Grantor & grantee indexes, 1831-1968.
    Soldiers register, 1861-1865.
Sheriff:
    Jail register, 1868-1885,1897-1938.
Surveyor:
    Surveyors records, 1820-1857.
Miscellaneous:
    Forest, Presbyterian Church, session minutes, 1869-1885.
    Marriage records, 1833-1865, by DAR.

**OHIO HISTORICAL SOCIETY: (MICROFILM)**
Clerk of Courts:
    Common Pleas journals, vA-C, 1833-1850.
    Chancery record, vB, 1842-1846.
    Judgment index, 1833-1867.
    Supreme Court complete record, 1837-1851.
    Supreme Court journal, 1836-1852.
    District Court journal, 1852-1857.
Commissioners:
    Journals & index, 1853-1903.
Probate Court:
    Final record, 1834-1848; 1853-1898.
    Will records, vG-J, 1901-1912.

Guardians' docket, v1-2, 1865-1889.
Administration docket, 1848.
Executors, administrators & guardians docket, 1873-1882.
Marriage records, v16-17, 1910-1918.
Recorder:
Deed records, v52-61, 1881-1886.
Miscellaneous:
Marriage records, 1833-1865, by DAR.

## CENSUS RECORDS (OHS,SLO,OGS,LDS)
1820-1880, 1900-1910; 1890 VETERANS; 1880,1900 SOUNDEX; 1910 MIRACODE

## AGRICULTURAL CENSUS SCHEDULES (OHS,SLO-mic)
1850,1860,1870,1880

## PRODUCTS OF INDUSTRY CENSUS SCHEDULE (OHS,SLO-mic)
1850,1870

## MORTALITY CENSUS SCHEDULES (OHS,SLO-mic)
1850,1860

## DEFECTIVE & DEPENDENT CENSUS SCHEDULES (OHS,SLO-mic)
1880

## NEWSPAPERS: [GUIDE TO OHIO NEWSPAPERS, 1793-1973]
Ada, Dunkirk, Kenton, Mt.Victory.

## TAX RECORDS (OHS & LDS)
1833-1838.

## GENEALOGICAL PERIODICAL ARTICLES
Bell, Carol Willsey. OHIO GENEALOGICAL PERIODICAL INDEX: A COUNTY GUIDE (Youngstown,
    OH: author, 6th ed., 1987)

## PUBLISHED SOURCES:
1983 HARDIN COUNTY OHIO HISTORY. (Kenton OH: Hardin Co Arch. & Hist Soc., 1983) 470p (OGS)
Biggs, Deb. GUIDE TO LOCAL GOVERNMENT RECORDS AT THE CENTER FOR ARCHIVAL COL-
    LECTIONS. (Bowling Green OH: Bowling Green State Univ, 1981) 104p (OGS)
Blue, Herbert T.O. CENTENNIAL HISTORY OF HARDIN COUNTY, OHIO. (Canton OH: Rogers-
    Miller Co., 1933) 180p (DAR,LDS)
Christian, Donna K. GUIDE TO NEWSPAPER HOLDINGS AT THE CENTER FOR ARCHIVAL COL-
    LECTIONS. (Bowling Green OH: Bowling Green State Univ, 1980) 64p (OGS)
CITY/COUNTY DIRECTORIES: check holdings of OHS & local public library.
Daughters of the American Revolution. BIBLE RECORDS AND FAMILY HISTORIES, ENTERED BY
    THE COURTESY OF FORT McARTHUR CHAPTER DAR. 1970. 76p (DAR,LDS)
Daughters of the American Revolution. MARRIAGE RECORDS OF HARDIN COUNTY OHIO FROM
    1833 TO 1865 INCLUSIVE. 1938. 200p. (SLO,DAR,LDS)
Drumm, Carl. A COMPLETE HISTORY OF THE SCIOTO MARSH, IN HARDIN COUNTY OHIO.
    1940. (Reprint, Evansville IN: Unigraphic, 1976) 94p (SLO,DAR,LDS)
FARM JOURNAL DIRECTORY OF HARDIN COUNTY, OHIO. 1916. (SLO)
Froyne, Culver P. HARDIN COUNTY CEMETERIES LISTED BY TOWNSHIP. (LDS)
HARDIN COUNTY, OHIO: A HISTORICAL UPDATE WITH FAMILY HISTORIES. (Kenton OH: Har-
    din Co.Arch. & Hist.Soc., 1983) 407p (LDS,SLO)
Hardesty, H.H. MILITARY HISTORY OF OHIO - HARDIN COUNTY EDITION. 1886/87. (OHS)
HARDIN COUNTY SCRAPBOOK. (news articles & obits) (OGS)

Hill, John W. LIFE SKETCHES - HILL - ADA, OHIO. (Ada OH: author, 19??) 58p (LDS)

HISTORY OF HARDIN COUNTY OHIO. (Chicago: Warner, Beers & Co., 1883) (Reprint, Evansville IN: Unigraphic, 1973) 1064p. (SLO,DAR,LDS)(RPI)

Howland, C.E. ATLAS OF HARDIN COUNTY OHIO. (Philadelphia: R.Sutton & Co., 1879) 53p (LDS,SLO,OHS)(RPI)

Kohler, M.L. TWENTIETH CENTURY HISTORY OF HARDIN COUNTY OHIO. (Chicago: Lewis Pub.Co.,1910) 898p. 2v. (LDS,SLO,DAR)(RPI)

Levinson, Marilyn. GUIDE TO NEWSPAPER HOLDINGS AT THE CENTER FOR ARCHIVAL COLLECTIONS. 2nd Edition. (Bowling Green OH: Bowling Green State Univ., 1987)

PORTRAIT AND BIOGRAPHICAL RECORD OF MARION AND HARDIN COUNTY OHIO. (Chicago: Chapman Pub.Co.,1895) 563p. (LDS,SLO,DAR)(RPI)

Scott, Beulah M. INDEX TO ATLAS OF HARDIN COUNTY OHIO BY HOWLAND, 1879. 53p (LDS)

Smith, Clifford N. FEDERAL LAND SERIES: A CALENDAR OF ARCHIVAL MATERIAL ON THE LAND PATENTS ISSUED BY THE U.S.GOVERNMENT, VOL.4, PT 2: GRANTS IN THE VIRGINIA MILITARY DISTRICT OF OHIO. (Chicago: American Library Assn., 1986) 306p

Smith, Clifford N. FEDERAL LAND SERIES: A CALENDAR OF ARCHIVAL MATERIAL ON THE LAND PATENTS ISSUED BY THE U.S.GOVERNMENT, VOL.4, PT 1: GRANTS IN THE VIRGINIA MILITARY DISTRICT OF OHIO. (Chicago: American Library Assn., 1982) 395p

Wagner, C.W. MISCELLANEOUS CEMETERY RECORDS OF ALLEN, LICKING, HARDIN, MADISON, PICKAWAY AND VINTON COUNTIES OHIO. (SLO)

Winter, Nevin O. HISTORY OF NORTHWEST OHIO. (Chicago: Lewis Pub.Co.,1917) 3v. (SLO,OHS)

# HARRISON COUNTY

| | |
|---|---|
| CREATED: | 1813 FROM JEFFERSON & TUSCARAWAS |
| COUNTY SEAT: | CADIZ 43907 |
| COURT HOUSE: | MAIN ST., CADIZ 43907 |
| LIBRARY: | 200 E. Market St., Cadiz 43907 |
| HISTORICAL SOCIETY: | 168 E. Market St., Cadiz 43907 |
| GENEALOGICAL SOCIETY: | HARRISON CO. CHAPTER, OGS |
| | 45507 Unionvale Rd., Cadiz 43907 |
| | publication: OUR HARRISON HERITAGE |
| HEALTH DEPARTMENT: | 943-B EAST MARKET, CADIZ 43907 |
| ARCHIVAL DISTRICT: | UNIVERSITY OF AKRON, AKRON, OHIO |
| | (see Folck's Guide to records) |
| LAND SURVEYS: | CONGRESS LANDS, SEVEN RANGES |
| | DOHRMAN GRANT |
| BOUNDED BY: | EAST:     JEFFERSON CO. |
| | NORTH:   CARROLL CO. |
| | WEST:     TUSCARAWAS CO. |
| | SOUTH:   BELMONT & GUERNSEY CO. |
| TOWNSHIPS: | Archer, Athens, Cadiz, Franklin, Freeport, German, Green, Monroe, Moorefield, North, Nottingham, Rumley, Short Creek, Stock, Washington. |

**COURT RECORDS: (LDS MICROFILM)**
Auditor:
    Tax duplicates, 1816-1828.
Commissioners:
    Journal, 1870-1905.
    Journal index, 1824-1909.
Probate Court:
    Birth records, v1-3, 1867-1971.
    Death records, 1867-1941.

    Marriage records, vA-K, 1813-1920.
    Marriage index to vB-C, 1828-1850.
    Will record, vA-E, 1813-1892.
    Index to wills, nd.
    Administration docket, 1813-1855.
    Accounts of exrs., adms. & grdns., 1826-1851.
    Guardians' docket, 1882-1913.
    Final record, vA-D, 1853-1887.
    Probate journal, vA-D, 1852-1887.
    Inventory & sales, vA-M, 1813-1887.
Recorder:
    Deed index, v1-3, 1812-1911.
    Deed records, vA-Z, 27-31, 1812-1882.
Sheriff:
    Jail register, 1913-1936.
Miscellaneous:
    Beech Spring Presby.Church, records, 1839-1868.
    Cadiz, First United Presby.Church, records, 1857-1888.
    Cadiz, Assoc.Reformed Church, records, 1827-1856.
    New Athens, Unity United Presby.church, minutes, 1813-1851,1838-1888.
    George Jenkins Papers, Short Creek Monthly Meeting 1820-1876. (WRHS)

**OHIO HISTORICAL SOCIETY: (MICROFILM)**
Commissioners:
    Journal, 1870-1905.
    Journal index, 1824-1909.
Sheriff:
    Jail register, 1913-1936.

**CENSUS RECORDS  (OHS,SLO,OGS,LDS)**
1820-1880, 1900-1910; 1890 VETERANS; 1880,1900 SOUNDEX; 1910 MIRACODE

**AGRICULTURAL CENSUS SCHEDULES  (OHS,SLO-mic)**
1850,1860,1870,1880

**PRODUCTS OF INDUSTRY CENSUS SCHEDULE  (OHS,SLO-mic)**
1850,1870

**MORTALITY CENSUS SCHEDULES (OHS,SLO-mic)**
1850,1860

**DEFECTIVE & DEPENDENT CENSUS SCHEDULES (OHS,SLO-mic)**
1880

**NEWSPAPERS: [GUIDE TO OHIO NEWSPAPERS, 1793-1973]**
Cadiz, Freeport, Scio.

**TAX RECORDS (OHS & LDS)**
1814,1816-1823,1825-1828,1835.

**GENEALOGICAL PERIODICAL ARTICLES**
Bell, Carol Willsey. OHIO GENEALOGICAL PERIODICAL INDEX: A COUNTY GUIDE (Youngstown,
    OH: author, 6th ed., 1987)

**PUBLISHED SOURCES:**

ABSTRACTS FROM CHURCH RECORD BOOKS OF REV. JOSEPH A. ROOF. (SLO,LDS)

Beebe, Mary H. HARRISON COUNTY OHIO 1862 LAND OWNERSHIP MAP AND PORTION OF THE 1803 PLAT OF THE DISTRICT OF STEUBENVILLE. (Ashland OH: author, 1987) 60p (OGS,LDS)

Bell, Carol W. OHIO LANDS: STEUBENVILLE LAND OFFICE RECORDS, 1800-1820. (Youngstown OH: author, 1983) 181p (OGS)

Bullock, Helen. HISTORY OF HARRISON COUNTY. 1961. 48p. (SLO)

Caldwell, John A. CALDWELL'S ATLAS OF HARRISON COUNTY, OHIO. (Condit OH: J.A.Caldwell, 1875) 139p (OGS,SLO,LDS)(RPI)

CITY/COUNTY DIRECTORIES: check holdings of OHS & local public library.

Cochran, Rev. Fred. FREEPORT PRESBYTERIAN CHURCH 1821-1971. (Freeport OH: author, 1971) 143p (OGS)

COMMEMORATIVE BIOGRAPHICAL RECORD OF THE COUNTIES OF HARRISON AND CAR-ROLL, OHIO. (Chicago: J.H.Beers CO., 1891) 1150p (SLO,DAR,LDS)

Daughters of the American Revolution. HARRISON COUNTY MARRIAGES: 1813 TO 1840 INCLUSIVE (copied from Hanna's Hist.Coll.) 200p (DAR)

DiThomas, Mary E. SOME NAMES OF PERSONS PRESENT IN HARRISON COUNTY OHIO BEFORE 1832. (OGS)

EARLY HISTORY OF TIPPECANOE, HARRISON COUNTY, OHIO. (OGS)

Eckley, Harvey J. & W.T.Perry. HISTORY OF CARROLL AND HARRISON COUNTIES OHIO (Chicago: Lewis Pub Co., 1921) 2v (LDS,LC,SLO,DAR)(RPI)

Folck, Linda. LOCAL GOVERNMENT RECORDS IN THE AMERICAN HISTORY RESEARCH CEN-TER AT THE UNIVERSITY OF AKRON. (Akron: U of Akron, 1982) 40p. (OGS)

Greer, Dorothea. MARRIAGE PERMISSIONS, HARRISON COUNTY, OHIO, 1813-1852. (Cadiz OH: author, 1986) 80p (LDS)

Greer, Dorothea. RECORDS OF INMATES IN THE HARRISON COUNTY OHIO INFIRMARY. (Cadiz OH: author, 1985) 21p (OGS,LDS)

Greer, Dorothea. SUPREME COURT CASES, HARRISON COUNTY, CADIZ, OHIO, 1814-1832. (Cadiz OH: author, 1985) 39p (OGS,LDS)

Hanna, Charles A. HISTORICAL COLLECTIONS OF HARRISON COUNTY OHIO. (New York: author, 1900) (Reprint, Evansville IN: Unigrqaphic, 1973) 636p (SLO,LDS,DAR)(RPI)

Hanna, Charles A. OHIO VALLEY GENEALOGIES, RELATING TO FAMILIES IN HARRISON, BEL-MONT & JEFFERSON COUNTIES OHIO. (New York: J.J.Little, 1900) 128p (LC,DAR)

Harrison Co Chapter OGS. MOOREFIELD AND NOTTINGHAM TOWNSHIPS CEMETERY BOOK (Cadiz: the society, 1987) 201p (LDS)

Harrison Co Chapter OGS. FRANKLIN, STOCK & WASHINGTON TOWNSHIP CEMETERIES. (Cadiz OH: the society, 1988?) 229p (OGS)

Harrison, J.T. STORY OF THE DINING FORK. (SLO)

McGavran, Samuel B. A BRIEF HISTORY OF HARRISON COUNTY. (Cadiz OH: Harrison Tribune, 1894) 55p (LDS,SLO)(RPI)

Poulson, Homer C. HISTORY OF THE VILLAGE OF DEERSVILLE OHIO 1815-1952. 1952. 169p (LDS,DAR,SLO)

PRESENTING HARRISON COUNTY! (FROM HARRISON COUNTY NEWS HERALD) (SLO)

Roof, Joseph A. BIRTHS, MARRIAGES, AND DEATHS TRANSCRIBED FROM CHURCH RECORD BOOKS OF REV.JOSEPH A. ROOF OF PICKAWAY COUNTY, OHIO (1834-1855): WITH RECORDS FROM TUSCARAWAS, HARRISON AND CARROLL COUNTIES OHIO; LEE AND VAN BUREN COUNTIES, IOWA. 1958. 95p (DAR,LDS)

Wallace, Charles B. THE YOUNG MR. GABLE [CLARK GABLE, ACTOR]. (Cadiz: Harrison Co Hist Soc, 1983) 59p (OGS)

Woodruff, Audrey W. 1850 CENSUS HARRISON COUNTY OHIO. (Springfield MO: author, 1963?) 30p (DAR)

# HENRY COUNTY

CREATED:                                1820 FROM SHELBY COUNTY
COUNTY SEAT:                            NAPOLEON 43545
COURT HOUSE:                            660 N. PERRY ST., NAPOLEON 43545
LIBRARY:                                310 W. CLINTON ST., NAPOLEON 43545
HISTORICAL SOCIETY:
GENEALOGICAL SOCIETY:                   HENRY CO. CHAPTER, OGS
                                        c/o PATRICK HENRY LIBRARY, DESHLER 43516
HEALTH DEPARTMENT:                      COURT HOUSE, 660 N.PERRY ST., NAPOLEON 43545
ARCHIVAL DISTRICT:                      BOWLING GREEN STATE UNIVERSITY, BOWLING GREEN
                                          (see Biggs' Guide to records)
LAND SURVEYS:                           CONGRESS LANDS, E & N OF 1ST PRIN.MERIDIAN
BOUNDED BY:                             EAST:      LUCAS & WOOD CO.
                                        NORTH:    FULTON CO.
                                        WEST:      DEFIANCE & WILLIAMS CO.
                                        SOUTH:    PUTNAM CO.
TOWNSHIPS:                              Barlow, Damascus, Flatrock, Freedom, Harrison,  Liberty, Marion,
                                        Monroe, Napoleon, Pleasant, Richfield, Ridgeville, Washington.

**SPECIAL NOTE:**                       A COURTHOUSE FIRE IN 1847 DESTROYED SOME RECORDS.

**COURT RECORDS: (LDS MICROFILM)**
Auditor:
    Tax duplicates, 1835-1838.
Clerk of Courts:
    Index to complete record, v1-3, 1847-1864.
    Complete record, v1-5, 1847-1873.
    Journal, vA,1-2, 1847-1870.
    District court record, 1852-1885.
    Supreme Court record, 1847-1853.
County Home:
    Register, 1870-1979.
Probate Court:
    Death records, v1-5, 1867-1908+
    Birth records, v1-5, 1867-1921
    Delayed birth records, dates vary.
    Marriage records, vA,1-14, 1847-1930.
    Will records, v1-10, 1852-1910.
    Probate journal, 1852-53, 1858-1882.
    Administration docket, 1847-1889.
    Guardians' docket, 1874-1882.
    General index, v1, 1847-1917.
    Naturalization records, 1852-1906.
Recorder:
    Deed records, v1-19, 1846-1874.
    General index to deeds, v1-97, n.d.
    Cemetery deed record, 1872-1976.
    Mortgage records, v1-19, 1847-1886.
    Index to mortgages, 1847-1902.
    Index to miscellaneous records, v1.
    Registration of veterans' graves, 1835-1976.
    Soldiers' discharge records, v1-3, 1865-1945.
    Articles of incorporation, 1874-1903.

Miscellaneous:
    Cemetery inscriptions.

**OHIO HISTORICAL SOCIETY: (MICROFILM)**
County Home:
    Register, 1870-1979.
Probate Court:
    Administration docket, 1847-1889.
    Guardians' docket, 1874-1882.
    General index, v1, 1847-1917.
    Will record, v8-10, 1899-1910.
    Naturalization records, 1852-1906.

**CENSUS RECORDS (OHS,SLO,OGS,LDS)**
1830-1880, 1900-1910; 1890 VETERANS; 1880,1900 SOUNDEX; 1910 MIRACODE

**AGRICULTURAL CENSUS SCHEDULES (OHS,SLO-mic)**
1850,1860,1870,1880

**PRODUCTS OF INDUSTRY CENSUS SCHEDULE (OHS,SLO-mic)**
1850,1870

**MORTALITY CENSUS SCHEDULES (OHS,SLO-mic)**
1850,1860

**DEFECTIVE & DEPENDENT CENSUS SCHEDULES (OHS,SLO-mic)**
1880

**NEWSPAPERS: [GUIDE TO OHIO NEWSPAPERS, 1793-1973]**
Deshler, Holgate, Liberty Center, Napoleon.

**TAX RECORDS (OHS & LDS)**
1835-1838.

**GENEALOGICAL PERIODICAL ARTICLES**
Bell, Carol Willsey. OHIO GENEALOGICAL PERIODICAL INDEX: A COUNTY GUIDE (Youngstown,
    OH: author, 6th ed., 1987)

**PUBLISHED SOURCES:**
Aldrich, Lewis C. HISTORY OF HENRY AND FULTON COUNTIES OHIO. (Syracuse NY: D.Mason
    & Co., 1888) 713p (LDS,LC,SLO,DAR) (RPI)
Biggs, Deb. GUIDE TO LOCAL GOVERNMENT RECORDS AT THE CENTER FOR ARCHIVAL COL-
    LECTIONS. (Bowling Green OH: Bowling Green State Univ, 1981) 104p (OGS)
Campbell, W.W. HISTORY OF HENRY COUNTY OHIO. 1905 (reprinted 1982 from HISTORY OF THE
    MAUMEE RIVER BASIN by Slocum) 330p (SLO)
Christian, Donna K. GUIDE TO NEWSPAPER HOLDINGS AT THE CENTER FOR ARCHIVAL COL-
    LECTIONS. (Bowling Green OH: Bowling Green State Univ, 1980) 64p (OGS)
CITY/COUNTY DIRECTORIES: check holdings of OHS & local public library.
Clegg, Michael, ed. DEFIANCE, FULTON, HENRY, PAULDING, PUTNAM, WILLIAMS & WOOD
    COUNTIES OHIO NEWSPAPER OBITUARY ABSTRACTS, 1838-1870 (OHIO NEWSPAPER SERIES
    VOL.5) (Ft.Wayne IN: author, 1987) 75p (OGS)
COMMEMORATIVE BIOGRAPHICAL RECORD OF NORTHWESTERN OHIO: INCLUDING THE
    COUNTIES OF DEFIANCE, HENRY, WILLIAMS & FULTON. (Chicago: J.H.Beers & Co., 1899)
    616p (LDS,OGS,SLO,DAR)(RPI)

Curtindale, Barbara R. HISTORY AND RECORDS OF HOPE LUTHERAN CHURCH, HAMLER, OHIO, 1879-PRESENT. (Lake orion MI: author, 1976) 2v (LDS,SLO)

Daughters of the American Revolution. MARRIAGE RECORDS, 1847-1859 BOOK A, HENRY COUNTY. (SLO)

Gebolys, Edith H. INSCRIPTIONS FROM STONES IN TEXAS CEMETERY, HENRY CO., TEXAS, OHIO. (LDS)

Glasbrenner, Helen. CEMETERY RECORDS IN PUTNAM AND HENRY COUNTIES, OHIO. 1979. 202p (LDS)

HAMLER, OHIO: 100 YEARS. 1975. (SLO)

HENRY COUNTY OHIO: A COLLECTION OF HISTORICAL SKETCHES AND FAMILY HISTORIES. (Napoleon OH: Henry Co Hist Soc., 1976-79). 3v. (SLO,DAR,LDS)

HOY FAMILY, HOY CEMETERY, HENRY COUNTY OHIO. nd. 4p. (OGS)

ITEMIZED DETAILED STATEMENT OF THE HENRY COUNTY (OHIO) WAR CHEST [w/ WWI Honor Roll] c.1918. 120p

Jacobs, Thelma R. CEMETERY INSCRIPTIONS, HENRY CEMETERY LOCATED ON STATE RT.65 AND COUNTY ROAD P. 1974. (LDS)

Knapp, Horace S. HISTORY OF THE MAUMEE VALLEY. (Toledo OH: author, 1872) 685p. (DAR,OHS,SLO)

Levinson, Marilyn. GUIDE TO NEWSPAPER HOLDINGS AT THE CENTER FOR ARCHIVAL COLLECTIONS. 2nd Edition. (Bowling Green OH: Bowling Green State Univ., 1987)

Maumee Valley Pioneer Assn. ADDRESSES, MEMORIALS, AND SKETCHES. 1900,1901. (SLO)

Seaman, Vashti. MISCELLANEOUS OHIO BIBLE AND CEMETERY RECORDS. (SLO)

Slentz, Roy S. ANNALS OF INWOOD FARM, 1983: & THE WASHINGTON STREET GANG, 1834-1984. (LDS)

Slentz, Roy S. SLENTZ, THE SCHOOLMASTER OF RIDGEVILLE CORNERS. (Napoleon OH: author, 1979) 154p (LDS)

Slentz, Roy S. SLENTZ: THE BLACK SWAMP SCHOOLMASTER. 1979. (LDS)

Slocum, C.E. HISTORY OF THE MAUMEE RIVER BASIN FROM THE EARLIEST ACCOUNT TO ITS ORGANIZATION INTO COUNTIES. 1905. 638p. (SLO)

Winter, Nevin O. HISTORY OF NORTHWEST OHIO. (Chicago: Lewis Pub.Co.,1917) 3v. (SLO,OHS)

# HIGHLAND COUNTY

| | |
|---|---|
| CREATED: | 1805 FROM ADAMS, CLERMONT & ROSS COUNTIES |
| COUNTY SEAT: | HILLSBORO 45133 |
| COURT HOUSE: | 105 NORTH HIGH ST., HILLSBORO 45133 |
| LIBRARY: | 10 WILLETTSVILLE PIKE, HILLSBORO 45133 |
| HISTORICAL SOCIETY: | 151 E. MAIN ST., HILLSBORO 45133 |
| GENEALOGICAL SOCIETY: | SOUTHERN OHIO GENEALOGICAL SOCIETY, PO BOX 414, HILLSBORO 45133 publication: ROOTS AND SHOOTS |
| HEALTH DEPARTMENT: | 135 NORTH HIGH ST., HILLSBORO 45133 (separate offices for Hillsboro City & Greenfield) |
| ARCHIVAL DISTRICT: | UNIVERSITY OF CINCINNATI, CINCINNATI |
| LAND SURVEYS: | VIRGINIA MILITARY DISTRICT |
| BOUNDED BY: | EAST:   PIKE & ROSS CO. |
| | NORTH:  CLINTON & FAYETTE CO. |
| | WEST:   BROWN & CLINTON CO. |
| | SOUTH:  ADAMS & BROWN CO. |
| TOWNSHIPS: | Brush Creek, Clay, Concord, Dodson, Fairfield, Hamer, Jackson, Liberty, Madison, New Market, Paint, Penn, Salem, Union, Washington, White Oak. |

**COURT RECORDS: (LDS MICROFILM)**
Auditor:
    Tax duplicates, 1816-1826.
Clerk of Courts:
    Common Pleas journal, v1-B, 1805-1811, 1808-1821, 1805-1854.
    Common Pleas record, v4,6-8, 1821,1836-1839,1840-1849.
    Chancery record, v1, 1849-1853.
    Common Pleas court docket, 1842-1847.
    Common Pleas criminal record, v1, 1850-1876.
    Supreme Court record, v1-3, 1806-1851.
    Poll books & tally sheets, 1806-1891.
    Indenture record, 1852-1859.
    Abstract of votes, 1880-1891.
    Register of blacks, 1828-1843.
Commissioners:
    Journal, 1811-1903.
    Index to journals, 1840-1903.
County Home:
    Infirmary record, 1909-1912.
Probate Court:
    Administration dockets, 1853-1913.
    Guardians docket, 1872-1906.
    Adm.,exr.,grdn. dockets 1852-1871.
    Birth records, v1-3, 1867-1909.
    Corrections of birth, v1-7, n.d.
    Death records, v1-2, 1868-1909.
    Will index, 1819-1968.
    Will records, v1-13, 1809-1902.
    Marriage index, 1808-1946.
    Marriage records, v1-14, 1805-1903.
    Accounts, v1-20, 1853-1899.
    Bonds, v1-7, 1850-1908.
    Journal record, vB-N, 1864-1901.
    Complete record, v1-14, 1852-1901.
    Naturalization records, 1879-1891.
Recorder:
    General index to deeds, 1804-1964.
    Deed records, v1-92, 1803-1901.
    General index to mortgages, 1859-1909.
    Soldiers' discharge records, 1864-1865.
Miscellaneous:
    Society of Friends:
    New Clear Creek school, 1882-1886,1891-1893.
    Fairfield Young People's Soc., minutes, 1896-1903.
    Fairfield Monthly Meeting, records, 1807-1941.
    Fairfield Quarterly meeting, records, 1815-1948.
    Fall Creek minutes & records, 1812-1854.
    Hardins Creek business meeting, 1947.
    Leesburg records, 1836-1974.
    Leesburg minutes, 1916-1949.
    New Lexington Sabbath school, 1885-1890.
    Rocky Spring Presby. Church baptisms, 1810-1836, by DAR.
    Birth registers of ...Highland Co...c1870-1907.
    Marriages by Rev.Smith, 1862-1900, by DAR.
    Marple Collection (news clippings), Leesburg, 1830-1954.

Cemetery records, State Library of Ohio collection.

## OHIO HISTORICAL SOCIETY: (MICROFILM)
Clerk of Courts:
Common Pleas journal, v1-B, 1805-1811, 1808-1821, 1805-1854.
Common Pleas record, v4,6-8, 1821,1836-1839,1840-1849.
Chancery record, v1, 1849-1853.
Common Pleas court docket, 1842-1847.
Common Pleas criminal record, v1, 1850-1876.
Supreme Court record, v1-3, 1806-1851.
Poll books & tally sheets, 1806-1891.
Indenture record, 1852-1859.
Abstract of votes, 1880-1891.
Register of blacks, 1828-1843.
Commissioners:
Journal, 1811-1903.
Index to journals, 1840-1903.
County Home:
Infirmary record, 1909-1912.
Miscellaneous:
Register of blacks in Ohio counties, 1828-1843.
Marriages, 1805-1820, by DAR.
Cemetery records of Auglaize,Highland & Mercer Cos., by DAR.
Cemetery records & inscriptions, by DAR.
Church records, by DAR.

## CENSUS RECORDS  (OHS,SLO,OGS,LDS)
1820-1880, 1900-1910; 1890 VETERANS; 1880,1900 SOUNDEX; 1910 MIRACODE

## AGRICULTURAL CENSUS SCHEDULES  (OHS,SLO-mic)
1850,1860,1870,1880

## PRODUCTS OF INDUSTRY CENSUS SCHEDULE  (OHS,SLO-mic)
1850,1870,1880

## MORTALITY CENSUS SCHEDULES (OHS,SLO-mic)
1850,1860

## DEFECTIVE & DEPENDENT CENSUS SCHEDULES (OHS,SLO-mic)
1880

## NEWSPAPERS: [GUIDE TO OHIO NEWSPAPERS, 1793-1973]
Greenfield, Hillsboro, Leesburg, Lynchburg.

## TAX RECORDS (OHS & LDS)
1806-1814,1816-1826,1835.

## GENEALOGICAL PERIODICAL ARTICLES
Bell, Carol Willsey. OHIO GENEALOGICAL PERIODICAL INDEX: A COUNTY GUIDE (Youngstown, OH: author, 6th ed., 1987)

## PUBLISHED SOURCES:
Adams, Marilyn. INDEX TO CIVIL WAR VETERANS & WIDOWS IN SOUTHERN OHIO, 1890 FEDERAL CENSUS (Cols,OH: Franklin Co Chapter OGS,1986) 84p
ATLAS OF HIGHLAND COUNTY OHIO. (H.C.Mead & Co., 1887) 70p

Ayres, E.J. HIGHLAND PIONEER SKETCHES AND FAMILY GENEALOGIES. 1971. 1077p. (SLO)

Ayres, E.J. HILLS OF HIGHLAND. 1971. 939p (SLO)

Ayres, Mrs. Edwin B. THE HILLSBORO STORY: 150 YEARS OF PROGRESS, 1807-1957. (Springfield OH: H.K.Skinner, 1957) 78p (LDS)

CITY/COUNTY DIRECTORIES: check holdings of OHS & local public library.

Core, Mrs. John. GREENFIELD OHIO CHURCH AND CEMETERY RECORD. (DAR,LDS)

Daughters of the American Revolution. CEMETERIES OF SOUTHERN OHIO. (SLO)

Daughters of the American Revolution. CEMETERY RECORDS, HIGHLAND COUNTY, OHIO, LIMES CEMETERY. (SLO)

Daughters of the American Revolution. CEMETERY RECORDS OF ROCKY SPRINGS PRESBYTERIAN CHURCH, HIGHLAND COUNTY, OHIO. (SLO)

Daughters of the American Revolution. OHIO CEMETERY RECORDS, AUGLAIZE, HIGHLAND AND MERCER COUNTIES. (SLO)

Daughters of the American Revolution. MARRIAGE RECORDS A-Z (1805-1820) & MARRIAGES BY REV.SMITH, 1862-1900, HIGHLAND COUNTY OHIO. (LDS,SLO)

Daughters of the American Revolution. ROCKY SPRING SESSION BOOK. 3v (SLO)

Genealogical Society, LDS Church. INDEX TO J.W.KLISE'S THE COUNTY OF HIGHLAND, 1902. 8p (LDS)

Genealogical Society, LDS Church. INDEX TO D.SCOTT'S HISTORY OF THE EARLY SETTLEMENT OF HIGHLAND COUNTY OHIO, 1890. 1954. 32p (LDS)

Harris, Frank R. A GREENE COUNTRIE TOWNE. (Greenfield OH: Greenfield Pub., 1954) 180p. (SLO,LDS,DAR)

Harris, Frank R. HOMETOWN CHRONICLES BASED ON THE CHRONICLES OF GREENFIELD AND THE COUNTY McARTHUR, 1870-1949 WITH ADDENDA TO 1955. (Greenfield OH: Greenfield Print & Pub Co, 1955) 246p (LDS)

Hinshaw, William Wade. ENCYCLOPEDIA OF AMERICAN QUAKER GENEALOGY, VOL.V, OHIO. (Baltimore: Genealogical Pub.Co., 1973) (SLO,OHS,LDS)

HISTORICAL DIRECTORY OF PRESBYTERIAN CHURCHES UNDER THE CARE OF G.W.H. SMITH. (SLO)

HISTORY OF ROSS AND HIGHLAND COUNTIES OHIO. (Cleveland: Williams Bros., 1880) 642p (LDS,SLO,DAR)(RPI)

HISTORY OF THE COUNTY OF HIGHLAND. 1878. 13p (SLO)

Hook, Glenn L. HISTORICAL DIRECTORY OF PRESBYTERIAN CHURCHES UNDER THE CARE OF G.W.H.SMITH, S.S. (Georgetown OH: author, 1976) 40p (LDS)

Huff, Truman C. MARRIAGE, BIRTH & DEATH RECORDS OF FAIRFIELD MONTHLY MEETING, LEESBURG, OHIO. 1966? (LDS)

Irwin, W.H. CENTENNIAL HISTORICAL SKETCHES OF GREENFIELD AND VICINITY. 1876. 16p (SLO,LDS)

Klise, J.W. THE COUNTY OF HIGHLAND, A HISTORY OF HIGHLAND COUNTY OHIO. (Madison Wi: Northwestern Hist Assn., 1902) 535p (LDS,SLO,DAR)(RPI)

Klise, J.W. STATE CENTENNIAL HISTORY OF HIGHLAND COUNTY OHIO, VOL.II. 1902. (Reprint, Hillsboro OH: So.Ohio Gen.Soc., 1980) 601p (OGS,LDS)

Lake, D.J. ATLAS OF HIGHLAND COUNTY OHIO. (Philadelphia: C.O.TITUS, 1871) (LDS,SLO)(RPI)

Lathrop, J.M. ATLAS OF HIGHLAND COUNTY OHIO. (Philadelphia: Mead, 1887) 82p (SLO)(RPI)

McBride, David N. & Jane. CEMETERY INSCRIPTIONS OF HIGHLAND COUNTY OHIO. (Hillsboro OH: author, 1972) 563p (LDS,OGS,SLO,DAR)

McBride, David N. & Jane. COMMON PLEAS COURT RECORDS OF HIGHLAND COUNTY OHIO. (Ann Arbor MI: Edwards Letter Shop, 1959) 295p (SLO,LDS,DAR)

McBride, David N. & Jane. MARRIAGE RECORDS OF HIGHLAND COUNTY OHIO 1805-1880. (Hillsboro OH: author, 1962, repr 1982) 398p (SLO,OGS,LDS,DAR)

McBride, David N. PERSONAL PROPERTY TAXPAYERS OF HIGHLAND COUNTY OHIO. (Hillsboro OH: author, 1980) 350p (LDS,DAR,SLO)

McBride, David N. & Jane. RECORDS OF THE RECORDERS OFFICE OF HIGHLAND COUNTY OHIO 1805-1850 (Ann Arbor: Edwards Bros., 1969) 566p (LDS,SLO,OHS,OGS,DAR)

McBride, David N. & Jane. WILLS, ADMINISTRATIONS, GUARDIANSHIPS AND ADOPTIONS OF HIGHLAND COUNTY OHIO, 1805-1880. (Ann Arbor: Edwards Bros., 1957) 340p (LDS,SLO,OGS,DAR)

MARPLE COLLECTION OBITUARY NOTES, LEESBURG, OHIO - HIGHLAND COUNTY. (SLO)

Martin, Alva W. HISTORY OF CLAY TOWNSHIP, HIGHLAND COUNTY OHIO, SESQUICENTEN-NIAL, 1805-1955. nd. 36p (LDS,SLO)

Morgan, Violet. FOLKLORE OF HIGHLAND COUNTY. 1946. 240p. (SLO,LDS) OBITUARY NOTES (NEWSPAPER CLIPPINGS) OF LEESBURG OHIO AND VICINITY 1830-1954 - MARPLE COL-LECTION. (Columbus OH: 1959) (LDS,SLO,DAR)

Scott, Daniel. A HISTORY OF THE EARLY SETTLEMENT OF HIGHLAND COUNTY OHIO. (Hillsboro OH: Hillsboro Gazette, 1890) 194p (LDS,DAR,SLO)(RPI)

Smith, Clifford N. FEDERAL LAND SERIES: A CALENDAR OF ARCHIVAL MATERIAL ON THE LAND PATENTS ISSUED BY THE U.S.GOVERNMENT, VOL.4, PT 1: GRANTS IN THE VIRGINIA MILITARY DISTRICT OF OHIO. (Chicago: American Library Assn.,1982) 395p

Smith, Clifford N. FEDERAL LAND SERIES: A CALENDAR OF ARCHIVAL MATERIAL ON THE LAND PATENTS ISSUED BY THE U.S.GOVERNMENT, VOL.4, PT 2: GRANTS IN THE VIRGINIA MILITARY DISTRICT OF OHIO. (Chicago: American Library Assn., 1986) 306p

Snider, Wayne L. ALL IN THE SAME SPACESHIP, PORTIONS OF AMERICAN NEGRO HISTORY IL-LUSTRATED IN HIGHLAND COUNTY, OHIO U.S.A. 1974. (SLO)

Southern Ohio Gen.Soc. BIRTH AND DEATH RECORDS OF HIGHLAND COUNTY OHIO, 1856-1857. (Hillsboro: the society, 198?) 80p. (LDS,SLO)

Southern Ohio Gen.Soc. EVERY NAME INDEX TO "HIGHLAND PIONEER SKETCHES AND FAMI-LY GENEALOGIES" BY AYERS. (Hillsboro: the society, 1981) 151p (LDS)

Southern Ohio Gen.Soc. EVERY NAME INDEX TO VETERANS' BURIAL RECORDS PREVIOUS TO WORLD WAR I, RECORDERS OFFICE, HIGHLAND COUNTY OHIO. (Hillsboro: the society, 1982) 30p (LDS,SLO)

Southern Ohio Gen.Soc. HISTORICAL AND DESCRIPTIVE REVIEW OF HIGHLAND COUNTY OHIO: A SOUVENIR EDITION OF THE NEW-HERALD, HILLSBORO OHIO, 1893. (Hillsboro: the society, 198?) 52p (LDS)

Southern Ohio Gen.Soc. INDEX TO HILLSBORO NEWS-HERALD, 1904. (Hillsboro: the society, nd)

Southern Ohio Gen.Soc. RECORD OF MILITARY SERVICE IN THE RECORDER'S OFFICE, HIGH-LAND COUNTY OHIO. (Hillsboro: the society, 198?) 28p (LDS)

SOUVENIR EDITION OF NEWS HERALD, 1893, HILLSBORO OHIO. (SLO)

Thompson, Eliza J. HILLSBORO CRUSADE SKETCHES AND FAMILY RECORDS. (Cincinnati: Cranston & Curts, c1896) 207p (LDS,DAR)

Thompson, James H. THE HISTORY OF THE COUNTY OF HIGHLAND IN THE STATE OF OHIO. (Hillsboro OH: Hillsboro Gazette, 1878) 132p (LDS,SLO,DAR)(RPI)

Turpin, Joan. REGISTER OF BLACK, MULATTO & POOR PERSONS IN FOUR OHIO COUNTIES, [CLINTON,HIGHLAND,LOGAN & ROSS] 1791-1861. (Bowie MD: Heritage Books, 1985) 44p (OHS,LDS)

Weidinger, Charlene M. ROCKY SPRING PRESBYTERIAN CHURCH SESSION BOOK, V.1-3, 1810-1867. (SLO,LDS,DAR)

Whitesell, Martha. ABSTRACTS OF BIOGRAPHIES IN HISTORY OF ROSS & HIGHLAND CO OHIO. (Indianapolis: Ye Olde Genealogie Shoppe, 1983) 4p

# HOCKING COUNTY

| | |
|---|---|
| CREATED: | 1818 FROM ATHENS, FAIRFIELD & ROSS COUNTIES |
| COUNTY SEAT: | LOGAN 43138 |
| COURT HOUSE: | 1 EAST MAIN ST., LOGAN 43138 |
| LIBRARY: | 10 N. WALNUT ST., LOGAN 43138 |
| HISTORICAL SOCIETY: | P.O.BOX 262, LOGAN 43138 |
| GENEALOGICAL SOCIETY: | none |

HEALTH DEPARTMENT: 605 SR#664, LOGAN 43138
                      (separate office for Logan city)
ARCHIVAL DISTRICT: OHIO UNIVERSITY, ATHENS
                      (see published Guide to records)
LAND SURVEYS: CONGRESS LANDS, OHIO RIVER SURVEY (SOUTH)
                      OHIO COMPANY
BOUNDED BY: EAST:     ATHENS CO.
                      NORTH: FAIRFIELD & PERRY CO.
                      WEST:   PICKAWAY & ROSS CO.
                      SOUTH:  VINTON CO.
TOWNSHIPS: Benton, Falls Gore, Good Hope, Green, Laurel, Marion, Perry, Salt Creek, Starr, Ward, Washington.

## COURT RECORDS: (LDS MICROFILM)
Auditor:
    Militia commutation & fund, 1818-1903.
    Volunteer relief fund, 1861-1865.
    Tax duplicates, 1819-1838.
Clerk of Courts:
    Supreme Court record, 1844-1859.
    Supreme Court appearance docket, 1837-1879
    Supreme Court minutes, 1844-1851.
    District Court minutes, 1852-1859.
    Minute docket, 1818-1840.
    Appearance docket, 1840-1860
    Complete record, civil, 1821-1851.
    Poll books & tally sheets, 1821-1870.
    Abstract of votes, 1828-1830,1844.
    Partition record, 1821-1833.
    Declarations of intentions to become citizens, 1906-1928.
    Estray records, 1818-1839.
Commissioners:
    Journal, 1818-1903.
Probate Court:
    Will records, v1, 1819-1846.
    Will records, transcribed, v1, 1819-1851.
    Will records, vA-C, 1852-1894.
    Death records, v1-4, 1867-1908.
    Birth records, v1-4, 1867-1908.
    Marriage records, vA-N, 1818-1919.
    Index to marriages, vA-C, 1818-1938.
    Administration docket, 1852-1895.
    Admin.,exrs.,grdns. docket, vC, 1874-1896.
    Appearance docket, vA-B, 1852-1895.
    Admin. letters & bonds, vA-C, 1852-1897.
    Executors' bonds, 1848-1897.
    Sale bills, vA-2, 1831-1862.
    Probate journal, v1-G, 1852-1887.
Recorder:
    Index to deeds, v1-4, 1818-1905.
    Deed records, vA-Z,1-6, 1818-1881.
Sheriff:
    Jail register, 1881-1927.
Miscellaneous:
    Logan, First Presby.Church, minutes, 1829-1887.

**OHIO HISTORICAL SOCIETY: (MICROFILM)**
Auditor:
   Militia commutation & fund, 1818-1903.
   Volunteer relief fund, 1861-1865.
Clerk of Courts:
   Supreme Court record, 1844-1859.
   Supreme Court appearance docket, 1837-1879
   Supreme Court minutes, 1844-1851.
   District Court minutes, 1852-1859.
   Minute docket, 1818-1840.
   Appearance docket, 1840-1860
   Complete record, civil, 1821-1851.
   Poll books & tally sheets, 1821-1870.
   Abstract of votes, 1828-1830,1844.
   Partition record, 1821-1833.
Commissioners:
   Journal, 1818-1903.
Sheriff:
   Jail register, 1881-1927.
Miscellaneous:
   Marriages, 1818-1865, by DAR.
   Cemetery records of Hocking & Vinton Cos., by DAR.

**CENSUS RECORDS (OHS,SLO,OGS,LDS)**
1820-1880, 1900-1910; 1890 VETERANS; 1880,1900 SOUNDEX; 1910 MIRACODE

**AGRICULTURAL CENSUS SCHEDULES (OHS,SLO-mic)**
1850,1860,1870,1880

**PRODUCTS OF INDUSTRY CENSUS SCHEDULE (OHS,SLO-mic)**
1850,1870

**MORTALITY CENSUS SCHEDULES (OHS,SLO-mic)**
1850,1860

**DEFECTIVE & DEPENDENT CENSUS SCHEDULES (OHS,SLO-mic)**
1880

**NEWSPAPERS: [GUIDE TO OHIO NEWSPAPERS, 1793-1973]**
Laurelville, Logan.

**TAX RECORDS (OHS & LDS)**
1819-1838.

**GENEALOGICAL PERIODICAL ARTICLES**
Bell, Carol Willsey. OHIO GENEALOGICAL PERIODICAL INDEX: A COUNTY GUIDE (Youngstown,
   OH: author, 6th ed., 1987)

**PUBLISHED SOURCES:**
Adams, Marilyn. INDEX TO CIVIL WAR VETERANS & WIDOWS IN SOUTHERN OHIO, 1890
   FEDERAL CENSUS (Cols,OH: Franklin Co Chapter OGS,1986) 84p
Atkinson, John H. ASBURY RIDGE: NEW ENGLAND OUTPOST. (Boston: Christopher Pub.House,
   c1950) 268p (LDS)
Bell, Carol W. 1821 TAX LIST FOR THE YEAR 1820, HOCKING COUNTY OHIO. 7p. (OHS)
CEMETERIES, FALLS GORE TOWNSHIP. (OHS)

CHURCHBOOK OF THE EMMANUEL EVANGELICAL LUTHERAN CONGREGATION, MARION TOWNSHIP, HOCKING COUNTY OHIO. (SLO,OHS)

CITY/COUNTY DIRECTORIES: check holdings of OHS & local public library.

Clark, Marie T. OHIO LANDS: CHILLICOTHE LAND OFFICE, 1800-1829. (Chillicothe: author, 1984) 144p (OGS,SLO,OHS)

Daughters of the American Revolution. CEMETERY RECORDS OF HOCKING AND VINTON CO., OHIO. 1953. 34p (DAR,LDS,SLO)

Daughters of the American Revolution. MARRIAGE RECORDS OF HOCKING COUNTY 1818-1865. 1946. 273p (SLO,DAR,LDS)

Daughters of the American Revolution. HOCKING COUNTY MISCELLANEA, VOL.1 [HOCKING CO DEATHS 1867-1869] 11p (SLO)

Daughters of the American Revolution. WILL ABSTRACTS, HOCKING COUNTY OHIO. 1977. 405p. (DAR)

Fairfield Co. Chapter OGS. CHURCHBOOK OF THE EMMANUEL EVANGELICAL LUTHERAN CONGREGATION, MARION TOWNSHIP, HOCKING COUNTY, OHIO. (Lancaster OH: the society, 1986) 1v (LDS)

Gable, Norma P. ABSTRACT OF WILLS, LOGAN, HOCKING COUNTY, OHIO, 1820-1851. 1981. 81p (DAR)

Harris, Charles H. THE HARRIS STORY. 1957. 329p (SLO)

HISTORY OF CHAUNCEY, OHIO. (SLO)

HISTORY OF HOCKING VALLEY OHIO. (Chicago: Interstate Pub Co., 1883) 1392p (LDS,SLO,OHS,DAR)

JOURNEY TO TOMORROW: LOGAN, OHIO 1816-1966. 1966. 84p (SLO)

Lake, D.J. ATLAS OF HOCKING COUNTY, OHIO. (Titus, Simmons, 1876) (OGS,SLO,LDS)(RPI)

LOGAN OHIO DIRECTORY. (Binghamton NY: Calkin-Kelly Directory Co., 1930) (LDS)

Murphy, James L. HOCKING COUNTY DEATH RECORDS, VOL.1, 1867-1883 (Columbus: author, 1986) 109p (SLO)

Ohio University. GUIDE TO LOCAL GOVERNMENT RECORDS AT OHIO UNIVERSITY. (Athens: OU Library, 1986) 61p.

Wells, Jim. JOURNEY TO TOMORROW: LOGAN, OHIO, 1816-1966. (Logan OH: Sesquicentennial Commission, 1966) 84p (LDS,SLO)

Whiteman, Jane. SURNAME INDEX TO THE HARRIS HISTORY BY C.H.HARRIS, 1957. (Tulsa OK: author, 1978)

Whiteman, Jane. SURNAME INDEX TO 1883 INTERSTATE PUB. HISTORY OF HOCKING VALLEY OHIO (Tulsa OK: author, 1980) 27p (LDS)

# HOLMES COUNTY

| | |
|---|---|
| CREATED: | 1824 FROM COSHOCTON, TUSCARAWAS & WAYNE COUNTY |
| SEAT: | MILLERSBURG 44654 |
| COURT HOUSE: | EAST JACKSON ST., MILLERSBURG 44654 |
| LIBRARY: | 10 W. JACKSON ST., MILLERSBURG 44654 |
| HISTORICAL SOCIETY: | 233 N. WASHINGTON ST., MILLERSBURG 44654 |
| GENEALOGICAL SOCIETY: | HOLMES CO. CHAPTER, OGS |
| | PO BOX 135, MILLERSBURG 44654 |
| | publication: HOLMES COUNTY HEIRS |
| HEALTH DEPARTMENT: | 2 HOSPITAL DRIVE, MILLERSBURG 44654 |
| ARCHIVAL DISTRICT: | UNIVERSITY OF AKRON, AKRON, OHIO |
| | (see Folck's Guide to records) |
| LAND SURVEYS: | CONGRESS LANDS, OHIO RIVER SURVEY (NORTH) |
| | UNITED STATES MILITARY DISTRICT |
| BOUNDED BY: | EAST:    TUSCARAWAS CO. |
| | NORTH:  STARK & WAYNE CO. |
| | WEST:    ASHLAND & KNOX CO. |

                              SOUTH:    COSHOCTON CO.
TOWNSHIPS:                    Berlin, Clark, Hardy, Killbuck, Knox, Mechanic, Monroe, Paint,
                              Prairie, Richland, Ripley, Salt Creek, Walnut Creek, Washington.

## COURT RECORDS: (LDS MICROFILM)
Auditor:
    Delinquent tax & land sale record, 1826-1855.
    Tax duplicates, 1825-1838.
Clerk of Courts:
    Supreme Court record, v1-3, 1826-1852.
    Supreme Court journal, 1826-1851.
    Common Pleas chancery records, v1-5, 1827-1852.
    Appearance dockets, v1-8, 1825-1852.
    Common Pleas journals, v1-9, 1825-1852.
    Naturalizations, 1840-1961.
Probate Court:
    Birth records, v1-11, 1867-1966.
    Death records, v1-3, 1867-1908.
    Marriage records, 1821-1939.
    General index to marriages, 1825-1954.
    Index to decedents estates, n.d.
    Index to wills, v1, 1825-1965.
    Record of wills, vA-4, 1833-1911.
    Naturalization index cards, A-Z, 1840-1940.
    Administrators & executors dockets & bonds, 1841-1886.
    Executors bonds, 1862-1897.
    Guardians bonds, 1849-1888.
    Guardians letters, 1857-1875.
    Probate journals, v1-8, 1852-1898.
    Miscellaneous index, no.1, n.d.
Recorder:
    General index to deeds, v1-10,1808-1941.
    Deed records, v1-81, 1825-1915.
    Soldiers' discharge records, v1-6, 1865-1959.
Miscellaneous:
    Berlin Presby. Church, records, 1852-1889.
    Mount Hope Presby.Church, session records, 1845-1854.
    Millersburg Presby.Church, session records, 1830-1858.

## OHIO HISTORICAL SOCIETY: (MICROFILM)
Auditor:
    Delinquent tax & land sale record, 1826-1855.
Clerk of Courts:
    Supreme Court record, v1-3, 1826-1852.
    Supreme Court journal, 1826-1851.
    Common Pleas chancery records, v1-5, 1827-1852.
    Appearance dockets, v1-8, 1825-1852.
    Common Pleas journals, v1-9, 1825-1852.
Probate Court:
    Naturalization index cards, A-Z, 1840-1940.

## CENSUS RECORDS  (OHS,SLO,OGS,LDS)
1830-1880, 1900-1910; 1890 VETERANS; 1880,1900 SOUNDEX; 1910 MIRACODE

**AGRICULTURAL CENSUS SCHEDULES  (OHS,SLO-mic)**
1850,1860,1870,1880

**PRODUCTS OF INDUSTRY CENSUS SCHEDULE  (OHS,SLO-mic)**
1850,1870

**MORTALITY CENSUS SCHEDULES (OHS,SLO-mic)**
1850,1860

**DEFECTIVE & DEPENDENT CENSUS SCHEDULES (OHS,SLO-mic)**
1880

**NEWSPAPERS: [GUIDE TO OHIO NEWSPAPERS, 1793-1973]**
Benton, Berlin, Millersburg, Winesburg.

**TAX RECORDS (OHS & LDS)**
1825-1832,1835,1837-1838.

**GENEALOGICAL PERIODICAL ARTICLES**
Bell, Carol Willsey. OHIO GENEALOGICAL PERIODICAL INDEX: A COUNTY GUIDE (Youngstown,
    OH: author, 6th ed., 1987)

**PUBLISHED SOURCES:**
Almendinger, F.W. HISTORICAL STUDY OF HOLMES COUNTY OHIO. 1962. 105p. (SLO)
Beachy, Leroy. CEMETERY DIRECTORY OF THE AMISH COMMUNITY IN EASTERN HOLMES AND
    ADJOINING COUNTIES IN OHIO. 1975. 200p (LDS)
Broglin, Jana. INDEX TO HOLMES COUNTY OHIO CEMETERY RECORDS COMPILED BY R.H. &
    MARGUERITE DICKINSON. (Swanton OH: author, nd) (OGS)
CALDWELL'S ATLAS OF HOLMES COUNTY, OHIO ILLUSTRATED. 1875. (OGS)
CITY/COUNTY DIRECTORIES: check holdings of OHS & local public library.
Cline, Catherine T. A HISTORY OF THE KILLBUCK AREA. 197? 43p (LDS)
COMMEMORATIVE BIOGRAPHICAL RECORD OF THE COUNTIES OF WAYNE AND HOLMES.
    (Chicago: J.H.Beers & Co.,1889) 836p (DAR,LDS,SLO)(RPI)
Cring, Henry. CALDWELL'S ATLAS OF HOLMES COUNTY OHIO. (Condit OH: J.A. Caldwell, 1875)
    105p (LDS,SLO)(RPI)
Cross, Harold E. OHIO AMISH GENEALOGY, HOLMES COUNTY AND VICINITY. (Baltimore: author,
    19??) 160p (LDS)
Daughters of the American Revolution. HOLMES COUNTY OHIO COURT RECORDS, 1825-1911. 1967.
    127p (DAR)
Daughters of the American Revolution. NOTES TAKEN BY JUDGE LESTER TAYLOR WHILE AP-
    PRAISING SCHOOL LANDS THAT GIVE US FREE PUBLIC SCHOOLS. (SLO)
Dickinson, Marguerite S. HOLMES COUNTY OHIO MARRIAGE RECORDS, 1875-1895 (SLO)
Dickinson, Marguerite S. HOLMES COUNTY OHIO MARRIAGE RECORDS, 1825-1854 (DAR,SLO)
Dickinson, Marguerite S. HOLMES COUNTY OHIO MARRIAGE RECORDS, 1854-1875 (SLO)
Dickinson, Marguerite S. HOLMES COUNTY OHIO CEMETERY RECORDS. (SLO)
Dickinson, Marguerite S. OBITUARIES HOLMES COUNTY OHIO TO 1895. (SLO)
Eberle, Maxine R. A BRIEF HISTORY OF CHURCHES AND MINISTERS IN AREA E (COSHOCTON,
    HOLMES, AND TUSCARAWAS COUNTIES), EASTERN OHIO ASSOCIATION OF THE OHIO
    CONFERENCE, UNITED CHURCH OF CHRIST. (Strasburg OH: Gordon Printing, 1976) 29p (DAR)
Egger, Donald. HOLMES COUNTY OHIO: FLASHES FROM THE PAST. (Millersburg? OH: Library
    Archives of Holmes Co.,1963) 75p (OGS,SLO,LDS)
Fair, Jayne C. HOLMES COUNTY OHIO COURT RECORDS, 1825-1911. (DAR,LDS)
Folck, Linda. LOCAL GOVERNMENT RECORDS IN THE AMERICAN HISTORY RESEARCH CEN-
    TER AT THE UNIVERSITY OF AKRON. (Akron: U of Akron, 1982) 40p. (OGS)
Garber, D.W. HOLMES COUNTY REBELLION. 1967. 19p. (SLO)

HISTORICAL ATLAS OF HOLMES COUNTY OHIO 1875 AND 1907. (SLO)

Holmes Co Chapter OGS. 1830 HOLMES COUNTY OHIO CENSUS INDEX. (Millersburg OH: the society, 1983) 13p (OGS,LDS)

HOLMES COUNTY OHIO 1830 CENSUS. (SLO)

Logsdon, Harry C. SILENT STREAMS - A HISTORICAL SKETCH OF DOUGHTY AND MILITARY VALLEYS IN MECHANIC & BERLIN TOWNSHIPS, HOLMES COUNTY, OHIO FROM 1800 TO 1950. (Millersburg OH: author, 1950) 81p (DAR,OGS)

MECHANIC TOWNSHIP SCHOOL RECORDS HOLMES COUNTY OHIO. 18p. (SLO)

Miller, Betty A. AMISH PIONEERS OF THE WALNUT CREEK VALLEY. (Wooster OH: Atkinson Printing, 1977) 31p (LDS)

Newton, G.F. HISTORY OF HOLMES COUNTY OHIO. 1889. 1953. 160p (SLO)

OHIO AMISH DIRECTORY OF HOLMES COUNTY AND VICINITY. (Baltimore: Johns Hopkins University School of Medicine, 1965) 262p (LDS)

Raber, Nellie M. DIGEST OF WILLS, HOLMES COUNTY, OHIO, SEPTEMBER 1825-MARCH, 1969. (Lakewood OH: author, 19??) 97p (LDS)

Raber, Nellie M. MARRIAGES HOLMES COUNTY OHIO, 1825-1865. (Lakewood OH: author, 19??) 2v, 568p (LDS,SLO)

Raber, Nellie M. THE MARRYING PARSONS OF HOLMES COUNTY, OHIO, 1825-1875. 40p (LDS)

SKETCH OF SOME EARLY SWISS SETTLERS OF HOLMES COUNTY, OHIO AND OF SOME OF THEIR DESCENDANTS, ESPECIALLY FLORIEN GIAUQUE. (LDS)

Smith, Arthur H. AN AUTHENTIC HISTORY OF WINESBURG, HOLMES COUNTY OHIO, INCLUDING A WINESBURG "WHO'S WHO". (Chicago: author, 1930) 87p (LDS)

Smith, Clifford N. FEDERAL LAND SERIES: A CALENDAR OF ARCHIVAL MATERIAL ON THE LAND PATENTS ISSUED BY THE U.S.GOVERNMENT, VOL.2: FEDERAL BOUNTY LAND WARRANTS OF THE AMERICAN REVOLUTION. (Chicago: American Library Assn., 1972) 416p

SOUVENIR: THE THIRTEENTH QUINQUENNIAL, WINESBURG, EX-WINESBURG REUNION. 1955. 36p (LDS)

Stiffler, Andrew J. STANDARD ATLAS OF HOLMES COUNTY. (Cincinnati: Standard Atlas Pub.Co.,1907) 141p (LDS,SLO)(RPI)

# HURON COUNTY

| | |
|---|---|
| CREATED: | 1815 FROM CUYAHOGA & PORTAGE COUNTIES |
| COUNTY SEAT: | NORWALK 44857 |
| COURT HOUSE: | 2 EAST MAIN ST., NORWALK 44857 |
| LIBRARY: | 46 W. MAIN ST., NORWALK 44857 |
| HISTORICAL SOCIETY: | FIRELANDS HISTORICAL SOCIETY, |
| | 4 CASE AVE., NORWALK 44857 |
| GENEALOGICAL SOCIETY: | HURON CO. CHAPTER OGS, |
| | 150 COLEMAN CT, NEW LONDON 44851 |
| HEALTH DEPARTMENT: | 180 MILAN AVE., PO BOX 188, NORWALK 44857 |
| | (separate offices for Norwalk city, Bellevue & Willard) |
| ARCHIVAL DISTRICT: | BOWLING GREEN STATE UNIVERSITY, BOWLING GREEN |
| | (see Biggs' Guide to records) |
| LAND SURVEYS: | FIRE LANDS |
| | CONNECTICUT WESTERN RESERVE |
| BOUNDED BY: | EAST:     LORAIN CO. |
| | NORTH:   ERIE CO. |
| | WEST:     SANDUSKY & SENECA CO. |
| | SOUTH:   ASHLAND, CRAWFORD & RICHLAND CO. |
| TOWNSHIPS: | Bronson, Clarksfield, Fairfield, Fitchville, Greenfield, Greenwich, Hartland, Lyme, New Haven, New London, Norwalk, Norwich, Peru, Richmond, Ridgefield, Ripley, Sherman, Townsend, Wakeman. |

## COURT RECORDS: (LDS MICROFILM)
Auditor:
Tax duplicates, 1816-1838.
Clerk of Courts:
Common Pleas appearance docket, 1818-1853.
Commissioners:
Infirmary records, 1848-1945.
Township trustees report of temporary relief, 1882-1898.
Probate Court:
Administrators & executors dockets, v1-3, 1852-1890.
Administrators & guardians record, v2, 1825-1832.
Admin. & Exec.docket, 1-4, 1852-1898.
Administrators' bonds & letters, v1-4, 1855-1891.
Birth records, v1-4, 1867-1908.
Birth registration & correction, v1-6, dates vary.
Civil docket, v1-3, 1852-1903.
Death records, 1867-1908.
Marriage records & index, v1-12, 1818-1919.
Record of licenses & permits, 1815-1828.
Will records, v1-9, 1828-1911.
Guardians' index, to 1900.
Guardian docket, v1-2, 1852-1904.
Guardian bonds, v1-2, 1855-1884.
Guardian appointments, v3-4, 1884-1894.
Executors' bonds & letters, v1-2, 1855-1888.
Final settlements, v1-8, 1851-1887.
Final records, v1-8, 1852-1889.
Journal, v19, 1851-1889.
Trial docket, 1889-1895.
Index to civil dockets, n.d.
Record of registered nurses, 1915.
Record of limited practitioners, 1916-1967.
Declaration & first papers, naturalization, 1859-1905.
Naturalization records, 1859-1905.
Index to administrators & executors dockets, 1852-1900.
Index to probate estates & guardians, 1815-1852.
Probate docket, admr., exec., & estates, v1-2, 1815-1822.
Probate docket, admrs. & grdns., 1849-1855.
Recorder:
Grantee & Grantor indexes, 1809-1900.
Deeds, old series, v1-23, 1809-1850.
Deeds, v1-59, 1850-1901.
Soldiers' discharge records, 1865-1931.
Miscellaneous:
Hartland Presby.Church, session minutes, 1838-1841.
Bellevue Meth.Epis.Church, records, 1852-1886. (WRHS)
Bellevue Zion United Church of Christ, records, 1861-1983.
Infirmary records, 1848-1945.
Cemetery inscriptions, State Library of Ohio collection.
Lyme Township First Presby.Church, sketch, 1871.
Lyme Township Congregational Church, records, 1787-1969.
Lyme Grange Cemetery inscriptions.


## OHIO HISTORICAL SOCIETY: (MICROFILM)
Clerk of Courts:

Common Pleas appearance docket, 1818-1853.
Probate Court:
  Index to administrators & executors dockets, 1852-1900.
  Administrators & executors dockets, v1-3, 1852-1890.
  Administrators & guardians record, v2, 1825-1832.
  Index to probate estates & guardians, 1815-1852.
  Probate docket, admr., exec., & estates, v1-2, 1815-1822.
  Probate docket, admrs. & grdns., 1849-1855.
  Will record, v10-12, 1903-1911.
Recorder:
  Deed records, 1809-1872.
  Grantee deed index, 1809-1900.
  Grantor deed index, 1809-1900.
  Soldiers' discharge records, 1865-1931.
Miscellaneous:
  Church records, 1837-1898, by DAR.
  Grave records, v1-3, by DAR.
  Tombstone inscriptions of Huron,Lawr.Lick.,Summit & Warren Co by DAR

**MANUSCRIPTS:**
Bellevue Meth.Epis.Church records, 1852-1886. (WRHS)
Huron & Lorain Baptist Assn. records, 1938-1947. (WRHS)
Receipt book, 1864, of draftees in Erie, Crawford, Huron, Ottawa, Sandusky & Seneca Counties Ohio
  who purchased substitutes. (OHS)

**CENSUS RECORDS  (OHS,SLO,OGS,LDS)**
1820-1880, 1900-1910; 1890 VETERANS; 1880,1900 SOUNDEX; 1910 MIRACODE

**AGRICULTURAL CENSUS SCHEDULES  (OHS,SLO-mic)**
1850,1860,1870,1880

**PRODUCTS OF INDUSTRY CENSUS SCHEDULE  (OHS,SLO-mic)**
1850,1870

**MORTALITY CENSUS SCHEDULES (OHS,SLO-mic)**
1850,1860

**DEFECTIVE & DEPENDENT CENSUS SCHEDULES (OHS,SLO-mic)**
1880

**NEWSPAPERS: [GUIDE TO OHIO NEWSPAPERS, 1793-1973]**
Bellevue, Chicago Jct., Clarksfield, Greenwich, Milan, Monroeville, New London, North Fairfield, Norwalk, Plymouth, Wakeman, Willard.

**TAX RECORDS (OHS & LDS)**
1816-1838.

**GENEALOGICAL PERIODICAL ARTICLES**
Bell, Carol Willsey. OHIO GENEALOGICAL PERIODICAL INDEX: A COUNTY GUIDE (Youngstown,
  OH: author, 6th ed., 1987)

**PUBLISHED SOURCES:**
Baughman, Abraham J. HISTORY OF HURON COUNTY. (Chicago: S.J.Clarke Pub.Co.,1909) 2v.
  (DAR,LDS,SLO)(RPI)

Beattie, A.M. HISTORY OF THE FIRST BAPTIST CHURCH OF NORWALK OHIO 1918 - CONTINUA-
TION by Tracy Patrick. 1968. 19p (OGS)

BEGINNING OF NORWALK. 190?. 63p (LDS)

Biggs, Deb. GUIDE TO LOCAL GOVERNMENT RECORDS AT THE CENTER FOR ARCHIVAL COL-
LECTIONS. (Bowling Green OH: B.G.State Univ, 1981) 104p (OGS)

Cherry, Marjorie. BLOCKHOUSES AND MILITARY POSTS OF THE FIRELANDS. (Shippensburg PA:
author, 1934) 94p (LDS,LC)

Christian, Donna K. GUIDE TO NEWSPAPER HOLDINGS AT THE CENTER FOR ARCHIVAL COL-
LECTIONS. (Bowling Green OH: Bowling Green State Univ, 1980) 64p (OGS)

CITY/COUNTY DIRECTORIES: check holdings of OHS & local public library.

COMMEMORATIVE BIOGRAPHICAL RECORD OF THE COUNTIES OF HURON AND LORAIN,
OHIO. (Chicago: J.H.Beers & Co., 1894) 2v (DAR,LDS,SLO)(RPI)

Daughters of the American Revolution. 1820 CENSUS OF HURON CO., OHIO.   1943. 153p
(DAR,LDS,SLO)

Daughters of the American Revolution. BIBLE AND FAMILY RECORDS FAIRFIELD, HANCOCK,
HURON, LORAIN, MAHONING AND WARREN COUNTIES. (SLO)

Daughters of the American Revolution. GRAVE RECORDS OF HURON COUNTY OHIO. 3v. (SLO,LDS)

Daughters of the American Revolution. HURON COUNTY WILLS TO 1852, VOLUME A. (SLO)

Daughters of the American Revolution. INDEX TO EXTANT HURON COUNTY ESTATE PAPERS,
1815-1852. (SLO)

Daughters of the American Revolution. MARRIAGE RECORDS HURON COUNTY OHIO 1816-1865.
3v. (DAR,SLO)

Daughters of the American Revolution. TOMBSTONE INSCRIPTIONS, HURON COUNTY, OHIO.
1943. 101p (DAR,SLO)

Daughters of the American Revolution. WILLARD AREA VETERANS BURIAL SITES. 1976. (SLO)

Duff, William A. HISTORY OF NORTH CENTRAL OHIO EMBRACING RICHLAND, ASHLAND,
WAYNE, MEDINA, LORAIN, HURON, AND KNOX COUNTIES. (Topeka KS: Historical Pub Co.,
1931) 3v (OHS,DAR)

Dush, Joseph F. HISTORY OF WILLARD, OHIO: WITH PIONEER SKETCHES OF NEW HAVEN,
GREENFIELD, NORWICH AND RICHMOND TOWNSHIPS. (Willard OH: author, 1974) 318p
(LDS)

Esker, Jerome A. MARRIAGE RECORDS OF HURON COUNTY OHIO, 1835-1846. (Norwalk OH:
author, 1939.) 126p (LDS)

Esker, Katie P. HURON COUNTY OHIO CENSUS OF 1820. (Washington: author, 1943) 177p (LDS,DAR)

Fedorchak, Catherine F. MINUTE BOOK OF GREENFIELD TOWNSHIP TRUSTEES, HURON COUN-
TY OHIO. (Crown Point IN: author, 1971) 110p (OGS,DAR)

Fire Lands Historical Society. FIRELANDS PIONEER, VOL.1, JUNE 1858-VOL.13, JULY 1878. (Norwalk OH: the society, 1858-1878) (LDS,SLO)

Fire Lands Historical Society. FIRELANDS PIONEER, Series 2, v.1-14, 1882-1937. (Norwalk OH: the
society, 1882-1937) (LDS)

Fire Lands Historical Society. FIRELANDS PIONEER, THIRD SERIES, VOL.1, 1980--. (LDS)

Fleming, May. HISTORY OF PLYMOUTH OHIO, 1815 TO 1930. 13p (LDS)

Foskett, Helen R. HISTORY OF NEW LONDON, OHIO, 1815-1941, WITH A BRIEF SUMMARY OF
RECENT HISTORY, 1941-1972. (New London OH: Public Library, 1976) 350p. (SLO,LDS)

GENEALOGICAL DATA RELATING TO WOMEN IN THE WESTERN RESERVE BEFORE 1840 (1850)
(Cleveland: Centennial Commission, 1943) (WRHS,LDS)

GRAVE RECORDS OF HURON COUNTY, OHIO. 3v. (SLO)

Griffin, Mrs. Kenneth E. GOLD RUSH DAYS, 1852-1853: FROM HURON COUNTY OHIO TO CALIFOR-
NIA. 1983. 119p (LDS)

Griffin, Paula P. DAY CEMETERY, NEW LONDON TWP., HURON CO., OHIO. 32p (LDS,SLO)

HISTORY OF THE BAPTIST CHURCH OF PERU OHIO, 1837-1898. (Peru OH: Peru Village Farm
Woman's Club, nd) (LDS,SLO)

HONOR ROLL OF HURON COUNTY, OHIO, 1917-1918. nd . 200p (OGS)

HURON COUNTY OHIO PLAT BOOK & INDEX OF OWNERS. (Town & Country Pub., 1973) 40p.
(OGS)

INDEX TO THE MICROFILM EDITION OF GENEALOGICAL DATA RELATING TO WOMEN IN THE WESTERN RESERVE BEFORE 1840. (Cleveland: Western Reserve His Soc., 1976) 226p (OGS,WRHS)

Jacobs, Thelma R. LYME GRANGE CEMETERY LOCATED ON STATE ROUTE 18 AND 20 AND YOUNG RD., LYME TOWNSHIP, OHIO. (LDS)

Keesy, William A. ROSTER OF RICHMOND SOLDIERS AND HISTORY OF RICHMOND TOWNSHIP. (Norwalk OH: Laning Co., 1908) 89p (LDS,SLO)

Lake, D.J. ATLAS OF HURON COUNTY OHIO. 1873. (SLO)(RPI)

Levinson, Marilyn. GUIDE TO NEWSPAPER HOLDINGS AT THE CENTER FOR ARCHIVAL COLLECTIONS. 2nd Edition. (Bowling Green OH: B.G.State Univ.,1987)

LYME TOWNSHIP: STRONG'S RIDGE, VOL.1, PIONEERS PROGRESS 1810-1835. (Bellevue OH: Historic Lyme Church Assn., 1973?. 44p.

LYME TOWNSHIP: THE WORLD GROWS SMALLER, 1836-1860, VOL.2 (Bellevue OH: Historic Lyme Church Assn., 1973?) 60p

Mesnard, H.W. ATLAS OF HURON COUNTY OHIO. (Cleveland OH: L.B.Mesnard, 1891) (LC,SLO)(RPI)

Meyers, Mrs.C.C. MARRIAGES PERFORMED BY REV.STEVENS...IN HURON CO OHIO...1825-1859 (Severna Park MD: author, 1959) 9p (LDS)

MILAN TOWNSHIP AND VILLAGE, ONE HUNDRED AND FIFTY YEARS: THE HISTORY OF OUR COMMUNITY... (Milan OH: Ledger Pub., 1959) 64p (LDS)

Norwalk Lions Club. SOUVENIR BOOK - NORWALK HOMECOMING & OHIO SESQUICENTENNIAL CELEBRATION. 1958. 72p. (OGS)

Norwalk Lions Club. SOUVENIR BOOK - NORWALK SESQUICENTENNIAL. 1967. 64p. (OGS)

NORWALK NEGROES - PIONEER DAYS TO 1967. A SESQUICENTENNIAL PUBLICATION. 1967. 21p. (OGS)

NORWALK OHIO DIRECTORY. (Binghamton NY: Calkin-Kelly Dir.Co., 1930-)(LDS)

Peru Village Farm Woman's Club. HISTORY OF THE BAPTIST CHURCH OF PERU, HURON COUNTY, OHIO. (LDS)

PICTURESQUE HURON OR HURON COUNTY OHIO AS SEEN THROUGH A CAMERA. (Bellevue OH: Historic Lyme Village Assn., 1896)(Reprint, Evansville IN: Unigraphic, 1978) 295p (DAR)

Robbins, Iona E. OLENA & HULL CEMETERIES, PERU-OLENA ROAD, BRONSON TOWNSHIP, HURON COUNTY OHIO. 1985. 52p (LDS)

Rowley, Charles S. THE VILLAGE OF NORTH FAIRFIELD AND A ROLLING STONE. (Baltimore: Genealogical Pub.Co., 1975) 109p

Rowley, Leverett A. NORTH FAIRFIELD OHIO: REMINISCENCES OF LIFE IN AN EARLY AMERICAN TOWN. (Baltimore: Genealogical Pub.Co., 1974) 101p

Ryan, James A. THE TOWN OF MILAN. (Sandusky OH: author, 1928) 96p (LDS)

Timman, Henry. VOLUME A, HURON COUNTY WILLS TO 1852. (Norwalk OH: author, 1960) 50p. (LDS,SLO)

Timman, Henry. JUST LIKE OLD TIMES-BOOK I 1972-1974. [NEWSPAPER ITEMS] (Norwalk OH: author, 1982) 142p (OGS,LDS,SLO)

Timman, Henry. JUST LIKE OLD TIMES-BOOK II [NEWSPAPER ITEMS] (Norwalk OH: author,1983) (OGS,LDS)

Timman, Henry. JUST LIKE OLD TIMES-BOOK III 1978-1980. [NEWSPAPER ITEMS] (Norwalk OH: author, 1984) 174p (OGS)

Timman, Henry. JUST LIKE OLD TIMES-BOOK IV 1981-1983. [NEWSPAPER ITEMS] (Norwalk OH: author, 1985) 175p (OGS)

Timman, Henry. NEWSPAPER ABSTRACTS, HURON COUNTY OHIO, 1822-1835. (Norwalk OH: author, 1974) 70p (OGS,LDS)

Upton, Harriet T. HISTORY OF THE WESTERN RESERVE (Chicago: Lewis Pub Co., 1910) 3v (SLO)

Weeks, Frank E. PIONEER HISTORY OF CLARKSFIELD. (Clarksfield OH: author, 1908) 163p. (LDS)

Western Reserve Hist.Soc. INDEX TO THE MICROFILM EDITION OF GENEALOGICAL DATA RELATING TO WOMEN IN THE WESTERN RESERVE PRE 1840. (Cleveland: the society, 1976) 226p (OGS,WRHS)

Wickham, Gertrude V.W. MEMORIAL TO THE PIONEER WOMEN OF THE WESTERN RESERVE. (Cleveland: Cleveland Centennial Commission, 1896+) 2v, repr 1981 (SLO)

WILLARD AREA MILITARY ROLLS AND VETERAN BURIAL RECORDS. (Willard OH: Bicentennial Congress, 1976) 47p (DAR)

Williams, J.H. HISTORICAL NOTES OF NORWALK, OHIO. 1941. 44,7p (DAR)

Williams, J.H. & O.Franz. NORWALK'S PUBLIC SCHOOLS - A NARRATIVE HISTORY. (Norwalk OH: Norwalk City School District, 1960) 96p (OGS)

Williams, William W. HISTORY OF THE FIRE LANDS, COMPRISING HURON AND ERIE COUNTIES, OHIO. (Cleveland: Press of Leader Printing Co., 1879) 524p (LC,DAR,SLO,LDS)(RPI)

# JACKSON COUNTY

| | |
|---|---|
| CREATED: | 1816 FROM ATHENS, GALLIA, ROSS & SCIOTO |
| COUNTY SEAT: | JACKSON 45640 |
| COURT HOUSE: | MAIN ST., JACKSON 45640 |
| LIBRARY: | 21 BROADWAY ST., JACKSON 45640 |
| HISTORICAL SOCIETY: | COALTON HIST.SOC., COALTON 45621 |
| GENEALOGICAL SOCIETY: | JACKSON CO. CHAPTER OGS, |
| | PO BOX 807, JACKSON 45640 |
| | publication: POPLAR ROW |
| HEALTH DEPARTMENT: | 200 MAIN ST., JACKSON 45640 |
| | (separate offices for Jackson City & Wellston) |
| ARCHIVAL DISTRICT: | OHIO UNIVERSITY, ATHENS |
| | (see published Guide to records) |
| LAND SURVEYS: | CONGRESS LANDS, OHIO RIVER SURVEY (SOUTH) |
| BOUNDED BY: | EAST: GALLIA & VINTON CO. |
| | NORTH: VINTON CO. |
| | WEST: PIKE & ROSS CO. |
| | SOUTH: GALLIA, LAWRENCE & SCIOTO CO. |
| TOWNSHIPS: | Bloomfield, Coal, Franklin, Hamilton, Jackson, Jefferson, Liberty, Lick, Madison, Milton, Scioto, Washington. |

## COURT RECORDS: (LDS MICROFILM)

Auditor:
  Tax duplicates, 1819-1838.
Clerk of Courts:
  Common Pleas journal, 1826-1856.
  Judgment docket, 1818.
  Common Pleas record, 1816-1852.
  Common Pleas record index, 1816-1904.
  District Court record, 1852-1858.
  Supreme Court journal, 1817-1851.
  Supreme Court record, 1818-1851.
Probate Court:
  Estates & trusts, general index refiled, 1819-1883.
  Wills, vA-B, 1819-1885.
  Death records, vA-C, 1867-1908.
  Birth records, vA-D, 1867-1908.
  Birth registrations & corrections, v1-8, 1941-1963.
  Marriage records, vA-O, 1816-1913.
  Aliens, declarations, v1, 1865-1906.
  General & judgment index, n.d.
  Naturalization records, v1-2, 1880-1906.
Recorder:
  Deed index, A-Z.
  Deeds, vA-Z, 1-9, 1816-1877.

Miscellaneous:
   Jackson Co. Oh. Dutch families 1847-1898.  (Hamilton Tp. school records & St. John's Ev. Luth.
      German Church, Hamilton Tp.)
   Marriages, 1816-1865, by DAR.

## OHIO HISTORICAL SOCIETY: (MICROFILM)
Clerk of Courts:
   Common Pleas journal, 1826-1856.
   Judgment docket, 1818.
   Common Pleas record, 1816-1852.
   Common Pleas record index, 1816-1904.
   District Court record, 1852-1858.
   Supreme Court journal, 1817-1851.
   Supreme Court record, 1818-1851.
Miscellaneous:
   Family & church records, by DAR.
   Marriage records, 1816-1868, by DAR.
   Manumissions of black & mulatto persons, 1816-1854. (in Mss.Div.)

## CENSUS RECORDS  (OHS,SLO,OGS,LDS)
1820-1880, 1900-1910; 1890 VETERANS; 1880,1900 SOUNDEX; 1910 MIRACODE

## AGRICULTURAL CENSUS SCHEDULES  (OHS,SLO-mic)
1850,1860,1870,1880

## PRODUCTS OF INDUSTRY CENSUS SCHEDULE  (OHS,SLO-mic)
1850,1870

## MORTALITY CENSUS SCHEDULES (OHS,SLO-mic)
1850,1860

## DEFECTIVE & DEPENDENT CENSUS SCHEDULES (OHS,SLO-mic)
1880

## NEWSPAPERS: [GUIDE TO OHIO NEWSPAPERS, 1793-1973]
Coalton, Jackson, Oak Hill, Wellston.

## TAX RECORDS (OHS & LDS)
1819-1838.

## GENEALOGICAL PERIODICAL ARTICLES
Bell, Carol Willsey. OHIO GENEALOGICAL PERIODICAL INDEX: A COUNTY GUIDE (Youngstown,
   OH: author, 6th ed., 1987)

## PUBLISHED SOURCES:
Adams, Marilyn. SOUTHERN OHIO TAXPAYERS IN THE 1820'S: GALLIA & JACKSON COS.OHIO.
   (Atlanta GA: Heritage Research, 1979) 53p (LDS,SLO)
Adams, Marilyn. INDEX TO CIVIL WAR VETERANS & WIDOWS IN SOUTHERN OHIO, 1890
   FEDERAL CENSUS (Cols,OH: Franklin Co Chapter OGS,1986)84p
Brill, H.E. THE STORY OF FINLEY CHAPEL. 1902. 61p. (SLO)
Carlyle, G.E. HISTORY OF THE PIONEER MEN AND PLANTS OF SOUTHERN OHIO. 1948. 52p.
   (SLO)
Clark, Marie T. OHIO LANDS: CHILLICOTHE LAND OFFICE, 1800-1829. (Chillicothe: author, 1984)
   144p (OGS,SLO,OHS)

Daughters of the American Revolution. MARRIAGE RECORDS JACKSON COUNTY OHIO 1818-1865. (SLO,LDS,DAR)

Davis, Dan T. EARLY HISTORY OF HOREB CHURCH. 1938. 40p (DAR)

Historical Records Survey. INVENTORY OF THE COUNTY ARCHIVES OF OHIO NO.40, JACKSON COUNTY. (Columbus: author, 1942) 269p (LDS,OHS,DAR)

HISTORY OF COALTON AND COAL TOWNSHIP OHIO SESQUICENTENNIAL, 1803-1953. (np: the committee, 1953) 85p (SLO,LDS)

HISTORY OF THE LOWER SCIOTO VALLEY OHIO. (Chicago: Interstate Pub.Co., 1884) 875p. (SLO,DAR)

Hixon, Frances. CEMETERY INSCRIPTIONS OF JACKSON COUNTY OHIO. (Baltimore MD: Gateway Press, 1982) 2v, 1224p (DAR,SLO,LDS)

Hixon, Frances. NATURALIZATIONS IN JACKSON COUNTY, OHIO 1860-1903. (np: author, 198?) 11p (LDS,SLO)

Hixon, Mary J. SOLDIERS BURIED IN JACKSON COUNTY, OHIO. (SLO)

Ingles, Wayne B. SYMMES CREEK: HISTORICAL EVENTS & STORIES OF THE SYMMES VALLEY., INCLUDING JACKSON, GALLIA & LAWRENCE COUNTIES. (Zanesville: author, 1976) (OHS,SLO)

Jackson Co.Chapter OGS. BIRTH AND DEATH RECORDS FOR BLOOMFIELD TOWNSHIP, JACKSON COUNTY, OHIO: TAKEN FROM ORIGINAL ASSESSORS' RECORDS. (Jackson OH: the society, 198?) 19,14p (LDS,SLO)

Jackson Co.Chapter OGS. BIRTH AND DEATH RECORDS FOR FRANKLIN TOWNSHIP, JACKSON COUNTY, OHIO: TAKEN FROM ORIGINAL ASSESSORS' RECORDS. (Jackson OH: the society, 198?) 21,12p (LDS,SLO)

Jackson Co.Chapter OGS. BIRTH AND DEATH RECORDS FOR HAMILTON TOWNSHIP, JACKSON COUNTY, OHIO: TAKEN FROM ORIGINAL ASSESSORS' RECORDS. (Jackson OH: the society, 198?) (LDS,SLO)

Jackson Co.Chapter OGS. BIRTH AND DEATH RECORDS FOR JACKSON TOWNSHIP, JACKSON COUNTY, OHIO: TAKEN FROM ORIGINAL ASSESSORS' RECORDS. (Jackson OH: the society, 198?) 38,20p (LDS,SLO)

Jackson Co.Chapter OGS. BIRTH AND DEATH RECORDS FOR JEFFERSON TOWNSHIP, JACKSON COUNTY, OHIO: TAKEN FROM ORIGINAL ASSESSORS' RECORDS. (Jackson OH: the society, 198?) 33,23p (LDS,SLO)

Jackson Co.Chapter OGS. BIRTH AND DEATH RECORDS FOR LIBERTY TOWNSHIP, JACKSON COUNTY, OHIO: TAKEN FROM ORIGINAL ASSESSORS' RECORDS. (Jackson OH: the society, 198?) 30,19p (LDS,SLO)

Jackson Co.Chapter OGS. BIRTH AND DEATH RECORDS FOR LICK TOWNSHIP, JACKSON COUNTY, OHIO: TAKEN FROM ORIGINAL ASSESSORS' RECORDS. (Jackson OH: the society, 198?) 60,42p (LDS,SLO)

Jackson Co.Chapter OGS. BIRTH AND DEATH RECORDS FOR MADISON TOWNSHIP, JACKSON COUNTY, OHIO: TAKEN FROM ORIGINAL ASSESSORS' RECORDS. (Jackson OH: the society, 198?) 33,21p (LDS,SLO)

Jackson Co.Chapter OGS. BIRTH AND DEATH RECORDS FOR MILTON TOWNSHIP, JACKSON COUNTY, OHIO: TAKEN FROM ORIGINAL ASSESSORS' RECORDS. (Jackson OH: the society, 198?) 67,44p (LDS,SLO)

Jackson Co.Chapter OGS. BIRTH AND DEATH RECORDS FOR SCIOTO TOWNSHIP, JACKSON COUNTY, OHIO: TAKEN FROM ORIGINAL ASSESSORS' RECORDS. (Jackson OH: the society, 198?) 11,11p (LDS,SLO)

Jackson Co.Chapter OGS. BIRTH AND DEATH RECORDS FOR WASHINGTON TOWNSHIP, JACKSON COUNTY, OHIO: TAKEN FROM ORIGINAL ASSESSORS' RECORDS. (Jackson OH: the society, 198?) 26,15p (LDS,SLO)

Jackson Co.Chapter OGS. BIRTH AND DEATH RECORDS FOR THE CITY OF JACKSON, JACKSON COUNTY, OHIO: TAKEN FROM ORIGINAL ASSESSORS' RECORDS. (Jackson OH: the society, 198?) 21,16p (LDS,SLO)

Jackson Co.Chapter OGS. BIRTH AND DEATH RECORDS FOR THE CITY OF WELLSTON, JACK-
SON COUNTY, OHIO: TAKEN FROM ORIGINAL ASSESSORS' RECORDS. (Jackson OH: the
society, 198?) 57,18p (LDS,SLO)

Jackson Co.Chapter OGS. INDEX TO THE 1875 ATLAS OF JACKSON COUNTY, OHIO. (Jackson OH:
the society, 198?) 28,5p (LDS)

Jones, Romaine A., ed. HISTORY OF JACKSON COUNTY. (Columbus OH: Heer, 1953) 91p (LDS,SLO)

Lake, D.J. ATLAS OF JACKSON COUNTY OHIO.(Phila.: Titus, Simmons & Titus, 1875)(Reprint, Athens
OH: Union Print.Co.,1975) 45p (OGS,LDS,SLO)(RPI)

Maxwell, Fay. INDEX TO EARLY JACKSON HISTORY. (Columbus OH: Maxwell Pub., 1976) 14p (LDS)

Morrow, F.C. HISTORY OF INDUSTRY IN JACKSON COUNTY OHIO. 1956. 291p. (SLO)

Ohio University. GUIDE TO LOCAL GOVERNMENT RECORDS AT OHIO UNIVERSITY. (Athens:
OU Library, 1986) 61p.

PORTRAIT AND BIOGRAPHICAL RECORD OF SCIOTO VALLEY, OHIO. (Chicago: no pub, 1894)
429p (DAR)

Riegel, Mayburt S. JACKSON COUNTY OHIO "DUTCH": SOME RECORDS FROM 1847 TO 1898.
1962.(SLO,LDS)

Roberts, E.O. HISTORY OF THE WELSH CHURCH, JACKSON, OHIO. (Utica NY: Griffiths, 1908)
(LDS)

Scott, Mrs. Ivan. 1860 CENSUS INDEX OF JACKSON COUNTY OHIO. (Columbus: author, 1979) 24p
(OGS)

Willard, Eugene B., ed. STANDARD HISTORY OF THE HANGING ROCK IRON REGION OF OHIO.
(Chicago?: Lewis Pub.Co., 1916) 2v. (SLO,LDS,DAR)

Williams, Daniel W. HISTORY OF JACKSON COUNTY OHIO. (Jackson OH: author, 1900). 188p
(SLO,LDS,DAR)(RPI)

# JEFFERSON COUNTY

| | |
|---|---|
| CREATED: | 1797 FROM WASHINGTON COUNTY |
| COUNTY SEAT: | STEUBENVILLE 43952 |
| COURT HOUSE: | 301 MARKET ST., STEUBENVILLE 43952 |
| LIBRARY: | 407 S. 4TH ST., STEUBENVILLE 43952 |
| HISTORICAL SOCIETY: | JEFFERSON COUNTY HISTORICAL ASSN., |
| | 426 FRANKLIN AVE., STEUBENVILLE 43952 |
| GENEALOGICAL SOCIETY: | JEFFERSON CO. CHAPTER, OGS, |
| | 109 MEADOW ROAD, WINTERSVILLE 43952 |
| HEALTH DEPARTMENT: | COURT HOUSE ANNEX, STEUBENVILLE 43952 |
| | (separate offices for Steubenville City, Mingo Junction & Toronto) |
| ARCHIVAL DISTRICT: | UNIVERSITY OF AKRON, AKRON, OHIO |
| | (see Folck's Guide to records) |
| LAND SURVEYS: | CONGRESS LANDS, SEVEN RANGES |
| BOUNDED BY: | EAST:   BROOKE & HANCOCK CO., W.VA. |
| | NORTH:  COLUMBIANA CO. |
| | WEST:   CARROLL & HARRISON CO. |
| | SOUTH:  BELMONT CO. |
| TOWNSHIPS: | Brush Creek, Cross Creek, Island Creek, Knox, Mount Pleasant, Ross, Salem, Saline, Smithfield, Spring field, Steubenville, Warren, Wayne, Wells. |

## COURT RECORDS: (LDS MICROFILM)
Auditor:
    Tax duplicates, 1816-1838.
Clerk of Courts:
    Common Pleas record, 1803-1851.
    Common Pleas civil action, 1879+.

Common Pleas civil docket, 1804-1854.
Civil appearance dockets, vA-K, 1804-1854.
Criminal appearance docket, 1896-1906,1926-1946.
Domestic relations [closed] 1956-1972.
Final record, civil, 1973-1981.
Judgments & suits index, v3-7, n.d.
Quadrennial enumeration, 1883-1907.
Commissioners:
Journal, 1808-1901.
Index to general journal, 1802-1908.
Probate Court:
Marriage licenses, v1-2, 1844-1886.
Marriage records, v1-24, 1803-1916.
Death records, v1-3, 1867-1908.
Birth records, v1-4, 1867-1908.
Record of wills, v1-9, 1798-1884.
Inventory of estates, v1-16, 1803-1889.
Administrators' dockets, v1-5, 1838-1895.
Executors' bonds, v1-3, 1849-1885.
Administrators' bonds, v1-3, 1849-1885.
Guardian bonds & letters, v1-5, 1867-1893.
Guardians' dockets, v1-3, 1838-1905.
Final record, v1-6, 1852-1888.
Probate Journal, v1-9, 1852-1887.
Naturalization record, 1823-1828, 1854-1904.
Recorder:
Deed index, grantor & grantee, v1-11, 1800-1939.
Deed records, vA-Z, A2-S2, 44-53, 1795-1881.
Miscellaneous:
East Springfield Presby.Church, register, 1865-1933.
Richmond United Presby.Church session minutes, 1852-1881.
Toronto, Island Creek Presby.Church, treasurer's records, 1818-1869.
Toronto, Island Creek Presby.Church, session records, 1826-1897.
Steubenville, Cross Creek Presby.Church, session minutes, 1839-1880.
Annapolis First Presby.Church, records, 1824-1854.
Richmond, Bacon Ridge Presby.Church, records, 1838-1872,1920-1931.
Steubenville, Herald-Star, Pioneer Edition, 1938.
George Jenkins Papers, 1788-1877. (WRHS)

## OHIO HISTORICAL SOCIETY: (MICROFILM)
Clerk of Courts:
Common Pleas record, 1803-1851.
Common Pleas civil action, 1879+.
Common Pleas civil docket, 1804-1854.
Criminal appearance docket, 1896-1906,1926-1946.
Domestic relations [closed] 1956-1972.
Final record, civil, 1973-1981.
Judgments & suits index, v3-7, n.d.
Quadrennial enumeration, 1883-1907.
Commissioners:
Journal, 1808-1901.
Index to general journal, 1802-1908.
Recorder:
Deed records, 1795-1881.
General index to deeds, 1800-1919, 1929-1941.

Miscellaneous:
  Marriage records, 1789-1839, by DAR.
  Quaker meeting records, by DAR.
  Society of Friends, minutes of the Ohio Yearly Meeting, Short Creek,
  (Mt.Pleasant), 1813-1831. (in Mss.Div.)

## MANUSCRIPTS:
Steubenville Female Seminary records, 1829-1836. (WRHS)
Steubenville Coal & Mining Co., records, 1856-1951 (payrolls) (OHS)
Richmond College records, 1872-1903. (WRHS)
Bates-Harrison Family papers, 1802-1856 (Quaker families) (OHS)

## CENSUS RECORDS  (OHS,SLO,OGS,LDS)
1820-1880, 1900-1910; 1890 VETERANS; 1880,1900 SOUNDEX; 1910 MIRACODE

## AGRICULTURAL CENSUS SCHEDULES  (OHS,SLO-mic)
1850,1860,1870,1880

## PRODUCTS OF INDUSTRY CENSUS SCHEDULE  (OHS,SLO-mic)
1850

## MORTALITY CENSUS SCHEDULES (OHS,SLO-mic)
1850,1860

## DEFECTIVE & DEPENDENT CENSUS SCHEDULES (OHS,SLO-mic)
1880

## QUADRENNIAL ENUMERATIONS (OHS)
1883,1887,1891,1895,1899,1903,1907.

## NEWSPAPERS: [GUIDE TO OHIO NEWSPAPERS, 1793-1973]
Carthage, Manhattan, Mount Pleasant, Richmond, Steubenville, Toronto.

## TAX RECORDS (OHS & LDS)
1806-1814,1816-1838.

## GENEALOGICAL PERIODICAL ARTICLES
Bell, Carol Willsey. OHIO GENEALOGICAL PERIODICAL INDEX: A COUNTY GUIDE (Youngstown,
  OH: author, 6th ed., 1987)

## PUBLISHED SOURCES:
1810-1960 SOUVENIR PROGRAM AND HISTORY SESQUICENTENNIAL CELEBRATION CALVARY
  METHODIST CHURCH, STEUBENVILLE, OHIO. (SLO)
Acton, Mrs. William. INDEX OF NAMES TO ATLAS OF JEFFERSON COUNTY OHIO BY BEERS,
  1871. (Steubenville: Jefferson Co Hist Assn., 1976) 25p (LDS)
Ashcraft, Reva & L.Francy. JEFFERSON COUNTY OHIO MARRIAGES, BOOK 5, 1838-1844. (Steuben-
  ville: Jefferson Co Hist Assn., 1982) 105p
ATLAS OF JEFFERSON COUNTY, OHIO. (New York: F.A.Beers, 1871)(Reprint, Steubenville OH: Jef-
  ferson Co.Hist.Assn., 1975) 37p (OGS,SLO)(RPI)
Baker, Wilma S. FATHER AND HIS TOWN: A STORY OF LIFE AT THE TURN OF THE CENTURY
  IN A SMALL OHIO RIVER TOWN. (Pittsburgh: University of Pittsburgh Press, 1961) 143p (LDS)
Bell, Carol W. OHIO LANDS: STEUBENVILLE LAND OFFICE RECORDS, 1800-1820. (Youngstown
  OH: author, 1983) 181p (OGS,LDS)
Burke, James L. & D.Bensch. MOUNT PLEASANT AND THE EARLY QUAKERS OF OHIO. (Colum-
  bus: Ohio Hist Soc., 1975) 45p (OHS,DAR,LDS)

Caldwell, John A. HISTORY OF BELMONT AND JEFFERSON COUNTIES, OHIO. (Wheeling WV: Historical Pub.Co., 1880) (Reprint, Evansville IN: Unigraphic, 1976) 611p (LC,SLO,OHS,OGS,LDS,DAR) (RPI)

CITY/COUNTY DIRECTORIES: check holdings of OHS & local public library.

Daughters of the American Revolution. THE FIRST FIFTY YEARS OF JEFFERSON COUNTY MARRIAGE BONDS, 1789-1839. 2v. (SLO,DAR,LDS)

Daughters of the American Revolution. METHODIST EPISCOPAL CHURCH 1869-1900. (SLO)

Daughters of the American Revolution. QUAKER BOOK OF RECORDS, WOMEN'S QUARTERLY MEETING FOR NEWGARDEN, JEFFERSON COUNTY, OHIO. (SLO)

DiThomas, Mary E. COURT APPOINTED AND CHOSEN GUARDIANS, JEFFERSON COUNTY OHIO, FROM COMMON PLEAS COURT JOURNALS TO 1818. (Mingo Junction OH: author, 1979) 7p (SLO)

DiThomas, Mary E. EARLY RESIDENCES STATED IN JEFFERSON COUNTY DEED ENTRIES, 1788 TO 1812. (SLO)

DiThomas, Mary E. ESTATE ADMINISTRATIONS, JEFFERSON COUNTY OHIO, FROM COMMON PLEAS COURT JOURNALS TO 1818.(Mingo Junction OH: author, 1979) 9p (SLO)

DiThomas, Mary E. WILL ABSTRACTS TAKEN FROM WILL BOOK ONE, 1798-1820, JEFFERSON COUNTY OHIO. (Mingo Junction OH: author, 1979?) 22p (SLO)

DiThomas, Mary E. WILL ABSTRACTS TAKEN FROM WILL BOOK TWO, 1821-1836, JEFFERSON COUNTY OHIO. (Mingo Junction OH: author, 1979) 24p (SLO)

Doyle, Joseph B. 20th CENTURY HISTORY OF STEUBENVILLE AND JEFFERSON COUNTY OHIO: AND REPRESENTATIVE CITIZENS. (Chicago: Richmond-Arnold Pub.Co., 1910) 1197p (SLO,OGS,OHS,DAR,LDS)(RPI)

Doyle, Joseph B. THE CHURCH IN EASTERN OHIO: A HISTORY WITH SPECIAL REFERENCE TO THE PARISHES OF ST.PAUL'S, STEUBENVILLE, ST.JAMES'S, CROSS CREEK, AND ST.STEPHEN'S, STEUBENVILLE. (Steubenville OH: H.C.Cook, 1914) 269p (LDS)

Filson & Sons. PHOTOGRAPHIC RECORD, STEUBENVILLE CITIZENS, 1897. (poster)

Folck, Linda. LOCAL GOVERNMENT RECORDS IN THE AMERICAN HISTORY RESEARCH CENTER AT THE UNIVERSITY OF AKRON. (Akron: U of Akron, 1982) 40p. (OGS)

Francy, Leila. DEATH RECORDS OF JEFFERSON COUNTY OHIO, BOOKS I-III, 1867-1908. (Toronto OH: author, 1985) 218p (LDS)

Francy, Leila. INVENTORY BOOKS I & II 1803-1816, ABSTRACTED, JEFFERSON COUNTY OHIO. (Toronto OH: author, 1983) 29p (LDS)

Francy, Leila. JEFFERSON COUNTY ACCOUNT RECORD BOOK 2, 1824-1832, INCLUD ING THE LEDGER OF DR. P.S.MASON. (Toronto OH: author, nd)

Francy, Leila & R.Ashcraft. JEFFERSON COUNTY WILL BOOK 3A, 1836-1844. (Toronto OH: author, 1986) 26p (LDS)

Francy, Leila. JEFFERSON COUNTY WILL BOOK 3B, 1846-1844. (Toronto OH: author, nd)

Francy, Leila. JEFFERSON COUNTY WILL BOOK 4, 1844-1853. (Toronto OH: author, 1985) 85p (LDS)

Francy, Leila. MARRIAGE RECORDS OF JEFFERSON COUNTY OHIO, BOOK 5, 1838-1844. (Steubenville: Jefferson Co Hist Assn., 1982) 105p (OGS,LDS,SLO)

Francy, Leila. MARRIAGE RECORDS OF JEFFERSON COUNTY OHIO, BOOK 6, 1844-1850. (Steubenville: Jefferson Co Hist Assn., 1985) 81p (OGS,SLO)

Gill, Lance D. THE 1870 CENSUS COMPILATION OF STEUBENVILLE AND JEFFERSON CO., OH. (Lordstown OH: author, 1987) 784p (WRHS)

Gould, Marcus T.C. REPORT OF THE TRIAL OF FRIENDS AT STEUBENVILLE, OHIO...1828. (Philadelphia: Jesper Harding, 1829) 300p (DAR)

Green, Karen M. PIONEER OHIO NEWSPAPERS, 1802-1818: GENEALOGICAL & HISTORICAL ABSTRACTS. (Galveston TX: Frontier Press, 1988) 362p (OGS)

Hanna, Charles A. OHIO VALLEY GENEALOGIES, RELATING TO FAMILIES IN HARRISON, BELMONT & JEFFERSON COUNTIES OHIO. (New York: J.J.Little, 1900) 128p (LC,DAR)

Harshman, Lida F. 1830 CENSUS INDEX OF JEFFERSON COUNTY OHIO. (Mineral Ridge OH: author, nd) 33p

Heald, Edward T. BEZALEEL WELLS, FOUNDER OF CANTON AND STUEBENVILLE OHIO. (Canton OH: Stark Co Hist Soc., 1948) (OHS)

Hinshaw, William Wade. ENCYCLOPEDIA OF AMERICAN QUAKER GENEALOGY, VOL.IV, OHIO. (Baltimore: Genealogical Pub.Co., 1973) 1424p (SLO,OHS,LDS)

HISTORY OF HILL TOP UNITED PRESBYTERIAN CHURCH: BEING THE HISTORIES OF ISLAND CREEK PRESBYTERIAN AND KNOXVILLE UNITED PRESBYTERIAN CHURCHES. 19?? 28p (LDS)

HISTORY OF THE UPPER OHIO VALLEY. [includes Jefferson & Belmont Cos.,OH & Brooke, Hancock & Marshall Cos.WVA] (Madison WI: Brant & Fuller, 1890). 2v. (SLO,LDS)

Humphreville, Elizabeth K. THE FIRST PRESBYTERIAN CHURCH, MT.PLEASANT, OHIO: FORMERLY THE INDIAN SHORT CREEK CONGREGATION. (Mt.Pleasant OH: Committee on History, 1948) 134p. (DAR)

Johnson, William C. NATURALIZATIONS FROM JEFFERSON COUNTY, OHIO COURT RECORDS, 1818-1879: INCLUDING DECLARATIONS OF INTENTION TO BE A CITIZEN, AND ADMISSIONS TO THE BAR. 1982. 7p (LDS)

McConnell, D.T. & F.Garrod. STEUBENVILLE: PAST, PRESENT AND FUTURE. 1872. 91p (SLO)

Powell, Esther W. TOMBSTONE INSCRIPTIONS AND FAMILY RECORDS OF JEFFERSON COUNTY OHIO. (Akron OH: author, 1967) 201p (SLO,OGS,DAR,LDS)

Richardson, Robert H. A TIME AND PLACE IN OHIO. (Tiltonsville OH: author, 1983) 365p (OGS,LDS,SLO)

Richardson, Robert H. THE DEEDS OF YORE JEFFERSON COUNTY OHIO 1795-1806. (Tiltonsville OH: author, 1982) 24p. (OGS)

Richardson, Robert H. TILTON TERRITORY: A HISTORICAL NARRATIVE, WARREN TWP., JEFFERSON COUNTY OHIO 1885-1838. (Tiltonsville: author, 1977) 300p. (SLO,OGS,LDS)

Roof, Joseph A. CHURCH RECORDS, 1834-1877. (LDS)

Schilling, Robert. HISTORICAL NOTES OF KNOX TOWNSHIP, JEFFERSON COUNTY, OHIO. 197?. 103p (LDS,SLO)

Sinclair, Dohrman. PIONEER COLLECTIONS OF JEFFERSON COUNTY OHIO. (Stephens City VA: Commercial Press, 1984) 190p (OGS,LDS)

Sinclair, Mary D. EARLY MARRIAGES JEFFERSON COUNTY OHIO 1789-1838 (Steubenville: D.Sinclair, 1982) 232p (OGS,DAR)

Sinclair, Mary D. JEFFERSON COUNTY OHIO DEATHS 1867-1907. (SLO)

Sinclair, Mary D. PIONEER DAYS - EARLY HISTORY OF JEFFERSON COUNTY OHIO. (Steubenville OH: author, 1962) 172p (OHS,LDS)

Sinclair, Mary D. PIONEER DAYS STEUBENVILLE OHIO. (Steubenville OH: author, 1962). 172p. (SLO,LDS,DAR)

UNION CEMETERY, INCORPORATED NOT-FOR-PROFIT 1854. (Steubenville OH: the cemetery, nd) 10p

Wiggins & McKillop. INDUSTRIES & RESOURCES OF OHIO: COLUMBIANA & JEFFERSON COUNTIES. c1881. (OHS)

Wintringer, Peggy. STEUBENVILLE IN EARLY DAYS. (Steubenville OH: Jefferson Co.Hist.Assn., 1985) 115p (LDS)

# KNOX COUNTY

| | |
|---|---|
| CREATED: | 1808 FROM FAIRFIELD COUNTY |
| COUNTY SEAT: | MT.VERNON 43050 |
| COURT HOUSE: | 111 EAST HIGH ST., MT.VERNON 43050 |
| LIBRARY: | 201 N. MULBERRY ST., MT.VERNON 43050 |
| HISTORICAL SOCIETY: | NEWARK RD., BEAM'S LAKE, MT.VERNON 43050 |
| GENEALOGICAL SOCIETY: | KNOX CO. CHAPTER, OGS |
| | PO BOX 1098, MT.VERNON 43050 |
| | publication: KNOX TREE CLIMBER |
| HEALTH DEPARTMENT: | 117 E.HIGH ST., MT.VERNON 43050 |
| | (separate office for Mt.Vernon city) |
| ARCHIVAL DISTRICT: | OHIO HISTORICAL SOCIETY, COLUMBUS |

| | |
|---|---|
| LAND SURVEYS: | UNITED STATES MILITARY DISTRICT |
| BOUNDED BY: | EAST: COSHOCTON & HOLMES CO. |
| | NORTH: ASHLAND & RICHLAND CO. |
| | WEST: DELAWARE & MORROW CO. |
| | SOUTH: LICKING CO. |
| TOWNSHIPS: | Berlin, Brown, Butler, Clay, Clinton, College, Harrison, Hilliar, Howard, Jackson, Jefferson, Liberty, Middlebury, Milford, Miller, Monroe, Morgan, Morris, Pike, Pleasant, Union, Wayne. |

## COURT RECORDS: (LDS MICROFILM)
Auditor:
  Tax duplicates, 1816-1838.
Clerk of Courts:
  Minutes, 1808-1853.
  Chancery record, vA-J, 1810-1854.
  Chancery & law index, vA, 1808-c1854.
  Supreme Court journal, vA, 1810-1851.
  Supreme Court law record, vA-C,E, 1812-1842,1848-1854.
  Supreme Court chancery record, vA-D, 1812-1862.
  Supreme Court, Owl Creek bank case, 1840.
  Common Pleas appearance docket, 1816-1855.
  Common Pleas minutes, vA-S, 1808-1853.
  General index, 1808-1854.
Probate Court:
  Marriages, 1808-1853, 1860-1912.
  Birth records, v1-4, 1867-1908.
  Death records, v1-4, 1867-1908.
  Will records, vA-N, 1808-1911.
  Estate records, vG-W, 1852-1887.
  Index to guardians, 1852-1922.
  Guardians' bonds, 1855-1876, 1879-1892.
  Probate record, 1849-1854.
  General index, administrators & executors, 1852-1914.
  Administrators' bonds, 1860-1888.
  Executors' bonds & letters, 1860-1896.
  Bonds, misc. & additional, 1861-1907.
  Naturalization of minors & soldiers, v2, 1880-1901.
  Naturalization, declaration of intent, 1860-1906.
  Naturalization record, 1860-1879, 1884-1885.
  Naturalization of aliens, 1880-1903.
  Ministers licenses, 1861-1878.
Recorder:
  Deed index, v1-13, 1808-1878
  Deed records, vA-Z, AA-ZZ, 51-52, 1808-1864.
  Plat books, v1-3, 1852-1949.
Miscellaneous:
  Martinsburg Presby.Church, session records, 1830-1880.
  Gambier, Harcourt Prot.Episc.Church, records, 1856-1919.

## OHIO HISTORICAL SOCIETY: (MICROFILM)
Clerk of Courts:
  Minutes, 1808-1853.
  Chancery record, vA-J, 1810-1854.
  Chancery & law index, vA, 1808-c1854.
  Supreme Court journal, vA, 1810-1851.

Supreme Court law record, vA-C,E, 1812-1842,1848-1854.
Supreme Court chancery record, vA-D, 1812-1862.
Supreme Court, Owl Creek bank case, 1840.
Common Pleas appearance docket, 1816-1855.
Probate Court:
Marriages, 1808-1853, 1847-1860,1860-1912.
Birth records, v1-4, 1867-1908.
Death records, v1-4, 1867-1908.
Will records, vA-N, 1808-1911.
Estate records, vG-W, 1852-1887.
Index to guardians, 1852-1922.
Guardians' bonds, 1855-1876, 1879-1892.
Probate record, 1849-1854.
General index, administrators & executors, 1852-1914.
Administrators' bonds, 1860-1888.
Executors' bonds & letters, 1860-1896.
Bonds, misc. & additional, 1861-1907.
Naturalization of minors & soldiers, v2, 1880-1901.
Naturalization, declaration of intent, 1860-1906.
Naturalization record, 1860-1879, 1884-1885,1880-1903.
Ministers licenses, 1861-1878.
Miscellaneous:
Marriages, c1812-c1865, by DAR.
Cemeteries of Guernsey,Knox,Morrow & Richlands Cos., by DAR.
Tombstone inscriptions of Fairfield,Knox,Lake & Perry Cos., by DAR.

**MANUSCRIPTS:**
Mt.Vernon Presbyterian Church, records, 1841-1843. (WRHS)

**CENSUS RECORDS  (OHS,SLO,OGS,LDS)**
1820-1880, 1900-1910; 1890 VETERANS; 1880,1900 SOUNDEX; 1910 MIRACODE

**AGRICULTURAL CENSUS SCHEDULES  (OHS,SLO-mic)**
1850,1860,1870,1880

**PRODUCTS OF INDUSTRY CENSUS SCHEDULE  (OHS,SLO-mic)**
1850

**MORTALITY CENSUS SCHEDULES (OHS,SLO-mic)**
1850,1860

**DEFECTIVE & DEPENDENT CENSUS SCHEDULES (OHS,SLO-mic)**
1880

**NEWSPAPERS: [GUIDE TO OHIO NEWSPAPERS, 1793-1973]**
Centerburg, Clinton, Fredericktown, Gambier, Mt.Vernon.

**TAX RECORDS (OHS & LDS)**
1809-1814,1816-1838.

**GENEALOGICAL PERIODICAL ARTICLES**
Bell, Carol Willsey. OHIO GENEALOGICAL PERIODICAL INDEX: A COUNTY GUIDE (Youngstown,
OH: author, 6th ed., 1987)

**PUBLISHED SOURCES:**

BIOGRAPHICAL RECORD OF KNOX COUNTY OHIO. (Chicago: Lewis Pub Co, 1902). 218p (SLO,LDS,DAR)(RPI)

Caldwell, John A. ATLAS OF KNOX COUNTY OHIO. (Philadelphia: E.R.Caldwell, 1896) 140p (SLO,LDS,DAR)(RPI)

Caldwell, J.A. & J.W.Starr. ATLAS OF KNOX COUNTY, OHIO. (Granville OH: authors, 1871) (Reprint, Knightstown IN: Mayhill Pubs., 1972) (OGS,LDS,DAR,SLO)(RPI)

CEMETERY IN MORRIS TOWNSHIP, KNOX COUNTY, OHIO. (LDS)

CITY/COUNTY DIRECTORIES: check holdings of OHS & local public library.

Daughters of the American Revolution. MARRIAGE RECORDS KNOX COUNTY OHIO 1810-1865. 3v. (SLO,LDS,DAR)

Daughters of the American Revolution. MISCELLANEOUS TOMBSTONE INSCRIPTIONS. 2v. (SLO)

DeLauder, Richard. KNOX COUNTY OHIO MARRIAGE INDEX 1860-1868. (Mt.Vernon OH: author, 1987) (OGS)

DeLauder, Richard. KNOX COUNTY OHIO BIRTH RECORDS, 1867-1908, A-MAR. (Mt. Vernon OH: author, 1987) (OGS)

Duff, William A. HISTORY OF NORTH CENTRAL OHIO: EMBRACING RICHLAND, ASHLAND, WAYNE, MEDINA, LORAIN, HURON, AND KNOX COUNTIES. (Topeka KS: Historical Pub Co., 1931) 3v (DAR,OHS)

Elliott, Mary Q. BIOGRAPHICAL SKETCHES OF KNOX COUNTY WRTIERS. 1937. 84p. (SLO)

Genealogical Society, LDS Church. INDEX TO NORTON'S HISTORY, 1862. 2p (LDS)

Genealogical Society, LDS Church. INDEX TO HILL'S HISTORY, 1881. 14p (LDS)

Hardesty, H.H. MILITARY HISTORY OF OHIO - KNOX COUNTY EDITION. 1886/87. (OHS)

Hill, Norman N. HISTORY OF KNOX COUNTY OHIO (Mt.Vernon OH: A.A. Graham & Co., 1881) 854p (DAR,SLO,OHS,LDS)(RPI)

Historical Records Survey. INVENTORY OF THE COUNTY ARCHIVES OF OHIO NO.42, KNOX COUNTY. (Columbus: author, 1939) 308p (OHS,LDS,DAR)

INDEX TO GRAVES, KENYON COLLEGE CEMETERY, MAY 23, 1938. (LDS)

James, Peggie S. 1860 CENSUS INDEX, KNOX COUNTY OHIO. (Munroe Falls OH: author, 1973) 66p (OGS,LDS)

JOHN WINTERRINGER'S LEDGER, MARTINSBURGH, KNOX CO., OHIO, OCTOBER 10TH, 1830. 10p (LDS)

Kelly, Laura E. MOUNT VERNON - KNOX COUNTY - OHIO; EARLY SETTLERS. 1954. 29p (LDS)

KNOX COUNTY OHIO BIRTH RECORDS, 1867-1908, LETTERS P-Z. (OGS)

Lorey, Frederick N. HISTORY OF KNOX COUNTY, OHIO, 1876-1976. (Mount Vernon OH: Knox Co.Hist.Soc., 1976) 514,35p (LDS)

Mark, Clara G. FRANKLIN COUNTY OHIO CEMETERY INSCRIPTIONS IN THE UNITED STATES MILITARY DISTRICT. 1948. (DAR,LDS)

Matusoff, Karen. CENTRAL OHIO LOCAL GOVERNMENT RECORDS AT THE OHIO HISTORICAL SOCIETY. (Columbus: Ohio Hist Soc., 1978) 38p (OGS)

Norton, Anthony B. HISTORY OF KNOX COUNTY OHIO. (Columbus: R.Nevins printer, 1862). 424p. (SLO,LDS,OGS,DAR)(RPI)

Raber, Nellie M. INDEX OF WILLS, FAIRFIELD COUNTY, KNOX COUNTY (1808-1855) AND TUS-CARAWAS COUNTY OHIO. (Lakewood OH: author, 1955) 77p (LDS)

Shewalter, Laura. REVOLUTIONARY ANCESTORS LIST [KNOX CO]. (SLO)

Smith, Clifford N. FEDERAL LAND SERIES: A CALENDAR OF ARCHIVAL MATERIAL ON THE LAND PATENTS ISSUED BY THE U.S.GOVERNMENT, VOL.2: FEDERAL BOUNTY LAND WARRANTS OF THE AMERICAN REVOLUTION. (Chicago: American Library Assn., 1972) 416p

Van Voorhis, C.L. CONDENSED STORY OF KNOX COUNTY. 21p (SLO)

Williams, Albert B. PAST AND PRESENT OF KNOX COUNTY OHIO. (Indianapolis: B.F.Bowen, 1912) 907p. 2v. (SLO,LDS,DAR)

# LAKE COUNTY

| | |
|---|---|
| CREATED: | 1840 FROM CUYAHOGA & GEAUGA COUNTIES |
| COUNTY SEAT: | PAINESVILLE 44077 |
| COURT HOUSE: | 47 N. PARK PLACE, PAINESVILLE 44077 |
| LIBRARY: | MORLEY LIBRARY, 184 PHELPS, PAINESVILLE 44077 |
| HISTORICAL SOCIETY: | 8610 MENTOR RD., KIRTLAND 44094 |
| GENEALOGICAL SOCIETY: | LAKE CO.CHAPTER, OGS |
| | 184 PHELPS ST., PAINESVILLE 44077 |
| | publication: LAKE COUNTY NEWSLETTER |
| HEALTH DEPARTMENT: | 105 MAIN ST., PO BOX 490, PAINESVILLE 44077 |
| | (separate offices for Painesville city, Eastlake, Wickliffe, Willoughby, Willowick, Mentor, Kirtland, Willoughby Hills & Mentor-on-the-Lake) |
| ARCHIVAL DISTRICT: | WESTERN RESERVE HIST.SOC., CLEVELAND |
| LAND SURVEYS: | CONNECTICUT WESTERN RESERVE |
| BOUNDED BY: | EAST:     ASHTABULA CO. |
| | NORTH:  LAKE ERIE |
| | WEST:    CUYAHOGA CO. |
| | SOUTH:  GEAUGA CO. |
| TOWNSHIPS: | Concord, Kirtland, Leroy, Madison, Mentor, Painesville, Perry, Willoughby. |

## COURT RECORDS: (LDS MICROFILM)
Assessor:
   Returns of personal property, 1849-1861.
Auditor:
   Bond book, 1840-1904.
   Record of taxable property, 1843-1846, 1852.
   Assessment of real property, 1859,1870.
   Returns of personal property, 1849,1852,1856,1859.
   School accounts, 1840-1906.
   Treasurer's tax duplicates, 1840-1871.
Board of Equalization:
   Minutes, 1852-1900.
Commissioners:
   Minutes, vA-D, 1840-1900.
Clerk of Courts:
   Appearance docket, 1853-1871.
   Chancery record, 1840-1853.
   Court journal, 1852-1884.
   Court docket, 1845-1852.
   Cost execution docket, 1855-1866.
   Cost bill docket, 1841-1854.
   Court records, vA-O, 1840-1873.
   Criminal record, 1840-1877.
   District Court records, 1845-1884.
   Execution docket, vA-G, 1840-1872.
   Index to journal, 1840-1877.
   Journal, vA-J, 1840-1880.
   Judgment docket, 1840-1854.
   Jury book, 1864-1876.
   Law record, 1852-1871.
   Record of bonds, 1840-1861.

Second trial docket, 1859-1883.
Supreme Court judgment docket, 1841-1882.
Supreme Court records, vA-B, 1841-1851.
Supreme Court chancery record, vA, 1841-1852.
Supreme Court journal, 1840-1852.
Supreme Court jury book, 1842-1858.
Witness record, 1847-1860.
Probate Court:
　Marriages, 1840-1923, 1952-1955.
　General index to marriages, 1840-1946.
　Births & deaths, v1-2, 1867-1909.
　Will records, 1853-1899.
　Adoption record, 1928-1931.
　Probate record, vA-E, 1840-1860.
　Final record, vA-M, 1843-1903.
　Probate journal, vA-H, 1852-1879.
　Inventories, 1886-1902.
　Civil dockets, 1853-1909.
　Criminal journal, vD-E, 1926-1940.
　Naturalization records, 1860-1884, 1887-1906.
　Cost bill record books, 1907-1929.
　Real estate records, 1840-1890.
　Jury book, 1853-1891.
　Administration docket, 1840-1885.
　Ministers' licenses, 1846-1885.
Recorder:
　Deeds, 1839-1937.
　Index to deeds, 1839-1950.
　Transfers of property, 1840-1874.
　Plat books, 1852-1951.
　List of personal property, 1840.
School Board:
　School enumeration records, 1842.
Sheriff:
　Sherriff's returns, 1840-1883.
Treasurer:
　List of lands for taxes, 1847-1872.
　List of delinquent taxes, 1847-1872.
Miscellaneous:
　Cemetery inscriptions, State Library of Ohio collection.
　Concord Twp. school board records, 1834-1837.
　Court docket of Charles B.Smythe, JP, 1838-1842.
　Grand River Presbytery minutes, 1814-1818,1829-1870. (WRHS)
　Grand River Baptist Assn., records, 1817-1842,1853-1871. (WRHS)
　Kirtland Presby.Church, minutes or ogranization, 1819. (WRHS)
　Kirtland Congreg.Church, subscription list, 1832. (WRHS)
　Kirtland Twp. trustee's minutes, 1817-1846.
　Kirtland Town Clerk, plat book, 1846.
　Lake Co. school board enumeration, 1842.
　Lake Co. Account book, 1824-1865.
　Leroy Twp. clerk's journal, 1820-1841.
　Leroy Twp. scholars, 1824-1860, poll books.
　Madison First Congreg.Church, minutes, 1814-1818. (WRHS)
　Madison Town Clerk, town records, 1867-1877,1883-1893.
　Mentor & Willoughby Baptist Church, records, 1836-1848. (WRHS)

Mentor Twp. Clerk's records, 1827-1838.
Mentor account book, 1824-1865.
Painesville Republican, 1836-1839.
Painesville Telegraph Weekly, 1822-1846.
Perry Twp. Trustee's records, 1815-1848. (WRHS)
Virginia A. Billings collection.
Willoughby Town Clerk's records, 1815-1874.(WRHS)

## OHIO HISTORICAL SOCIETY: (MICROFILM)
Clerk of Courts:
Common Pleas chancery record, 1840-1852.
Supreme Court chancery record, 1841-1852.
Supreme Court index, 1840.
Supreme Court journal, 1840-1852.
Supreme Court record, 1841-1849.
Probate Court:
Administration docket, 1840-1885.
Wills, 1896-1899.
Miscellaneous:
Connecticut Land Co., Western Reserve land draft, 1795-1809.
Marriages, 1840-1865, by DAR.
Bible records & wills, by DAR.
Cemetery & tombstone inscriptions, by DAR.
Tombstone inscriptions of Knox,Fairfield,Lake & Perry Cos., by DAR.

## MANUSCRIPTS:
Jonathan Goldsmith papers, 1804-1858, Painesville acct.book. (WRHS)
Hedrick E.Paine family papers, 1788-1941, acct.books. (WRHS)
John M.Henderson papers, Willoughby JP, 1834-1850. (WRHS)
Willoughby Temperance Society, records, 1836-1842. (WRHS)
Mentor & Willoughby Plains temperance society, records, 1839-1842. (WRHS)

## CENSUS RECORDS  (OHS,SLO,OGS,LDS)
1840-1880, 1900-1910; 1890 VETERANS; 1880,1900 SOUNDEX; 1910 MIRACODE

## AGRICULTURAL CENSUS SCHEDULES  (OHS,SLO-mic)
1850,1860,1870,1880

## PRODUCTS OF INDUSTRY CENSUS SCHEDULE  (OHS,SLO-mic)
1850

## MORTALITY CENSUS SCHEDULES (OHS,SLO-mic)
1850,1860

## DEFECTIVE & DEPENDENT CENSUS SCHEDULES (OHS,SLO-mic)
1880

## NEWSPAPERS: [GUIDE TO OHIO NEWSPAPERS, 1793-1973]
Fairport Harbor, Kirtland, Madison, Mentor, Painesville, Perry, Willoughby, Willowick.

## TAX RECORDS (OHS & LDS)
none listed; see parent counties.

## GENEALOGICAL PERIODICAL ARTICLES
Bell, Carol Willsey. OHIO GENEALOGICAL PERIODICAL INDEX: A COUNTY GUIDE (Youngstown, OH: author, 6th ed., 1987)

## PUBLISHED SOURCES:
1857 LANDOWNERS' MAPS: GEAUGA AND LAKE COUNTIES OHIO. (Painesville OH: Lake & Geauga Chapters OGS, 1985) 66p (OGS)

Anthony, Elnor. 1859,1860,1861 TAX EVALUATION BOOK. (OGS)

Backman, Milton V. A PROFILE OF LATTER-DAY SAINTS OF KIRTLAND, OHIO, AND MEMBERS OF ZION'S CAMP: VITAL STATISTICS AND SOURCES. (Provo UT: Brigham Young Univ., 1983) 164p (LDS)

Bell, Carol W. ABSTRACTS FROM BIOGRAPHIES IN HISTORY OF NORTH EASTERN OHIO by John S. Stewart, 1935. (Indianapolis: Ye Olde Genealogie Shoppe, 1983)

BIOGRAPHICAL HISTORY OF NORTHEASTERN OHIO EMBRACING THE COUNTIES OF ASHTABULA, GEAUGA AND LAKE. (Chicago: Lewis Pub Co., 1893) 1028p (LDS, DAR,OHS,LDS)(RPI)

Blakeslee, Joel. SKETCHES OF THE EARLY HISTORY OF MADISON. 1863? (LDS)

CENTENNIAL HISTORY WITH DIRECTORY AND LIST OF OFFICERS OF THE METHODIST EPISCOPAL CHURCH PAINESVILLE OHIO. (SLO)

CITY/COUNTY DIRECTORIES: check holdings of OHS & local public library.

Clark, Neva S. INDEX FOR 1840 POPULATION CENSUS FOR LAWRENCE & LAKE COUNTIES OHIO. np, 1976. 22p (OGS)

Cobb, Phillip L. INSCRIPTIONS IN WILLOUGHBY CENTER CEMETERY. (LDS)

Collacott, Margaret O. INDEX FOR HISTORY OF GEAUGA AND LAKE COUNTIES, OHIO. (Mentor OH: Lake Co.Hist.Soc., 1964)(Reprint, Evansville IN: Unigraphic, 1973) 100p (LDS)

Crary, Christopher G. PIONEER AND PERSONAL REMINISCENCES. (Marshalltown IA: Marshall Printing, 1893) 105p (LDS)

Daughters of the American Revolution. ASSESSOR'S RETURN OF TAXABLE PROPERTY IN LAKE COUNTY, OHIO, FOR THE YEARS 1859 TO 1861. 1980? 257p (DAR)

Daughters of the American Revolution. BIBLE RECORDS AND WILLS, LAKE COUNTY OHIO. (SLO,LDS)

Daughters of the American Revolution. CEMETERY INSCRIPTIONS, LAKE COUNTY OHIO. 2v. (SLO,DAR)

Daughters of the American Revolution. EARLY SEMINARIES. 1958. (SLO)

Daughters of the American Revolution. JUSTICE PEACE OLD BOOK, 1855-1896. 1979. 160p (DAR)

Daughters of the American Revolution. LAKE COUNTY OHIO INFIRMARY RECORDS, 1852-1896, 1896-1911. (SLO,DAR)

Daughters of the American Revolution. MARRIAGE RECORDS, 1840-1865. 131p (DAR,LDS)

Daughters of the American Revolution. MISCELLANEOUS RECORDS OF LAKE COUNTY OHIO. 1974. 1v (DAR)

Daughters of the American Revolution. RECORD OF BURIALS, PAINESVILLE, LAKE COUNTY, OHIO. 1971. 263p (DAR)

Daughters of the American Revolution. RECORD OF THE REVOLUTIONARY SOLDIERS BURIED IN LAKE COUNTY OHIO. 1902. 94p (LDS,SLO)

Daughters of the American Revolution. RECORDS OF LEROY TOWNSHIP, LAKE COUNTY OHIO: BOOK NO.1. 1972? 109p (DAR)

Daughters of the American Revolution. REGISTER OF INMATES, LAKE COUNTY OHIO INFIRMARY 1855-1973. (SLO,DAR)

Daughters of the American Revolution. REVOLUTIONARY SOLDIERS, ALPHABETIZED ANCESTRAL LISTS OF CHAPTERS (SLO,DAR)

Daughters of the American Revolution. THE LAND AROUND YOU, A STORY OF LAKE COUNTY OHIO. 1952. 28p (SLO,DAR)

Daughters of the American Revolution. TOMBSTONE INSCRIPTIONS: CEMETERIES IN MENTOR, PERRY & WILLOUGHBY TOWNSHIPS, LAKE COUNTY, OHIO. 1959. 113p (DAR,SLO)

Federal Writers Program. LAKE COUNTY HISTORY. (Cleveland: Western Reserve Hist.Soc., 1940,1941)
     100p (DAR)
Federal Writers Program. LAKE COUNTY LANDMARKS. (Columbus: Ohio Hist.Soc., 1940) 35p (DAR)
Ferris, E.J. HISTORY OF THE LITTLE MOUNTAIN FROM 1810 TO 1887. (Painesville OH: Painesville
     Advertiser, 1887) 34p (LDS)
Freeborn, Robert J. HISTORY OF ST.JAMES PARISH, PAINESVILLE, OHIO (1824-1924): AND HIS-
     TORY OF PAINESVILLE, 1824. 1924? 34p (DAR)
GENEALOGICAL DATA RELATING TO WOMEN IN THE WESTERN RESERVE BEFORE 1840 (1850)
     (Cleveland: Centennial Commission, 1943) (WRHS,LDS)
Hawley, Emma W. CEMETERY RECORDS OF LAKE COUNTY OHIO. (Cleveland OH: author, nd)
     22p (LDS)
Historical Records Survey. INVENTORY OF THE COUNTY ARCHIVES OF OHIO, NO.43, LAKE
     COUNTY. (Columbus: author, 1941. 273p (OHS,LDS,DAR)
HISTORY OF FAIRPORT HARBOR OHIO, 1976. (Fairport Harbor OH: Bicentennial Committee, 1976)
     304p (LDS)
HISTORY OF GEAUGA AND LAKE COUNTIES OHIO. (Philadelphia: Williams Bros., 1878) 259p
     (LC,SLO,LDS,DAR)(RPI)
INDEX TO THE MICROFILM EDITION OF GENEALOGICAL DATA RELATING TO WOMEN IN
     THE WESTERN RESERVE BEFORE 1840. (Cleveland: Western Reserve His Soc., 1976) 226p (OGS)
Kerr, Daniel. MAP OF THE TOWN OF PAINESVILLE AND ITS ENVIRONS, GEAUGA CO OHIO.
     1836. (LDS)
LAKE COUNTY AND GEAUGA COUNTY OHIO MARRIAGES, VOL.II, 1817-1825, 550 MARRIAGES.
     [from New Haven CT Hist.Soc.] 22p (LDS)
LAKE COUNTY'S 125TH ANNIVERSARY SOUVENIR ALBUM, 1840-1965. (Painesville OH: Telegraph,
     1965) 96p (LDS)
Lake County Chapter OGS. 1840 LAKE COUNTY LANDOWNER MAP INDEX. 1978. (SLO)
Lake County Historical Society. EARLY MILLS & HISTORICAL LANDMARKS OF LAKE COUNTY.
     (Mentor OH: author, 1971) (LDS)
Lake County Historical Society. KIRTLAND FILE. (LDS)
Lake County Historical Society. PAINESVILLE FILE. (LDS)
LAKE COUNTY HISTORY. 1941. 100p. (SLO)
Lake, D.J. ATLAS OF LAKE AND GEAUGA COUNTIES. (Philadelphia, Titus,Simmons &
     Titus,1874)(Reprint, Evansville IN: Unigraphic, 1973) 95p (LDS,SLO,DAR) (RPI)
Launius, Roger D. THE KIRTLAND TEMPLE: A HISTORICAL NARRATIVE. (Independence MO:
     Herald Pub.House, 1986) 216p (LDS)
MAP OF OLD BURYING GROUND SHOWING LOCATIONS OF BURIED TOMBSTONES. (LDS)
Mathews, S.H. MAP OF GEAUGA AND LAKE COUNTIES (Philadelphia: author, 1857) 13 maps. (LDS)
Merrell, Fred E. LAKE COUNTY OBSERVES OHIO'S SESQUICENTENNIAL: 1803-1953 OFFICIAL
     HANDBOOK. (np: the committee, 1953) 32p (DAR)
NEW CENTURY ATLAS OF LAKE COUNTY OHIO (Philadelphia: Century Map Co., 1915) 127p (LDS)
Phillips, Vernon S. LAKE COUNTY AND GEAUGA COUNTY OHIO MARRIAGES. (Akron OH: author,
     1934?) 2v (LC,LDS,DAR)
Prusha, Anne B. A HISTORY OF KIRTLAND, OHIO. (Mentor OH: Lakeland Community College Press,
     1982) 130p (LDS)
Rolf, Eleanor G. WILLOUGHBY TOWNSHIP SCHOOLS: THE FIRST ONE HUNDRED YEARS, 1829-
     1929. (Willoughby OH: Bd. of Educ., 1978) 1v (LDS)
Selby, Robert E. LAKE COUNTY OHIO MARRIAGE RECORDS, 1840-1851. (Kokomo IN: Selby Pub.,
     1983) 65p (LDS)
Shepherd, Paula H. KIRTLAND HERITAGE. (Kirtland OH: Printing Assoc., 1984) 93p (LDS,SLO)
Sherman, E.H. LAKE COUNTY OHIO CEMETERY INSCRIPTIONS. (Painesville OH: author, 1929)
     172p,410p. (LDS)
Smith, A.G. INTERESTING TALE OF OLD GEAUGA AND THE MORMONS AS TOLD IN AN
     ORIGINAL WAY BY A.G.SMITH, LAKE COUNTY'S HISTORIAN. (Telegraph-Republican, 1910)
     2p (LDS)
Smith, Percy K. FIRST SETTLERS OF LAKE COUNTY. 1963. 19p. (SLO)

Stark, Alexander C. NEW CENTURY ATLAS OF LAKE COUNTY, OHIO. (Philadelphia: Century Map Co., 1915) 127p (LDS)

Stebbins, Judy J. GUIDE TO THE PAINESVILLE TELEGRAPH, 1822-1829: NEWSPAPER ABSTRACTS WITH INDEXES. (Willoughby OH: Genealogical Research, 1982) 375p (LDS)

Steed, Mildred E. ANCESTRAL TRAIL, DEC.21, 1974-FEB.28, 1976. (articles in Painesville Telegraph) (LDS)

Steed, Mildred H. SOLDIERS & WIDOWS OF THE AMERICAN REVOLUTION WHO LIVED IN LAKE COUNTY OHIO. (Cleveland OH: B.M.Blackmur, 1985) 270p (GH)

Stewart, John S. HISTORY OF NORTHEASTERN OHIO. (Indianapolis: Historical Pub Co., 1935) 3v. (SLO)

Stranahan, H.B. ATLAS OF LAKE COUNTY OHIO.(Cleveland: author, 1898) 114p. (SLO,LDS)(RPI)

Towne, Jeannette & Ernest L. LAKE COUNTY, PAINESVILLE, OHIO, PROBATE COURT MARRIAGE RECORDS: FEB.22,1862 TO SEPT.11, 1904. (Painesville OH: authors, 1979) 240p (OGS)

Trucksis, Theresa. A GUIDE TO LOCAL HISTORICAL MATERIALS IN THE LIBRARIES OF NORTH-EASTERN OHIO. (Youngstown OH: NE Oh Libr.Assn., 1977) 72p (Yo PL)

Turo, Nancy P. KIRTLAND TOWNSHIP RECORDS. 1969. 1v. (LDS)

Tuttle, N.A. METHODISM IN PERRY, OHIO. (SLO)

UNION LIST OF BOOKS ON GENEALOGY AND LOCAL HISTORY FOUND IN LAKE COUNTY OHIO LIBRARIES. 43p (LDS)

Upton, Harriet T. HISTORY OF THE WESTERN RESERVE (Chicago: Lewis Pub Co., 1910) 3v (SLO)

Waldorf, Lula R. THE STORY OF ONE HUNDRED YEARS: FIRST BAPTIST CHURCH, PAINESVILLE, OHIO (1836-1936). 1936? 22p (DAR)

Western Reserve Hist.Soc. HISTORY HALL: A TRIBUTE TO THE MEMORY OF PIONEER SETTLERS AND OTHERS, ERECTED BY THE LAKE COUNTY AND WESTERN RESERVE MONUMENTAL ASSOCIATION, LAKE COUNTY AGRICULTURAL SOCIETY GROUNDS, PAINESVILLE, OHIO, SEPTEMBER 8, 1914. (Cleveland OH: the society, 1983) 13p (LDS,WRHS)

Western Reserve Hist.Soc. INDEX TO THE MICROFILM EDITION OF GENEALOGICAL DATA RELATING TO WOMEN IN THE WESTERN RESERVE PRE 1840. (Cleveland: the society, 1976) 226p (OGS,WRHS)

Wickham, Gertrude V.W. MEMORIAL TO THE PIONEER WOMEN OF THE WESTERN RESERVE. (Cleveland: Cleveland Centennial Commission, 1896+) 2v, repr 1981 (SLO)

# LAWRENCE COUNTY

| | |
|---|---|
| CREATED: | 1815 FROM GALLIA & SCIOTO COUNTIES |
| COUNTY SEAT: | IRONTON 45638 |
| COURT HOUSE: | 5TH & PARK, IRONTON 45638 |
| LIBRARY: | 321 S. 4TH ST., IRONTON 45638 |
| HISTORICAL SOCIETY: | 506 S. 6TH ST., IRONTON 45638 |
| GENEALOGICAL SOCIETY: | LAWRENCE CO. CHAPTER OGS, |
| | PO BOX 945, IRONTON 45638 |
| | publication: LAWCO LORE |
| HEALTH DEPARTMENT: | 2120 SOUTH 8TH ST., IRONTON 45638 |
| | (separate office for Ironton city) |
| ARCHIVAL DISTRICT: | OHIO UNIVERSITY, ATHENS |
| | (see published Guide to records) |
| LAND SURVEYS: | CONGRESS LANDS, OHIO RIVER SURVEY (SOUTH) |
| BOUNDED BY: | EAST:  CABELL CO., W.VA. |
| | NORTH:  GALLIA & JACKSON CO. |
| | WEST:  SCIOTO CO. |
| | SOUTH:  CABELL & WAYNE CO.W.VA. & GREENUP KY. |
| TOWNSHIPS: | Aid, Decatur, Elizabeth, Fayette, Hamilton, Lawrence, Mason, Perry, Rome, Symmes, Union, Upper, Washington, Windsor. |

**COURT RECORDS: (LDS MICROFILM)**
Auditor:
> Tax duplicates, 1820-1838.
> Militia roll, 1863-1865.
> Commutation record, 1864.
> Ohio National Guard members, 1865.
> Enumeration of school-aged youth, 1861-1880.
> Enumeration of blacks, 1863.
> Enumeration of soldiers & sailors, 1895.

Childrens Home:
> Register, 1874-1951.

Clerk of Courts:
> Common Pleas complete records, 1845-1851.
> Appearance docket, 1819-1856.
> Chancery record, 1843-1853.
> Common Pleas general index, 1817-1861.
> Common Pleas journal, 1817-1851.
> Common Pleas record, 1819-1821,1825-1835,1840-1845.
> Common Pleas term record, 1819-1839.
> District Court record, 1853-1858.
> Quadrennial enumeration, 1891-1907.
> Supreme Court record, 1846-1850.

Commissioners:
> Journal, 1817-1904.

County Home:
> Infirmary record, 1888-1915.
> Infirmary register, 1876-1930.

Probate Court:
> Birth records, 1867-1908.
> Birth registrations & corrections, v1-15, dates vary.
> Death records, 1867-1908.
> Marriage records, v1-22, 1817-1909.
> Index to marriage records, 1895-1914.
> Probate journals, v1-5, 1852-1878
> Wills, 1846-1883.
> Declaration of intention, 1877-1888.
> Naturalizations, 1880-1906.

Recorder:
> Index to deeds, v1-2, 1818-1876.
> Deeds, v1-33, 1818-1876.
> Military discharges, & index, 1861-1919.

Sheriff:
> Jail register, 1867-1923.

Miscellaneous:
> Burlington, Congregational Presby.Church, records, 1828-1839.
> Ohio National Guard, 15th Independent Battery, members, 1865.
> Militia enrollment book, 1861: Lawrence County.
> Cemetery records, State Library of Ohio collection.
> Marriages, 1817-1839, by DAR.

**OHIO HISTORICAL SOCIETY: (MICROFILM)**
Auditor:
> Militia roll, 1863-1865.
> Commutation record, 1864.
> Ohio National Guard members, 1865.

Enumeration of school-aged youth, 1861-1880.
Enumeration of blacks, 1863.
Enumeration of soldiers & sailors, 1895.
Childrens Home:
Register, 1874-1951.
Clerk of Courts:
Common Pleas complete records, 1845-1851.
Appearance docket, 1819-1856.
Chancery record, 1843-1853.
Common Pleas general index, 1817-1861.
Common Pleas journal, 1817-1851.
Common Pleas record, 1819-1821,1825-1835,1840-1845.
Common Pleas term record, 1819-1839.
District Court record, 1853-1858.
Quadrennial enumeration, 1891-1907.
Supreme Court record, 1846-1850.
Commissioners:
Journal, 1817-1904.
County Home:
Infirmary record, 1888-1915.
Infirmary register, 1876-1930.
Probate Court:
Declaration of intention, 1877-1888.
Naturalizations, 1880-1906.
Recorder:
Military discharges, & index, 1861-1919.
Sheriff:
Jail register, 1867-1923.
Miscellaneous:
Marriage records, 1823-1839, by DAR.
Marriage records of Lawrence & Fulton Cos., 1817-1822, by DAR.
Cemetery records, by DAR.
Tombstone inscriptions, by DAR.

**CENSUS RECORDS (OHS,SLO,OGS,LDS)**
1820-1880, 1900-1910; 1890 VETERANS; 1880,1900 SOUNDEX; 1910 MIRACODE

**AGRICULTURAL CENSUS SCHEDULES (OHS,SLO-mic)**
1850,1860,1870,1880

**PRODUCTS OF INDUSTRY CENSUS SCHEDULE (OHS,SLO-mic)**
1850

**MORTALITY CENSUS SCHEDULES (OHS,SLO-mic)**
1850,1860

**DEFECTIVE & DEPENDENT CENSUS SCHEDULES (OHS,SLO-mic)**
1880

**NEWSPAPERS: [GUIDE TO OHIO NEWSPAPERS, 1793-1973]**
Ironton.

**TAX RECORDS (OHS & LDS)**
1818,1820-1838.

## GENEALOGICAL PERIODICAL ARTICLES
Bell, Carol Willsey. OHIO GENEALOGICAL PERIODICAL INDEX: A COUNTY GUIDE (Youngstown, OH: author, 6th ed., 1987)

## PUBLISHED SOURCES:
Adams, Marilyn. INDEX TO CIVIL WAR VETERANS & WIDOWS IN SOUTHERN OHIO, 1890 FEDERAL CENSUS (Cols,OH: Franklin Co Chapter OGS,1986) 84p
Adams, Marilyn. SOUTHERN OHIO TAXPAYERS IN THE 1820s: SCIOTO, LAWRENCE AND PIKE COUNTIES.(Atlanta GA: Heritage Research, 1981) 61p (OGS,SLO)
Bester, Louis C. GENEALOGY, LAWRENCE COUNTY, IRONTON, OHIO. 2v. (SLO)
Brown, Paul M. A STORY ABOUT LAWRENCE COUNTY OHIO. (Huntington WV, 1966) 80p (SLO)
Caulley, Thomas A. LAWRENCE COUNTY OHIO MILITARY LISTS FROM THE IRONTON REGISTER. (O'Fallen MO: author, 1981) 49p (OGS)
CEMETERIES, WINDSOR TOWNSHIP. (OHS)
CITY/COUNTY DIRECTORIES: check holdings of OHS & local public library.
Clark, Marie T. OHIO LANDS: CHILLICOTHE LAND OFFICE, 1800-1829. (Chillicothe: author, 1984) 144p (OGS,SLO,OHS)
Clark, Neva S. INDEX FOR 1840 POPULATION CENSUS FOR LAWRENCE & LAKE COUNTIES OHIO. np, 1976. 22p (OGS)
COMBINED ATLAS OF LAWRENCE COUNTY, 1882 & 1887. (OHS)
Daughters of the American Revolution. LAWRENCE CO. OHIO CEMETERY RECORDS, VOL.1. 1951. 37p (DAR,LDS)
Daughters of the American Revolution. LAWRENCE CO.OHIO GENEALOGIES. 1951. 255p (DAR,LDS)
Daughters of the American Revolution. LAWRENCE COUNTY MARRIAGE RECORDS. (DAR,LDS)

Daughters of the American Revolution. TOMBSTONE INSCRIPTIONS HURON, LAWRENCE, LICK-ING, SUMMIT, AND WARREN COUNTIES, OHIO. (SLO)
Douthit, Ruth L. LAWRENCE COUNTY MARRIAGES 1823-1839. 20p. (SLO)
Hamner, Mary P. LAWRENCE COUNTY OHIO NATURALIZATIONS. (SLO)
Hardesty, H.H. MILITARY HISTORY OF OHIO - LAWRENCE COUNTY EDITION. 1886/87. (OHS)
Hardesty, H.H. HISTORICAL HAND-ATLAS AND HISTORIES OF LAWRENCE AND GALLIA COUN-TIES OHIO, 1882.(repr 1985) (SLO,OGS)(RPI)
HISTORY OF OHIO BAPTIST CHURCH, 1804-1895. (SLO)
HUNTINGTON WEST VIRGINIA CITY DIRECTORY...INCLUDING...CHESAPEAKE OHIO. (Pit-tsburgh PA: R.L.Polk & Co., 1930-) (LDS)
Ingles, Wayne B. SYMMES CREEK: HISTORICAL EVENTS & STORIES OF THE SYMMES VALLEY., INCLUDING JACKSON, GALLIA & LAWRENCE COUNTIES. (Zanesville: author, 1976) (OHS,SLO)
IRONTON CITY DIRECTORY. (Columbus: R.L.Polk & Co., 1930-) (LDS)
Jewell, Mrs. Walter. INSCRIPTIONS FROM FIRST BAPTIST CHURCH CEMETERY NEAR NEW LEX-INGTON, NORTHUP, McCALL, FULLER, & BLAKE CEMETERIES. (Arlington VA: author, nd) 13p (LDS)
Jones, John L.E. LAWRENCE TOWNSHIP CEMETERY INSCRIPTIONS, LAWRENCE COUNTY OHIO. (Ironton OH: Lawrence Co Chapter OGS,1984?) 50p (OGS,LDS)
Jones, John L.E. NAME LIST OF LAWRENCE COUNTY OHIO RESIDENTS FROM 1820 FEDERAL CENSUS AND 1818 & 1821 TAX LISTS. (Ironton OH: Lawrence Co Chapter OGS, 1984) 15p (OGS,SLO,OHS,LDS)
Jones, John L.E. ROME CEMETERY INSCRIPTIONS, LAWRENCE COUNTY OHIO. (Ironton OH: Lawrence Co Chapter OGS, 1987) 69p (OGS)
Jones, John L.E. THE FEDERAL CENSUS OF 1820 FOR LAWRENCE COUNTY OHIO. (Ironton OH: Lawrence Co Chapter OGS, 1984) 11p (OGS,LDS)
Jones, John L.E. WINDSOR TOWNSHIP CEMETERY INSCRIPTIONS, LAWRENCE COUNTY OHIO. (Ironton OH: Lawrence Co Chapter OGS, 1986) 74p (OGS)
Lake, D.J. ATLAS OF LAWRENCE COUNTY OHIO. 1887. (SLO)(RPI)
LAWRENCE COUNTY MISCELLANEA, VOL.I. (SLO)

Myers, James C. & Mary L. CEMETERIES OF AID TOWNSHIP, LAWRENCE COUNTY, OHIO. (Gallipolis OH: Gallia Co.Hist.Soc., 1983) 31p (LDS,SLO)

Myers, James C. & Mary L. CEMETERIES OF MASON TOWNSHIP, LAWRENCE COUNTY, OHIO. (Gallipolis OH: Gallia Co.Hist.Soc., 1982) 55p (LDS,SLO)

Ohio University. GUIDE TO LOCAL GOVERNMENT RECORDS AT OHIO UNIVERSITY. (Athens: OU Library, 1986) 61p.

Rutman, Neil. CEMETERY TOMBSTONE INSCRIPTIONS, LAWRENCE COUNTY, OHIO. 1979. 14p. (LDS)

Scherer, Lois D. REMINISCENCES BY REV.JOHN KELLEY, "IRONTON REGISTER" 1854. [Lawrence & Scioto Cos] (Franklin Furnace OH: author, 1984) 33p (OGS)

Shoemaker, Caryn R. LAWRENCE COUNTY, OHIO 1880 CENSUS INDEX (Minford OH: author, 1984) 97p. (LDS)

STORY OF THE GLORIOUS PAST ONE HUNDRED YEARS: 1849-1949, IRONTON, OHIO CENTENNIAL OFFICIAL SOUVENIR. (Ironton OH: Centennial Commission, 1949) 78p (LDS)

STORY ABOUT LAWRENCE COUNTY OHIO. 1966. 80p. (SLO)

Templeton, Marjorie. INDEX TO LAWRENCE COUNTY OHIO GENEALOGIES. 1952. (DAR)

Templeton, Marjorie. LAWRENCE COUNTY CEMETERY RECORDS. (np: author, 1949-50) 37p (SLO,DAR.LDS)

Walton, Thomas A. RECOLLECTIONS OF THE EARLY RESIDENTS OF ROME TOWNSHIP IN LAWRENCE COUNTY, OHIO. (Ironton OH: Ironton Register, 1874) (LDS)

WIGGINS AND WEAVER'S OHIO RIVER DIRECTORY FOR 1871-1872: EMBRACING...IRON TON... (Cleveland OH: authors, 1872) 419p (LDS)

Willard, Eugene B. STANDARD HISTORY OF THE HANGING ROCK IRON REGION OF OHIO. (Lewis Pub Co.,1916) 2v. 1356p. (SLO,DAR,LDS)

# LICKING COUNTY

| | |
|---|---|
| CREATED: | 1808 FROM FAIRFIELD COUNTY |
| COUNTY SEAT: | NEWARK 43055 |
| COURT HOUSE: | NO STREET ADDRESS, NEWARK 43055 |
| LIBRARY: | 88 W. CHURCH ST., NEWARK 43055 |
| HISTORICAL SOCIETY: | PO BOX 785, NEWARK 43055 |
| GENEALOGICAL SOCIETY: | LICKING CO. CHAPTER OGS, |
| | PO BOX 4037, NEWARK 43055-8037 |
| | publication: LICKING LANTERN |
| HEALTH DEPARTMENT: | 675 PRICE RD., NEWARK 43055 |
| | (separate offices for Newark City, Heath & Reynoldsburg) |
| ARCHIVAL DISTRICT: | OHIO HISTORICAL SOCIETY, COLUMBUS |
| LAND SURVEYS: | UNITED STATES MILITARY DISTRICT |
| | REFUGEE TRACT |
| BOUNDED BY: | EAST:     COSHOCTON & MUSKINGUM CO. |
| | NORTH:  KNOX CO. |
| | WEST:     DELAWARE & FRANKLIN CO. |
| | SOUTH:   FAIRFIELD & PERRY CO. |
| TOWNSHIPS: | Bennington, Bowling Green, Burlington, Eden, Etna, Fallsbury, Franklin, Granville, Hanover, Harrison, Hartford, Hopewell, Jersey, Liberty, Licking, Lima, McKean, Madison, Mary Ann, Monroe, Newark, Newton, Perry, St.Albans, Union, Washington. |
| SPECIAL NOTE: | A COURTHOUSE FIRE IN 1875 DESTROYED MANY RECORDS. |

## COURT RECORDS: (LDS MICROFILM)
Auditor:
    Duplicate tax records, 1834,1840.

Tax duplicates, 1816-1838.
Soldiers' burial, 1909-1923.
Clerk of Courts:
    Supreme Court docket, 1834-1844.
    Supreme Court journals & records, 1811-1812,1823-1841, 1841-1851.
    Supreme Court chancery record, vC-D, 1842-1856.
    Supreme Court law record, 1839-1845.
    Supreme Court & Common Pleas court docket, 1814-1825.
    Chancery index, n.d.
    Chancery record, vB-E,O-V, 1819-1854.
    Appearance docket, 1822-1827.
    Court records, 1809-1811.
    Journal, 1816-1819.
    Partition of land, 1816-1912.
    Law record, 1811-1834,1837-1851.
    Common Pleas appearance docket, 1819-1822.
    Common Pleas docket, 1814-1825.
    Common Pleas general index, vA, n.d.
    Common Pleas journal, 1813-1815,1819-1852.
Probate Court:
    Marriage records, v1-20, 1875-1933.
    Index to transcribed marriages, v1, 1808-1879.
    Death records, v1-3, 1875-1908.
    Birth records, v1-4, 1875-1908;registrations & corrections, v1-15.
    Transcribed burnt records, 1867-1875.
    Administration application letters, 1875-1897.
    Will records, vF-H, 1875-1898.
    Index to wills, 1875-1915.
    Index to civil cases, 1875-1917.
    Civil appearance dockets, v4-5, 1875-1891.
    Index to administrators & executors, 1875-1915.
    Executors' docket, v1, 1875-1885.
    Administrators' docket, v1, 1875-1885.
    Guardians' docket, v1, 1875-1885.
    Administrators' & executors' docket, v2-4, 1877-1889.
    Guardians' docket, v2, 1882-1892.
    Record of guardians' inventories, v1, 1877-1913.
    Guardians' bonds & letters, v1-2, 1875-1895.
    Appointment of guardians, v1-2, 1875-1895.
    Letters of administration, 1875-1886.
    Administrators' bonds & letters, 1874-1890.
    Probate journal, v1-4, 1875-1888.
    Inventory & sale bill, v1-6, 1875-1888.
    Complete record, v1-5, 1875-1888.
    Naturalization records, 1867-1906.
Recorder:
    Grantor & grantee index, 1808-1892, 1957-1964.
    Deeds, transcribed, vA-Z,AA-UU,49-179,597-610, 1800-1901,1965-1966.
Sheriff:
    Jail register, 1875-1888,1895-1918.
Miscellaneous:
    Brownsville United Presby.Church, session minutes, 1855-1880.
    Homer Presby.Church, session minutes, 1846-1899.
    Johnstown Presby.Church, session records, 1835-1862.
    Newark, First Presby.German Salems Church, records, 1857-1901.

Newark Second Presby.Church, trustees minutes, 1838-1859.
Newark Second Presby.Church, session records, 1836-1890.
Pataskala, South Fork Presby.Church, session records, 1837-1856.
Utica First Presby.Church, session records, 1838-1891.
Utica First Presby.Church, Women's Missionary Soc., 1875-1881.
Marriages, 1808-1816, by DAR.
Cemetery inscriptions by Johnstown Genealogical Society.

## OHIO HISTORICAL SOCIETY: (MICROFILM)
Auditor:
Soldiers' burial, 1909-1923.
Board of Health:
Board minutes, 1853-1865.
Clerk of Courts:
Chancery record & index, 1819-1824.
Chancery record, 1849-1850.
Supreme Court journal, v1, 1841-1851.
Supreme Court law record, 1839-1845.
Supreme Court chancery record, 1842-1856.
Law record, 1811-1834,1837-1851.
Supreme Court & Common Pleas court docket, 1814-1825.
Common Pleas appearance docket, 1819-1822.
Common Pleas docket, 1814-1825.
Common Pleas general index, vA, n.d.
Common Pleas journal, 1813-1815,1819-1852.
Commissioners:
Journal & index, 1855-1904.
County Home:
Infirmary journal, 1901-1942.
Probate Court:
Naturalization, 1867-1906.
Sheriff:
Jail register, 1875-1888,1895-1918.
City of Newark, Clerk of Council:
Contracts, 1960-1965.
Ordinances, 1824-1867.
Personnel files, 1963-1967.
Resolutions, 1924-1956.
Warrants, purchase orders, 1965-1968.
Miscellaneous:
Marriages, 1808-1816, by DAR.
Tombstone inscriptions, by DAR.

## MANUSCRIPTS:
Licking Land Co. Records, 1804-1806. (WRHS)
Licking Co.Pioneer, Historical & Antiquarian Soc., 1803-1899. (WRHS)
Wm.Robertson & Sons records, Utica Mill. (WRHS)

## CENSUS RECORDS (OHS,SLO,OGS,LDS)
1820-1880, 1900-1910; 1890 VETERANS; 1880,1900 SOUNDEX; 1910 MIRACODE

## AGRICULTURAL CENSUS SCHEDULES (OHS,SLO-mic)
1850,1860,1870,1880

PRODUCTS OF INDUSTRY CENSUS SCHEDULE  (OHS,SLO-mic)
1850

MORTALITY CENSUS SCHEDULES (OHS,SLO-mic)
1850,1860

DEFECTIVE & DEPENDENT CENSUS SCHEDULES (OHS,SLO-mic)
1880

NEWSPAPERS: [GUIDE TO OHIO NEWSPAPERS, 1793-1973]
Granville, Hanover, Newark, Pataskala, Utica.

TAX RECORDS (OHS & LDS)
1809-1814,1816-1838.

GENEALOGICAL PERIODICAL ARTICLES
Bell, Carol Willsey. OHIO GENEALOGICAL PERIODICAL INDEX: A COUNTY GUIDE (Youngstown
    OH: author, 6th ed., 1987)

PUBLISHED SOURCES:
Amner, Mary. DEATH NOTICES IN THE GRANVILLE TIMES, 1880-1941. (Kent OH: author, 1976)
    181p (ad)
Arms, Walter F. CALDWELL'S ILLUSTRATED HISTORICAL ATLAS. (Newark, Ohio: J.A.Caldwell,
    1880?) 183p (LC)
Barcus, Polly & M.Francis. LICKING COUNTY OHIO TRANSCRIBED MARRIAGES 1808-1875.
    (Newark OH: Licking Co Chapter OGS, 1984) 158p (OGS,SLO)
Beers, F.W. ATLAS OF LICKING COUNTY OHIO. (New York: Beers, Soule, 1866)(Reprint, Knightstown
    IN: Mayhill Pubs., 1970) 32p (LDS,SLO)(RPI)
Brister, E.M. CENTENNIAL HISTORY OF THE CITY OF NEWARK AND LICKING COUNTY OHIO.
    (Chicago: S.J.Clarke & Co., 1909) 2v. (SLO,DAR,LDS)(RPI)
BRISTER'S CENTENNIAL HISTORY OF THE CITY OF NEWARK AND LICKING COUNTY OHIO.
    INDEX VOLS.I & II. (Newark OH: Licking Co Chapter OGS, 1981) 107p (OGS)
Bushnell, Henry. THE HISTORY OF GRANVILLE, LICKING COUNTY OHIO. (Columbus: Press of
    Hann & Adair, 1889) (Reprint, Evansville IN: Unigraphic, 1976) 372p (DAR,OGS,LDS,SLO)(RPI)
CITY/COUNTY DIRECTORIES: check holdings of OHS & local public library.
COMBINATION ATLAS OF LICKING COUNTY OHIO, Beers, 1866 & L.H.Everts ATLAS, 1875.
    (Knightstown IN: Mayhill Pubs., 1971) (SLO,LDS)
Daughters of the American Revolution. CEMETERY RECORDS OF FAIRFIELD, PERRY, PICKAWAY
    AND LICKING COUNTIES OHIO. 1967? 54p (DAR,LDS,SLO)
Daughters of the American Revolution. LICKING COUNTY OHIO TOMBSTONE INSCRIPTIONS OF
    OLD FREDONIA CEMETERY. (SLO,LDS)
Daughters of the American Revolution. PROBATE COURT MARRIAGE RECORDS, LAKE COUNTY
    1840-1865 & LICKING COUNTY, 1808-1816. 1938? 131p (DAR,LDS)
Daughters of the American Revolution. TOMBSTONE INSCRIPTIONS HURON, LAWRENCE, LICK-
    ING, SUMMIT AND WARREN COUNTIES, OHIO. (SLO)
Evans, Robert. THE WELSH HILLS. 145p. (SLO)
Everts, L.H. COMBINATION ATLAS MAP OF LICKING COUNTY OHIO. (Philadelphia: author, 1875)
    137p (LDS)(RPI)
Everts, L.H. HISTORY AND ATLAS, LICKING COUNTY OHIO, 1875. (Newark OH: Licking Co Chap-
    ter OGS, 1975) 202p (DAR)
Everts, L.H. NEW HISTORICAL ATLAS OF LICKING COUNTY OHIO. 1875. (OGS)
FIRST PRESBYTERIAN CHURCH, GRANVILLE, OHIO: A HISTORY OF THE CHURCH FROM 1805-
    1955. (Granville OH: the church, 1955) 89p (LDS)
Granville Public Library. DIGGING UP YOUR ANCESTORS: BIBLIOGRAPHY OF THE GENEALOGY
    & LOCAL HISTORY COLLECTION OF THE GRANVILLE PUBLIC LIBRARY. c1974. 6p

Hardesty, H.H. MILITARY HISTORY OF OHIO - LICKING COUNTY EDITION. 1886/87. (OHS)

Hayes, Ellen. WILD TURKEYS AND TALLOW CANDLES. (Boston: Four Seas Co., 1920) 163p (DAR)

Hervey, H.M. HISTORICAL SKETCHES OF THE PRESBYTERIAN CHURCHES LICKING COUNTY OHIO. (SLO)

Hill, Norman N. HISTORY OF LICKING COUNTY OHIO, ITS PAST AND PRESENT. (Newark OH: A.A.Graham & Co., 1881) 822p (LDS,SLO,OHS,OGS,DAR)(RPI)

Horst, Mrs. Gus. FIRST PRESBYTERIAN GERMAN SALEMS CHURCH, NEWARK OHIO, 1857-1901. 1975. 64p (LDS)

Horst, Mrs. Gus. ST. JOHN'S GERMAN EVANGELICAL PROTESTANT CHURCH, NEWARK OHIO, ORGANIZED 1841, RECORDS 1837-1857. 28p (LDS)

Imlay, Arlene. ST. FRANCIS DE SALES CHURCH RECORDS, 1844-1884, LICKING COUNTY OHIO. 1979. 79p (LDS,SLO)

Johnstown Genealogy Society. CEMETERY INSCRIPTIONS ENDING JUNE 1970, JERSEY TOWNSHIP. (Johnstown OH: the society, 1971) 24p (LDS,SLO)

Johnstown Genealogy Society. CEMETERY INSCRIPTIONS ENDING JUNE 1970, ST.ALBANS TOWNSHIP. (Johnstown OH: the society, 1970) 35p (LDS,SLO)

Johnstown Genealogy Society. CEMETERY INSCRIPTIONS ENDING JUNE 1970, NEWTON TOWNSHIP. (Johnstown OH: the society, 1971) 77p (LDS,SLO)

Johnstown Genealogy Society. CEMETERY INSCRIPTIONS ENDING JUNE 1970, MARY ANN, MADISON TOWNSHIPS (Johnstown OH: the society, 1971) 22p (LDS,SLO)

Johnstown Genealogy Society. CEMETERY INSCRIPTIONS ENDING JUNE 1970, BENNINGTON & McKEAN TOWNSHIPS. (Johnstown OH: the society, 1971) 28p (LDS,SLO)

Johnstown Genealogy Society. CEMETERY INSCRIPTIONS ENDING MAR 1971, LIMA TOWNSHIP. (Johnstown OH: the society, 1971) 39p (LDS,SLO)

Johnstown Genealogy Society. CEMETERY INSCRIPTIONS ENDING JUNE 1970, LICKING TOWNSHIP. (Johnstown OH: the society, 1971) 24p (LDS,SLO)

Johnstown Genealogy Society. CEMETERY INSCRIPTIONS ENDING OCTOBER 1970, LIBERTY TOWNSHIP. (Johnstown OH: the society, 1970) 17p (LDS,SLO)

Johnstown Genealogy Society. CEMETERY INSCRIPTIONS ENDING JUNE 1970, NEWARK TOWNSHIP. (Johnstown OH: the society, 1971) 33p (LDS,SLO)

Johnstown Genealogy Society. CEMETERY INSCRIPTIONS ENDING JUNE 1970, HOPEWELL TOWNSHIP. (Johnstown OH: the society, 1971) 23p (LDS,SLO)

Johnstown Genealogy Society. CEMETERY INSCRIPTIONS ENDING JUNE 1970, HARTFORD TOWNSHIP. (Johnstown OH: the society, 1971) 19p (LDS,SLO)

Johnstown Genealogy Society. CEMETERY INSCRIPTIONS ENDING JUNE 1970, GRANVILLE TOWNSHIP. (Johnstown OH: the society, 1971) 77p (LDS,DAR,SLO)

Johnstown Genealogy Society. CEMETERY INSCRIPTIONS ENDING OCTOBER 1970, MONROE TOWNSHIP. (Johnstown OH: the society, 1970) 64p (LDS,SLO)

Johnstown Genealogy Society. CEMETERY INSCRIPTIONS ENDING JUNE 1970, WASHINGTON, EDEN TOWNSHIPS. (Johnstown OH: the society, 1971) 33p (LDS)

Johnstown Genealogy Society. CEMETERY INSCRIPTIONS ENDING JUNE 1970, FALLSBURY, PERRY TOWNSHIPS. (Johnstown OH: the society, 1971) 22p (LDS)

Johnstown Genealogy Society. CEMETERY INSCRIPTIONS ENDING JUNE 1970, UNION TOWNSHIP. (Johnstown OH: the society, 1971) 24p (LDS,SLO)

Johnstown Genealogy Society. CEMETERY INSCRIPTIONS ENDING JUNE 1970, BURLINGTON TOWNSHIP. (Johnstown OH: the society, 1971) 26p (LDS,SLO)

Johnstown Genealogy Society. CEMETERY INSCRIPTIONS ENDING JUNE 1970, HARRISON, ETNA TOWNSHIPS. (Johnstown OH: the society, 1971) 32p (LDS)

Johnstown Genealogy Society. CEMETERY INSCRIPTIONS ENDING JUNE 1970, BOWLING GREEN, FRANKLIN TOWNSHIPS. (Johnstown OH: the society, 1971) 25p (LDS,SLO)

Johnstown Genealogy Society. GREEN HILL CEMETERY INSCRIPTIONS: ADDITION TO MONROE TWP., LICKING CO OHIO (Johnstown OH: the society, nd) 65-66p (LDS,SLO)

Johnstown Genealogy Society. INDEX FOR LICKING COUNTY HISTORY BY HILL, 1881. (Johnstown OH: the society, 1973?)

Johnstown Genealogy Society. NEWARK CEDAR HILL CEMETERY, NEWARK OHIO, 1850-1909.
   (Johnstown OH: the society, 1972) 53,250p (LDS)
King, Florence M. FAMOUS AND IN-FAMOUS PEOPLE OF OLD NEWARK. 1925. (SLO)
Lewis, Thomas W. SOUTHEASTERN OHIO AND THE MUSKINGUM VALLEY, 1788-1928: COVER-
   ING ATHENS, BELMONT, COSHOCTON, GUERNSEY, LICKING, MEIGS, MONROE, MORGAN,
   MUSKINGUM, NOBLE, PERRY AND WASHINGTON COUNTIES. (Chicago: S.J.Clarke Co.,1928)
   3v. (SLO,DAR,OHS)
Licking Co Chapter OGS. 1820 CENSUS, LICKING COUNTY OHIO. (Newark OH: the society, 1979)
   43p (OGS,SLO)
Licking Co Chapter OGS. 1830 CENSUS, HOPEWELL TOWNSHIP, LICKING COUNTY OHIO.
   (Newark OH: the society, nd)
Licking Co Chapter OGS. 1860 CENSUS LICKING COUNTY OHIO PART I (Burl, McKean, Wash,
   Eden, Fall, Mary, Perry, Newton Tps) (Newark OH: the society, nd) (OGS)
Licking Co Chapter OGS. 1860 CENSUS LICKING COUNTY OHIO PART IV. (Newark Tp) (Newark
   OH: the society,nd) (OGS)
Licking Co Chapter OGS. 1860 CENSUS LICKING COUNTY OHIO PART II. (Mad, Han, Fra, Hope,
   Lick & Bowl Tps) (Newark OH: the society, nd) (OGS)
Licking Co Chapter OGS. 1860 CENSUS LICKING COUNTY OHIO PART III. (Granville Tp) (Newark
   OH: the society, nd) (OGS)
Licking Co Chapter OGS. INDEX - CENTENNIAL HISTORY OF THE CITY OF NEWARK & LICK-
   ING CO OHIO by E.M.P.Brister. (Newark OH: the society, nd)
Licking Co Chapter OGS. INDEX OF THE 1834 LICKING CO OHIO TAX DUPLICATE. (Newark OH:
   the society, nd) (OGS)
Licking Co Chapter OGS. LICKING COUNTY OHIO CEMETERIES - PERRY TOWNSHIP. (Newark
   OH: the society, 1984) 68p (OGS)
Licking Co Chapter OGS. LICKING COUNTY OHIO MARRIAGES 1808-1875. (Newark OH: the society,
   1984) 158p (OGS,LDS)
Licking Co Chapter OGS. LICKING COUNTY OHIO 1982: A COLLECTION OF HISTORICAL
   SKETCHES AND FAMILY HISTORIES. (Newark OH: the society, 1982) 2v (OGS,LDS,SLO)
Licking Co Chapter OGS. LICKING COUNTY OHIO PROBATE RECORDS 1828-1904. (Newark OH:
   the society, 1975) 174p (OGS,SLO)
Licking Co Chapter OGS. ST.FRANCES DE SALES CHURCH RECORDS, 1844-1884. (Newark OH: the
   society, nd) (OGS)
LICKING COUNTY OHIO, AMERICAN REVOLUTION BICENTENNIAL, 1776-1976: BICENTEN-
   NIAL HISTORICAL PUBLICATION, TOWNSHIPS OF ETNA, HARRISON, JERSEY, LIMA, PATAS-
   KALA. 1976. 336p (LDS)
Mark, Clara G. FRANKLIN COUNTY OHIO CEMETERY INSCRIPTIONS IN THE UNITED STATES
   MILITARY DISTRICT. 1948. (DAR,LDS)
Matusoff, Karen. CENTRAL OHIO LOCAL GOVERNMENT RECORDS AT THE OHIO HISTORICAL
   SOCIETY. (Columbus: Ohio Hist Soc., 1978) 38p. (OGS)
Maxwell, Fay. INDEX TO LICKING COUNTY MARRIAGES 1808-1822. (Columbus OH: Ohio Geneal-
   ogy Center, 1977) 23p (LDS)
Maxwell, Fay. LICKING COUNTY RECORDS COLLECTION: LANDGRANTS, MARRIAGES, WILLS,
   MAPS... (Columbus OH: Ohio Genealogy Center, 1985) 83p (LDS)
MEMORIAL RECORD OF LICKING COUNTY OHIO. (Chicago: Record Pub Co., 1894) 526p
   (DAR,LDS,SLO)(RPI)
Obetz, Genevieve M. THE FIRST REGULAR BAPTIST CHURCH AND OTHER BAPTIST CHURCHES
   OF COLUMBUS AND CENTRAL OHIO, 1825-1884. (Columbus: Franklin Co.Chapter OGS, 1984)
   69p (LDS)
Park, Samuel. NOTES OF THE EARLY HISTORY OF UNION TOWNSHIP, LICKING COUNTY OHIO.
   (Terre Haute IN: O.U.Smith & Co., 1870) 56p (LDS,SLO)
PEOPLE MAKE THE DIFFERENCE, BICENTENNIAL HISTORICAL PUBLICATION, TOWNSHIPS
   OF ETNA, HARRISON, JERSEY, LIMA, PATASKALA. (SLO)
Pheneger, Diane. INDEX 1834 LICKING COUNTY OHIO TAX DUPLICATE. 1981. (SLO)

Price, Robert. ALEXANDRIA AND ST.ALBANS TOWNSHIP, LICKING COUNTY OHIO. (Alexandria OH: Alexandria Community Council, 1952) 248p. (SLO,LDS)

Rugg, John D. EVERY-NAME INDEX TO ETNA AND KIRKERSVILLE. 1976. 7p (LDS)

Schaff, Morris. ETNA AND KIRKERSVILLE, 1905 & THE HISTORY OF GRANVILLE, LICKING COUNTY OHIO by Henry Bushnell, 1889. (Reprint, Newark OH: Licking Co Chapter OGS, c1977) (SLO,LDS,DAR)

Scott, Harry B. & K.Skutski. THE HANOVER STORY, THE SAGA OF AN AMERICAN VILLAGE. (Ann Arbor: Braun-Brumfield, 1972) 259p (OGS,LDS,SLO)

SESSIONAL RECORDS OF THE PRESBYTERIAN CHURCH OF JERSEY, LICKING COUNTY, OHIO. (SLO)

Shepardson, Leora N. LICKING COUNTY OHIO, SHARON WELSH METHODIST CHURCH, SHARON VALLEY, NEAR GRANVILLE, OHIO. (DAR,LDS)

Simpson, Joseph. THE STORY OF BUCKEYE LAKE. 1912. 104p. (SLO)

Smith, Clifford N. FEDERAL LAND SERIES: A CALENDAR OF ARCHIVAL MATERIAL ON THE LAND PATENTS ISSUED BY THE U.S.GOVERNMENT, VOL.2: FEDERAL BOUNTY LAND WARRANTS OF THE AMERICAN REVOLUTION. (Chicago: American Library Assn., 1972) 416p

Smucker, Isaac. AN ACCOUNT OF THE CELEBRATION OF AMERICAN INDEPENDENCE AT CLAY LICK BY THE LICKING COUNTY PIONEERS. (Newark OH: Clark & King, 1869) 35p (DAR)

Smucker, Isaac. CENTENNIAL HISTORY OF LICKING COUNTY OHIO & MEMORIAL RECORD OF LICKING COUNTY OHIO, 1894. (Reprint, Newark OH: Licking Co Chapter OGS, c1977) (SLO,LDS)(RPI)

Smucker, Isaac. HISTORY OF THE WELSH SETTLEMENTS IN LICKING COUNTY OHIO. (Newark OH: Wilson & Clark, nd, c1869) 22p (LDS)

Smucker, Isaac. OUR PIONEERS: BEING BIOGRAPHICAL SKETCHES OF...HUGHES,RATLIFF, GREEN,PITZER,VAN BUSKIRK,STADDEN & ELLIOTT. (Newark OH: Clark & King, 1872) 33p (DAR,LDS)

Smythe, Brandt G. EARLY RECOLLECTIONS OF NEWARK. (Newark OH: E.Hite Pubs., 1940) 134p (DAR)

Tharp, Robert. A HISTORY OF HARRISON CHAPEL CHURCH 1844-1982. (Pataskala OH: author, 1982) 21p. (OGS,SLO)

TRIENNIAL ATLAS & PLAT BOOK, LICKING COUNTY, OHIO. (Rockford IL: Rockford Map Pubs., 1969) 59p (LDS)

Utter, William T. GRANVILLE, THE STORY OF AN OHIO VILLAGE. (Granville OH: Granville Hist.Soc., Denison University, 1956) 347p. (SLO,LDS)

Wagner, C.W. MISCELLANEOUS CEMETERY RECORDS OF ALLEN, LICKING, HARDIN, MADISON, PICKAWAY AND VINTON COUNTIES OHIO. (SLO)

Wagy, Ollie. 1820 CENSUS OF LICKING COUNTY OHIO. (Afton OK: author, 1963) 6,32p (LDS,DAR)

White, Alfred. HISTORY OF FLETCHER CHAPEL, METHODIST EPISCOPAL CHURCH. (SLO)

Yon, Paul D. GUIDE TO OHIO COUNTY & MUNICIPAL GOVERNMENT RECORDS. (Columbus: Ohio Hist Soc., 1973) 216p (OHS)

# LOGAN COUNTY

| | |
|---|---|
| CREATED: | 1818 FROM CHAMPAIGN COUNTY |
| COUNTY SEAT: | BELLEFONTAINE 43311 |
| COURT HOUSE: | MAIN ST., BELLEFONTAINE 43311 |
| LIBRARY: | MAIN & SANDUSKY, BELLEFONTAINE 43311 |
| HISTORICAL SOCIETY: | W.CHILLICOTHE & SEYMORE ST., BELLEFONTAINE 43311 |
| GENEALOGICAL SOCIETY: | LOGAN CO. GENEALOGICAL SOCIETY. PO BOX 36, BELLEFONTAINE 43311 library: 521 E.COLUMBUS ST. publication: BRANCHES & TWIGS |

HEALTH DEPARTMENT:          815 SOUTH MAIN ST., BELLEFONTAINE 43311
                            (separate office for Bellefontaine city)
ARCHIVAL DISTRICT:          WRIGHT STATE UNIVERSITY, DAYTON
                            (see Leggett's Guide to records)
LAND SURVEYS:               CONGRESS LANDS, E & S OF 1ST PRIN.MERIDIAN
                            VIRGINIA MILITARY DISTRICT
                            CONGRESS LANDS, BETWEEN THE MIAMI RIVER
BOUNDED BY:                 EAST:    UNION CO.
                            NORTH:   AUGLAIZE & HARDIN CO.
                            WEST:    AUGLAIZE & SHELBY CO.
                            SOUTH:   CHAMPAIGN CO.
TOWNSHIPS:                  Bloomfield, Bokes Creek, Harrison, Jefferson, Lake, Liberty,
                            McArthur, Miami, Monroe, Perry, Pleasant,  Richland, Rush Creek,
                            Stokes, Union, Washington, Zane.

## COURT RECORDS: (LDS MICROFILM)
Auditor:
    Tax duplicates, 1818-1838.
Childrens' Home:
    Record of inmates, 1886-1934.
Clerk of Courts:
    Chancery record, 1849-1857.
    Civil docket, 1818-1855.
    Civil journal, 1818-1854.
    Common Pleas general index, 1819-1894.
    Supreme Court record, 1820-1851.
    Supreme Court naturalizations, 1828-1884.
    District Court record, 1851-1866.
    Register of blacks, 1824-1857.
    Register of free blacks, 1804-1857.
    Manumission record, 1843-1857.
County Home:
    Record of inmates, 1850-1978.
Probate Court:
    Applications of birth records, v1-15, 1941-1967.
    Birth & death records, 1940.
    Registration of birth, 1941-1942.
    Birth records, 1867-1908.
    Death records, 1867-1908.
    Marriage certificates, 1818-1842.
    Marriage records, vA-V, 1818-1966.
    Will records, vA-Z,A1-A9, 1851-1966.
    Final record, 1909-1944.
    Administration dockets, vA-G, 1818-1852.
    Administrators' docket, v1-16, 1852-1967.
    Administrators' & executors' record, 1916-1929.
    Accounts & settlements, vA-Z, 27-39,1852-1958.
    Guardian docket, vA-E, 1879-1967.
    Guardian records, v5-10, 1952-1967.
    Guardian bonds, vE, 1900-1913.
    Guardians account records, vG-M, 1893-1942.
    Guardian settlement, vA-F, 1862-1890.
    Guardian appointments, v1-3, 1911-1944.
    Guardians' bonds, 1904-1937.
    Probate journals, vA-Z,1-29, 1852-1967.

Naturalization records, 1860-1880,1881-1906.
Recorder:
Military discharges, 1865-1963.
General index to mortgages, v1-16, n.d.
Mortgage record, 1849-1852.
Deed records, vAZ,27-91, 1810-1900.
General index to deeds, 1810-1967.
Miscellaneous:
Goshen monthly meeting, Soc. of Friends, minutes, 1828-1848.
Bellefontaine United Presby.Church, session minutes, 1853-1886.
Northwood United Presby.Church, session minutes, 1859-1876.
Rushsylvania United Presby.Church, session minutes, 1875-1888.
Zanesfield Presby.Church, session minutes, 1853-1952.

## OHIO HISTORICAL SOCIETY: (MICROFILM)
Childrens' Home:
Record of inmates, 1886-1934.
Clerk of Courts:
Chancery record, 1849-1857.
Civil docket, 1818-1855.
Civil journal, 1818-1854.
Common Pleas general index, 1819-1894.
Supreme Court record, 1820-1866.
District Court record, 1851-1866.
Register of blacks, 1824-1857.
Register of free blacks, 1804-1857.
Manumission record, 1843-1857.
Supreme Court naturalizations, 1828-1884.
County Home:
Record of inmates, 1850-1978.
Probate Court:
Naturalizations, 1860-1880.
Miscellaneous:
Marriage records of Lake, Licking & Logan Cos., 1818-1834, by DAR.
Joseph Dickinson & family, by DAR.

## MANUSCRIPTS:
John D.Inskeep diaries, E.Liberty & Bellefontaine, 1861-1865. (OHS)

## CENSUS RECORDS  (OHS,SLO,OGS,LDS)
1820-1880, 1900-1910; 1890 VETERANS; 1880,1900 SOUNDEX; 1910 MIRACODE

## AGRICULTURAL CENSUS SCHEDULES  (OHS,SLO-mic)
1850,1860,1870,1880

## PRODUCTS OF INDUSTRY CENSUS SCHEDULE  (OHS,SLO-mic)
1850

## MORTALITY CENSUS SCHEDULES (OHS,SLO-mic)
1850,1860

## DEFECTIVE & DEPENDENT CENSUS SCHEDULES (OHS,SLO-mic)
1880

**NEWSPAPERS: [GUIDE TO OHIO NEWSPAPERS, 1793-1973]**
Belle Center, Bellefontaine, Degraff, East Liberty, Huntsville, Russells Point, West Liberty, West Mansfield.

**TAX RECORDS (OHS & LDS)**
1818-1838.

**GENEALOGICAL PERIODICAL ARTICLES**
Bell, Carol Willsey. OHIO GENEALOGICAL PERIODICAL INDEX: A COUNTY GUIDE (Youngstown OH: author, 6th ed., 1987)

**PUBLISHED SOURCES:**
Adams, Barbara. MEMORIAL RECORDS OF SHELBY COUNTY, OHIO, 1819-1975. [incl. some Logan Co. cemeteries] (Baltimore: Gateway Press, 1977) 668p (LDS)
Antrim, Joshua. CHAMPAIGN AND LOGAN COUNTIES, OHIO EARLY VOTERS LISTS. (Bellefontaine OH: Press Printing Co., 1872) 17p (LDS,DAR)(RPI)
Antrim, Joshua. THE HISTORY OF CHAMPAIGN AND LOGAN COUNTIES, FROM THEIR FIRST SETTLEMENT. (Bellefontaine OH: Press Printing Co., 1872) 460p (LDS,SLO)
Berry, Ellen T. & David A. EARLY OHIO SETTLERS: PURCHASERS OF LAND IN SOUTHWESTERN OHIO, 1800-1840. (Baltimore: Genealogical Pub.Co., 1986) 372p (OGS,SLO,OHS)
CITY/COUNTY DIRECTORIES: check holdings of OHS & local public library.
DAILY SCHOOL REGISTER OF JAMES M. EBRITE 1866-1886, ADAMS & LOGAN CO. OHIO. 1952-3. (SLO,LDS)
Daughters of the American Revolution. DAILY SCHOOL REGISTER OF JAMES M. EBRITE, 1866-1886: ADAMS & LOGAN COUNTY OHIO. 1952-53. 45p (DAR)
Daughters of the American Revolution. LOGAN COUNTY OHIO MARRIAGES, 1818-1846. 1977. 124p (SLO,DAR,LDS)
Daughters of the American Revolution. PROBATE COURT MARRIAGE RECORDS: LAKE COUNTY 1840-1865, LICKING COUNTY, 1808-1816, & LOGAN COUNTY, 1818-1834. 1938? 131p (DAR)
Grandi, Bud. OLD TIME PHOTO ALBUM OF INDIAN LAKE. (SLO)
Haller, Stephen E. & P.Nolan. FIRST STOP FOR LOCAL HISTORY RESEARCH. A GUIDE TO COUNTY RECORDS PRESERVED AT WRIGHT STATE UNIVERSITY ARCHIVES AND SPECIAL COLLECTIONS. 1976. 21p.
Hardesty, H.H. MILITARY HISTORY OF OHIO - LOGAN COUNTY EDITION. 1886/87. (OHS)
Hinshaw, William Wade. ENCYCLOPEDIA OF AMERICAN QUAKER GENEALOGY, VOL.IV, OHIO. (Baltimore: Genealogical Pub.Co., 1973) 1424p (SLO,OHS,LDS)
HISTORY OF LOGAN COUNTY AND OHIO. (Chicago: O.L.Baskin, 1880) 840p (LDS,DAR,SLO)(RPI)
HISTORY OF THE FIRST PRESBYTERIAN CHURCH OF BELLEFONTAINE OHIO...35TH ANNIVERSARY. (Bellefontaine OH: Press of the Index Printing & Pub Co., 1900) 278p (LDS,DAR)
Hover, John C. MEMOIRS OF THE MIAMI VALLEY. (Chicago: Robert O. Law Co.,1919). 3v. (OHS,SLO)
Kennedy, Robert P. THE HISTORICAL REVIEW OF LOGAN COUNTY OHIO. (Chicago: S.J.Clarke Pub., 1903) 823p (LDS,SLO,DAR)(RPI)
Lambert, Marguerite. DEATH NOTICES FROM OHIO NEWSPAPERS 1830-1872. (SLO)
Leggett, Nancy G. & D.E.Smith. A GUIDE TO LOCAL GOVERNMENT RECORDS AND NEWSPAPERS PRESERVED AT THE DEPARTMENT OF ARCHIVES AND SPECIAL COLLECTIONS WRIGHT STATE UNIVERSITY. (Dayton OH: Wright State U., 1987)
Logan Co. Gen.Soc. LOGAN COUNTY OHIO 1982: A COLLECTION OF HISTORICAL SKETCHES AND FAMILY HISTORIES. (Bellefontaine OH: the society, 1983) 538p (LDS,SLO)
McCormick, Virginia E. A LOGAN COUNTY DIARY. (Worthington OH: author, 1979) 90p (OGS,SLO)
Marmon, Herman C. LOGAN COUNTY OHIO SESQUICENTENNIAL, 1818-1968. (Bellefontaine OH: Sesquicentennial Committee, 1968) 9p (LDS)
PORTRAIT & BIOGRAPHICAL RECORD OF AUGLAIZE, LOGAN & SHELBY COUNTIES, OHIO. (Chicago: Chapman Bros., 1892) 593p (LC,SLO,DAR,LDS)
Skinner, H.K. HISTORIC WEST LIBERTY OHIO. 1967. 51p (SLO)
Smith, William E. HISTORY OF SOUTHWESTERN OHIO, THE MIAMI VALLEYS. 1963. 3v. (SLO)

Stewart, David J. COMBINATION ATLAS MAP OF LOGAN COUNTY OHIO. 1875.(Reprint, Evansville IN: Unigraphic, 1976) 44p (OGS,SLO,DAR)(RPI)
Thompson, N.J. HOMETOWN, USA. nd. 102p. (SLO)
Turpin, Joan. REGISTER OF BLACK, MULATTO & POOR PERSONS IN FOUR OHIO COUNTIES, [CLINTON,HIGHLAND,LOGAN & ROSS] 1791-1861. (Bowie MD: Heritage Books, 1985) 44p (OHS)
Wiggins & McKillop's DIRECTORY OF CHAMPAIGN COUNTY FOR 1878-9 [incl. Logan, Miami & Shelby Co]. (Wellsville OH: author, 1878. (DAR)

# LORAIN COUNTY

| | |
|---|---|
| CREATED: | 1824 FROM CUYAHOGA, HURON & MEDINA COUNTY |
| COUNTY SEAT: | ELYRIA 44035 |
| COURT HOUSE: | 226 MIDDLE AVE., ELYRIA 44035 |
| LIBRARY: | 320 WASHINGTON AVE., ELYRIA 44035 |
| HISTORICAL SOCIETY: | 509 WASHINGTON AVE., ELYRIA 44035 |
| GENEALOGICAL SOCIETY: | LORAIN CO. CHAPTER OGS, |
| | PO BOX 865, ELYRIA 44036-0865 |
| | publication: LORAIN COUNTY RESEARCHER |
| | BLACK RIVER GENEALOGISTS, |
| | c/o LORAIN PUBLIC LIBRARY, 6th & Reid Ave |
| | WELLINGTON GENEALOGICAL WORKSHOP, |
| | c/o WELLINGTON TOWN HALL, WELLINGTON |
| HEALTH DEPARTMENT: | 9880 S.MURRAY RIDGE RD., ELYRIA 44035 |
| | (separate offices for Lorain city, Elyria, Vermilion, Oberlin, Amherst, Avon, Avon Lake, North Ridge & Sheffield Lake) |
| ARCHIVAL DISTRICT: | WESTERN RESERVE HIST.SOC., CLEVELAND |
| LAND SURVEYS: | CONNECTICUT WESTERN RESERVE |
| BOUNDED BY: | EAST: CUYAHOGA & MEDINA CO. |
| | NORTH: LAKE ERIE |
| | WEST: ERIE & HURON CO. |
| | SOUTH: ASHLAND & MEDINA CO. |
| TOWNSHIPS: | Amherst, Avon, Avon Lake, Black River, Brighton, Brownhelm, Camden, Carlisle, Columbia, Eaton, Elyria, Grafton, Henrietta, Huntington, La Grange, Penfield, Pittsfield, Ridgeville, Rochester, Russia, Sheffield, Wellington. |

## COURT RECORDS: (LDS MICROFILM)
Auditor:
    Tax duplicates, 1824-1838.
Clerk of Courts:
    General index to civil dockets, 1914-1945.
    Supreme Court record, 1826-1847.
    Common Pleas record, 1824-1847.
    Common Pleas journal, 1832-1845.
Probate Court:
    Death records, 1867-1908.
    Birth registration & correction, 1941-1942.
    Birth records, 1867-1908.
    Marriage index, A-Z, 1824-1884.
    Marriage license application, 1824-1875, 1875-1901.
    Marriage records, 1925-1932.
    Record of wills, 1840-1904
    Probate docket records, 1913-1960.
    Probate journal, 1852-1902.

Guardianship & trustee bonds & letters, 1854-1925.
Index to letters of administration, 1914-1949.
Record of final settlement accounts, 1938.
Miscellaneous:
Elyria First Baptist Church, Women's Home Mission, records, 1887-1900.
Cemetery records, State Library of Ohio collection.

## OHIO HISTORICAL SOCIETY: (MICROFILM)
Clerk of Courts:
Common Pleas record, 1824-1847.
Common Pleas journal, 1832-1845.
Supreme Court record, vA, 1826-1847.
Probate Court:
Birth records, 1867-1908.
Death records, 1867-1889.
Marriage index, 1824-1884.
Marriage applications, 1875-1901.
Marriage index, 1824-1884.
Miscellaneous:
Marriages, 1824-1865, by DAR.
Cemeteries of Cuyahoga & Lorain Cos., by DAR.
Cemetery inscriptions, by DAR.
Connecticut Land Co., Western Reserve land draft, 1795-1809.

## MANUSCRIPTS:
Black River Tp. records, 1817-1848. (WRHS)
Huron & Lorain Baptist Assn. records, 1938-1947. (WRHS)
George W. Stanley docket book, 1837-1841. (WRHS)
Hattie Cowing papers (Rev.War & War 1812 soldiers). (WRHS)

## CENSUS RECORDS  (OHS,SLO,OGS,LDS)
1830-1880, 1900-1910; 1890 VETERANS; 1880,1900 SOUNDEX; 1910 MIRACODE

## AGRICULTURAL CENSUS SCHEDULES  (OHS,SLO-mic)
1850,1860,1880

## PRODUCTS OF INDUSTRY CENSUS SCHEDULE  (OHS,SLO-mic)
1850

## MORTALITY CENSUS SCHEDULES (OHS,SLO-mic)
1850,1860

## DEFECTIVE & DEPENDENT CENSUS SCHEDULES (OHS,SLO-mic)
1880

## NEWSPAPERS: [GUIDE TO OHIO NEWSPAPERS, 1793-1973]
Amherst, Avon Lake, Elyria, Lorain, North Amherst, North Ridgeville, Oberlin, Wellington.

## TAX RECORDS (OHS & LDS)
1824-1838.

## GENEALOGICAL PERIODICAL ARTICLES
Bell, Carol Willsey. OHIO GENEALOGICAL PERIODICAL INDEX: A COUNTY GUIDE (Youngstown
OH: author, 6th ed., 1987)

**PUBLISHED SOURCES:**

1875-1975 CENTENNIAL YEAR, ST.PETER'S PARISH, NORTH RIDGEVILLE OHIO. (N. Ridgeville OH: the church, 1975) 51p (OGS)

American Atlas Co. ATLAS AND DIRECTORY OF LORAIN COUNTY. 1897. (SLO)(RPI)

AMHERST SESQUICENTENNIAL, AUGUST 1-8, 1964: HISTORY OF AMHERST, 1814-1964. 1984. 57p (LDS)

Armstrong, Robert G. AMHERST'S STORY. (Amherst OH: Old Home Week Committee, 1914) 224p (SLO,LDS)

Bigglestone, William E. THEY STOPPED IN OBERLIN, BLACK RESIDENTS AND VISITORS OF THE NINETEENTH CENTURY. 1981. 252p. (SLO)

Black River Genealogists. LORAIN, OHIO 1903 & THE TORNADO. (Lorain OH: the society, nd)

Boynton, Washington W. THE EARLY HISTORY OF LORAIN COUNTY. (Elyria: Lorain County Agricultural Society, 1876) 65p (LDS,DAR,SLO)(RPI)

Burrell, Doris. SHEFFIELD, OHIO. (Elyria OH: Lorain Co Metro Park District, 1971) 22p (DAR)

Carruthers, Glenn A. NON-MILITARY DEATH NOTICES FROM THE LORAIN COUNTY NEWS, 1860-1867. 1983. 54p (LDS)

Chamberlain, Gladys E. CEMETERY INSCRIPTIONS, ROCHESTER TOWNSHIP, LORAIN COUNTY, OHIO. (SLO,LDS)

CITY/COUNTY DIRECTORIES: check holdings of OHS & local public library.

COMMEMORATIVE BIOGRAPHICAL RECORD OF THE COUNTIES OF HURON AND LORAIN OHIO. (Chicago: J.H.Beers & Co., 1894) 2v (LDS,SLO,DAR)(RPI)

Cunningham, Dan & Sue. BRIEF HISTORY OF SACRED HEART CHURCH, OBERLIN OHIO, BASED ON THE ADMINISTRATIONS OF ITS PASTORS. (Oberlin OH: authors, 1980) 17p (OGS)

Darmstadt, Mrs. H.F. CEMETERY RECORDS, LORAIN COUNTY OHIO: COLUMBIA TOWNSHIP CEMETERY, AVON LAKE CEMETERY. (DAR,LDS)

Daughters of the American Revolution. ABSTRACTS OF WILLS FROM PROBATE COURT RECORDS LORAIN COUNTY OHIO, 1824-1865. 1962. 114p (DAR,SLO)

Daughters of the American Revolution. BIBLE AND FAMILY RECORDS, FAIRFIELD, HANCOCK, HURON, LORAIN, MAHONING AND WARREN COUNTIES OHIO. (SLO)

Daughters of the American Revolution. CEMETERY INSCRIPTIONS, ROCHESTER TOWNSHIP, LORAIN COUNTY, OHIO. (SLO)

Daughters of the American Revolution. CEMETERY RECORDS, LORAIN COUNTY OHIO, COLUMBIA TOWNSHIP AND AVON LAKE CEMETERIES. (SLO)

Daughters of the American Revolution. COMMON PLEAS COURT JOURNALS, COURT HOUSE, ELYRIA OHIO. (SLO)

Daughters of the American Revolution. FIRST TAX LISTS OF REAL ESTATE AND PERSONAL PROPERTY, YEAR 1824, LORAIN COUNTY OHIO. 1970. 41p (DAR,SLO)

Daughters of the American Revolution. MARRIAGE RECORDS OF LORAIN COUNTY OHIO, 1824-1865. (Elyria OH: author, 1942-44) 4v (LDS,DAR,SLO)

Daughters of the American Revolution. REVOLUTIONARY SOLDIERS, ALPHABETIZED ANCESTRAL LISTS OF CHAPTERS, D.A.R. OHIO 1958-1959. (SLO)

Daughters of the American Revolution. REVOLUTIONARY SOLDIERS WHO LIVED OR ARE BURIED IN LORAIN COUNTY OHIO. 1976. 87p (DAR)

Daughters of the American Revolution. SOME CEMETERY RECORDS OF CUYAHOGA, FULTON, MEDINA, LORAIN & WAYNE COUNTIES. 1938. 175p (DAR,LDS)

Dillman, A.G. OBITUARY INDEX TO ELYRIA OHIO NEWSPAPERS. (SLO)

Duff, William A. HISTORY OF NORTH CENTRAL OHIO EMBRACING RICHLAND, ASHLAND, WAYNE, MEDINA, LORAIN, HURON AND KNOX COUNTIES. (Topeka KS: Historical Pub Co., 1931) 3v (OHS,DAR)

EATON MEMORIES: HISTORY OF EATON TOWNSHIP, LORAIN COUNTY OHIO. (Eaton Tp. Hist Soc., 1983) 100p

Elyria Chapter D.A.R. REVOLUTIONARY SOLDIERS WHO LIVED OR ARE BURIED IN LORAIN COUNTY OHIO. (Elyria: author, 1975-76) np (OHS)

Fairchild, James H. EARLY SETTLEMENT AND HISTORY OF BROWNHELM. (Oberlin OH: The News Office, 1867) 24p (LDS)

GENEALOGICAL DATA RELATING TO WOMEN IN THE WESTERN RESERVE BEFORE 1840 (1850)
(Cleveland: Centennial Commission, 1943) (WRHS,LDS)

Gray, Mary P. EARLY RECORDS OF LORAIN COUNTY, OHIO: ABSTRACTS OF WILLS AND ES-
TATES, YEARS 1824-1847. (DAR,LDS)

Griffith, Maryann P. LAGRANGE CEMETERY: LOCATION ON RT.303 ABOUT 1 MILE EAST OF
LAGRANGE, LORAIN COUNTY OHIO. (LDS)

Hardesty, H.H. MILITARY HISTORY OF OHIO, LORAIN COUNTY EDITION. 1885. (OHS)

Historical Records Survey. INVENTORY OF THE COUNTY ARCHIVES OF OHIO NO.47, LORAIN
COUNTY. (Cleveland: author, 1941) 376p (LDS,OHS,DAR)

HISTORY OF LORAIN COUNTY OHIO. (Philadelphia: Williams Bros., 1879)(Reprint, Evansville IN:
Unigraphic, 1973) 373p (LDS,SLO)(RPI)

INDEX TO THE MICROFILM EDITION OF GENEALOGICAL DATA RELATING TO WOMEN IN
THE WESTERN RESERVE BEFORE 1840. 1940. (Cleveland: Western Reserve Hist Soc., 1976) 226p
(WRHS,LDS)

Jamison, Charles T. HISTORY OF WELLINGTON OHIO. (Wellington OH: Kings Daughters, 1930) 32p
(OGS)

Lake, D.J. ATLAS OF LORAIN COUNTY, OHIO. 1874. (Reprint, Evansville IN: Unigraphic, 1974) 73,71p
(LDS,OGS,SLO)(RPI)

LORAIN CITY DIRECTORY. (Cleveland OH: R.L. Polk & Co., 1931-) (LDS)

Lorain Co. Chapter OGS. PICTURESQUE ELYRIA, 1903. (Elyria OH: the society, nd)

Lorain Co. Chapter OGS. 1850 LORAIN COUNTY CENSUS INDEX. (Elyria OH: the society, 1972) 51p
(DAR)

Lorain Co. Historical Society. CEMETERY INSCRIPTIONS OF LORAIN COUNTY OHIO. (Elyria OH:
the society, 1980) 528p (OGS,DAR,LDS,SLO)

Lorain Co. Historical Society. ELYRIA SESQUICENTENNIAL. (Elyria OH: the society, nd)

Lorain Co. Historical Society. INDEX TO THE CENSUS OF 1850 FOR LORAIN COUNTY OHIO. (Elyria
OH: the society, 1972) 51p (LDS,SLO)

Lorain Co. Historical Society. LORAIN COUNTY SESQUICENTENNIAL. (Elyria OH: American Multi-
Service, 1974) 112p (OGS)

Lorain Co. Historical Society. MARRIAGES LORAIN COUNTY 1824-1865. (Elyria OH: the society,
1980)

Painter, Dorothy. A HISTORY OF THE RIDGEVILLE TOWN HALL. (North Ridgeville: Hist.Soc., 1982)
23p. (OGS)

Painter, Dorothy. LORAIN COUNTY, 1827. (N.Ridgeville OH: author, 1975) 26p (OGS)

Painter, Dorothy. RIDGEVILLE: WYLLYS TERRELL'S MEMOIRS OF EARLY RIDGEVILLE.
(N.Ridgeville OH: author, 1976) 108p (OGS)

Phillips, Wilbur H. OBERLIN COLONY: THE STORY OF A CENTURY. (Oberlin OH: Oberlin Printing
Co., 1933) 328p (LDS)

Reefy, E.L. HOMES AND GARDENS OF EARLY ELYRIA. 1947. 102p. (SLO)

SACRED HEART CHURCH, OBERLIN, OHIO. (Oberlin OH: Sacred Heart Parish Council, nd) 28p
(OGS)

Saye, Amy M. EARLY SETTLEMENT OF COLUMBIA AND RIDGEVILLE. 1969? 41p (DAR)

Shipherd, Jacob R. HISTORY OF THE OBERLIN-WELLINGTON RESCUE, 1859. 1859? 280p (LDS)

Upton, Harriet T. HISTORY OF THE WESTERN RESERVE (Chicago: Lewis Pub.Co., 1910) 3v (SLO)

Webber, A.R. EARLY HISTORY OF ELYRIA AND HER PEOPLE. (Elyria OH: Caxton Press, 1930) 326p
(LDS,DAR)

Webster, Frederick. LEGENDS OF THE INDIAN HOLLOW ROAD. (Elyria OH: Lorain Co Chapter
OGS, 1987) 36p

Weeks, Frank E. PIONEER HISTORY OF CAMDEN TOWNSHIP, LORAIN COUNTY, OHIO. (Akron
OH: Wellington Genealogical Workshop, 1982) 102p (LDS,SLO)

Western Reserve Hist.Soc. INDEX TO THE MICROFILM EDITION OF GENEALOGICAL DATA
RELATING TO WOMEN IN THE WESTERN RESERVE PRE 1840. (Cleveland: the society, 1976)
226p (OGS,WRHS)

Wickham, Gertrude V.W. MEMORIAL TO THE PIONEER WOMEN OF THE WESTERN RESERVE.
(Cleveland: Cleveland Centennial Commission, 1896+) 2v (SLO)

Williams Brothers. HISTORY OF LORAIN COUNTY OHIO. 1879. (Reprint, Elyria OH: Lorain Co Chapter OGS, 1973?) 373p (LDS)

Wright, George F. A STANDARD HISTORY OF LORAIN COUNTY OHIO. (Chicago: Lewis Pub Co., 1916) 2v (LDS,DAR)

YEAR BOOK OF THE SECOND CONGREGATIONAL CHURCH, OBERLIN OHIO, FOR YEAR ENDING OCT.6, 1890. (Oberlin OH: Oberlin News Press, 1891-1892) 36,43p (LDS)

Yon, Paul D. GUIDE TO OHIO COUNTY & MUNICIPAL GOVERNMENT RECORDS. (Columbus: Ohio Hist.Soc., 1973) 216p (OHS)

# LUCAS COUNTY

| | |
|---|---|
| CREATED: | 1835 FROM HENRY, SANDUSKY & WOOD COUNTIES |
| COUNTY SEAT: | TOLEDO 43624 |
| COURT HOUSE: | 700 ADAMS ST., TOLEDO 43624 |
| LIBRARY: | 325 MICHIGAN AVE., TOLEDO 43624 |
| HISTORICAL SOCIETY: | MAUMEE VALLEY HISTORICAL SOCIETY, |
| | 1031 RIVER RD., MAUMEE 43537 |
| GENEALOGICAL SOCIETY: | LUCAS CO. CHAPTER OGS, |
| | c/o TOLEDO-LUCAS CO.PUBLIC LIBRARY |
| | 325 MICHIGAN AVE., TOLEDO 43624 |
| | publication: FORT INDUSTRY REFLECTIONS |
| | NORTHWEST OHIO GENEALOGICAL SOCIETY, |
| | PO BOX 17066, TOLEDO 43615-0566 |
| HEALTH DEPARTMENT: | 635 NORTH ERIE ST., TOLEDO 43624 |
| | (separate offices for Toledo City, Maumee, Oregon & Sylvania) |
| ARCHIVAL DISTRICT: | BOWLING GREEN STATE UNIVERSITY, BOWLING GREEN |
| | (see Biggs' Guide to records) |
| LAND SURVEYS: | MICHIGAN SURVEY |
| | CONGRESS LANDS, E & N OF 1ST PRIN.MERIDIAN |
| | 12 MILE SQUARE RESERVE |
| BOUNDED BY: | EAST:      LAKE ERIE |
| | NORTH:   LENAWEE & MONROE CO., MICHIGAN |
| | WEST:     FULTON & HENRY CO. |
| | SOUTH:   OTTAWA & WOOD CO. |
| TOWNSHIPS: | Adams, Harding, Jerusalem, Monclova, Oregon, Providence, Richfield, Spencer, Springfield, Swanton, Sylvania, Washington, Waterville, Waynesfield. |

## COURT RECORDS: (LDS MICROFILM)
Auditor:
    Tax record, 1836-1838.
Clerk of Courts:
    Supreme court chancery record, v1-3, 1838-1854.
    Supreme court complete record, v1-3, 1837-1854.
    District court chancery record, v2, 1852-1855.
    Civil journal, v1-10, 1835-1856.
    Chancery records, v1-8, 1836-1856.
    Appearance docket, v1-2, 1838-1853.
Probate Court:
    Will records, v1-27, 1835-1903.
    Index to estates, 1891-1959.
    Record of births, v1-8, 1867-1908.
    Record of deaths, v1-5, 1868-1908.
    Marriage records, v1-19, 1835-1909.

    Index to marriage records, 1835-1911.
    Guardians' general index, 1891-1939.
    Guardians' bonds, 1874-1890.
    Guardianship index, 1891-1970.
    Index to administrators, n.d.
    Estate records, v1-14, 1852-1890.
    Civil dockets, v1-4, 1852-1903.
    Appearance dockets, v1-2, 1836-1853.
    Administrators' & executors' bonds & letters, 1859-1891.
    Letters testamentary, 1879-1890.
    Executors', administrators' & guardians' bonds, 1859-1875.
    Assignments, v1-5, 1877-1893.
    Real estate records, v1-14, 1852-1886.
    Journal, v1-19, 1852-1890.
Recorder:
    Deed records, 1821-1881.
    Index to deed records, 1808-1902.
Miscellaneous:
    Maumee, First Presby.Church, minutes 1820-1969.
    Toledo, Fifth Presby.Church, Women's Missionary Soc., 1890-1895.
    Toledo, Epworth United Methodist Church, records, 1894-1959.
    Toledo, Salem United Brethren Church, records, 1873-1901.
    Toledo, Forest Cemetery, lot burials, 1869-1969.
    Northwestern Ohio Gen.Soc., compiled cemetery records.

## OHIO HISTORICAL SOCIETY: (MICROFILM)
Clerk of Courts:
    Common Pleas appearance docket, v1-2, 1838-1853.
    Chancery record, v1-8, 1836-1853.
    Supreme Court journal, v1, 1837-1855.
    Supreme Court chancery record, 1838-1855.
    Supreme Court complete record, 1837-1854.
Miscellaneous:
    Marriage records, 1835-1866, by DAR.
    Bible & family records & letters, by DAR.

## MANUSCRIPTS:
George W. Stanley docket book, 1837-1841. (WRHS)

## CENSUS RECORDS  (OHS,SLO,OGS,LDS)
1840-1880, 1900-1910; 1890 VETERANS; 1880,1900 SOUNDEX; 1910 MIRACODE

## AGRICULTURAL CENSUS SCHEDULES  (OHS,SLO-mic)
1850,1860,1880

## PRODUCTS OF INDUSTRY CENSUS SCHEDULE  (OHS,SLO-mic)
1850

## MORTALITY CENSUS SCHEDULES (OHS,SLO-mic)
1850,1860

## DEFECTIVE & DEPENDENT CENSUS SCHEDULES (OHS,SLO-mic)
1880

**NEWSPAPERS: [GUIDE TO OHIO NEWSPAPERS, 1793-1973]**
Maumee, Oregon, Rossford, Sylvania, Toledo, Waterville, Whitehouse.

**TAX RECORDS (OHS & LDS)**
1836-1838.

**GENEALOGICAL PERIODICAL ARTICLES**
Bell, Carol Willsey. OHIO GENEALOGICAL PERIODICAL INDEX: A COUNTY GUIDE (Youngstown
OH: author, 6th ed., 1987)

**PUBLISHED SOURCES:**
Andreas & Baskin. AN ILLUSTRATED ATLAS OF LUCAS COUNTY AND PART OF WOOD COUN-
TY, OHIO. 1875. (OGS,SLO)(RPI)
Biggs, Deb. GUIDE TO LOCAL GOVERNMENT RECORDS AT THE CENTER FOR ARCHIVAL COL-
LECTIONS. (Bowling Green OH: Bowling Green State Univ, 1981) 104p (OGS)
Blaine, Harry S. ABSTRACTS OF LUCAS COUNTY OHIO WILLS, V1-6 INCLUSIVE, TO YEAR 1874.
(Toledo: Assn. of Histl. & Ancestral Societies & Histl. Soc. of NW Ohio, 1954) 129p (SLO,LDS,DAR)
Blaine, Harry S. RECOLLECTIONS OF OLD ATTICA AND TOLEDO. 125p. (SLO)
Bower, Harriet C. GRAVESTONE RECORDS OF LUCAS AND FULTON COUNTIES SITUATED
SOUTH OF LENAWEE COUNTY MICHIGAN TO OLD STATE LINE. (DAR,LDS)
Christian, Donna K. GUIDE TO NEWSPAPER HOLDINGS AT THE CENTER FOR ARCHIVAL COL-
LECTIONS. (Bowling Green OH: B.G.State Univ, 1980) 64p (OGS)
CITY/COUNTY DIRECTORIES: check holdings of OHS & local public library.
Daughters of the American Revolution. BIBLE RECORDS, COPIES OF DIARIES, LETTERS AND
NEWSPAPER NOTICES. 1943. (SLO,LDS,DAR)
Daughters of the American Revolution. GRAVESTONE RECORDS OF LUCAS AND FULTON COUN-
TIES. 1944-1951. 278p (DAR)
Daughters of the American Revolution. LUCAS COUNTY OHIO MARRIAGE RECORDS, 1835-1866.
2v. (SLO,LDS,DAR)
Daughters of the American Revolution. MARRIAGE RECORDS (A TO L) LUCAS COUNTY UP TO
1866 INCL. 1938? 172p (DAR)
Downes, Randall C. LUCAS COUNTY HISTORICAL SERIES, 1948. 646p. (SLO)
Doyle, John H. A STORY OF EARLY TOLEDO: HISTORICAL FACTS AND INCIDENTS OF THE
EARLY DAYS OF THE CITY AND ENVIRONS. (Bowling Green OH: C.S.VanTassel, c1919) 135p
(DAR)
Fassett, Josephine. HISTORY OF OREGON AND JERUSALEM: THE STORY OF TWO COMMUNITIES.
194?. 349p (LDS)
Harrison, John M. THE BLADE OF TOLEDO, THE FIRST 150 YEARS. (Toledo OH: Toledo Blade Co.,
1985) 374p
Harrison, Kay. OAKWOOD CEMETERY INSCRIPTIONS. (LDS)
Historical Records Survey. INVENTORY OF THE COUNTY ARCHIVES OF OHIO NO.48, LUCAS
COUNTY. (Columbus: author, 1937) 148p (LDS,OHS,DAR)
HISTORY OF THE LOWER SCIOTO VALLEY OHIO. 1884. 3v. (SLO)
Huffman, June. THE PROVIDENCE RECORD 1981: A COMPREHENSIVE ACCOUNT OF
PROVIDENCE TWP. LUCAS CO OHIO. (Defiance OH: Hubbard Co., 1982) 136p. (LDS,SLO)
Killits, John M. TOLEDO AND LUCAS COUNTY OHIO, 1623-1923. (Chicago: S.J. Clarke Pub Co, 1923)
3v (LDS,SLO,DAR)
Knapp, Horace S. HISTORY OF THE MAUMEE VALLEY. (Toledo OH: author, 1872) 685p.
(DAR,OHS,SLO)
Levinson, Marilyn. GUIDE TO NEWSPAPER HOLDINGS AT THE CENTER FOR ARCHIVAL COL-
LECTIONS. 2nd Edition. (Bowling Green OH: B.G.State Univ., 1987)
Maumee Valley Pioneer Assn. ADDRESSES, MEMORIALS, AND SKETCHES. 1900, 1901. (SLO)
Mettler, Peter J. CHRONIK DES DEUTSCHEN PIONIER-VEREINS VON TOLEDO, OHIO: SAMMT
EINER KURZEN GESCHICHTE DER ERSTEN DEUTSCHEN ANSIEDLER IN TOLEDO UND

LUCAS COUNTY UND DER NEKROLOGE DER VERSTORBENEN MITGLIEDER DES VEREINS. (Toledo OH: Gilsdorf Printing, 1898) 115p (LDS)

Mosier-Porter, Tana. TOLEDO PROFILE: A SESQUICENTENNIAL HISTORY. (Toledo OH: Toledo-Lucas Co.Pub.Lib., 1987) 146p

Northwest Ohio Genealogical Society. CEMETERIES OF LUCAS COUNTY OHIO. 3v.(SLO,LDS)

Northwest Ohio Genealogical Society. LUCAS COUNTY OHIO MARRIAGE RECORDS, 1835 TO 1858. (Toledo OH: the society, 1984) 63p (DAR)

Northwest Ohio Genealogical Society. TOMBSTONE INSCRIPTIONS OF LUCAS COUNTY, OHIO, VOL.1. (Toledo OH: the society, 1988) 350p

PORTRAIT AND BIOGRAPHICAL RECORDS OF CITY OF TOLEDO AND LUCAS AND WOOD COUNTIES OHIO. (Chicago: Chapman Pub.Co.,1895) 523p (LDS,SLO,DAR)(RPI)

Read, Helen H. MINISTERS AND JUSTICES OF THE PEACE, LUCAS COUNTY, OHIO, 1835-1858. 1984. 10p (LDS)

Scribner, Harvey. MEMOIRS OF LUCAS COUNTY AND THE CITY OF TOLEDO. (Madison WI: Western Histl Assn., 1910) 2v (DAR,SLO,LDS)(RPI)

Smith, John A. THE HISTORY OF MAUMEE, 1748-1926. (Toledo: H.M.Schmit, 1924) 226p (LDS)

ST.PETRI EVANGELICAL LUTHERAN CHURCH, TOLEDO, OHIO, 100, FEBRUARY 11, 1874-FEBRUARY 11, 1974. 1974. 24p (LDS)

TOLEDO CITY DIRECTORY. (Toledo: Toledo Directory Co., 1913,1916,1917, 1923,1940,1941) (LDS)

Van Tassel, Charles S. STORY OF THE MAUMEE VALLEY, TOLEDO AND THE SANDUSKY REGION. (Chicago: S.J.Clarke Pub Co., 1929) 4v. (LDS)

Waggoner, Clark. HISTORY OF THE CITY OF TOLEDO AND LUCAS COUNTY OHIO. (New York: Munsell & Co., 1888) 2v (DAR,LDS,SLO)(RPI)

Whelan, Florence S. A FEW RECORDS OF LUCAS CO., OHIO AND RAISIN, LENAWEE CO., MICH., AS KEPT BY URIEL SPENCER AND NATHAN SPENCER. 1940? 48p (DAR)

Wiley, Marilyn P. ADAMS TOWNSHIP. 1984. 2v (LDS)

Winter, Nevin O. HISTORY OF NORTHWEST OHIO. (Chicago: Lewis Pub.Co.,1917) 3v. (SLO,OHS)

Yon, Paul D. GUIDE TO OHIO COUNTY & MUNICIPAL GOVERNMENT RECORDS. (Columbus: Ohio Hist.Soc., 1973) 216p (OHS)

# MADISON COUNTY

| | |
|---|---|
| CREATED: | 1810 FROM FRANKLIN COUNTY |
| COUNTY SEAT: | LONDON 43140 |
| COURT HOUSE: | MAIN & HIGH ST., LONDON 43140 |
| LIBRARY: | 20 E.FIRST ST., LONDON 43140 |
| HISTORICAL SOCIETY: | PO BOX 124, LONDON 43140 |
| GENEALOGICAL SOCIETY: | MADISON CO. CHAPTER OGS, |
| | PO BOX 102, LONDON 43140 |
| | publication: MADISONIAN |
| HEALTH DEPARTMENT: | 61 EAST HIGH ST., LONDON 43140 |
| | (separate office for London city) |
| ARCHIVAL DISTRICT: | OHIO HISTORICAL SOCIETY, COLUMBUS |
| LAND SURVEYS: | VIRGINIA MILITARY DISTRICT |
| BOUNDED BY: | EAST:    FRANKLIN & PICKAWAY CO. |
| | NORTH:  UNION CO. |
| | WEST:    CHAMPAIGN & CLARK CO. |
| | SOUTH:   FAYETTE, GREENE & PICKAWAY CO. |
| TOWNSHIPS: | Canaan, Darby, Deer Creek, Fairfield, Jefferson, Monroe, Oak Run, Paint, Pike, Pleasant, Range, Somerford, Stokes, Union. |

**COURT RECORDS: (LDS MICROFILM)**
Auditor:
    Military commutation record, 1865.

Tax duplicates, 1816-1838.
Clerk of Courts:
  Common Pleas complete record, 1839-1842,1840,1848-1853.
  Common Pleas journal, v1, 1810-1817, 1834.
  Common Pleas appearance docket, 1841-1856.
  Common Pleas chancery record, 1841-1856.
  Common Pleas general index, 1810-1880.
  Common Pleas minutes, 1821-1852.
  Supreme Court journal, v1, 1846-1886.
  Supreme Court record, 1823-1859.
Commissioners:
  Journal & index, 1810-1903.
  Soldiers' burial record, 1900-1927.
County Home:
  Register of inmates, v1, 1868-1885.
Probate Court:
  Record of wills, v1-39, 1810-1967.
  Death records, 1888-1895.
  Birth records, 1867-1908.
  Marriage records, vA-B, 1-18, 1810-1967.
  Journals, v1-56, 1852-1965.
  Accounts, vA-H, 9-12, 1850-1901.
  Final record, v1-3,5, 1884-1914,1922-1928.
  Final record of accounts, vA-I, 10-12, 1850-1860,1871-1901.
  Administrators' bonds & letters, 1869-1904.
  Executors' bonds, 1857-1900.
  Record of bonds, 1844-1881.
  Guardians' bonds, 1857-1932.
  Inventories, 1877-1929.
  Civil docket, 1860-1890.
  Naturalization papers, 1860-1888.
  Land records, vA-D,5-29, 1852-1964.
Recorder:
  Record of war veterans' graves.
  Record of soldiers' & sailors' discharges, 1865-1967.
  Record of cemetery grave deeds, 1880-1967.
  Index to deeds, 1A-10B, 1810-1955.
  Deeds, v1-90, 1810-1922.
  Cemetery deed records, v1-2, 1880-1967.
Sheriff:
  Jail register, 1875-1928.
Miscellaneous:
  Plain City, Lower Liberty Presby.Church, session books, 1821-1930.

**OHIO HISTORICAL SOCIETY: (MICROFILM)**
Auditor:
  Military commutation record, 1865.
Clerk of Courts:
  Common Pleas complete record, 1839-1842,1840,1848-1853.
  Common Pleas journal, v1, 1810-1817, 1834.
  Common Pleas appearance docket, 1841-1856.
  Common Pleas chancery record, 1841-1856.
  Common Pleas general index, 1810-1880.
  Common Pleas minutes, 1821-1852.
  Supreme Court journal, v1, 1846-1886.

Supreme Court record, 1823-1859.
Commissioners:
    Journal & index, 1810-1903.
    Soldiers' burial record, 1900-1927.
County Home:
    Register of inmates, v1, 1868-1885.
Sheriff:
    Jail register, 1875-1928.
Miscellaneous:
    Marriage records, 1810-1865, by DAR.
    Bible records & deed abstracts, 1814-1866.
    Cemeteries, by DAR.
    Tombstone inscriptions, by DAR.

CENSUS RECORDS  (OHS,SLO,OGS,LDS)
1820-1880, 1900-1910; 1890 VETERANS; 1880,1900 SOUNDEX; 1910 MIRACODE

AGRICULTURAL CENSUS SCHEDULES  (OHS,SLO-mic)
1850,1860,1880

PRODUCTS OF INDUSTRY CENSUS SCHEDULE  (OHS,SLO-mic)
1850

MORTALITY CENSUS SCHEDULES (OHS,SLO-mic)
1850,1860

DEFECTIVE & DEPENDENT CENSUS SCHEDULES (OHS,SLO-mic)
1880

NEWSPAPERS: [GUIDE TO OHIO NEWSPAPERS, 1793-1973]
London, Mount Sterling, Plain City, West Jefferson.

TAX RECORDS (OHS & LDS)
1810-1814,1816-1838.

GENEALOGICAL PERIODICAL ARTICLES
Bell, Carol Willsey. OHIO GENEALOGICAL PERIODICAL INDEX: A COUNTY GUIDE (Youngstown
    OH: author, 6th ed., 1987)

PUBLISHED SOURCES:
Baynes, Gerald A. FROM HOSTELRY TO HOME TO HOSTELRY: A HISTORY OF THE RED BRICK
    AT LA FAYETTE, MADISON COUNTY OHIO. (np: Madison Press, 1968) 13p (LDS)
Bradley, Raymond K. TOMBSTONE INSCRIPTIONS OF "BILLY" BRADLEY CEMETERY. 6p. (SLO,LDS)
Bryan, Chester E. HISTORY OF MADISON COUNTY, OHIO: ITS PEOPLE, INDUSTRIES, AND IN-
    STITUTIONS. (Indianapolis: B.F.Bowen, 1915) 942p (DAR,LDS)
Carl, Martha T. ABSTRACTS OF DEEDS OF MADISON COUNTY, OHIO: BIBLE RECORDS, KENT
    AND CARPENTER FAMILIES. (SLO,LDS)
CITY/COUNTY DIRECTORIES: check holdings of OHS & local public library.
Clark, William P. BRIEF HISTORY OF ST.PATRICKS PARISH, LONDON, OHIO. (London OH: Madison
    Press, 1937) 74p (LDS)
Cring, Henry. CALDWELL'S ATLAS OF MADISON COUNTY OHIO. (Condit OH: J.A.Caldwell, 1875)
    (Reprint, Evansville IN: Unigraphic, 1973) 103p (LDS,SLO)(RPI)
Daughters of the American Revolution. ABSTRACT OF DEEDS AND BIBLE RECORDS FOR MADISON
    COUNTY OHIO. (SLO,DAR)
Daughters of the American Revolution. BIBLE RECORDS, MADISON COUNTY OHIO. (SLO,LDS)

Daughters of the American Revolution. CEMETERY INSCRIPTIONS MISCELLANEOUS VOLUME OHIO, V.2. (SLO)

Daughters of the American Revolution. CEMETERY RECORDS BROWN, CUYAHOGA, MADISON, MEDINA, LORAIN AND SHELBY COUNTIES OHIO. (SLO)

Daughters of the American Revolution. GRAVESTONE INSCRIPTIONS IN COUNTIES SURROUND-ING PICKAWAY COUNTY OHIO. (SLO,LDS)

Daughters of the American Revolution. MARRIAGE RECORDS, MADISON COUNTY OHIO, 1810-1865. 2v. (SLO,LDS,DAR)

Daughters of the American Revolution. TOMBSTONE INSCRIPTIONS OF CEMETERIES IN MADISON COUNTY OHIO. (SLO,LDS)

Dennison, Rachel E. GENEALOGICAL INDEX TO CALDWELL'S ATLAS OF MADISON COUNTY, OHIO, 1875, BY HENRY CRING. (London OH: Madison Co Chapter OGS, 1982) 95p (LDS,SLO)

Dennison, Rachel E. LONDON, COUNTY SEAT OF MADISON COUNTY OHIO, TOWN PLAT, DEED RECORDS. 1983. (SLO)

Haney, Nellie. SOME OF THE OLD CEMETERIES IN RANGE TOWNSHIP, MADISON CO., OHIO. (SLO,LDS)

Historical Records Survey. INVENTORY OF THE COUNTY ARCHIVES OF OHIO: MADISON COUN-TY. (Columbus: author, 1941) 263p (DAR,LDS)

HISTORY OF MADISON COUNTY OHIO, CONTAINING A HISTORY OF THE COUNTY. (Chicago: W.H.Beers & Co., 1883) (Reprint, Evansville IN: Unigraphic, 1972) (LDS,DAR,SLO)(RPI)

Kinnear, Robert B. TRANSCRIPT OF DIARIES OF STEPHEN A. KINNEAR, 1862,1863, 1879. (Colum-bus OH: author, 1974) 199p (LDS)

Madison County Bicentennial Committee. A CHRONICLE OF OUR TIME...'SEVENTY SIX.' (SLO)

Madison Co. Historical Society. ODDS AND ENDS PICKED UP FROM REMOTE CORNERS AND CUBBYHOLES OF HISTORY THROUGHOUT MADISON COUNTY... (Mt. Sterling OH: author, 1968-) v. (LDS,SLO)

Mathews, M.P. RECORD OF BIRTHS IN MADISON, FAYETTE, PICKAWAY COUNTIES OHIO 1866-1884. (SLO)

Matusoff, Karen. CENTRAL OHIO LOCAL GOVERNMENT RECORDS AT THE OHIO HISTORICAL SOCIETY. (Columbus: Ohio Hist Soc., 1978) 38p. (OGS)

PORTRAIT AND BIOGRAPHICAL RECORD OF FAYETTE, PICKAWAY AND MADISON COUNTIES OHIO. (Chicago: Chapman Bros., 1892) 877p (LDS,DAR,SLO,LC)(RPI)

Rankin, Maude P. CEMETERY RECORDS, FAYETTE CO., OHIO, V.3, WASHINGTON COURT HOUSE CITY CEMETERY WITH A FEW FROM SURROUNDING COUNTIES. (DAR,LDS)

Robinson, Elizabeth. ONE HUNDRED AND FIFTY YEARS OF THE PRESBYTERIAN CHURCH OF PLAIN CITY, OHIO. (n.p.: The Christian Education Committee, 1953) 33p (DAR)

Robinson, Mrs. James L. AN ABSTRACT - LOWER LIBERTY PRESBYTERIAN CHURCH 1821-1930, MADISON COUNTY OHIO. (Plain City OH: author, 1982) 69p (OGS)

Smith, Clifford N. FEDERAL LAND SERIES: A CALENDAR OF ARCHIVAL MATERIAL ON THE LAND PATENTS ISSUED BY THE U.S.GOVERNMENT, VOL.4, PT 1: GRANTS IN THE VIRGINIA MILITARY DISTRICT OF OHIO. (Chicago: American Library Assn., 1982) 395p

Smith, Clifford N. FEDERAL LAND SERIES: A CALENDAR OF ARCHIVAL MATERIAL ON THE LAND PATENTS ISSUED BY THE U.S.GOVERNMENT, VOL.4, PT 2: GRANTS IN THE VIRGINIA MILITARY DISTRICT OF OHIO. (Chicago: American Library Assn., 1986) 306p

Wagner, C.W. MISCELLANEOUS CEMETERY RECORDS OF ALLEN,LICKING,HAR-DIN,MADISON,PICKAWAY, VINTON COUNTIES OHIO. (SLO)

# MAHONING COUNTY

CREATED: 1846 FROM COLUMBIANA & TRUMBULL COS.
COUNTY SEAT: YOUNGSTOWN 44501
COURT HOUSE: 120 MARKET ST., YOUNGSTOWN 44503
LIBRARY: 305 WICK AVE., YOUNGSTOWN 44503

HISTORICAL SOCIETY:          MAHONING VALLEY HISTORICAL SOCIETY,
                             648 WICK AVE., YOUNGSTOWN 44502
GENEALOGICAL SOCIETY:        MAHONING CO. CHAPTER OGS,
                             c/o 3430 REBECCA DR., CANFIELD 44406
                             publication: MAHONING MEANDERINGS
HEALTH DEPARTMENT:           CITY BLDG., 26 S.PHELPS ST., YOUNGSTOWN 44503
                             (separate offices for Canfield, Sebring, Campbell, Struthers
                             & Alliance)
ARCHIVAL DISTRICT:           UNIVERSITY OF AKRON, AKRON, OHIO
                             (see Folck's Guide to records)
LAND SURVEYS:                CONGRESS LANDS, OHIO RIVER SURVEY (NORTH)
                             CONNECTICUT WESTERN RESERVE
BOUNDED BY:                  EAST:    LAWRENCE CO., PENNSYLVANIA
                             NORTH:   TRUMBULL CO.
                             WEST:    PORTAGE & STARK CO.
                             SOUTH:   COLUMBIANA CO.
TOWNSHIPS:                   Austintown, Beaver, Berlin, Boardman, Canfield, Coitsville, Ells-
                             worth, Goshen, Green, Jackson, Milton, Poland, Smith, Springfield,
                             Youngstown.

## COURT RECORDS: (LDS MICROFILM)
Clerk of Courts:
    Civil record, 1847-1867.
    Supreme Court record, 1848-1851.
County Home:
    Infirmary record, 1855-1859.
Probate Court:
    Record of wills, 1846-1909.
    Register of births, deaths & marriages, 1856-1857.
    Birth & death records, 1864 [?1867?]-1908.
    Marriage records, v1-35, 1852-1916.
    Marriage licenses, 1852-1861.
    Marriage certificates, 1846-1851.
    Index to marriage record, v1, 1852-1872.
    Naturalization records, 1873-1906.
    Administrators & executors index, 1846-1946.
    General index to guardians, assignees & trustees dockets, vA-B.
    General index to guardians & trustees, 1846-1946.
    Administration docket, v1-3,7-8, 1846-1868,1881-1891.
    Guardians docket, v1-4, 1846-1891.
    Civil docket, vA-E, 1853-1886.
    Adm., exr., grdn. bonds, 1864-1871.
    Guardians bonds & letters, v3, 1875-1886.
    Inventory records, 1848-1886.
    Probate journal, v1-21, 1852-1886.
    Final records, vA,C-F,H-J,L-O,Q-Y, 1853-1888.
Recorder:
    Index to transcribed deeds, vA-B, 1795-1845.
    Index to deeds, v1-9, 1846-1901.
    Deeds transcribed from Col. & Trum. Cos., 1795-1845.
    Deeds, v1-48, 1837-1885.
    Soldiers' discharge records, 1861-1909.
Miscellaneous:
    Youngstown, Belmont Ave.Presby.Church, treasurers records, 1882-86.
    Canfield, Presby.Church, records, 1804-1860. (WRHS)

Cemetery records, State Library of Ohio collection.
Manuscript history of Canfield, c1860. (WRHS)
David Simon's Tagebuch, 1853-1856. (WRHS)
Canfield Twp. Trustee records, 1805-1809. (WRHS)
Youngstown, LDS Church, members, 1948-1952.

## OHIO HISTORICAL SOCIETY: (MICROFILM)
Clerk of Courts:
Civil record, 1847-1867.
Supreme Court record, 1848-1851.
County Home:
Infirmary record, 1855-1859.
Probate Court:
Record of wills, 1887-1909.
Recorder:
Soldiers' discharge records, 1861-1909.
Record of deeds, 1881-1885.
Miscellaneous:
Connecticut Land Co., Western Reserve land draft, 1795-1809.
Marriage, birth, death & cemetery records, 1846-1865, by DAR.
Wills, Columbiana, Mahoning & Trumbull Cos., 1803-1850, by DAR.
Early records of people & places, by DAR.
Youngstown City Directories, 1872-1944, 1947-1973.

## CENSUS RECORDS (OHS,SLO,OGS,LDS)
1850-1880, 1900-1910; 1890 VETERANS; 1880,1900 SOUNDEX; 1910 MIRACODE

## AGRICULTURAL CENSUS SCHEDULES (OHS,SLO-mic)
1850,1860,1880

## PRODUCTS OF INDUSTRY CENSUS SCHEDULE (OHS,SLO-mic)
1850

## MORTALITY CENSUS SCHEDULES (OHS,SLO-mic)
1850,1860

## DEFECTIVE & DEPENDENT CENSUS SCHEDULES (OHS,SLO-mic)
1880

## NEWSPAPERS: [GUIDE TO OHIO NEWSPAPERS, 1793-1973]
Austintown, Boardman, Campbell, Canfield, Lowellville, Poland, Sebring, Struthers, Youngstown.

## TAX RECORDS (OHS & LDS)
none listed; see parent counties.

## GENEALOGICAL PERIODICAL ARTICLES
Bell, Carol Willsey. OHIO GENEALOGICAL PERIODICAL INDEX: A COUNTY GUIDE (Youngstown, OH: author, 6th ed., 1987)

## PUBLISHED SOURCES:
Aley, Howard C. BICENTENNIAL HISTORY OF MAHONING COUNTY OHIO. (Youngstown OH: Bicentennial Commission, 1975) 589p (Yo Pub Lib)
Aley, Howard C. INTERESTING PEOPLE OF OUR COMMUNITY...EMBRACING MAHONING, TRUMBULL & COLUMBIANA COUNTIES OHIO (Youngstown OH: author, 1948) 173p (OHS)

Aley, Howard C. THE BEGINNINGS OF OUR COMMUNITY...EMBRACING MAHONING, TRUM-
BULL & COLUMBIANA COUNTIES OHIO (Youngstown OH: author, 1950) 247p (OHS)

Aley, Howard C. THE FIRST HUNDRED YEARS. THE CENTENNIAL HISTORY OF THE MAHON-
ING COUNTY AGRICULTURAL SOCIETY. (Youngstown OH: United Printing Co., 1946) 113p.
(OHS)

Aley, Howard C. THE STORY OF OUR COMMUNITY...EMBRACING MAHONING, TRUMBULL &
COLUMBIANA COUNTIES OHIO (Youngstown OH: author, 1954) 263p

Aley, Howard C. THE TIME OF YOUR LIFE. THE ONE HUNDRED TWENTY-FIFTH ANNIVERSARY
HISTORY OF THE MAHONING COUNTY AGRICULTURAL SOCIETY. (Boardman OH: Web
Graphics, 1971) 82p (OHS)

Aley, Howard C. UNDERSTANDING THE RESOURCES OF OUR COMMUNITY...EMBRACING
MAHONING, TRUMBULL & COLUMBIANA COUNTIES OHIO. (Youngstown OH: author, 1951)
193p

ANNUAL BUSINESS REVIEW OF MAHONING COUNTY. (Canton OH: Review Pub Co., 1887) (OHS)

APPLEBY CO'S RURAL MAIL DIRECTORY. (Saginaw MI: author, 1906) (OHS)

Askue, Mabel. FIRST PRESBYTERIAN CHURCH OF YOUNGSTOWN, RECORDS, 1812-1832.
(Youngstown OH: author, 1930) 6p (Yo Pub Lib)

ATLAS OF MAHONING CO OHIO by D.J.LAKE, 1874 & ATLAS OF SURVEYS OF MAHONING CO
OHIO by A.H.Mueller 1899-1900. (Knightstown IN: Unigraphic, 1974) (OGS,SLO)

Baldwin, Henry R. WILLS OF COLUMBIANA, MAHONING AND TRUMBULL COUNTIES OHIO.
(SLO,LDS)

Baldwin, Henry R. OLDEST INSCRIPTIONS, WITH REVOLUTIONARY AND WAR OF 1812
RECORDS, OF THE CEMETERIES OF OHIO & PENNSYLVANIA. (Yo Pub Lib, SLO,LDS)

Baldwin, Henry R. THE BALDWIN COLLECTION, OWNED BY YOUNGSTOWN PUBLIC LIBRARY.
(Yo Pub Lib,Ft.Wayne Pub Lib, WRHS)

Bell, Carol W. MAHONING COUNTY OHIO 1845 TAX LIST, COMPILED FROM THE RECORDS OF
COLUMBIANA & TRUMBULL COUNTIES. (Youngstown OH: author, 1973) 85p (OGS,LDS,OHS)

Bell, Carol W. ABSTRACTS FROM BIOGRAPHIES IN HISTORY OF NORTH EASTERN OHIO by John
S. Stewart, 1935. (Indianapolis: Ye Olde Genealogie Shoppe, 1983)

Bell, Carol W. OHIO LANDS: STEUBENVILLE LAND OFFICE RECORDS, 1800-1820. (Youngstown
OH: author, 1983) 181p (OGS)

Bell, Carol W. & M.M.Simon. INDEX TO "20TH CENTURY HISTORY OF YOUNGSTOWN" BY
SANDERSON, 1907. (Youngstown OH: authors, 1972) 121p (Yo Pub Lib)

BICENTENNIAL HISTORY OF BEAVER TOWNSHIP 1976. (North Lima OH: Bicentennial Committee, 1976) 111p (Yo Pub Lib)

BICENTENNIAL USA 1776-1976: THE HISTORY OF ELLSWORTH-BERLIN TOWNSHIPS. (North
Jackson OH: Layman Printing, 1976) 160p (Yo Pub Lib)

BIOGRAPHICAL HISTORY OF NORTHEASTERN OHIO EMBRACING THE COUNTIES OF ASH-
TABULA, TRUMBULL AND MAHONING. (Chicago: Lewis Pub.Co.,1893) 735p
(DAR,SLO,LDS,OHS)

Bishara, Judy, et al, ed. ST. MARON PARISH, YOUNGSTOWN OHIO, 1911-1986.
(Youngstown OH: the church, 1986?) (OGS)

Butler, Joseph G. Jr. YOUNGSTOWN AND THE MAHONING VALLEY OHIO. (Chicago: American
Histl Soc, 1921) 3v (Yo Pub Lib, OHS,LDS,DAR,SLO)

Butler, Joseph G. Jr. YOUNGSTOWN AND THE MAHONING VALLEY: ILLUSTRATED (SPECIAL
LIMITED EDITION). (Chicago: American Historical Society, nd) 282p (Warren Pub.Lib.)

CITY/COUNTY DIRECTORIES: check holdings of OHS & local public library.

Cochran, Fred. 150TH ANNIVERSARY OF ELLSWORTH PRESBYTERIAN CHURCH, 1818-1968. (Yo
Pub Lib)

DAMASCUS THROUGH THE YEARS, 1808-1958. (Yo Pub Lib)

Daughters of the American Revolution. COURT, CHURCH, AND FAMILY RECORDS OF MAHON-
ING & COLUMBIANA COUNTIES OF OHIO. 1943. 119p (DAR)

Daughters of the American Revolution. EARLY CEMETERY RECORDS (ARRANGED BY TOWNSHIPS)
MAHONING COUNTY, OHIO. 1951. 73p (DAR)

Daughters of the American Revolution. EARLY RECORDS OF PEOPLE & PLACES (CEMETERY, FAMILY & BIBLE RECORDS) IN THE COUNTIES OF COLUMBIANA, MAHONING, PORTAGE, STARK. 1963. 161p (LDS,DAR)

Daughters of the American Revolution. MARRIAGE RECORDS AND REGISTRY OF BIRTHS, MAHONING COUNTY OHIO, 1846-1865. (SLO,LDS,DAR)

Daughters of the American Revolution. RECORDS OF ADMINISTRATORS, DEATHS, MARRIAGES, ETC., COLLECTED FROM MAHONING VALLEY NEWSPAPERS 1839-1863. (SLO,OHS)

Davis, Harry P. HISTORICAL COLLECTIONS OF SPRINGFIELD TOWNSHIP, MAHONING COUNTY OHIO. (New Middletown OH: author, 1939, repr 1976) (Yo Pub Lib)

Davis, Mabel. LINKS: HISTORY OF SPRINGFIELD TOWNSHIP (Columbiana OH: Village Print Shop, 1977) 123p (Yo Pub Lib)

Folck, Linda. LOCAL GOVERNMENT RECORDS IN THE AMERICAN HISTORY RESEARCH CENTER AT THE UNIVERSITY OF AKRON. (Akron: U of Akron, 1982) 40p. (OGS)

Galida, Edward. MILL CREEK PARK, YOUNGSTOWN, OHIO. (Youngstown OH: author, 1941) 104p (Yo Pub Lib,SLO)

Galida, Florence. FASCINATING HISTORY OF THE CITY OF CAMPBELL. (State College PA: Jostens, 1976) 268p (Yo Pub Lib)

Genco, Nancy, ed. HISTORY OF NEW SPRINGFIELD, MAHONING COUNTY OHIO. 1976. 48p (Yo Pub Lib)

Gutknecht, William J. ATLAS OF MAHONING COUNTY OHIO AND PART OF TRUMBULL COUNTY OHIO. (Youngstown OH: author, c1915) (OHS)

Hardesty, H.H. MILITARY HISTORY OF OHIO: MAHONING COUNTY EDITION, 1889. (Youngstown State U)

Higley, George. YOUNGSTOWN, AN INTIMATE HISTORY. (Youngstown OH: United Printing Co., 1953) 172p (Yo Pub Lib)

Hinshaw, William Wade. ENCYCLOPEDIA OF AMERICAN QUAKER GENEALOGY, VOL.IV, OHIO. (Baltimore: Genealogical Pub.Co., 1973) 1424p (SLO,OHS,LDS)

HISTORICAL HIGHLIGHTS OF POLAND (Poland OH: Centennial Committee, 1966) np (Yo Pub Lib)

HISTORY OF ST.JOHN'S EPISCOPAL CHURCH, YOUNGSTOWN OHIO. (Youngstown OH: Greenwood School Supply, 1898) 94p (Yo St Univ)

HISTORY OF THE POLICE DEPARTMENT, YOUNGSTOWN OHIO (Youngstown OH: Board of Safety, 1906) 152p (Yo Pub Lib)

HISTORY OF TRUMBULL AND MAHONING COUNTIES OHIO. (Chicago: H.Z.Williams, 1882) 2v.(SLO,OGS,OHS,LDS,DAR)(RPI)

Hixson, W.W. PLAT BOOK OF MAHONING COUNTY OHIO. (Rockford IL: author, nd) (OHS)

INDEX TO THE MICROFILM EDITION OF GENEALOGICAL DATA RELATING TO WOMEN IN THE WESTERN RESERVE BEFORE 1840. 1940. (Cleveland: Western Reserve Hist Soc, 1976) 226p (OGS)

Karsnak, Joyce. THE FOUR CORNERS: A HISTORY OF PETERSBURG OHIO. (Columbiana OH: Village Print Shoppe, 1976) 37p (Yo Pub Lib)

Lake, D.J. ATLAS OF MAHONING COUNTY OHIO. (Philadelphia: Titus,Simmons & Titus, 1874)(Reprint, Evansville IN: Unigraphic, 1974) 95p (OHS)(RPI)

LaLumia & Moore. THAT'S THE WAY IT WAS -- HISTORICAL HIGHLIGHTS OF BOARDMAN TOWNSHIP. (Youngstown OH: author, 1976) 117p (Yo Pub Lib)

Lamond, Richard C. A HISTORY OF HILLMAN LODGE NO.481, F & AM 1874-1974. (np: author, 1974) 96p

Mahoning Co Chapter OGS. MAHONING COUNTY OHIO - GUARDIANSHIP RECORDS VOL.1, 1846-1860. (Youngstown OH: the society, 1987) 60p (OGS)

Mahoning Co Chapter OGS. MAHONING COUNTY OHIO NATURALIZATION PROCEEDINGS: PRE 1870 IMMIGRANTS. (Youngstown OH: the society, 1987) 51p

Mahoning Co Chapter OGS. WILLS AND ADMINISTRATIONS ABSTRACTS, 1846-1856, VOL.I. (Youngstown OH: the society, 1979) 145p (OGS,SLO)

Mahoning Valley Historical Society. HISTORICAL COLLECTIONS OF THE MAHONING VALLEY. 1876. 524p. (Yo Pub Lib, SLO, OHS,DAR)

Mahoning Valley Historical Society. PIONEER REUNIONS OF THE MAHONING VALLEY, 1874-75 (Youngstown OH: the society,1876) 120p (Yo Pub Lib, OHS)

Mansfield, Ira F. OHIO AND PENNSYLVANIA REMINISCENCES. [Mahoning & Columbiana Co] (Beaver Falls PA: Tribune Printing Co., 1916) 204p (OHS)

Martin, Calvin C. THE REHOBOTH CONGREGATION: A HISTORY OF THE EARLY PRESBYTERIANS IN WEATHERSFIELD, AUSTINTOWN AND JACKSON TWPS. nd. 15p (Yo Pub Lib)

Melnick, John C. THE GREEN CATHEDRAL: HISTORY OF MILL CREEK PARK. (Youngstown OH: author, 1976)

Melnick, John C. HISTORY OF MEDICINE IN YOUNGSTOWN AND THE MAHONING VALLEY OHIO. (Youngstown OH: author, 1973) 121p (Yo Pub Lib,OHS)

Meredith, W.Fenton. THINK ON THESE THINGS: AN APPRECIATION OF HISTORIC ST.JAMES EPISCOPAL CHURCH, BOARDMAN OHIO. (Youngstown OH: author, 1969) 183p (Yo Pub Lib)

Mueller, A.H. Co. ATLAS OF SURVEYS OF MAHONING COUNTY OHIO. (Philadelphia: author, 1899-1900)(Reprint, Evansville IN: Unigraphic, 1974) 30p. (LDS,OHS)

Price, Carolyn & Forrest. NORTH JACKSON TOWNSHIP CEMETERY, MAHONING COUNTY, NORTH JACKSON, OHIO: INCLUDES OLD UNION CHURCH CEMETERY (LUTHERAN & REFORMED) (Akron OH: authors, 198?) 78p (LDS)

RECORDS OF THE VOTES OF THE INHABITANTS OF THE TOWNSHIP OF COITSVILLE, TRUMBULL CO OHIO, 6 APR 1807. (Yo Pub Lib)

Reynolds, Irene. EAST GOSHEN CEMETERY INSCRIPTIONS, BELOIT OHIO. (Beloit OH: author, 1982) 13p. (OGS)

Sanderson, Thomas W. 20TH CENTURY HISTORY OF YOUNGSTOWN AND MAHONING COUNTY OHIO AND REPRESENTATIVE CITIZENS. (Chicago: Biographical Pub Co., 1907) 1030p (Yo Pub Lib,SLO,LDS,OHS,DAR)(RPI)

Scott, Eva. ABSTRACTS OF MAHONING CO WILLS FROM RECORDS OF COLUMBIANA & TRUMBULL COUNTIES OHIO. (Youngstown OH: author, nd) 73p

Scott, Eva. REGISTER OF BIRTHS AND DEATHS FOR THE YEAR ENDING 1 MARCH 1857, MAHONING CO OHIO. (Youngstown OH: author, nd) 19p (Yo Pub Lib)

Shinn, Donna V. EVERYNAME INDEX TO HISTORY OF THE WESTERN RESERVE BY HARRIET T. UPTON, 1910. (np, author, 1983) 76p (Yo Pub Lib)

Simon, Bernice H. EARLY HISTORY & CHURCH REGISTER...SWEDISH MISSION CHURCH OF YOUNGSTOWN OH 1886-1930. (Canfield OH: author, 1986) 128p (LDS)

Simon, Bernice H. EVERY NAME INDEX TO HISTORY OF YOUNGSTOWN & THE MAHONING VALLEY OH by J.G.Butler, 1921 (Canfield OH: author, 1986) 84p

Simon, Bernice H. EVERY NAME INDEX TO GENEALOGICAL & FAMILY HISTORY OF EASTERN OHIO by E.Summers, 1903. (Canfield OH: author, 1986)

Simon, Margaret M. BOARDMAN DUTCH CHURCH BAPTISMAL REGISTER OF THE BETHLEHEM LUTHERAN & REFORMED CHURCH, BOARDMAN TOWNSHIP, MAHONING COUNTY OHIO, 1816-1858. (Boardman OH: author, 1978) 41p (OGS,LDS)

Simon, Margaret M. CANFIELD TOWNSHIP CEMETERY AND DEATH RECORDS, MAHONING COUNTY OHIO. (Canfield OH: Mahoning Co Chapter OGS, 1983) 148p (OGS,Yo Pub Lib,LDS)

Simon, Margaret M. DAVID SIMON'S TAGEBUCH, 1853-1856, MAHONING CO OHIO. (Cleveland: Western Reserve Hist Soc, 1974) (LDS,WRHS)

Simon, Margaret M. GOOD HOPE CHURCH RECORDS OF GERMAN LUTHERAN & REFORMED CONGREGATIONS, BEAVER TP, MAHONING CO OH 1815-1895 (Boardman, OH: author, 1986) 112p (OGS,LDS)

Simon, Margaret M. MAHONING COUNTY OHIO NEWSPAPER OBITUARY ABSTRACTS 1843-1870 (OHIO NEWSPAPER ABSTRACTS SERIES VOL.3) (Ft.Wayne IN: M.Clegg,ed. 1983) 78p (OGS,LDS,SLO)

Simonton, Nellie H. REFORMED & LUTHERAN CHURCH OF SPRINGFIELD TOWNSHIP, BAPTISMS. (np: author, nd) 94p (Yo Pub Lib,DAR)

Sittig, Kay. MARION G. FOWLER'S NOTES ON THE HISTORY OF CANFIELD OHIO. (np:author, 1975) 68p (Yo Pub Lib)

Skardon, Alvin W. STEEL VALLEY UNIVERSITY: THE ORIGIN OF YOUNGSTOWN STATE. (Youngstown OH: Youngstown State University, 1983) 288p (Yo Pub Lib, YSU)

Society of Friends. Ohio Yearly Meeting, Damascus. OBSERVING OUR 150TH YEARLY MEETING: OHIO QUAKER SESQUI-CENTENNIAL, 1812-1962. (Damascus OH: the church, 1962) 111p (LDS)

Stewart, John S. HISTORY OF NORTHEASTERN OHIO. (Indianapolis: Historical Pub Co., 1935) 3v. (SLO)

Summers, Ewing. GENEALOGICAL AND FAMILY HISTORY OF EASTERN OHIO ILLUSTRATED. (New York: Lewis Pub Co., 1903) (Yo Pub Lib, OHS)(RPI)

Trucksis, Theresa. A GUIDE TO LOCAL HISTORICAL MATERIALS IN THE LIBRARIES OF NORTHEASTERN OHIO. (Youngstown OH: NE Oh Libr.Assn., 1977) 72p (YoPL)

Truesdale, Jackson. SCRAPS OF HISTORY [CANFIELD] AS PUBLISHED IN THE MAHONING DISPATCH 1897-1900. (np: Youngstown Public Library, nd) 150p (Yo Pub Lib)

Tuttle, H.A. HISTORY OF SMITH TOWNSHIP, MAHONING COUNTY OHIO. (OHS)

Ulrich, Richard. AN EARLY HISTORY OF CANFIELD, 1776-1876. (Canfield OH: Canfield Hist Soc, 1980) 102p (Yo Pub Lib)

Upton, Harriet T. HISTORY OF THE WESTERN RESERVE (Chicago: Lewis Pub Co., 1910) 3v (SLO)

W.P.A. YOUNGSTOWN VINDICATOR INDEX, 1933-1939. (Yo Pub Lib, OHS)

Wadsworth, Frederick. MANUSCRIPT HISTORY OF CANFIELD, TRUMBULL COUNTY OHIO, CA.1860. (Cleveland: Western Reserve Hist Soc, 1974) (LDS,WRHS)

Washburn, George W. CIVIL WAR SOLDIERS BURIED IN MAHONING COUNTY CEMETERIES. (SLO)

Western Reserve Hist.Soc. INDEX TO THE MICROFILM EDITION OF GENEALOGICAL DATA RELATING TO WOMEN IN THE WESTERN RESERVE PRE 1840. (Cleveland: the society, 1976) 226p (OGS,WRHS)

Wickham, Gertrude V.W. MEMORIAL TO THE PIONEER WOMEN OF THE WESTERN RESERVE. (Cleveland: Cleveland Centennial Commission, 1896+) 2v, repr 1981 (SLO)

WIGGINS & McKILLOP'S DIRECTORY OF THE MAHONING AND SHENANGO VALLEYS. (Cleveland: author, 1875) (OHS)

Yon, Paul D. GUIDE TO OHIO COUNTY & MUNICIPAL GOVERNMENT RECORDS. (Columbus: Ohio Hist Soc, 1973) 216p (OHS)

Youngstown Public Library. 1860 MAHONING COUNTY CENSUS INDEX. 1940. (YoPub Lib)

# MARION COUNTY

| | |
|---|---|
| CREATED: | 1820 FROM DELAWARE COUNTY |
| COUNTY SEAT: | MARION 43302 |
| COURT HOUSE: | MAIN & CENTER ST., MARION 43302 |
| LIBRARY: | 445 E. CHURCH ST., MARION 43302 |
| HISTORICAL SOCIETY: | PO BOX 169, MARION OH 43302 |
| GENEALOGICAL SOCIETY: | MARION CO. CHAPTER OGS, |
| | PO BOX 844, MARION 43302 |
| | publication: MARION MEMORIES |
| HEALTH DEPARTMENT: | COUNTY: 98 McKINLEY PARK DR., MARION 43302 |
| | CITY:233 W.CENTER ST., MARION 43302 |
| ARCHIVAL DISTRICT: | OHIO HISTORICAL SOCIETY, COLUMBUS |
| LAND SURVEYS: | CONGRESS LANDS, E & S OF 1ST PRIN.MERIDIAN |
| | VIRGINIA MILITARY DISTRICT |
| | UNITED STATES MILITARY DISTRICT |
| BOUNDED BY: | EAST:    MORROW CO. |
| | NORTH:   CRAWFORD & WYANDOT CO. |
| | WEST:    HARDIN CO. |
| | SOUTH:   DELAWARE & UNION CO. |
| TOWNSHIPS: | Big Island, Bowling Green, Claridon, Grand, Grand Prairie, Green Camp, Marion, Montgomery, Pleasant, Prospect, Richland, Salt Rock, Scott, Tully, Waldo. |

## COURT RECORDS: (LDS MICROFILM)
Auditor:
   Tax duplicates, 1824-1838.
Clerk of Courts:
   Common Pleas chancery record, 1824-1861.
   Common Pleas general index, n.d.
   Common Pleas journal, 1829-1856.
   Common Pleas record, 1824-1855.
   Supreme Court journal, 1847-1883.
   Supreme Court record, 1825-1866.
Probate Court:
   Adoption records, 1923-1948.
   Birth records, v1-3, 1867-1908.
   Birth registrations, dates vary.
   Death records, 1867-1908.
   Marriage index, v1-4, 1824-1964.
   Marriage records, v1-40, 1824-1964.
   General index to records, n.d.
   Will records, 1825-1924.
   Probate journal, 1852-1911.
   Probate records, grdns. bonds & applications, 1879-1950.
   Index to land sales & estates, n.d.
   Naturalization records, 1859-1905.
Recorder:
   Index to deeds, vA-XYZ, 1828-1954.
   Deeds, v1-100, 1821-1904.
   Special index to deeds (church,cemetery), 1828-1870.
   General index to mortgages, v1-4,A-Z, 1828-1969.
   Mortgage records, v51-100, 1900-1927.
   Mortgage index to companies, v1-4, 1821-1969.
   Town plats, 1821-1880.
   Record of soldiers' & sailors' discharge, 1865-1970.
Miscellaneous:
   Cemetery records, State Library of Ohio collection.

## OHIO HISTORICAL SOCIETY: (MICROFILM)
Clerk of Courts:
   Common Pleas chancery record, 1824-1861.
   Common Pleas general index, n.d.
   Common Pleas journal, 1829-1856.
   Common Pleas record, 1824-1855.
   Supreme Court journal, 1847-1883.
   Supreme Court record, 1825-1866.
Commissioners:
   Journal, 1824-1902.
   Index to journals, 1875-1904.
County Engineer:
   Ditch plat book, c1886-c1956.
   Ditch profiles, c1907-1945.
County Home:
   Infirmary record, 1913-1924.
Probate Court:
   Ministers' licenses, 1861-1976.
   Index to births, 1867-1908.
   Birth records, v1-3, 1867-1908.

Death records, 1867-1908.
General index to marriages, 1824-1964.
Marriage record, v1-24, 1824-1939.
Recorder:
Deed records, v1-166, 1821-1925.
General index to deeds, 1828-1954.
Index to mortgages, 1828-1969.
Mortgage record, v1-165, 1850-1941.
Soldiers' discharges, v1-15, 1865-1970.
Special index to deeds (church,school etc) 1826-1870.
Town plats, 1821-1876.
Miscellaneous:
Marriages, v1-2, 1824-1865, by DAR.
Bible records, by DAR.
Grave records, by DAR.

## CENSUS RECORDS (OHS,SLO,OGS,LDS)
1830-1880, 1900-1910; 1890 VETERANS; 1880,1900 SOUNDEX; 1910 MIRACODE

## AGRICULTURAL CENSUS SCHEDULES (OHS,SLO-mic)
1850,1860,1880

## PRODUCTS OF INDUSTRY CENSUS SCHEDULE (OHS,SLO-mic)
1850

## MORTALITY CENSUS SCHEDULES (OHS,SLO-mic)
1850,1860

## DEFECTIVE & DEPENDENT CENSUS SCHEDULES (OHS,SLO-mic)
1880

## NEWSPAPERS: [GUIDE TO OHIO NEWSPAPERS, 1793-1973]
La Rue, Marion, Prospect.

## TAX RECORDS (OHS & LDS)
1824-1838.

## GENEALOGICAL PERIODICAL ARTICLES
Bell, Carol Willsey. OHIO GENEALOGICAL PERIODICAL INDEX: A COUNTY GUIDE (Youngstown, OH: author, 6th ed., 1987)

## PUBLISHED SOURCES:
ATLAS AND PLAT BOOK, MARION COUNTY, OHIO, 1973. (Rockford IL: Rockford Map Pub., 1973) 38p (LDS)
CITY/COUNTY DIRECTORIES: check holdings of OHS & local public library.
Crist, A.C. THE HISTORY OF MARION PRESBYTERY: ITS CHURCHES, ELDERS, MINISTERS, ETC. 1908. 352p (DAR,LDS)
Daughters of the American Revolution. BIBLE RECORDS OF THE CAPT. WILLIAM HENDRICKS CHAPTER, MARION OHIO. 1963. 167p (SLO,LDS)
Daughters of the American Revolution. GRAVE RECORDS FROM MARION COUNTY OHIO CEMETERIES. 1947. 104p (SLO,LDS)
Daughters of the American Revolution. MARRIAGE RECORDS OF MARION COUNTY OHIO, 1824-1865, A-Z, VOLS.1-2. 1963. (SLO,LDS,DAR)
Drake, Tom E. FUNERAL DIRECTORS RECORDS OF MR. TOM E. DRAKE AND MR. FRED GEHM, PROSPECT, OHIO, 1907-1921. 2v. (SLO)

FIRST CHURCH OF THE BRETHREN, MARION OHIO - 60TH ANNIVERSARY, 1918-1978. 12p (OGS)

Hardesty, H.H. MILITARY HISTORY OF OHIO - MARION COUNTY EDITION. 1886/87. (OHS)

Hartline, David L. SOLDIERS OF MARION COUNTY OHIO 1776-1900. (Marion OH: author, 1972) 250p (SLO,LDS,OHS,OGS,DAR)

HISTORY OF GREEN CAMP, OHIO, 1838-1938. (Green Camp OH: Centennial Committee, 1938) 31,50p (DAR)

HISTORY OF MARION COUNTY OHIO. (Chicago: Leggett Conway & Co., 1883) 1031p (OGS,DAR,SLO,LDS)(RPI)

Howland, H.G. ATLAS OF MARION COUNTY, OHIO. (Philadelphia: Harrison, Sutton & Hare, 1878) (Reprint, Evansville IN: Unigraphic, 1974) 128p (DAR,LDS,OGS,SLO)(RPI)

Jacoby, J.Wilbur. HISTORY OF MARION COUNTY OHIO. (Chicago: Biographical Pub.Co.,1907)(Reprint, Evansville IN: Unigraphic, 1976) 834p.(SLO,DAR,LDS) (RPI)

Leeka, Ora E. GRAVE RECORDS FROM MARION COUNTY, OHIO, CEMETERIES. 1947. 106p (DAR,LDS)

MARION CITY DIRECTORY, INCLUDING MARION COUNTY TAXPAYERS. (Columbus: R.L.Polk & Co., 1931-) v. (LDS)

Marion Co Chapter OGS. 1850 CENSUS OF MARION COUNTY OHIO. (Marion OH: the society, 1982) 259p (OGS)

Marion Co Chapter OGS. 1852 LANDOWNERS MAP, MARION COUNTY. (Marion OH: the society,nd)

Marion Co Chapter OGS. 1880 MARION COUNTY OHIO CENSUS INDEX. (Marion OH: the society, nd) 60p (OGS)

Marion Co Chapter OGS. CEMETERY INSCRIPTIONS OF MARION COUNTY OHIO: LISTING IN-SCRIPTIONS FROM 115 MARION COUNTY CEMETERIES WITH 15 TOWNSHIP HISTORIES AND MAPS. (Marion OH: the society, 1985) 358p (LDS,OGS)

Marion Co Chapter OGS. EARLY MARION COUNTY COURTHOUSE RECORDS. (Marion OH: the society, nd) 87p (OGS)

Marion Co Chapter OGS. FUNERAL DIRECTORS RECORDS OF DRAKE & GEHM, PROSPECT OHIO, VOL.I, 1907-1914. (Marion OH: the society, 1980) 41p (OGS)

Marion Co Chapter OGS. MARION COUNTY TOMBSTONE INSCRIPTIONS. (Marion OH: author, nd) 245p (OGS)

Marion Co Chapter OGS. MARION COUNTY FAMILIES - TERRITORIAL DAYS TO PRESENT. (Marion OH: the society, nd) 552p (OGS)

Marion Co Chapter OGS. PROSPECT OHIO FUNERAL RECORDS VOL.I. (Marion OH: the society, nd)

Marion Co Chapter OGS. PROSPECT OHIO FUNERAL RECORDS VOL.II, 1914-1921. (Marion OH: author, 1982) 37p.(OGS)

Marion Co Chapter OGS. SOME EARLY COURT RECORDS - MARION COUNTY OHIO. (Marion OH: the society,1982) 116p. (OGS,LDS,SLO)

Marion Co Chapter OGS. SURNAME LIST FROM MEMBERS' 5 GENERATION CHARTS. INDEXED. VOL.II. (Marion OH: the society, nd) (OGS)

Marion Co Chapter OGS. SURNAME LIST FROM MEMBERS' 5 GENERATION CHARTS. INDEXED. VOL.I. (Marion OH: the society, nd) (OGS)

Marion Co Chapter OGS. TOMBSTONE INSCRIPTIONS OF THE CALEDONIA AND CLAIRDON CEMETERIES, CLARIDON TOWNSHIP, MARION COUNTY OHIO. (Marion OH: the society, 1987) 90p (OGS)

Marion Co.Historical Society. MARION COUNTY 1979 HISTORY. (Marion OH: the society, 1979) (SLO,LDS)

MARION COUNTY BANK, 100 YEARS OF GROWTH...A BRIEF HISTORY OF MARION COUNTY OHIO. (SLO)

Marshall, Maxine. EARLY NEWSPAPERS, MARION CO OHIO 1828-1842. (Marion OH: author, 1983) 102p (OGS,LDS)

Marshall, Maxine. SOLDIERS' & SAILORS' MEMORIAL CHAPEL, MARION CEMETERY, MARION OHIO. (Marion OH: author, 1981) 43p (OGS,LDS,SLO)

Matusoff, Karen. CENTRAL OHIO LOCAL GOVERNMENT RECORDS AT THE OHIO HISTORICAL SOCIETY. (Columbus: Ohio Hist Soc., 1978) 38p. (OGS)

PORTRAIT AND BIOGRAPHICAL RECORD OF MARION AND HARDIN COUNTIES OHIO. (Chicago: Chapman Pub.Co.,1895) 563p. (LDS,SLO,DAR)(RPI)

Potts, Allen L. RECORDS FROM MEEKER & UNION CEMETERIES ABT 1819 TO 1960 AND OBITUARY NOTICES TAKEN FROM LOCAL NEWSPAPERS. (Marion OH: author, 1960) 63p (LDS)

Powell, Esther W. TOMBSTONE INSCRIPTIONS AND OTHER RECORDS OF DELAWARE COUNTY OHIO, INCLUDING PORTIONS OF MORROW AND MARION COUNTIES. (Akron OH: author, 1972) 448p (OGS,LDS,SLO,DAR)

Rayburn, E.E. CEMETERIES OF SOUTHERN OHIO. (SLO)

Smith, Clifford N. FEDERAL LAND SERIES: A CALENDAR OF ARCHIVAL MATERIAL ON THE LAND PATENTS ISSUED BY THE U.S.GOVERNMENT, VOL.2: FEDERAL BOUNTY LAND WARRANTS OF THE AMERICAN REVOLUTION. (Chicago: American Library Assn., 1972) 416p

Smith, Clifford N. FEDERAL LAND SERIES: A CALENDAR OF ARCHIVAL MATERIAL ON THE LAND PATENTS ISSUED BY THE U.S.GOVERNMENT, VOL.4, PT 1: GRANTS IN THE VIRGINIA MILITARY DISTRICT OF OHIO. (Chicago: American Library Assn., 1982) 395p

Smith, Clifford N. FEDERAL LAND SERIES: A CALENDAR OF ARCHIVAL MATERIAL ON THE LAND PATENTS ISSUED BY THE U.S.GOVERNMENT, VOL.4, PT 2: GRANTS IN THE VIRGINIA MILITARY DISTRICT OF OHIO. (Chicago: American Library Assn., 1986) 306p

Wilson, Sylvia & Ruth. BIOGRAPHIES OF MANY RESIDENTS OF MARION COUNTY AND REVIEW OF THE HISTORY OF MARION COUNTY. (Galion OH: Wilson Printing Co., 1950) 370p (ad)

Winter, Nevin O. HISTORY OF NORTHWEST OHIO. (Chicago: Lewis Pub Co.,1917) 3v. (SLO,OHS)

# MEDINA COUNTY

| | |
|---|---|
| CREATED: | 1812 FROM PORTAGE COUNTY |
| COUNTY SEAT: | MEDINA 44256 |
| COURT HOUSE: | 93 PUBLIC SQUARE, MEDINA 44256 |
| LIBRARY: | 210 S. BROADWAY, MEDINA 44256 |
| HISTORICAL SOCIETY: | 231 E. WASHINGTON ST., MEDINA 44256 |
| GENEALOGICAL SOCIETY: | MEDINA COUNTY CHAPTER OGS, PO BOX 804, MEDINA 44250 |
| HEALTH DEPARTMENT: | 246 NORTHLAND DR., PO BOX 1033, MEDINA 44256 (separate offices for Medina City, Brunswick, Wadsworth & Rittman) |
| ARCHIVAL DISTRICT: | WESTERN RESERVE HIST.SOC., CLEVELAND |
| LAND SURVEYS: | CONNECTICUT WESTERN RESERVE |
| BOUNDED BY: | EAST:     SUMMIT CO. |
| | NORTH:   CUYAHOGA & LORAIN CO. |
| | WEST:    ASHLAND & LORAIN CO. |
| | SOUTH:   WAYNE CO. |
| TOWNSHIPS: | Brunswick, Chatham, Granger, Guilford, Harrisville, Hinckley, Homer, Lafayette, Litchfield, Liverpool, Medina, Montville, Sharon, Spencer, Wadsworth, Westfield, York. |

## COURT RECORDS: (LDS MICROFILM)
Auditor:
  Tax duplicates, 1819-1838.
Clerk of Courts:
  Common Pleas execution dockets, vA-I, 1818-1852.
  Supreme Court record, 1820-1842.
  Supreme Court docket, 1834-1849.
Probate Court:
  Birth & death records, 1867-1909
  Delayed & corrected birth records, dates vary.
  Marriage records, 1818-1965.

Marriage records card file index.
Birth records card file, 1867-1909.
Probate journal, vA-Z, A1-26, 1852-1949.
Probate docket, v1-2, 1833-1852.
Probate records, old, 1818-1861.
Will records, vA-Z,1-7, 1862-1949.
Civil docket, vA-F, 1852-1888.
Miscellaneous records, vA-F, 1873-1907.
Recorder:
    Deed records, vA-BB,1-26, 1818-1871.
    Deed index, v1-9, 1818-1871.
    Land sales, final record, vA-Z, 1852-1931.
Miscellaneous:
    Guilford Presby.Church, records, 1834-1854.
    Lafayette, First Presby.Church, records, 1853-1883. (WRHS)

## OHIO HISTORICAL SOCIETY: (MICROFILM)
Clerk of Courts:
    Common Pleas dockets, vA-I, 1818-1852.
    Supreme Court record, 1820-1842.
    Supreme Court docket, 1834-1849.
Miscellaneous:
    Connecticut Land Co., Western Reserve land draft, 1795-1809.
    Marriage records, 1818-1865, by DAR.
    Cemeteries of Brown, Cuya.,Lor.,Mad.,Medina & Shelby Cos., by DAR.

## CENSUS RECORDS  (OHS,SLO,OGS,LDS)
1820-1880, 1900-1910; 1890 VETERANS; 1880,1900 SOUNDEX; 1910 MIRACODE

## AGRICULTURAL CENSUS SCHEDULES  (OHS,SLO-mic)
1850,1860,1880

## PRODUCTS OF INDUSTRY CENSUS SCHEDULE  (OHS,SLO-mic)
1850

## MORTALITY CENSUS SCHEDULES (OHS,SLO-mic)
1850,1860

## DEFECTIVE & DEPENDENT CENSUS SCHEDULES (OHS,SLO-mic)
1880

## NEWSPAPERS: [GUIDE TO OHIO NEWSPAPERS, 1793-1973]
Chippewa Lake, Lodi, Medina, Rittman, Seville, Wadsworth.

## TAX RECORDS (OHS & LDS)
1819-1838.

## GENEALOGICAL PERIODICAL ARTICLES
Bell, Carol Willsey. OHIO GENEALOGICAL PERIODICAL INDEX: A COUNTY GUIDE (Youngstown,
    OH: author, 6th ed., 1987)

## PUBLISHED SOURCES:
ATLAS AND DIRECTORY OF MEDINA COUNTY OHIO. (Cleveland: American Atlas Co., 1897) 143p
    (OGS,LDS,SLO)(RPI)

Brown, Edward. WADSWORTH MEMORIAL; CONTAINING AN ACCOUNT ...OF THE 60TH AN-
NIVERSARY. (Wadsworth: Steam Printing House, 1875) 232p (LDS,SLO)
CITY/COUNTY DIRECTORIES: check holdings of OHS & local public library.
Clegg, Michael. TAX RECORDS OF PORTAGE, SUMMIT AND PORTIONS OF MEDINA COUNTY
OHIO, 1808-1820. (Mansfield: Ohio Gen Soc, 1979) 58p (OGS,LDS)
COMBINATION ATLAS MAP OF MEDINA COUNTY OHIO. 1874 repr 1972. (OGS)
Coolman, Ford & R.Kreider. THE MENNONITE CEMETERIES OF MEDINA COUNTY WITH A BRIEF
HISTORICAL SKETCH OF THE CHURCHES. (Medina: author, 1971) 137p (OGS)
Daughters of the American Revolution. BROWN, CUYAHOGA, MADISON, MEDINA, LORAIN AND
SHELBY COUNTIES OHIO CEMETERY RECORDS. (SLO)
Daughters of the American Revolution. CEMETERY RECORDS, LIVERPOOL TOWNSHIP, MEDINA
COUNTY, OHIO. 1976? 179p (DAR,SLO)
Daughters of the American Revolution. MARRIAGE RECORDS 1818-1865 MEDINA COUNTY OHIO.
1936-37. 2v (DAR,SLO,LDS)
Daughters of the American Revolution. MEDINA COUNTY CEMETERIES. (SLO)
Daughters of the American Revolution. SOME CEMETERY RECORDS OF CUYAHOGA, FULTON,
MEDINA, LORAIN & WAYNE COUNTIES. 1838. 175p (DAR,SLO,LDS)
Duff, William A. HISTORY OF NORTH CENTRAL OHIO EMBRACING RICHLAND, ASHLAND,
WAYNE, MEDINA, LORAIN, HURON, AND KNOX COUNTIES (Topeka KS:
Historical Pub Co., 1931) 3v (OHS,DAR)
Ensworth, Ruth. EARLY SHARON TOWNSHIP. 1981. 256p. (SLO)
Everts, L.H. COMBINATION ATLAS MAP OF MEDINA COUNTY OHIO. (Chicago: Everts, 1874)
(Reprint, Evansville IN: Unigraphic, 1972) 143p (DAR,LDS, SLO)
GENEALOGICAL DATA RELATING TO WOMEN IN THE WESTERN RESERVE BEFORE 1840 (1850)
(Cleveland: Centennial Commission, 1943) (LDS)
Hardesty, H.H. MILITARY HISTORY OF OHIO - MEDINA COUNTY EDITION. 1886/87. (OHS)
Harter, Mrs. Bert. GERMAN REFORMED & LUTHERAN CHURCH RECORDS, BAPTISMS, DEATHS
FROM WAYNE, STARK, MEDINA & SUMMIT COUNTIES, TRANSLATED FROM THE GER-
MAN. (Doylestown OH: author, 1962)
HISTORY OF MEDINA COUNTY. (Fostoria OH: Gray Print.Co., 1948) 419p (LDS)
HISTORY OF MEDINA COUNTY OHIO. (Chicago: Baskin & Battey, 1881) (Reprint, Evansville IN:
Unigraphic, 1972) 922p (DAR,SLO,LDS)(RPI)
INDEX TO THE MICROFILM EDITION OF GENEALOGICAL DATA RELATING TO WOMEN IN
THE WESTERN RESERVE BEFORE 1840. 1940. (Cleveland: Western Reserve Hist Soc, 1976) 226p
(WHRS)
Lee, Charles R. HISTORY OF WALNUT GROVE CEMETERY. (Naples FL: Neapolitan Pub., 1970) 123p
(LDS)
McKINNEY RECORDS (U.S.CENSUS FOR 1820-1830) 1966? (LDS)
Medina Co Genealogical Society. TOMBSTONE INSCRIPTIONS FROM THE CEMETERIES IN
MEDINA COUNTY, OHIO, 1983: WHISPERS FROM THE PAST. (Evansville IN: Unigraphic, 1984)
476,114p (SLO,SLO)
Medina Co Historical Society. HISTORY OF MEDINA COUNTY. (Fostoria OH: Gray Printing, c1948)
419p (LDS,DAR)
Medina Senior High School. HISTORICAL HIGHLIGHTS OF MEDINA. 1966. 211p. (SLO,LDS)
Murray, Zola F. SEVILLE, OHIO: 1816-1941. (Wadsworth OH: Banner Press, 1941) 85p (DAR)
Northrop, Nira B. PIONEER HISTORY OF MEDINA COUNTY. (Medina: G.Redway, printer, 1861)
(Reprint, Evansville IN: Unigraphic, 1972) 224p (DAR, LDS,SLO)(RPI)
Schapiro, Eleanor. WADSWORTH: CENTER TO CITY. (Wadsworth OH: Banner Press, 1938) 203p
(SLO,DAR)
Schapiro, Eleanor. WADSWORTH HERITAGE. (Wadsworth OH: Wadsworth Newsbanner, 1964) 392p
(LDS)
Shewalter, Laura. REVOLUTIONARY ANCESTORS LISTS. (SLO)
Upton, Harriet T. HISTORY OF THE WESTERN RESERVE (Chicago: Lewis Pub Co., 1910) 3v (SLO)
Vaughn, Helen & R. Ensworth. EARLY SHARON TOWNSHIP. (Medina OH: authors, 1984) 256p (OGS)
Wadsworth High School. WADSWORTH, CENTER TO CITY. 1938. 204p. (SLO)

**TAX RECORDS (OHS & LDS)**
1820-1838.

**GENEALOGICAL PERIODICAL ARTICLES**
Bell, Carol Willsey. OHIO GENEALOGICAL PERIODICAL INDEX: A COUNTY GUIDE (Youngstown,
OH: author, 6th ed., 1987)

**PUBLISHED SOURCES:**
1969 MEIGS COUNTY OHIO ATLAS AND PLAT BOOK. (Rockford IL: Rockford Map Pub., 1969) 38p
(OGS)
Berry, Ellen T. & David. EARLY OHIO SETTLERS: PURCHASERS OF LAND IN SOUTHEASTERN
OHIO, 1800-1840. (Baltimore: Genealogical Pub.Co., 1984) 129p (OHS,SLO,OGS,DAR)
CITY/COUNTY DIRECTORIES: check holdings of OHS & local public library.
Daughters of the American Revolution. CEMETERY RECORDS AND MARRIAGES 1812-1866, MEIGS
COUNTY OHIO. (np: author, 1963) (LDS,SLO)
Daughters of the American Revolution. EARLY INHABITANTS OF MEIGS COUNTY OHIO 1800-1883.
1r mic (SLO)
Daughters of the American Revolution. FREEWILL BAPTIST CHURCH, MEIGS COUNTY OHIO. 1975.
131p (DAR,SLO)
Daughters of the American Revolution. MARRIAGE RECORDS, MEIGS COUNTY OHIO 1812-1866.
1936? 2v. (SLO,LDS,DAR)
Daughters of the American Revolution. MEIGS COUNTY OHIO CEMETERIES. (SLO)
Daughters of the American Revolution. MEIGS COUNTY'S EARLY RELIGIOUS HERITAGE. 1975. 97p
(DAR,SLO)
Daughters of the American Revolution. MIDDLEPORT HILL CEMETERY, MEIGS COUNTY OHIO.
(SLO,LDS)
Daughters of the American Revolution. SCIPIO TOWNSHIP, MEIGS COUNTY OHIO. 1941. 138p.
(SLO)
Ervin, Edgar. PIONEER HISTORY OF MEIGS COUNTY OHIO TO 1949, INCLUDING MASONIC HIS-
TORY OF THE SAME PERIOD. (np: author, 1954?) 514p (DAR,LDS, SLO)
Evans, James M. HARDESTY'S HISTORICAL AND GEOGRAPHICAL ENCYCLOPEDIA & 1867 TAX
MAP OF MEIGS COUNTY OHIO. (Pomeroy OH: Meigs Co Hist Soc., 1982) (OGS)
HARDESTY'S HISTORICAL AND GEOGRAPHICAL ENCYCLOPEDIA, ILLUSTRATED. (Chicago:
H.H.Hardesty & Co., 1883) 40p (LDS)
Harris, Charles H. THE HARRIS STORY. 1957. 329p (SLO)
Hill, Agnes C. TUPPERS PLAINS AND THE SURROUNDING AREA OF OLIVE AND ORANGE
TOWNSHIPS: STORIES AND PICTURES OF THE YESTERDAYS. (np: author, 1985) 184p (LDS)
HISTORY OF MEIGS, VINTON, GALLIA AND ATHENS COUNTIES FROM NEWSPAPER CLIPPINGS
FROM THE DYE COLLECTION. 1959. (LDS,SLO)
HISTORY OF THE UPPER OHIO VALLEY. (Madison WI: Brant & Fuller, 1891) 929p, 2v (SLO)
HISTORY OF TUPPERS PLAINS, OHIO, AND SURROUNDING AREAS OF OLIVE AND ORANGE
TOWNSHIPS. (SLO)
ILLUSTRATED HISTORICAL & BUSINESS REVIEW OF MEIGS & GALLIA COUNTIES OHIO.
(Coshocton: Union Pub Co., 1891) (OHS)
Larkin, Stillman C. THE PIONEER HISTORY OF MEIGS COUNTY. 1908. (Reprint, Pomeroy OH: Meigs
Co Hist Soc.,1982) 208p (DAR,OGS,SLO,LDS)(RPI)
Lewis, Thomas W. SOUTHEASTERN OHIO AND THE MUSKINGUM VALLEY, 1788-1928: COVER-
ING ATHENS, BELMONT, COSHOCTON, GUERNSEY, LICKING, MEIGS, MONROE, MORGAN,
MUSKINGUM, NOBLE, PERRY AND WASHINGTON COUNTIES. (Chicago: S.J.Clarke Co.,1928)
3v. (SLO,DAR,OHS)
Madson, Mabel B. OLD BIRAM CEMETERY BURIALS, HAZAEL, LEBANON TWP., MEIGS CO.,
OHIO. (LDS)
MEIGS COUNTY OHIO FROM HARDESTY'S HISTORICAL AND GEOGRAPHICAL EN-
CYCLOPEDIA, 1883. (Pomeroy OH: Meigs Co.Pioneer & Hist.Soc., 1982) 1v (SLO)

MEIGS COUNTY OHIO HISTORY BOOK. (Pomeroy OH: Meigs Co Pioneer & Hist.Soc., 1979) 514p (DAR,OGS,LDS,SLO)

Meigs Co.Chapter OGS. MEIGS COUNTY OHIO LETART TWP CEMETERY RECORDS. (Racine OH: the society, 1986) 121p (OGS)

Meigs Co.Pioneer & Hist.Society. POLL RECORDS OF MEIGS COUNTY. (Columbus OH: Inskeep Bros., 1985) 134p (LDS)

Ohio University. GUIDE TO LOCAL GOVERNMENT RECORDS AT OHIO UNIVERSITY. (Athens: OU Library, 1986) 61p.

OUTLINE MAP AND HISTORY OF MEIGS COUNTY OHIO CONTAINING BIOGRAPHICAL SKETCHES FROM HADESTY'S HISTORICAL AND GEOGRAPHICAL ENCYCLOPEDIA. (Chicago: 1883) 40p (LDS)(RPI)

Pierce, Homer C. MEIGS COUNTY OHIO 1820 CENSUS. (Minerva OH: Pierce Enterprises, nd)

Pierce, Homer C. MEIGS COUNTY OHIO 1830 CENSUS. (Minerva OH: Pierce Enterprises, nd)

Pierce, Homer C. MEIGS COUNTY OHIO 1840 CENSUS. (Minerva OH: Pierce Enterprises, nd)

Pierce, Homer C. MEIGS COUNTY OHIO MARRIAGE BOOKS 1 & 2, 1819-1862. (Minerva OH: Pierce Enterprises, 1977) 136p

POLL RECORDS OF MEIGS COUNTY OHIO. (SLO)

Slaughter, Ray. INDEX 1870 CENSUS MEIGS COUNTY OHIO. (OHS)

Taylor, Charles B. EARLY HISTORY AND WAR RECORD OF WILKESVILLE AND SALEM. 1874. 89p. (SLO)

Tolson, Grace C. OLD GRAVESTONE READINGS, LETART FALLS CEMETERY, MEIGS COUNTY OHIO. (SLO,LDS)

Whiteman, Jane. EVERY NAME INDEX TO HISTORY OF MEIGS COUNTY OHIO & HARDESTY'S ENCYCLOPEDIA, 1883. (Tulsa OK: author, 1982) np

Whiteman, Jane. EVERY NAME INDEX TO A BRIEF HISTORY OF BEDFORD TP (MEIGS CO OH) BY D.B.STORY, 1894. (Tulsa OK: author, 1983) 14p (LDS)

Whiteman, Jane. EVERY-NAME INDEX TO HISTORY OF MEIGS CO OHIO BY JAMES M. EVANS & HARDESTY'S HIST. & GEOG.ENCY., 1883 (Tulsa OK: author, 1982) 50p (LDS)

Whiteman, Jane. SURNAME INDEX TO "THE HARRIS HISTORY" BY C.H.HARRIS 1957. (Tulsa OK: author, 1978)

Whiteman, Jane. SURNAME INDEX TO 1883 INTERSTATE PUB. HISTORY OF HOCKING VALLEY OHIO (Tulsa OK: author, nd) 27p

Whiteman, Jane. SURNAME INDEX TO HISTORY OF THE UPPER OHIO VALLEY, Brant & Fuller, 1891.

WIGGINS & WEAVER'S OHIO RIVER DIRECTORY FOR 1871-1872: EMBRACING...POMEROY... (Cleveland: authors, 1872) 419p (LDS)

## MERCER COUNTY

| | |
|---|---|
| CREATED: | 1820 FROM DARKE COUNTY |
| COUNTY SEAT: | CELINA 45822 |
| COURT HOUSE: | MAIN ST., CELINA 45822 |
| LIBRARY: | 303 N. MAIN ST., CELINA 45822 |
| HISTORICAL SOCIETY: | 130 E. MARKET ST., CELINA 45822 |
| GENEALOGICAL SOCIETY: | MERCER CO. CHAPTER OGS, |
| | PO BOX 437, CELINA 45822 |
| | publication: MERCER COUNTY MONITOR |
| HEALTH DEPARTMENT: | 311 SOUTH MAIN, LOWER LEVEL, CELINA 45822 |
| | (separate office for Celina city) |
| ARCHIVAL DISTRICT: | WRIGHT STATE UNIVERSITY, DAYTON |
| | (see Leggett's Guide to records) |
| LAND SURVEYS: | CONGRESS LANDS, E & S OF 1ST PRIN.MERIDIAN |
| | CONGRESS LANDS, MIAMI RIVER SURVEY |

BOUNDED BY:                  EAST:     AUGLAIZE CO
                             NORTH:    VAN WERT CO
                             WEST:     ADAMS & JAY CO., INDIANA
                             SOUTH:    DARKE CO
TOWNSHIPS:                   Black Creek, Butler, Center, Dublin, Franklin,  Gibson, Granville,
                             Hopewell, Jefferson, Liberty, Marion, Recovery, Union, Washington.

## COURT RECORDS: (LDS MICROFILM)
Auditor:
    Tax duplicates, 1826-1838.
Clerk of Courts:
    Administrators docket, 1829-1851.
    Record of estates, 1838-1851.
    Common Pleas chancery record, 1838-1857.
    Common Pleas civil docket, minutes, 1824-1861.
    Civil minutes journal, 1824-1852.
    Common Pleas general index, 1826-1871;judgment index, 1824-1871.
    Common Pleas naturalization register, 1852-1860.
    Naturalizations, 1838-1839.
    Supreme Court chancery record, 1847-1852.
    Supreme Court minutes, 1825-1867.
    Supreme Court record, 1834-1873.
County Home:
    Inmates, 1888-1938.
Probate Court:
    Marriage records, vA-E,3-10, 1838-1916.
    Birth records, v1-4, 1867-1908.
    Death records, v1-2, 1867-1908.
    Record of wills, v1-8, 1825-1902.
    Admin., exrs., & grdns. bonds, vA, 1824-1892.
    Probate journal, v1-10, 1852-1886.
    Final record, v1-8, 1852-1891.
    Civil dockets, v1-24, 1852-1971.
    Ministers' licenses & marriage bans, v1-3, 1870-1966.
    Naturalization records, 1848-1903.
Recorder:
    Deeds, vA-Y, 2-9, 1823-1866.
Miscellaneous:
    Cemetery records, State Library of Ohio collection.

## OHIO HISTORICAL SOCIETY: (MICROFILM)
Clerk of Courts:
    Supreme Court chancery record, vA, 1837-1852.
    Supreme Court minutes, 1825-1867.
    Supreme Court record, vA-B, 1834-1873.
    Common Pleas chancery record, vB-E, 1838-1857.
    Civil docket minute book, 1824-1836,1840-1861.
    Civil minutes journal, vA-D, 1824-1852.
    General index, 1826-1871.
    Judgment index, 1824-1871.
County Home:
    Record of inmates, 1888-1938.
Miscellaneous:
    Marriage records, 1838-1880, by DAR.
    Cemetery records, by DAR.

**CENSUS RECORDS (OHS,SLO,OGS,LDS)**
1820-1880, 1900-1910; 1890 VETERANS; 1880,1900 SOUNDEX; 1910 MIRACODE

**AGRICULTURAL CENSUS SCHEDULES (OHS,SLO-mic)**
1850,1860,1880

**PRODUCTS OF INDUSTRY CENSUS SCHEDULE (OHS,SLO-mic)**
1850,1880

**MORTALITY CENSUS SCHEDULES (OHS,SLO-mic)**
1850,1860

**DEFECTIVE & DEPENDENT CENSUS SCHEDULES (OHS,SLO-mic)**
1880

**NEWSPAPERS: [GUIDE TO OHIO NEWSPAPERS, 1793-1973]**
Celina, Coldwater, Fort Recovery.

**TAX RECORDS (OHS & LDS)**
1826-1838.

**GENEALOGICAL PERIODICAL ARTICLES**
Bell, Carol Willsey. OHIO GENEALOGICAL PERIODICAL INDEX: A COUNTY GUIDE (Youngstown, OH: author, 6th ed., 1987)

**PUBLISHED SOURCES:**
Alig, Joyce. A HISTORY OF SAINT HENRY OHIO 1836-1971, 135 YEARS. (np: author, 1972) 200p (OHS)
Alig, Joyce, ed. MERCER COUNTY, OHIO HISTORY. 1978. (SLO)
Alig, Joyce L. CELINA OHIO SESQUICENTENNIAL, 1834-1984. (Celina OH: Mercer Co.Hist.Soc., 1984) 76p (LDS)
Barber, Celia B. HISTORY OF HAMILTON BETHEL METHODIST CHURCH: LOCATED IN SECTION 35, UNION TOWNSHIP. (DAR,LDS)
Berry, Ellen T. & David A. EARLY OHIO SETTLERS: PURCHASERS OF LAND IN SOUTHWESTERN OHIO, 1800-1840. (Baltimore: Genealogical Pub.Co., 1986) 372p (OGS,SLO,OHS)
CITY/COUNTY DIRECTORIES: check holdings of OHS & local public library.
Daughters of the American Revolution. AUGLAIZE, HIGHLAND AND MERCER COUNTIES OHIO CEMETERY RECORDS. (SLO)
Daughters of the American Revolution. CEMETERY RECORDS OF SHELBY COUNTY, OHIO: AND OF FRANKLIN TOWNSHIP, MERCER COUNTY, OHIO. 1974. (DAR)
Daughters of the American Revolution. HISTORY OF HAMILTON BETHEL METHODIST CHURCH, MERCER COUNTY OHIO. (SLO)
Daughters of the American Revolution. MARRIAGE RECORDS, MERCER COUNTY 1838-1880 & LAWRENCE COUNTY 1817-1822. (SLO,LDS,DAR)
Daughters of the American Revolution. OHIO CEMETERY RECORDS: COUNTIES OF AUGLAIZE, HIGHLAND, AND MERCER. 1953. 68p (DAR,LDS)
Daughters of the American Revolution. OHIO CHURCH HISTORIES AND RECORDS (incl. Hamilton Bethel Methodist Church, Mercer Co.) 1949-1953. (DAR)
Fecher, Con J. ANCESTRAL PORTRAITS OF OHIO SETTLERS. (Dayton OH: Univ. of Dayton Press, 1980) 321p (OGS,LDS)
Gerlach, Dominic B. HISTORY OF ST.JOSEPH PARISH, R.R.1, FORT RECOVERY, OHIO. (Carthagena OH: Messenger Press, 1961) 85p (LDS)

Haller, Stephen E. & P.Nolan. FIRST STOP FOR LOCAL HISTORY RESEARCH. A GUIDE TO COUNTY RECORDS PRESERVED AT WRIGHT STATE UNIVERSITY ARCHIVES AND SPECIAL COLLECTIONS. 1976. 21p.

Hamilton, William. HISTORY OF THE EARLY SETTLEMENTS OF UNION, CENTER AND DUBLIN TOWNSHIPS, MERCER COUNTY OHIO. 1876. 26p. (SLO)

HISTORY OF VAN WERT AND MERCER COUNTIES OHIO. (Wapakoneta OH: R.Sutton & Co., 1882) 488p (DAR,LDS,SLO)(RPI)

Knapp, Horace S. HISTORY OF THE MAUMEE VALLEY. (Toledo OH: author, 1872) 685p. (DAR,OHS,SLO)

Lacy, Roy. CEMETERY RECORDS OF SHELBY COUNTY OHIO AND OF FRANKLIN TOWNSHIP, MERCER COUNTY OHIO. (SLO)

Leggett, Nancy G. & D.E.Smith. A GUIDE TO LOCAL GOVERNMENT RECORDS AND NEWSPAPERS PRESERVED AT THE DEPARTMENT OF ARCHIVES AND SPECIAL COLLECTIONS WRIGHT STATE UNIVERSITY. (Dayton OH: Wright State U., 1987)

Lutz. ATLAS OF MERCER COUNTY OHIO. 1900 (OGS,SLO)(RPI)

Mercer Co Chapter OGS. MERCER COUNTY OHIO CEMETERY INSCRIPTIONS, VOL.I. JEFFERSON TWP. (Celina OH: the society, 1984) 167p (OGS,LDS)

Mercer Co Chapter OGS. MERCER COUNTY OHIO CEMETERY INSCRIPTIONS, VOL.II. (Celina OH: the society, 1986) 97p (OGS,LDS)

Mercer Co Chapter OGS. MERCER COUNTY OHIO CEMETERY INSCRIPTIONS, VOL.III CENTER & UNION TWPS. (Celina OH: the society, 1988) 115p (OGS)

Mercer Co Chapter OGS. MERCER COUNTY OHIO CEMETERY INSCRIPTIONS, VOL.IV, BUTLER, FRANKLIN & WASHINGTON TWPS. (Celina OH: the society, 1988)(OGS)

Mercer Co Chapter OGS. MERCER COUNTY, OHIO 1880 CENSUS INDEX (Celina, OH: the society, 1985) 55p. (OGS,LDS)

Mercer Co. Historical Society. MERCER COUNTY OHIO HISTORY, 1978. (Celina OH: the society, 1980) 976p (LDS)

Mohneke, Edward H. TOMBSTONE INSCRIPTIONS, OHIO AND INDIANA. (Grand Rapids MI: author, 1937) 87p (LDS)

PORTRAIT AND BIOGRAPHICAL RECORD OF MERCER AND VAN WERT COUNTIES OHIO. (Chicago: A.W.Bowen & Co., 1896) (Reprint, Evansville IN: Unigraphic, 1971) 909p (LDS,SLO,DAR)

Scranton, S.S. HISTORY OF MERCER COUNTY OHIO AND REPRESENTATIVE CITIZENS. (Chicago: Biographical Pub Co., 1907) 751p (LDS,SLO)(RPI)

Winter, Nevin O. HISTORY OF NORTHWEST OHIO. (Chicago: Lewis Pub Co.,1917) 3v. (SLO,OHS)

# MIAMI COUNTY

| | |
|---|---|
| CREATED: | 1807 FROM MONTGOMERY COUNTY |
| COUNTY SEAT: | TROY 45373 |
| COURT HOUSE: | MIAMI CO. SAFETY BUILDING, TROY 45373 |
| LIBRARY: | 419 W. MAIN ST., TROY 45373 |
| HISTORICAL SOCIETY: | PO BOX 407, TIPP CITY 45371 |
| GENEALOGICAL SOCIETY: | MIAMI CO. CHAPTER OGS, |
| | PO BOX 407, TIPP CITY 45371 |
| HEALTH DEPARTMENT: | 3232 N.COUNTY RD. 25A, BOX 677, TROY 45373 |
| | (separate offices for Troy city, Tipp City, & Piqua) |
| ARCHIVAL DISTRICT: | WRIGHT STATE UNIVERSITY, DAYTON |
| | (see Leggett's Guide to records) |
| LAND SURVEYS: | CONGRESS LANDS, MIAMI RIVER SURVEY |
| | CONGRESS LANDS, BETWEEN THE MIAMI RIVER SURVEY |
| BOUNDED BY: | EAST: CHAMPAIGN & CLARK CO. |
| | NORTH: SHELBY CO. |
| | WEST: DARKE CO. |
| | SOUTH: MONTGOMERY CO. |

TOWNSHIPS:                    Bethel, Brown, Concord, Elizabeth, Lost Creek, Monroe, Newberry,
                              Newton, Spring Creek, Staunton, Union, Washington.

## COURT RECORDS: (LDS MICROFILM)
Auditor:
    Enumeration of school-aged youth, 1851-1911.
    Militia rolls, 1863-1865.
    Militia poll book, 1863-1865.
    Commutation receipts, Lost Creek Tp.,1864.
    Tax duplicates, 1816-1838.
    Militia records, 1857-1864.
Board of Elections:
    Poll books, tally sheets, 1817-1902.
Childrens' Home:
    Record of indentures, 1880-1904.
    Inmates, 1879-1939.
    Trustees journal, 1879-1931.
Clerk of Courts:
    Appearance docket, 1811-1815,1850-1858.
    Execution docket, 1836-1842.
    Chancery record, v1-4, 1840-1858.
    Civil minutes journal, v1-15, 1807-1853.
    Common Pleas general index, 1807-1853.
    Manumission record, 1834-1847.
    Supreme Court record, vA-C, 1808-1857.
    Supreme Court docket & minutes, 1807-1838.
    Quadrennial enumeration, 1827,1835.
    Poll books & tally sheets, abstract of votes, 1817-1902.
    Register of free blacks, 1804-1857.
County Home:
    Record of inmates, 1842-1927.
    Director's minutes, 1890-1910.
Ohio Childrens' Home:
    Record of inmates, 1879-1939.
Probate Court:
    Index to marriages, v1-9, 1807-1968.
    Marriage records, vA1-F, v1-44, 1807-1860, 1871-1968.
    Will record, 1807-1902.
    Death record, v1-4, 1867-1908.
    Birth record, v1-4, 1853-1908.
    Birth registration, v1-23, 1941-1965.
    Admin. & exrs. journal, v39-40, 1966-1968.
    Probate journal, v1-82, 1855-1968.
    Guardian bonds, v1-33, 1807-1968.
    Administration guardian docket, v1-10, 1833-1968.
    Docket, settlement, v1-38, 1874-1966.
    Settlement of accounts, v8-108, 1871-1968.
    Naturalization record, 1st papers, 1860-1904.
    Naturalization record, 2nd papers, 1860-1906.
Recorder:
    Direct index to deeds, vA-Z, 1809-1863.
    General index to deeds, v3-28, 1809-1968.
    Deed records, v1-118, 1807-1902.
    Index to mortgages, v1-26, 1833-1963.
    Mortgage record, v1-3, 1837-1851.

Soldiers' discharge record, 1864-1918.
Sheriff:
    Jail register, 1882-1920.
Miscellaneous:
    Pleasant Hill Presby.Church, session records, 1818-1870.
    Honey Creek Baptist Church, records, 1811-1844. (WRHS)
    Mill Creek Monthly Meeting of Friends, records, 1808-1860.
    West Branch Monthly Meeting, records, 1807-1906.
    Union Monthly Meeting, records, 1813-1921.
    West Branch Quarterly meeting, records, 1812-1855.
    Cemetery records, State Library of Ohio collection.

## OHIO HISTORICAL SOCIETY: (MICROFILM)
Auditor:
    Enumeration of school-aged youth, 1851-1911.
    Militia rolls, 1863-1865.
    Commutation receipts, Lost Creek Tp.,1864.
    Militia records, 1857-1864.
Childrens' Home:
    Record of indentures, 1880-1904.
    Inmates, 1879-1939.
    Trustees journal, 1879-1931.
Clerk of Courts:
    Appearance docket, 1811-1815,1850-1858.
    Execution docket, 1836-1842.
    Chancery record, v1-4, 1840-1858.
    Civil minutes journal, v1-15, 1807-1853.
    Common Pleas general index, 1807-1853.
    Manumission record, 1834-1847.
    Supreme Court record, vA-C, 1808-1857.
    Supreme Court docket & minutes, 1807-1838.
    Quadrennial enumeration, 1827,1835.
    Poll books & tally sheets, abstract of votes, 1817-1902.
    Register of free blacks, 1804-1857.
County Home:
    Record of inmates, 1842-1927.
    Director's minutes, 1890-1910.
Ohio Childrens' Home:
    Record of inmates, 1879-1939.
Probate Court:
    Naturalization record, 1st papers, 1860-1904.
    Naturalization record, 2nd papers, 1860-1906.
Recorder:
    Soldiers' discharge record, v1-2, 1861-1918.
Sheriff:
    Jail register, 1882-1920.
Tipp City City Council:
    Minutes, 1851-1978.
    Ordinance record, 1858-1978.
    Original ordinances, 1932-1978.
    Planning commission minutes, 1954-1977.
    Fire company minutes, 1874-1952.
Miscellaneous:
    Marriages, 1807-1866, by DAR.
    Cemetery records, by DAR.

Society of Friends, Mill Creek Women's meeting, 1824-1852 &
West Branch women's meeting, 1838-1873. (in Mss.Div.)
Brown Tp., 3rd School Dist. minutes, 1853-1884.
Piqua City Directories, 1875-1907.

**CENSUS RECORDS (OHS,SLO,OGS,LDS)**
1820-1880, 1900-1910; 1890 VETERANS; 1880,1900 SOUNDEX; 1910 MIRACODE

**AGRICULTURAL CENSUS SCHEDULES (OHS,SLO-mic)**
1850,1860,1880

**PRODUCTS OF INDUSTRY CENSUS SCHEDULE (OHS,SLO-mic)**
1850,1880

**MORTALITY CENSUS SCHEDULES (OHS,SLO-mic)**
1850,1860

**DEFECTIVE & DEPENDENT CENSUS SCHEDULES (OHS,SLO-mic)**
1880

**NEWSPAPERS: [GUIDE TO OHIO NEWSPAPERS, 1793-1973]**
Bradford, Covington, Piqua, Tipp City, Troy, West Milton.

**TAX RECORDS (OHS & LDS)**
1810-1814,1816-1838.

**GENEALOGICAL PERIODICAL ARTICLES**
Bell, Carol Willsey. OHIO GENEALOGICAL PERIODICAL INDEX: A COUNTY GUIDE (Youngstown
   OH: author, 6th ed., 1987)

**PUBLISHED SOURCES:**
1875 ATLAS OF MIAMI COUNTY OHIO & 1894 ATLAS OF MIAMI COUNTY OHIO. (Reprint, Van-
   dalia OH: Miami Co Hist Soc.,1973) (SLO)
Adams, Barbara. MEMORIAL RECORDS OF SHELBY COUNTY, OHIO, 1819-1975. (Bal-
   timore: Gateway Press, 1977) 668p (LDS)
ATLAS OF MIAMI COUNTY OHIO. 1871. (SLO)
Berry, Ellen T. & David A. EARLY OHIO SETTLERS: PURCHASERS OF LAND IN SOUTHWESTERN
   OHIO, 1800-1840. (Baltimore: Genealogical Pub.Co., 1986) 372p (OGS,SLO,OHS)
Bosserman, Joseph H., Sr. CEMETERY INSCRIPTIONS OF NEWBERRY TOWNSHIP, MIAMI COUN-
   TY OHIO. (Covington OH: author, nd) (OGS)
Brien, Lindsay M. A GENEALOGICAL INDEX OF PIONEERS IN THE MIAMI VALLEY OHIO: MIAMI,
   MONTGOMERY, PREBLE AND WARREN COUNTIES OHIO. (Dayton: Colonial Dames of
   America, 1970) 196p (LDS,DAR)
Brien, Lindsay M. INDEX TO MIAMI VALLEY RECORDS, MIAMI COUNTY CEMETERY RECORDS,
   V.5. (SLO)
Brien, Lindsay M. MARRIAGES BUTLER CO., GREENE CO., MIAMI CO., PREBLE CO., AND WAR-
   REN CO. (LDS)
Brien, Lindsay M. MIAMI COUNTY CEMETERY RECORDS. (np: author, nd) 177p (LDS,DAR)
Brien, Lindsay M. MIAMI VALLEY WILL ABSTRACTS FROM THE COUNTIES OF MIAMI,
   MONTGOMERY, WARREN AND PREBLE IN THE STATE OF OHIO, 1803-1850. 177p (SLO,DAR)
Brien, Lindsay M. MIAMI VALLEY RECORDS, VOL.VI, QUAKER RECORDS. (Dayton OH: Miami
   Valley Gen Soc, 1986) 121p (OGS)
Brien, Lindsay M. MIAMI VALLEY RECORDS, 5v (SLO) OUR FOREFATHERS ... GENEALOGY OF
   MIAMI VALLEY FAMILIES. 1r mic. (SLO)
CITY/COUNTY DIRECTORIES: check holdings of OHS & local public library.

Daughters of the American Revolution. BIBLE RECORDS OF DARKE, MIAMI AND MONTGOMERY COUNTIES OHIO. (SLO)

Daughters of the American Revolution. CEMETERY RECORDS, MIAMI COUNTY OHIO. (SLO,LDS)

Daughters of the American Revolution. MARRIAGE RECORDS, MIAMI COUNTY OHIO, 1807-1866. 3v. (SLO,DAR)

Daughters of the American Revolution. OHIO BIBLE RECORDS: CONCERNING FAMILIES OF CRAWFORD, DARKE, FAIRFIELD, MIAMI, MONTGOMERY, PICKAWAY, PREBLE AND SHELBY COUNTIES. 1970. 126p (DAR)

Daughters of the American Revolution. SOLDIERS OF THE AMERICAN REVOLUTION, LIVED, DIED, BURIED IN MIAMI COUNTY. (SLO)

Davis, Eileen & J.Ireton. QUAKER RECORDS OF THE MIAMI VALLEY OF OHIO. 1980. (SLO)

Everts, L.H. ILLUSTRATED HISTORICAL ATLAS OF MIAMI COUNTY OHIO. (Philadelphia: author, 1875) 53p (OGS,DAR)(RPI)

Floyd, Marjorie D. EVERY NAME INDEX TO MIAMI VALLEY OHIO PIONEERS BY LINDSAY M. BRIEN. (Dayton OH: author, 1980) 38p (LDS)

GENEALOGICAL AND BIOGRAPHICAL RECORD OF MIAMI COUNTY OHIO. COMPENDIUM OF NATIONAL BIOGRAPHY. (Chicago: Lewis Pub Co., 1900) 914p (LDS,SLO) (RPI)

Haller, Stephen E. & P.Nolan. FIRST STOP FOR LOCAL HISTORY RESEARCH. A GUIDE TO COUNTY RECORDS PRESERVED AT WRIGHT STATE UNIVERSITY ARCHIVES AND SPECIAL COLLECTIONS. 1976. 21p.

Haller, Stephen E. & R.H.Smith. REGISTER OF BLACKS IN THE MIAMI VALLEY OHIO 1804-1857. (Dayton: Wright State University, nd) (SLO)

Harbaugh, Thomas C. CENTENNIAL HISTORY, TROY, PIQUA AND MIAMI COUNTY OHIO AND REPRESENTATIVE CITIZENS. (Chicago: Richmond-Arnold Pub Co., 1909) 857p (DAR,LDS,SLO)(RPI)

Hardesty, H.H. MILITARY HISTORY OF OHIO - MIAMI COUNTY EDITION. 1886/87. (OHS)

Hill, Leonard U. HISTORY OF MIAMI COUNTY OHIO, 1807-1953. (Columbus: F.J. Heer, c1953) 403p. (SLO,DAR,LDS)

Hill, L.U. REPRODUCTION OF A SCRAPBOOK FROM NEWSPAPER ARTICLES ON LOCAL AND REGIONAL HISTORY 1948-1970. 1970. 156p. (SLO,OGS)

Hinshaw, William Wade. ENCYCLOPEDIA OF AMERICAN QUAKER GENEALOGY, VOL.V, OHIO. (Baltimore: Genealogical Pub.Co., 1973) (SLO,OHS,LDS)

HISTORY OF MIAMI COUNTY OHIO. (Chicago: W.H.Beers & Co.,1880) 880p (LDS,SLO,DAR) (RPI)

HISTORY OF MIAMI QUARTERLY MEETING OF THE RELIGIOUS SOCIETY OF FRIENDS, 1809-1828. (SLO)

HISTORY OF WEST BRANCH QUARTERLY MEETING OF SOCIETY OF FRIENDS, WEST MILTON, OHIO,1807-1957. 1957? 74p. (SLO,DAR,LDS)

Kinder, W.R. HISTORIC NOTES OF MIAMI COUNTY OHIO. 1953. 213p. (SLO)

Lake, D.J. ATLAS OF MIAMI COUNTY OHIO. 1875. (RPI)

Leggett, Nancy G. & D.E.Smith. A GUIDE TO LOCAL GOVERNMENT RECORDS AND NEWSPAPERS PRESERVED AT THE DEPARTMENT OF ARCHIVES AND SPECIAL COLLECTIONS WRIGHT STATE UNIVERSITY. (Dayton OH: Wright State U., 1987)

McKENDREE'S HOME-COMING: ON ITS NINETY-SIXTH ANNIVERSARY. 1908. 75p (DAR)

McKinney, Louise W. EARLY HISTORY OF PIQUA. 1920? 73p (DAR)

MEMOIRS OF THE MIAMI VALLEY OHIO. (Chicago: Robert O.Law Co.,1919) 3v (OHS,SLO)

MIAMI COUNTY SOLDIERS OF THE REVOLUTION, 1776. (Troy OH: Troy American Bicentennial Commission, 1976?) 33p (LDS)

Miller, E.Irene. HISTORY OF MIAMI COUNTY, OHIO. (Tipp City OH: Miami Co. Hist.Soc., 1982) 584p (DAR,LDS)

Miller, Marcus. ROOTS BY THE RIVER: THE HISTORY, DOCTRINE AND PRACTICE OF THE OLD GERMAN BAPTIST BRETHREN IN MIAMI COUNTY OHIO. (Covington OH: Hammer Graphics, 1973) 256p (LDS)

Mote, Luke S. EARLY SETTLEMENT OF FRIENDS IN THE MIAMI VALLEY. 1961. (SLO)

Pemberton, M.H. ORIGINAL LAND ENTRIES, UNION TOWNSHIP, MIAMI COUNTY OHIO. (SLO)

Pouget, Luella R. CEMETERY INSCRIPTIONS FROM MONTGOMERY, MIAMI, PREBLE AND DARKE COUNTIES OHIO. (LDS)

Rayner, John A. THE FIRST CENTURY OF PIQUA OHIO. (Piqua OH: Magee Bros. Pub.Co.,1916) 372p. (SLO,DAR)

Rerick Bros. THE COUNTY OF MIAMI: AN IMPERIAL ATLAS AND ART FOLIO. (np: Rerick Bros., 1894)(Reprint, Evansville IN: Unigraphic, 1973) 102p (SLO,LDS)(RPI)

Short, Anita. LAND PATENT RECORDS MIAMI COUNTY. (np: author, 1973) 40p (LDS,SLO)

Short, Anita. OHIO BIBLE RECORDS CONCERNING THE FAMILIES OF CRAWFORD, DARKE,FAIR-FIELD,MIAMI,MONTGOMERY,PICKAWAY,PREBLE & SHELBY COUNTIES OHIO. (SLO)

Short, Anita. OHIO BIBLE RECORDS. (SLO)

Smith, W.E. HISTORY OF SOUTHWESTERN OHIO, THE MIAMI VALLEYS, 1917. 3v. (SLO)

Sterrett, Frank M. A HISTORY OF MIAMI COUNTY. (Troy OH: Montgomery Printing Co., 1917) 676p (DAR,LDS,SLO)

Trostel, Scott D. BRADFORD, THE RAILROAD TOWN: A RAILROAD TOWN HISTORY OF BRAD-FORD, OHIO. (Fletcher OH: Cam-Tech Pub., 1987) 152p (LDS)

TROY OHIO OF YESTERDAY AND TOMORROW. (Troy OH: Historical Society of Troy, 197?) 128p (LDS)

Troy American Bicentennial Committee. MIAMI COUNTY SOLDIERS OF THE REVOLUTION. (Troy OH: author, nd) 33p

Vicory, Jacqueline. MILO UNION LIST OF GENEALOGIES IN THE LIBRARIES OF CHAMPAIGN, CLARK, DARKE, GREENE, MIAMI, MONTGOMERY AND PREBLE COUNTIES, OHIO. (Dayton OH: Miami Valley Library Organization, 1977) 122p (LDS)

Welsh, E.B. RECORDS OF THE PROCEEDINGS OF THE SESSION OF THE CONGREGATION OF PLEASANT HILL: 1818-1870. (LDS)

WEST MILTON'S SESQUI-CENTENNIAL 1807-1957. (np: Historical Committee, nd) 127p (LDS,SLO,DAR)

Wheeler. TROY OHIO IN THE 19TH CENTURY. 1970.

WIGGINS & McKILLOP'S DIRECTORY OF CHAMPAIGN COUNTY FOR 1878-9 [incl. Miami Couny] (Wellsville OH: Wiggins & McKillop, 1878) 125p (DAR)

# MONROE COUNTY

CREATED: 1813 FROM BELMONT, GUERNSEY & WASHINGTON
COUNTY SEAT: WOODSFIELD 43793
COURT HOUSE: MAIN ST., WOODSFIELD 43793
LIBRARY: 101 N. MAIN ST., WOODSFIELD 43793
HISTORICAL SOCIETY: PO BOX 538, WOODSFIELD 43793.
GENEALOGICAL SOCIETY: MONROE CO CHAPTER OGS, & MONROE CO H.S.
PO BOX 538, WOODSFIELD 43793
publication: MONROE COUNTY HERITAGE
HEALTH DEPARTMENT: ROUTE #1, BOX 141-A,WOODSFIELD 43793
ARCHIVAL DISTRICT: OHIO UNIVERSITY, ATHENS
(see published Guide to records)
LAND SURVEYS: CONGRESS LANDS, SEVEN RANGES
BOUNDED BY: EAST: MARSHALL & WETZEL CO., W.VA.
NORTH: BELMONT CO.
WEST: NOBLE CO.
SOUTH: WASHINGTON CO. & TYLER CO., W.VA.
TOWNSHIPS: Adams, Benton, Bethel, Center, Franklin, Green, Jackson, Lee, Malaga, Ohio, Perry, Salem, Seneca, Summit, Sunsbury, Switzerland, Washington, Wayne.

SPECIAL NOTE: COURTHOUSE FIRES IN 1840 & 1867 DESTROYED MANY RECORDS.

**COURT RECORDS: (LDS MICROFILM)**
Auditor:
   Tax duplicates, 1816-1838.
Clerk of Courts:
   Common Pleas appearance docket, 1822-1853.
   Common Pleas chancery record, 1834-1856.
   Common Pleas complete record, 1822-1847.
   Common Pleas general index, direct & reverse, 1818-1846.
   Common Pleas journal, 1822-1854.
   Common Pleas law record index, 1818-1857.
   District Court minutes, 1852-1865.
   Supreme Court appearance docket, 1832-1852.
   Supreme Court minutes, 1820-1850.
   Supreme Court record, 1825-1850.
County Home:
   Infirmary register, 1855-1978.
Probate Court:
   Birth records, 1867-1908.
   Death records, 1867-1908.
   Marriage records, 1866-1917.
Recorder:
   Deeds, general index, 1836-1968.
   Deeds, vA-37, 1840-1881.
Miscellaneous:
   Beallsville Presby.Church, records, 1847-1862.
   Woodsfield, First Presby.Church, session minutes, 1866-1899.
   East Woodsfield, Presby. Church, records, 1850-1864.
   Hannibal, Zion Evangelical Church, records, 1855-1886.
   Cemetery records, State Library of Ohio collection.

**OHIO HISTORICAL SOCIETY: (MICROFILM)**
Clerk of Courts:
   Common Pleas appearance docket, 1822-1853.
   Common Pleas chancery record, 1834-1856.
   Common Pleas complete record, 1822-1847.
   Common Pleas general index, direct & reverse, 1818-1846.
   Common Pleas journal, 1822-1854.
   Common Pleas law record index, 1818-1857.
   District Court minutes, 1852-1865.
   Supreme Court appearance docket, 1832-1852.
   Supreme Court minutes, 1820-1850.
   Supreme Court record, 1825-1850.
County Home:
   Infirmary register, 1855-1978.
Miscellaneous:
   Cemetery records, by DAR.

**CENSUS RECORDS  (OHS,SLO,OGS,LDS)**
1820-1880, 1900-1910; 1890 VETERANS; 1880,1900 SOUNDEX; 1910 MIRACODE

**AGRICULTURAL CENSUS SCHEDULES  (OHS,SLO-mic)**
1850,1860,1880

**PRODUCTS OF INDUSTRY CENSUS SCHEDULE (OHS,SLO-mic)**
1850,1880

**MORTALITY CENSUS SCHEDULES (OHS,SLO-mic)**
1850,1860

**DEFECTIVE & DEPENDENT CENSUS SCHEDULES (OHS,SLO-mic)**
1880

**NEWSPAPERS: [GUIDE TO OHIO NEWSPAPERS, 1793-1973]**
Clarington, Woodsfield.

**TAX RECORDS (OHS & LDS)**
1816-1838.

**GENEALOGICAL PERIODICAL ARTICLES**
Bell, Carol Willsey. OHIO GENEALOGICAL PERIODICAL INDEX: A COUNTY GUIDE (Youngstown
    OH: author, 6th ed., 1987)

**PUBLISHED SOURCES:**
Berry, Ellen T. & David. EARLY OHIO SETTLERS: PURCHASERS OF LAND IN SOUTHEASTERN
    OHIO, 1800-1840. (Balümore: Genealogical Pub.Co., 1984) 129p (OHS,SLO,OGS,DAR)
Byers, Arley. BENT, ZIG-ZAG & CROOKED: A NARROW GAUGE RAILROAD. (Woodsfield OH:
    Monroe Co Hist Soc, nd) 231p
CALDWELL'S ATLAS OF MONROE CO OH. (Mount Vernon OH: Atlas Pub.Co.,1898) (Reprint,
    Evansville IN: 1975) 254p (OGS,OHS,LDS,SLO)(RPI)
CEMETERY RECORDS OF WASHINGTON AND MONROE COUNTIES OHIO. (Marietta: Campus
    Martius Museum, nd) 259p (OHS)
CITY/COUNTY DIRECTORIES: check holdings of OHS & local public library.
COMBINED HISTORY OF MONROE COUNTY OHIO, H.H.HARDESTY & CO., 1882, AND
    CALDWELL'S ATLAS OF MONROE COUNTY, OHIO. (Woodsfield OH: Monroe Co.Hist.Soc.,
    198?) 1v (LDS)
COMMISSIONERS' JOURNAL, 1815-1835. (SLO)
Cranmer, G.L. HISTORY OF THE UPPER OHIO VALLEY. (Madison WI: Brant & Fuller, 1890,1891)
    (OHS,SLO)
Daughters of the American Revolution. FOUR MONROE COUNTY OHIO CEMETERIES. (SLO,LDS)
Daughters of the American Revolution. MISCELLANEOUS OHIO CEMETERIES, VOL.I. (SLO,LDS)
Davis, Wilma. THE FEDERAL CENSUS OF 1860 FOR MONROE COUNTY OHIO. (Washington DC:
    author, 1967) 594p (LDS,SLO,OHS,OGS,DAR)
Davis, Wilma. THE FEDERAL CENSUS OF 1850 FOR MONROE COUNTY OHIO. (Washington DC:
    author, 1965) 603p (LDS,SLO,OHS,OGS)
Fedorchak, Catharine F. CHURCH BOOK OF GERMAN EVANGELICAL SALEM CHURCH, MON-
    ROE COUNTY OHIO [1853-1963]. 1984. 67p (LDS)
Fedorchak, Catharine F. MONROE COUNTY OHIO GENEALOGICAL RECORDS. 1960-1975. 12v.
    (Gary IN: author, 1960-75) (SLO,LDS,OHS,DAR)
Fedorchak, Catharine F. FAMILY RESEARCH IN MONROE COUNTY OHIO. 214p (LDS)
Hardesty, H.H. HISTORICAL HAND ATLAS AND HISTORY OF MONROE COUNTY. (Chicago: author,
    1882) (OHS,SLO)(RPI)
Hardesty's HISTORY OF MONROE COUNTY OHIO, 1882 (Reprint, Woodsfield OH: Monroe Co Hist
    Soc, 1984)
HISTORY OF MONROE COUNTY, 1813. (Woodsfield OH: Chamber of Commerce, 198?) 39p (LDS)
HIXSON, W.W. PLAT BOOK OF MONROE COUNTY OHIO. (Rockford IL: author, nd) (OHS)
Hunter, William F. SKETCHES OF MONROE COUNTY. 1860. 7p. (OHS)
Kopp, Rita. MINI-ATLAS OF LANDOWNERS: 1869 MAP OF MONROE COUNTY OHIO. (Ashland
    OH: author, 1985) 50p (OGS,SLO,LDS)

Kopp, Rita. SPIRIT OF DEMOCRACY, A MONROE COUNTY OHIO NEWSPAPER ABSTRACT OF OBITS 1892-1895. (Ashland OH: author, 1982?) 23p (OGS)

Kopp, Rita. SPIRIT OF DEMOCRACY, A MONROE COUNTY OHIO NEWSPAPER ABSTRACT OF OBITS 1909-1912. (Ashland OH: author, 1982?) 40p (OGS)

Kopp, Rita. SPIRIT OF DEMOCRACY, A MONROE COUNTY OHIO NEWSPAPER ABSTRACT OF OBITS 1912-1914. (Ashland OH: author, 1982?) 51p (OGS)

Kopp, Rita. SPIRIT OF DEMOCRACY, A MONROE COUNTY OHIO NEWSPAPER ABSTRACT OF OBITS 1914-1916. (Ashland OH: author, 1982) 79p (OGS)

Kopp, Rita. SPIRIT OF DEMOCRACY, A MONROE COUNTY OHIO NEWSPAPER ABSTRACT OF OBITS 1916-1917. (Ashland OH: author, 1982) (OGS)

Lewis, Thomas W. SOUTHEASTERN OHIO AND THE MUSKINGUM VALLEY, 1788-1928: COVER-ING ATHENS, BELMONT, COSHOCTON, GUERNSEY, LICKING, MEIGS, MONROE, MORGAN, MUSKINGUM, NOBLE, PERRY AND WASHINGTON COUNTIES. (Chicago: S.J.Clarke Co.,1928) 3v. (SLO,DAR,OHS)

Monroe Co. Historical Society. CALAIS CEMETERY BOOK. (Woodsfield OH: the society, nd)

Monroe Co. Historical Society. HARDESTY'S HISTORY OF MONROE COUNTY (1882) & CALDWELL'S ATLAS OF MONROE COUNTY (1898). (Reprint, Woodsfield OH: the society, nd) 2v in 1.

Monroe Co. Historical Society. INDEX TO BENT, ZIG ZAG & CROOKED: A NARROW GAUGE RAIL-ROAD BY ARLEY BYERS. (Woodsfield OH: the society, nd)

Monroe Co. Historical Society. INDEX TO THE MONROE COUNTY OHIO TAX DUPLICATE, 1833 & 1835. (Woodsfield OH: the society, nd) 35p

Monroe Co. Historical Society. MONROE COUNTY CHURCH RECORDS, ZION EVANGELICAL CHURCH, OHIO TOWNSHIP, HANNIBAL [1855-1886]. (Woodsfield OH: the society, 1983) 68p (LDS)

Monroe Co. Historical Society. MONROE COUNTY OHIO (CHAPTER FROM HOWE'S HISTORICAL COLLECTIONS OF OHIO). (Woodsfield OH: the society, 1983) (LDS)

MONROE COUNTY REPUBLICAN. SOUVENIR OF WOODSFIELD & MONROE COUNTY. 1906. (OHS,SLO)

Mozena, J.Francis. MOUNT UNION CEMETERY AND MOUNT VERNON CEMETERY, MONROE COUNTY OHIO. (SLO)

Neiswonger, Shirley. MONROE COUNTY OHIO MARRIAGE RECORDS 1867-1877. (Beallsville OH: author, nd) 103p

Ohio University. GUIDE TO LOCAL GOVERNMENT RECORDS AT OHIO UNIVERSITY. (Athens OH: OU Library, 1986) 61p.

Sloan, Pam. RECEIPTS, REMEDIES & REMEMBRANCES (OF MONROE COUNTY). (Woodsfield OH: Monroe Co Hist Soc., c1976)

Warthman, Hubert. QUAKER CEMETERY, SEC.29, MALAGA TWP., MONROE COUNTY OHIO. (Livonia MI: author, 1982) 18p. (OGS,LDS)

Whiteman, Jane. SURNAME INDEX TO HISTORY OF THE UPPER OHIO VALLEY, Brant & Fuller, 1891.

Wolf, Carolyn. MONROE COUNTY OHIO: THE FIRST TWENTY YEARS - COMMISSIONERS JOUR-NAL 1815-1835. (Woodsfield OH: Monroe Co Hist Soc, nd) 120p

Wolf, Carolyn. NINE COMMUNITIES OF MONROE COUNTY OHIO - A HISTORY. (Woodsfield OH: Monroe Co Hist Soc, 1984) 176p (OGS,LDS,SLO)

Woodsfield Chamber of Commerce. HISTORY OF MONROE COUNTY OHIO. (Woodsfield OH: author, 1964) 39p

# MONTGOMERY COUNTY

| | |
|---|---|
| CREATED: | 1803 FROM HAMILTON & WAYNE CO., MICHIGAN |
| COUNTY SEAT: | DAYTON 45402 |
| COURT HOUSE: | 41 N.PERRY ST., DAYTON 45422 |
| LIBRARIES: | 215 E. THIRD ST., DAYTON 45402 |
| | WRIGHT STATE UNIVERSITY LIBRARY, DAYTON |

| | |
|---|---|
| HISTORICAL SOCIETY: | OLD COURT HOUSE, 3RD & MAIN, DAYTON 45402 |
| GENEALOGICAL SOCIETY: | MONTGOMERY CO. CHAPTER OGS, |
| | PO BOX 1584, DAYTON 45401 |
| | publication: NEWSLETTER |
| | MIAMI VALLEY CHAPTER OGS, |
| | PO BOX 1364, DAYTON 45401 |
| | publication: GENEALOGICAL AIDS BULLETIN |
| HEALTH DEPARTMENT: | ADM.BLDG., 451 W.3RD ST., DAYTON 45422 |
| | (separate offices for Dayton City, Miamisburg, Kettering, |
| | Vandalia, Moraine, West Carrollton, Centerville, Trotwood, |
| | Englewood, Germantown, Huber Hts., Union City & Oakwood) |
| ARCHIVAL DISTRICT: | WRIGHT STATE UNIVERSITY, DAYTON |
| | (see Leggett's Guide to records) |
| LAND SURVEYS: | CONGRESS LANDS, MIAMI RIVER SURVEY |
| | CONGRESS LANDS, BETWEEN THE MIAMI RIVER SURVEY |
| BOUNDED BY: | EAST: CLARK & GREENE CO. |
| | NORTH: DARKE & MIAMI CO. |
| | WEST: PREBLE CO. |
| | SOUTH: BUTLER & WARREN CO. |
| TOWNSHIPS: | Butler, Clay, German, Harrison, Jackson, Jefferson, Madison, Mad |
| | River, Miami, Perry, Randolph, Van Buren, Washington, Wayne. |

## COURT RECORDS: (LDS MICROFILM)
Auditor:
>Real estate tax duplicates, 1820-1850.
>Tax duplicates, 1798-1809; 1816-1838; 1820-1845, 1850.

Board of Railroad Appraisers:
>Record, 1891-1909.

Childrens' Home:
>Death record, 1877-1924.
>Minutes of trustees, 1867-1917.
>Indentures, 1867-1908.
>Inmates, 1867-1912.

Clerk of Courts:
>Appearance dockets, 1835-1900.
>Chancery records, vA-N, 1824-1854.
>Circuit Court journal, 1885-1912.
>Civil docket, 1803-1836.
>Common Pleas law record, 1803-1901.
>District court & journal, 1852-1883.
>Executions, vA-1--H-1.
>General index, v1-7, 1876-1900.
>Judgment index, v1-7, 1857-1901.
>Minutes, vB-34, 1815-1901.
>Naturalization records, 1818-1916.
>Register of free blacks, 1804-1857.
>Supreme Court blotter, vB-C, 1825-1851.
>Supreme Court minutes, vA-C, 1803-1851.
>Supreme Court record, vA-G, 1804-1853.
>Superior Court general index, v1-2, 1882-1886.
>Superior Court judgment index, 1856-1887.
>Superior Court minutes, 1856-1882.
>Superior Court record, v1-49, 1856-1886.

Commissioners:
>Burial of indigent soldiers, 1884-1902.

Journals, 1804-1953.
County Home:
    Infirmary directors minutes, 1826-1873,1900-1912.
    Birth & death record, v1-2, 1886-1969.
    Index, register of inmates, 1888-1892.
    Infirmary & insane record, 1829-1890.
    Register of inmates, 1888-1892; sane inmates, 1892-1908.
Probate Court:
    Birth record index, 1867-1910.
    Record of births, 1867-1909.
    Record of deaths, 1866-1909.
    General index, admin. & exec., 1803-1894.
    General index, assignment, 1803-1900.
    General index, civil, 1803-1939.
    General index, guardians & trustees, 1803-1900.
    General index, marriages, v1-11, 1803-1913.
    Marriage affidavits, 1824-1834,1848-1857.
    Marriage records, 1803-1910.
    Probate civil journal, 1852-1886.
    Probate civil record, 1856-1886.
    Probate will record, 1805-1910.
    Naturalization records, 1st papers, v1-6, 1859-1906.
    Naturalization records, 2nd papers, v1-16, 1859-1906.
    Naturalization records, minors, v1-7, 1862-1906.
Recorder:
    Deed records, vB-227, 1805-1900.
    Soldiers' discharge record, 1865-1917.
Sheriff:
    Jail register, 1920-1921.
Soldiers' Relief Commission:
    U.S.Military Home, Dayton, Inmate record, 1867-1888.
    Payment record, 1890-1896.
    Relief commission minutes, 1893-1921.
    Minutes, 1946-1950.
Miscellaneous:
    Admin., chancery, court, census, marriage & tax records (Gen.Soc.Pa.)
    Dayton courts, Greencastle Cem., misc.records. (Gen.Soc.Pa.)
    German, Jefferson, Jackson & Miami Twp. records. (Gen.Soc.Pa.)
    Shiloh Presby.Church, session records, 1873-1877.
    Dayton, Third St.Presby.Church, records, 1839-1871.
    Dayton, First Presby.Church, records, 1817-1886.
    Amity, United Presby.Church, records, 1877-1899.
    Dayton, City Workhouse, register & blotter, 1876-1916.
    Eugene Wierbach genealogy collection, 1924-1974.
    Dayton, old cemetery epitaphs, 1805-1899, Amer.Jewish Archives.
    Dayton, Police Dept., register, 1908-1910.
    Dayton, Twp. Clerk, indenture record of minors, 1838-1883.
    Church records, congregations in Montgomery Co., Ohio.

## OHIO HISTORICAL SOCIETY: (MICROFILM)
Auditor:
    Real estate tax duplicates, 1820-1850.
Board of Railroad Appraisers:
    Record, 1891-1909.

Childrens' Home:
    Death record, 1877-1924.
    Minutes of trustees, 1867-1917.
    Indentures, 1867-1908.
    Inmates, 1867-1912.
Clerk of Courts:
    Appearance dockets
    Chancery records, vA-N, 1824-1854.
    Circuit Court journal, 1885-1912.
    Civil docket
    Common Pleas law record, 1803-1901.
    District court & journal, 1852-1883.
    Executions, vA-1--H-1.
    General index, v1-7, 1876-1900.
    Judgment index, v1-7, 1857-1901.
    Minutes, vB-34, 1815-1901.
    Naturalization records, 1818-1916.
    Register of free blacks, 1804-1857.
    Supreme Court blotter, vB-C, 1825-1851.
    Supreme Court minutes, vA-C, 1803-1851.
    Supreme Court record, vA-G, 1804-1853.
    Superior Court general index, v1-2, 1882-1886.
    Superior Court judgment index, 1856-1887.
    Superior Court minutes, 1856-1882.
    Superior Court record, v1-49, 1856-1896.
Commissioners:
    Burial of indigent soldiers, 1884-1902.
    Journals, 1804-1953.
County Home:
    Infirmary directors minutes, 1826-1873,1900-1912.
    Birth & death record, v1-2, 1886-1969.
    Index, register of inmates, 1888-1892.
    Infirmary & insane record, 1829-1890.
    Register of inmates, 1888-1892.
    Register of sane inmates, 1892-1908.
Probate Court:
    Birth record index, 1867-1910.
    Record of births, 1867-1909.
    Record of deaths, 1866-1909.
    General index, admin. & exec., 1803-1894.
    General index, assignment, 1803-1900.
    General index, civil, 1803-1939.
    General index, guardians & trustees, 1803-1900.
    General index, marriages, v1-11, 1803-1913.
    Marriage affidavits, 1824-1834,1848-1857.
    Marriage records, 1803-1910.
    Probate civil journal, 1852-1886.
    Probate civil record, 1856-1886.
    Probate will record, 1805-1910.
    Naturalization records, 1st papers, v1-6, 1859-1906.
    Naturalization records, 2nd papers, v1-16, 1859-1906.
    Naturalization records, minors, v1-7, 1862-1906.
Recorder:
    Soldiers' discharge record, 1865-1917.

Sheriff:
    Jail register, 1920-1921.
Soldiers' Relief Commission:
    U.S.Military Home, Dayton, Inmate record, 1867-1888.
    Payment record, 1890-1896.
    Relief commission minutes, 1893-1921.
    Minutes, 1946-1950.
    City of Centerville City Council:
    Minutes, 1960-1978.
    Planning commission minutes, 1947-1959.
    Original resolutions, 1939-1972.
    Resolution record, 1939-1978.
    Original ordinances, 1939-1972.
    Ordinance record, 1963-1978.
    Minutes of council, 1926-1979.
City of Dayton:
    City manager files, 1914-1936.
City of Kettering:
    Board of construction review minutes, 1955-1976.
    Board of housing appeals, minutes, 1966-1975.
    Board of plumbers examiners, minutes, 1957-1976.
    Building inspection, board of zoning appeals, 1953-1974.
    Building inspection, board of zoning appeals, 1954-1975.
    Building permits, 1953-1974.
    Electrical permits, A-Z; plumbing permits, A-Z.
    City council minutes, 1953-1974;improvements, 1969-1974.
    City council ordinances, 1953-1974.
    Planning commission appeals, 1962-1973.
    Resolutions, 1953-1974.
    Zoning cases & code amendments, 1953-1975.
    Finance Dept., payroll journal, 1953-1974; payroll records, 1960-1975.
    Personnel Dept., Action, A-Z.
    Planning division minutes, 1953-1976.
    Police Dept. arrest records, 1966-1974.
    Police Dept. scrapbook, 1955-1976.
    Police reports, blueprints, 1965-1972.
Village of New Lebanon Council:
    Fire Assn. fire run record, 1930-1945.
    Fire Assn. minutes, 1934-1964.
    Resolution record, 1879-1978.
    Ordinance record, 1878-1978.
    Minutes, 1878-1978.
    Board of public affairs minutes, 1936-1978.
City of Trotwood City Council:
    Indexed resolutions & ordinances, 1903-1939,1950-1968.
    Resolutions, 1933-1978; ordinances, 1901-1978.
    Ordinance & resolution book, 1901-1903.
    Board of zoning appeals, 1966-1975.
    Minutes of planning commission, 1951-1979.
    Council minutes, 1901-1979.
City of West Carrollton City Council:
    Minutes of council, 1887-1978.
    Ordinance record, 1887-1978; resolutions, 1978.
    Record of resolutions, 1969-1978.
    Planning commission record, 1960-1978.

Board of zoning appeals, 1963-1978.
Board of zoning appeals minutes, 1978.
Van Buren Township:
Incorporations, 1936-1970.
Minutes, 1921-1953.
Miscellaneous:
Deed, tax & cemetery records, by DAR.
Emmanuel's Evan.Luth.Church, Germantown, records, 1809-1933.

**CENSUS RECORDS (OHS,SLO,OGS,LDS)**
1820-1880, 1900-1910; 1890 VETERANS; 1880,1900 SOUNDEX; 1910 MIRACODE

**AGRICULTURAL CENSUS SCHEDULES (OHS,SLO-mic)**
1850,1860,1880

**PRODUCTS OF INDUSTRY CENSUS SCHEDULE (OHS,SLO-mic)**
1850,1880

**MORTALITY CENSUS SCHEDULES (OHS,SLO-mic)**
1850,1860

**DEFECTIVE & DEPENDENT CENSUS SCHEDULES (OHS,SLO-mic)**
1880

**NEWSPAPERS: [GUIDE TO OHIO NEWSPAPERS, 1793-1973]**
Brookville, Centerville, Dayton, Englewood, Farmersville, Germantown, Kettering, Miamisburg, New Lebanon, Trotwood, Vandalia, West Carollton.

**TAX RECORDS (OHS & LDS)**
1806-1808,1810-1814,1816-1838.

**MANUSCRIPTS:**
Dayton, First Regular Baptist Church, records, 1840-1846. (WRHS)
Germantown, St.John's Reformed Church, records, 1844-1884. (OHS)

**GENEALOGICAL PERIODICAL ARTICLES**
Bell, Carol Willsey. OHIO GENEALOGICAL PERIODICAL INDEX: A COUNTY GUIDE (Youngstown OH: author, 6th ed., 1987)

**PUBLISHED SOURCES:**
Barron, William P. THE FLOOD OF MARCH 1913, THE MIAMI CONSERVANCY DISTRICT, AND THE EFFECT ON THE VILLAGE OF OSBORN OHIO. (Willard OH: Family Heritage Pubs., 1983) 64p (LDS)
Becker, Carl M. A BIBLIOGRAPHY OF SOURCES FOR DAYTON OHIO 1850-1950: COOPERATIVE DAYTON HISTORY PROJECT. (Dayton: Wright State U, 1971) 209p (OHS,LDS)
Berry, Ellen T. & David A. EARLY OHIO SETTLERS: PURCHASERS OF LAND IN SOUTHWESTERN OHIO, 1800-1840. (Baltimore: Genealogical Pub.Co., 1986) 372p (OGS,SLO,OHS)
Bigger, William H. OUR CREATIVE YEARS: A HISTORY OF THE SUGAR CREEK UNITED PRES-BYTERIAN CHURCH, DAYTON, OHIO, 1784-1954. 1955? 36p (DAR)
Bowman, Donald R. ATLAS OF MONTGOMERY COUNTY OHIO BY TOWNSHIPS. (Brookville OH: author, 1976) 17p (OGS)
Bowman, Donald R. ATLAS OF MONTGOMERY COUNTY OHIO BY TOWNSHIPS C.1830. (Brookville OH: author, 1975) 15p (OGS)
Bowman, Donald R. CEMETERY ATLAS OF MONTGOMERY COUNTY OHIO BY TOWNSHIPS. (Brookville OH: author, 1976) 45p (OGS)

Brien, Lindsay M. CEMETERY RECORDS OF MONTGOMERY COUNTY, OHIO. 1962. 209p (DAR,LDS)

Brien, Lindsay M. A GENEALOGICAL INDEX OF PIONEERS IN THE MIAMI VALLEY OHIO: MIAMI, MONTGOMERY, PREBLE AND WARREN COUNTIES OHIO. (Dayton: Colonial Dames of America, 1970) 196p (LDS,DAR)

Brien, Lindsay M. AN INDEX OF WILLS AND ADMINISTRATIONS, 1803-1893: MONTGOMERY COUNTY OHIO. 1957. 112p (DAR,LDS)

Brien, Lindsay M. INDEX TO MIAMI VALLEY RECORDS, MIAMI COUNTY CEMETERY RECORDS, V.5. (SLO)

Brien, Lindsay M. MIAMI COUNTY CEMETERY RECORDS. nd. 177p (LDS)

Brien, Lindsay M. MIAMI VALLEY WILL ABSTRACTS FROM THE COUNTIES OF MIAMI, MONTGOMERY, WARREN AND PREBLE IN THE STATE OF OHIO. 1940. (SLO,DAR,LDS)

Brien, Lindsay M. OUR FOREFATHERS ... GENEALOGY OF MIAMI VALLEY FAMILIES. 1r mic. (SLO)

Brien, Lindsay M. MIAMI VALLEY RECORDS, VOL.VI, QUAKER RECORDS. (Dayton OH: Miami Valley Gen Soc, 1986) 121p (OGS)

Brien, Lindsay M. MIAMI VALLEY RECORDS, 5v (SLO)

Brien, Lindsay M. MONTGOMERY COUNTY OHIO MARRIAGES 1803-1851 VOLS II & III. (Reprints, Dayton OH: Miami Valley Gen Soc, 1986) 376p (OGS)

Brien, Lindsay M. QUAKER RECORDS MONTGOMERY COUNTY OHIO. (West Milton OH: Miami Valley Gen.Soc., 1986) 121p (LDS)

Brien, Lindsay M. REGISTER OF MARRIAGE CERTIFICATES RECORDED IN MONTGOMERY COUNTY OHIO, JULY 26, 1803 TO JULY 20, 1851. (LDS)

Burba, Howard L. MIAMI VALLEY LOCAL HISTORY AND VARIOUS OTHER SUBJECTS, 1921-1937. (Columbus: Ohio Hist.Soc., 1974) (LDS)

Caffrey, Joanne T. VETERAN SOLDIERS OF MONTGOMERY COUNTY OHIO, 1862-1885. (Bellbrook OH: author, 1986) 112p (LDS)

CITY/COUNTY DIRECTORIES: check holdings of OHS & local public library.

COMBINATION ATLAS MAP OF MONTGOMERY COUNTY, OHIO. (np: L.H.Everts, 1875)(Reprint, Evansville IN: Unigraphic, 1972) 172p (LDS,OGS,SLO)

Conover, Charlotte. DAYTON AND MONTGOMERY COUNTY, RESOURCES AND PEOPLE. (New York: Lewis Histl Pub Co., 1932) 4v. (LDS,DAR)

Conover, Charlotte. SOME DAYTON SAINTS AND PROPHETS. (Dayton OH: author, 1907) 286p (DAR)

Conover, Charlotte. STORY OF DAYTON, OHIO (Dayton: Otterbein Prs., 1917) 251p (DAR,LDS,SLO)

Conover, Frank. CENTENNIAL PORTRAIT AND BIOGRAPHICAL RECORD OF THE CITY OF DAYTON AND OF MONTGOMERY COUNTY OHIO. (np: A.W.Bowen & Co., 1897) 1310p (DAR,LDS,SLO)(RPI)

Daughters of the American Revolution. 1820 FEDERAL CENSUS OF MONTGOMERY COUNTY OHIO: WITH INDEX. 1949. 83p (DAR)

Daughters of the American Revolution. BIBLE RECORDS OF DARKE, MIAMI AND MONTGOMERY COUNTIES OHIO. (SLO)

Daughters of the American Revolution. INDEX TO DEED BOOKS B & C, 1805-1813, MONTGOMERY COUNTY OHIO. (SLO,LDS)

Daughters of the American Revolution. INSCRIPTIONS HOPEWELL CEMETERY, PRESBYTERIAN, MONTGOMERY COUNTY OHIO. (SLO)

Daughters of the American Revolution. MARRIAGE RECORDS, MONTGOMERY COUNTY OHIO, 1803-1852. 3v. (SLO,DAR,LDS)

Daughters of the American Revolution. MONTGOMERY COUNTY OHIO DEEDS AND TAX RECORDS. (SLO)

Daughters of the American Revolution. OHIO BIBLE RECORDS: CONCERNING FAMILIES OF CRAW-FORD, DARKE, FAIRFIELD, MIAMI, MONTGOMERY, PICKAWAY, PREBLE AND SHELBY COUNTIES. 1970. 126p (DAR)

Daughters of the American Revolution. OHIO CHURCH RECORDS: STILLWATER EVANGELICAL LUTHERAN CHURCH RECORDS AND ST.PAUL'S EVANGELICAL LUTHERAN CHURCH RECORDS; PLEASANT VIEW, OHIO, MONTGOMERY COUNTY, BUTLER TOWNSHIP. 1972. 112p (DAR)

Davis, Eileen & J.Ireton. QUAKER RECORDS OF THE MIAMI VALLEY OF OHIO. 1980. (SLO)

DAYTON CITY DIRECTORY. (Cincinnati: Williams Directory Co., 1940) (LDS)

Drury, Augustus W. HISTORY OF THE CITY OF DAYTON AND MONTGOMERY COUNTY OHIO. (Chicago: S.J.Clarke Pub Co., 1909) 2v. (LDS,SLO,DAR)(RPI)

Edgar, John F. PIONEER LIFE IN DAYTON AND VICINITY, 1796-1840. (Dayton: W.J.Shuey, 1896) 265p (LDS,SLO,DAR)

EMMANUEL'S EVANGELICAL LUTHERAN CHURCH, GERMANTOWN, OHIO, SESQUICENTEN-NIAL CELEBRATION, JULY 30, 1959. (Germantown OH: the church, 1959) 36p (LDS)

Floyd, Marjorie D. EVERY NAME INDEX TO MIAMI VALLEY OHIO PIONEERS BY LINDSAY M. BRIEN. (Dayton OH: author, 1980) 38p (LDS)

Fox, John H. GRAVESTONE INSCRIPTIONS, OHIO. 197? 10p (LDS)

Fullerton, Richard D. 99 YEARS OF DAYTON PHOTOGRAPHERS. (Dayton: author, 1982) 48p. (OGS,LDS)

Funk, Nellis R. A PICTORIAL HISTORY OF THE GREAT DAYTON FLOOD: MARCH 25,26,27, 1913. (Dayton OH: Otterbein Press, 1913) 63p (DAR)

Haller, Stephen E. & P.Nolan. FIRST STOP FOR LOCAL HISTORY RESEARCH. A GUIDE TO COUN-TY RECORDS PRESERVED AT WRIGHT STATE UNIVERSITY ARCHIVES AND SPECIAL COL-LECTIONS. 1976. 21p.

Heck, Earl L. THE HISTORY OF ENGLEWOOD AND RANDOLPH TOWNSHIPS MONTGOMERY COUNTY OHIO. (np, 1960) 96,24p (LDS,SLO)

Heeter, Ken J. INDEX TO THE MAP OF MONTGOMERY COUNTY OHIO. (Knightstown IN: Book-mark, 1975) 23p (LDS)

Heins, Gustavus. MAP OF MONTGOMERY COUNTY OHIO. (np: author, 1851)(Reprint, Knightstown IN: Bookmark, 1974) 15p (LDS)

Hentz, John P. HISTORY OF THE EVANGELICAL LUTHERAN CONGREGATION IN GERMAN-TOWN, OHIO; AND BIOGRAPHIES OF ITS PASTORS AND FOUNDERS. (Dayton OH: Christian Pub.House, 1882) 102p (LDS,SLO)

Hentz, John P. TWIN VALLEY; ITS SETTLEMENT AND SUBSEQUENT HISTORY, 1798-1882. (Dayton: Christian Pub House, 1883) 288p (LDS,DAR)

Historical Records Survey. INVENTORY OF THE COUNTY ARCHIVES OF OHIO NO.57, MONTGOMERY COUNTY. (Columbus: author, 1941) 345p (OHS,LDS)

HISTORY OF DAYTON OHIO, WITH PORTRAITS AND BIOGRAPHICAL SKETCHES. (Dayton: United Brethren Pub House, 1889) 728p (LDS,SLO,DAR)

HISTORY OF MONTGOMERY COUNTY OHIO. (Chicago: W.H.Beers & Co., 1882) 2v. (LDS,SLO,DAR)(RPI)

HISTORY OF ST.JACOB'S LUTHERAN CHURCH, MIAMISBURG, OHIO: DEDICATION CENTEN-NIAL, 1964. 33p (LDS)

HISTORY OF WAYNE TOWNSHIP 1810 TO PRESENT. (Dayton: Wayne Tp. Bicentennial Commission, 1976) (OHS)

HOMETOWN HERITAGE, WEST CARROLLTON, OHIO. 1976. (SLO)

Houser, Howard R. A SENSE OF PLACE IN CENTERVILLE AND WASHINGTON TOWNSHIP OHIO. (Centerville OH: Hist Soc., 1977?) 238p (SLO)

INDEX TO CITY OF DAYTON, OHIO BIRTHS, VOL.I & II, 1867-1881. (SLO)

Leggett, Nancy G. & D.E.Smith. A GUIDE TO LOCAL GOVERNMENT RECORDS AND NEWSPAPERS PRESERVED AT THE DEPARTMENT OF ARCHIVES AND SPECIAL COLLECTIONS WRIGHT STATE UNIVERSITY. (Dayton OH: Wright State U., 1987)

Light, Esther. MIAMISBURG; THE FIRST ONE HUNDRED FIFTY YEARS. (Miamisburg OH: Lions Club, c1968) 206p (LDS)

MEMOIRS OF THE MIAMI VALLEY OHIO. (Chicago: Robert O.Law Co.,1919) 3v (OHS,SLO)

Montgomery Co Chapter OGS. 1850 DAYTON CITY DIRECTORY. 133p (Reprint, Dayton OH: the society, 1987)

Montgomery Co Chapter OGS. CEMETERY INSCRIPTIONS PLUS MONTGOMERY CO OHIO VOL.I-3. [Mad River & Wayne Tps; Washington Tp; Van Buren Tp] (Dayton: the society, 1982+) (LDS,OGS,SLO)

Montgomery Co Chapter OGS. COMPLETE NAME INDEX TO JOHN EDGAR'S 1896 "PIONEER LIFE IN DAYTON & VICINITY" (Dayton: the society, 1976) 35p (OGS)

Montgomery Co Chapter OGS. INDEX TO MONTGOMERY COUNTY INFIRMARY BIRTH AND
    DEATH RECORDS, 1886-1907. (Dayton: the society, 1982) 14p (OGS,LDS,SLO)
Montgomery Co Chapter OGS. MONTGOMERY COUNTY OHIO CEMETERY INSCRIPTIONS VOL.III.
    [Van Buren Tp] (Dayton: the society, 1984) 326p (OGS)
Montgomery Co Chapter OGS. ODELL'S DAYTON DIRECTORY AND BUSINESS ADVERTISER WITH
    A SKETCH OF THE HISTORY OF THE CITY. (Dayton: the society, 1988) 133p (OGS)
MONTGOMERY COUNTY OHIO RECORDS. (Philadelphia: Gen Soc of Pa, nd) 4r mic (LDS)
MONTGOMERY COUNTY OHIO TOWNSHIPS 1900 FEDERAL CENSUS [EXCLUDING DAYTON &
    VETERAN'S HOME] (Brookville OH: Brookville Hist Soc., nd) 610p (OGS)
OLD GERMAN BAPTIST CHURCH MINUTES OF THE YEARLY MEETING OF THE BRETHREN OF
    THE OLD GERMAN BAPTIST CHURCH: WOLF CREEK CHURCH, NEAR BROOKVILLE.
    (Dayton OH: Christian Pub.House, 1882) 8p (LDS)
Pouget, Luella R. CEMETERY INSCRIPTIONS FROM MONTGOMERY, MIAMI, PREBLE AND
    DARKE? COUNTIES, OHIO. (LDS)
Schlipf, Patricia. INDEX TO CITY OF DAYTON, DEATHS, 1867-1873. 1984. (SLO) Shilt, Rose & A.Gil-
    bert. MONTGOMERY COUNTY OHIO ADMINISTRATIONS AND WILLS, 1805-1850, GUAR-
    DIANS, 1805-1850. (np: author, 1985) 210p (LDS)
Shilt, Rose & A.Gilbert. MONTGOMERY COUNTY OHIO 1850 CENSUS. (West Alexandria OH: A.Gil-
    bert, 1985) 343p (LDS)
Short, Anita. OHIO BIBLE RECORDS CONCERNING FAMILIES OF CRAWFORD, DARKE, FAIR-
    FIELD, MIAMI, MONTGOMERY, PICKAWAY, PREBLE AND SHELBY COUNTIES. (SLO)
Short, Anita. OHIO BIBLE RECORDS. (SLO)
Siebert, Albert F. BRIEF HISTORY OF EMMANUEL'S EVANGELICAL LUTHERAN CHURCH, GER-
    MANTOWN, OHIO, FOR ITS CENTENNIAL, A.D., 1809-A.D.1909. (Germantown OH: author,
    1909) 60p (LDS)
Smith, William E. HISTORY OF SOUTHWESTERN OHIO, THE MIAMI VALLEYS. 1964. 3v. (SLO)
Steele, Robert W. EARLY DAYTON; WITH IMPORTANT FACTS AND INCIDENTS, 1796-1896. (Dayton
    OH: W.J.Shuey, 1896) 247p (LDS,SLO,DAR)
SULPHUR GROVE UNITED METHODIST CHURCH: CENTENNIAL PICTORIAL DIRECTORY, 1871-
    1971. 1971. 30p (DAR)
TRIENNIAL ATLAS & PLAT BOOK, MONTGOMERY COUNTY OHIO. (Rockford IL: Rockford Map
    Pubs., 1971) 26p (LDS)
Vicory, Jacqueline. MILO UNION LIST OF GENEALOGIES IN THE LIBRARIES OF CHAMPAIGN,
    CLARK, DARKE, GREENE, MIAMI, MONTGOMERY AND PREBLE COUNTIES, OHIO. (Dayton
    OH: Miami Valley Library Organization, 1977) 122p (LDS)
Wright State University Library. AN INDEX TO NATURALIZATION RECORDS FROM
    MONTGOMERY COUNTY OHIO 1803-1931. (Dayton OH: author, 1987?)
Wyllie, Stanley. A GUIDE TO GENEALOGICAL MATERIALS IN THE DAYTON & MONTGOMERY
    COUNTY OHIO PUBLIC LIBRARY. (Dayton OH: Public Library, 1982) 27p. (OGS,LDS)
Yon, Paul D. GUIDE TO OHIO COUNTY & MUNICIPAL GOVERNMENT RECORDS. (Columbus:
    Ohio Hist Soc., 1973) 216p (OHS)

# MORGAN COUNTY

| | |
|---|---|
| CREATED: | 1817 FROM GUERNSEY, MUSKINGUM & WASHINGTON |
| COUNTY SEAT: | McCONNELSVILLE 43756 |
| COURT HOUSE: | 19  E. MAIN ST., McCONNELSVILLE 43756 |
| LIBRARIES: | 358 E. MAIN ST., McCONNELSVILLE 43756 |
| HISTORICAL SOCIETY: | 142 E. MAIN ST., McCONNELSVILLE 43756 |
| GENEALOGICAL SOCIETY: | MORGAN COUNTY CHAPTER, OGS, |
| | PO BOX 418, McCONNELSVILLE 43756 |
| | publication: MORGAN LINKS |
| HEALTH DEPARTMENT: | 4275 NO.STATE RTE.376 NW, McCONNELSVILLE 43756 |

| | |
|---|---|
| ARCHIVAL DISTRICT: | OHIO UNIVERSITY, ATHENS |
| | (see published Guide to records) |
| LAND SURVEYS: | CONGRESS LANDS, OHIO RIVER SURVEY (SOUTH) |
| | OHIO COMPANY |
| | DONATION TRACT |
| BOUNDED BY: | EAST:   NOBLE & WASHINGTON CO. |
| | NORTH:  MUSKINGUM CO. |
| | WEST:   PERRY CO. |
| | SOUTH:  ATHENS & WASHINGTON CO. |
| TOWNSHIPS: | Bloom, Bristol, Center, Deerfield, Homer, Malta,  Manchester, |
| | Marion, Meigsville, Morgan, Penn, Union, Windsor, York. |

## COURT RECORDS: (LDS MICROFILM)
Auditor:
> Tax duplicates, 1833,1840-41,1846-1849;1820-1838.
> Land assessments, 1859,1870.

Clerk of Courts:
> Index to appearance dockets, 1819-1860.
> Appearance dockets, vA-G,I, 1819-1848,1851-1853.
> Common Pleas minutes, vA-I, 1819-1852.
> Common Pleas record, vA-L, 1819-1853.

Probate Court:
> Birth records, v1-3, 1867-1908.
> Death records, v1-2, 1867-1908.
> Index to death records, v3, 1867-1962.
> Will records, vO-3, 1820-1887.
> Index to wills, 1819-1953.
> Marriage license index, 1840-1867.
> Marriage records, vA-J, 1819-1923.
> Estate docket, vA, 1838-1856.
> Executors' docket, vB-C, 1857-1884.
> Administration docket, vC-D, 1870-1894.
> Guardians' docket, vC-D, 1870-1894.
> Probate appearance docket, vA-B, 1852-1885.
> Civil docket, vC, 1885-1894.
> Administrators' bonds, 1821-1892.
> Executors' bonds, 1870-1892.
> Guardians' bonds, 1849-1870.
> Court journal, vA-I, 1852-1886.
> Inventories, v1-6, 1853-1888.
> Sale bills of estates, v1-3, 1853-1887.
> Final record, vA-F, 1852-1891.
> Naturalization record, 1861-1892.

Recorder:
> Grantor & grantee index to deeds, vA-Z, 1795-1895.
> Deed records, vA-Z, 1-27, 1819-1881.

Miscellaneous:
> Windsor, Baptist church records, 1818-1904.
> Enrollment of militia, May 1867, Morgan Co.
> Records of Carl L.Wagner, Lutheran minister, Eagleport, 1920-1965.

## OHIO HISTORICAL SOCIETY: (MICROFILM)
Miscellaneous:
> Death records, 1867-1896, by DAR.
> Marriage records, 1819-1862, by DAR.

**CENSUS RECORDS (OHS,SLO,OGS,LDS)**
1820-1880, 1900-1910; 1890 VETERANS; 1880,1900 SOUNDEX; 1910 MIRACODE

**AGRICULTURAL CENSUS SCHEDULES (OHS,SLO-mic)**
1850,1860,1880

**PRODUCTS OF INDUSTRY CENSUS SCHEDULE (OHS,SLO-mic)**
1850,1880

**MORTALITY CENSUS SCHEDULES (OHS,SLO-mic)**
1850,1860

**DEFECTIVE & DEPENDENT CENSUS SCHEDULES (OHS,SLO-mic)**
1880

**NEWSPAPERS: [GUIDE TO OHIO NEWSPAPERS, 1793-1973]**
Chesterhill, McConnelsville, Malta.

**TAX RECORDS (OHS & LDS)**
1820-1838.

**GENEALOGICAL PERIODICAL ARTICLES**
Bell, Carol Willsey. OHIO GENEALOGICAL PERIODICAL INDEX: A COUNTY GUIDE (Youngstown OH: author, 6th ed., 1987)

**PUBLISHED SOURCES:**
Berry, Ellen T. & David. EARLY OHIO SETTLERS: PURCHASERS OF LAND IN SOUTHEASTERN OHIO, 1800-1840. (Baltimore: Genealogical Pub.Co., 1984) 129p (OHS,SLO,OGS,DAR)
CITY/COUNTY DIRECTORIES: check holdings of OHS & local public library.
Daughters of the American Revolution. EARLY DEATHS OF MORGAN COUNTY OHIO, 1867-1896. 1945. 85p. (SLO,LDS,DAR)
Daughters of the American Revolution. EARLY MARRIAGES OF MORGAN COUNTY OHIO, 1819-1864. 1963. 2v. (SLO,LDS,DAR)
DEERFIELD UNITED PRESBYTERIAN CHURCH, SESQUI-CENTENNIAL 1821-1971. 1971. 13p (OGS)
Gaylord, James M. HISTORICAL REMINISCENCES OF MORGAN COUNTY OHIO. (McConnelsville OH: Morgan Co Hist Soc., 1984) 92p (OGS,SLO,LDS)
Gerlach, Elmer & B. Blackburn. INDEX 1980 HISTORY OF MORGAN COUNTY OHIO. (McConnelsville OH: Morgan Co Hist Soc, 1985) 164p (OGS)
Gerlach, Elmer & Katherine. MEIGS CEMETERY RECORDS, BRISTOL TP., MORGAN COUNTY OHIO. (McConnelsville OH: author, 1980) 15p. (OGS)
Gerlach, Elmer. THE VETERANS OF WORLD WAR II, MORGAN COUNTY OHIO (McConnelsville OH: Morgan Co Chapter OGS) 183p (OGS,OHS,LDS)
Hardesty, H.H. MILITARY HISTORY OF OHIO - MORGAN COUNTY EDITION. 1886/87. (OHS)
Hinshaw, William Wade. ENCYCLOPEDIA OF AMERICAN QUAKER GENEALOGY, VOL.IV, OHIO. (Baltimore: Genealogical Pub.Co., 1973) 1424p (SLO,OHS,LDS)
Lake, D.J. ATLAS OF MORGAN COUNTY, OHIO. (Philadelphia: Titus, Simmons & Titus, 1875)(Reprint, McConnelsville OH: Morgan Co Hist Soc.,1976) 57p (DAR,LDS,OGS)(RPI)
Lewis, Thomas W. SOUTHEASTERN OHIO AND THE MUSKINGUM VALLEY, 1788-1928: COVERING ATHENS, BELMONT, COSHOCTON, GUERNSEY, LICKING, MEIGS, MONROE, MORGAN, MUSKINGUM, NOBLE, PERRY AND WASHINGTON COUNTIES. (Chicago: S.J.Clarke Co.,1928) 3v. (SLO,DAR,OHS)
McConnelsville Sesquicentennial Committee. McCONNELSVILLE OHIO 1817-1967. 1967. 73p. (SLO)
Morgan Co Chapter OGS. CEMETERIES OF CENTER & MANCHESTER TOWNSHIPS. (McConnelsville OH: the society, 1982) 55p (OGS,LDS,SLO)

Morgan Co Chapter OGS. CEMETERIES OF DEERFIELD & UNION TOWNSHIPS, MORGAN COUNTY OHIO (McConnelsville OH: the society, 1982,1983) 73p (OGS,LDS)

Morgan Co Chapter OGS. CEMETERIES OF HOMER & MARION TOWNSHIPS, MORGAN COUNTY OHIO (McConnelsville OH: the society, 1982) (OGS,LDS,SLO)

Morgan Co Chapter OGS. CEMETERIES OF MALTA & MORGAN TOWNSHIPS, MORGAN COUNTY OHIO. (McConnelsville OH: the society, 1982) 142p (OGS,LDS,SLO)

Morgan Co Chapter OGS. CEMETERIES OF PENN & WINDSOR TOWNSHIPS. (McConnelsville OH: the society, 1985) 101p (OGS,LDS,SLO)

Morgan Co Chapter OGS. CEMETERIES OF BLOOM & YORK TOWNSHIPS, MORGAN COUNTY OHIO (McConnelsville OH: the society, 1982) 56p (OGS,LDS,SLO)

Morgan Co Chapter OGS. CEMETERIES OF BRISTOL-MEIGSVILLE TOWNSHIPS,MORGAN COUNTY OHIO. (McConnelsville OH: the society, 1982) 71p (OGS,LDS,SLO)

Morgan Co Chapter OGS. GENEALOGICAL EXTRACTS FROM MORGAN COUNTY NATURALIZATION RECORDS.[1819-1899] (McConnelsville OH: the society, 1982) 50p (OGS,LDS,SLO)

Morgan Co Chapter OGS. INDEX, 1980 HISTORY OF MORGAN COUNTY OHIO. (McConnelsville OH: the society, 1980) 164p (LDS)

Morgan Co Chapter OGS. MARRIAGES IN MORGAN COUNTY OHIO VOL.A, 1819-1841 (Malta OH: the society, 1983) 113p (OGS)

Morgan Co Chapter OGS. MARRIAGES IN MORGAN COUNTY OHIO VOL.B, 1841-1853. (McConnelsville OH: the society, 1984) 60p (OGS,OHS,SLO,LDS)

Morgan Co Chapter OGS. MARRIAGES IN MORGAN COUNTY OHIO VOL.C, 1853-1867. (McConnelsville OH: the society, 1985) 69p (OGS,SLO)

Morgan Co Chapter OGS. MORGAN CO OHIO INDEX TO THE 1900 POPULATION CENSUS SCHEDULES (McConnellsville OH: the society, 1986) 20p

Morgan Co Chapter OGS. MORGAN COUNTY OHIO 1850 FEDERAL POPULATION CENSUS. (McConnelsville OH: the society, 1988) 746p (OGS)

Morgan Co Chapter OGS. MORGAN COUNTY OHIO 1880 CENSUS INDEX. (McConnelsville OH: the society, 1986) 54p (OGS,LDS)

Morgan Co Chapter OGS. MORGAN COUNTY OHIO MARRIAGE BOOK E, 1869-1878. (McConnelsville OH: the society, 1987) 55p (OGS)

Morgan Co. Historical Society. THE HISTORY OF MORGAN COUNTY, OHIO, 1980. (McConnelsville OH: The Society, 1980) 336p (DAR,SLO)

Murray. ATLAS OF MORGAN COUNTY, OHIO. 1902. (SLO)(RPI)

Ohio University. GUIDE TO LOCAL GOVERNMENT RECORDS AT OHIO UNIVERSITY. (Athens OH: OU Library, 1986) 61p.

Robertson, Charles. HISTORY OF MORGAN COUNTY. (Chicago: L.H.Watkins & Co., 1886) 538p (McConnelsville OH: Morgan Co Hist Soc., nd) (OGS,SLO,LDS) (RPI)

Schneider, Norris F. THE MUSKINGUM RIVER: A HISTORY AND GUIDE. (Columbus: Ohio Hist.Soc., 1968) 48p (LDS)

Slaughter, Raymond D. INDEX 1900 CENSUS OF MORGAN COUNTY, OHIO. (SLO)

Walker, Richard. A COMPLETE LIST OF TOMBSTONE INSCRIPTIONS OF WINDSOR TOWNSHIP, MORGAN COUNTY, OH: AND ALL NEARBY CEMETERIES. 1979. 66p (DAR)

Weller, Robert. MORGAN COUNTY OHIO CEMETERY INSCRIPTIONS, YORK TOWNSHIP. (Springfield OH: author, 1981) (OGS,SLO)

Yocum, E.G. HIGH ON A HILL. 1953. 103p. (SLO)

# MORROW COUNTY

CREATED:            1848 FROM RICHLAND COUNTY
COUNTY SEAT:        MT.GILEAD 43338
COURT HOUSE:        EAST HIGH ST., MT.GILEAD 43338
LIBRARIES:          EAST HIGH ST., MT.GILEAD 43338
HISTORICAL SOCIETY: 619 W. MARION RD., MT.GILEAD 43338

GENEALOGICAL SOCIETY:     MORROW COUNTY CHAPTER, OGS,
                          PO BOX 401, MT.GILEAD 43338
HEALTH DEPARTMENT:        COURT HOUSE, MOUNT GILEAD 43338
ARCHIVAL DISTRICT:        OHIO HISTORICAL SOCIETY, COLUMBUS
LAND SURVEYS:             CONGRESS LANDS, E & S OF 1ST PRIN.MERIDIAN
                          CONGRESS LANDS, OHIO RIVER SURVEY (NORTH)
                          UNITED STATES MILITARY DISTRICT
BOUNDED BY:               EAST:     KNOX & RICHLAND CO.
                          NORTH:    CRAWFORD & RICHLAND CO.
                          WEST:     MARION CO.
                          SOUTH:    DELAWARE CO.
TOWNSHIPS:                Bennington, Canaan, Cardington, Chester, Congress, Franklin,
                          Gilead, Harmony, Lincoln, North Bloomfield, Perry, Peru, South
                          Bloomfield, Troy, Washington, Westfield.

## COURT RECORDS: (LDS MICROFILM)
Auditor:
    Quadrennial enumeration, 1895-1907.
Clerk of Courts:
    Chancery record, v1-4, 1848-1858.
    Supreme Court journal, v1, 1849-1875.
    Supreme Court complete record, 1849-1861.
    Common Pleas appearance docket, v2-3, 1851-1856.
    Common Pleas journal, v1-2, 1848-1852.
    Quadrennial enumeration, 1875-1879,1891-1903.
Probate Court:
    Marriage records, v1A-8, 1848-1926.
    Birth records, v1-2, 1867-1908.
    Birth registration & corrections, v1-6, dates vary.
    Death records, 1867-1909.
    Index to probate court, v1, 1848-1950.
    Wills, v1-7, 1848-1903.
    Guardian index, v1, 1848-1950.
    Guardian docket, v1-4, 1848-1914.
    Probate journal, v1-16, 1852-1900.
    Naturalization records, 1861-1902.
Recorder:
    Grantor & grantee index to deeds, v1-2, 1848-1896.
    Deeds, v1-23, 1848-1871.
Miscellaneous:
    Alum Creek Monthly Meeting of Friends, records, 1828-1865.

## OHIO HISTORICAL SOCIETY: (MICROFILM)
Auditor:
    Quadrennial enumeration, 1895-1907.
Clerk of Courts:
    Chancery record, v1-4, 1848-1858.
    Supreme Court journal, v1, 1849-1875.
    Supreme Court complete record, 1849-1861.
    Common Pleas appearance docket, v2-3, 1851-1856.
    Common Pleas journal, v1-2, 1848-1852.
    Quadrennial enumeration, 1875-1879,1891-1903.
Miscellaneous:
    Cemetery records, by DAR.

**CENSUS RECORDS (OHS,SLO,OGS,LDS)**
1850-1880, 1900-1910; 1890 VETERANS; 1880,1900 SOUNDEX; 1910 MIRACODE

**AGRICULTURAL CENSUS SCHEDULES (OHS,SLO-mic)**
1860,1880

**PRODUCTS OF INDUSTRY CENSUS SCHEDULE (OHS,SLO-mic)**
1850,1860,1880

**MORTALITY CENSUS SCHEDULES (OHS,SLO-mic)**
1850,1860

**DEFECTIVE & DEPENDENT CENSUS SCHEDULES (OHS,SLO-mic)**
1880

**QUADRENNIAL ENUMERATIONS: (OHS)**
1867,1871,1875,1879,1883,1891,1895,1899,1903,1907.

**NEWSPAPERS: [GUIDE TO OHIO NEWSPAPERS, 1793-1973]**
Blooming Grove, Cardington, Fulton, Iberia, Mount Gilead, Williamsport.

**TAX RECORDS (OHS & LDS)**
none listed; see parent counties.

**GENEALOGICAL PERIODICAL ARTICLES**
Bell, Carol Willsey. OHIO GENEALOGICAL PERIODICAL INDEX: A COUNTY GUIDE (Youngstown
   OH: author, 6th ed., 1987)

**PUBLISHED SOURCES:**
150th ANNIVERSARY OF JOHNSVILLE OHIO SESQUICENTENNIAL 1834. (Johnsville OH: Volun-
   teer Fire Dept., 1984) 144p (OGS)
Battle, J.H. & W.H.Perrin. HISTORY OF MORROW COUNTY OHIO. (Chicago: O.L. Baskin & Co.,
   1880) 838p (SLO,OHS)(RPI)
Baughman, Abraham J. HISTORY OF MORROW COUNTY, OHIO: A NARRATIVE ACCOUNT OF
   ITS HISTORICAL PROGRESS, ITS PEOPLE, AND ITS PRINCIPAL INTERESTS. (Chicago: Lewis
   Pub.Co., 1911) 2v (DAR,LDS)
Benedict, Aaron. HISTORY OF PERU TOWNSHIP, MORROW COUNTY OHIO. (Mt.Gilead OH: Sen-
   tinel Printing House, 1897) 54p. (LDS,OGS)
Bouic, Margaret M. GENEALOGICAL INDEX OF DELAWARE, UNION AND MORROW COUNTIES.
   (SLO,OGS)
Buck, Thaddeus. ATLAS OF MORROW COUNTY OHIO. 1901. (OGS,SLO)
Buck. ATLAS OF MORROW COUNTY OHIO. 1871. (SLO)(RPI)
CEMETERY INSCRIPTIONS KNOX, MORROW, RICHLAND AND GUERNSEY COUNTIES OHIO.
   1r mic (SLO)
CHESTERVILLE UNITED METHODIST CHURCH SESQUICENTENNIAL CELEBRATION, 1833-1983.
   (SLO)
CITY/COUNTY DIRECTORIES: check holdings of OHS & local public library.
Crist, A.C. THE HISTORY OF THE MARION PRESBYTERY: ITS CHURCHES, ELDERS, MINISTERS,
   MISSIONARY SOCIETIES, ETC. 1908. 352p (DAR)
Hardesty, H.H. MILITARY HISTORY OF OHIO - MORROW COUNTY EDITION. 1886/87. (OHS)
HISTORICAL PROGRAM, MORROW COUNTY CENTENNIAL, 1848-1948. (SLO)
HISTORY OF MORROW COUNTY AND OHIO. (Chicago: O.L.Baskin & Co., 1880) 838p
   (DAR,LDS,SLO)
L.D.S. UNION CEMETERY RECORDS, MORROW COUNTY OHIO. 1956. (LDS)

Main, Florence D. HISTORY OF PERU TOWNSHIP, MORROW COUNTY, OHIO. (Mt. Gilead OH: Sentinel Printing House, 1897) 54p (LDS)
Matusoff, Karen. CENTRAL OHIO LOCAL GOVERNMENT RECORDS AT THE OHIO HISTORICAL SOCIETY. (Columbus: Ohio Hist Soc., 1978) 38p. (OGS)
MEMORIAL RECORD OF THE COUNTIES OF DELAWARE, UNION AND MORROW. (Chicago: Lewis Pub Co., 1895) 501p. (LDS,SLO,OHS,OGS,DAR)(RPI)
Morrow Co Chapter OGS. MORROW COUNTY OHIO TOMBSTONE INSCRIPTIONS VOL.I. (Perry & Troy Twps) (Mt.Gilead OH: the society, 1986) 86p (OGS,LDS)
Powell, Esther W. TOMBSTONE INSCRIPTIONS AND OTHER RECORDS OF DELAWARE COUNTY OHIO, INCLUDING PORTIONS OF MORROW AND MARION COUNTIES. (Akron OH: author, 1972) 448p (OGS,LDS,SLO,DAR)
Smith, Bertha. MORROW COUNTY MARRIAGES 1848-1854. (np: author, nd) 1v. (LDS,SLO)
Smith, Clifford N. FEDERAL LAND SERIES: A CALENDAR OF ARCHIVAL MATERIAL ON THE LAND PATENTS ISSUED BY THE U.S.GOVERNMENT, VOL.2: FEDERAL BOUNTY LAND WARRANTS OF THE AMERICAN REVOLUTION. (Chicago: American Library Assn., 1972) 416p

# MUSKINGUM COUNTY

| | |
|---|---|
| CREATED: | 1804 FROM FAIRFIELD & WASHINGTON COUNTIES |
| COUNTY SEAT: | ZANESVILLE 43701 |
| COURT HOUSE: | MAIN ST., ZANESVILLE 43701 |
| LIBRARIES: | 220 N. FIFTH ST., ZANESVILLE 43701 |
| HISTORICAL SOCIETY: | PO BOX 2201, ZANESVILLE 43701 |
| GENEALOGICAL SOCIETY: | MUSKINGUM COUNTY CHAPTER, OGS, |
| | PO BOX 3066, ZANESVILLE 43701 |
| | publication: MUSKINGUM |
| HEALTH DEPARTMENT: | 421 MAIN ST., ZANESVILLE 43701 |
| | (separate office for Zanesville city) |
| ARCHIVAL DISTRICT: | OHIO UNIVERSITY, ATHENS |
| | (see published Guide to records) |
| LAND SURVEYS: | UNITED STATES MILITARY DISTRICT |
| | CONGRESS LANDS, OHIO RIVER SURVEY (SOUTH) |
| | ZANE'S TRACTS |
| BOUNDED BY: | EAST:    GUERNSEY & NOBLE CO. |
| | NORTH:  COSHOCTON CO. |
| | WEST:    LICKING CO. |
| | SOUTH:  MORGAN & PERRY CO. |
| TOWNSHIPS: | Adams, Blue Rock, Brush Creek, Clay, Fall, Harrison, Highland, Hopewell, Jackson, Jefferson, Licking, Madison, Meigs, Monroe, Muskingum, Newton, Perry, Rich Hill, Salem, Salt Creek, Springfield, Union, Washington, Wayne. |

**COURT RECORDS: (LDS MICROFILM)**
Auditor:
    Civil War veteran record, c1881-1920.
    Tax duplicates, 1816-1834.
Clerk of Courts:
    Common Pleas appearance docket, 1812-1852.
    Common Pleas chancery index, 1824-1852.
    Common Pleas complete record, 1808-1822.
    Common Pleas complete record index, 1804-1853.
    Common Pleas minutes, 1814-1853.
    Common Pleas court record, 1820-1852.
    Supreme Court appearance docket, 1813-1851.

Supreme Court minutes, 1816-1852.
Supreme Court record, 1805-1851.
Abstract of votes, 1878-1892.
Commissioners:
Journal, 1808-1900.
Index to journals, 1859-1904.
County Home:
Board minutes, 1908,1912.
Probate Court:
Marriages, 1804-1917.
Death records, v1-4, 1867-1908.
Birth records, v1-5, 1867-1909.
General index to probate records, 1912-1948.
Final record of court cases, v1-9, 1852-1885.
Administration docket, vA-C, 1-5, 1830-1889.
Guardians' docket, vA-B,1-5, 1816-1898.
Will records, guard., admin., vA-C, 1804-1843.
Will records, vD,1-7, 1843-1890.
Executors' bond record, vA-B, 1867-1900.
Journal docket, v1-14, 1852-1887.
Motion docket, 1947-1958.
Record of licensed ministers, c1804-1841.
Naturalization records, 1860-1905.
Recorder:
Grantor & grantee index to deeds, 1803-1907.
Deed records, vA-Z, 1-72, 1800-1881.
Sheriff:
Jail register, 1868-1925.
Miscellaneous:
Adams Mills, Madison Presby.Church, records, 1837-1885.
Dresden, First Presby.Church, records, 1828-1892.
Madison Tp., St.Matthew's Episc.Church, register, 1837-1965.
New Concord, Presby.Church, records, 1804-1898.
New Concord, Pleasant Hill Presby.Church, records, 1818-1882.
Norwich, Presby.Church, records, 1828-1870.
Zanesville, First Presby.Church, records, 1896-1909.
Zanesville, First Presby.Church, communicants, early to 1883.
Cemetery records, State Library of Ohio collection.
Records kept by Rev.Carl L.Wagner, Lutheran minister, 1920-1965.

## OHIO HISTORICAL SOCIETY: (MICROFILM)
Auditor:
Civil War veteran record, c1881-1920.
Clerk of Courts:
Common Pleas appearance docket, 1812-1852.
Common Pleas chancery index, 1824-1852.
Common Pleas complete record, 1808-1822.
Common Pleas complete record index, 1804-1853.
Common Pleas minutes, 1814-1853.
Common Pleas court record, 1820-1852.
Supreme Court appearance docket, 1813-1851.
Supreme Court minutes, 1816-1852.
Supreme Court record, 1805-1851.
Abstract of votes, 1878-1892.

Commissioners:
  Journal, 1808-1900.
  Index to journals, 1859-1904.
County Home:
  Board minutes, 1908,1912.
Sheriff:
  Jail register, 1868-1925.
Miscellaneous:
  Marriage records, 1804-1897, by DAR.
  Index to wills & guardianships, 1804-1901, by DAR.
  Tax records, 1806-1810, by DAR.

## CENSUS RECORDS  (OHS,SLO,OGS,LDS)
1820-1880, 1900-1910; 1890 VETERANS; 1880,1900 SOUNDEX; 1910 MIRACODE

## AGRICULTURAL CENSUS SCHEDULES  (OHS,SLO-mic)
1860,1880

## PRODUCTS OF INDUSTRY CENSUS SCHEDULE  (OHS,SLO-mic)
1850,1860,1880

## MORTALITY CENSUS SCHEDULES (OHS,SLO-mic)
1850,1860

## DEFECTIVE & DEPENDENT CENSUS SCHEDULES (OHS,SLO-mic)
1880

## NEWSPAPERS: [GUIDE TO OHIO NEWSPAPERS, 1793-1973]
Adamsville, Dresden, Frazeyburg, New Concord, Putnam, Zanesville.

## TAX RECORDS (OHS & LDS)
1806-1814,1816-1838.

## GENEALOGICAL PERIODICAL ARTICLES
Bell, Carol Willsey. OHIO GENEALOGICAL PERIODICAL INDEX: A COUNTY GUIDE (Youngstown
  OH: author, 6th ed., 1987)

## PUBLISHED SOURCES: [OUZ = OHIO UNIVERSITY, Zanesville]
Adamsville H.S.Alumni Assn. ADAMSVILLE HIGH SCHOOL HISTORY AND BIOGRAPHY 1894-
  1966. (Zanesville OH: author, 1966) 108p (OGS)
Barnes, Charles E. BIOGRAPHICAL MEMORIES OF MUSKINGUM COUNTY OHIO. (OUZ)
Barnes, Charles E. HISTORICAL SKETCH OF SECOND PRESBYTERIAN CHURCH, ZANESVILLE
  OHIO, 1852-1897. (OUZ)
Beers, F.W. ATLAS OF MUSKINGUM COUNTY, OHIO. (New York: Beers, Soule, 1866) (Reprint,
  Knightstown IN: Bookmark,1973) 48p (LDS,OGS,SLO,DAR) (RPI)
Bell, Carol W. (Flavell) MUSKINGUM COUNTY OHIO GENEALOGICAL GUIDE. (Youngstown OH:
  author, 1979) 46p (SLO,OGS,OHS,LDS)
Bell, Carol W. TABLE OF CONTENTS TO CEMETERY INSCRIPTIONS COPIED BY MUSKINGUM
  CHAPTER D.A.R. (Columbus: author, 1975) 6p. (OHS)
Berry, Ellen T. & David. EARLY OHIO SETTLERS: PURCHASERS OF LAND IN SOUTHEASTERN
  OHIO, 1800-1840. (Baltimore: Genealogical Pub.Co., 1984) 129p (OHS,SLO,OGS,DAR)
BIOGRAPHICAL AND HISTORICAL MEMOIRS OF MUSKINGUM COUNTY OHIO. (Chicago:
  Goodspeed Pub Co., 1892) 620p. (DAR,LDS,SLO)(RPI)
Buell, Wyllys. A MAP OF THE COUNTY OF MUSKINGUM IN THE STATE OF OHIO. 1833. (Reprint,
  Zanesville OH: Verna Cordray Pubs., 198?) (LDS)

Cassel, A.F. 1851 ZANESVILLE CITY DIRECTORY. (Zanesville: Muskingum Co Chapter OGS, 1981) 119p. (OGS)

Chamberlin, Mrs. Verne. HISTORY & RECORD OF MUSKINGUM PRESBYTERIAN CHURCH & CEMETERY, MUSKINGUM TOWNSHIP, 1819-1886. (Wooster OH: author, 1972) (OHS)

CITY/COUNTY DIRECTORIES: check holdings at OHS & local public library.

Daughters of the American Revolution. BIBLE AND CEMETERY RECORDS, 1966-67. (SLO)

Daughters of the American Revolution. CEMETERIES OF MUSKINGUM COUNTY OHIO, V.1 & 2. (SLO,DAR)

Daughters of the American Revolution. CEMETERY INSCRIPTIONS, MISCELLANEOUS VOLUME, OHIO, 1957-1958, VOL.2.(SLO)

Daughters of the American Revolution. FAMILY AND CHURCH RECORDS OF MUSKINGUM COUNTY OHIO. (SLO,DAR)

Daughters of the American Revolution. OHIO CEMETERY AND BIBLE RECORDS. (SLO)

Daughters of the American Revolution. SOME CHURCH AND SCHOOL RECORDS OF MUSKINGUM COUNTY OHIO, 1811-1955. (SLO)

Daughters of the American Revolution. TAX DUPLICATES OF CLARK AND MUSKINGUM COUNTY. 1974. 1v (DAR)

Daughters of the American Revolution. WOODLAWN CEMETERY, MUSKINGUM COUNTY OHIO. (SLO,DAR)

Dickson, Shirley A. DR.CALVIN CONANT LEDGERS, PUTNAM OHIO. (Zanesville OH: author, 1986) 56p (OGS)

Everhart, J.F. HISTORY OF MUSKINGUM COUNTY OHIO. (cOLUMBUS oh: AUTHOR, 1882) (Reprint, Evansville IN: Unigraphic, 1974) 440,87p. (OGS,SLO,LDS,DAR)(RPI)

Everts, L.H. COMBINATION ATLAS OF MUSKINGUM COUNTY OHIO. (Philadelphia: Everts Pub Co., 1875) (DAR,OHS,SLO)(RPI)

Federal Writers Project. ZANESVILLE AND MUSKINGUM COUNTY OHIO. (Zanesville: author, 1937) (OHS)

GENERAL BUSINESS REVIEW OF MUSKINGUM COUNTY OHIO FOR 1890. (Newark OH: American Pub Co, 1890) (OHS)

Gerlach, Elmer. OAK GROVE: A PIONEER COMMUNITY. 1983. (SLO)

Gobel, Irma. COPY OF DUPLICATE TAX RECORD 1806, 1807, 1810. (Roseville OH: author, nd) (OHS,SLO,LDS)

Gobel, Irma B. INDEX OF MEN AND WOMEN IN HISTORY OF MUSKINGUM COUNTY OHIO WITH ILLUSTRATIONS AND BIOGRAPHICAL SKETCHES [EVERHART]... (DAR,LDS)

Gobel, Irma. INDEX TO WILLS AND GUARDIANSHIP RECORDS 1804-1901 OF MUSKINGUM COUNTY OHIO. (Roseville OH: author, nd) (SLO,LDS)

Gobel, Irma. MUSKINGUM COUNTY OHIO MARRIAGES, 1804-1897. (Roseville OH: author, nd) 5v. (OHS,SLO,LDS)

Hargrove, Sylvia & H.Yinger. MUSKINGUM COUNTY FOOTPRINTS, VOL.1. (Zanesville OH: authors, 1984) 56p  (OGS,OHS,LDS)

Hargrove, Sylvia & H.Yinger. MUSKINGUM COUNTY FOOTPRINTS, VOL.2. (Zanesville OH: authors, 1984) 60p (OGS,OHS,LDS)

Hargrove, Sylvia & H.Yinger. MUSKINGUM COUNTY FOOTPRINTS, VOL.3. (Zanesville OH: authors, 1985) 58p (OGS,OHS,LDS)

Hargrove, Sylvia & H.Yinger. MUSKINGUM COUNTY FOOTPRINTS, VOL.4. (Zanesville OH: authors, 1985) 60p (OGS,OHS,LDS)

Hargrove, Sylvia & H.Yinger. MUSKINGUM COUNTY FOOTPRINTS, VOL.5. (Zanesville OH: authors, 1986) 60p (OGS,OHS,LDS)

Hargrove, Sylvia & H.Yinger. MUSKINGUM COUNTY FOOTPRINTS, VOL.6. (Zanesville OH: authors, 1986) 62p (OGS,OHS)

Hargrove, Sylvia & H.Yinger. MUSKINGUM COUNTY FOOTPRINTS, VOL.7. (Zanesville OH: authors, 1987) 70p (OGS,OHS)

Hargrove, Sylvia & H.Yinger. MUSKINGUM COUNTY FOOTPRINTS, VOL.8. (Zanesville OH: authors, 1987) 132p (OGS,OHS)

Hixson, H.H. PLAT BOOK OF MUSKINGUM COUNTY OHIO. (Rockford IL: author, nd) (OHS)

INDEX TO GUARDIAN BOOK A, 1816-1848, MUSKINGUM COUNTY PROBATE COURT, OHIO. 197?. 17p (LDS)

King, John W. THE SILENT DEAD OR ROLL OF HONOR. 1866. (OHS)

Klaiber, Teresa. NEW CONCORD OHIO 1833-1902. (New Concord OH: author, 1984) 155p (OGS,LDS)

L.D.S. MUSKINGUM COUNTY OHIO CEMETERY RECORDS. (Salt Lake City: author, 1949) 1v. (LDS)

Lewis, Thomas W. SOUTHEASTERN OHIO AND THE MUSKINGUM VALLEY, 1788-1928: COVERING ATHENS, BELMONT, COSHOCTON, GUERNSEY, LICKING, MEIGS, MONROE, MORGAN, MUSKINGUM, NOBLE, PERRY AND WASHINGTON COUNTIES. (Chicago: S.J.Clarke Co.,1928) 3v. (SLO,DAR,OHS,LDS)

Lewis, Thomas W. ZANESVILLE AND MUSKINGUM COUNTY OHIO. (Chicago: S.J. Clarke Pub Co, 1927) 3v. (LDS,OHS,SLO,DAR)

Lewis, Thomas W. ZANESVILLE IN THE FLOOD OF 1913. (Zanesville OH: A.E. Starr, 1913) 94p (LDS)

Louden, John R. THE FIRST 75 YEARS OF FIRST UNITED PRESBYTERIAN CHURCH, ZANESVILLE OHIO. (OUZ)

Martin, Terry. HISTORY OF ZANESVILLE AND ITS BLACK COMMUNITY. (OUZ)

McCutcheon, Mrs. Richard. MUSKINGUM COUNTY CEMETERY RECORDS. (Zanesville: author, nd) 5v. (OHS,SLO)

Midwest Specialities. MUSKINGUM COUNTY HONOR ROLL DIRECTORY. (Zanesville OH: author, 1945) (OHS)

Mitchener, C.H. OHIO ANNALS: HISTORIC EVENTS IN THE TUSCARAWAS AND MUSKINGUM VALLEYS AND IN OTHER PORTIONS OF THE STATE OF OHIO. (Dayton OH: Thomas W. Odell, 1876) 358p (DAR)

MUSKINGUM ANNALS-NUMBER ONE. (Zanesville OH: Muskingum Valley Archaeological Survey, 1985) 124p (OGS)

Muskingum Co Chapter OGS. ANNALS OF ADAMS TOWNSHIP, MUSKINGUM COUNTY, OHIO. 1984. (SLO)

Muskingum Co Chapter OGS. CEMETERY INSCRIPTIONS OF UNION TOWNSHIP, MUSKINGUM COUNTY OHIO. (Zanesville OH: the society, 1986) 134p (OGS, SLO,LDS)

Muskingum Co Chapter OGS. CEMETERY INSCRIPTIONS OF HOPEWELL, LICKING AND MUSKINGUM TOWNSHIPS, MUSKINGUM COUNTY OHIO. (Zanesville OH: the society, 1983) 96p (LDS,SLO)

Muskingum Co Chapter OGS. CEMETERY INSCRIPTIONS OF WAYNE TOWNSHIP. (Zanesville OH: the society, 1982) 97p. (OGS,LDS,SLO)

Muskingum Co Chapter OGS. CEMETERY INSCRIPTIONS OF SPRINGFIELD TOWNSHIP. (Zanesville OH: the society, 1977) 7p,3p. (OGS)

Muskingum Co Chapter OGS. CEMETERY INSCRIPTIONS OF BLUE ROCK AND SALT CREEK TOWNSHIPS. (Zanesville OH: the society, 1983) 49p (OGS,LDS)

Muskingum Co Chapter OGS. CEMETERY INSCRIPTIONS OF CASS & JACKSON TOWNSHIPS OF MUSKINGUM COUNTY OHIO. (Zanesville OH: the society, 1986) 109p (OGS,SLO,LDS)

Muskingum Co Chapter OGS. CEMETERY INSCRIPTIONS OF JEFFERSON AND MADISON TOWNSHIPS, MUSKINGUM COUNTY OHIO. (Zanesville OH: the society, nd) 80p (OGS,LDS)

Muskingum Co Chapter OGS. CEMETERY INSCRIPTIONS OF NEWTON AND SPRINGFIELD TOWNSHIPS, MUSKINGUM COUNTY, OHIO. (Zanesville OH: the society, 1983) 116p (LDS)

Muskingum Co Chapter OGS. CEMETERY INSCRIPTIONS OF MEIGS AND RICH HILL TOWNSHIPS. (Zanesville OH: the society, 1981) 112p (LDS,SLO)

Muskingum Co Chapter OGS. CEMETERY INSCRIPTIONS OF BRUSH CREEK, CLAY AND HARRISON TOWNSHIPS, MUSKINGUM COUNTY OHIO. (Zanesville OH: the society, 1984) 114p (OGS,LDS)

Muskingum Co Chapter OGS. CEMETERY INSCRIPTIONS OF FALLS TOWNSHIP. (Zanesville OH: the society, 1982) 181p. (OGS,LDS,SLO)

Muskingum Co Chapter OGS. CEMETERY INSCRIPTIONS OF PERRY & WASHINGTON TWPS., MUSKINGUM CO OH (Zanesville OH: the society, 1986) 105p (OGS,LDS)

Muskingum Co Chapter OGS. MUSKINGUM COUNTY OHIO CEMETERY LIST AND MAP. (Zanesville OH: the society, 198?) 3p (LDS)

Muskingum Co Chapter OGS. FIRST FAMILIES OF MUSKINGUM COUNTY OHIO OFFICIAL ROSTER 1982 & 1983. (Zanesville OH: the society, 1984) 71p (OGS,LDS)

Muskingum Co Chapter OGS. GENEALOGICAL GLEANINGS FROM HIGHLAND & MONROE TOWNSHIPS, MUSKINGUM COUNTY OHIO. (Zanesville OH: the society, 1985) 1v (LDS)

Muskingum Co Chapter OGS. INTERMENT RECORDS OF GREENWOOD CEMETERY, ZANESVILLE OHIO, VOLS.I-IV. (Zanesville OH: the society, nd) (OGS,OHS)

Muskingum Co Chapter OGS. MUSKINGUM COUNTY OHIO MARRIAGES BOOK I, 1803-1818. (Zanesville OH: the society, 1977) 80p (OGS,DAR,LDS)

Muskingum Co Chapter OGS. MUSKINGUM COUNTY OHIO MARRIAGES BOOK II, 1818-1835. (Zanesville OH: the society, 1977) 298p (OGS,DAR,LDS)

Muskingum Co Chapter OGS. MUSKINGUM COUNTY OHIO MARRIAGES BOOK III, 1835-1848. (Zanesville OH: the society, 1980) 230p (OGS,DAR,LDS)

Muskingum Co Chapter OGS. MUSKINGUM COUNTY OHIO MARRIAGES BOOK IV, 1848-1865. (Zanesville OH: the society, 1983) 207p (OGS,LDS)

Muskingum Co Chapter OGS. MUSKINGUM COUNTY OHIO MARRIAGES BOOK V, 1865-1869. (Zanesville OH: the society, 1983) 68p (LDS,OGS,DAR)

Muskingum Co Chapter OGS. RECORDS OF EARLY JURORS, JUSTICE OF THE PEACE, AND SCHOOL LAND LEASES FOR MUSKINGUM COUNTY OHIO. (Zanesville OH: the society, 1985) 1v (LDS)

Muskingum Co Chapter OGS. SCRIPTS AND TRANSCRIPTS OF SALEM TOWNSHIP, MUSKINGUM COUNTY OHIO. (Zanesville OH: the society, 1985) 145p (LDS)

Muskingum Co Chapter OGS. ZANESVILLE BUSINESS DIRECTORY, AND CITY GUIDE, FOR 1851. (Zanesville OH: A.F.Cassel, 1851) (Reprint, Zanesville OH: the society, 1981) 120p (LDS,SLO)

MUSKINGUM COUNTY OHIO WILLS 1804-1852. 2r mic. (SLO)

Muskingum Valley Archaeological Survey. MUSKINGUM ANNALS, Vol.1. (Zanesville OH: the survey, 1985) (LDS)

Myers, Bernadine. MUSKINGUM CO. OHIO, EVERHART'S HISTORY INDEX, 1882. (Malta OH: author, 1985) 90p (OGS)

Ohio University. GUIDE TO LOCAL GOVERNMENT RECORDS AT OHIO UNIVERSITY. (Athens OH: OU Library, 1986) 61p.

Owen, Elizabeth T. WAS THE FRIENDSHIP OF THE IROQUOIS WORTH A 'YOHA' TO THE MUSKINGUM SETTLERS? (Beverly OH: author, 1932) 23p (DAR)

Schneider, Norris F. BIBLIOGRAPHY OF ZANESVILLE AND MUSKINGUM COUNTY OHIO. (Zanesville OH: author, 1941) 23p. Addenda, 1942, 4p. (OHS)

Schneider, Norris F. CENTENNIAL HISTORY OF ROLLING PLAINS UNITED METHODIST CHURCH, MUSKINGUM COUNTY OHIO. (Zanesville: author, 1971) 8p. (OHS)

Schneider, Norris F. HISTORIC HOMES OF ZANESVILLE OHIO. (Zanesville OH: Mathes Printing Co., 1970) 32p. (OHS)

Schneider, Norris F. LODGE OF AMITY, NO.5, F & AM, ZANESVILLE OHIO 1805-1955. (Zanesville OH: Lodge of Amity, 1955) 153p. (OHS)

Schneider, Norris F. MUSKINGUM COUNTY MEN AND WOMEN IN WORLD WAR II. (Zanesville OH: Times Recorder, 1947) 511p. (OHS,OGS,LDS)

Schneider, Norris F. MUSKINGUM RIVER COVERED BRIDGES. (Zanesville: Southern Ohio Covered Bridge Assn., 1971) 20p. (OHS)

Schneider, Norris F. MUSKINGUM VALLEY GUNSMITHS. (Zanesville OH: Muskingum Co Gun Collectors Assn., 1961) 40p. (OHS)

Schneider, Norris F. MY HOME - ZANESVILLE AND MUSKINGUM COUNTY. A SHORT HISTORY FOR SCHOOLS. (Zanesville OH: Board of Educ., 1949) 67p.(OHS)

Schneider, Norris F. TAVERNS ON ZANE'S TRACE. (Zanesville OH: Chamber of Commerce, 1975) 35p. (OHS)

Schneider, Norris F. THE FIRST BAPTIST CHURCH, ZANESVILLE OHIO, 1821-1971. (Zanesville OH: author, 1971) 8p. (OHS)

Schneider, Norris F. THE MUSKINGUM RIVER: A HISTORY AND GUIDE. (Columbus: Ohio Hist Soc., c1968) 48p. (OHS,LDS,DAR)

Schneider, Norris F. THE NATIONAL ROAD: MAIN STREET OF AMERICA. (Columbus: Ohio Hist Soc, 1975) 40p. (OHS)

Schneider, Norris F. Y-BRIDGE CITY, THE STORY OF ZANESVILLE AND MUSKINGUM COUNTY OHIO. 1950. (Zanesville OH: Muskingum Co Chapter OGS, 1983) 407p (OGS,LDS,SLO)

Schneider, Norris F. ZANE'S TRACE. (Zanesville OH: Chamber of Commerce, 1947) 32p. (OHS,DAR)

Schneider, Norris F. ZANESVILLE AND MUSKINGUM COUNTY IN WORLD WAR II. 9v. (OHS,DAR)

Schneider, Norris F. ZANESVILLE AND MUSKINGUM COUNTY BICENTENNIAL MILITARY MEMORIAL HISTORY. (Zanesville OH: Pioneer & Hist Soc of Muskingum Co, 1976) 28p. (OHS,LDS)

Schneider, Norris F. ZANESVILLE ART POTTERY IN COLOR. (Leon IA: Mid America Book Co., 1968) 52p. (OHS)

Schneider, Norris F. ZANESVILLE ART POTTERY. (Zanesville OH: author, 1963) 27p. (OHS,SLO)

Schneider, Norris F. ZANESVILLE OHIO. FIRST UNITED PRESBYTERIAN CHURCH. THE FIRST 75 YEARS. (Zanesville OH: author, 1965) 24p. (OHS)

Schneider, Norris F. ZANESVILLE STORIES. (SCRAPBOOKS) 1939-1968. (OHS,SLO)

Schneider, Norris F. ZANESVILLE STORIES: A SUBJECT INDEX. (SLO,LDS)

Shewalter, Laura. REVOLUTIONARY ANCESTORS LIST. (SLO)

Smith, Clifford N. FEDERAL LAND SERIES: A CALENDAR OF ARCHIVAL MATERIAL ON THE LAND PATENTS ISSUED BY THE U.S.GOVERNMENT, VOL.2: FEDERAL BOUNTY LAND WARRANTS OF THE AMERICAN REVOLUTION. (Chicago: American Library Assn., 1972) 416p

ST.PAUL'S LUTHERAN CEMETERY: PERRY TWP., MUSKINGUM COUNTY OHIO. 1980? 26p (DAR)

Sutor, John H. PAST AND PRESENT OF CITY OF ZANESVILLE AND MUSKINGUM COUNTY OHIO. (Chicago: S.J.Clarke, 1905) 845p (OHS,SLO,DAR)(RPI)

WILLIAMS' ZANESVILLE DIRECTORY, CITY GUIDE & BUSINESS MIRROR FOR 1860-61. (Zanesville OH: Adams Fletcher, 1860) 147p (DAR)

ZANE'S TRACE COMMEMORATION. (Zanesville OH: Zanesville Area Chamber of Commerce, 1974) 32p (LDS)

# NOBLE COUNTY

| | |
|---|---|
| CREATED: | 1851 FROM GUERNSEY, MORGAN & WASHINGTON |
| COUNTY SEAT: | CALDWELL 43724 |
| COURT HOUSE: | 400 COURT HOUSE SQUARE, CALDWELL 43724 |
| LIBRARIES: | PUBLIC LIBRARY, COURT HOUSE, CALDWELL 43724 |
| HISTORICAL SOCIETY: | PO BOX 511, CALDWELL 43724 |
| GENEALOGICAL SOCIETY: | NOBLE COUNTY CHAPTER, OGS, |
| | PO BOX 444, CALDWELL 43724 |
| | publication: NCCOGS |
| HEALTH DEPARTMENT: | P.O.BOX 345, CALDWELL 43724 |
| ARCHIVAL DISTRICT: | OHIO UNIVERSITY, ATHENS |
| | (see published Guide to records) |
| LAND SURVEYS: | CONGRESS LANDS, OHIO RIVER SURVEY (SOUTH) |
| | CONGRESS LANDS, SEVEN RANGES |
| BOUNDED BY: | EAST:   BELMONT & MONROE CO. |
| | NORTH:  GUERNSEY CO. |
| | WEST:   MORGAN & MUSKINGUM CO. |
| | SOUTH:  WASHINGTON CO. |
| TOWNSHIPS: | Beaver, Brookfield, Buffalo, Center, Elk, Enoch,  Jackson, Jefferson, Marion, Noble, Olive, Seneca, Sharon, Stock, Wayne. |

**COURT RECORDS: (LDS MICROFILM)**

Clerk of Courts:

Common Pleas appearance docket, 1851-1857.

Common Pleas chancery record, 1851-1859.

Common Pleas journal, 1851-1852.
Common Pleas law record, 1851-1855.
Probate Court:
Index to files, 1851-1973.
Birth records, v1-5, 1867-1972.
Death records, v1-4, 1867-1909.
Marriage records, v1-11, 1851-1917.
General index to marriages, v1-3, 1851-1973.
Administrators bonds, v1-4, 1852-1889.
Guardians' bonds, v1-3, 1852-1893.
Guardians' docket, 1852-1904.
Guardians' settlement record, v1-8, 1864-1893.
Settlement records, v1-10, 1852-1889.
Will records, v1-3, 1851-1895.
Probate journal, v1-8, 1852-1888.
Inventory and sales book vA, 1851-1858.
Inventory record, v2-9, 1858-1888.
Ministers' license record, 1860-1880.
Recorder:
Deed records, v1-33, 1851-1887.
General index to deeds, 1851-1900.
Military discharges, 1861-1913.

## OHIO HISTORICAL SOCIETY: (MICROFILM)
Clerk of Courts:
Common Pleas appearance docket, 1851-1857.
Common Pleas chancery record, 1851-1859.
Common Pleas journal, 1851-1852.
Common Pleas law record, 1851-1855.
Recorder:
Military discharges, 1861-1913.
Miscellaneous:
Marriage records, 1852-1865, by DAR.

## CENSUS RECORDS (OHS,SLO,OGS,LDS)
1860-1880, 1900-1910; 1890 VETERANS; 1880,1900 SOUNDEX; 1910 MIRACODE

## AGRICULTURAL CENSUS SCHEDULES (OHS,SLO-mic)
1860,1880

## PRODUCTS OF INDUSTRY CENSUS SCHEDULE (OHS,SLO-mic)
1860,1880

## MORTALITY CENSUS SCHEDULES (OHS,SLO-mic)
1860

## NEWSPAPERS: [GUIDE TO OHIO NEWSPAPERS, 1793-1973]
Caldwell, Sarahsville.

## TAX RECORDS (OHS & LDS)
none listed; see parent counties.

## GENEALOGICAL PERIODICAL ARTICLES
Bell, Carol Willsey. OHIO GENEALOGICAL PERIODICAL INDEX: A COUNTY GUIDE (Youngstown
OH: author, 6th ed., 1987)

**PUBLISHED SOURCES:**

Archer, George W. AN EVERYNAME PERSONAL AND NON-PERSONAL INDEX...FOR IL-
LUSTRATED ATLAS OF NOBLE COUNTY OHIO, 1876. (Caldwell OH: Noble Co Chapter OGS,
1987) 48p (OGS,LC)

Blake, Lois. WILL ABSTRACTS OF NOBLE COUNTY OHIO, 1851-1901, v.1-4. 1977. 137p. (SLO,DAR)

Blake, Lois. CENSUS INDEX 1860 NOBLE COUNTY OHIO & 1850 INDEX OF TOWNSHIPS TAKEN
TO FORM NOBLE COUNTY. (Caldwell OH: Noble Co Chapter OGS, 1986) 92p (OGS,LC,LDS)

Booher, Emma R. A HISTORY OF MT.EPHRAIM UNITED METHODIST CHURCH, MT. EPHRAIM
OHIO 1820-1980. (Zanesville OH: author, 1980) 78p. (OGS,LDS)

CITY/COUNTY DIRECTORIES: check holdings at OHS & local public library.

Cochran, Wes. 1860 CENSUS OF NOBLE COUNTY. (Parkersburg WV: author, 1985) 269p (OGS,LDS)

Daughters of the American Revolution. BIBLE RECORDS OF NOBLE COUNTY OHIO. 1974. 100p.
(SLO,DAR,LDS)

Daughters of the American Revolution. NOBLE COUNTY MARRIAGES 1852-1900. 1974. 403p.
(SLO,LDS,DAR)

Daughters of the American Revolution. NOBLE COUNTY OHIO CHURCH RECORDS. 1975.
(SLO,DAR)

Daughters of the American Revolution. OBITUARIES, NOBLE COUNTY OHIO. 1976. 128p. (SLO,DAR)

Eynon, Nola. NOBLE COUNTY SOLDIERS, NOBLE COUNTY OHIO. 1966. 20p. (SLO,LDS)

Eynon, Nola. MARRIAGES OF NOBLE COUNTY OHIO, 1851-1871. nd. (SLO,LDS)

Eynon, Nola. NOBLE COUNTY CEMETERIES. (Cambridge OH: author, 1965) 198p (SLO,LDS,LC)

HISTORY OF MT. ZION EVANGELICAL LUTHERAN CHURCH. (SLO)

HISTORY OF NOBLE COUNTY, OHIO, WITH PORTRAITS AND BIOGRAPHICAL SKETCHES OF
SOME OF ITS PIONEERS AND PROMINENT MEN. (Chicago: L.H.Watkins & Co., 1887) (Reprint,
Caldwell OH: Noble Co.Hist.Soc., 1987) 597p (SLO,LDS,DAR) (RPI)

ILLUSTRATED ATLAS OF NOBLE COUNTY, OHIO. 1876. (OGS,SLO)

LaHue, William O. THE CARLISLE STORY. 1984. (SLO)

Lewis, Thomas W. SOUTHEASTERN OHIO AND THE MUSKINGUM VALLEY, 1788-1928: COVER-
ING ATHENS, BELMONT, COSHOCTON, GUERNSEY, LICKING, MEIGS, MONROE, MORGAN,
MUSKINGUM, NOBLE, PERRY AND WASHINGTON COUNTIES. (Chicago: S.J.Clarke Co.,1928)
3v. (SLO,DAR,OHS)

Linicome, James. PIONEER LIFE HISTORY. (Caldwell OH: Noble Co Chapter OGS, n.d.)

Martin, Frank. THE COUNTY OF NOBLE. 1904. (SLO)(RPI)

Miller, Fran. MT.TABOR CEMETERY INSCRIPTIONS, STOCK TOWNSHIP. (Caldwell OH: author,
1987?) 30p

Noble Co Chapter OGS. CENTER TOWNSHIP CEMETERY INSCRIPTIONS. (Caldwell OH: the society,
n.d.)

Noble Co Chapter OGS. EARLY NOBLE COUNTY OHIO MARRIAGES 1851-1865. (Caldwell OH: the
society, 1984) 102p (OGS,LC)

Noble Co Chapter OGS. FRATERNAL & PATRIOTIC SOCIETIES OF NOBLE COUNTY OHIO 1859-
1909. (Caldwell OH: the society, 1986) 57p (OGS)

Noble Co Chapter OGS. INDEX TO THE 1876 ATLAS OF NOBLE COUNTY. (Caldwell OH: the society,
n.d.)

Noble Co Chapter OGS. NOBLE COUNTY OHIO CEMETERY INSCRIPTIONS, BOOK I, SHARON
TOWNSHIP. (Caldwell OH: the society, 1984) 52p (OGS,OHS,LC,LDS)

Noble Co Chapter OGS. NOBLE COUNTY OHIO CEMETERY INSCRIPTIONS, BOOK II, OLIVE
TOWNSHIP. (Caldwell OH: the society, 1985) 202p (LDS)

Noble Co Chapter OGS. NOBLE TOWNSHIP, NOBLE COUNTY OHIO CEMETERY BOOK III.
(Caldwell OH: the society, 1985) 97p (OGS,OHS,LC,LDS)

Noble Co Chapter OGS. NOBLE COUNTY OHIO CEMETERY INSCRIPTIONS, BOOK IV. JACKSON
TOWNSHIP. (Caldwell OH: the society, 1986) 75p (OGS,LC,LDS)

Noble Co Chapter OGS. NOBLE COUNTY OHIO CENSUS INDEX 1860. (Caldwell OH: the society,
n.d.)

Noble Co Chapter OGS. NOBLE COUNTY OHIO CENSUS INDEX 1870 & 1880. (Caldwell OH: the
society, 1986) 102p

Noble Co Chapter OGS. NOBLE COUNTY OHIO NATURALIZATIONS. (Caldwell OH: the society, n.d.)

Noble Co Chapter OGS. OLIVE TOWNSHIP CEMETERY RECORDS. (Caldwell OH: the society, n.d.)

Ohio University. GUIDE TO LOCAL GOVERNMENT RECORDS AT OHIO UNIVERSITY. (Athens: OU Library, 1986) 61p.

Ratcliffe, Susan K. CHURCH RECORD OF THE DEXTER CITY CHARGE: CAMBRIDGE DISTRICT, METHODIST EPISCOPAL CHURCH, EAST OHIO CONFERENCE, 1893-1905, AND HISTORICAL RECORD, 1871-1890. (Delaware OH: author, 1977) 157p (DAR)

Smith, Clifford N. FEDERAL LAND SERIES: A CALENDAR OF ARCHIVAL MATERIAL ON THE LAND PATENTS ISSUED BY THE U.S.GOVERNMENT, VOL.2: FEDERAL BOUNTY LAND WAR-RANTS OF THE AMERICAN REVOLUTION. (Chicago: American Library Assn., 1972) 416p

Swann, Mary L. INDEX TO NOBLE COUNTY CEMETERIES, NOBLE COUNTY OHIO, BY NOLA R. EYNON. 230p (LDS)

W.P.A. MARRIAGE RECORDS OF NOBLE COUNTY OHIO, 1852-1865. 1939. 197p. (SLO)

Wall, B. etal. ILLUSTRATED ATLAS OF NOBLE COUNTY OHIO. (Philadelphia: Wall, Mann & Hall, 1876) (Reprint, Evansville IN: Unigraphic, 1977) 95p (DAR,LC)

# OTTAWA COUNTY

| | |
|---|---|
| CREATED: | 1840 FROM ERIE, LUCAS & SANDUSKY COUNTIES |
| COUNTY SEAT: | PORT CLINTON 43452 |
| COURT HOUSE: | MADISON & FOURTH ST., PORT CLINTON 43452 |
| LIBRARIES: | 310 MADISON ST., PORT CLINTON 43452 |
| HISTORICAL SOCIETY: | 4392 E. LEDGE AVE., PORT CLINTON 43452 |
| GENEALOGICAL SOCIETY: | OTTAWA COUNTY CHAPTER, OGS, PO BOX 193, PORT CLINTON 43452 |
| HEALTH DEPARTMENT: | 315 MADISON ST., PORT CLINTON 43452 (separate office for Port Clinton city) |
| ARCHIVAL DISTRICT: | BOWLING GREEN STATE UNIVERSITY, BOWLING GREEN (see Biggs' Guide to records) |
| LAND SURVEYS: | CONGRESS LANDS, E & N OF 1ST PRIN.MERIDIAN FIRE LANDS CONNECTICUT WESTERN RESERVE |
| BOUNDED BY: | EAST: LAKE ERIE NORTH: LAKE ERIE & LUCAS CO. WEST: WOOD CO. SOUTH: SANDUSKY CO. |
| TOWNSHIPS: | Allen, Bay, Benton, Carroll, Clay, Danbury, Erie, Harris, Portage, Salem, Van Rensselaer. |

## COURT RECORDS: (LDS MICROFILM)

Assessor:
Quadrennial enumerations, 1899,1903,1907.
Carroll Tp., list of males aged 18-45 in 1857.
Soldiers' record, through Spanish American War.
Enumeration of volunteers, 1862-1877.
Births & deaths by assessors, 1889-1908.

Auditor:
Enumeration of youth, 1835-1868,1871-1889,1891-1908.
School directors' reports, 1840-1856.
Burial record of indigent soldiers, 1885-1930.

Clerk of Courts:
Supreme Court journal, 1841-1884.
Supreme Court complete record, v1, 1843-1872.

Common Pleas appearance docket & index, v1, 1840-1858.
Common Pleas journal, 1840-1857.
Chancery record, v1, 1841-1854.
Poll book & tally sheets of elections, 1847-1887.
Record of justices' & mayors' oaths, 1861-1946.
Jury & witness books, 1857-1918.
Commissioners:
Record of bonds of public officers, 1840-1885.
Probate Court:
Administrators docket, v1, 1876-1909.
Birth records, v1-2, 1867-1908.
Birth registration & correction, v1-19, dates vary.
Civil records, vA-N, 1860-1912.
Death record, 1869-1908.
Guardians' docket, v1, 1880-1932.
General index to births, 1867-1908.
Journal, vA-D, 1852-1891.
Probate general index, 1853-1915.
Complete record, vA-P, 1854-1912.
Marriage records, vA-5, 1840-1930.
Will records, vA-D, 1853-1912.
Probate bonds & letters, 1852-1900.
General index to probate records, 1840-1961.
Naturalization records, 1851-1872,1877-1903.
Recorder:
Grantor & grantee index to deeds, 1820-1900.
Deeds transcribed from Sandusky, Erie & Lucas Co., 1820-1841.
Deed records, vA-Z,29-57,1840-1903.
Index to mortgages, v1-3.
Land transfer book, 1866-1870.
Geographical index to deeds, 1900-1967.
Soldiers' discharge record, 1865-1912.
Miscellaneous:
Cemetery records by Northwestern Ohio Genealogical Society.
Oak Harbor, St.Pauls United Church of Christ, records, 1879-1979.
Port Clinton, St.John's Lutheran Church, records, 1875-1977.
Port Clinton, St.Thomas Episcopal Church, records, 1896-1982.
Port Clinton, Trinity United Meth-Episc.Church, records, 1854-1924.

## OHIO HISTORICAL SOCIETY: (MICROFILM)
Clerk of Courts:
Supreme Court journal, 1841-1884.
Supreme Court complete record, v1, 1843-1872.
Common Pleas appearance docket & index, v1, 1840-1858.
Common Pleas journal, 1840-1857.
Chancery record, v1, 1841-1854.
Probate Court:
Administrators docket, v1, 1876-1909.
Guardians' docket, v1, 1880-1932.
General index to births, 1867-1908.
Probate general index, 1853-1915.
Will record, vC-F, 1889-1912.
Complete record, vA-P, 1854-1912.
Recorder:
Soldiers' discharge records, 1865-1912.

Miscellaneous:
  Marriage records, 1840-1880, by DAR.

**CENSUS RECORDS  (OHS,SLO,OGS,LDS)**
1840-1880, 1900-1910; 1890 VETERANS; 1880,1900 SOUNDEX; 1910 MIRACODE

**AGRICULTURAL CENSUS SCHEDULES  (OHS,SLO-mic)**
1860,1880

**PRODUCTS OF INDUSTRY CENSUS SCHEDULE  (OHS,SLO-mic)**
1850,1860,1880

**MORTALITY CENSUS SCHEDULES (OHS,SLO-mic)**
1850,1860

**NEWSPAPERS: [GUIDE TO OHIO NEWSPAPERS, 1793-1973]**
Elmore, Genoa, Lakeside, Marblehead, Oakharbor, Port Clinton.

**TAX RECORDS (OHS & LDS)**
none listed; see parent counties.

**MANUSCRIPTS:**
Receipt book, 1864, of draftees in Erie, Crawford, Huron, Ottawa, Sandusky & Seneca Counties Ohio
  who purchased substitutes. (OHS)

**GENEALOGICAL PERIODICAL ARTICLES**
Bell, Carol Willsey. OHIO GENEALOGICAL PERIODICAL INDEX: A COUNTY GUIDE (Youngstown
  OH: author, 6th ed., 1987)

**PUBLISHED SOURCES:**
ATLAS OF OTTAWA COUNTY OHIO. 1900. (SLO)
Biggs, Deb. GUIDE TO LOCAL GOVERNMENT RECORDS AT THE CENTER FOR ARCHIVAL COL-
  LECTIONS. (Bowling Green OH: Bowling Green State Univ, 1981) 104p (OGS)
Christian, Donna K. GUIDE TO NEWSPAPER HOLDINGS AT THE CENTER FOR ARCHIVAL COL-
  LECTIONS. (Bowling Green OH: Bowling Green State Univ, 1980) 64p (OGS)
CITY/COUNTY DIRECTORIES: check holdings at OHS & local public library.
Clegg, Michael, ed. OTTAWA, SANDUSKY AND SENECA COUNTIES OHIO NEWSPAPER
  OBITUARY ABSTRACTS 1836-1870 [OHIO NEWSPAPER ABSTRACTS SERIES VOL.4] (Ft.Wayne
  IN: author, 1985) 92p (OGS,LDS)
COMMEMORATIVE BIOGRAPHICAL RECORD OF THE COUNTIES OF SANDUSKY AND OTTAWA
  OHIO. (Chicago: J.H.Beers & Co., 1896) 854p. (LC,SLO,LDS,DAR)(RPI)
Daughters of the American Revolution. CEMETERY INSCRIPTIONS OF OTTAWA COUNTY OHIO.
  (SLO)
Daughters of the American Revolution. RECORD OF MARRIAGES IN OTTAWA COUNTY OHIO,
  1840-1880. (SLO,LDS,DAR)
DIRECTORY OF ALL BUSINESS AND PROFESSIONAL MEN OF SANDUSKY AND OTTAWA COUN-
  TIES OHIO. (Conneaut OH: Watson & Dorman, 1896) 91p (OHS)
Durr, Eleanor. LAKESIDE, OHIO: FIRST 100 YEARS. (New York: Carlton Press, c1973) 230p (DAR,LDS)
Fouke, W.L. HISTORY OF GENOA AND CLAY TOWNSHIP, 1835-1935. 48p (LDS)
Frohman, Charles E. PUT-IN-BAY: ITS HISTORY. (Columbus OH: Ohio Hist.Soc., 1971) 156p (LDS)
Gebolys, Edith H. CEMETERY LOCATED SAND RD. NEAR CEMETERY RD. WHICH IS ALSO
  KNOWN AS CATAWBA ISLAND, OTTAWA CO., OHIO. (LDS)
Hardesty, H.H. ILLUSTRATED HISTORICAL ATLAS OF OTTAWA CO OHIO. (Chicago:
  author,1874)(Reprint, Knightstown IN: Bookmark, 1974) 116p (OGS,LC,
  SLO,LDS)(RPI)

Kern, J. & S.Rice. RECORDS OF ST.JOSEPH'S CATHOLIC CHURCH, OAK HARBOR, OTTAWA COUN-
TY, OHIO. 5v. (SLO)
Knapp, Horace S. HISTORY OF THE MAUMEE VALLEY. (Toledo OH: author, 1872) 685p.
(DAR,OHS,SLO)
Levinson, Marilyn. GUIDE TO NEWSPAPER HOLDINGS AT THE CENTER FOR ARCHIVAL COL-
LECTIONS. 2nd Edition. (Bowling Green OH: Bowling Green State Univ., 1987)
Luebke, Grace. ELMORE, OHIO, A HISTORY PRESERVED. (Evansville IN: Unigraphic, 1975) 380p.
(SLO,DAR)
Maizuk, Ruth. THE PUT-IN-THE-BAY STORY. 48p. (SLO)
Neipp, Morton. OAK HARBOR 1820-1920. 1972. 165p. (SLO)
Northwestern Ohio Gen.Soc. CEMETERY INSCRIPTIONS, OTTAWA COUNTY OHIO. 1974. (LDS)
O.G.S. CEMETERIES OF DEFIANCE, OTTAWA, AND WOOD COUNTIES OHIO. (SLO)
Ottawa Co Chapter OGS. CEMETERY INSCRIPTIONS OF OTTAWA COUNTY OHIO. (Mansfield OH:
Ohio Gen Soc., 1976) 223p (OGS,LDS,SLO)
Ottawa Co Chapter OGS. DEATH RECORDS FROM THE PROBATE COURT, OTTAWA COUNTY
OHIO, 1869-1908. (Port Clinton OH: author, 1981) 111p (OGS)
Ottawa Co Chapter OGS. THE HISTORY OF OTTAWA COUNTY OHIO AND ITS FAMILIES. (Port
Clinton OH: author, 1985) 282p (OGS)
Reinhart, Mary E. ST.JOSEPH CEMETERY IN ERIE TOWNSHIP, 1800-1859,1885-1935. (SLO)
Ross, Harry H. ENCHANTING ISLES OF ERIE: HISTORIC SKETCHES. (np: author, 1949) 80p (LDS)
Shepard, O.L. STORY OF LAKESIDE. (Lakeside OH: Lakeside Assn., 1923) 99p (LDS)
SOUVENIR BOOK PUBLISHED ON THE OCCASION OF THE COMPLETION OF THE NEW OUR
LADY OF LOURDES CHURCH, GENOA, OHIO, MAY 1955. (Genoa OH: the church, 1955) 54p
(LDS)
Winter, Nevin O. HISTORY OF NORTHWEST OHIO. (Chicago: Lewis Pub.Co.,1917) 3v. (SLO,OHS)

# PAULDING COUNTY

CREATED:                      1820 FROM DARKE COUNTY
COUNTY SEAT:                  PAULDING 45879
COURT HOUSE:                  N.WILLIAMS ST., PAULDING 45879
LIBRARIES:                    205 S. MAIN ST., PAULDING 45879
HISTORICAL SOCIETY:           CITY HALL, NORTH MAIN ST., ANTWERP 45813
GENEALOGICAL SOCIETY:         PAULDING COUNTY CHAPTER OGS,
                              c/o PUBLIC LIBRARY, PAULDING 45679
HEALTH DEPARTMENT:            101 W.PERRY ST., PAULDING 45879
ARCHIVAL DISTRICT:            BOWLING GREEN STATE UNIVERSITY, BOWLING GREEN
                              (see Biggs' Guide to records)
LAND SURVEYS:                 CONGRESS LANDS, E & N OF 1ST PRIN.MERIDIAN
BOUNDED BY:                   EAST:     PUTNAM CO.
                              NORTH:    DEFIANCE CO.
                              WEST:     ALLEN CO., INDIANA
                              SOUTH:    VAN WERT CO.
TOWNSHIPS:                    Auglaize, Benton, Blue Creek, Brown, Carryall, Crane, Emerald,
                              Harrison, Jackson, Latty, Paulding, Washington.

**COURT RECORDS: (LDS MICROFILM)**
Clerk of Courts:
    Court records, 1839-1846
    Chancery records, 1840-1866.
Probate Court:
    Record of deaths, v1-4, 1867-1908.
    Record of births, v1-5, 1867-1908.
    Will records, v1-3, 1852-1903.

Index to wills deposited, 1852-1972.
Marriage records, v1-13, 1839-1952.
General index, v1, 1839-1969.
Appearance docket, v1, 1852-1884.
Administration docket, v1, 1879-1898.
Civil docket, v1-2, 1852-1898.
Docket, 1842-1849, 1865-1888.
Minutes, 1852-1855.
Journal, v1-3, 1842-1856.
Probate journal, v1-6, 1852-1885.
Admr. & exrs. bonds & letters, v1, 1872-1891.
Guardians' bonds & letters, v1, 1871-1891.
Inventories & sale bills, v1-5, 1852-1890.
Record of accounts, v1-5, 1860-1887.
Final records, v1-5, 1852-1886.
Naturalization records, v1, 1860-1903.
Recorder:
Soldiers' discharge record, v1-2, 1862-1928.
Record of war veterans' graves, v1, 1862-1972.
Grantee & grantor index to deeds, v1-10, 1835-1960.
General index to deeds, v2, 1866-1900.
Deeds, v1-30, 1835-1881.
Deed register, v6-10, 1913-1940.
Miscellaneous:
Cecil, Immaculate Conception Church, records, 1868-1964.
Paulding, St.Joseph's Catholic Church, records, 1900-1983.

**OHIO HISTORICAL SOCIETY: (MICROFILM)**
(none listed)

**CENSUS RECORDS (OHS,SLO,OGS,LDS)**
1830-1880, 1900-1910; 1890 VETERANS; 1880,1900 SOUNDEX; 1910 MIRACODE

**AGRICULTURAL CENSUS SCHEDULES (OHS,SLO-mic)**
1860,1880

**PRODUCTS OF INDUSTRY CENSUS SCHEDULE (OHS,SLO-mic)**
1850,1860,1880

**MORTALITY CENSUS SCHEDULES (OHS,SLO-mic)**
1850,1860

**NEWSPAPERS: [GUIDE TO OHIO NEWSPAPERS, 1793-1973]**
Antwerp, Grover Hill, Paulding, Payne.

**TAX RECORDS (OHS & LDS)**
none listed; see parent counties.

**GENEALOGICAL PERIODICAL ARTICLES**
Bell, Carol Willsey. OHIO GENEALOGICAL PERIODICAL INDEX: A COUNTY GUIDE (Youngstown OH: author, 6th ed., 1987)

**PUBLISHED SOURCES:**
Biggs, Deb. GUIDE TO LOCAL GOVERNMENT RECORDS AT THE CENTER FOR ARCHIVAL COLLECTIONS. (Bowling Green OH: Bowling Green State Univ, 1981) 104p (OGS)

CENTURY OF PROGRESS, ANTWERP, OHIO, 1841-1941: OFFICIAL PROGRAM. 1941. 61p (LDS)

Christian, Donna K. GUIDE TO NEWSPAPER HOLDINGS AT THE CENTER FOR ARCHIVAL COL-LECTIONS. (Bowling Green OH: Bowling Green State Univ, 1980) 64p (OGS)

Clegg, Michael, ed. DEFIANCE, FULTON, HENRY, PAULDING, PUTNAM, WILLIAMS & WOOD COUNTIES OHIO NEWSPAPER OBITUARY ABSTRACTS, 1838-1870 (OHIO NEWSPAPER SERIES VOL.5) (Ft.Wayne IN: author, 1987) 75p (OGS)

Hardesty, W.S. REPRESENTATIVE CITIZENS OF PAULDING COUNTY. (Toledo OH: author, 1902) 403p (DAR,LDS)

Knapp, Horace S. HISTORY OF THE MAUMEE VALLEY. (Toledo OH: author, 1872) 685p. (DAR,SLO)

Levinson, Marilyn. GUIDE TO NEWSPAPER HOLDINGS AT THE CENTER FOR ARCHIVAL COL-LECTIONS. 2nd Edition. (Bowling Green OH: Bowling Green State Univ., 1987)

Morrow, Oliver. HISTORICAL ATLAS OF PAULDING CO OHIO. (Madison WI: Western Pub., 1892)(Reprint, Dallas TX: John Taylor Pub., 1978) 109p (LDS,DAR,OGS,SLO,LC)(RPI)

Ogle, George A. & Co. STANDARD ATLAS OF PAULDING COUNTY, OHIO, INCLUDING A PLAT BOOK OF THE VILLAGES, CITIES AND TOWNSHIPS OF THE COUNTY. (Chicago: author, 1917) 55p (LC)

PAULDING COUNTY OHIO WILLS 1852?-1873? & MARRIAGES, 1839-1879. 1r mic. (SLO,LDS)

Price, Don H. HISTORY OF PAULDING, THE MEN WHO BUILT THE TOWN, 1880-1920. (Paulding OH: author, c1975) 127p (DAR,OHS,LDS,LC)

Temple, Sandra K. HISTORIC ANTWERP. (Antwerp OH: Antwerp Bee-Argus, 1966) 23p (DAR)

Winter, Nevin O. HISTORY OF NORTHWEST OHIO. (Chicago: Lewis Pub.Co.,1917) 3v. (SLO,OHS)

# PERRY COUNTY

| | |
|---|---|
| CREATED: | 1818 FROM FAIRFIELD, MUSKINGUM & WASHINGTON |
| COUNTY SEAT: | NEW LEXINGTON 43764 |
| COURT HOUSE: | 105 N. MAIN ST., NEW LEXINGTON 43764 |
| LIBRARIES: | 113 S. MAIN ST., NEW LEXINGTON 43764 |
| HISTORICAL SOCIETY: | c/o JAMES SMITH, GLENFORD 43739 |
| GENEALOGICAL SOCIETY: | PERRY COUNTY CHAPTER, OGS, |
| | PO BOX 275, JUNCTION CITY 43748 |
| | publication: PERRY COUNTY HEIRLINES |
| HEALTH DEPARTMENT: | 121 W.BROWN, PO BOX 230, NEW LEXINGTON 43764 |
| ARCHIVAL DISTRICT: | OHIO UNIVERSITY, ATHENS |
| | (see published Guide to records) |
| LAND SURVEYS: | CONGRESS LANDS, OHIO RIVER SURVEY (SOUTH) |
| | REFUGEE TRACT |
| BOUNDED BY: | EAST: MORGAN & MUSKINGUM CO. |
| | NORTH: LICKING & MUSKINGUM CO. |
| | WEST: FAIRFIELD CO. |
| | SOUTH: ATHENS & HOCKING CO. |
| TOWNSHIPS: | Bearfield, Clayton, Coal, Harrison, Hopewell, Jackson, Madison, Monday Creek, Monroe, Pike, Pleasant, Reading, Salt Lick, Thorn. |

**COURT RECORDS: (LDS MICROFILM)**
Auditor:
Tax duplicates, 1819-1838.
License book, 1837-1849.
Quadrennial enumeration, 1847-1871,1879-1887.
Commutation record, 1865.
Militia rolls, 1863.
Enumeration of soldiers & marines, 1863-1864.
Enumeration of school-aged youth, 1864-1880.

Enumeration of deaf, dumb, etc., 1861-1878.
Childrens' Home:
    History, 1885-1927.
    Register, 1885-1918.
    Journal, 1885-1921.
Clerk of Courts:
    Supreme Court appearance dockets, 1838-1852.
    Supreme Court minutes, 1837-1850.
    Supreme Court record, 1819-1850.
    General index, 1840-1866.
    Appearance docket, vA-J, 1818-1852.
    Common Pleas minutes, vA-L, 1818-1854.
    Chancery record, 1821-1841,1842-1856.
    Journal vK-L, 1849-1854.
    Minutes Probate, 1837-1847.
    Abstract of votes, 1822-1882.
    Poll books & tally sheets, 1822-1892.
    Law record, 1818-1852.
    Poll books & land sale, c1830.
    District Court record, 1852.
Commissioners:
    Journal & index, 1818-1902.
    Officers report, 1850-1860.
County Home:
    Infirmary records, 1853-1963.
Probate Court:
    Marriage records, v1-14, 1818-1916.
    Index to marriages, 1818-1914.
    Record of deaths, v1-3, 1867-1908.
    Record of births, v1-4, 1867-1908.
    Record of wills, v2-4, 1817-1886.
    Inventory record of estates, vC-12, 1840-1887.
    Probate court minutes, 1837-1850.
    Administration docket, 1819-1903.
    Civil docket, 1852-1905.
    Guardians' docket, 1848-1910.
    Probate journal, v1-7, 1852-1888.
    Naturalization records, 1859-1906.
    Index to naturalization records, n.d.
Recorder:
    Military discharges, 1863-1918.
    Deed index, 1818-1886.
    Deed records, vA-25, 1818-1881.
Miscellaneous:
    Highland Meeting, Society of Friends, records, 1887-1951.
    Oakfield, Presbyterian Church, records, 1855-1899.
    Cemetery records, State Library of Ohio collection.

## OHIO HISTORICAL SOCIETY: (MICROFILM)
Auditor:
    License book, 1837-1849.
    Quadrennial enumeration, 1847-1871,1879-1887.
    Commutation record, 1865.
    Militia rolls, 1863.
    Enumeration of soldiers & marines, 1863-1864.

  Enumeration of school-aged youth, 1864-1880.
  Enumeration of deaf, dumb, etc., 1861-1878.
Childrens' Home:
  History, 1885-1927.
  Register, 1885-1918.
  Journal, 1885-1921.
Clerk of Courts:
  Supreme Court appearance dockets, 1838-1852.
  Supreme Court minutes, 1837-1850.
  Supreme Court record, 1819-1850.
  General index, 1840-1866.
  Appearance docket, vA-J, 1818-1852.
  Common Pleas minutes, vA-L, 1818-1854.
  Chancery record, 1821-1841,1842-1856.
  Minutes Probate, 1837-1847.
  Abstract of votes, 1822-1882.
  Poll books & tally sheets, 1822-1892.
  Law record, 1818-1852.
  Poll books & land sale, c1830.
Commissioners:
  Journal & index, 1818-1902.
  Officers' report, 1850-1860.
County Home:
  Infirmary records, 1853-1963.
Probate Court:
  Minutes, 1847-1852.
Sheriff:
  Jail register, 1876-1927.
Miscellaneous:
  Cemetery inscriptions, by DAR.
  Tombstone inscriptions of Fair.,Knox,Lake & Perry Cos., by DAR.
  Marriage records, 1818-1878, by DAR.

**CENSUS RECORDS  (OHS,SLO,OGS,LDS)**
1820-1880, 1900-1910; 1890 VETERANS; 1880,1900 SOUNDEX; 1910 MIRACODE

**AGRICULTURAL CENSUS SCHEDULES  (OHS,SLO-mic)**
1860,1880

**PRODUCTS OF INDUSTRY CENSUS SCHEDULE  (OHS,SLO-mic)**
1850,1860,1880

**MORTALITY CENSUS SCHEDULES (OHS,SLO-mic)**
1850,1860

**NEWSPAPERS: [GUIDE TO OHIO NEWSPAPERS, 1793-1973]**
Corning, Crooksville, New Lexington, New Straitsville, Shawnee, Somerset, Thornville.

**TAX RECORDS (OHS & LDS)**
1819-1838.

**MANUSCRIPTS:**
New Straitsville, United States Hotel register, 1885-1886. (OHS)
Somerset, W.E.Finck letterbooks, 1858-59,1862-63. (OHS)

## GENEALOGICAL PERIODICAL ARTICLES

Bell, Carol Willsey. OHIO GENEALOGICAL PERIODICAL INDEX: A COUNTY GUIDE (Youngstown OH: author, 6th ed., 1987)

## PUBLISHED SOURCES:

Berry, Ellen T. & David. EARLY OHIO SETTLERS: PURCHASERS OF LAND IN SOUTHEASTERN OHIO, 1800-1840. (Baltimore: Genealogical Pub.Co., 1984) 129p (OHS,SLO,OGS,DAR)

BIOGRAPHICAL RECORD OF FAIRFIELD AND PERRY COUNTIES OHIO. 1902. 483p. (SLO)

CITY/COUNTY DIRECTORIES: check holdings of OHS & local public library.

Clark, Marie T. OHIO LANDS: CHILLICOTHE LAND OFFICE, 1800-1829. (Chillicothe: author, 1984) 144p (OGS,SLO,OHS)

Colburn, Ephraim S. 1883 HISTORY OF PERRY COUNTY OHIO, PAST AND PRESENT. (Reprint, Knightstown IN: Bookmark, 1977) 596,92p (LC)

Collier, Jean S. CEMETERY INSCRIPTIONS, PERRY COUNTY OHIO. (Columbus OH: author, 1978) 176p (OGS,SLO)

Collier, Jean S. CEMETERY INSCRIPTIONS OF PERRY COUNTY, OHIO - TWO VOLUMES, 1979-1980. (Columbus: author, 1980) 155p (OGS,SLO)

Collier, Jean S. SHAWNEE CEMETERY, PERRY COUNTY OHIO. (Columbus OH: author, 1981) 65p.(OGS,SLO)

Daughters of the American Revolution. CEMETERY RECORDS OF FAIRFIELD, PERRY, PICKAWAY & LICKING COUNTIES OHIO. 1967? 54p (DAR,SLO,LDS)

Daughters of the American Revolution. PERRY COUNTY OHIO CEMETERIES. 1959. 31,15p. (OHS,LDS)

Daughters of the American Revolution. PERRY AND FAIRFIELD COUNTY CEMETERY RECORDS. 1959. 1v (DAR)

Daughters of the American Revolution. TOMBSTONE INSCRIPTIONS, FIVE CEMETERIES IN PERRY COUNTY. (SLO)

Daughters of the American Revolution. TWELVE OHIO COUNTIES. (SLO)

Davidson, James T. HIGHWAY MAP OF PERRY COUNTY OHIO. (New Lexington OH: author, 1960) (LDS)

Fedorchak, Mrs. John. SOMERSET OHIO CEMETERY INSCRIPTIONS FROM EVANGELICAL LUTHERAN CEMETERY. (Gary IN: author, 1958) 5p. (LDS,SLO)

Gibson, R.M. HISTORY OF SHAWNEE. (OHS)

Graham, Albert A. [HISTORY OF] FAIRFIELD AND PERRY COUNTIES, OHIO. (Chicago: W.H.Beers & Co., 1883) 1186p (DAR,LC,SLO,LDS,OHS)(RPI)

Hillis, L.B. THE BOOK OF PERRY COUNTY; AN HISTORIC INDUSTRIAL PORTFOLIO. (New Lexington OH: New Lexington Herald, 1909) 43p (OHS,LC)

HISTORY OF THE ST.PAUL UNITED CHURCH OF CHRIST, GLENFORD OHIO. (SLO)

Hixson, W.W. PLAT BOOK OF PERRY COUNTY OHIO. (Rockford IL: author, nd) (OHS)

Jewell, Mrs. Walter. INSCRIPTIONS FROM FIRST BAPTIST CHURCH CEMETERY NEAR NEW LEXINGTON. (Arlington VA: author, nd) 13p. (LDS)

Lake, D.J. ATLAS OF PERRY COUNTY OHIO. (Philadelphia: Titus, Simmons & Titus, 1875)(Reprint, np: Historical Soc. of Perry Co., 1976) 61p (LC,LDS,OGS,OHS,SLO)(RPI)

Lewis, Thomas W. SOUTHEASTERN OHIO AND THE MUSKINGUM VALLEY, 1788-1928: COVERING ATHENS, BELMONT, COSHOCTON, GUERNSEY, LICKING, MEIGS, MONROE, MORGAN, MUSKINGUM, NOBLE, PERRY AND WASHINGTON COUNTIES. (Chicago: S.J.Clarke Co.,1928) 3v. (SLO,DAR,OHS)

McClintock, C.L. INDEX TO MAPLEWOOD CEMETERY NEW LEXINGTON PERRY COUNTY OHIO. (SLO)

McClintock, Calvin J. ABSTRACTS OF WILLS OF PERRY COUNTY OHIO, VOL.B. nd. 28p. (SLO)

Martzolff, Clement L. HISTORY OF PERRY COUNTY OHIO. (New Lexington OH: Ward & Weiland, 1902) 195p. (LC,OHS,SLO,LDS,DAR)(RPI)

Ohio University. GUIDE TO LOCAL GOVERNMENT RECORDS AT OHIO UNIVERSITY. (Athens: OU Library, 1986) 61p.

Perry Co. Chapter OGS. 1870 PERRY COUNTY OHIO CENSUS INDEX. (New Lexington, OH: the society, 1984) 33p (OGS,SLO)

Perry Co. Chapter OGS. PERRY CO., OHIO, THORN TWP. CEMETERIES. (Junction City OH: the society, 1985) 167p (LDS)

Perry Co. Chapter OGS. PERRY COUNTY OHIO INFIRMARY RECORDS 1853-1910. (Junction City OH: the society, 1983) 82p. (OGS,SLO)

Perry Co. Chapter OGS. PERRY COUNTY OHIO THORN TWP. CEMETERIES, VOL.I. (Junction City OH: the society, nd) 167p (OGS)

Perry Co. Chapter OGS. PERRY COUNTY OHIO DEATH RECORDS: EARLY YEARS, VOL.I, 1867-? (Junction City OH: the society, 1986) 428p (OGS,OHS,SLO)

Perry Co.Historical Society. HISTORY OF PERRY COUNTY OHIO: ILLUSTRATED 1980. (Paoli PA: the society, 1980) 304p (LDS)

PERRY COUNTY OHIO WILLS 1817-1852. 1r mic. (SLO,LDS)

PERRY COUNTY OHIO CHURCH RECORDS. 1r mic. (SLO)

Rankin, Maude P. PERRY AND FAIRFIELD COS. OHIO CEMETERY RECORDS. (DAR,LDS)

Rugg, John D. EVERY-NAME INDEX TO HISTORY OF PERRY COUNTY OHIO. 1975. 4p (LDS)

Scott, Margaret & M.Mollenkamp. 1870 PERRY COUNTY OHIO CENSUS INDEX. (Junction City OH: authors, 1984) 33p (LDS)

Selby, Robert E. PERRY COUNTY OHIO MARRIAGE RECORDS, 1818-1830. (Kokomo IN: Selby Pub., 1983) 37p (LDS)

Seymour, Nada M. MARRIAGES PERRY COUNTY OHIO 1818-1878. (Washington DC: author, 1954) 3v. (LDS,DAR)

THESE ROLLING HILLS; NEW LEXINGTON-PERRY COUNTY OHIO SESQUI-CENTENNIAL, 1817-1967. (New Lexington OH, 1967) 24p (OHS)

Wagner, Charles W. INSCRIPTIONS FROM THE OLD BAPTIST CEMETERY WEST OF THORNVILLE AND THE LUTHERAN-REFORMED CEMETERY IN THORNVILLE, THORN TOWNSHIP, PERRY COUNTY, OHIO. (DAR,LDS,SLO)

# PICKAWAY COUNTY

| | |
|---|---|
| CREATED: | 1810 FROM FAIRFIELD, FRANKLIN & ROSS |
| COUNTY SEAT: | CIRCLEVILLE 43113 |
| COURT HOUSE: | S.COURT ST., CIRCILEVILLE 43113 |
| LIBRARIES: | 165 E. MAIN ST., CIRCLEVILLE 43113 |
| HISTORICAL SOCIETY: | PO BOX 85, CIRCLEVILLE 43113 |
| | publication: PICKAWAY QUARTERLY |
| GENEALOGICAL SOCIETY: | NONE KNOWN |
| HEALTH DEPARTMENT: | BERGER HOSP., 610 N.PICKAWAY ST., |
| | CIRCLEVILLE 43113 |
| ARCHIVAL DISTRICT: | OHIO HISTORICAL SOCIETY, COLUMBUS |
| LAND SURVEYS: | VIRGINIA MILITARY DISTRICT |
| BOUNDED BY: | EAST:     FAIRFIELD & HOCKING CO. |
| | NORTH:  FRANKLIN CO. |
| | WEST:    FAYETTE & MADISON CO. |
| | SOUTH:   ROSS CO. |
| TOWNSHIPS: | Circleville, Darby, Deer Creek, Harrison, Jackson, Madison, Monroe, Muhlenburg, Perry, Pickaway, Scioto, Walnut, Washington, Wayne. |

**COURT RECORDS: (LDS MICROFILM)**

Auditor:
Tax duplicates, 1816-1838.
Enumeration of school-aged youth, 1829-1894.
Quadrennial enumeration, 1863,1891-1899.

Childrens' Home:
Admittance record, 1906-1923.

Clerk of Courts:

Chancery record, 1843-1857.
Common Pleas complete record, 1810-1842.
Common Pleas criminal journal, 1813-1816.
Common Pleas order book, 1810-1854.
Common Pleas appearance docket, 1824-1832, 1835-1853.
Supreme Court appearance docket, 1819-1852.
Supreme Court order book, 1810-1852.
Supreme Court complete record, 1811-1851.
Commissioners:
    Journals, 1810-1969.
County Home:
    Register, 1873-1965.
Probate Court:
    Births & deaths, v1-3, 1867-1908.
    Index to births & deaths, v1-3, 1867-1908.
    Marriages, v1-7, 1810-1878.
    Wills, v1-5, 1810-1884.
    Guardians' bonds & letters, v1,3, 1856-1886.
Recorder:
    Grantor & grantee index to deeds, 1810-1916.
    Deed records, vA-J, 11-45, 1810-1877.
Sheriff:
    Jail register, 1861-1880.
Miscellaneous:
    Tarlton, Cumberland Presby.Church, Sunday school records, 1879-1882.
    Cemetery records, State Library of Ohio collection.

## OHIO HISTORICAL SOCIETY: (MICROFILM)
Auditor:
    Enumeration of school-aged youth, 1829-1894.
    Quadrennial enumeration, 1863,1891-1899.
Childrens' Home:
    Admittance record, 1906-1923.
Clerk of Courts:
    Chancery record, 1843-1857.
    Common Pleas complete record, 1810-1842.
    Common Pleas criminal journal, 1813-1816.
    Common Pleas order book, 1810-1854.
    Common Pleas appearance docket, 1824-1832, 1835-1853.
    Supreme Court appearance docket, 1819-1852.
    Supreme Court order book, 1810-1852.
    Supreme Court complete record, 1811-1851.
Commissioners:
    Journals, 1810-1969.
County Home:
    Register, 1873-1965.
Sheriff:
    Jail register, 1861-1880.
Miscellaneous:
    Marriage records, 1812-1861, by DAR.
    Cemetery inscriptions, by DAR.
    Abstract of wills, 1808-1892, by DAR.
    Virginia Military landgrants, by DAR.

**CENSUS RECORDS (OHS,SLO,OGS,LDS)**
1820-1880, 1900-1910; 1890 VETERANS; 1880,1900 SOUNDEX; 1910 MIRACODE

**AGRICULTURAL CENSUS SCHEDULES (OHS,SLO-mic)**
1860,1880

**PRODUCTS OF INDUSTRY CENSUS SCHEDULE (OHS,SLO-mic)**
1850,1860,1880

**MORTALITY CENSUS SCHEDULES (OHS,SLO-mic)**
1850,1860

**NEWSPAPERS: [GUIDE TO OHIO NEWSPAPERS, 1793-1973]**
Ashville, Circleville, New Holland, Williamsport.

**TAX RECORDS (OHS & LDS)**
1810-1814,1816-1838.

**MANUSCRIPTS:**
Circleville, Trinity Evang.-Luth. Brotherhood, records, 1915-1923. (WRHS)
Morgan, Ledger & daybook of Benj. Bailey, 1797-1824, 1836-1863. (OHS)
Tarlton Meeting House subscribers, 1830. (OHS)

**GENEALOGICAL PERIODICAL ARTICLES**
Bell, Carol Willsey. OHIO GENEALOGICAL PERIODICAL INDEX: A COUNTY GUIDE (Youngstown
    OH: author, 6th ed., 1987)

**PUBLISHED SOURCES:**
A BRIEF HISTORY OF PICKAWAY COUNTY TO ACCOMPANY WHEELER'S MAP. (Circleville OH:
    Pickaway Co Hist Soc., 1973) 22p. (OHS)
Clark, Marie T. OHIO LANDS: CHILLICOTHE LAND OFFICE, 1800-1829. (Chillicothe OH: author,
    1984) 144p (OGS,SLO,OHS)
CIRCLVEVILLE REMINISCENCES: A DESCRIPTION OF CIRCLEVILLE, OHIO, 1825-1840, ALSO AN
    ACCOUNT OF THE 115 YEAR OLD SISTER OF COMMODORE OLIVER HAZARD PERRY. (Chil-
    licothe OH: D.K.Webb, 1944) 40p (LDS)
CITY/COUNTY DIRECTORIES: check holdings of OHS & local public library.
Daughters of the American Revolution. ABSTRACTS OF WILLS PICKAWAY COUNTY OHIO, 1808-
    1892, V.1. 1942. 118p. (SLO,LDS,DAR)
Daughters of the American Revolution. BIBLE RECORDS OF CUYAHOGA AND PICKAWAY COUN-
    TIES, WILLS OF DEFIANCE COUNTY. (SLO,LDS)
Daughters of the American Revolution. CEMETERY RECORDS: FAIRFIELD, PICKAWAY, ROSS,
    FRANKLIN COUNTY OHIO. 1953. 33p (DAR,LDS,SLO)
Daughters of the American Revolution. CEMETERY RECORDS OF FAIRFIELD, PERRY, PICKAWAY
    & LICKING COUNTY OHIO. 1967? 54p (DAR,SLO)
Daughters of the American Revolution. FAIRFIELD CO.OHIO (CEMETERIES OF PERRY, PICKAWAY
    & LICKING COS) (DAR,LDS)
Daughters of the American Revolution. GRAVESTONE INSCRIPTIONS IN COUNTIES SURROUND-
    ING PICKAWAY. (SLO)
Daughters of the American Revolution. INSCRIPTIONS FROM GRAVESTONES PICKAWAY COUN-
    TY OHIO. 1936. 120p (SLO,OHS,DAR)
Daughters of the American Revolution. MARRIAGE RECORDS PICKAWAY COUNTY OHIO BOOK
    1-5. 3v. (SLO,LDS,DAR)
Daughters of the American Revolution. OHIO BIBLE RECORDS: CONCERNING FAMILIES OF CRAW-
    FORD, DARKE, FAIRFIELD, MIAMI, MONTGOMERY, PICKAWAY, PREBLE AND SHELBY
    COUNTIES. 1970. 126p (DAR)

Daughters of the American Revolution. RECORDS FROM 78 BIBLES FOR FAYETTE, PICKAWAY AND ALLEN COUNTIES OHIO. (SLO)

Daughters of the American Revolution. THREE OLD CEMETERIES ALONG ZANE'S TRACE IN SALT CREEK TOWNSHIP, PICKAWAY COUNTY OHIO. 1961. 94p (SLO,LDS,DAR)

Daughters of the American Revolution. VIRGINIA MILITARY LAND GRANTS OF PICKAWAY COUNTY OHIO. 1951-53. 70p (DAR,SLO,LDS)

Dolle, Genevieve. ABSTRACTS FROM CHURCH RECORD BOOKS OF REV.JOSEPH A. ROOF, 1834-1855. 1958. (SLO,OHS,LDS)

Drake, Paul. THE DAY BOOK OF DR. WILLIAM K. DRAKE FOR THE PERIOD 1841-1856 [PICK-AWAY, DELAWARE & HANCOCK COS]. (Crab Orchard TN: author, 1984) 105p (OGS)

HISTORY OF FRANKLIN AND PICKAWAY COUNTIES, OHIO. (Cleveland: Williams Bros., 1880) 593p. (OHS,OGS,LDS,SLO,LC,DAR)(RPI)

Hixson, W.W. PLAT BOOK OF PICKAWAY COUNTY OHIO. (Rockford IL: author, nd) (OHS)

Johnson, P.R. CLASSIFIED BUSINESS AND PROFESSIONAL DIRECTORY OF PROMINENT TOWNS AND CITIES OF OHIO AND EASTERN INDIANA. (Columbus OH: Berlin Printing, 1899) 303p (LDS)

King, Mrs. Orion. EARLY CONGRESSIONAL LAND GRANTS OF PICKAWAY COUNTY, 1801-1815. (SLO)

Kinnear, Robert B. TRANSCRIPT OF DIARIES OF STEPHEN A. KINNEAR, 1862,1863,1879. (Columbus OH: author, 1974) 199p (LDS)

Kusel, Mary. JOHN FRY FARM CEMETERY, PICKAWAY COUNTY OHIO. (Salt Lake City: author, 1972) 8p. (LDS)

Lake, D.J. ATLAS OF PICKAWAY COUNTY OHIO. (Philadelphia: C.O.Titus, 1871) 57p (OHS,SLO)(RPI)

Mathews, M.P. RECORD OF BIRTHS IN MADISON,FAYETTE AND PICKAWAY COUNTIES OHIO, 1866-1884. (SLO)

Matusoff, Karen. CENTRAL OHIO LOCAL GOVERNMENT RECORDS AT THE OHIO HISTORICAL SOCIETY. (Columbus: Ohio Hist Soc., 1978) 38p. (OGS)

Morgan, J.B.F. THE RISE AND PROGRESS OF THE DEER CREEK SETTLEMENT. 1889. 90p. (SLO)

Pickaway County Assessor. QUADRENNIAL APPRAISEMENT OF PICKAWAY TOWNSHIP, PICK-AWAY COUNTY OHIO. (Circleville OH: author, 1910) 5p. (OHS)

Pickaway Co.Hist.Soc. INDEX, HISTORY OF FRANKLIN AND PICKAWAY COUNTIES, OHIO. (Circleville OH: the society, 198?) 158p (LDS)

PORTRAIT AND BIOGRAPHICAL RECORD OF FAYETTE, PICKAWAY AND MADISON COUNTIES, OHIO. (Chicago: Chapman Bros., 1892) 877p (LC,SLO,LDS,DAR)(RPI)

Reichelderfer, Laura A. A GENEALOGY OF SOME PIONEER FAMILIES ORIGINATING IN PICK-AWAY COUNTY OHIO AND VICINITY. (Delaware OH: M.R.Werkman, 1966?) 63p (DAR,LDS)

Roof, Joseph A. BIRTHS, MARRIAGES, AND DEATHS TRANSCRIBED FROM CHURCH RECORD BOOKS OF REV. JOSEPH A. ROOF OF PICKAWAY COUNTY OHIO (1834-1855): WITH RECORDS FROM TUSCARAWAS, HARRISON, AND CARROLL COUNTIES, OHIO. 1958.95p (DAR,LDS)

Short, Anita. OHIO BIBLE RECORDS CONCERNING THE FAMILIES OF CRAWFORD, DARKE,FAIR-FIELD,MIAMI,MONTGOMERY,PICKAWAY,PREBLE AND SHELBY COUNTIES OHIO. (SLO)

Smith, Clifford N. FEDERAL LAND SERIES: A CALENDAR OF ARCHIVAL MATERIAL ON THE LAND PATENTS ISSUED BY THE U.S.GOVERNMENT, VOL.4, PT 1 :GRANTS IN THE VIRGINIA MILITARY DISTRICT OF OHIO. (Chicago: American Library Assn., 1982) 395p

Smith, Clifford N. FEDERAL LAND SERIES: A CALENDAR OF ARCHIVAL MATERIAL ON THE LAND PATENTS ISSUED BY THE U.S.GOVERNMENT, VOL.4, PT 2 :GRANTS IN THE VIRGINIA MILITARY DISTRICT OF OHIO. (Chicago: American Library Assn., 1986) 306p

Van Cleaf, A.R. HISTORY OF PICKAWAY COUNTY OHIO AND REPRESENTATIVE CITIZENS. (Chicago: Biographical Pub.Co.,1906) 882p (DAR,SLO,OGS,OHS,LDS)(RPI)

Wagner, C.W. MISCELLANEOUS CEMETERY RECORDS OF ALLEN,LICKING,HAR-DIN,MADISON,PICKAWAY,VINTON COUNTIES OHIO. (SLO)

Welsh, Gene A. PRAIRIE VIEW CEMETERY, SALTCREEK TOWNSHIP, PICKAWAY COUNTY, OHIO. 1983. (SLO)

Welsh, Gene A. ST.JOSEPH CEMETERY, CIRCLEVILLE, OHIO, PICKAWAY COUNTY, OHIO. 1983. (SLO)

Welsh, Gene A. SPRINGLAWN CEMETERY, DEERCREEK TOWNSHIP, PICKAWAY COUNTY, OHIO. 1983. (SLO)

Welsh, Gene A. CEMETERY INSCRIPTIONS OF DARBYVILLE CEMETERY, MUHLENBURG TWP., PICKAWAY COUNTY. 1982. (SLO)

Welsh, Gene A. HARRISON TOWNSHIP CEMETERY, PICKAWAY COUNTY, OHIO CEMETERY INSCRIPTIONS. (SLO)

Wertman, Mildred O. THE DEMOCRACY OF PICKAWAY COUNTY IN THE CIVIL WAR. 1932. 78p (OHS)

Wilder, Mary. EARLY INDUSTRIES OF PICKAWAY COUNTY. (Chillicothe OH: author, nd) 7p. (OHS)

WILLIAMS' CIRCLEVILLE AND LANCASTER DIRECTORY, CITY GUIDE AND BUSINESS MIRROR, VOLUME 1, 1859-60. (Circleville OH: L.N.Olds, 1859) 124,72p (LDS)

WORLD'S WAR NEWS OF OHIO, PICKAWAY COUNTY. 1917-1919. (OHS)

# PIKE COUNTY

| | |
|---|---|
| CREATED: | 1815 FROM ADAMS, ROSS & SCIOTO |
| COUNTY SEAT: | WAVERLY 45690 |
| COURT HOUSE: | SECOND ST., WAVERLY 45690 |
| LIBRARIES: | 111 N. HIGH ST., WAVERLY 45690 |
| HISTORICAL SOCIETY: | NONE LISTED |
| GENEALOGICAL SOCIETY: | PIKE COUNTY CHAPTER OGS, |
| | PO BOX 224, WAVERLY 45690 |
| | publication: NEWSLETTER |
| HEALTH DEPARTMENT: | 229 VALLEYVIEW DR., WAVERLY 45690 |
| ARCHIVAL DISTRICT: | OHIO UNIVERSITY, ATHENS |
| | (see published Guide to records) |
| LAND SURVEYS: | VIRGINIA MILITARY DISTRICT |
| | CONGRESS LANDS, OHIO RIVER SURVEY (SOUTH) |
| BOUNDED BY: | EAST: JACKSON CO. |
| | NORTH: ROSS CO. |
| | WEST: HIGHLAND CO. |
| | SOUTH: ADAMS & SCIOTO CO. |
| TOWNSHIPS: | Beaver, Benton, Camp Creek, Jackson, Marion, Mifflin, Newton, Pee Pee, Perry, Preble, Scioto, Seal, Sunfish, Union. |

## COURT RECORDS: (LDS MICROFILM)
Auditor:
    Tax duplicates, 1816-1838.
Childrens' Home:
    Register, 1882-1957,1967-1970.
Clerk of Courts:
    Complete record, vA-C, 1815-1840,1843-1855.
    Appearance docket, 1828-1853.
    Ferry & tavern license record, 1816-1877.
    Marriage record, 1815-1817.
    Supreme Court record, vA-B, 1818-1849.
    Supreme Court minutes, v1-2, 1815-1851.
    District Court record, 1852-1856.
    District Court minutes, 1852-1874.
    Clerk's docket, 1815-1836.
    General index, 1815-1941.
    Chancery record, vE-G, 1835-1855.
    Common Pleas minutes, v1-9, 1815-1859.
Commissioners:

Journal & index, 1815-1905.
County Home:
    Register, 1882-1938.
    Directors' minutes, 1878-1917.
Probate Court:
    Death records, 1867-1908.
    Birth records, v1-4, 1867-1908.
    Marriage records, v1-7, 1815-1913.
    Index to marriages, v1-3.
    Wills, 1817-1884.
Recorder:
    Grantor & grantee index to deeds, v1-3, 1799-1884.
    Deed records, v1-24, 1799-1877.
Sheriff:
    Jail register, 1873-1929.
Miscellaneous:
    Piketon, Presby.Church, register, 1832-1880.
    Waverly, First Presby.Church, session minutes, 1881-1899.
    Waverly, First Presby.Church, women's missionary, 1890-1894.
    Cemetery records, State Library of Ohio collection.

**OHIO HISTORICAL SOCIETY: (MICROFILM)**
Childrens' Home:
    Register, 1882-1957,1967-1970.
Clerk of Courts:
    Complete record, vA-C, 1815-1840,1843-1855.
    Appearance docket, 1828-1853.
    Ferry & tavern license record, 1816-1877.
    Marriage record, 1815-1817.
    Supreme Court record, vA-B, 1818-1849.
    Supreme Court minutes, v1-2, 1815-1851.
    District Court record, 1852-1856.
    District Court minutes, 1852-1874.
    Clerk's docket, 1815-1836.
    General index, 1815-1941.
    Chancery record, vE-G, 1835-1855.
    Common Pleas minutes, v1-9, 1815-1859.
Commissioners:
    Journal & index, 1815-1905.
County Home:
    Register, 1882-1938.
    Directors' minutes, 1878-1917.
Probate Court:
    Marriages, 1815-1817.
Sheriff:
    Jail register, 1873-1929.
Miscellaneous:
    Marriage records, 1815-1857, by DAR.

**CENSUS RECORDS  (OHS,SLO,OGS,LDS)**
1820-1880, 1900-1910; 1890 VETERANS; 1880,1900 SOUNDEX; 1910 MIRACODE

**AGRICULTURAL CENSUS SCHEDULES  (OHS,SLO-mic)**
1860,1880

**PRODUCTS OF INDUSTRY CENSUS SCHEDULE (OHS,SLO-mic)**
1850,1860,1880

**MORTALITY CENSUS SCHEDULES (OHS,SLO-mic)**
1850,1860

**NEWSPAPERS: [GUIDE TO OHIO NEWSPAPERS, 1793-1973]**
Flat, Piketon, Waverly.

**TAX RECORDS (OHS & LDS)**
1816-1838.

**GENEALOGICAL PERIODICAL ARTICLES**
Bell, Carol Willsey. OHIO GENEALOGICAL PERIODICAL INDEX: A COUNTY GUIDE (Youngstown
    OH: author, 6th ed., 1987)

**PUBLISHED SOURCES:**
1870 CENSUS INDEX OF PIKE COUNTY. (SLO)
75 YEARS WITH PIKE COUNTY, OHIO. (SLO)
Adams, Marilyn. INDEX TO CIVIL WAR VETERANS & WIDOWS IN SOUTHERN OHIO, 1890
    FEDERAL CENSUS (Cols,OH: Franklin Co Chapter OGS,1986) 84p
Adams, Marilyn. SOUTHERN OHIO TAXPAYERS IN THE 1820s: SCIOTO, LAWRENCE AND PIKE
    COUNTIES.(Atlanta GA: Heritage Research, 1981) 61p (OGS,LDS,SLO)
BEAVER VALLEY PIONEERS, 1800-1947. 1r mic (SLO)
Brenig, David A. THE PIKE COUNTY WAR BOOK. n.d. (OHS)
Brill, H.E. BEAVER VALLEY PIONEERS, PIKE COUNTY, OHIO, 1800-1947. HISTORICAL SKETCH &
    GENEALOGIES OF MORE THAN 100 FAMILIES. (Oklahoma City OK: Consolidated Pub.Co.,
    1947) 208p (LDS,OHS)
Carrigan, M.J. LIFE AND REMINISCENCES OF HON. JAMES EMMITT (1806-1895) AS REVISED BY
    HIMSELF. (Chillicothe OH: Peerless Prtg., 1888) 624p (OHS)
CITY/COUNTY DIRECTORIES: check holdings of OHS & local public library.
Clark, Marie T. OHIO LANDS: CHILLICOTHE LAND OFFICE, 1800-1829. (Chillicothe: author, 1984)
    144p (OGS,SLO,OHS)
Daughters of the American Revolution. PIKE COUNTY OHIO COURT RECORD OF MARRIAGE,
    VOL.1-2, FROM MAY 4, 1815 TO NOVEMBER 8, 1857. 80p (LDS,SLO,DAR)
Daughters of the American Revolution. PIKE COUNTY OHIO COURT RECORDS OF MARRIAGE
    1815-1851. 2v. (SLO)
Daughters of the American Revolution. PIKE COUNTY OHIO MARRIAGES AND WILLS. (SLO)
Daughters of the American Revolution. PIKE COUNTY RECORDS. 1973. 42,38p (DAR,LDS)
Dixon, Editha H. PIKE COUNTY OHIO COURT RECORDS OF MARRIAGE 1815-1857. (DAR,LDS)
Historical Records Survey. INVENTORY OF THE COUNTY ARCHIVES OF OHIO, NO.66, PIKE COUN-
    TY. (Columbus OH: author, 1942) 296p (OHS,LDS,DAR)
HISTORY OF THE LOWER SCIOTO VALLEY, OHIO, WITH BIOGRAPHIES OF REPRESENTATIVE
    CITIZENS. (Chicago: Interstate Pub.Co., 1884) 875p (OHS,DAR,SLO)
Hixson, W.W. PLAT BOOK OF PIKE COUNTY OHIO. (Rockford IL: author, n.d.) (OHS)
McCormick, Mrs. Harold. HISTORY OF PIKE COUNTY. (Waverly OH: Commissioners of Pike Co.,
    1958) 42p (LDS,OHS,SLO)
Ohio University. GUIDE TO LOCAL GOVERNMENT RECORDS AT OHIO UNIVERSITY. (Athens:
    OU Library, 1986) 61p.
Pike Co Chapter OGS. SEAL TOWNSHIP CEMETERIES, PIKE CO.OHIO. (Waverly OH: the society,
    1986) 127p (OGS,OHS,SLO)
Pike Co Chapter OGS. TOMBSTONE INSCRIPTIONS EVERGREEN UNION CEMETERY, PIKE COUN-
    TY, WAVERY OHIO. (Waverly OH: the society, 1978) 331p (LDS,SLO)
PIKE COUNTY OHIO DEATH RECORDS, 1867-1908. 1r mic (SLO)

PORTRAIT AND BIOGRAPHICAL RECORD OF SCIOTO VALLEY OHIO. (Chicago: no pub, 1894) 429p (DAR)

Rand, McNally & Co. MAP OF PIKE COUNTY OHIO. (Chicago: author, c1912) (OHS)

Rankin, Maude P. CEMETERY RECORDS, FAYETTE CO., OHIO, V.3, WASHINGTON COURT HOUSE CITY CEMETERY WITH A FEW FROM SURROUNDING COUNTIES. (DAR,LDS)

Rankin, Maude P. ROSS COUNTY OHIO, PIKE COUNTY OHIO, CEMETERIES. (LDS)

Scott, Ivan R. CENSUS INDEX OF PIKE COUNTY OHIO, 1870. (Columbus OH: author, 1974) 38p (LDS)

Southern Ohio Gen.Soc. INDEX TO BIRTHS AND DEATHS, PERRY TOWNSHIP, PIKE COUNTY OHIO, 1914-1928. (Hillsboro: the society, nd) 15p (LDS,SLO)

Smith, Clifford N. FEDERAL LAND SERIES: A CALENDAR OF ARCHIVAL MATERIAL ON THE LAND PATENTS ISSUED BY THE U.S.GOVERNMENT, VOL.4, PT 1: GRANTS IN THE VIRGINIA MILITARY DISTRICT OF OHIO. (Chicago: American Library Assn., 1982) 395p

Smith, Clifford N. FEDERAL LAND SERIES: A CALENDAR OF ARCHIVAL MATERIAL ON THE LAND PATENTS ISSUED BY THE U.S.GOVERNMENT, VOL.4, PT 2: GRANTS IN THE VIRGINIA MILITARY DISTRICT OF OHIO. (Chicago: American Library Assn., 1986) 306p

Waverly First National Bank. THE STORY OF A COUNTY THAT GREW, AND A BANK THAT PROSPERED WITH IT. (Waverly OH: author, 1951) 43p (OHS)

# PORTAGE COUNTY

| | |
|---|---|
| CREATED: | 1808 FROM TRUMBULL COUNTY |
| COUNTY SEAT: | RAVENNA 44266 |
| COURT HOUSE: | 203 W. MAIN ST., RAVENNA 44266 |
| LIBRARIES: | 167 E. MAIN ST., RAVENNA 44266 |
| HISTORICAL SOCIETY: | 6549 N. CHESTNUT ST., RAVENNA 44266 |
| GENEALOGICAL SOCIETY: | PORTAGE COUNTY CHAPTER OGS, |
| | 6252 N. SPRING ST., RAVENNA 44266 |
| | publication: PORTAGE PATH TO GENEALOGY |
| HEALTH DEPARTMENT: | 651 MIDDLEBURY RD., KENT 44240 |
| | (separate offices for Kent City, Aurora, Streetsboro & Ravenna) |
| ARCHIVAL DISTRICT: | UNIVERSITY OF AKRON, AKRON, OHIO |
| | (see Folck's Guide to records) |
| LAND SURVEYS: | CONNECTICUT WESTERN RESERVE |
| BOUNDED BY: | EAST: MAHONING & TRUMBULL CO. |
| | NORTH: GEAUGA CO. |
| | WEST: SUMMIT CO. |
| | SOUTH: STARK CO. |
| TOWNSHIPS: | Atwater, Aurora, Brimfield, Charlestown, Deerfield, Edinburg, Franklin, Freedom, Hiram, Mantua, Nelson, Palmyra, Paris, Randolph, Ravenna, Rootstown, Shalersville, Streetsboro, Suffield, Windham. |

## COURT RECORDS: (LDS MICROFILM)

Auditor:
    Tax duplicates, 1816-1838.
Clerk of Courts:
    Chancery record, 1835-1847,1851-1853.
    Civil docket, 1809-1855.
    Supreme Court record, 1823-1851.
County Home:
    Register, 1840-1913.
Probate Court:
    Marriage records, v1-16, 1808-1917.
    Will records, 1823-1918.

Birth & death records, v1-3, 1867-1908.
Administrators' bonds & letters, v1-2, 1872-1887.
Record of civil cases, v1-2, 1852-1856, 1878-1894.
Probate journal, v9-15, 1877-1886.
Probate record, v3-9, 1821-1884.
Probate docket, v1-2,4,6, 1819-1853, 1856-1868,1876-1889.
Administration docket, v3,5,7, 1848-1889.
Guardians' docket, v1-4, 1819-1888.
Guardians' records, 1872-1890.
Guardians' records, 1832-1849,1865-1884.
Guardianship appointments, v1-5, 1832-1884.
Probate civil docket, v1-2, 1862-1886.
Probate record, 1803-1815,1819-1834,1852-1867.
Executors' bonds & letters, v1-2, 1874-1892.
Record of inventories, v3-9, 1862-1886.
Naturalization records, 1859-1906.
Recorder:
Index to deeds, 1795-1917.
Deeds transcribed from Trumbull Co., 1795-1796.
Deed records, vA-126, 1807-1881.
Miscellaneous:
Ravenna, OHIO STAR, 1830-1833.
Franklin Township, First Congregational Church, records, 1819-1898.
Garrettsville, Church of Christ, records, 1889-1902.
Garrettsville Baptist Church, records, 1808-1860.
Garrettsville United Disciples of Christ, records, 1834-1863.
Randolph First Congregational Church, records, 1846-1899.
Streetsboro Congregational Church, records, 1833-1881.
Cemetery records, State Library of Ohio collection.
Mahoning Baptist Assn., minutes, 1820-1827.
Ravenna, Stage office book, 1833-1849.
[see Manuscripts]

## OHIO HISTORICAL SOCIETY: (MICROFILM)
Clerk of Courts:
Chancery record, 1835-1847,1851-1853.
Civil docket, 1809-1855.
Supreme Court record, 1823-1851.
County Home:
Register, 1840-1913.
Probate Court:
Guardians' records, 1832-1849,1865-1884.
Probate record, 1803-1815,1819-1834,1852-1867.
Will records, 1886-1918.
Recorder:
Index to deeds, 1795-1917.
Deed records, 1795-1881.
Miscellaneous:
Connecticut Land Co., Western Reserve land draft, 1795-1809.
Marriage records, A-J only, 1808-1865, by DAR.
Bible & baptismal records, by DAR.
Bible records, by DAR.
Cemetery records, census 1831, church & soldiers, marriages diary
1812-1829, by DAR.
Early records of people and places, by DAR.

John Brown (abolitionist) papers.

## CENSUS RECORDS (OHS,SLO,OGS,LDS)
1820-1880, 1900-1910; 1890 VETERANS; 1880,1900 SOUNDEX; 1910 MIRACODE

## AGRICULTURAL CENSUS SCHEDULES (OHS,SLO-mic)
1860,1880

## PRODUCTS OF INDUSTRY CENSUS SCHEDULE (OHS,SLO-mic)
1850,1860,1880

## MORTALITY CENSUS SCHEDULES (OHS,SLO-mic)
1850,1860

## NEWSPAPERS: [GUIDE TO OHIO NEWSPAPERS, 1793-1973]
Aurora, Garrettsville, Kent, Mantua, Ravenna.

## TAX RECORDS (OHS & LDS)
1808-1814,1816-1838.

## MANUSCRIPTS: [WRHS ITEMS ALSO ON LDS MICROFILM]
Franklin, First Congreg.Church, records, 1819-1898. (WRHS)
Brimfield, First Universalist Church, records, 1839-1922. (WRHS)
Portage Co.Bible Society, Ravenna, records, 1853-1908. (WRHS)
Randolph, First Congreg.Church, records, 1846-1899. (WRHS)
Ravenna, Stage office records, 1833-1866. (WRHS)
Charlestown, M-E Church, records, 1867-1902. (WRHS)
Ravenna, M-E Church, records, 1843-1905. (WRHS)
Ravenna, Disciples Church Ladies Aid Soc., records, 1872-1876. (WRHS)
Garrettsville, Church of Christ, records, 1889-1902. (WRHS)
Garrettsville, Baptist Church records, 1808-1860. (WRHS)
John Harmon family papers, c1800-1872 (poll books, docket books) (WRHS)
Streetsboro, Congreg.Church, records, 1833-1881. (WRHS)
Streetsboro, 1st Calvanistic Congreg. Soc., records, 1836-1875. (WRHS)
Streetsboro, Presby. Church woman's soc. records, 1896-1905. (WRHS)
George Prichard Acct. Book, Hiram, 1832-1867. (WRHS)
Mantua, Gilbert & King blacksmith shop, ledger, 1866-1892. (OHS)
Garrettsville, General store ledger, 1834-1838. (OHS)
Freedom, Wm. Gardner ledger, 1828-1850. (OHS)
Mantua, Calvin White daybook, 1835-1836. (OHS)
Edinburg, GAR post #377, minute book, 1889-1900. (OHS)

## GENEALOGICAL PERIODICAL ARTICLES
Bell, Carol Willsey. OHIO GENEALOGICAL PERIODICAL INDEX: A COUNTY GUIDE (Youngstown OH: author, 6th ed., 1987)

## PUBLISHED SOURCES:
Archer, Cathaline A. BECKET SONS IN A MASSACHUSETTS SETTLEMENT OF NEW CONNEC-TICUT. (Northford CT: L.W.Gibbons, 1953) 58p (DAR)
Bell, Carol W. ABSTRACTS FROM BIOGRAPHIES IN HISTORY OF NORTH EASTERN OHIO by John S. Stewart, 1935. (Indianapolis: Ye Olde Genealogie Shoppe, 1983)
Brown, R.C. HISTORY OF PORTAGE COUNTY OHIO. (Chicago: Warner, Beers, 1885)(Reprint, Ravenna OH: Portage Co.Hist.Soc.,1972) 927p (SLO,LDS)
Cackler, Christian. RECOLLECTIONS OF AN OLD SETTLER: STORIES OF KENT AND VICINITY IN PIONEER TIMES. 1874.(Reprint, Kent OH: Portage Co. Hist.Soc., 1963) 60p (DAR,LDS)

CEMETERY INSCRIPTIONS, PORTAGE COUNTY OHIO. 1r mic. (SLO)

CITY/COUNTY DIRECTORIES: check holdings of OHS & local public library.

Clegg, Michael,ed. PORTAGE COUNTY OHIO NEWSPAPER OBITUARY ABSTRACTS 1825-1870. [OHIO NEWSPAPER ABSTRACTS SERIES VOL.2] (Ft.Wayne IN: author, 1982) 100p (OGS,LDS,SLO)

Clegg, Michael. TAX RECORDS OF PORTAGE, SUMMIT AND PORTIONS OF MEDINA COUNTY OHIO, 1808-1820. (Mansfield: Ohio Gen Soc, 1979) 58p (OGS,LDS)

COMBINED ATLAS OF THE WORLD, WITH SPECIAL MAPS OF PORTAGE, SUMMIT AND MEDINA COUNTIES OHIO, TOGETHER WITH CONDENSED HISTORIES OF THE SAME. (Philadelphia: Everts, Stewart & Co., 1874) (OHS)

Daughters of the American Revolution. BIBLE RECORDS: RAVENNA, PORTAGE COUNTY OHIO. 1956. 167p. (DAR,SLO,LDS)

Daughters of the American Revolution. CENSUS RECORDS 1831-1835-1889 PORTAGE COUNTY OHIO (INCLUDES JOHN SEWARD'S WEDDING DIARY, 1812-1829) (SLO)

Daughters of the American Revolution. EARLY MARRIAGE BONDS OF PORTAGE COUNTY OHIO. 1937. 2v. (SLO,LDS)

Daughters of the American Revolution. EARLY RECORDS OF PLACES AND PEOPLE IN COLUMBIANA, MAHONING, PORTAGE & STARK COUNTIES OHIO. 1941. 160p. (LDS,OHS,DAR,SLO)

Daughters of the American Revolution. PORTAGE COUNTY OHIO RECORDS. 1951-1953. 52p (DAR,SLO)

Dawson, William J. THE AURORA STORY. 1949. 79p (LDS)

Dickinson, Walter J. PIONEER HISTORY, 1802-1865: AN INTERESTING RECORD OF RANDOLPH TOWNSHIP. (Ravenna OH: H.W.Widener, 1953) 163p (DAR)

Everts, L.H. COMBINATION ATLAS MAP OF PORTAGE CO OHIO. (Chicago: author, 1874) (LDS,OHS,OGS,SLO) (RPI)

Folck, Linda. LOCAL GOVERNMENT RECORDS IN THE AMERICAN HISTORY RESEARCH CENTER AT THE UNIVERSITY OF AKRON. (Akron: U of Akron, 1982) 40p. (OGS)

GENEALOGICAL DATA RELATING TO WOMEN IN THE WESTERN RESERVE BEFORE 1840 (1850) (Cleveland: Centennial Commission, 1943) (OHS,LDS,WRHS)

Grismer, Karl H. THE HISTORY OF KENT: HISTORICAL AND BIOGRAPHICAL. (Kent OH: Courier Tribune, 1932) 296p (DAR,LDS)

Hardesty, H.H. MILITARY HISTORY OF OHIO - PORTAGE COUNTY EDITION. 1886/87. (Warren Pub.Lib.)

HISTORY OF PORTAGE COUNTY OHIO. (Chicago: Warner Beers & Co.,1885) 927p (OHS,LDS,DAR) (RPI)

Hixson, W.W. PLAT BOOK OF PORTAGE COUNTY OHIO. (Rockford IL: author, nd) (OHS)

Holm, James B. PORTAGE HERITAGE: A HISTORY OF PORTAGE COUNTY OHIO. (Ravenna OH: Portage Co.Hist.Soc., 1957) 824p (DAR,OHS,LDS,LC)

Holm, Sarah E. THE STATELY MANSION: A HISTORY OF THE UNITED CHURCH OF CHRIST OF KENT. (Kent OH:, author, 1969) 131p (DAR)

James, Peggie S. PORTAGE AND SUMMIT COUNTY PIONEER ASSOCIATION. (Munroe Falls OH: author, 1972) 52p (LDS,SLO)

Johnson, William C. ENUMERATION OF YOUTH AND PARTIAL CENSUS FOR SCHOOL DISTRICTS IN PORTAGE COUNTY OHIO 1832-1838. (Kent OH: Kent State Univ, 1982) (OGS)

Johnson, William C. NATURALIZATIONS FROM PORTAGE COUNTY, OHIO COURT RECORDS, 1816-1878: INCLUDING ADMISSIONS TO THE BAR, AND REVOLUTIONARY WAR PENSION APPLICATIONS. 1983. 9p (LDS)

Kettering, Leon C.W. TRANSACTIONS OF THE EVANGELICAL PROTESTANT TRINITY CHURCH. [STARK & PORTAGE COS] (Toledo OH: author, 1952) 30p (OGS)

Myers, Merrible E. PORTAGE COUNTY OHIO CENSUS RECORDS, 1835,1839, CEMETERY RECORDS, CHURCH RECORDS; SOLDIERS, 1776-1812. (LDS)

NEW HISTORICAL ATLAS OF PORTAGE COUNTY OHIO. 1875. (SLO)

Pfaff, Elmer F. REDISCOVERING MANTUA: THE FIRST 100 YEARS OF SURVIVAL, 1799-1899 (Mantua OH: Mage in Nation Co., 1985) 199p (LDS)

Portage Co.Hist.Soc. 1874-1978 BICENTENNIAL ATLAS OF PORTAGE COUNTY OHIO. (Ravenna OH: the society, 1978) 1v (LDS,SLO)
Portage Co.Hist.Soc. HISTORY OF PORTAGE COUNTY OHIO. (Ravenna OH: the society, 1972) 927,187p (LC)
PORTAGE COUNTY OHIO MARRIAGES, 1807-1865, A-Z. 1r mic. (SLO)
PORTRAIT AND BIOGRAPHICAL RECORD OF PORTAGE AND SUMMIT COUNTIES OHIO. (Logansport IN: A.W.Bowen & Co., 1898) 988p (LC,DAR,SLO,OHS,LDS) (RPI)
Powell, Esther W. CHURCH AND CEMETERY RECORDS OF EVANGELICAL PROTESTANT TRINITY CHURCH IN PLAIN TOWNSHIP. 1973. (OGS)
SEMI-CENTENNIAL CELEBRATION OF WINDHAM, PORTAGE COUNTY, OHIO. 1861. 80p (SLO)
Stevenson, Mrs. John. BIBLE RECORDS, RAVENNA, PORTAGE COUNTY OHIO. (DAR,LDS)
Stewart, John S. HISTORY OF NORTHEASTERN OHIO. (Indianapolis: Historical Pub Co., 1935) 3v. (SLO)
Stranahan, H.B. ATLAS OF PORTAGE COUNTY OHIO. (Cleveland: author, 1900) 83p (SLO,OHS) (RPI)
Tallmadge Hist.Soc. HISTORY OF TALLMADGE OHIO 1807-1957. (Tallmadge OH: the society, 1957?) 135p
Trucksis, Theresa. A GUIDE TO LOCAL HISTORICAL MATERIALS IN THE LIBRARIES OF NORTH-EASTERN OHIO. (Youngstown OH: NE Oh Libr.Assn., 1977) 72p (Yo PL)
Tuttle, H.A. PORTAGE COUNTY IN THE WORLD WAR. 1918. (OHS)
Upton, Harriet T. HISTORY OF THE WESTERN RESERVE (Chicago: Lewis Pub Co., 1910) 3v (SLO)
Western Reserve Hist.Soc. INDEX TO THE MICROFILM EDITION OF GENEALOGICAL DATA RELATING TO WOMEN IN THE WESTERN RESERVE PRE 1840. (Cleveland: the society, 1976) 226p (OGS,WRHS)
Wickham, Gertrude V.W. MEMORIAL TO THE PIONEER WOMEN OF THE WESTERN RESERVE.(Cleveland: Cleveland Centennial Commission, 1896+) 2v, repr 1981 (SLO)

# PREBLE COUNTY

| | |
|---|---|
| CREATED: | 1808 FROM BUTLER & MONTGOMERY |
| COUNTY SEAT: | EATON 45320 |
| COURT HOUSE: | 100 E. MAIN ST., EATON 45320 |
| LIBRARIES: | 301 N. BARRON ST., EATON 45320 |
| HISTORICAL SOCIETY: | RT.4, SWARTSEL RD., EATON 45320 |
| GENEALOGICAL SOCIETY: | PREBLE CO. CHAPTER OGS, |
| | 301 N.BARRON ST., EATON OH 45320 |
| | publication: PREBLE'S PRIDE |
| HEALTH DEPARTMENT: | CO.OFF.BLDG., 119 S.BARRON ST., EATON 45320 |
| | (separate office for Eaton city) |
| ARCHIVAL DISTRICT: | WRIGHT STATE UNIVERSITY, DAYTON |
| | (see Leggett's Guide to records) |
| LAND SURVEYS: | CONGRESS LANDS, MIAMI RIVER SURVEY |
| BOUNDED BY: | EAST:     MONTGOMERY CO. |
| | NORTH:  DARKE CO. |
| | WEST:    UNION & WAYNE CO., INDIANA |
| | SOUTH:  BUTLER CO. |
| TOWNSHIPS: | Dixon, Gasper, Gratis, Harrison, Israel, Jackson, Jefferson, Lanier, Monroe, Somers, Twin, Washington. |

**COURT RECORDS: (LDS MICROFILM)**
Auditor:
    Tax duplicates, 1816-1838.
Children's Home:
    Record of inmates, 1884-1946.
Clerk of Courts:

Chancery records, vF-Y, 1827-1853.
General Index, 1808-1852.
Civil minutes journal, v1-4, 1808-1853.
Supreme Court index, 1817-1856.
Supreme Court records, vA-D, 1817-1856.
County Home:
    Record of inmates, 1838-1904.
Probate Court:
    Birth records, v1-4, 1867-1908.
    Death records, v1-3, 1867-1908.
    Marriages, vA,1-7, 1808-1903.
    Marriage index, 1808-1859.
    Wills, v1,B-H, 1808-1901.
    Journal, v3-24, 1858-1901.
    Administrators & executors docket, v1-4, 1880-1905.
    Record of accounts, v3-30, 1861-1899.
Recorder:
    Soldiers' discharge record, 1865-1917.
    Index to deeds, v1-Z, 1805-1963.
    Deed records, v1-104, 1808-1900.
    Mortgage index, v1-3, 1884-1886.
    Mortgages, v1, 1833-1863.
Miscellaneous:
    Westfield Monthly Meeting, minutes, 1821-1942.
    Elk Hicksite Monthly Meeting, minutes, 1828-1840.
    Elk Monthly Meeting, records, scat. 1809-1949.
    Eaton Presby.Church, session records, 1870.
    Cemetery records, State Library of Ohio collection.

## OHIO HISTORICAL SOCIETY: (MICROFILM)
Childrens' Home:
    Record of inmates, 1884-1946.
Clerk of Courts:
    Chancery record, vF-Y, 1827-1853.
    Civil minutes journal, v1-4, 1808-1853.
    General index, 1808-1852.
    Supreme Court index, 1817-1856.
    Supreme Court record, vA-D, 1817-1856.
County Home:
    Record of inmates, 1838-1904.
City of Eaton City Council:
    Council minutes, 1872-1975.
    Record of resolutions, 1953-1975.
    Ordinances & resolutions, 1913-1922.
    Ordinance record, 1913-1976.
Miscellaneous:
    Cemetery records, by DAR.

## CENSUS RECORDS  (OHS,SLO,OGS,LDS)
1820-1880, 1900-1910; 1890 VETERANS; 1880,1900 SOUNDEX; 1910 MIRACODE

## AGRICULTURAL CENSUS SCHEDULES  (OHS,SLO-mic)
1860,1880

**PRODUCTS OF INDUSTRY CENSUS SCHEDULE (OHS,SLO-mic)**
1850,1860,1880

**MORTALITY CENSUS SCHEDULES (OHS,SLO-mic)**
1850,1860

**NEWSPAPERS: [GUIDE TO OHIO NEWSPAPERS, 1793-1973]**
Camden, Eaton, Eldorado, Lewisburg, New Paris, West Alexandria.

**TAX RECORDS (OHS & LDS)**
1810-1814,1816-1838.

**MANUSCRIPTS:**
Second Creek New Hope Baptist Church, records, 1836-1881. (WRHS)

**GENEALOGICAL PERIODICAL ARTICLES**
Bell, Carol Willsey. OHIO GENEALOGICAL PERIODICAL INDEX: A COUNTY GUIDE (Youngstown
    OH: author, 6th ed., 1987)

**PUBLISHED SOURCES:**
Berry, Ellen T. & David A. EARLY OHIO SETTLERS: PURCHASERS OF LAND IN SOUTHWESTERN
    OHIO, 1800-1840. (Baltimore: Genealogical Pub.Co., 1986) 372p (OGS,SLO,OHS)
BIOGRAPHICAL HISTORY OF PREBLE CO OHIO: COMPENDIUM OF NATIONAL BIOGRAPHY.
    (Chicago: Lewis Pub.Co., 1900) 573p (LDS,LC,OHS,SLO) (RPI)
Borradaile, Charlotte & A.Gilbert. PREBLE COUNTY OHIO BIRTHS VOL.IV 1897-1908. (West
    Alexandria OH: author, 1985) 96p (OGS)
Borradaile, Charlotte & A.Gilbert. PREBLE COUNTY OHIO BIRTHS VOL.II 1877-1886. (West Alexandria
    OH: author, 1984) 103p (OGS)
Borradaile, Charlotte & A.Gilbert. PREBLE COUNTY OHIO BIRTHS VOL.I 1867-1876. (West Alexandria
    OH: author, 1984) 96p (OGS)
Brien, Lindsay M. CEMETERY RECORDS, PART OF BUTLER COUNTY, GREENE COUNTY, PREBLE
    COUNTY. [MIAMI VALLEY RECORDS v6] 155p (LDS)
Brien, Lindsay M. A GENEALOGICAL INDEX OF PIONEERS IN THE MIAMI VALLEY OHIO: MIAMI,
    MONTGOMERY, PREBLE AND WARREN COUNTIES OHIO. (Dayton: Colonial Dames of
    America, 1970) 196p (LDS,DAR)
Brien, Lindsay M. INDEX TO MIAMI VALLEY RECORDS, MIAMI COUNTY CEMETERY RECORDS,
    V.5. (SLO)
Brien, Lindsay M. MIAMI COUNTY CEMETERY RECORDS. (np: author, nd) 177p (LDS)
Brien, Lindsay M. MIAMI VALLEY WILL ABSTRACTS FROM THE COUNTIES OF MIAMI,
    MONTGOMERY, WARREN AND PREBLE IN THE STATE OF OHIO. (SLO,DAR,LDS)
Brien, Lindsay M. MIAMI VALLEY RECORDS, VOL.VI, QUAKER RECORDS. (Dayton OH: Miami
    Valley Gen Soc, 1986) 121p (OGS)
Brien, Lindsay M. MIAMI VALLEY RECORDS, 5v (SLO,LDS)
Brien, Lindsay M. OUR FOREFATHERS ... GENEALOGY OF MIAMI VALLEY FAMILIES. (SLO)
Brooke, Mary G. HISTORIC EATON AND FORT SAINT CLAIR. (Eaton OH: author, 1930) 42p
    (DAR,SLO)
Brubaker, Joan. ABSTRACTS FROM THE EATON DEMOCRAT, PREBLE COUNTY OHIO, 1872-1877,
    VOL.I. (West Alexandria OH: author, 1979) 76p (OGS,LDS,SLO)
Brubaker, Joan. ABSTRACTS FROM THE EATON DEMOCRAT, EATON, PREBLE COUNTY, OHIO,
    1877-1881, VOL.II. (West Alexandria OH: author, 1980) 120p. (OGS,LDS)
Brubaker, Joan. ABSTRACTS FROM THE EATON DEMOCRAT, EATON, PREBLE COUNTY, OHIO,
    1883-1887, VOL.III. (West Alexandria OH: author, 1980) 120p. (OGS,LDS,SLO)
Brubaker, Joan. ABSTRACTS FROM THE EATON DEMOCRAT, EATON, PREBLE COUNTY, OHIO,
    1888-1891, VOL.IV. (West Alexandria OH: author, 1983) 78p.(OGS,SLO)

Brubaker, Joan. CEMETERY INSCRIPTIONS, PREBLE COUNTY, OHIO, VOL.I & II. (Eaton OH: Preble Co Gen.Club, 1980) 87p (OGS,LDS)

Brubaker, Joan. CEMETERY INSCRIPTIONS, PREBLE COUNTY OHIO, VOL.III. (West Alexandria OH: author, 1983) 72p (OGS)

Brubaker, Joan. DUPLICATE OF THE LAND TAX OF PREBLE COUNTY, OHIO, 1820. (West Alexandria OH: author, 1981) 41p (LDS)

Brubaker, Joan. OBITUARY ABSTRACTS, EATON OHIO PAPERS, 1850-1890. (West Alexandria OH: author, 1981) 181p (OGS)

Brubaker, Joan. OBITUARY ABSTRACTS, PREBLE COUNTY PAPERS, 1877-1895. (West Alexandria OH: author, 1983) 227p. (OGS)

Brubaker, Joan. OBITUARY ABSTRACTS 1896-1900 FROM PREBLE COUNTY OHIO NEWSPAPERS, VOLUME III. (West Alexandria OH: author, 1985) 188p (OGS)

Brubaker, Joan. PREBLE COUNTY OH LAND RECORDS 1821-1828 (West Alexandria OH: author, 1987?) np

Brubaker, Joan. PREBLE COUNTY OHIO 1860 CENSUS. (West Alexandria OH: author, nd) (OGS)

Brubaker, Joan. PREBLE COUNTY OHIO 1870 CENSUS. (West Alexandria OH: author, 1982) 256p (OGS)

Brubaker, Joan. PREBLE COUNTY OHIO 1880 CENSUS. (West Alexandria OH: author, nd) 304p (OGS)

Brubaker, Joan. PREBLE COUNTY OHIO 1900 CENSUS. (West Alexandria OH: author, nd) (OGS)

Brubaker, Joan. PREBLE COUNTY OHIO 1910 CENSUS INDEX. (Utica KY: McDowell Pubs., 1984) 252p (OGS)

Brubaker, Joan. PREBLE COUNTY OHIO BIRTHS 1867-1876. (West Alexandria OH: author, nd) (OGS)

Brubaker, Joan. PREBLE COUNTY OHIO BIRTHS VOL.II 1877-1886. (West Alexandria OH: author, 1984) 103p (OGS)

Brubaker, Joan. PREBLE COUNTY OHIO BIRTHS, VOLUME III, 1887-1896. (West Alexandria OH: author, 1985) 87p (OGS)

Brubaker, Joan. PREBLE COUNTY OHIO BIRTHS VOL.IV 1897-1908. (West Alexandria OH: author, 1985) 96p (OGS)

Brubaker, Joan. PREBLE COUNTY OHIO MARRIAGES 1860-1898. (West Alexandria OH: author, nd) (OGS)

Brubaker, Joan. WEST ALEXANDRIA FIRST BRETHREN CHURCH 1885-1985. (West Alexandria OH: Women's Missionary Society, 1986) 35p (OGS)

CAMDEN SESQUICENTENNIAL SOUVENIR HISTORY BOOK, 1818-1968. 48p (SLO)

CEMETERIES OF PREBLE COUNTY OHIO. 1r mic (SLO)

CITY/COUNTY DIRECTORIES: check holdings of OHS & local public library.

Craig, Robert D. PREBLE COUNTY OHIO CEMETERY INSCRIPTIONS. (Cincinnati OH: author, 1963) 36p (OHS)

Curry, John C. CEMETERY RECORD, PREBLE COUNTY, WASHINGTON TOWNSHIP, OHIO: OLD CEMETERY LOCATED ON CREEKSIDE FARM. 2p (LDS)

Daughters of the American Revolution. CEMETERY INSCRIPTIONS PREBLE COUNTY OHIO. (Illinois: Martha Ibbetson Chapter, 1970) (DAR,SLO,LDS)

Daughters of the American Revolution. CEMETERIES OF PREBLE COUNTY OHIO. 68p. (DAR,LDS)

Daughters of the American Revolution. EARLY CHURCHES AND CEMETERIES OF PREBLE COUNTY 1807-1900. 1941. 25p (OHS,SLO)

Daughters of the American Revolution. OBITUARY ABSTRACTS FROM PREBLE COUNTY NEWSPAPERS IN PREBLE COUNTY OHIO, VOLUME II. (Utica KY: McDowell Pubs., 1983) 227p (DAR)

Daughters of the American Revolution. OHIO BIBLE RECORDS. (SLO)

Daughters of the American Revolution. PREBLE COUNTY OHIO CEMETERY INSCRIPTIONS. 1969. 94p. (DAR,LDS,SLO)

Daughters of the American Revolution. PREBLE COUNTY OHIO MARRIAGE RECORDS, 1808-1860. 3v. (DAR)

DIRECTORY OF PREBLE COUNTY OHIO. HISTORICAL SKETCHES AND BIOGRAPHIES OF EMINENT PIONEERS. (Eaton OH: B.F.Morgan, 1875) (LDS,SLO)

Dunham, J.R. PLAT BOOK OF PREBLE COUNTY OHIO, COMPILED FROM COUNTY RECORDS AND ACTUAL SURVEYS. (Des Moines IA: Northwest Pub.Co., 1912) 61p (OHS)

Floyd, Marjorie D. EVERY NAME INDEX TO MIAMI VALLEY OHIO PIONEERS BY LINDSAY M. BRIEN. (Dayton OH: author, 1980) 38p (LDS)

Gilbert, Audrey. OBITUARY ABSTRACTS, 1850-1900. (West Alexandria OH: author, 1981) 3v (LDS,SLO)

Gilbert, Audrey. ABSTRACTS FROM EARLY EATON OHIO NEWSPAPERS, 1825-1850. (West Alexandria OH: author, 1988?) 90p

Gilbert, Audrey. PREBLE COUNTY OHIO MARRIAGES 1860-1898. (West Alexandria OH: author, 1981) 159p (OGS,LDS,SLO)

Gilbert, Audrey. PREBLE COUNTY OHIO PERSONAL PROPERTY TAX LIST 1827-1834. (West Alexandria OH: author, 1987) 134p (OGS)

Gilbert, Audrey. PREBLE COUNTY OHIO, 1860 CENSUS. (West Alexandria OH: author, 1981) 269,13p (LDS)

Gilbert, Audrey. 1870 PREBLE COUNTY OHIO CENSUS. (Owensboro KY: McDowell Pubs., 1982) 256,17p (LDS)

Gilbert, Audrey. PREBLE COUNTY OHIO, THE 1900 FEDERAL CENSUS. (Owensboro KY: Cook & McDowell Pubs., 1980) 357p (OGS,LDS)

Gilbert, Audrey. PREBLE COUNTY OHIO BIRTHS, 1867-1908. (Utica KY: McDowell Pubs., 198?) 4v (LDS,SLO)

Gilbert, Audrey. WEST ALEXANDRIA FIRST BRETHREN CHURCH, 1885-1985. (Utica KY: McDowell Pubs., 1985) 35p (LDS)

GRATIS SESQUICENTENNIAL SOUVENIR: HISTORY BOOK, 1817-1967. (Gratis OH: committee, 1967) (LDS)

Haller, Stephen E. & P.Nolan. FIRST STOP FOR LOCAL HISTORY RESEARCH. A GUIDE TO COUNTY RECORDS PRESERVED AT WRIGHT STATE UNIVERSITY ARCHIVES AND SPECIAL COLLECTIONS. 1976. 21p.

Hillis, L.B. SOUVENIR, PREBLE COUNTY OHIO. (Eaton OH: Eaton Herald, 1908) 32p (OHS)

Hinshaw, William Wade. ENCYCLOPEDIA OF AMERICAN QUAKER GENEALOGY, VOL.V, OHIO. (Baltimore: Genealogical Pub.Co., 1973) (SLO,OHS,LDS)

HISTORY OF PREBLE COUNTY OHIO: WITH ILLUSTRATIONS AND BIOGRAPHICAL SKETCHES. (Cleveland: H.Z.Williams & Co., 1881) 337,106p (LDS,OHS,SLO,LC) (RPI)

Irwin, Homer H. INSCRIPTIONS TAKEN FROM GRAVE MARKERS IN THE BEECHWOOD CEMETERY, RISING SUN. (Elmhurst IL: author, 1966) 15p (OHS)

JUDICIARY RECORDS, 1869-1894, ISRAEL TOWNSHIP, PREBLE COUNTY OHIO. 260p. (OGS)

Lake, D.J. ATLAS OF PREBLE COUNTY OHIO. (Philadelphia: Lake, Griffing etal, 1871) 49p (LDS,SLO,OHS) (RPI)

Leggett, Nancy G. & D.E.Smith. A GUIDE TO LOCAL GOVERNMENT RECORDS AND NEWSPAPERS PRESERVED AT THE DEPARTMENT OF ARCHIVES AND SPECIAL COLLECTIONS WRIGHT STATE UNIVERSITY. (Dayton OH: Wright State U., 1987)

Lowry, Robert E. HISTORY OF PREBLE COUNTY, OHIO, HER PEOPLE, INDUSTRIES AND INSTITUTIONS. (Indianapolis: B.F.Bowen & CO., 1915)(Reprint, Owensboro KY: Cook & McDowell, 1981) 938p (LDS,OHS,SLO,LC)

Montgomery Co.Chapter OGS. INDEX TO PREBLE COUNTY NATURALIZATION RECORDS, COMMON PLEAS COURT MINUTES, 1808-1852. (Dayton OH: the society, 1985?) 3p (LDS)

Morgan, B.J. DIRECTORY OF PREBLE COUNTY OHIO FOR 1875: HISTORICAL SKETCHES AND BIOGRAPHIES OF EMINENT PIONEERS. (Eaton OH: Preble Co.Hist.Soc., 1975) (DAR)

OUR CHURCH HERITAGE: THE FIRST BRETHREN CHURCH, GRATIS, OHIO. (Middletown OH: Perry, 1969) 144p (LDS)

Pouget, Luella R. CEMETERY INSCRIPTIONS FROM MONTGOMERY, MIAMI, PREBLE AND DARKE? COUNTIES OHIO. (LDS)

Preble Co. Chapter OGS. RESEARCHER'S GUIDE TO PREBLE COUNTY OHIO. (Eaton OH: the society, 1987) 260p

Preble Co.Historical Society. COMPOSITE COLLECTION OF CADASTRAL MAPS OF PREBLE COUNTY OHIO. (Eaton OH: the society, 197?) 376p (LDS,SLO)

Railsback, Mildred H. HISTORICAL CEMETERIES OF PREBLE COUNTY. (Eaton OH: author, 1947) 17p (OHS)

Rost, Grace A. & B.Norberg. ROSELAWN & LOWER CEMETERY, 1887-1940, LEWISBURG, PREBLE COUNTY OHIO. (Ogden UT: authors, 1962) 60p (LDS)

Runyon, Grace C. HISTORICAL FACTS ON PREBLE COUNTY: AND DAUGHTERS OF THE AMERICAN REVOLUTION SOCIETY. (Eaton OH: author, 1945) 122p (DAR,OHS,LC,SLO)

Runyon, Grace C. PREBLE COUNTY PIONEERS. (Eaton OH: author, 1939) 54p (SLO,DAR)

Schlotterbeck, Seth. HISTORY AND PROGRAM LEWISBURG AREA SESQUICENTENNIAL CELEBRATION. 1968. 100p. (DAR)

Shilt, Rose. PREBLE COUNTY OHIO 1850 CENSUS. (Mansfield OH: Ohio Gen Soc,1974) 195p (OGS,OHS,SLO,LDS)

Short, Anita. DUPLICATE OF THE LAND TAX OF PREBLE COUNTY OHIO FOR THE YEARS 1820 AND 1821. (Arcanum OH: author, 1975. 140p (DAR,OHS)

Short, Anita. PREBLE COUNTY OHIO COMMON PLEAS COURT RECORDS, 1810-1850. (Arcanum OH: author, 1970) 142p (OGS,DAR,LDS,OHS)

Short, Anita & R.Bowers. PREBLE COUNTY OHIO CEMETERY INSCRIPTIONS, VOL.I. (Arcanum OH: author, 1969) 100p (OGS,DAR,LDS,OHS)

Short, Anita & R.Bowers. PREBLE COUNTY OHIO DEED RECORDS, 1808-1821. 1978. (SLO)

Short, Anita & R.Bowers. PREBLE COUNTY OHIO WILL ABSTRACTS, VOL.I, 1808-1836. (Arcanum OH: author, 1967) 37p (OGS,DAR,OHS,SLO)

Short, Anita & R.Bowers. PREBLE COUNTY OHIO WILL ABSTRACTS, VOL.II, 1836-1854. (Arcanum OH: author, 1973) 33p (OGS,OHS,SLO)

Short, Anita & R.Bowers. PREBLE COUNTY OHIO MARRIAGE RECORDS, VOL.I,1808-1830. (Arcanum OH: author, 1966) 65p (OGS,LDS,OHS)

Short, Anita & R.Bowers. PREBLE COUNTY OHIO MARRIAGE RECORDS, VOL.2, 1831-1840. (Arcanum OH: author, 1967.) 58p (OGS,LDS,OHS)

Short, Anita & R.Bowers. PREBLE COUNTY OHIO MARRIAGE RECORDS, VOL.3, 1841-1859. (Arcanum OH: author, 1973) 144p (OGS,LDS,OHS)

Short, Anita & R.Bowers. PREBLE COUNTY OHIO RECORDS. (Arcanum OH: author, 1973) 144p (DAR)

Short, Anita & R.Bowers. UNITED STATES LAND ENTRIES FROM PREBLE COUNTY OHIO. (Greenville OH: author, 1968) 25p (DAR,LDS,OHS,SLO)

Slevin, Ruth. PREBLE COUNTY OHIO MARRIAGES: 1808-1859. 1965. 1v. (DAR,SLO)

Smith, William E. HISTORY OF SOUTHWESTERN OHIO: THE MIAMI VALLEYS. 1917. 3v (SLO)

Snyder, Mrs. Kenneth. PREBLE COUNTY OHIO MUNICIPAL RECORDS, 1850-1860. (SLO)

Titus, C.O. ATLAS OF PREBLE CO OHIO (Philadelphia: author, 1871) 49p (LC,OGS)(RPI)

Vicory, Jacqueline. MILO UNION LIST OF GENEALOGIES IN THE LIBRARIES OF CHAMPAIGN, CLARK, DARKE, GREENE, MIAMI, MONTGOMERY AND PREBLE COUNTIES OHIO. (Dayton OH: Miami Valley Libr. Organization, 1977) 122p (LDS)

WEST ALEXANDRIA OHIO SESQUI-CENTENNIAL BOOK - CELEBRATING 150 YEARS 1836-1986. 1986. 107p. (OGS)

# PUTNAM COUNTY

| | |
|---|---|
| CREATED: | 1808 FROM SHELBY COUNTY |
| COUNTY SEAT: | OTTAWA 45875 |
| COURT HOUSE: | MAIN ST., OTTAWA 45875 |
| LIBRARIES: | 364 E. MAIN ST., OTTAWA 45875 |
| HISTORICAL SOCIETY: | PO BOX 260, KALIDA 45853 |
| GENEALOGICAL SOCIETY: | PUTNAM COUNTY CHAPTER OGS, PO BOX 405, OTTAWA 45875 publication: PUTNAM PASTFINDER |
| HEALTH DEPARTMENT: | 336 E.MAIN ST., OTTAWA 45875-1946 |

| | |
|---|---|
| ARCHIVAL DISTRICT: | BOWLING GREEN STATE UNIVERSITY, BOWLING GREEN |
| | (see Biggs' Guide to records) |
| LAND SURVEYS: | CONGRESS LANDS, E & N OF 1ST PRIN.MERIDIAN |
| | CONGRESS LANDS, E & S OF 1ST PRIN.MERIDIAN |
| BOUNDED BY: | EAST:    HANCOCK CO. |
| | NORTH:  DEFIANCE & HENRY CO. |
| | WEST:    PAULDING & VAN WERT CO. |
| | SOUTH:   ALLEN CO. |
| TOWNSHIPS: | Blanchard, Greensburg, Jackson, Jennings, Liberty, Monroe, Monterey, Ottawa, Palmer, Perry, Pleasant, Riley, Sugar Creek, Union, Van Buren. |

| | |
|---|---|
| **SPECIAL NOTE:** | A FIRE IN 1864 DESTROYED THE COURT HOUSE. |

**COURT RECORDS: (LDS MICROFILM)**
Clerk of Courts:
   Common Pleas appearance docket, 1848-1861.
   Common Pleas journal, v1-3, 1834-1857.
   Common Pleas court records, 1835-1867.
   Judgment index, 1835-1867.
   Chancery record v2, 1850-1860.
County Engineer:
   Plat book, 1962.
County Home:
   Register, 1869-1927.
Probate Court:
   Marriage records, 1834-1916.
   Index to marriage records, 1834-1927.
   Birth records, 1857-1920.
   Index to birth records, 1854-1920.
   Death records, v1-2, 1867-1920.
   Index to death records, v1, 1867-1920.
   Will records, vA-G, 1835-1910.
   Index to will record, v1, 1835-1973.
   Guardians' docket, v1, 1880-1943.
   Guardians' settlements, v1-3, 1882-1898.
   Naturalization intention & final, 1860-1905.
   Naturalization records, 1854-1883.
   Administration docket 1880-1890.
   Admr. & Exr. settlements, v1-2, 1882-1893.
   Journal of settlements, v1-2, 1875-1900.
   Final record of accounts, vA-D, 1853-1879.
   Probate journal, vA-G, 1853-1889.
   General index, 1837-1963.
Recorder:
   General index to deeds, 1830-1951.
   Deed records, v1-49, 1830-1892.
   Record of soldiers' discharges, v1-2, 1861-65.
Miscellaneous:
   Swiss Mennonite Church records of Putnam Co., c1835-1903.
   Pandora, Grace Mennonite Church minutes, 1893-1928.
   Columbus Grove, Rockport Presby.Church, records, 1850-1879.

**OHIO HISTORICAL SOCIETY: (MICROFILM)**
Clerk of Courts:

Common Pleas appearance docket, 1848-1861.
Common Pleas journal, v1-3, 1834-1857.
Judgment index, 1835-1867.
Chancery record v2, 1850-1860.
County Home:
   Register, 1869-1927.
Probate Court:
   Index to death records, v1, 1859-1920.
   Guardians' docket, v1, 1880-1943.
   Will record, vH-1, 1902-1910.
   Naturalization intention & final, 1860-1905.
Recorder:
   Deed records, v39-40,43-49, 1881-1892.

**CENSUS RECORDS (OHS,SLO,OGS,LDS)**
1830-1880, 1900-1910; 1890 VETERANS; 1880,1900 SOUNDEX; 1910 MIRACODE

**AGRICULTURAL CENSUS SCHEDULES (OHS,SLO-mic)**
1860

**PRODUCTS OF INDUSTRY CENSUS SCHEDULE (OHS,SLO-mic)**
1850,1860,1880

**MORTALITY CENSUS SCHEDULES (OHS,SLO-mic)**
1850,1860

**NEWSPAPERS: [GUIDE TO OHIO NEWSPAPERS, 1793-1973]**
Columbus Grove, Continental, Kalida, Leipsic, Ottawa, Pandora.

**TAX RECORDS (OHS & LDS)**
1834-1838.

**MANUSCRIPTS:**
George D. Kinder papers (incl. court records) 1830-1903. (OHS)

**GENEALOGICAL PERIODICAL ARTICLES**
Bell, Carol Willsey. OHIO GENEALOGICAL PERIODICAL INDEX: A COUNTY GUIDE (Youngstown
   OH: author, 6th ed., 1987)

**PUBLISHED SOURCES:**
Biggs, Deb. GUIDE TO LOCAL GOVERNMENT RECORDS AT THE CENTER FOR ARCHIVAL COL-
   LECTIONS. (Bowling Green OH: Bowling Green State Univ, 1981) 104p (OGS)
Calvin, Marguerite C. DEATH, ADMINISTRATION, MARRIAGE, AND MISCELLANEOUS NOTICES
   FROM THE KALIDA VENTURE, PUTNAM COUNTY OHIO 1845-1854. (Ottawa OH: Putnam Co
   District Library, 1987) 48p (OGS)
Calvin, Marguerite C. LIST OF LETTERS AT THE POST OFFICE IN KALIDA, PUTNAM COUNTY
   OHIO, FROM THE KALIDA VENTURE 1845-1854. (Ottawa OH: Putnam Co District Library, 1987)
   13p (OGS)
Calvin, Marguerite C. PEOPLE AND PLACES - PUTNAM COUNTY OHIO. (Ottawa OH: author, 1981)
   232p (LC,LDS,SLO)
Christian, Donna K. GUIDE TO NEWSPAPER HOLDINGS AT THE CENTER FOR ARCHIVAL COL-
   LECTIONS. (Bowling Green OH: Bowling Green State Univ, 1980) 64p (OGS)
CITY/COUNTY DIRECTORIES: check holdings of OHS & local public library.

Clegg, Michael, ed. DEFIANCE, FULTON, HENRY, PAULDING, PUTNAM, WILLIAMS & WOOD COUNTIES OHIO NEWSPAPER OBITUARY ABSTRACTS, 1838-1870 (OHIO NEWSPAPER SERIES VOL.5) (Ft.Wayne IN: author, 1987) 75p (OGS)

Daughters of the American Revolution. MARRIAGE RECORDS PUTNAM COUNTY OHIO. 1959-1966. (DAR,SLO)

Daughters of the American Revolution. PUTNAM COUNTY OHIO 1834-1934. (SLO) Echelbarger, Rae. ONE HUNDREDTH ANNIVERSARY OF TRINITY METHODIST CHURCH, OTTAWA OHIO 1855-1955.

Gazette Printing Co. TEN YEARS IN PUTNAM COUNTY 1890-1900, OTTAWA OHIO.

Glasbrenner, Helen. CEMETERY RECORDS IN PUTNAM AND HENRY COUNTIES, OHIO. 1979. 202p (LDS)

Gratz, Delbert L. HISTORICAL AND GENEALOGICAL SKETCH OF THE SWISS MENNONITES OF ALLEN AND PUTNAM COUNTIES, OHIO. 1940. (OHS)

Gunchel, John E. THE EARLY HISTORY OF THE MAUMEE VALLEY. (Toledo: Hadley Printing Co., 1902)

Hardesty, H.H. HISTORICAL HAND ATLAS OF PUTNAM COUNTY OHIO. (Chicago: author, 1880) (SLO,OHS) (RPI)

HISTORY OF PUTNAM COUNTY OHIO: CONTAINING OUTLINE MAP... (Chicago: H.H. Hardesty, 1976) 65p (LDS)

HISTORY OF THE OTTAWA RIVER CHURCH 1860-1960. 20p (SLO)

Hixson, W.W. PLAT BOOK OF PUTNAM COUNTY OHIO. (Rockford IL: author, nd) (OHS)

IMMACULATE CONCEPTION PARISH, OTTOVILLE, OHIO SOUVENIR OF THE DIAMOND JUBILEE, 1848-1923. (Ottoville OH: the parish, 1923) 121p (LDS)

Kinder, George D. HISTORY OF PUTNAM COUNTY OHIO. (Indianapolis: B.F.Bowen & Co., 1915) 1465p (OHS,LDS)

Knapp, Horace S. HISTORY OF THE MAUMEE VALLEY. (Toledo OH: author, 1872) 685p. (DAR,OHS,SLO)

Levinson, Marilyn. GUIDE TO NEWSPAPER HOLDINGS AT THE CENTER FOR ARCHIVAL COLLECTIONS. 2nd Edition. (Bowling Green OH: Bowling Green State Univ., 1987)

Northwestern Ohio Gen.Soc. CEMETERY RECORDS. (LDS)

PIONEER REMINESCENCES, BOOK I SENTINEL, OTTAWA, 1878; BOOK II, GAZETTE PRINT, 1887.

PLAT BOOK, PUTNAM COUNTY, OHIO. 1962. (LDS)

PORTRAIT AND BIOGRAPHICAL RECORD OF ALLEN AND PUTNAM COUNTIES OHIO. (Chicago: A.W.Bowen & Co., 1896) 609p (OHS,DAR,LDS,SLO)

PUTNAM COUNTY ATLAS 1895 COMBINED WITH PUTNAM COUNTY HISTORY 1880 (OGS,LDS,SLO)

Putnam Co Chapter OGS. PUTNAM CO OHIO CEMETERIES, MONROE TOWNSHIP, VOL.ONE (Ottawa OH: the society, 1986) 61p (OGS,LDS)

Putnam Co Chapter OGS. PUTNAM COUNTY OHIO CEMETERIES, JENNINGS TOWNSHIP, VOLUME TWO. (Ottawa OH: the society, 1987) 59p (OGS,LDS)

Putnam County Pioneer Assn. CENTENNIAL HISTORY, 1873-1973. (Columbus Grove OH: Heffner Printing, 1973) 159p (DAR,OHS,LDS,SLO)

Putnam County Sesquicentennial Committee. PUTNAM COUNTY PROGRESSES, 1803-1953. (Ottawa OH: the committee, 1953)

Rust, Orton. HISTORY OF WEST CENTRAL OHIO. (Indianapolis: Historical Pub Co., 1914) 3v

ST. JOHN'S CATHOLIC CEMETERY, PUTNAM COUNTY, OHIO. (SLO)

Seitz, D.W. & D.C.Talbot. ATLAS OF PUTNAM COUNTY OHIO. (Ottawa OH: authors, 1895)(Reprint, Evansville IN: Unigraphic, 1976) 133,39p (SLO,OHS,LDS) (RPI)

Sheeley, Mary L., ed. PUTNAM COUNTY OHIO ONE ROOM SCHOOLS. (Kalida OH: Putnam Co.Hist.Soc., 1985) 720,102p (LDS)

Slocum, Charles E. HISTORY OF THE MAUMEE RIVER BASIN. (Indianapolis: Bowen & Slocum, 1905) 638p (SLO)

Sommers, Edwin. PUTNAM COUNTY CENTENNIAL HISTORY, 1834-1934. (Ottawa OH: Centennial Committee, 1934) 176p (SLO,OHS,LDS)

Turnwald, Rita. HISTORY OF ST.MARY'S PARISH & SURROUNDING COUNTY AS TRANSLATED
    FROM DER DEMOKRAT, A GERMAN LANGUAGE NEWSPAPER PUBLISHED AT OTTAWA
    OHIO, 1887-1918. (Ottawa OH?: author, 1972)
Van Tassel, C.S. STORY OF THE MAUMEE VALLEY, TOLEDO & THE SANDUSKY REGION. (Chicago:
    S.J.Clarke Pub Co., 1929) 2v (OHS)
Winter, Nevin O. HISTORY OF NORTHWEST OHIO. (Chicago: Lewis Pub.Co., 1917) 3v (SLO,OHS)

# RICHLAND COUNTY

| | |
|---|---|
| CREATED: | 1808 FROM FAIRFIELD COUNTY |
| COUNTY SEAT: | MANSFIELD 44902 |
| COURT HOUSE: | 50 PARK AVE.WEST, MANSFIELD 44902 |
| LIBRARIES: | 43 W. THIRD ST., MANSFIELD 44902 |
| HISTORICAL SOCIETY: | 403 RICHLAND TRUST BLDG., MANSFIELD 44902 |
| GENEALOGICAL | OHIO GENEALOGICAL SOCIETY (STATE HEADQUARTERS) |
| SOCIETIES: | PO BOX 2625, MANSFIELD 44906 |
| | RICHLAND CO. CHAPTER, OGS, |
| | PO BOX 3154, LEXINGTON 44904 |
| | publication: THE PASTFINDER |
| HEALTH DEPARTMENT: | 600 WEST 3RD ST., MANSFIELD 44906 |
| | (separate offices for Mansfield city, Shelby & Crestline) |
| ARCHIVAL DISTRICT: | UNIVERSITY OF AKRON, AKRON, OHIO |
| | (see Folck's Guide to records) |
| LAND SURVEYS: | CONGRESS LANDS, OHIO RIVER SURVEY (NORTH) |
| BOUNDED BY: | EAST: ASHLAND CO. |
| | NORTH: HURON CO. |
| | WEST: CRAWFORD CO. |
| | SOUTH: KNOX & MORROW CO. |
| TOWNSHIPS: | Blooming Grove, Butler, Cass, Franklin, Jackson, Jefferson, Madison, Mifflin, Monroe, Perry, Plymouth, Sandusky, Sharon, Springfield, Troy, Washington, Weller, Worthington. |

## COURT RECORDS: (LDS MICROFILM)
Auditor:
    Tax duplicates, 1816-1838.
Childrens' Home:
    Indentures, 1883-1900.
    Minutes, 1880-1917.
Clerk of Courts:
    Chancery records, v1-10, 1822-1852.
    Index to journals, v1-27, 1820-1850.
    Common Pleas journals, v2-19, 1822-1852.
    Law record & index, 1819-1853.
Commissioners:
    Journal, 1816-1826, 1872-1903.
Probate Court:
    Birth records, alphabetical, 1856-1909.
    Register of births, 1893-1908.
    Mortality records, 1890-1908.
    Marriage records, v1-29, 1813-1930.
    Direct & reverse index to marriages, 1815-1940.
    Probate record & court journal, 1852-1874.
    Probate journal, v1-13, 1852-1886.
    Guardians' record & index, 1846-1905.

Will records, v1/2-13, 1816-1903.
Inventory records, v1-11, 1863-1884.
Administration index (docket) v1-3, 1837-1890.
Administration record, 1813-1885.
Administrators' & executors' bond record, v1-8, 1849-1891.
Naturalization records, final, v1-2, 1892-1906.
Naturalization intention, v1-3, 1852-1906.
General index to miscellaneous records, 1813-1900.
Recorder:
Grantee & grantor index to deeds, v1-7, 1814-1927.
Deed records, v1-140, 1814-1913.
Miscellaneous:
Plymouth, Assoc. Reformed Church, treas. records, 1831-1864.
Plymouth, Assoc. Reformed Church, session minutes, 1834-1856.
Lexington, First United Presby.Church, records, 1832-1983.
Mansield, First United Methodist Church, records, 1853-1982.
Register of Pastor David Hall, Mansfield, 1868-1874.
Cemetery records, State Library of Ohio collection.
Cemetery records, by LDS Church.
Mansfield, Ohio State Reformatory, admissions, 1896-1917.
Index of admissions, 1918-1954.

## OHIO HISTORICAL SOCIETY: (MICROFILM)

Childrens' Home:
Indentures, 1883-1900.
Minutes, 1880-1917.
Clerk of Courts:
Chancery records, v1-10, 1822-1852.
Index to journals, v1-27, 1820-1850.
Common Pleas journals, v2-19, 1822-1852.
Law record & index, 1819-1853.
Commissioners:
Journal, 1816-1826, 1872-1903.
Probate Court:
Naturalization records, final, v1-2, 1892-1906.
Naturalization intention, v1-3, 1852-1906.
Miscellaneous:
Commissioners' journals, 1813-1816, by DAR.
Marriages, v1-2, 1813-1864, by DAR.
Wills & administration record, 1813-1823, by DAR.
Cemetery records, by DAR.
Cemetery records of Knox,Guernsey,Morrow & Richland Cos., by DAR.

## CENSUS RECORDS (OHS,SLO,OGS,LDS)
1820-1880, 1900-1910; 1890 VETERANS; 1880,1900 SOUNDEX; 1910 MIRACODE

## AGRICULTURAL CENSUS SCHEDULES (OHS,SLO-mic)
1860

## PRODUCTS OF INDUSTRY CENSUS SCHEDULE (OHS,SLO-mic)
1850,1860,1870,1880

## MORTALITY CENSUS SCHEDULES (OHS,SLO-mic)
1850,1860

**NEWSPAPERS: [GUIDE TO OHIO NEWSPAPERS, 1793-1973]**
Bellville, Butler, Mansfield, Ontario, Plymouth, Shelby.

**TAX RECORDS (OHS & LDS)**
1814,1816-1838.

**MANUSCRIPTS:**
Eliza Bailey Paxton Diary, 1842. (OHS)
Lexington, Geo. W. Bowland saddle shop ledger, 1832-1851. (OHS)

**GENEALOGICAL PERIODICAL ARTICLES**
Bell, Carol Willsey. OHIO GENEALOGICAL PERIODICAL INDEX: A COUNTY GUIDE (Youngstown
    OH: author, 6th ed., 1987)

**PUBLISHED SOURCES:**
Andreas, A.T. ATLAS MAP OF RICHLAND COUNTY, OHIO. (Chicago: author, 1873) (Reprint,
    Evansville IN: Unigraphic, 1977) (LDS,OHS,DAR,OGS,LC) (RPI)
Atwater, Francis. HISTORY OF THE TOWN OF PLYMOUTH, CONNECTICUT...ALSO A SKETCH OF
    PLYMOUTH, OHIO, SETTLED BY LOCAL FAMILIES. (Meridan CT: Journal Pub.Co., c1895) 441p
    (DAR,LDS)
Bailey, A. THE HERALD'S DIRECTORY TO MANSFIELD, OHIO, 1883-84. 1883. (SLO)
Baughman, A.J. A CENTENNIAL BIOGRAPHICAL HISTORY OF RICHLAND & ASHLAND COUN-
    TIES OHIO. (Chicago: Lewis Pub.Co.,1901)(Reprint, Lexington OH: Richland Co Chapter OGS,
    1983). (LDS,LC,OHS,DAR,OGS,SLO)(RPI)
Baughman, A.J. HISTORY OF RICHLAND COUNTY OHIO. (Chicago: S.J.Clarke Pub.Co.,1908) 2v.
    (OGS,OHS,DAR,SLO,LDS) (RPI)
Brinkerhoff, Jacob. EARLY SETTLEMENT OF RICHLAND COUNTY OHIO AND DIRECTORY OF
    RESIDENTS...IN 1873. 24p (LDS)
Bristor, John H. HISTORY OF THE SCHOOLS OF MANSFIELD, OHIO. 1964. (SLO)
Budd, Anne D. RICHLAND COUNTY OHIO ABSTRACTS OF WILLS 1813-1873. (Mansfield OH: Ohio
    Gen Soc, 1974) 241p (OGS,SLO,OHS,DAR,LDS)
CEMETERIES - KNOX, RICHLAND, GUERNSEY & MORROW COUNTIES. 1r mic (SLO)
CEMETERY RECORDS OF RICHLAND COUNTY OHIO. 1961-1963. 4v (LDS)
CENTENNIAL FOURTH OF JULY, 1876. (Mansfield OH: np, 1876) (LDS)
CENTENNIAL HISTORY OF ST.PAUL'S LUTHERAN CHURCH, UNITED LUTHERAN CHURCH IN
    AMERICA, LUCAS, OHIO: ORGANIZED MAY 16, 1846, CENTENNIAL CELEBRATION MAY,
    19-26,1946. 16p (LDS)
CITY/COUNTY DIRECTORIES: check holdings of OHS & local public library.
COMBINED ATLASES OF RICHLAND COUNTY, OHIO, 1873-1896. (SLO)
COUNTY OF RICHLAND OHIO. IMPERIAL ATLAS & ART FOLIO. 1896.(OGS)(RPI)
Daughters of the American Revolution. BIRTH CERTIFICATES OF RICHLAND COUNTY OHIO. 1940?
    39p (DAR,SLO,LDS)
Daughters of the American Revolution. A COPY OF THE FIRST COMMISSIONERS' JOURNAL OF
    RICHLAND COUNTY, OHIO, FROM 1813 TO 1816. 1940. 33p (DAR,LDS,SLO)
Daughters of the American Revolution. DATA ON CEMETERIES IN RICHLAND COUNTY OHIO:
    WITH RECORDS OF FIRST BURIALS AND LOCATION OF CEMETERIES. 1940. 23p (DAR,LDS)
Daughters of the American Revolution. DEATH CERTIFICATES, RICHLAND COUNTY, OHIO: 1856-
    1870. 1940? 9p (DAR,LDS)
Daughters of the American Revolution. EARLY CHURCH HISTORY OF MANSFIELD. 1938. 42p (SLO)
Daughters of the American Revolution. FIRST WILLS AND ADMINISTRATION RECORDS. (SLO)
Daughters of the American Revolution. RECORDS OF RICHLAND COUNTY OHIO: MARRIAGES
    1813-1864, WILLS, 1813-1823. (DAR,LDS)
Daughters of the American Revolution. RICHLAND COUNTY OHIO MARRIAGES. 1936. 2v
    (DAR,SLO)

Daughters of the American Revolution. RICHLAND COUNTY OHIO REVOLUTIONARY SOLDIERS RECORDS. 40p (LDS)

Daughters of the American Revolution. RICHLAND COUNTY RECORDS. 2v (SLO)

Daughters of the American Revolution. WILLS DEFIANCE, RICHLAND, MAHONING COUNTIES. 1936? 200p (DAR)

Dirlam, H.Kenneth. YOUR LAND AND MY LAND: A BRIEF STORY ABOUT RICHLAND COUNTY OHIO. (Mansfield OH: Richland Co.Hist.Soc., 1963) 14p (OHS)

Dirlam, H.Kenneth. BITS OF HISTORY FROM TALKS HERE & THERE, 2nd Ed. (Mansfield OH: Richland Co.Hist.Soc., 1965) 1v (OHS,SLO,LDS)

Duff, William A. HISTORY OF NORTH CENTRAL OHIO EMBRACING RICHLAND, ASHLAND, WAYNE, MEDINA, LORAIN, HURON, AND KNOX COUNTIES. (Topeka KS: Historical Pub Co., 1931) 3v (OHS,DAR)

Fisher, David G. RECORDS OF FIRST ENGLISH EVANGELICAL LUTHERAN CHURCH, CRESTLINE OHIO 1854-1935. [CRAWFORD & RICHLAND COS.] (Columbus OH: author, 1979) 95p (OGS,SLO)

Fleming, May. HISTORY OF PLYMOUTH, OHIO, 1815 TO 1930. 1965. 13p (LDS,SLO)

Folck, Linda. LOCAL GOVERNMENT RECORDS IN THE AMERICAN HISTORY RESEARCH CENTER AT THE UNIVERSITY OF AKRON. (Akron: U of Akron, 1982) 40p. (OGS)

Frank, Henrietta A. A HISTORY OF THE MANY CHURCHES OF MANSFIELD OHIO. 1938. 50p (DAR)

Frank, Henrietta A. REVOLUTIONARY SOLDIERS, RECORDS OF RICHLAND COUNTY OHIO. 1940? 40p (DAR,LDS)

Grace Episcopal Church. OUR FIRST HUNDRED YEARS: GRACE EPISCOPAL CHURCH, MANSFIELD, OHIO. (Mansfield OH: the church, nd) 147p (DAR,SLO)

Graham, A.A. HISTORY OF RICHLAND COUNTY OHIO. (Mansfield OH: author, 1880) (Reprint, Lexington OH: Richland Co Chapter OGS, 1972) 938p (OGS,DAR,SLO,LDS,LC)(RPI)

HARDESTY'S HISTORICAL & GENEALOGICAL ENCYCLOPEDIA, SPECIAL MILITARY HISTORY OF RICHLAND COUNTY OHIO. (New York: H.H.Hardesty, 1885) 532p (OGS,OHS)

Hixson, W.W. PLAT BOOK OF RICHLAND COUNTY OHIO. n.d. (OHS)

Johnson, P.R. CLASSIFIED BUSINESS AND PROFESSIONAL DIRECTORY OF PROMINENT TOWNS AND CITIES OF OHIO AND EASTERN INDIANA. (Columbus OH: Berlin Printing, 1899) 303p (LDS)

Keene, Mrs. Howard N. HISTORY, THE FIRST CONGREGATIONAL CHURCH, 1835-1960. 42p (LDS)

Kinton, Maxine L. 1880 FEDERAL POPULATIONS CENSUS, RICHLAND COUNTY, OHIO, INDEX (Lexington OH: Richland Co Chapter OGS,1986) 103pp. (OGS,LDS)

Kinton, Maxine L. RICHLAND COUNTY OHIO DEEDS - UNITED STATES TO ORIGINAL OWNER. (Mansfield OH: author, 1982) 21p. (OGS,LDS)

Kinton, Maxine L. RICHLAND COUNTY OHIO NATURALIZATIONS. (Mansfield OH: author, 1986) 58,159p (LDS)

LEXINGTON AREA OHIO SESQUICENTENNIAL HISTORICAL PROGRAM 1814-1964. (Lexington OH: the committee, 1964) 52p (OGS,LDS)

M'Gaw, James F. PHILIP SEYMOUR: OR, PIONEER LIFE IN RICHLAND COUNTY OHIO. (Mansfield OH: R.Brickerhoff, 1858) 279p (DAR,LDS)

McConnell, George E. SOME CEMETERIES OF RICHLAND COUNTY OHIO. n.d. 3p (OHS,LDS)

MANSFIELD CITY DIRECTORIES, 1908-1909. (LDS)

NEWSPAPER CLIPPINGS AND MEMORABILIA, JEFFERSON TOWNSHIP, RICHLAND COUNTY OHIO. [SCRAPBOOK] 75p (OGS)

Raber, Nellie M. INDEX OF FIRST WILLS OF RICHLAND CO., OHIO, 1813-1855. (Kokomo IN: Selby Pub.Co., 1984) 58p (LDS)

Rerick Brothers. THE COUNTY OF RICHLAND OHIO; AN IMPERIAL ATLAS. (Richmond IN: authors, 1896)(Reprint, Evansville IN: Unigraphic, 1977) 109p (OHS,SLO,LDS)

Richland Co Chapter OGS. BIOGRAPHICAL HISTORY OF RICHLAND COUNTY, OHIO. 1983. 278p (SLO)

Richland Co Chapter OGS. COMBINED ATLASES OF RICHLAND COUNTY OHIO, 1873 & 1896. (Reprint, Lexington OH: the society, 1977) (OGS)

Richland Co Chapter OGS. LEXINGTON SESQUICENTENNIAL PICTORIAL BOOKLET. (LDS)

Richland Co Chapter OGS. MANSFIELD 175TH BIRTHDAY PICTORIAL BOOKLET. (LDS)

Richland Co Chapter OGS. RICHLAND COUNTY OHIO CEMETERY RECORDS. (Lexington OH: the society, 1981) 501p (OGS,DAR,OHS,SLO)

Richland Co Chapter OGS. 1880 FEDERAL POPULATION CENSUS, RICHLAND COUNTY OHIO, INDEX. (Lexington OH: the society, 1986) 103p (OGS)

Richland Co.Hist.Soc. PROCEEDINGS OF THE RICHLAND COUNTY HISTORICAL SOCIETY. (Mansfield OH: the society, 1905-) (LDS)

Richland Co.Hist.Soc. THE UNDERGROUND RAILROAD IN RICHLAND COUNTY: ACTUAL EXPERIENCES OF UNDERGROUND RAILROAD CONDUCTORS AND OTHER HITHERTO UNPUBLISHED MATERIAL. (Mansfield OH: the society, 1963?) 1v (LDS)

RICHLAND COUNTY OHIO 1982 PLAT BOOK. (Mansfield OH: Farmers Production Credit Assn., 1982) 56p. (OGS)

SCRAPBOOK - RICHLAND AND ASHLAND COUNTY OHIO. [OBITS, c1880-1900] 109p. (OGS)

SCRAPBOOK OF CLIPPINGS, 1904-1905, RICHLAND COUNTY OHIO. 283p (OGS)

SCRAPBOOK OF NEWSPAPER ARTICLES WHICH APPEARD IN "THE OHIO LIBERAL" BY R.BRINKERHOFF, c1860s. (OHS)

Urban, Mrs. Ernest. RECORDS OF THE ENGLISH EVANGELICAL LUTHERAN CONGREGATION OF MANSFIELD OHIO. [1849-1882] (Mansfield OH: author, 1982) 122p. (OGS)

Wilkinson, Raymond M. THE BEGINNING...SHELBY, OHIO: SOME HIGHLIGHTS OF ITS EARLY HISTORY. 1976. 125p (DAR)

WORLD'S WAR NEWS OF OHIO (RICHLAND COUNTY EDITION) 1918-1919. (OHS)

# ROSS COUNTY

| | |
|---|---|
| CREATED: | 1798 FROM ADAMS & WASHINGTON COUNTIES |
| COUNTY SEAT: | CHILLICOTHE 45601 |
| COURT HOUSE: | corner PAINT & MAIN ST., CHILLICOTHE 45601 |
| LIBRARIES: | 140-146 S. PAINT ST., CHILLICOTHE 45601 |
| HISTORICAL SOCIETY: | 45 W. 5TH AVE., CHILLICOTHE 45601 |
| GENEALOGICAL SOCIETY: | ROSS CO. CHAPTER OGS, |
| | PO BOX 395, CHILLICOTHE 45601 |
| | publication: NEWSLETTER |
| HEALTH DEPARTMENT: | 425 CHESTNUT ST., CHILLICOTHE 45601 |
| | (separate office for Chillicothe city) |
| ARCHIVAL DISTRICT: | OHIO UNIVERSITY, ATHENS |
| | (see published Guide to records) |
| LAND SURVEYS: | VIRGINIA MILITARY DISTRICT |
| | CONGRESS LANDS, OHIO RIVER SURVEY (SOUTH) |
| | ZANE'S TRACTS |
| BOUNDED BY: | EAST: HOCKING & VINTON CO. |
| | NORTH: PICKAWAY CO. |
| | WEST: FAYETTE & HIGHLAND CO. |
| | SOUTH: JACKSON & PIKE CO. |
| TOWNSHIPS: | Buckskin, Colerain, Concord, Deerfield, Franklin, Green, Harrison, Huntington, Jefferson, Liberty, Paint, Paxton, Scioto, Springfield, Twin, Union. |

**COURT RECORDS: (LDS MICROFILM)**

Auditor:

   Tax duplicates, 1808,1810,1816-1838,1865.

   Military commutations, 1864.

Clerk of Courts:

   Register of blacks in Ohio counties, 1804-1855.

   Common Pleas general index, c1830-1870.

Common Pleas order book, 1798-1811.
Common Pleas court record, 1804-1813.
Common Pleas complete record, 1803-1852.
Supreme Court record, 1803-1847.
Clerk's bar docket, 1896-1899.
Execution docket, 1807-1819,1802-1806.
Chancery & partition records, 1824-1852.
Jury book, 1875-1885,1885-1893.
Justice commissions, 1830-1855.
Record of commission, notary publics, 1858-1886.
Rule docket, 1810-1818.
Witness books, 1803-1829,1852-1859.
Quarter sessions appearance docket, 1799-1844.
Estrays records, 1805-1823,1862-1918.
Tavern licenses, 1815-1839.
Commissioners:
Journal, 1861-1904.
Index to journals, 1875-1901.
Order book, 1809-1846.
Probate Court:
Will records, vA-H, 1797-1879.
Marriage records, vA-9, 1798-1910.
Index to marriages, 1803-1852.
Marriage affidavits, 1853-1876.
Death records & index, 1867-1908.
Birth records & index, 1867-1908.
Corrected & omitted births, v1-19, c1870-1960.
General index, A-Z, v1-2, 1801-1887.
Administration docket, v1, 1853-1861.
Administrators & exrs.docket, v2, 1881-1896.
Admr., exr.& guardians docket, v1, 1874-1895.
Testamentary docket, 1816-1853.
Administration bonds, v1-4, 1849-1882.
Administrators appointments, 1882-1886.
Executors bonds & letters, v1-2, 1849-1881.
Executors appointments, 1882-1891.
Guardians bonds, v1-2, 1849-1876.
Appointment of guardians, 1876-1889.
Probate journal, v1-12, 1853-1886.
Naturalization records, 1851-1906.
Recorder:
Veterans grave registration, 1790-1920.
Index to deed records, 1797-1900.
Deeds, v1-200, 1798-1925.
Chillicothe city index, 1899-1945.
Towns & villages index, 1900-1923.
Sectional land, 1923-1937.
Military discharges, 1861-1918.
Sheriff:
Jail register, 1881-1910.
Miscellaneous:
Bourneville Presby.Church, records, 1888-1898.
Chillicothe Memorial Presby.Church, records, 1869-1883.
Buckskin Presby.Church, session book, 1804-1822, 1838-1863.
Chillicothe First New Jerusalem Society, records, 1838-1879.

Concord Presby.Church, records, 1804-1820.
Chillicothe, THE SCIOTO GAZETTE, 1802-1803.
Londonderry Monthly Meeting, minutes, 1871-1948.
Abel Larkin family papers, 1790-1895. (WRHS)
Cemetery records, State Library of Ohio collection.

**OHIO HISTORICAL SOCIETY: (MICROFILM)**
Auditor:
    Military commutations, 1864.
Clerk of Courts:
    Register of blacks in Ohio counties, 1804-1855.
    Common Pleas general index, c1830-1870.
    Common Pleas order book, 1798-1803.
    Common Pleas complete record, 1803-1852.
    Supreme Court record, 1805-1843.
Commissioners:
    Journal, 1861-1904.
    Index to journals, 1875-1901.
    Order book, 1809-1846.
Recorder:
    Military discharges, 1861-1918.
Sheriff:
    Jail register, 1881-1910.
Miscellaneous:
    Abstracts of wills (1797-1845) and estates (1798-1903) by DAR.
    Index to marriage records, 1798-1890, by DAR.
    Marriage records, 1798-1890, by DAR.
    Presbyterian church records, South Salem, by DAR.
    Tombstone inscriptions of Ross Co. & other counties, by DAR.
    Shanton Cemetery, North Union Tp., by DAR.

**CENSUS RECORDS  (OHS,SLO,OGS,LDS)**
1820-1880, 1900-1910; 1890 VETERANS; 1880,1900 SOUNDEX; 1910 MIRACODE

**AGRICULTURAL CENSUS SCHEDULES  (OHS,SLO-mic)**
1850,1860

**PRODUCTS OF INDUSTRY CENSUS SCHEDULE  (OHS,SLO-mic)**
1850,1860,1870,1880

**MORTALITY CENSUS SCHEDULES (OHS,SLO-mic)**
1850,1860

**NEWSPAPERS: [GUIDE TO OHIO NEWSPAPERS, 1793-1973]**
Adelphi, Bainbridge, Chillicothe, Kingston.

**TAX RECORDS (OHS & LDS)**
1800,1801,1806-1814,1816-1838.

**MANUSCRIPTS:**
Bainbridge, N.Smith tavern ledger, 1826-1830. (OHS)
Bainbridge, J.G.White general store daybook, 1830-1855. (OHS)
Bainbridge, C.B. Cobb general store ledger, 1840-41, 1844-48. (OHS)
Bourneville, Straight-Outs Club, members, 1840. (OHS)
Chillicothe First New Jerusalem Society, records, 1838-1879. (WRHS)

Chillicothe Meth.-Prot. Church, records, 1854-1861. (WRHS)
Robert Harper's riflemen, record book, Apr-Jly 1813. (OHS)
Abel Larkin family papers (incl.Sheriff rec. & Meth-Prot.church) (WRHS)

## GENEALOGICAL PERIODICAL ARTICLES
Bell, Carol Willsey. OHIO GENEALOGICAL PERIODICAL INDEX: A COUNTY GUIDE (Youngstown, OH: author, 6th ed., 1987)

## PUBLISHED SOURCES:
ABSTRACTS OF LAND RECORDS. 1r mic. (SLO)
ABSTRACT OF WILLS, ROSS COUNTY, OHIO, 1798-1848. (LDS)
Adams, Marilyn. INDEX TO CIVIL WAR VETERANS & WIDOWS IN SOUTHERN OHIO, 1890 FEDERAL CENSUS (Cols,OH: Franklin Co Chapter OGS,1986)84p
AN ABSTRACT OF WILLS, ROSS COUNTY, OHIO, 1798-1848. n.d. 82p (LDS)
Bennett, Henry H. STATE CENTENNIAL HISTORY OF ROSS COUNTY. (Madison WI: Selwyn A.Brant, 1902) (Reprint, Chillicothe OH: Ross Co Chapter OGS, 1981) 845p (SLO,OGS,LC,LDS,OHS)(RPI)
BICENTENNIAL ATLAS OF ROSS COUNTY, OHIO, 1776-1976. (Chillicothe OH: Bicentennial Commission, 1976) 37p (LC,LDS,OGS)
Blosser, Katherine D. ROSS COUNTY OHIO TOMBSTONE RECORDS OF PERSONS BORN IN 1800 OR EARLIER. 1958? 117p (DAR,LDS)
CENTENNIAL 1855-1955 OF THE PRESBYTERIAN CHURCH, SOUTH SALEM, OHIO. (SLO)
CHILLICOTHE AND ROSS COUNTY. (Columbus OH: F.J.Heer, 1938) 91p (LC)
CHILLICOTHE, OHIO'S FIRST CAPITAL. (Chillicothe OH: Civic Assn., 1941) 31p (LDS)
Chillicothe News-Advertiser. CENTENNIAL EDITION, 16 NOV 1931. (LDS)
CITY/COUNTY DIRECTORIES: check holdings of OHS & local public library.
Clark, Marie T. OHIO LANDS: CHILLICOTHE LAND OFFICE, 1800-1829. (Chillicothe: author, 1984) 148p (OGS,SLO,OHS,LDS)
Clark, Marie T. OHIO LANDS: SOUTH OF THE INDIAN BOUNDARY LINE. (Chillicothe: author, 1984) 145p (OGS,LDS)
Clark, Marie T. TOMBSTONE INSCRIPTIONS OF GRANDVIEW CEMETERY, CHILLICOTHE, OHIO, ROSS COUNTY. (Evansville IN: Unigraphic, 1972) 439p (LDS,SLO)
Clark, Marie T. VETERANS' GRAVES REGISTRATION, V1-3. (LDS)
Clarksburg High School. THE RISE AND PROGRESS OF THE DEER CREEK SETTLEMENT. (Chillicothe: Alumni Assn., 1984) 90p (LDS)
Cokanougher, Ralph W. GRAVESTONE INSCRIPTIONS IN ROSS COUNTY OHIO. 2v (New Holland OH: author, 1979) 61p (OGS,LDS,SLO)
Core, Mrs. John. GREENFIELD OHIO CHURCH AND CEMETERY RECORD. (DAR,LDS)
COUNTY OF ROSS: A HISTORY OF ROSS COUNTY OHIO FROM THE EARLIEST DAYS... (Madison WI: S.A.Brant, 1902) 736p (LDS)
Crouse, David E. HISTORY OF KINGSTON AND RURAL VICINITY, PUBLISHED IN CELEBRATION OF THE CENTENNIAL ANNIVERSARY. (Kingston OH: committee, 1934) 106p (OHS)
Daughters of the American Revolution. ABSTRACTS OF WILL BOOKS A,B,C & D, ROSS COUNTY OHIO: INCLUDING RECORDS OF ADMINISTRATION OF ESTATES. 1961. (SLO,DAR)
Daughters of the American Revolution. CHURCH RECORDS (BUCKSKIN CHURCH AT SOUTH SALEM SESSION RECORDS, WITH BAPTISMS c1802-1820). (SLO,LDS)
Daughters of the American Revolution. CEMETERY RECORDS: FAIRFIELD, PICKAWAY, ROSS & FRANKLIN COUNTY OHIO. 1953. 33p (DAR,LDS)
Daughters of the American Revolution. FAMILIY GENEALOGIES OF THE JULIANA WHITE CHAPTER, DAR. (SLO)
Daughters of the American Revolution. FIRST SESSION BOOK AND THIRD SESSION BOOK OF THE BUCKSKIN-SALEM PRESBYTERIAN CHURCH AT SOUTH SALEM, ROSS COUNTY OHIO. (SLO,DAR)
Daughters of the American Revolution. FOURTH SESSION BOOK OF THE BUCKSKINSALEM PRESBYTERIAN CHURCH AT SOUTH SALEM, ROSS COUNTY OHIO. (SLO,DAR)

Daughters of the American Revolution. GRAVESTONE INSCRIPTIONS IN COUNTIES SURROUND-ING PICKAWAY. (SLO)

Daughters of the American Revolution. MARRIAGE RECORDS, ROSS COUNTY OHIO, 1798-1890. 8v (SLO,LDS,DAR)

Daughters of the American Revolution. OHIO FAMILY RECORDS (CEMETERIES AND GRAVES OF EARLY SETTLERS BORN BEFORE 1860 & BURIED IN ROSS COUNTY)(SLO)

Daughters of the American Revolution. PISGAH PRESBYTERIAN CHURCH OF ROSS COUNTY OHIO, GENERAL EARLY RECORDS, 1810-1850; CONCORD CHURCH NEAR LATTAVILLE; & BUCKSKIN CHURCH. 1957. (DAR,LDS)

Daughters of the American Revolution. TOMBSTONE RECORDS OF PERSONS BORN IN 1800 OR EARLIER, ROSS COUNTY, OHIO. (SLO)

Daughters of the American Revolution. WILL ABSTRACTS, CHURCH & CEMETERY RECORDS, ROSS COUNTY OHIO. 1963. (SLO,LDS)

DEEDS, FAIRFIELD AND ROSS COUNTIES, OHIO (FRANKLIN COUNTY TODAY) 1r mic (SLO)

Dolle, Mrs. Percy A. ROSS COUNTY OHIO REVOLUTIONARY SOLDIERS. 1960. (SLO)

Evans, Lyle S. STANDARD HISTORY OF ROSS COUNTY OHIO. (Chicago: Lewis Pub.Co., 1917) 2v. (Reprint, Chillicothe OH: Ross Co Chapter OGS, 1987) (LDS,SLO,OHS,DAR,LC)

Federal Writers Project, Ohio. CHILLICOTHE AND ROSS COUNTY. (Chillicothe OH: authors, 1938) 91p (OHS,SLO,DAR)

Finley, Isaac J. PIONEER RECORD AND REMINISCENCES OF THE EARLY SETTLERS AND SET-TLEMENT OF ROSS COUNTY OHIO. (Cincinnati: R.Clarke & Co.,1871) 148p (LC,OHS,LDS,SLO,DAR) (RPI)

Galbraith, Robert C. THE HISTORY OF THE CHILLICOTHE PRESBYTERY, FROM ITS ORGANIZA-TION IN 1799-1899. (Chillicothe OH: Scioto Gazette Job Office, 1889) 431p (LDS,DAR)

Galloway, William A. OLD CHILLICOTHE: SHAWNEE AND PIONEER HISTORY. (Xenia OH: Buck-eye Press, 1934) (Reprint, Evansville IN: Unigraphic, 1974) 336p (LDS)

Gough, Joy. CHILLICOTHE FIRST CAPITAL GUIDEBOOK. 1980. 32p.

Gould, H.T. & Co. ILLUSTRATED ATLAS OF ROSS COUNTY OHIO. (Columbus: author, 1875) (Reprint, Chillicothe OH: Ross Co Chapter OGS, 1975) 83p (LC,OHS,OGS,SLO)(RPI)

Grabb, John R. THE CANAL - ITS RISE AND FALL IN ROSS COUNTY. (Chillicothe OH: Ross Co Chapter OGS, 1985) 50p

Gragg, Rodney. BOURNEVILLE OHIO STORY. (Chillicothe OH: Ross Co Chapter OGS, 1973) 21p (OGS,LDS)

Grady, Herbert. MITCHELL CEMETERY INSCRIPTIONS, BOURNEVILLE, ROSS COUNTY OHIO. 1p. (LDS)

Green, Karen M. PIONEER OHIO NEWSPAPERS, 1793-1810: GENEALOGICAL & HISTORICAL ABSTRACTS. (Galveston TX: Frontier Press, 1986) 383p (OGS)

Green, Karen M. PIONEER OHIO NEWSPAPERS, 1802-1818: GENEALOGICAL & HISTORICAL ABSTRACTS. (Galveston TX: Frontier Press, 1988) 362p (OGS)

Hardesty, H.H. MILITARY HISTORY OF OHIO - ROSS COUNTY EDITION. 1886/87. (OHS)

Historical Records Survey. INVENTORY OF THE COUNTY ARCHIVES OF OHIO, NO.71, ROSS COUNTY. (Columbus: author, 1939) 307p (LDS,OHS,DAR)

HISTORY OF ROSS AND HIGHLAND COUNTIES, OHIO, WITH ILLUSTRATIONS AND BIOGRAPHICAL SKETCHES. (Cleveland: Williams Bros., 1880) 532p (DAR,LC,LDS,OHS,SLO)

Hixson, W.W. PLAT BOOK OF ROSS COUNTY OHIO. (Rockford IL: author, n.d.) (OHS)

Johnson, P.R. CLASSIFIED BUSINESS AND PROFESSIONAL DIRECTORY OF PROMINENT TOWNS AND CITIES OF OHIO AND EASTERN INDIANA. (Columbus OH: Berlin Printing, 1899) 303p (LDS)

King, Mrs. Orion. GRAVESTONE INSCRIPTIONS IN COUNTIES SURROUNDING PICKAWAY. (SLO,LDS)

Kingston Area Historical Society. HISTORY OF KINGSTON OHIO. (Kingston OH: the society, 1984) 109p.109p (LDS)

McDonald, John. WESTERN SKETCHES. 1852.(Reprint, Chillicothe OH: Ross Co Chapter OGS, 1979) 260p

McKell, David. ROSS COUNTY'S LITTLE KNOWN INDIAN YEARS, 1752-1774. (Chillicothe: Ross Co.Hist.Soc., 1942) 12p (OHS)
Mark, Clara. CEMETERY RECORDS [ROSS CO., OHIO]. 1948. 21p (DAR)
MILITARY HISTORY OF OHIO, ROSS COUNTY EDITION. 1886-1887. (OHS)
Morgan, J.B.F. THE RISE AND PROGRESS OF THE DEERCREEK SETTLEMENT. (Chillicothe OH: Ross Co Chapter OGS, 1984) 90p (OGS)
Ohio University. GUIDE TO LOCAL GOVERNMENT RECORDS AT OHIO UNIVERSITY. (Athens: OU Library, 1986) 61p.
Pemberton, H.C. REVOLUTIONARY SOLDIERS, ROSS COUNTY OHIO. COMPILED FROM OBITUARY NOTICES IN NEWSPAPERS, PENSION RECORDS AND OHIO ROSTER. n.d.1v.(OHS)
Prestel, Mrs. G.K. BISHOP HILL METHODIST CHURCH CEMETERY, HUNTINGTON TOWNSHIP, OHIO. (Tacoma WA: author, n.d.) 6p (LDS)
Provolt, Lois. ORIGINAL INVENTORY BOOK, 1798-1801: INVENTORIES AND APPRAISEMENTS OF THE GOODS, CHATTELS, RIGHTS AND CREDITS OF DECEASED PERSONS OF ROSS COUNTY IN THE TERRITORY OF THE UNITED STATES OF AMERICA NORTHWEST OF THE OHIO. 197? 4p (LDS)
Provolt, Lois. THE LIST OF MARRIAGES FOR ROSS COUNTY OHIO FOR THE YEARS 1798-1803 AND FOR THE YEARS 1808-1809. (Trinidad CA: author, nd) 18p (OGS)
Raber, Nellie M. WAUGH CEMETERY RECORDS, BUCKSKIN TWP., ROSS COUNTY OHIO. (Columbia City IN: author, 1964) 7p (LDS)
Rankin, Jane T. HIXON CEMETERY, BUCKSKIN TOWNSHIP, ROSS CO., OHIO. (LDS)
Rankin, Maude P. CEMETERY RECORDS, FAYETTE CO., OHIO, V.3, WASHINGTON COURT HOUSE CITY CEMETERY WITH A FEW FROM SURROUNDING COUNTIES. (DAR,LDS)
Rankin, Maude P. ROSS COUNTY, OHIO, PIKE COUNTY, OHIO CEMETERIES; EARLY MARRIAGES OF ROSS CO., OHIO. (LDS)
Rankin, Maude P. SESSION RECORDS AND CEMETERY INSCRIPTIONS OF CONCORD CHURCH, ROSS COUNTY, OHIO. (LDS)
Renick, L.W. CHE-LE-CO-THE: GLIMPSES OF YESTERDAY. (Chillicothe OH: author, 1896) 261p (SLO,DAR,LDS)
Robinson, George Jr. ABSTRACT OF WILL BOOKS, A,B,C AND D, INCLUDING RECORDS OF ADMINISTRATION OF ESTATES. (DAR,LDS)
ROSS COUNTY OHIO CEMETERY RECORDS, SPARGUSVILLE CEMETERY. (SLO)
Ross Co Chapter OGS. ROSS COUNTY OHIO FAMILY BIBLE RECORDS, VOL.I. (Chillicothe OH: the society, 1984) 149p (OGS,OHS,LDS,SLO)
Ross Co Chapter OGS. ROSS COUNTY OHIO FAMILIES, BICENTENNIAL EDITION [VOL.I] (Chillicothe OH: the society, 1976) (SLO,DAR,LDS)
Ross Co Chapter OGS. ROSS COUNTY OHIO FAMILIES VOL.II. (Chillicothe OH: the society, 1979) 720p (OGS,OHS,LDS,SLO)
Ross Co Chapter OGS. ROSS COUNTY OHIO FAMILIES, VOL.III. (Chillicothe OH: the society, 1982) 627p (OGS,OHS,LDS,SLO)
Ross Co Chapter OGS. TOMBSTONE INSCRIPTIONS OF GREEN TWP., ROSS CO OHIO (Chillicothe OH: the society, 1986) 140p (OGS,OHS,LDS)
Smith, Clifford N. FEDERAL LAND SERIES: A CALENDAR OF ARCHIVAL MATERIAL ON THE LAND PATENTS ISSUED BY THE U.S.GOVERNMENT, VOL.4, PT 1: GRANTS IN THE VIRGINIA MILITARY DISTRICT OF OHIO. (Chicago: American Library Assn., 1982) 395p
Smith, Clifford N. FEDERAL LAND SERIES: A CALENDAR OF ARCHIVAL MATERIAL ON THE LAND PATENTS ISSUED BY THE U.S.GOVERNMENT, VOL.4, PT 2: GRANTS IN THE VIRGINIA MILITARY DISTRICT OF OHIO. (Chicago: American Library Assn., 1986) 306p
SOUTH SALEM PRESBY.CHURCH SESQUI-CENTENNIAL ANNIVERSARY, 1802-1952.(SLO)
Turpin, Joan. REGISTER OF BLACK, MULATTO & POOR PERSONS IN FOUR OHIO COUNTIES, [CLINTON,HIGHLAND,LOGAN & ROSS] 1791-1861. (Bowie MD: Heritage Books, 1985) 44p (OHS,LDS)
Williams Brothers. HISTORY OF ROSS AND HIGHLAND COUNTIES OHIO. 1880. (Reprint, Chillicothe OH: Ross Co Chapter OGS, 1972) 640p (SLO)(RPI)

Works Projects Administration, Ohio. CHILLICOTH, OHIO'S FIRST CAPITAL. (Chillicothe OH: Civic
    Assn., c1941) 31p (DAR)
WORLD'S WAR NEWS OHIO OHIO, ROSS COUNTY, 1918-1919. (OHS)
Yon, Paul D. GUIDE TO OHIO COUNTY AND MUNICIPAL GOVERNMENT RECORDS FOR URBAN
    RESEARCH. (Columbus: Ohio Hist Soc., 1973) 216p.(OHS)

# SANDUSKY COUNTY

| | |
|---|---|
| CREATED: | 1820 FROM HURON CO. |
| COUNTY SEAT: | FREMONT 43420 |
| COURT HOUSE: | 100 N.PARK AVE., FREMONT 43420 |
| LIBRARIES: | 423 CROGHAN ST., FREMONT 43420 |
| | RUTHERFORD B. HAYES LIBRARY, |
| | 1337 HAYES AVE., FREMONT 43420 |
| HISTORICAL SOCIETY: | c/o HAYES LIBRARY, FREMONT 43420 |
| GENEALOGICAL SOCIETY: | SANDUSKY COUNTY KINHUNTERS, |
| | 1337 HAYES AVE., FREMONT 43420 |
| | publication: KITH AND KIN |
| HEALTH DEPARTMENT: | 108 S.PARK AVE., FREMONT 43420 |
| | (separate offices for Fremont city, Clyde & Bellevue) |
| ARCHIVAL DISTRICT: | BOWLING GREEN STATE UNIVERSITY, BOWLING GREEN |
| | (see Biggs' Guide to records) |
| LAND SURVEYS: | CONGRESS LANDS, E & N OF 1ST PRIN.MERIDIAN |
| | TWO MILE SQUARE RESERVE, 1805 |
| BOUNDED BY: | EAST:    ERIE & HURON CO. |
| | NORTH:  OTTAWA CO. & LAKE ERIE |
| | WEST:    WOOD CO. |
| | SOUTH:   SENECA CO. |
| TOWNSHIPS: | Ballville, Green Creek, Jackson, Madison, Rice, Riley, Sandusky, Scott, |
| | Townsend, Washington, Woodville, York. |

**COURT RECORDS: (LDS MICROFILM)**
Auditor:
    Tax duplicates, 1823-1838.
Clerk of Courts:
    Appearance docket, 1821-1849.
    Chancery records, v1-8, 1826-1856.
    Common Pleas journal, v1-7, 1820-1856.
    Common Pleas record, 1827-1838.
    District Court record, 1852-1856.
    Execution docket, 1841-1854.
    Journal, v1-8, 1827-1861.
    Naturalizations, 1830-1860.
    Supreme Court law record, v2-4, 1837-1846.
    Supreme Court record, v5, 1846-1847.
    Supreme Court & district court record, 1848-1856.
    Supreme Court journals, 1823-1851.
    Supreme Court appearance docket, 1838-1857.
    Supreme Court witness record, 1838-1857.
County Home:
    Infirmary register, v1, 1882-1936.
Probate Court:
    Administration docket, v34, 1837-1842.
    Administration record, v1-2, 1820-1841.

Administrators bonds & letters, 1852-1888.
Marriages, vA-37, 1820-1967.
Index to marriages, n.d.
Record of births & deaths, v1-4, 1867-1916.
Records of the Probate Court, #1--4450, 1820-1911.
Record of wills, vA-50, 1836-1959.
Index to wills, v.1
General index, 1820-1965.
Guardians docket, v1, 1880-1901.
Guardians bonds & letters, 1852-1857.
Executors bonds & letters, 1852-1886.
Journal, vA-H, 1852-1886.
Final record, v1-19, 1852-1910.
Naturalizations, declarations of aliens, 1830-1854,1859-1906.
Index to final record of naturalizations, 1857-1907.
Naturalization record of minors, 1859-1912.
Naturalization record of aliens, 1875-1905.
Naturalization final record, 1875-1902.
Naturalization record, 2nd papers, 1902-1903.
Probate packets, #1-4450.
Recorder:
Index to deeds, 1822-1902.
Deeds, vA-74, 1822-1902.
Soldiers' discharge, 1865-1937.
Miscellaneous:
Cemetery records by Northwestern Ohio Genealogical Society.
Clyde, McPherson Cemetery record & burial record.
Helena, Shiloh United Methodist Church, records, 1822-1895.

## OHIO HISTORICAL SOCIETY: (MICROFILM)
Clerk of Courts:
Chancery record, v5-8, 1845-1856.
Common Pleas journal, v1-7, 1820-1856.
Common Pleas record, 1827-1838.
District Court record, 1852-1856.
Supreme Court law record, v2-4, 1837-1846.
Supreme Court record, v5, 1846-1847.
Supreme Court & district court record, 1848-1856.
Supreme Court journals, 1823-1851.
Supreme Court appearance docket, 1838-1857.
Supreme Court witness record, 1838-1857.
County Home:
Infirmary register, v1, 1882-1936.
Probate Court:
Administration docket, v34, 1837-1842.
Administration record, v1-2, 1820-1841.
Final record, v1-19, 1852-1910.
Naturalizations, declarations of aliens, 1830-1854,1859-1906.
Index to final record of naturalizations, 1857-1907.
Naturalization record of minors, 1859-1912.
Naturalization record of aliens, 1875-1905.
Naturalization final record, 1875-1902.
Naturalization record, 2nd papers, 1902-1903.
Recorder:
Soldiers' discharge, 1865-1937.

Deed index, 1822-1902.
Deed records, 1822-1902.
Miscellaneous:
Marriage records, 1820-1870, by DAR.
Cemetery inscriptions & Rev.soldiers' burial, by DAR.

## CENSUS RECORDS (OHS,SLO,OGS,LDS)
1820-1880, 1900-1910; 1890 VETERANS; 1880,1900 SOUNDEX; 1910 MIRACODE

## AGRICULTURAL CENSUS SCHEDULES (OHS,SLO-mic)
1850,1860

## PRODUCTS OF INDUSTRY CENSUS SCHEDULE (OHS,SLO-mic)
1850,1860,1870,1880

## MORTALITY CENSUS SCHEDULES (OHS,SLO-mic)
1850,1860

## NEWSPAPERS: [GUIDE TO OHIO NEWSPAPERS, 1793-1973]
Clyde, Fremont, Gibsonburg, Lower Sandusky, Woodville.

## TAX RECORDS (OHS & LDS)
1823-1838.

## MANUSCRIPTS:
Receipt book, 1864, of draftees in Erie, Crawford, Huron, Ottawa, Sandusky & Seneca Counties Ohio
who purchased substitutes. (OHS)

## GENEALOGICAL PERIODICAL ARTICLES
Bell, Carol Willsey. OHIO GENEALOGICAL PERIODICAL INDEX: A COUNTY GUIDE (Youngstown,
OH: author, 6th ed., 1987)

## PUBLISHED SOURCES:
Biggs, Deb. GUIDE TO LOCAL GOVERNMENT RECORDS AT THE CENTER FOR ARCHIVAL COL-
LECTIONS. (Bowling Green OH: Bowling Green State Univ, 1981) 104p (OGS)
Bowland, James M. PIONEER RECOLLECTIONS OF THE EARLY 30'S AND 40'S IN SANDUSKY
COUNTY OHIO. (Fremont OH: Muchmore & Sons Print., 1930) 31p (OHS)
Burgner, Jacob. LOWER SANDUSKY CEMETERY, FREMONT OHIO. (Philadelphia: E.E.Brownell, 1943)
14p (DAR,SLO,LDS)
CENTENARY HISTORY OF FIRST PRESBYTERIAN CHURCH, FREMONT OHIO, 1833-1933. 1933.
37p (SLO,DAR)
Chilcote, Mary F. INDEX TO HISTORY OF SANDUSKY COUNTY OHIO BY EVERETT. (Evansville
IN: Unigraphic, 1972) 87p (LDS)
Christian, Donna K. GUIDE TO NEWSPAPER HOLDINGS AT THE CENTER FOR ARCHIVAL COL-
LECTIONS. (Bowling Green OH: Bowling Green State Univ, 1980) 64p (OGS)
CITY/COUNTY DIRECTORIES: check holdings of OHS & local public library.
Clegg, Michael, ed. OTTAWA, SANDUSKY AND SENECA COUNTIES OHIO NEWSPAPER
OBITUARY ABSTRACTS 1836-1870 [OHIO NEWSPAPER ABSTRACTS SERIES VOL.4] (Ft.Wayne
IN: author, 1985) 92p (OGS,LDS)
COMMEMORATIVE BIOGRAPHICAL RECORD OF THE COUNTY OF SANDUSKY & OTTAWA
OHIO. (Chicago: J.H.Beers & Co.,1896) 854p (OHS,LDS,SLO,DAR)(RPI)
Conner, Margaret & N.Goodpaster. OHIO SOLDIERS (incl Soldiers from the Revolution and War of
1812 buried in Sandusky Co.) 1950-1964. 1v (DAR)
Daughters of the American Revolution. EARLY MARRIAGE RECORDS OF SANDUSKY COUNTY
OHIO. 1936. 2v. (SLO,DAR,LDS)

Daughters of the American Revolution. OLD CEMETERY, FREMONT OHIO. (SLO)

Daughters of the American Revolution. RECORDS OF REVOLUTIONARY SOLDIERS' GRAVES. (SLO,LDS)

DIRECTORY & YEAR BOOK OF THE OLD FIRST CHURCH, SANDUSKY OHIO. 1938. 56p (SLO)

DIRECTORY OF ALL BUSINESS AND PROFESSIONAL MEN OF SANDUSKY AND OTTAWA COUNTIES OHIO. (Conneaut OH: Watson & Dorman, 1896) 91p (OHS)

Everett, Homer. HISTORY OF SANDUSKY COUNTY OHIO: WITH PORTRAITS AND BIOGRAPHIES OF PROMINENT CITIZENS AND PIONEERS. (Cleveland OH: H.Z.Williams & Bro., 1882)(Reprint,Evansville IN: Unigraphic, 1972) 834p (LDS,SLO,OHS,LC)(RPI)

Everts, Stewart & Co. HISTORICAL ATLAS OF SANDUSKY COUNTY OHIO. 1874.(Reprint, Knightstown IN: Bookmark, 1974) 96p (LC,SLO,OHS,OGS)(RPI)

FARM JOURNAL ILLUSTRATED RURAL DIRECTORY OF SANDUSKY COUNTY, OHIO. (Philadelphia: Wilmer Atkinson Co., n.d.) (LC)

Federal Writers Program, Ohio. FREMONT AND SANDUSKY COUNTY. (Columbus: Ohio State Arch.& Hist.Soc., 1940) 115p (OHS,DAR,SLO,LC,LDS)

Hansen, Helen M. AT HOME IN EARLY SANDUSKY. 1975. 101p. (SLO)

Hayes Memorial Methodist Church. ONE CENTURY AND A QUARTER OF HISTORY. (Fremont OH: author, 1947). 45p (SLO)

HISTORY OF SANDUSKY COUNTY, OHIO: WITH PORTRAITS AND BIOGRAPHIES OF PROMINENT CITIZENS AND PIONEERS. 1882. (Reprint, Evansville IN: Unigraphic, 1972) 834p (DAR,SLO,LDS,OHS)

Hixson, W.W. PLAT BOOK OF SANDUSKY COUNTY OHIO. (Rockport IL: author, n.d.) (OHS)

Hopple, William H. THE COUNTY OF SANDUSKY, OHIO. (Fremont OH: author, 1898) 83p (OHS,SLO)

Johnson, P.R. CLASSIFIED BUSINESS AND PROFESSIONAL DIRECTORY OF PROMINENT TOWNS AND CITIES OF OHIO AND EASTERN INDIANA. (Columbus: Berlin Printing Co., 1899) 303p (LDS)

Keeler, Lucy E. OLD FORT SANDOSKI OF 1745 AND THE "SANDUSKY COUNTRY." (Columbus: author, 1908) (OHS)

Keeler, Lucy E. A GUIDE TO LOCAL HISTORY OF FREMONT OHIO PRIOR TO 1860. (Columbus: Fred J. Heer, 1905) 28p. (SLO,DAR,LDS)

Knapp, Horace S. HISTORY OF THE MAUMEE VALLEY. (Toledo OH: author, 1872) 685p. (DAR,OHS,SLO)

Levinson, Marilyn. GUIDE TO NEWSPAPER HOLDINGS AT THE CENTER FOR ARCHIVAL COLLECTIONS. 2nd Edition. (Bowling Green OH: Bowling Green State Univ., 1987)

Luebke, Grace, ed. BLACK SWAMP HERITAGE, 1987. (LDS)

McGrady, L.J. PIONEER RECOLLECTIONS OF THE EIGHTEEN TWENTIES IN SANDUSKY COUNTY, OHIO, AS NARRATED BY MRS. CATHERINE HAWK TILLOTSON. (Toledo OH: author, 1984) 27p

Marshall, Emogene N. EARLY METHODISM IN SANDUSKY: A BRIEF HISTORY OF THE ACTIVITIES OF THE METHODIST EPISCOPAL CHURCH IN SANDUSKY AND VICINITY. 1930? 28p (DAR)

Meek, Basil. EVOLUTION OF SANDUSKY COUNTY OHIO. (Columbus OH: author, 1915) 19p. (SLO,OHS,LC)

Meek, Basil. TWENTIETH CENTURY HISTORY OF SANDUSKY COUNTY OHIO AND REPRESENTATIVE CITIZENS. (Chicago: Richmond-Arnold Pub.Co., 1909) 934p (LDS,DAR,SLO,OHS) (RPI)

Northwestern Ohio Gen.Soc. CEMETERY INSCRIPTIONS. (LDS)

PROCEEDINGS AT THE UNVEILING OF THE SOLDIER'S MONUMENT ON THE SITE OF FORT STEPHENSON, FREMONT, OHIO. (Fremont OH: Democratic Messenger, 1885) 123p (LDS,OHS)

SANDUSKY COUNTY GAZETTEER AND DIRECTORY FOR 1869. (Sandusky OH: A.Bailey, 1869) 152p (OHS)

Scott, Beulah M. INDEX OF COMBINATION ATLAS MAP OF SANDUSKY COUNTY OHIO BY EVERTS, 1874. 1971. 43p (LDS)

Sims, James R & Janet L. SANDUSKY COUNTY OHIO CEMETERIES. (Arvada CO: Ancestor Pubs., 1979) (LDS,SLO)

Slocum, Charles E. HISTORY OF THE MAUMEE RIVER BASIN. (Defiance OH: author, 1905) 638p
    (DAR,SLO)
Smith, S.Winifred. GRACE EVANGELICAL LUTHERAN CHURCH, FREMONT. (Columbus:Ohio
    Hist.Soc., 1948) 5p (LDS)
TAD GENEALOGICAL BOOK AND MICROFILM LIST FOR SANDUSKY COUNTY OHIO. (SLO)
Tillotson, Catherine H. PIONEER RECOLLECTIONS OF THE EIGHTEEN TWENTIES IN SANDUS-
    KY COUNTY OHIO. (Toledo OH: L.J.McGrady, 1984) 27p (LDS)
Van Tassel, Charles S. STORY OF THE MAUMEE VALLEY, TOLEDO AND THE SANDUSKY REGION.
    (Chicago: S.V.Clarke Pub.Co., 1929) 4v (OHS)
Whirlpool Parade. THESE THINGS STAY BY YOU (CLYDE, OHIO, HISTORY). 1968. 56p (SLO)
Winter, Nevin O. HISTORY OF NORTHWEST OHIO. (Chicago: Lewis Pub Co., 1917) 3v. (SLO,OHS)

# SCIOTO COUNTY

CREATED:                        1803 FROM ADAMS COUNTY
COUNTY SEAT:                    PORTSMOUTH 45662
COURT HOUSE:                    602 7TH ST., PORTSMOUTH 45662
LIBRARIES:                      1220 GALLIA ST., PORTSMOUTH 45662
HISTORICAL SOCIETY:             PO BOX 1810, PORTSMOUTH 45662
GENEALOGICAL SOCIETY:           SCIOTO COUNTY CHAPTER OGS,
                                    PO BOX 812, PORTSMOUTH 45662
                                    publication: NEWSLETTER
HEALTH DEPARTMENT:              COURT HOUSE, PORTSMOUTH 45662
                                    (separate office for Portsmouth city)
ARCHIVAL DISTRICT:              OHIO UNIVERSITY, ATHENS
                                    (see published Guide to records)
LAND SURVEYS:                   VIRGINIA MILITARY DISTRICT
                                CONGRESS LANDS, OHIO RIVER SURVEY (SOUTH)
                                FRENCH GRANTS
BOUNDED BY:                     EAST:    LAWRENCE CO.
                                NORTH:   JACKSON & PIKE CO.
                                WEST:    ADAMS CO.
                                SOUTH:   GREENUP & LEWIS CO., KENTUCKY
TOWNSHIPS:                      Bloom, Brush Creek, Clay, Green, Harrison, Jefferson, Madison, Mor-
                                gan, Nile, Porter, Rarden, Rush, Union, Valley, Vernon, Washington.

## COURT RECORDS: (LDS MICROFILM)
Auditor:
    Enumeration of soldiers and sailors, 1900.
    Tax duplicates, 1816-1838.
Clerk of Courts:
    Common Pleas appearance docket 1835-1855.
    Common Pleas appearance docket index, 1810-1811.
    Common Pleas minutes, 1829-1857.
    Common Pleas chancery records, vC-F, 1839-1855.
    Common Pleas complete record, 1810-1852.
    Common Pleas journal, 1810-1811,1814-1851.
    Common Pleas minutes, 1829-1857.
    Supreme Court record, 1809-1857.
    Supreme Court chancery record, 1821-1847.
Commissioners:
    Record, 1812-1906.
    Index to proceedings, 1812-1893.

County Home:
    Register of inmates, 1871-1896.
    Record of proceedings, 1909-1912.
Probate Court:
    Wills, 1810-1876.
    Birth records, vO-5, 1856-1908.
    Birth registrations, v6-24, dates vary.
    Death records, 1856-1908.
    Marriages, vA-15, 1804-1911.
    Naturalization record, 1879-1900.
    Declarations for naturalization, 1859-1870.
Recorder:
    Grantee & grantor index, v1-3, 1855-1876.
    Deed records, vA-24, 1803-1876.

**OHIO HISTORICAL SOCIETY: (MICROFILM)**
Auditor:
    Enumeration of soldiers and sailors, 1900.
    Tax duplicates, 1806-1814,1816-1838.
Clerk of Courts:
    Common Pleas appearance docket 1835-1855.
    Common Pleas appearance docket index, 1810-1811.
    Common Pleas minutes, 1829-1857.
    Common Pleas chancery records, vC-F, 1839-1855.
    Common Pleas complete record, 1810-1852.
    Common Pleas journal, 1810-1811,1814-1851.
    Common Pleas minutes, 1829-1857.
    Supreme Court record, 1809-1857.
    Supreme Court chancery record, 1821-1847.
Commissioners:
    Record, 1812-1906.
    Index to proceedings, 1812-1893.
County Home:
    Register of inmates, 1871-1896.
    Record of proceedings, 1909-1912.
Miscellaneous:
    Marriage records, 1804-1865, by DAR.

**CENSUS RECORDS (OHS,SLO,OGS,LDS)**
1820-1880, 1900-1910; 1890 VETERANS; 1880,1900 SOUNDEX; 1910 MIRACODE

**AGRICULTURAL CENSUS SCHEDULES (OHS,SLO-mic)**
1850,1860

**PRODUCTS OF INDUSTRY CENSUS SCHEDULE (OHS,SLO-mic)**
1850,1860,1870,1880

**MORTALITY CENSUS SCHEDULES (OHS,SLO-mic)**
1850,1860

**NEWSPAPERS: [GUIDE TO OHIO NEWSPAPERS, 1793-1973]**
Portsmouth.

**TAX RECORDS (OHS & LDS)**
1806-1814,1816-1838.

**MANUSCRIPTS:**
Franklin Junior Furnace Co., ledger, 1846-1848. (OHS)
Sciotoville, Free Will Baptist Church, records, 1819-1916. (OHS)

**GENEALOGICAL PERIODICAL ARTICLES**
Bell, Carol Willsey. OHIO GENEALOGICAL PERIODICAL INDEX: A COUNTY GUIDE (Youngstown, OH: author, 6th ed., 1987)

**PUBLISHED SOURCES:**
Adams, Marilyn. INDEX TO CIVIL WAR VETERANS & WIDOWS IN SOUTHERN OHIO, 1890 FEDERAL CENSUS (Cols,OH: Franklin Co Chapter OGS,1986)84p
Adams, Marilyn. SOUTHERN OHIO TAXPAYERS IN THE 1820s: SCIOTO, LAWRENCE AND PIKE COUNTIES.(Atlanta GA: Heritage Research, 1981) 61p (OGS,LDS,SLO)
Adkins, Tom. A BACKWARD GLANCE: THE LUCASVILLE OHIO AREA, 1819-1919, VOL.I. (Lucasville OH: Lucasville Area Hist Soc., 1987) 108p (ad)
Bannon, Henry T. SCIOTO SKETCHES. (Chicago: A.C.McClurg & Co., 1920) 86p.(SLO,OHS,LC)
Bannon, Henry T. STORIES OLD AND OFTEN TOLD, BEING CHRONICLES OF SCIOTO COUNTY OHIO. (Baltimore: Waverly Press, 1927) 275p (OHS,LC)
Barton & Gibbs. MAP OF SCIOTO COUNTY OHIO, 1875. (OHS)
CEMETERY INSCRIPTIONS, GREENLAWN CEMETERY. (OHS)
CEMETERY INSCRIPTIONS, BLOOM & PORTER TWPS. (OHS)
CEMETERY INSCRIPTIONS, MADISON & HARRISON TWPS. (OHS)
CITY/COUNTY DIRECTORIES: check holdings of OHS & local public library.
Clark, Marie T. OHIO LANDS: CHILLICOTHE LAND OFFICE, 1800-1829. (Chillicothe: author, 1984) 144p (OGS,SLO,OHS)
Copley, Raymond. TOMBSTONE INSCRIPTIONS, SCIOTO COUNTY, OHIO (FOR THE) OHIOANA LIBRARY. (Chillicothe OH: Scioto Valley Folk Research Project, 1962) (LDS)
Daughters of the American Revolution. CEMETERIES OF SOUTHERN OHIO. (SLO,LDS)
Daughters of the American Revolution. TOMBSTONE INSCRIPTIONS, SCIOTO COUNTY OHIO. (SLO)
Daughters of the American Revolution. EARLY MARRIAGE BONDS 1804-1865. 3v.(LDS,SLO,DAR)
Evans, Nelson W. HISTORY OF SCIOTO COUNTY OHIO, TOGETHER WITH A PIONEER RECORD OF SOUTHERN OHIO. (Portsmouth OH: author, 1903) 1302p (DAR,OHS,SLO,LC,LDS)(RPI)
Flechtner, Myron. GALLIPOLIS - ACCOUNT OF THE FRENCH 500 AND THE TOWN THEY ESTABLISHED. 1940.
Historical Records Survey. INVENTORY OF THE COUNTY ARCHIVES OF OHIO, NO.73, SCIOTO COUNTY OHIO. (Columbus: author, 1938) 236p (LDS,OHS,DAR)
HISTORY OF SCIOTO COUNTY OHIO 1986. (Portsmouth OH: Portsmouth Area Recognition Society, 1986) 697p (OGS,DAR)
HISTORY OF THE LOWER SCIOTO VALLEY. (Chicago: Interstate Pub.Co., 1884) 875p (LC,OHS,SLO) (RPI)
Hixson, W.W. PLAT BOOK OF SCIOTO COUNTY OHIO. (Rockford IL: author, n.d.) (OHS)
Jarrells, Wilma. CEMETERY INSCRIPTIONS OF RUSH TOWNSHIP, SCIOTO COUNTY OHIO. 1981. 141p. (SLO)
Keyes, James. PIONEERS OF SCIOTO COUNTY OHIO. (Portsmouth OH: author, 1880) (Reprint, Portsmouth OH: Scioto Co.Chapter OGS, 1988) 60p. (SLO,OHS,DAR,LDS) (RPI)
Lewis, Carolyn. MAP OF SCIOTO COUNTY OHIO 1875. (Dayton OH: author, 1983) 41p. (OGS,DAR,LDS,SLO)
Ohio University. GUIDE TO LOCAL GOVERNMENT RECORDS AT OHIO UNIVERSITY. (Athens: OU Library, 1986) 61p.
PORTRAIT AND BIOGRAPHICAL RECORD OF THE SCIOTO VALLEY OHIO. (Chicago: Lewis Pub.Co.,1894) 429p (LC,DAR,LDS)
Pruden, M.M. PRUDEN'S COMBINED BUSINESS DIRECTORY AND GAZETTEER: EMBRACING...PORTSMOUTH...1899-1900. (Charleston WV: Pruden Pub.Co., 1900) 353p (LDS)

Ramsey, Virgil. GRAVESTONE INSCRIPTIONS OF SCIOTO COUNTY OHIO, VOL.6, BLOOM TOWNSHIP. 1981. 77p (LDS)

Scherer, Lois D. REMINISCENCES BY REV.JOHN KELLEY, "IRONTON REGISTER" 1854. [Lawrence & Scioto Cos] (Franklin Furnace OH: author, 1984) 33p (OGS)

Scioto Co Chapter OGS. 1870 SCIOTO COUNTY OHIO CENSUS INDEX. (Lucasville OH: the society, 1979) 50p (OGS,LDS,SLO)

Scott, Ivan & Meg. 1880 SCIOTO CO. OHIO CENSUS INDEX (Columbus, OH: author, 1975) 74p.

Shoemaker, Caryn R. GRAVESTONE INSCRIPTIONS OF SCIOTO COUNTY OHIO, VOL.1, MADISON AND HARRISON TOWNSHIPS. (Minford OH: author, 1978) 88p.(LDS)

Shoemaker, Caryn R. GRAVESTONE INSCRIPTIONS OF SCIOTO COUNTY OHIO, VOL.2, JEFFERSON AND VALLEY TOWNSHIPS. (Minford OH: author, 1979) 93p.(LDS)

Shoemaker, Caryn R. GRAVESTONE INSCRIPTIONS OF SCIOTO COUNTY OHIO, VOL.3, PORTER TOWNSHIP (EXCLUDES MEMORIAL BURIAL PARK). (Minford OH: author, 1980) 49p.(LDS,SLO)

Shoemaker, Caryn R. CEMETERY INSCRIPTIONS OF SCIOTO COUNTY OHIO, VOL.4: VERNON TOWNSHIP. (Minford OH: author, 1980) 34p (OGS,LDS,SLO)

Shoemaker, Caryn R. CEMETERY INSCRIPTIONS OF SCIOTO COUNTY OHIO: VOL.5: GREEN TOWNSHIP. (Minford OH: author, 1980) 63p (OGS,LDS,SLO)

Shoemaker, Caryn R. etal. GRAVESTONE INSCRIPTIONS OF SCIOTO COUNTY OHIO, VOL.6, BLOOM TOWNSHIP. (Minford OH: author, 1980) 77p. (SLO)

Shoemaker, Caryn R. etal. CEMETERY INSCRIPTIONS OF SCIOTO COUNTY OHIO, VOL.7, MORGAN TOWNSHIP. 1981. 34p. (SLO)

Shoemaker, Caryn R. etal. GRAVESTONE INSCRIPTIONS OF SCIOTO COUNTY OHIO, VOL.8, RARDEN TOWNSHIP. (Minford OH: author, 1981) 66p. (SLO)

Shoemaker, Caryn R. etal. GRAVESTONE INSCRIPTIONS OF SCIOTO COUNTY OHIO, VOL.9, CLAY TOWNSHIP. (Minford OH: author, 1984) 33p. (LDS,SLO)

Shoemaker, Caryn R. etal. GRAVESTONE INSCRIPTIONS OF SCIOTO COUNTY OHIO, VOL.10, NILE TOWNSHIP. (Minford OH: author, 1984) 100p (OGS)

Shoemaker, Caryn R. EARLY COURT RECORDS OF SCIOTO COUNTY OHIO. (Minford OH: author, 1979) 152p. (OHS,OGS,LDS,SLO)

Shoemaker, Caryn R. EARLY COURT RECORDS OF SCIOTO COUNTY OHIO, VOLUME 2. (Minford OH: author, 1981) 127p. (SLO)

Shoemaker, Caryn R. SELECTED ABSTRACTS FROM COMMON PLEAS AND CHANCERY COMPLETE RECORDS - SCIOTO COUNTY OHIO (1810-1875). (Minford OH: author, 1985) 235p (OGS,SLO,OHS,LDS)

Shoemaker, Caryn R. etal. CEMETERY LOCATIONS OF SCIOTO COUNTY OHIO. (Minford OH: authors, 1978) 21p.

Shoemaker, Caryn R. & B.Rudity. MARRIAGE RECORDS OF SCIOTO COUNTY OHIO 1803-1860. (Baltimore MD: Genealogical Pub.Co., 1987) 195p (OGS,LDS)

Smith, Clifford N. FEDERAL LAND SERIES: A CALENDAR OF ARCHIVAL MATERIAL ON THE LAND PATENTS ISSUED BY THE U.S.GOVERNMENT, VOL.4, PT 1: GRANTS IN THE VIRGINIA MILITARY DISTRICT OF OHIO. (Chicago: Amer.Libr.Assn.,1982)

Smith, Clifford N. FEDERAL LAND SERIES: A CALENDAR OF ARCHIVAL MATERIAL ON THE LAND PATENTS ISSUED BY THE U.S.GOVERNMENT, VOL.4, PT 2: GRANTS IN THE VIRGINIA MILITARY DISTRICT OF OHIO. (Chicago: Amer.Libr.Assn.,1986) TOMBSTONE INSCRIPTIONS, SCIOTO COUNTY OHIO. 1r mic (SLO)

Vastine, Roy E. SCIOTO A COUNTY HISTORY (Portsmouth OH: Knauff Graphics, 1986) 260p (OGS,LDS)

WIGGINS AND WEAVER'S OHIO RIVER DIRECTORY FOR 1871-1872: EMBRACING. . . PORTSMOUTH. . . (Cleveland OH: authors, 1872) 419p (LDS)

Willard, Eugene. A STANDARD HISTORY OF THE HANGING ROCK IRON REGION, OHIO. (Chicago: Lewis Pub.Co., 1916) 2v. (SLO,OHS,DAR,SLO,LC,LDS)

WORLD'S WAR NEWS OF OHIO, SCIOTO COUNTY OHIO. 1917-1918. (OHS)

# SENECA COUNTY

CREATED: 1820 FROM HURON COUNTY
COUNTY SEAT: TIFFIN 44883
COURT HOUSE: (no street address) TIFFIN 44883
LIBRARIES: 77 JEFFERSON ST., TIFFIN 44883
HISTORICAL SOCIETY: PO BOX 253, TIFFIN 44883
GENEALOGICAL SOCIETY: SENECA CO. CHAPTER OGS,
PO BOX 841, TIFFIN 44883
publication: SENECA SEARCHERS
HEALTH DEPARTMENT: 3140 S.ST.RTE.100, TIFFIN 44883
(separate offices for Tiffin city & Fostoria)
ARCHIVAL DISTRICT: BOWLING GREEN STATE UNIVERSITY, BOWLING GREEN
(see Biggs' Guide to records)
LAND SURVEYS: CONGRESS LANDS, E & N OF 1ST PRIN.MERIDIAN
BOUNDED BY: EAST: HURON CO.
NORTH: SANDUSKY CO.
WEST: HANCOCK & WOOD CO.
SOUTH: CRAWFORD & WYANDOT CO.
TOWNSHIPS: Adams, Big Spring, Bloom, Clinton, Eden, Hopewell, Jackson,
Liberty, Loudon, Pleasant, Reed, Scipio, Seneca, Thompson, Venice.

SPECIAL NOTE: A COURTHOUSE FIRE IN 1841 DESTROYED SOME RECORDS.

## COURT RECORDS: (LDS MICROFILM)
Auditor:
    Burial record of indigent soldiers, 1885-1930.
    Quadrennial enumeration, 1899,1903.
    Soldiers & sailors relief record, 1908-1918, 1933-1944.
    Tax duplicates, 1826-1838,1841-1850.
Clerk of Courts:
    Jury book, 1882-1911; witness book, 1889-1911.
    Record of mayor's certificates of election, 1877-1903.
    Commission records, 1841-1861.
    Naturalization records, 1852-1930.
    Chancery record v2-9, 1835-1853.
    Chancery record index, 1824-1858.
    Supreme Court & district court journal, index, 1826-1884.
    Supreme Court journal, v1, 1825-1843.
    District Court journal, v2, 1851-1877.
    Supreme Court record, v2-3, 1843-1855.
    Common Pleas journal, v1-5,7, 1834-1850,1852-1854.
    General index to files, 1825-1914.
County Home:
    Infirmary record, 1881-1966.
Probate Court:
    Marriages, v2-20, 1841-1951.
    Index to marriages, v1-4, 1841-1930.
    Marriage licenses, 1841-1861.
    Will records, v1-11, 1828-1910.
    Index to wills, v1-18.
    Birth record, 1879-1909.
    Birth & death records, 1867-1905.
    Death record, 1879-1908.

Birth registration, delayed births, v1-18, dates vary.
Naturalization records, 1859-1905.
Record of deaths & some births, 1905-1908.
List of jurors, 1889-1903.
Civil docket, v1-2, 1852-1886.
Civil record, v1, 1853-1874.
General index to files, 1906-1963.
General index to wills, 1828-1964.
Civil record, v1-18, 1853-1912.
Bond records, v1-3, 1849-1869.
Probate journal, v1-10, 1852-1887.
Reform school records, 1885-1886.
Recorder:
Deed records, v1-137, 1822-1902.
Index to deeds v1-7,1821-1889.
Soldiers' discharge record, 1865-1951.
Index to original entries, 1821-1926.
Miscellaneous:
Bascom, United Methodist Church, records, 1834-1983.
Melmore, Presby.Church, records, 1828-1907.
Old Fort United Methodist Church, records, 1882-1969.
Old Fort Evangelical United Brethren Church, records, 1934-1964.
Republic, St.Jacob's Reformed Church, records, 1843-1960.
Seneca Township, Evangelical Jerusalem Church, records, 1842-1914.
Tiffin, First Presby.Church, records, 1831-1930.
Tiffin, St.John's United Church of Christ, records, 1836-1983.
Tiffin, St.Paul's Methodist Church, records, 1882-1983.
Tiffin, Trinity United Church of Christ, records, 1833-1951.
Scipio Twp. Clerk's record book, 1837-1841.
Cemetery records, State Library of Ohio collection.

## OHIO HISTORICAL SOCIETY: (MICROFILM)
Clerk of Courts:
Chancery record v2-9, 1835-1853.
Chancery record index, 1824-1858.
Supreme Court & district court journal, index, 1826-1884.
Supreme Court journal, v1, 1825-1843.
District Court journal, v2, 1851-1877.
Supreme Court record, v2-3, 1843-1855.
Common Pleas journal, v1-5,7, 1834-1850,1852-1854.
General index to files, 1825-1914.
County Home:
Infirmary record, 1881-1966.
Probate Court:
Civil record, v1-18, 1853-1912.
Will record, v12-16, 1901-1910.
Recorder:
Soldiers' discharge record, 1865-1951.
Index to original entries, 1821-1926.
Deed index, v1-6, 1821-1889.
Miscellaneous:
Marriage records, 1841-1867, by DAR.
Tombstone inscriptions, by DAR.

**CENSUS RECORDS (OHS,SLO,OGS,LDS)**
1830-1880, 1900-1910; 1890 VETERANS; 1880,1900 SOUNDEX; 1910 MIRACODE

**AGRICULTURAL CENSUS SCHEDULES (OHS,SLO-mic)**
1850,1870

**PRODUCTS OF INDUSTRY CENSUS SCHEDULE (OHS,SLO-mic)**
1850,1860,1870,1880

**MORTALITY CENSUS SCHEDULES (OHS,SLO-mic)**
1850,1860,1870 [1870 PUBLISHED *OHIO RECORDS & PIONEER FAMILIES* v24 p25]

**NEWSPAPERS: [GUIDE TO OHIO NEWSPAPERS, 1793-1973]**
Attica, Bloomsville, Fostoria, Green Springs, Kansas, Republic, Tiffin.

**TAX RECORDS (OHS & LDS)**
1826-1838.

**MANUSCRIPTS:**
Receipt book, 1864, of draftees in Erie, Crawford, Huron, Ottawa, Sandusky & Seneca Counties Ohio
    who purchased substitutes. (OHS)
Republic, St.Jacob's Reformed Church, records, 1843-1960. (Hayes Lib)

**GENEALOGICAL PERIODICAL ARTICLES**
Bell, Carol Willsey. OHIO GENEALOGICAL PERIODICAL INDEX: A COUNTY GUIDE (Youngstown,
    OH: author, 6th ed., 1987)

**PUBLISHED SOURCES:**
Barnes, Myron B. BETWEEN THE EIGHTIES - TIFFIN OHIO 1880-1980. (Tiffin OH: Seneca Co Museum
    Fdn., 1982) 328p. (OGS,LDS,SLO)
Baughman, A.J. HISTORY OF SENECA COUNTY OHIO: ITS HISTORICAL PROGRESS, ITS PEOPLE
    AND ITS PRINCIPAL INTERESTS. (Chicago: Lewis Pub.Co., 1911) 2v (OHS,LC,DAR)
Biggs, Deb. GUIDE TO LOCAL GOVERNMENT RECORDS AT THE CENTER FOR ARCHIVAL COL-
    LECTIONS. (Bowling Green OH: Bowling Green State Univ, 1981) 104p (OGS)
Blain, Harry. LACON - A FORGOTTEN OHIO HAMLET. nd. 6p (OGS)
Butterfield, Consul W. HISTORY OF SENECA COUNTY. (Sandusky OH: D.Campbell & Sons, 1848)
    245p. (SLO,LDS,OHS,LC,SLO)
CENTENNIAL BIOGRAPHICAL HISTORY OF SENECA COUNTY. (Chicago: Lewis Pub.Co., 1902)
    757p (LDS,DAR,SLO,OHS) (RPI)
Christian, Donna K. GUIDE TO NEWSPAPER HOLDINGS AT THE CENTER FOR ARCHIVAL COL-
    LECTIONS. (Bowling Green OH: Bowling Green State Univ, 1980) 64p (OGS)
CITY/COUNTY DIRECTORIES: check holdings of OHS & local public library.
Clegg, Michael, ed. OTTAWA, SANDUSKY AND SENECA COUNTIES OHIO NEWSPAPER
    OBITUARY ABSTRACTS 1836-1870 [OHIO NEWSPAPER ABSTRACTS SERIES VOL.4] (Ft.Wayne
    IN: author, 1985) 92p (OGS,LDS)
Daughters of the American Revolution. CEMETERY INSCRIPTIONS. (SLO,LDS)
Daughters of the American Revolution. SENECA COUNTY OHIO TOMBSTONE INSCRIPTIONS.
    (SLO,LDS,OHS,DAR)
Daughters of the American Revolution. MARRIAGE RECORDS, 1841-1865. 2v (SLO,LDS,DAR)
Daughters of the American Revolution. EARLY STATE AND LOCAL HISTORY. 1915. 246p. (DAR,SLO)
Dildine, Frank. HISTORY OF TIFFIN AND SENECA COUNTY OHIO [FROM WILDERNESS TO CITY,
    V.1] 1930? 53p (OHS)
Emerine, Andrew. FOSTORIA HIGHLIGHS: OF SOME OF THE OCCURRENCES IN FOSTORIA
    DURING THE PAST 120 YEARS, IN CONJUNCTION WITH FOSTORIA'S 100 YEARS ANNIVER-
    SARY CELEBRATION, 1954. (Fostoria OH: First National Bank, 1954) 32p (LDS)

Ernsberger, C.S. A HISTORY OF THE WITTENBERG SYNOD OF THE GENERAL SYNOD, OF THE EVANGELICAL LUTHERAN CHURCH, 1847-1916: TOGETHER WITH A BRIEF SKETCH OF EACH CONGREGATION OF THE SYNOD. (Columbus OH: Wittenberg Synod, 1917) 582p (LDS)

Gibson, Martha M. REMINISCENCES OF THE EARLY DAYS OF TIFFIN, OHIO. 1967. 48p (DAR)

Historical Records Survey. INVENTORY OF THE COUNTY ARCHIVES OF OHIO, NO.74, SENECA COUNTY. (Columbus: author, 1942) 340p (LDS,OHS,DAR)

HISTORY OF SENECA COUNTY OHIO. (Chicago: Beers & Co., 1886) 1069p (SLO,LDS,OHS,DAR) (RPI)

Hixson, W.W. PLAT BOOK OF SENECA COUNTY OHIO. (Rockford IL: author, n.d.) (OHS)

Knapp, Horace S. HISTORY OF THE MAUMEE VALLEY. (Toledo OH: author, 1872) 685p. (DAR,OHS,SLO)

Lang, William. HISTORY OF SENECA COUNTY OHIO. (Springfield OH: Transcript Printing Co., 1880) 691p (SLO,LDS,OHS,LC) (RPI)

Levinson, Marilyn. GUIDE TO NEWSPAPER HOLDINGS AT THE CENTER FOR ARCHIVAL COLLECTIONS. 2nd Edition. (Bowling Green OH: Bowling Green State Univ., 1987)

Luebke, Grace. BLACK SWAMP HERITAGE, VOL.7, 1987. (LDS)

Murray, Melvin L. THE RETURN TO RISDON: HISTORY OF THE METHODIST CHURCH FOSTORIA OHIO, 1833-1900. 1968. 39p. (SLO,LDS)

Northwestern Ohio Gen.Soc. CEMETERY INSCRIPTIONS. (LDS)

Rawson, Abel. ADDRESS OF HON. ABEL RAWSON, BEFORE THE SENECA CO. PIONEER ASSOCIATION, NOVEMBER 6, 1869. (Tiffin OH: Star Printing House, 1869) (LC)

Rerick Brothers. THE COUNTY OF SENECA OHIO. (Richmond IN: author, 1896) 84p (LC,OHS,SLO)

Seneca Co Chapter OGS. ANCESTRAL PIONEER MEN AND WOMEN OF SENECA COUNTY OHIO. (Tiffin OH: the society, 1987) 24p

Seneca Co Chapter OGS. SENECA COUNTY CEMETERY INSCRIPTIONS. (Tiffin OH: the society, 1987) 1075p (OGS)

Seneca Co Chapter OGS. SENECA COUNTY OHIO BIBLE RECORDS VOL.I. (Tiffin: the society, 1983) np (OGS,SLO)

Stewart, David J. COMBINATION ATLAS OF SENECA COUNTY OHIO. (Philadelphia:author, 1874) 57p (SLO,LDS,OHS,DAR,LC)(RPI)

Van Tassel, Charles S. STORY OF THE MAUMEE VALLEY, TOLEDO AND THE SANDUSKY REGION. (Chicago: S.V.Clarke Pub.Co., 1929) 4v (OHS)

Von Harten, Inez G. INDEX OF HISTORY OF SENECA COUNTY OHIO. 16p (LDS)

Winter, Nevin O. HISTORY OF NORTHWEST OHIO. (Chicago: Lewis Pub.Co., 1917) 3v. (SLO,OHS)

# SHELBY COUNTY

| | |
|---|---|
| CREATED: | 1819 FROM MIAMI COUNTY |
| COUNTY SEAT: | SIDNEY 45365 |
| COURT HOUSE: | (no street address) SIDNEY 45365 |
| LIBRARIES: | 230 E. NORTH ST., SIDNEY 45365 |
| HISTORICAL SOCIETY: | PO BOX 253, SIDNEY 45365 |
| GENEALOGICAL SOCIETY: | SHELBY CO. GENEALOGICAL SOCIETY, |
| | c/o 17755 ST.RT.47, SIDNEY 45365 |
| | publication: SHELBYANA |
| HEALTH DEPARTMENT: | COURT HOUSE, SIDNEY 45365 |
| | (separate office for Sidney city) |
| ARCHIVAL DISTRICT: | WRIGHT STATE UNIVERSITY, DAYTON |
| | (see Leggett's Guide to records) |
| LAND SURVEYS: | CONGRESS LANDS, E & S OF 1ST PRIN.MERIDIAN |
| | CONGRESS LANDS, MIAMI RIVER SURVEY |
| | CONGRESS LANDS, BETWEEN THE MIAMI RIVER SURVEY |
| BOUNDED BY: | EAST:    CHAMPAIGN & LOGAN CO. |
| | NORTH:  AUGLAIZE CO. |

WEST:       DARKE & MERCER CO.
SOUTH:      MIAMI CO.

TOWNSHIPS:                Clinton, Cynthian, Dinsmore, Franklin, Green, Jackson, Loramie,
                         McLean, Orange, Perry, Salem, Turtle Creek, Van Buren, Washington.

## COURT RECORDS: (LDS MICROFILM)

Assessor:
    Register of births, deaths and marriages, 1857-1858.
Auditor:
    Indigent soldiers' burial record, 1885-1886.
    Blind pension records, 1923-1936.
    Tax duplicates, 1820-1838.
    Record of commutations, 1864-1865.
Childrens' Home:
    Record of inmates, 1897-1910.
    Trustees minutes, 1896-1921.
Clerk of Courts:
    Criminal case files, 1819-1914.
    Chancery record, v1-4, 1839-1857.
    Civil docket, v1-3, 1824-1853.
    Civil minutes journal, v1-8, 1819-1854.
    General index, v1-2, 1818-1857.
    Index to appearance docket, v1, 1824-1853.
    Naturalization record, 1843-1861.
    Register of births, deaths & marriages, 1857-1858.
    Supreme Court index, 1823-1859.
    Supreme Court minutes, 1820-1856.
    Supreme Court record, v1-2, 1823-1859.
    District Court journal, 1857-1887.
    Circuit Court journal, 1885-1912.
    Quadrennial enumeration, 1819-1875.
    Poll books & tally sheets, 1819-1874.
    Soldiers' poll books & ballots, 1863-1865.
County Home:
    Infirmary record, 1878-1918.
    Record of inmates, 1866-1947.
Probate Court:
    Administrator & executor dockets, v103, 1851-1911.
    Marriage records, v1-9, 1824-1904.
    Birth records, v1-3, 1867-1908.
    Death records, 1867-1904.
    Guardian docket, v1-2, 1859-1919.
    Admr. exr & grdn settlements, v1-3, 1851-1905.
    Administrators bonds & letters, v1-3, 1862-1901.
    Journal of appointments, 1875-1916.
    Probate minute book, v1-10, 1852-1901.
    Wills, v1-5, 1825-1902.
    Guardian bonds & letters, v1-3, 1862-1902.
    Naturalization records, 1843-1905.
Railroad Appraisers:
    Appraisal record, 1891-1910.
Recorder:
    Deed records, vA-78, 1819-1904.
    Index to deeds, 1822-1966.
    Mortgages, v1-3, 1837-1854.

Index to mortgages, v1-8, 1835-1908.
Record of soldiers discharges, 1865-1917.
Sheriff:
Jail register, 1879-1923.
Soldiers' Relief:
Commission minutes, 1887-1947.

## OHIO HISTORICAL SOCIETY: (MICROFILM)
Auditor:
Indigent soldiers' burial record, 1885-1886.
Blind pension records, 1923-1936.
Record of commutations, 1864-1865.
Childrens' Home:
Record of inmates, 1897-1910.
Trustees minutes, 1896-1921.
Clerk of Courts:
Criminal case files, 1819-1914.
Chancery record, v1-4, 1839-1857.
Civil docket, v1-3, 1824-1853.
Civil minutes journal, v1-8, 1819-1854.
General index, v1-2, 1818-1857.
Index to appearance docket, v1, 1824-1853.
Naturalization record, 1843-1861.
Register of births, deaths & marriages, 1857-1858.
Supreme Court index, 1823-1859.
Supreme Court minutes, 1820-1856.
Supreme Court record, v1-2, 1823-1859.
District Court journal, 1857-1887.
Circuit Court journal, 1885-1912.
Quadrennial enumeration, 1819-1875.
Poll books & tally sheets, 1819-1874.
Soldiers' poll books & ballots, 1863-1865.
County Home:
Infirmary record, 1878-1918.
Record of inmates, 1866-1947.
Railroad Appraisers:
Appraisal record, 1891-1910.
Sheriff:
Jail register, 1879-1923.
Soldiers' Relief:
Commission minutes, 1887-1947.
Miscellaneous:
Marriage records, 1825-1865, by DAR.
Cemeteries of Brown, Cuya.,Lor.,Mad.,Med & Shelby Cos., by DAR.
Gravestone records, 1807-1858, by DAR.

## CENSUS RECORDS (OHS,SLO,OGS,LDS)
1820-1880, 1900-1910; 1890 VETERANS; 1880,1900 SOUNDEX; 1910 MIRACODE

## AGRICULTURAL CENSUS SCHEDULES (OHS,SLO-mic)
1850,1870

## PRODUCTS OF INDUSTRY CENSUS SCHEDULE (OHS,SLO-mic)
1850,1860,1870,1880

MORTALITY CENSUS SCHEDULES (OHS,SLO-mic)
1850,1860

NEWSPAPERS: [GUIDE TO OHIO NEWSPAPERS, 1793-1973]
Botkins, Fort Loramie, Jackson Center, Sidney.

TAX RECORDS (OHS & LDS)
1820-1838.

GENEALOGICAL PERIODICAL ARTICLES
Bell, Carol Willsey. OHIO GENEALOGICAL PERIODICAL INDEX: A COUNTY GUIDE (Youngstown,
   OH: author, 6th ed., 1987)

PUBLISHED SOURCES:
Adams, Barbara. MARRIAGE RECORDS OF SHELBY COUNTY OHIO, 1819-1899. (Baltimore MD:
   Gateway Press, 1981-83) 2v (LDS,SLO)
Adams, Barbara & G.Mozley. MEMORIAL RECORDS OF SHELBY COUNTY OHIO, 1819-1975. (Sid-
   ney OH: authors, 1975) 668p (LDS,DAR,SLO)
ATLAS AND DIRECTORY OF SHELBY COUNTY OHIO, 1875 & 1900.(Reprint, Evansville IN:
   Unigraphic, 1975) 53,130p (LC,SLO)
Berry, Ellen T. & David A. EARLY OHIO SETTLERS: PURCHASERS OF LAND IN SOUTHWESTERN
   OHIO, 1800-1840. (Baltimore: Genealogical Pub.Co., 1986) 372p (OGS,SLO,OHS)
Bigot, Wilhelm P. ANNALS OF ST.MICHAEL'S PARISH IN LORAMIE (BERLIN) SHELBY COUNTY
   OHIO IN THE ARCHDIOCESE OF CINCINNATI FROM 1838-1903. (Sidney OH: Anzeiger, 1907)
   217,332p (LDS,DAR,SLO)
CITY/COUNTY DIRECTORIES: check holdings of OHS & local public library.
COMBINATION ATLAS MAP OF SHELBY COUNTY OHIO. (np: Page & Smith, 1875) 77p
   (OGS,LDS)(RPI)
Daughters of the American Revolution. OHIO BIBLE RECORDS CRAWFORD, SHELBY... COUNTIES.
   (SLO,DAR)
Daughters of the American Revolution. CEMETERY RECORDS OF BROWN, CUYAHOGA...SHELBY
   COUNTIES. (SLO,DAR)
Daughters of the American Revolution. CEMETERY RECORDS OF SHELBY COUNTY OHIO AND
   OF FRANKLIN TOWNSHIP, MERCER COUNTY, OHIO. 1974. 1v (DAR)
Daughters of the American Revolution. MARRIAGE RECORDS, SHELBY COUNTY OHIO. 2v.
   (SLO,LDS,DAR)
Daughters of the American Revolution. SHELBY AND MERCER COUNTY OHIO CEMETERY
   RECORDS. (SLO)
Daughters of the American Revolution. TWELVE OHIO COUNTIES. (SLO)
Haller, Stephen E. & P.Nolan. FIRST STOP FOR LOCAL HISTORY RESEARCH. A GUIDE TO COUN-
   TY RECORDS PRESERVED AT WRIGHT STATE UNIVERSITY ARCHIVES AND SPECIAL COL-
   LECTIONS. 1976. 21p.
HISTORY OF SHELBY COUNTY OHIO. (Philadelphia: R.Sutton, 1883)(Reprint, Shelby Co.Hist.Soc.,
   1963) 406p (SLO,DAR,LDS) (RPI)
Hitchcock, A. HISTORY OF SHELBY COUNTY OHIO AND REPRESENTATIVE CITIZENS. (Chicago:
   Richmond-Arnold Pub.Co., 1913) 862p. (SLO,LDS,DAR)
Hover, John C. MEMOIRS OF THE MIAMI VALLEY. (Robert O. Law, 1919) 3v (SLO)
Johnson, P.R. CLASSIFIED BUSINESS AND PROFESSIONAL DIRECTORY OF PROMINENT TOWNS
   AND CITIES OF OHIO AND EASTERN INDIANA. (Columbus OH: Berling Printing Co., 1899)
   303p (LDS)
Leggett, Nancy G. & D.E.Smith. A GUIDE TO LOCAL GOVERNMENT RECORDS AND NEWSPAPERS
   PRESERVED AT THE DEPARTMENT OF ARCHIVES AND SPECIAL COLLECTIONS WRIGHT
   STATE UNIVERSITY. (Dayton OH: Wright State U., 1987)
MEMOIRS OF THE MIAMI VALLEY OHIO. (Chicago: Robert O.Law Co.,1919) 3v (OHS,SLO)
Mohneke, Edward H. TOMBSTONE INSCRIPTIONS, OHIO AND INDIANA. 1937. 87p (LDS)

OLD GRAVES FOUND IN SHELBY COUNTY OHIO. (SLO)
PORTRAIT & BIOGRAPHICAL RECORD OF AUGLAIZE, LOGAN & SHELBY COUNTIES, OHIO. (Chicago: Chapman Bros., 1892) 593p (LC,LDS,DAR,SLO)
Shelby County Historical Society. HISTORY OF SHELBY COUNTY OHIO c1883. 1968. 374p (SLO,LC)
SHELBY COUNTY OHIO SPANISH-AMERICAN WAR VOLUNTEERS NELSON, BROWN & THOMPSON BATTALION. (SLO)
Smith, William. HISTORY OF SOUTHWESTERN OHIO, THE MIAMI VALLEYS. 1964. 3v. (SLO)
Wallace, Lenna T. AN INDEX TO NATURALIZATION RECORDS FROM SHELBY COUNTY OHIO, 1814-1906. (Dayton OH: Wright State University, 1986?) 19p (LDS)
WIGGINS AND McKILLOP'S DIRECTORY OF CHAMPAIGN COUNTY FOR 1878-9 [INCLUDES SHELBY COUNTY]. (Wellsville OH: authors, 1878) (DAR)

# STARK COUNTY

CREATED:                1808 FROM COLUMBIANA COUNTY
COUNTY SEAT:            CANTON 44702
COURT HOUSE:           CENTRAL PLAZA, CANTON 44702
LIBRARIES:             715 MARKET AVE.NORTH, CANTON 44702
HISTORICAL SOCIETY:    PO BOX 483, CANTON 44701
GENEALOGICAL           STARK CO. CHAPTER OGS,
SOCIETIES:                 7300 WOODCREST NE, CANTON 44721
                           publication: TREE CLIMBER
                       ALLIANCE CHAPTER OGS,
                           PO BOX 3630, ALLIANCE 44601
                           publication: TAGS NEWSLETTER
HEALTH DEPARTMENT:     209 W.TUSCARAWAS ST., CANTON 44702
                           (separate offices for Canton city, Louisville, North Canton, Massillon & Alliance)
ARCHIVAL DISTRICT:     UNIVERSITY OF AKRON, AKRON, OHIO
                           (see Folck's Guide to records)
LAND SURVEYS:          CONGRESS LANDS, SEVEN RANGES
                       CONGRESS LANDS, OHIO RIVER SURVEY (NORTH)
BOUNDED BY:            EAST:     COLUMBIANA & MAHONING CO.
                       NORTH:    PORTAGE & SUMMIT CO.
                       WEST:     WAYNE CO.
                       SOUTH:    CARROLL & TUSCARAWAS CO.
TOWNSHIPS:             Bethlehem, Canton, Jackson, Lake, Lawrence, Lexington, Marlboro, Nimishillen, Osnaburg, Paris, Perry, Pike, Plain, Sandy, Sugar Creek, Tuscarawas, Washington.

## COURT RECORDS: (LDS MICROFILM)
Auditor:
    Tax duplicates, 1816-1838.
    Military enrollment, 1865.
    Enumeration of school-aged youth, 1862.
Clerk of Courts:
    Supreme Court records, vA-D, 1810-1849.
    Common Pleas court index, v1-3, 1810-1866.
    Common Pleas journal, vA-U, 1809-1852.
    Common Pleas appearance dockets, vA-W, 1809-1852.
    Supreme Court appearance docket, 1834-1868.
    Poll books & tally sheets, Lake Tp., 1858-1876.
Probate Court:
    Administration dockets, vA-G, 1810-1890.

Guardians dockets, vA-E, 1816-1891.
Administrators & guardians bonds, vA-C, 1849-1868.
Guardians records, vB-K, 1850-1888.
Letters of guardianship, 1873-1888.
Guardians bonds, 1868-1891.
Journal, bA-K, 1852-1886.
Administration records, vB-41, 1817-1887.
Inventories & sale bills, v1-5, 1880-1886.
Will records, vA-H, 1811-1888.
Index to wills, v1, 1811-1943.
Naturalizations, 1861-1903.
Birth records, v1-6, 1867-1908.
Death records, v1-4, 1867-1908.
Marriage records, vA-26, 1809-1916.
Index to marriages, 1809-1972.
Recorder:
Land records, 1809-1906.
Miscellaneous:
Canal Fulton, First Presby.Church, records, 1826-1842.
Canton, LDS Church, members, 1927-1957.
Marlboro Township, St.Peter's Reformed Church, register, 1897-1934.
Minerva, Presbyterian Church, session minutes, 1851-1896.
Uniontown, Associate Reformed Church, minutes, 1865-1881.

## OHIO HISTORICAL SOCIETY: (MICROFILM)
Auditor:
Military enrollment, 1865.
Enumeration of school-aged youth, 1862.
Clerk of Courts:
Common Pleas Supreme Court records, vA-D, 1810-1849.
Common Pleas court index, v1-3, 1810-1866.
Common Pleas journal, vA-U, 1809-1852.
Common Pleas appearance dockets, vA-W, 1809-1852.
Supreme Court appearance docket, 1834-1868.
Poll books & tally sheets, Lake Tp., 1858-1876.
Miscellaneous:
Index to marriages, 1808-1865, by DAR.
Marriage records, 1808-1865, by DAR.
Index to wills, 1809-1890, by DAR.
Bible records, by DAR.
Births, deaths & marriages, by DAR.
Church records, by DAR.
Early records of people & places, by DAR.
Cemetery records, by DAR.

## CENSUS RECORDS  (OHS,SLO,OGS,LDS)
1820-1880, 1900-1910; 1890 VETERANS; 1880,1900 SOUNDEX; 1910 MIRACODE

## AGRICULTURAL CENSUS SCHEDULES  (OHS,SLO-mic)
1850,1870

## PRODUCTS OF INDUSTRY CENSUS SCHEDULE  (OHS,SLO-mic)
1850,1860,1870,1880

## MORTALITY CENSUS SCHEDULES (OHS,SLO-mic)
1850,1860

## NEWSPAPERS: [GUIDE TO OHIO NEWSPAPERS, 1793-1973]
Alliance, Canal Fulton, Canton, East Canton, Hartville, Louisville, Magnolia, Massillon, Minerva, North Canton, Waynesburg.

## TAX RECORDS (OHS & LDS)
1810-1814,1816-1838.

## GENEALOGICAL PERIODICAL ARTICLES
Bell, Carol Willsey. OHIO GENEALOGICAL PERIODICAL INDEX: A COUNTY GUIDE (Youngstown, OH: author, 6th ed., 1987)

## PUBLISHED SOURCES:
ALLIANCE CENTENNIAL SOUVENIR BOOK: PROGRAM OF EVENTS, AUG.27 TO SEPT.2, 1950. 1950. 89p (LDS)

Alliance Genealogical Society, OGS. EARLY MARRIAGES OF STARK COUNTY OHIO, 1809-1840. (Alliance OH: author, 1986) 149p (OGS,LDS)

Armstrong, Mary A. THE PEOPLE IN THEIR TIME VOL.1 & 2 [Limaville] (Limaville OH: author, 1977-1983) (LC)

ATLAS OF STARK COUNTY OHIO. 1896. (OGS)

Basner, Ruth H. THE NORTH CANTON HERITAGE. (North Canton OH: Heritage Society of No.Canton, 1972) 312p (DAR,SLO)

Beers, Frederick W. ATLAS OF STARK COUNTY OHIO. 1870. (OGS,SLO)(RPI)

Bell, Carol W. ABSTRACTS FROM BIOGRAPHIES IN HISTORY OF NORTH EASTERN OHIO by John S. Stewart, 1935. (Indianapolis: Ye Olde Genealogie Shoppe, 1983)

Bell, Carol W. OHIO LANDS: STEUBENVILLE LAND OFFICE RECORDS, 1800-1820. (Youngstown OH: author, 1983) 181p (OGS)

Blue, H.T.O. HISTORY OF STARK COUNTY OHIO. (Chicago: S.J.Clarke Co., 1928) 3v. (LC,OHS,LDS,DAR)

Bollinger, Theodore P. HISTORY OF THE FIRST REFORMED CHURCH, CANTON, OHIO. (Cleveland: Central Pub.House, 19??) 208p (LDS)

CITY/COUNTY DIRECTORIES: check holdings of OHS & local public library.

Danner, John. OLD LANDMARKS OF CANTON AND STARK COUNTY OHIO. (Logansport IN: B.F.Bowen, 1904) 1511p (OGS,SLO,LC,LDS,DAR)

Daughters of the American Revolution. ADMINISTRATION RECORDS, STARK COUNTY & WILLS. (SLO,LDS,DAR)

Daughters of the American Revolution. STARK COUNTY OHIO BIBLE, CHURCH AND FAMILY RECORDS. (DAR,LDS)

Daughters of the American Revolution. BIBLE RECORDS OF FAMILIES. (SLO)

Daughters of the American Revolution. BICENTENNIAL HISTORY OF THE MINERVA AREA FAMILIES. 2v (SLO)

Daughters of the American Revolution. CEMETERY RECORDS, STARK CO.OHIO. 4v. (SLO)

Daughters of the American Revolution. EARLY CHURCH AND BIBLE RECORDS, COLUMBIANA... AND STARK COUNTIES. (SLO,DAR)

Daughters of the American Revolution. EARLY RECORDS OF PLACES AND PEOPLE IN THE FOLLOWING COUNTIES OF OHIO: COLUMBIANA, MAHONING, PORTAGE, STARK. 1941. 160p (DAR)

Daughters of the American Revolution. EARLY RECORDS OF THE HOLY TRINITY LUTHERAN CHURCH, CANTON, OHIO AND EMMANUEL'S UNITED CHURCH OF CHRIST, DOYLESTOWN, OHIO. (SLO,DAR)

Daughters of the American Revolution. INDEX OF WILLS, STARK COUNTY. (SLO)

Daughters of the American Revolution. MARRIAGE RECORDS, STARK COUNTY OHIO. 4v. (SLO,LDS,DAR)

Daughters of the American Revolution. RECORDS OF ZION LUTHERAN CHURCH OF NORTH CANTON OHIO. (SLO)

Daughters of the American Revolution. SOLDIERS OF THE AMERICAN REVOLUTION BURIED IN STARK COUNTY OHIO. 1982. (SLO)

Daughters of the American Revolution. ST.TIMOTHY'S EPISCOPAL CHURCH, MASSILLON, OHIO, BAPTISM, MARRIAGE & BURIAL RECORDS, 1837-1851. (SLO,LDS)

Daughters of the American Revolution. TRINITY LUTHERAN CHURCH, CANTON, OHIO. (SLO)

Daughters of the American Revolution. ZION LUTHERAN AND REFORMED CHURCH, NORTH CANTON, OHIO. (SLO,DAR)

Everts, L.H. & Co. COMBINATION ATLAS MAP OF STARK COUNTY OHIO. 1875. (Reprint, Knightstown IN: Bookmark, 1974) 121p (LDS,OGS,SLO,LC,DAR)(RPI)

Ferguson, H.Clay. MARRIAGES PERFORMED BY REV.H.CLAY FERGUSON AT EMSWORTH, PA., 1887-1889; CANTON, OHIO, 1890-1900; PHILADELPHIA, 1901-1938. (LDS)

Ferguson, H.Clay. RECORDS OF PERSONS UNITING WITH THE PRESBYTERIAN CHURCH UNDER THE MINISTRY OF REV.H.CLAY FERGUSON AT EMSWORTH, PA., 1885-1890; CANTON, OHIO, FIRST PRESBYTERIAN CHURCH, 1890-1901; PHILADELPHIA, 1901-1939, INCLUDES BAPTISMS. (LDS)

FIRESTONE PARK PRESBYTERIAN CHURCH DIRECTORY. (Lexington OH: 20th Century, 1975) 28p (OGS)

First Baptist Church, Canton. THE SEVENTY-FIFTH ANNIVERSARY CELEBRATION OF THE FIRST BAPTIST CHURCH OF CANTON, OHIO. (Canton: the church, 1924) 16p (LDS)

First Presbyterian Church, Canton. THE CENTENNIAL CELEBRATION OF THE FIRST PRESBYTERIAN CHURCH OF CANTON, OHIO, 1821-1921. 24p (LDS)

Fisher, Clay C. NAVARRE, A LITTLE TOWN AND ITS PEOPLE. (Navarre OH: author, 1976) 200p (LDS)

Folck, Linda. LOCAL GOVERNMENT RECORDS IN THE AMERICAN HISTORY RESEARCH CENTER AT THE UNIVERSITY OF AKRON. (Akron: U of Akron, 1982) 40p. (OGS)

Fritzsche, Elizabeth K. MT.ZION REFORMED AND LUTHERAN CHURCH, NORTH CANTON, OHIO, STARK COUNTY: BIRTHS, BAPTISMS, DEATHS (1812-1865) (SLO,LDS)

GREENTOWN, OHIO SESQUICENTENNIAL, 1816-1966. 35p (LDS)

Hardesty, H.H. MILITARY HISTORY OF OHIO - STARK COUNTY EDITION. 1886/87. (OHS)

Harter, Mrs. Bert. GERMAN REFORMED & LUTHERAN CHURCH RECORDS, BAPTISMS, DEATHS FROM WAYNE, STARK, MEDINA & SUMMIT COUNTIES, TRANSLATED FROM THE GERMAN. (Doylestown OH: author, 1962)

Harter, Fayne E. CHURCH RECORDS OF THE EVANGELICAL AND REFORMED CHURCH, NAVARRE, OHIO (FORMERLY GERMAN LUTHERAN AND REFORMED) 1835-1911. (Grabill IN: author, 1967) 75p (LDS)

Harter, Mary. EARLY RECORDS OF HOLY TRINITY LUTHERAN CHURCH, CANTON, OHIO AND EMANUEL'S UNITED CHURCH OF CHRIST, DOYLESTOWN, OHIO. (DAR,LDS)

Heald, Edward T. BEZALEEL WELLS, FOUNDER OF CANTON & STEUBENVILLE OHIO. (Canton: Stark Co Hist.Soc., 1948) (SLO)

Heald, Edward T. HISTORY OF STARK COUNTY OHIO.[a digest of his 6 vol. "Stark Co Story"] (Canton OH: Stark Co Hist.Soc., 1963) 183p (LC,OGS)

Heald, Edward T. THE STARK COUNTY STORY. (Canton OH: author, 1949-50) 6v (SLO,LC) (OHS)

Hinshaw, William Wade. ENCYCLOPEDIA OF AMERICAN QUAKER GENEALOGY, VOL.IV, OHIO. (Baltimore: Genealogical Pub.Co., 1973) 1424p (SLO,OHS,LDS)

Historical Records Survey. INVENTORY OF THE COUNTY ARCHIVES OF OHIO, NO.76, STARK COUNTY (CANTON). (Columbus OH: author, 1940) 345p (LDS)

Kane, Ruth. WHEAT, GLASS, STONE AND STEEL: THE STORY OF MASSILLON. (Massillon OH: Sesquicentennial Committee, 1976) 194p (LDS)

Kauffman, William J. ATLAS OF STARK COUNTY OHIO. (Canton OH: Ohio Map and Atlas Co.,1896) 190p (LDS,SLO)

Kettering, Leon C.W. TRANSACTIONS OF THE EVANGELICAL PROTESTANT TRINITY CHURCH. [STARK & PORTAGE COS] (Toledo OH: author, 1952) 30p (OGS)

Knipfer, Eileen M. SOLDIERS OF THE AMERICAN REVOLUTION BURIED IN STARK COUNTY OHIO. 1982. 103p (DAR)

Kuhns, William T. MEMORIES OF OLD CANTON: AND MY PERSONAL RECOLLECTIONS OF WILLIAM McKINLEY. 1937. 64p (DAR)

Lehman, John H. STANDARD HISTORY OF STARK COUNTY OHIO. (Chicago: Lewis Pub.Co., 1939?) 3v. (DAR,SLO)(RPI)

Mann, Clyde. HISTORY OF WAYNESBURG, OHIO: IN COMMEMORATION OF 1833-1933 CENTENNIAL & HOMECOMING. (Waynesburg OH: Centennial Committee, 1933) 16p (LDS)

MINUTES OF THE CENTENNIAL MEETING OF THE WOOSTER BAPTIST ASSOCIATION: BAPTIST CHURCH, MASSILLON OHIO. 1939. 28p (DAR)

NAVARRE, OHIO SESQUICENTENNIAL: 1806-1956. (Navarre OH: committee, 1956) 56p (DAR)

PARIS OHIO SESQUI-CENTENNIAL 1814-1964. (Chicago: Lewis Pub., 1964) 56p (LDS,OGS)

Perrin, William H. HISTORY OF STARK COUNTY OHIO. (Chicago: Baskin & Battey, 1881) (Reprint, Evansville IN: Unigraphic, 1977) 1012p (OGS,SLO,DAR,LC,LDS)

PORTRAIT AND BIOGRAPHICAL RECORD OF STARK COUNTY OHIO. (Chicago: Chapman Bros., 1892) 524p (SLO,LDS,DAR)(RPI)

Powell, Esther W. STARK COUNTY OHIO: EARLY CHURCH RECORDS AND CEMETERIES. (Akron OH: author, 1973) 269p (OGS,OHS,LDS,DAR)

Rodman Public Library. OHIO GENEALOGICAL & BIOGRAPHICAL RESOURCES AVAILABLE AT RODMAN PUBLIC LIBRARY. (Alliance OH: author, 1982) 74p. (OGS)

Schapiro, E. WADSWORTH HERITAGE. 1964. 392p. (SLO)

Shallenberger, Eliza H. STARK COUNTY AND ITS PIONEERS. (Cambridge IL: B.W.Seaton, printer, 1876) 327p (LC)

Skinner, Bessie V.R. MASSILLON ONCE UPON A TIME. (Massillon OH: Independent Pub.Co., 1928) 74p (DAR)

Smith, Mrs.Barton. UPON THESE HILLS - "MASSILLON'S BEGINNINGS AND EARLY DAYS". 1962. 72p. (SLO,DAR)

Stark Co Chapter OGS. 1870 CENSUS INDEX, STARK COUNTY OHIO. (Canton OH: the society, 1988?) (OGS)

Stark Co Chapter OGS. 1880 CENSUS INDEX OF STARK COUNTY, OHIO (Canton OH: the society, 1985). 69pp. (OGS,LDS)

Stark Co Chapter OGS. ANCESTOR CHARTS: STARK COUNTY OHIO CHARTER MEMBERS. (Canton OH: the society, 1987) 357p (OGS)

Stark Co Chapter OGS. CEMETERY INSCRIPTIONS, STARK COUNTY OHIO, VOL.I LEXINGTON, WASHINGTON, PARIS & MARLBORO TOWNSHIPS. (Canton OH: the society, 1982) 419p (OGS,LDS,DAR,SLO)

Stark Co Chapter OGS. CEMETERY INSCRIPTIONS, STARK COUNTY OHIO, VOL.II NIMISHILLEN, OSNABURG, SANDY, PIKE, BETHLEHEM & SUGAR CREEK TOWNSHIPS. (Canton OH: the society, 1982) 398p (OGS,LDS,DAR,SLO)

Stark Co Chapter OGS. CEMETERY INSCRIPTIONS, STARK COUNTY OHIO, VOL.III TUSCARAWAS, LAWRENCE & JACKSON TOWNSHIPS. (Canton OH: the society, 1983) 419p (OGS,LDS,DAR,SLO)

Stark Co Chapter OGS. CEMETERY INSCRIPTIONS, STARK COUNTY OHIO, VOL.IV LAKE & PLAIN TOWNSHIPS. (Canton OH: the society, 1984) 425p (OGS,LDS)

Stark Co Chapter OGS. CEMETERY INSCRIPTIONS, STARK COUNTY OHIO, VOL.V PLAIN & CANTON TOWNSHIPS. (Canton OH: the society, 1984) 379p (OGS,LDS)

Stark Co Chapter OGS. CEMETERY INSCRIPTIONS, STARK COUNTY OHIO, VOL.VI PERRY TOWNSHIP. (Canton OH: the society, 1985) 397p (OGS,LDS,DAR,SLO)

Stark Co Chapter OGS. CEMETERY INSCRIPTIONS, STARK COUNTY OHIO, VOL.VII WEST LAWN CEMETERY, CANTON. (Canton OH: the society, 1986) 369p (OGS,LDS,DAR,SLO

Stark Co.Historical Society. CEMETERY RECORDS, STARK COUNTY, OHIO. (Canton: the society, 1963) 3v (LDS,DAR)

Stewart, John S. HISTORY OF NORTHEASTERN OHIO. (Indianapolis: Historical Pub Co., 1935) 3v. (SLO)

Waltenbaugh, Mrs. Charles. BIBLE RECORDS OF FAMILIES, STARK COUNTY OHIO. (SLO,LDS)

Waltenbaugh, Mrs. Charles. TRINITY LUTHERAN CHURCH, CANTON, OHIO: BIRTHS, BAPTISMS, DEATHS, MARRIAGES (1838-1870) (SLO,LDS)

Waltenbaugh, Mrs. Charles. ZION LUTHERAN AND ZION REFORMED CHURCH AT NORTH CANTON, OHIO (1863-1882). (SLO,LDS)

Wess, Mrs. Samuel. ZION LUTHERAN CHURCH, NO.CANTON, OHIO (1821-1841) (SLO,LDS,DAR)

Wiles, Virginia C. THE BICENTENNIAL BIOGRAPHICAL HISTORY OF MINERVA AREA FAMILIES. 1976. 2v (DAR)

Yon, Paul D. GUIDE TO OHIO COUNTY & MUNICIPAL GOVERNMENT RECORDS. (Columbus: Ohio Hist Soc, 1973) 216p (OHS)

# SUMMIT COUNTY

| | |
|---|---|
| CREATED: | 1840 FROM MEDINA, PORTAGE & STARK |
| COUNTY SEAT: | AKRON 44308 |
| COURT HOUSE: | 209 S.HIGH ST., AKRON 44308 |
| LIBRARIES: | AKRON & SUMMIT COUNTY PUBLIC LIBRARY, 55 S. MAIN ST., AKRON 44326 |
| HISTORICAL SOCIETY: | 550 COPLEY RD., AKRON 44320 |
| GENEALOGICAL SOCIETY: | SUMMIT COUNTY CHAPTER OGS, PO BOX 2232, AKRON 44309 publication: THE HIGHPOINT |
| HEALTH DEPARTMENT: | 1100 GRAHAM CIRCLE, CUYAHOGA FALLS 44224 |
| AKRON: | 177 S.BROADWAY, AKRON 44308 (separate offices for Cuyahoga Falls, Tallmadge, Stow, Norton, Twinsburg, Fairlawn, Macedonia & Barberton) |
| ARCHIVAL DISTRICT: | UNIVERSITY OF AKRON, AKRON, OHIO (see Folck's Guide to records) |
| LAND SURVEYS: | CONNECTICUT WESTERN RESERVE CONGRESS LANDS, OHIO RIVER SURVEY (NORTH) |
| BOUNDED BY: | EAST: PORTAGE CO. NORTH: CUYAHOGA CO. WEST: MEDINA CO. SOUTH: STARK & WAYNE CO. |
| TOWNSHIPS: | Bath, Boston, Copley, Coventry, Franklin, Green, Hudson, Macedonia, Northfield, Northhampton, Norton, Portage, Richfield, Sagamore, Springfield, Stow, Tallmadge, Twinsburg. |
| SPECIAL NOTE: | Microfilm copies of many Probate Court records may be purchased by individuals or libraries. This is unique to Summit County, and is the result of exceptional cooperation with the Summit County Chapter, O.G.S. |

## COURT RECORDS: (LDS MICROFILM)

Auditor:
   Enlistment & enrollment of militia, 1857-1865.
   Commutation receipts, 1864.
Clerk of Courts:
   Common Pleas journals, 1842-1852.
   Plaintiff index, v1, 1840-1870.
   Common Pleas civil dockets, v2-12, 1840-1852.
   Supreme Court minutes, v1, 1842-1851.
   Supreme Court record, v1, 1842-1846.
Commissioners:
   Bounty receipts, 1864.

Probate Court:
    Will books, v8-21, 1887-1909.
    Probate journal, v1-16, 1852-1886.
    Index to estates, 1841-1944.
    Index to administration dockets, 1846-1944.
    Will books, b1-21, 1839-1909.
    Birth records, v1-4, 1866-1908.
    Marriage records, vA-26, 1840-1916.
    Marriage index, 1840-1843.
    Death records, & index, v1-3, 1870-1908.
    Naturalizations, decl. of intent, v1-3, 1883-1906.
    Naturalization final record, v1-10, 1859-1906.
    Naturalization records certificates, v1-4, 1884-1903.
    Guardians dockets, v1-3, 1840-1886.
    Guardians appointments, v6, 1881-1885.
Recorder:
    Grantor & Grantee index, 1840-1914.
    Deed records, v1-124, 1840-1895.
Miscellaneous:
    Pastor's register for private use, 1888-1891 (R.C.Zartman, Evang-Ref)
    Akron, Temple Israel Hebrew Congregation, minutes, 1865-1968.
    The High Schurch: 150th Anniversary, Emmanuel United Church of Christ, Doylestown, 1817-1867.
    Springfield Tp. Presby. Church, records, 1809-1938.

## OHIO HISTORICAL SOCIETY: (MICROFILM)
Auditor:
    Enlistment & enrollment, 1857-1865.
    Commutation receipts, 1864.
Clerk of Courts:
    Common Pleas journals, 1842-1852.
    Plaintiff index, v1, 1840-1870.
    Common Pleas civil dockets, v2-12, 1840-1852.
    Supreme Court minutes, v1, 1842-1851.
    Supreme Court record, v1, 1842-1846.
Commissioners:
    Bounty receipts, 1864.
Probate Court:
    Will books, v8-21, 1887-1909.
    Naturalizations, decl. of intent, v1-3, 1883-1906.
    Naturalization final record, v1-10, 1859-1906.
    Naturalization records certificates, v1-4, 1884-1903.
Miscellaneous:
    Connecticut Land Co., Western Reserve land draft, 1795-1809.
    Marriages, 1840-1865, by DAR.
    Bible records & cemetery inscriptions, by DAR.
    Tombstone inscriptions, by DAR.
    Law, wills & bible records, by DAR.
    Tombstones & cemetery inscriptions, by DAR.

## CENSUS RECORDS  (OHS,SLO,OGS,LDS)
1840-1880, 1900-1910; 1890 VETERANS; 1880,1900 SOUNDEX; 1910 MIRACODE

## AGRICULTURAL CENSUS SCHEDULES  (OHS,SLO-mic)
1850,1870

**PRODUCTS OF INDUSTRY CENSUS SCHEDULE (OHS,SLO-mic)**
1850,1860,1870,1880

**MORTALITY CENSUS SCHEDULES (OHS,SLO-mic)**
1850,1860

**NEWSPAPERS: [GUIDE TO OHIO NEWSPAPERS, 1793-1973]**
Akron, Barberton, Cuyahoga Falls, Hudson, Northfield, Stow, Tallmadge, Twinsburg.

**TAX RECORDS (OHS & LDS)**
none listed; see parent counties.

**GENEALOGICAL PERIODICAL ARTICLES**
Bell, Carol Willsey. OHIO GENEALOGICAL PERIODICAL INDEX: A COUNTY GUIDE (Youngstown, OH: author, 6th ed., 1987)

**PUBLISHED SOURCES:**
1950 RECORD OF OLD HOUSES OF HUDSON OHIO. 1950. (SLO)
Akron Map & Atlas Co. ILLUSTRATED SUMMIT COUNTY OHIO ATLAS. 1891 (OGS,SLO)
AKRON BEACON JOURNAL 100 HISTORIC PAGES (1852-1976) 1976. 111p (OGS)
Akron Turner Club. CENTENNIAL ANNIVERSARY OF THE AKRON TURNER CLUB 1885-1985. 1985. (OGS)
Alliance Genealogical Society OGS. EARLY MARRIAGES OF STARK COUNTY, OHIO, 1809-1840: IN-CLUDES GREEN & FRANKLIN TOWNSHIPS OF SUMMIT COUNTY. (Alliance OH: the society, 1986) 149p (LDS)
Alling, Ethan. LOCUST GROVE CEMETERY, TWINSBURGH. 1963. 40p (DAR)
Atwater, George P. ANNALS OF A PARISH: A CHRONICAL OF THE FOUNDING AND OF THE GROWN AND DEVELOPMENT OF THE CHURCH OF OUR SAVIOR, AKRON, OHIO. (np: author, 1928) 67p (LDS)
Barnholth, William I. THE CUYAHOGA-TUSCARAWAS PORTAGE: A DOCUMENTARY HISTORY. (Akron OH: Summit Co.Hist.Soc., 1954) 28p (DAR,LDS)
Bell, Carol W. OHIO LANDS: STEUBENVILLE LAND OFFICE RECORDS, 1800-1820. (Youngstown OH: author, 1983) 181p (OGS)
Bierce, Lucius V. HISTORICAL REMINISCENCES OF SUMMIT COUNTY OHIO. (Akron OH: T. & H.G.Canfield, 1854) 157p (LC,DAR,SLO,LDS)(RPI)
Caccamo, James F. HUDSON (OHIO) CENSUS INDEX 1910. (Hudson OH: Hudson Library & Hist.Assn., 1984) 34p (OGS)
Caccamo, James F. INDEX TO 1900 OHIO CENSUS FOR HUDSON OHIO. (Hudson: Hudson Hist Soc, 1984) 16p (OGS)
Caccamo, James F. INDEX TO THE 1870 FEDERAL POPULATION CENSUS OF 1870 FOR HUDSON, OHIO. (Hudson: Hudson Hist Soc, 1982) 14p. (OGS)
Carter, Lena M. & R.T.Cross. TWINSBURG, OHIO, 1817-1917. (Twinsburg OH: Samuel Bissell Memorial Libr.Assn., 1917) 533p (DAR)
Case, Lora. HUDSON OF LONG AGO. (Hudson OH: Hudson Independent, 1897) 70p. (SLO,LDS)
CITY/COUNTY DIRECTORIES: check holdings of OHS & local public library.
Clegg, Michael. TAX RECORDS OF PORTAGE, SUMMIT AND PORTIONS OF MEDINA COUNTY OHIO, 1808-1820. (Mansfield: Ohio Gen Soc, 1979) 58p (OGS,LDS)
COMBINATION ATLAS MAP OF SUMMIT COUNTY OHIO. (Philadelphia: Tackabury, Mead & Moffett, 1874) (Reprint, Evansville IN: Unigraphic, 1972) 139p (LDS,OGS,LC)
Daughters of the American Revolution. BIBLE RECORDS, SUMMIT COUNTY OHIO. (SLO,DAR)
Daughters of the American Revolution. BIBLE, BAPTISMAL RECORDS. (SLO)
Daughters of the American Revolution. CEMETERY INSCRIPTIONS, COPLEY TOWNSHIP, SUMMIT COUNTY OHIO. (SLO,LDS,DAR)
Daughters of the American Revolution. CEMETERY INSCRIPTIONS, SUMMIT COUNTY OHIO. (SLO,LDS)

Daughters of the American Revolution. EARLY RECORDS, LAWS, WILLS, BIBLE. (LDS,SLO,DAR)

Daughters of the American Revolution. MARRIAGE RECORDS, SUMMIT COUNTY OHIO, 1840-1865. 3v. (SLO,LDS,DAR)

Daughters of the American Revolution. TOMBSTONE INSCRIPTIONS, HURON, SUMMIT...COUNTIES OHIO. (SLO)

Daughters of the American Revolution. TOMBSTONE INSCRIPTIONS, BATH TOWNSHIP, SUMMIT COUNTY OHIO. (SLO,LDS,DAR)

Dibbert, Roderic B. FAITH OF OUR FATHERS: THE STORY OF THE BRONSON FAMILY AND THEIR CHURCH. (Akron OH: DeKoven Fdn., 1985) 16p (LDS)

District Historical Society of Medina, Summit, and Wayne Counties. FIRST REPORT, CONTAINING THE CONSTITUTION AND ACCOUNT OF THE ORGANIZATION OF THE SOCIETY. 1877-1878. 42p (LDS)

Doyle, William. CENTENNIAL HISTORY OF SUMMIT COUNTY. (Chicago: Biographical Pub.Co.,1908) 1115p (DAR,SLO,LDS) (RPI)

Fairchild, Thomas B. A HISTORY OF THE TOWN OF CUYAHOGA FALLS, SUMMIT COUNTY OHIO. 1876. (Akron OH: Old Book Store, 1968?) 39p. (DAR,SLO)

Folck, Linda. LOCAL GOVERNMENT RECORDS IN THE AMERICAN HISTORY RESEARCH CENTER AT THE UNIVERSITY OF AKRON. (Akron: U of Akron, 1982) 40p. (OGS)

Fox, John H. GRAVESTONE INSCRIPTIONS, OHIO. 197? 10p (LDS)

GENEALOGICAL DATA RELATING TO WOMEN IN THE WESTERN RESERVE BEFORE 1840 (1850) (Cleveland: Centennial Commission, 1943) (WRHS,LDS)

Gillespie, Bob. NOSTALGIA - PORTAGE LAKES, HIGHLIGHTS AND ANCEDOTES FROM "THE PORTAGE LAKES WEEKLY." (Akron OH: author, 1975) 106p (OGS)

Grismer, Karl H.. AKRON & SUMMIT COUNTY OHIO. (Akron OH: Summit Co.Hist. Soc., 1952) 834p (LC,LDS,DAR,SLO) (RPI)

Hardesty, H.H. MILITARY HISTORY OF OHIO - SUMMIT COUNTY EDITION. 1886/87. (OHS)

Harter, Mrs. Bert. GERMAN REFORMED & LUTHERAN CHURCH RECORDS, BAPTISMS, DEATHS FROM WAYNE, STARK, MEDINA & SUMMIT COUNTIES, TRANSLATED FROM THE GERMAN. (Doylestown OH: author, 1962)

Heintz, Calvin W. THE COPPACAW STORY: A HISTORY OF CUYAHOGA FALLS, OHIO. (Cuyahoga Falls OH: Summit Pub., 1962?) 92p (LDS)

HISTORICAL ATLAS OF SUMMIT CO OHIO. (Philadelphia: Tackaberry, Mead & Moffett, 1874) 140p (RPI)

Historical Records Survey. INVENTORY OF THE COUNTY ARCHIVES OF OHIO: SUMMIT COUNTY, AKRON. (Columbus OH: author, 1941) 322p (DAR,LDS,OHS)

Hudson Library & Historical Society. MINUTES OF THE FIRST CONGREGATIONAL CHURCH, HUDSON, OHIO, 1802-1837. 45p. (SLO)

Hudson Library & Historical Society. A SHORT HISTORY OF HUDSON, OHIO. (Hudson OH: the society, 1975) 49p (LDS)

Izant, Grace G. HUDSON'S HERITAGE: A CHRONICLE OF THE FOUNDING AND THE FLOWERING OF THE VILLAGE OF HUDSON, OHIO. (Kent OH: Kent State University Press, 1985) 278p (OGS,LDS)

James, Peggie S. PORTAGE & SUMMIT COUNTY PIONEER ASSOCIATION: ORGANIZED 1874. (Munroe Falls OH: author, 1972) 52p (LDS)

James, Peggie S. STOW OHIO: SHADOWS OF ITS PAST. (Ann Arbor: Edwards Bros., 1972) 307p (LDS,SLO)

Johnson, William C. ENUMERATION OF YOUTH AND PARTIAL CENSUS FOR SCHOOL DISTRICTS IN PORTAGE COUNTY OHIO, 1832-1838. (Kent OH: American Historical Research Center, 1982) 1v (LDS)

Kenfield, Scott D. AKRON AND SUMMIT COUNTY OHIO, 1825-1929. (Chicago: S.J.Clarke Pub.Co., 1928) 3v (LDS)

Kovatch, Marilyn & L.St.John. SUMMIT COUNTY OHIO DEATH RECORDS, VOL.III, 1876-1878 AND SCATTERED RECORDS, 1900-1902. (Akron OH: Summit Co Chapter OGS, 1986) 61p (OGS)

Lane, Samuel. FIFTY YEARS AND OVER OF AKRON AND SUMMIT COUNTY OHIO. (Akron OH: Beacon Job Dept., 1892) 1167p. (LC,LDS,DAR,SLO)(RPI)

Lawrence, Frank. ABOUT OLD TALLMADGE. (Tallmadge OH: Tallmadge Hist Soc., 1984) 54p (OGS,LDS)

McCormick, Alexander S. THE HISTORY OF MEDICINE IN SUMMIT COUNTY, OHIO. (New York: Hobson Book Press, 1946) 145p (LC)

Nichols, Kenneth. YESTERDAY'S AKRON: THE FIRST 150 YEARS. (Miami FL: E.A. Seemann Pub., 1975) 120p (LDS)

Olin, Oscar E. AKRON AND ENVIRONS, HISTORICAL, BIOGRAPHICAL, GENEALOGICAL. (Chicago: Lewis Pub.Co., 1917) 708p (LDS)

Olin, Oscar E. CENTENNIAL HISTORY OF AKRON, OHIO. (Akron OH: Summit Co Hist.Soc.,1925) 666p (DAR)

Perrin, William. HISTORY OF SUMMIT COUNTY OHIO. (Chicago: Baskin & Battey, 1881) 1050p. (LC,LDS,SLO,DAR)(RPI)

PORTRAIT AND BIOGRAPHICAL RECORD OF PORTAGE AND SUMMIT COUNTIES OHIO. (Logansport IN: A.W.Bowen, 1898) 988p (LC,LDS,SLO,DAR)(RPI)

PROCEEDINGS IN COMMEMORATION OF THE FIFTIETH ANNIVERSARY OF THE SETTLEMENT OF TALLMADGE. 1857. 109p. (SLO)

Randall, Emilius. HISTORICAL SKETCH OF THE SETTLEMENT OF TALLMADGE OHIO. 1908. 34p. (SLO)

Samuel Bissell Memorial Library of Twinsburg. TWINSBURG, OHIO, 1817-1917. 1917. 528p. (SLO)

St. John, Loretta. SUMMIT COUNTY OHIO DEATHS [1866-1878,1900-1902] 1970,1972. 2v (LDS,DAR,SLO)

Summit Co Chapter OGS. INDEX TO FIFTY YEARS AND OVER IN AKRON AND SUMMIT COUNTY BY SAMUEL LANE, 1892. (Akron: the society, 1986) 192p (OGS,LDS)

Summit Co Chapter OGS. SUMMIT COUNTY CEMETERY RECORDS, VOL.I, BATH, COPLEY, NORTON. (Akron: the society, 1979) 100p (OGS,LDS,SLO)

Summit Co Chapter OGS. SUMMIT COUNTY CEMETERY RECORDS, VOL.II, GREEN, FRANKLIN (Akron: the society, 1980) 126p (OGS,LDS,SLO)

Summit Co Chapter OGS. SUMMIT COUNTY CEMETERY RECORDS, VOL.III, COVENTRY TOWNSHIP. (Akron: the society, 1985) 79p (OGS,LDS)

Summit Co Chapter OGS. SUMMIT COUNTY CEMETERY RECORDS, VOL.IV, MOUNT HOPE CEMETERY, AKRON. (Akron: the society, 198?) (OGS,LDS)

Summit Co Chapter OGS. SUMMIT COUNTY WILL INDEX 1840-1902 (Akron: the society, nd) 55p (OGS)

Summit Co Chapter OGS. SUMMIT COUNTY DEATH RECORDS 1876-1878,1900-1902 (Akron: the society, nd) 64p (OGS)

Summit Co. Historical Society. A CENTENNIAL HISTORY OF AKRON, 1825-1925. 1925. 666p. (SLO)

SUMMIT COUNTY OHIO [ATLAS]. 1910. (SLO)

Tackaberry, Mead & Moffett. COMBINATION ATLAS MAP OF SUMMIT COUNTY. 1874. (SLO)

Tallmadge Hist. Society. A HISTORY OF TALLMADGE OHIO. 1957. 136p. (SLO)

Twinsburg Hist. Society. HISTORY OF TWINSBURG, OHIO, 1817-1967. 59p.(SLO) TWINSBURG OHIO, 1817-1917. (Twinsburg OH: Champlin Press, 1917) 533p (LDS)

Upton, Harriet T. HISTORY OF THE WESTERN RESERVE (Chicago: Lewis Pub Co., 1910) 3v (SLO)

Welsh, Marilyn & L.St.John. INDEX TO TWINSBURG OHIO HISTORY, 1817-1917, GENEALOGIES PART II. (Uniontown OH: author, 1972) 81p.

Welsh, Marilyn & L.St.John. SUMMIT COUNTY DEATH RECORDS VOL.II, 1873-1876. (Uniontown OH: author, nd) 69p. (OGS)

Welsh, Marilyn & L.St.John. SUMMIT COUNTY DEATH RECORDS VOL.I,1866-1872. (Uniontown OH: author, nd) 55p. (OGS)

Western Reserve Hist.Soc. INDEX TO THE MICROFILM EDITION OF GENEALOGICAL DATA RELATING TO WOMEN IN THE WESTERN RESERVE PRE 1840. (Cleveland: the society, 1976) 226p (OGS,WRHS)

Whittlesey, Charles. A SKETCH AND THE SETTLEMENT AND PROGRESS OF THE TOWNSHIP OF TALLMADGE. 1842. 29p. (SLO)

Wickham, Gertrude V.W. MEMORIAL TO THE PIONEER WOMEN OF THE WESTERN RESERVE. (Cleveland: Cleveland Centennial Commission, 1896+) 2v, repr 1981 (SLO)

Yon, Paul D. GUIDE TO OHIO COUNTY AND MUNICIPAL GOVERNMENT RECORDS FOR URBAN RESEARCH. (Columbus: Ohio Hist Soc., 1973) 216p.(OHS)

# TRUMBULL COUNTY

| | |
|---|---|
| CREATED: | 1800 FROM JEFFERSON OH & WAYNE CO. MICH. |
| COUNTY SEAT: | WARREN 44481 |
| COURT HOUSE: | 161 HIGH ST.NW, WARREN 44481 |
| LIBRARY: | WARREN-TRUMBULL COUNTY PUBLIC LIBRARY, 444 MAHONING AVE NW, WARREN 44483 |
| HISTORICAL SOCIETY: | 309 SOUTH ST. SE, WARREN 44483 |
| GENEALOGICAL SOCIETY: | TRUMBULL CO CHAPTER OGS, PO BOX 309, WARREN 44483 publication: ANCESTRY TRAILS |
| HEALTH DEPARTMENT: | 418 MAIN AVE SW, WARREN 44481 (separate offices for Warren city, Niles, Hubbard, Newton Falls, Cortland & Girard) |
| ARCHIVAL DISTRICT: | WESTERN RESERVE HIST.SOC., CLEVELAND |
| LAND SURVEYS: | CONNECTICUT WESTERN RESERVE |
| BOUNDED BY: | EAST: MERCER CO., PENNSYLVANIA |
| | NORTH: ASHTABULA CO. |
| | WEST: PORTAGE CO. |
| | SOUTH: MAHONING CO. |
| TOWNSHIPS: | Bazetta, Bloomfield, Braceville, Bristol, Brookfield, Champion, Farmington, Fowler, Greene, Gustavus, Hartford, Howland, Hubbard, Johnston, Kinsman, Liberty, Lordstown, Mecca, Mesopotamia, Newton, Southington, Vernon, Vienna, Warren, Weathersfield. |
| SPECIAL NOTE: | A COURTHOUSE FIRE IN 1895 DESTROYED SOME RECORDS. |

## COURT RECORDS: (LDS MICROFILM)
Auditor:
  School enumeration & account records, 1831-1913.
  Tax duplicates, 1816-1838.
  Township land list, 1808.
  Enumeration of school aged youth, Hartford Tp., 1851.
  Enumeration of taxable persons, 1808.
Clerk of Courts:
  Supreme Court journal, 1807-1841.
  Indentures, 1824-1869.
Commissioners:
  Journal, 1837-1899 & Index, 1877-1908.
Probate Court:
  Administrators, exrs, grdns. bonds & letters, v1-2, 1853-1863.
  Guardians bonds & letters, v2-4, 1863-1899.
  Executors bonds & letters, v2, 1868-1886.
  Administrators bonds & letters, v4, 1885-1893.
  Index to estates to 1921.
  Probate docket, v1-10, 1837-1883.
  Probate journal, v1-20, 1852-1887.
  Probate records, v1-18, 1803-1853.
  Will records, v1-9, 1841-1886.
  Marriage certificates, 1817-1820.
  Marriage licenses, 1816-1891.

Marriage records, v1-19, 1803-1916.
Birth records, v1-4, 1867-1908.
Death records, v1-3, 1867-1908.
Administration docket, v11, 1882-1885.
Civil docket, v1-7, 1852-1886.
Guardians docket v1, 1839-1859; v1, 1882-1895.
Inventories, bills of sale, v1-12, 1853-1887.
Inventories, appraisements, v13-16, 1882-1890.
Probate final record, v1-19, 1853-1883.
Petitions to sell land, v1-15, 1852-1887.

Recorder:
Deed index, transcribed from Mahoning Co.,1795-1845.
Deed records transcribed from Mahoning Co., 1795-1845.
Index to deeds transcribed from Summit Co., 1795-1840.
Record of indentured children, 1824-1869.
Soldiers discharge, 1861-1919.
Western Reserve land draft, 1795-1809.

Miscellaneous:
Brookfield, LDS Church, members, 1868-1876.
Mahoning Baptist Assn., minutes, 1820-1827.
Farmington, United Presby.& Congreg.Church, records, 1817-1869.
J.P.docket book of Benj.Morse, Geauga & Trum.Co., 1805-1809.
David Simon's school records, 1831-1842.
Pastor's records, Lucian J. Mayer, Sharon Charge in Mercer Co., Pa & Trumbull Co., OH, 1864-1866, Evang.-Reformed.
Plat map of Vienna Cemetery, with name index.

## OHIO HISTORICAL SOCIETY: (MICROFILM)
Auditor:
School enumeration & account records, 1831-1913.
Township land list, 1808.
Enumeration of school aged youth, Hartford Tp., 1851.
Enumeration of taxable persons, 1808.

Common Pleas:
Indentures, 1824-1869.

Commissioners:
Journal, 1837-1899 & Index, 1877-1908.

Recorder:
Soldiers discharge, 1861-1919.
Western Reserve land draft, 1795-1809.

Miscellaneous:
Marriages, 1803-1865, by DAR.
Births, Marriages & Deaths, by DAR.
Cemetery records & War of 1812, by DAR.
Will records, 1803-1850, by DAR.
Connecticut Land Co., Western Reserve land draft, 1795-1809.
Bible & Family records of Trumbull Co Ohio, by DAR.
Census of Pioneer Women of Trumbull & Ashtabula Co. Ohio, by DAR.

## CENSUS RECORDS  (OHS,SLO,OGS,LDS)
1820-1880, 1900-1910; 1890 VETERANS; 1880,1900 SOUNDEX; 1910 MIRACODE

## AGRICULTURAL CENSUS SCHEDULES  (OHS,SLO-mic)
1850,1870

**PRODUCTS OF INDUSTRY CENSUS SCHEDULE (OHS,SLO-mic)**
1850,1860,1870,1880

**MORTALITY CENSUS SCHEDULES (OHS,SLO-mic)**
1850,1860

**NEWSPAPERS: [GUIDE TO OHIO NEWSPAPERS, 1793-1973]**
Cortland, Girard, Hartford, Hubbard, Kinsman, Newton Falls, Niles, Warren.

**TAX RECORDS (OHS & LDS)**
1806-1814,1816-1838.

**GENEALOGICAL PERIODICAL ARTICLES**
Bell, Carol Willsey. OHIO GENEALOGICAL PERIODICAL INDEX: A COUNTY GUIDE (Youngstown,
   OH: author, 6th ed., 1987)

**PUBLISHED SOURCES:**
Aley, Howard C. INTERESTING PEOPLE OF OUR COMMUNITY...EMBRACING MAHONING,
   TRUMBULL & COLUMBIANA COUNTIES OHIO (Youngstown OH: author, 1948) 173p
Aley, Howard C. THE BEGINNINGS OF OUR COMMUNITY...EMBRACING MAHONING, TRUM-
   BULL & COLUMBIANA COUNTIES OHIO (Youngstown OH: author, 1950) 247p
Aley, Howard C. THE STORY OF OUR COMMUNITY...EMBRACING MAHONING, TRUMBULL &
   COLUMBIANA COUNTIES OHIO (Youngstown OH: author, 1954) 263p
Aley, Howard C. UNDERSTANDING THE RESOURCES OF OUR COMMUNITY...EMBRACING
   MAHONING, TRUMBULL & COLUMBIANA COUNTIES OHIO. (Youngstown OH: author, 1951)
   193p
Allen, Ruth, ed. TRUMBULL COUNTY OHIO CADASTRAL OR LAND OWNER MAPS 1830-1840-
   1850. (Warren OH: Trumbull Co Chapter OGS, 1985) 156p. (OGS,LDS)
Allison, Grace C. COVERED BRIDGES OF NILES IN TRUMBULL COUNTY OHIO. (Niles OH: Niles
   Hist.Soc., nd)
Allison, Grace C. HEATON'S TOWN [articles about history, people, places & past events of Niles OH)
   (Niles OH: Niles Hist.Soc., nd)
Allison, Grace C. HISTORY OF HOWLAND SPRINGS. (Warren OH: author, 1983) 72p)
American Atlas Co. ATLAS AND DIRECTORY OF TRUMBULL COUNTY OHIO. (Cleveland: author,
   1899)(Reprint, Evansville IN: Unigraphic, 1979) 236p (SLO,LC,LDS) (RPI)
Baldwin, Henry R. OLDEST INSCRIPTIONS WITH REVOLUTIONARY AND WAR OF 1812 RECORDS
   OF TRUMBULL....CO. OHIO. (SLO,LDS)
Baldwin, Henry R. WILLS OF COLUMBIANA, MAHONING AND TRUMBULL COUNTIES OHIO.
   (SLO,LDS)
Bell, Carol W. ABSTRACTS FROM BIOGRAPHIES IN HISTORY OF NORTH EASTERN OHIO by John
   S. Stewart, 1935. (Indianapolis: Ye Olde Genealogie Shoppe, 1983)
Benton, Frank. WEST MECCA UNITED METHODIST CHURCH, WEST MECCA OHIO, 1835-1972.
   1972.
BIOGRAPHICAL HISTORY OF NORTHEASTERN OHIO EMBRACING THE COUNTIES OF ASH-
   TABULA, TRUMBULL AND MAHONING. (Chicago: Lewis Pub.Co.,1893) 735p
   (DAR,LDS,LC,SLO)
Butler, Joseph G. Jr. HISTORY OF YOUNGSTOWN AND THE MAHONING VALLEY OHIO. (Chicago:
   American Histl Soc, 1921) 3v (Yo Pub Lib, OHS,LDS)
Case, Leonard. EARLY SETTLEMENT OF WARREN, TRUMBULL COUNTY OHIO. (Warren: Hist Soc
   Tract, 1876) (Reprint, Cleveland: G.Alison & A.Nolan, 1974). 34p. (LDS)
CITY/COUNTY DIRECTORIES: check holdings of OHS & local public library.
Clark, Hazel V. MESOPOTAMIA: BETWEEN TWO RIVERS, 1798-1900. (Warren OH: Trumbull
   Co.Hist.Soc., 1957) 52p (DAR)
Clegg, Michael, ed. TRUMBULL COUNTY OHIO NEWSPAPER OBITUARY ABSTRACTS 1812-1870.
   [OHIO NEWSPAPER ABSTRACTS SERIES VOL.I] (Ft.Wayne IN: author, 1981) 146p. (OGS,SLO)

Daughters of the American Revolution. BROWNLEE MANUSCRIPTS OF TRUMBULL COUNTY OHIO [Kinsman, Vernon, Hartford, Fowler, Hubbard]. 1961. 287p. (WTCPL)

Daughters of the American Revolution. EARLY MARRIAGE BONDS, 1803-1865. (SLO,LDS,DAR)

Daughters of the American Revolution. GENERAL INDEX OF NAMES FROM THE INDEXES OF VOLUMES 1 THRU 12 OF THE EARLY PROBATE RECORDS OF TRUMBULL COUNTY, OHIO, 1803-1843. (SLO)

Daughters of the American Revolution. RECORDS OF MARRIAGES (1815-1874) AND BAPTISMS (1816-1874) METHODIST CHURCH CHARGES IN FOWLER, VIENNA, BAZETTA, BROCKWAY MILLS, HARTFORD, BROOKFIELD, TRUMBULL CO., OHIO. (DAR,LDS)

Daughters of the American Revolution. INDEX TO TWENTIETH CENTURY HISTORY OF TRUMBULL COUNTY OHIO, VOL.1 & 2 BY HARRIET TAYLOR UPTON. 1963. (SLO)

Davis, Florence. KINSMAN MEMORIES, 1799-1970. (Warren OH: Trumbull Co.Hist.Soc., 1970) 52p (LDS)

Drohan, Rev.N.J. HISTORY OF HUBBARD OHIO, 1798-1907. (Hubbard OH: author, 1907) (WCTPL,YoPL)

Everts, Louis H. COMBINATION ATLAS MAP OF TRUMBULL COUNTY, OHIO. (Chicago: author,1874) (Reprint, Knightstown IN: Bookmark, 1974) 132p (LDS,LC,OGS,SLO)(RPI)

Everts, L.H. HISTORICAL ATLAS OF TRUMBULL COUNTY OHIO. 1875. (SLO)

Federal Writers Project. WARREN AND TRUMBULL COUNTY. (sp: Western Reserve Hist.Celebration Committee, 1938) 60p (DAR)

Fiedler, George E. A HISTORICAL STORY OF EAST HUBBARD (TOWNSHIP) AND PARTS OF HUBBARD AND PENNSYLVANIA. (Youngstown OH: author, 1976) 150p. (Yo PL)

Fowler, Fred E. VARIOUS BIRTHS, MARRIAGES & DEATHS IN EASTERN TRUMBULL COUNTY. (Brookfield OH: author, 1949) 81p. (SLO,LDS,WTCPL)

GENEALOGICAL DATA RELATING TO WOMEN IN THE WESTERN RESERVE BEFORE 1840 (1850) (Cleveland: Centennial Commission, 1943) (LDS,WRHS)

Gutknecht, William J. ATLAS OF MAHONING COUNTY OHIO AND PART OF TRUMBULL COUNTY OHIO. (Youngstown OH: author, c1915) 104p (LC,OHS)

Historical Records Survey. INVENTORY OF THE COUNTY ARCHIVES OF OHIO, NO.78, TRUMBULL COUNTY (WARREN). (Columbus: author, 1937) 128p (LDS,DAR,OHS)

HISTORY OF TRUMBULL AND MAHONING COUNTIES OHIO. (Chicago: H.Z.Williams, 1882)(Reprint, Evansville IN: Unigraphic, 1972) 2v. (LDS,SLO,LC,OGS,OHS,DAR)(RPI)

Hoskins, Mary C. THE GREENE STORY, 1817-1963. (Warren: Trumbull Co Hist.Soc., 1963) 97p (SLO,DAR)

Hoskins, Mary C. THE GUSTAVUS STORY, 1800-1965. (Warren: Trumbull Co Hist.Soc.,1965) 95p. (DAR,SLO)

Kachur, Thomas. HISTORICAL COLLECTIONS BAZETTA TWP., CORTLAND OHIO. (Cortland OH: author, 1983) 675p (OGS,LDS,SLO)

Lyman, Lima. LYMAN'S HISTORIES AND STORIES OF NEWTON FALLS, TRUMBULL COUNTY OHIO. (Chicago: Adams Press, 1970) 133p

Mahoning Valley Historical Society. HISTORICAL COLLECTIONS OF THE MAHONING VALLEY. 1876. 524p. (SLO)

MAKERS OF WARREN. (Warren OH: Warren Tribune Chronicle, 1930) 40p (LDS)

MANUALS FOR THE FIRST PRESBYTERIAN CHURCH IN WARREN, OHIO 1850-1872. 1979. (SLO)

Mathews, Elsie H. JUSTICES OF THE PEACE OF TRUMBULL COUNTY OHIO 1800-1865. 1976. 8p.(SLO,WTCPL)

Meyers, Mrs.C.C. MARRIAGES PERFORMED BY REV.STEVENS IN TOMPKINS AND GENESSEE COUNTIES NY, HURON, TRUMBULL AND CUYAHOGA COUNTIES OHIO, AND A FEW IN MICHIGAN AND TENNESSEE, 1825-1859. 9p (LDS)

Sells, Grace R. THE HISTORY OF BRACEVILLE TOWNSHIP, TRUMBULL COUNTY. 1976. 152p

Simon, Bernice H. NAME INDEX FOR GENEALOGICAL AND FAMILY HISTORY OF EASTERN OHIO by E.Summers, 1903. (Chagrin Falls OH: author, 1973) 28p (Yo Pub Lib)

Stewart, John S. HISTORY OF NORTHEASTERN OHIO. (Indianapolis: Historical Pub Co., 1935) 3v. (SLO)

Strong, Doris W. FEDERAL CENSUS RECORDS FOR TRUMBULL COUNTY OHIO, 1820. (Washington: Guild Pub.Co., 1946) 125,23p (LDS,SLO,DAR)

Summers, Ewing. GENEALOGICAL AND FAMILY HISTORY OF EASTERN OHIO ILLUSTRATED. (New York: Lewis Pub Co., 1903) (Yo Pub Lib, OHS)

THE CHRONICLE - WARREN, OHIO 1906. (Warren OH: Trumbull Co Hist Soc., nd) 45p (OGS)

Trucksis, Theresa. A GUIDE TO LOCAL HISTORICAL MATERIALS IN THE LIBRARIES OF NORTH-EASTERN OHIO.(Youngstown OH: NE Oh Libr.Assn., 1977) 72p (YoPL)

Trumbull Co Chapter OGS. ABSTRACTS OF PROBATE RECORDS TRUMBULL COUNTY OHIO 1803-1843. (Warren: the society, 1986) 282p (OGS)

Trumbull Co Chapter OGS. TRUMBULL COUNTY OHIO CEMETERY INSCRIPTIONS 1800-1930. (Warren: the society, 1983) 422p. (OGS,LDS,SLO)

Trumbull Co Chapter OGS. TRUMBULL COUNTY OHIO EARLY MARRIAGES 1800-1865. (Warren: the society, 1973) 94p

TRUMBULL COUNTY MISCELLANEA, VOL.1: BIRTH CERTIFICATES,1911-1914.21p (SLO)

Ulam, Norman & Mary. NATURALIZATIONS IN TRUMBULL COUNTY OHIO 1800-1870. (Warren: Trumbull Co Chapter OGS, 1983) 72p. (OGS,LDS,SLO)

Upton, Harriet T. A 20TH CENTURY HISTORY OF TRUMBULL COUNTY OHIO. (Chicago: Lewis Pub.Co.,1909) 2v. (Reprint, Warren OH: Western Reserve Chapter DAC,1983) (OGS,LC,LDS,DAR,SLO)(RPI)

Upton, Harriet T. HISTORY OF THE WESTERN RESERVE (Chicago: Lewis Pub Co., 1910) 3v (DAR,SLO)(RPI)

Western Reserve Hist.Soc. INDEX TO THE MICROFILM EDITION OF GENEALOGICAL DATA RELATING TO WOMEN IN THE WESTERN RESERVE PRE 1840. (Cleveland: the society, 1976) 226p (OGS,WRHS)

Wickham, Gertrude V.W. MEMORIAL TO THE PIONEER WOMEN OF THE WESTERN RESERVE. (Cleveland: Cleveland Centennial Commission, 1896+) 2v.(SLO)

Winnagle, Grace M. CEMETERY RECORDS OF TRUMBULL COUNTY OHIO. 4v (LDS,DAR)

Winnagle, Grace M. CENSUS OF PIONEER WOMEN OF TRUMBULL COUNTY OHIO WHO CAME TO, OR WERE BORN IN THE COUNTY BEFORE 1850: FOR THE TOWNSHIPS OF BRACEVILLE, CHAMPION, FARMINGTON, GREENE, GUSTAVUS, HARTFORD, HUBBARD, JOHNSTON, KINSMAN, LORDSTOWN, MECCA, MESOPOTAMIA. (LDS)

Winnagle, Grace M. EARLY MARRIAGES OF TRUMBULL COUNTY OHIO,1800-1865.(SLO)

Winnagle, Grace M. GENEALOGICAL DATA IN BIBLES & FAMILY RECORDS.(LDS,DAR)

Winnagle, Grace M. INDEX TO PROPERTY DEEDS OF TRUMBULL COUNTY, OHIO, VOLUME A THROUGH Z, 1800-1831. 1984. (SLO)

Yon, Paul D. GUIDE TO OHIO COUNTY AND MUNICIPAL GOVERNMENT RECORDS FOR URBAN RESEARCH. (Columbus: Ohio Hist Soc., 1973) 216p. (OHS)

# TUSCARAWAS COUNTY

| | |
|---|---|
| CREATED: | 1808 FROM MUSKINGUM COUNTY |
| COUNTY SEAT: | NEW PHILADELPHIA 44663 |
| COURT HOUSE: | PUBLIC SQUARE, NEW PHILADELPHIA 44663 |
| LIBRARY: | 121 FAIR AVE. NW, NEW PHILADELPHIA 44663 |
| HISTORICAL SOCIETY: | TUSCARAWAS CO. HISTORICAL SOCIETY, PO BOX 462, NEW PHILADELPHIA 44663 |
| | RAGERSVILLE HISTORICAL SOCIETY, PO BOX 6, SUGARCREEK 44681 |
| GENEALOGICAL SOCIETY: | TUSCARAWAS CO CHAPTER OGS, PO BOX 141, NEW PHILADELPHIA 44663 publication: PIONEER FOOTPRINTS |
| HEALTH DEPARTMENT: | 897 E.IRON AVE., PO BOX 443, DOVER 44622 (separate offices for Dover city, Uhrichsville & New Philadelphia) |

ARCHIVAL DISTRICT:          UNIVERSITY OF AKRON, AKRON, OHIO
LAND SURVEYS:               CONGRESS LANDS, SEVEN RANGES
                            UNITED STATES MILITARY DISTRICT
                            MORAVIAN INDIAN GRANT
                            DOHRMAN GRANT
BOUNDED BY:                 EAST:    CARROLL & HARRISON CO.
                            NORTH:   STARK CO.
                            WEST:    COSHOCTON & HOLMES CO.
                            SOUTH:   GUERNSEY CO.
TOWNSHIPS:                  Auburn, Bucks, Clay, Dover, Fairfield, Franklin, Goshen, Jefferson,
                            Lawrence, Mill, Oxford, Perry, Rush, Salem, Sandy, Sugar Creek,
                            Union, Warren, Warwick, Washington, Wayne, York.

## COURT RECORDS: (LDS MICROFILM)
Auditor:
    Tax duplicates, 1816-1838.
Clerk of Courts:
    Supreme Court journal, v2, 1842-1851.
    Supreme Court record, v2-4, 1827-1852.
    Common Pleas court, index to plaintiffs, v1-2, 1808-1870.
    Common Pleas court, index to defendants, v1-2, 1808-1870.
    Common Pleas journal, v2-10, 1819-1853.
    Common Pleas appearance docket, v1-10, 1819-1852.
    Common Pleas chancery record, v1-9, 1813,1817,1821-1852.
    Law record, 1808-1854.
Commissioners:
    Journal, 1808-1901.
County Home:
    Minutes, 1862-1912.
Probate Court:
    Administration dockets, 1817-1978.
    Appearance dockets, v1-21, 1852-1970.
    General index to files, 1808-1938.
    Birth records, v1-5, 1867-1908.
    Birth registrations, 1941-1966.
    Death records, v1-3, 1867-1908.
    Executor bonds, v1-2, 1854-1893.
    Guardianship dockets, v1-13, 1832-1977.
    Guardians letters, 1843-1898.
    Guardians bonds, 1882-1881.
    Guardian record, v1-2, 1858-1892.
    Probate journals, 1852-1887.
    Marriage records & index, v1-18, 1808-1917.
    Marriage record index, v7-10, 1872-1898.
    Marriage records, v7-46, 1872-1978.
    Naturalization record, v1-10, 1854-1906.
    Probate case files, 1904-1932, 182 reels.
    Will record, v1-16, 1809-1909.
Sheriff:
    Jail register, 1904-1929.

## OHIO HISTORICAL SOCIETY: (MICROFILM)
Clerk of Courts:
    Supreme Court journal, v2, 1842-1851.
    Supreme Court record, v2-4, 1827-1852.

Common Pleas court, index to plaintiffs, v1-2, 1808-1870.
Common Pleas court, index to defendants, v1-2, 1808-1870.
Common Pleas journal, v2-10, 1819-1853.
Common Pleas appearance docket, v1-10, 1819-1852.
Common Pleas chancery record, v1-9, 1813,1817,1821-1852.
Law record, 1808-1854.
Commissioners:
    Journal, 1808-1901.
County Home:
    Minutes, 1862-1912.
Probate Court:
    Administration dockets, 1817-1978.
    Appearance dockets, v1-21, 1852-1970.
    General index to files, 1808-1890.
    Birth records, v1-7, 1867-1966.
    Birth registrations, 1941-1966.
    Death records, v1-4, 1867-1966.
    Guardianship dockets, v1-13, 1832-1977.
    Probate journals, 1852-1969.
    Marriage records & index, v1-6, 1808-1872.
    Marriage record index, v7-10, 1872-1898.
    Marriage records, v7-46, 1872-1978.
    Naturalization record, v1-10, 1854-1906.
    Probate case files, 1904-1932, 182 reels.
    Will record, v1-65, 1809-1953.
Sheriff:
    Jail register, 1904-1929.
Miscellaneous:
    Marriages, 1812-1865, by DAR.
    Anna Beuter's Register of births at Zoar, 1851-1880. (in Mss.Div.)

## CENSUS RECORDS (OHS,SLO,OGS,LDS)
1820-1880, 1900-1910; 1890 VETERANS; 1880,1900 SOUNDEX; 1910 MIRACODE

## AGRICULTURAL CENSUS SCHEDULES (OHS,SLO-mic)
1850,1870

## PRODUCTS OF INDUSTRY CENSUS SCHEDULE (OHS,SLO-mic)
1850,1860,1870,1880

## MORTALITY CENSUS SCHEDULES (OHS,SLO-mic)
1850,1860

## NEWSPAPERS: [GUIDE TO OHIO NEWSPAPERS, 1793-1973]
Cancal Dover, Dennison, Dover, Gnaddenhutten, Mineral City, Mineral Point, New Philadelphia, New-comerstown, Strasburg, Sugarcreek, Uhrichsville, Zoar.

## TAX RECORDS (OHS & LDS)
1810-1814,1816-1838.

## GENEALOGICAL PERIODICAL ARTICLES
Bell, Carol Willsey. OHIO GENEALOGICAL PERIODICAL INDEX: A COUNTY GUIDE (Youngstown,
    OH: author, 6th ed., 1987)

## PUBLISHED SOURCES:

Beachy, Leroy. CEMETERY DIRECTORY OF THE AMISH COMMUNITY IN EASTERN HOLMES AND ADJOINING COUNTIES IN OHIO. (np: author, 1975) 200p (LDS)

Bell, Carol W. OHIO LANDS: STEUBENVILLE LAND OFFICE RECORDS, 1800-1820. (Youngstown OH: author, 1983) 181p (OGS)

CITY/COUNTY DIRECTORIES: check holdings of OHS & local public library.

Daughters of the American Revolution. WILLS: GEAUGA AND TUSCARAWAS COUNTIES, OHIO (ETC). 1977. 100p (DAR)

Dickinson, Marguerite S. MARRIAGES OF TUSCARAWAS COUNTY. (SLO,LDS,DAR)

Dolle, Genevieve M. ABSTRACTS FROM CHURCH RECORD BOOK OF REV. JOSEPH A. ROOF. (SLO,LDS,DAR)

Dougherty, George W. REMINISCENCE OF NEW PHILADELPHIA, OHIO, FORTY YEARS AGO AND SKETCHES OF TUSCARAWAS COUNTY AND THE EARLY SETTLERS. 1888. 16p (SLO)

Eberle, Maxine. AUBURN TWP., TUSCARAWAS COUNTY OHIO ST.JOHN'S EVANGELICAL 1879-1929. (Sugarcreek OH: Ragersville Hist Soc., 1982) 34p (LDS,SLO)

Eberle, Maxine. BALTIC, BUCKS TWP., TUSCARAWAS COUNTY OHIO ZION'S EVANGELICAL 1856-1918. (Sugarcreek OH: Ragersville Hist Soc., 1983) 77p (LDS)

Eberle, Maxine. BRIEF HISTORY OF CHURCHES AND MINISTERS IN AREA E. (COSHOCTON, HOLMES AND TUSCARAWAS COUNTIES) EASTERN OHIO ASSOCIATION OF THE OHIO CONFERENCE, UNITED CHURCH OF CHRIST. (Strasburg OH: Gordon Printing, 1976) 29p (DAR)

Eberle, Maxine. BUCKS TWP., TUSCARAWAS COUNTY OHIO ST.PAUL'S EVANGELICAL (RENNER'S) 1849-1878. (Sugarcreek OH: Ragersville Hist Soc., 1982) 48p (SLO)

Eberle, Maxine. BEERSHEBA MORAVIAN CHURCH BOOK, CLAY TOWNSHIP, 1850+. (Sugarcreek OH: author, 1987) 109p

Eberle, Maxine. BUCKS TWP., TUSCARAWAS COUNTY OHIO ST.PAUL'S EVANGELICAL (RENNER'S) 1879-1939. (Sugarcreek OH: Ragersville Hist Soc., nd) 81p

Eberle, Maxine. CHURCH RECORD BOOK FOR HIGH GERMAN REFORMED & EV-LUTH JERUSALEM'S CHURCH, STONE CREEK, 1811-1880 & JERUSALEM REF CONGR YORK TP 1903-1930 (Sugarcreek OH: Ragersville Hist Soc., 1984) 139p (LDS)

Eberle, Maxine. CHURCH RECORDS BOOK FOR FIAT ST.PETERS CONGREGATION, BUCKS TP., TUSC CO OHIO, 1849-1936 AND FOR SALEM'S REFORMED CONGREGATION, BAKERSVILLE, COSHOCTON CO OHIO, 1892-1946. (Sugarcreek OH: Ragersville Hist Soc., 1981,1984) 182p (LDS,SLO)

Eberle, Maxine. CLAY TOWNSHIP, TUSCARAWAS COUNTY OHIO - BRETHREN'S (MORAVIAN) CONGREGATION, BEGUN IN 1805. (Sugarcreek OH: Ragersville Hist.Soc., 1987) 109p

Eberle, Maxine. DOVER TOWNSHIP, TUSCARAWAS COUNTY OHIO - SALEM'S EVANGELICAL CONGREGATION, 1879-1917. (Sugarcreek OH: Ragersville Hist.Soc., 1987) 43p

Eberle, Maxine. DUNDEE, WAYNE TOWNSHIP, TUSCARAWAS COUNTY OHIO - THE GERMAN REFORMED CONGREGATION, 1861-1891. (Sugarcreek OH: Ragersville Hist.Soc., 1986) 24p (LDS)

Eberle, Maxine. JEFFERSON TOWNSHIP, TUSCARAWAS COUNTY OHIO - ST.JACOB'S REFORMED CONGREGATION, BEGUN IN 1856. (Sugarcreek OH: Ragersville Hist.Soc., 1987) 45p

Eberle, Maxine. JERUSALEM'S, YORK TWP., TUSCARAWAS COUNTY OHIO REFORMED, LUTHERAN, EVANGELICAL 1811-1880. (Sugarcreek OH: Ragersville Hist Soc., nd) 145p

Eberle, Maxine. KIRCHENBUCH DER DEUTSCHEN EVANGELISCHEN ST.JOHANNES GEMEINDE IN CANAL DOVER, TUSCARAWAS CO., OHIO, 1846-1902. (Sugarcreek OH: Ragersville Hist.Soc., 1985) 264p (LDS)

Eberle, Maxine. KIRCHENBUCH DER ERSTEN HOCHDEUTSCH-REFORMIERTEN GEMEINDE ZU RAGERSVILLE, TUSCARAWAS CO., OHIO. (Sugarcreek OH: Ragersville Hist.Soc., 1986) 163p (LDS)

Eberle, Maxine. KIRCHENBUCH DER EV.REF.ZIONS GEMEINDE IN RAGERSVILLE, TUSCARAWAS CO., OHIO, BEGUN 1893. (Sugarcreek OH: Ragersville Hist. Soc., 1986) 163p

Eberle, Maxine. KIRCHENBUCH FUR DIE EVANGELISCHE ZIONS GEMEINDE IN ROWVILLE, TUSCARAWAS COUNTY, OHIO, 1856-1918. (Sugarcreek OH: Ragersville Hist.Soc., 1983) (SLO)

Eberle, Maxine. PORT WASHINGTON, SALEM TWP.,TUSCARAWAS COUNTY OHIO ST.PAUL'S EVANGELICAL 1852-1876. (Sugarcreek OH: Ragersville Hist Soc., 1984) 112p (LDS,SLO)

Eberle, Maxine. RAGERSVILLE OHIO CEMETERY. (Sugarcreek OH: Ragersville Hist.Soc., 1978) 50p (LDS,DAR)

Eberle, Maxine. SHANESVILLE (NOW SUGARCREEK) TUSCARWAS COUNTY OHIO FIRST GERMAN REFORMED 1847-1898. (Sugarcreek OH: Ragersville Hist.Soc., 1981) 61p (LDS,SLO)

Eberle, Maxine. CHURCHBOOK FOR THE GERMAN UNITED EVANGELICAL LUTHERAN AND THE GERMAN REFORMED ZIONS CONGREGATION, UPPER STONECREEK, JEFFERSON TOWNSHIP, TUSCARAWAS COUNTY, OHIO, 1849-1889. (Sugarcreek OH: Ragersville Hist Soc., 1983) 99p (SLO)

Eberle, Maxine. STONECREEK, JEFFERSON TWP., TUSCARAWAS COUNTY OHIO FRIEDEN'S EVANGELICAL AND ZION'S REFORMED, 1890-1941 AND CHURCHBOOK, THE ZION'S REFORMED CONGREGATION, 1890-1925, PHILLIPSBURG, JEFFERSON TOWNSHIP, TUSCARAWAS COUNTY OHIO. (Sugarcreek OH: Ragersville Hist Soc., 1984) 118p (LDS,SLO)

Everts, L.H. COMBINATION ATLAS MAP OF TUSCARAWAS COUNTY OHIO. (Philadelphia: Litt.Levers, 1875) (Reprint, Strasburg OH: Gordon Print., 1973) 79p (LC,OGS,LDS,SLO)(RPI)

Federal Writers' Project. GUIDE TO TUSCARAWAS COUNTY, OHIO. (Columbus OH: author, 1939) 119p. (DAR,SLO)

Folck, Linda. LOCAL GOVERNMENT RECORDS IN THE AMERICAN HISTORY RESEARCH CENTER AT THE UNIVERSITY OF AKRON. (Akron: U of Akron, 1982) 40p. (OGS)

GRACE UNITED CHURCH OF CHRIST, STONE CREEK, OHIO, 125TH ANNIVERSARY, OCTOBER 13, 1974. (Stone Creek OH: the church, 1974) (LDS)

Gramley, Richard M. FORT LAURENS 1778-9, THE ARCHAELOGICAL RECORD. 1978. 100p.

Hagloch, Henry C. THE HISTORY OF TUSCARAWAS COUNTY OHIO. (Dover OH: Dover Hist.Soc., 1956) 212p (LDS)

Hinds, R.W. EARLY DUTCH VALLEY HISTORY: PRINTED IN "THE FREEPORT PRESS" APRIL & MAY 1954. (OGS)

HISTORY OF SOME OHIO CHURCHES, 1916-1929 [MORAVIAN CHURCH, NEW PHILADELPHIA]. (DAR)

HISTORY OF TUSCARAWAS COUNTY OHIO. (Chicago: Warner Beers, 1884) 1007p (DAR,LC,LDS,OGS,OHS,SLO)(RPI)

HISTORY OF OLD ST.PETERS, LAWRENCE TWP., TUSCARAWAS COUNTY OHIO.

INDEX TO A JUSTICE OF THE PEACE DOCKET: FOR JOSEPH ORR SCOTT WHO RESIDED AT NEW CUMBERLAND OHIO IN THE 1840'S. 1980? 7p (LDS)

INDIAN LORE OF THE MUSKINGUM HEADWATERS OF THE OHIO, 1972.

Kaiser, Peter H. HISTORY OF DUTCH VALLEY AND OTHER PAPERS. (news clippings) (SLO)

Lenhart, Rev.John M. THE HISTORY OF OLD SAINT PETER'S. 196? 135p (OGS,LDS,DAR,SLO)

LOCAL HISTORY, OUR UNIQUE HERITAGE (New Philadelphia OH: AIRS Project, 1972) 14p

Lohrman, Herbert. HISTORY OF EARLY TUSCARAWAS COUNTY OHIO FOR THE SCHOOLS. (New Philadelphia OH: Acme Printing Co.,1930) 54p. (LC,SLO)

Lohrman, Herbert P. VALLEY OF THE TUSCARAWAS. (Dover OH: Ohio Hills Pubs., 1972) 78p (LC)

Mansfield, J.B. THE HISTORY OF TUSCARAWAS COUNTY OHIO. (Strasburg OH: Gordon Print, 1974) 84p (LC)

Mitchener, C.H. OHIO ANNALS AND HISTORIC EVENTS IN THE TUSCARAWAS AND MUSKINGUM VALLEYS. (Dayton OH: Thomas W. Odell, 1876) 358p. (SLO,DAR)

OHIO ANNALS, HISTORIC EVENTS IN THE TUSCARAWAS & MUSKINGUM VALLEYS, 1876.

PORTRAIT AND BIOGRAPHICAL RECORD OF TUSCARAWAS COUNTY OHIO. (Chicago: C.O.Owen & Co., 1895) 507p (DAR,LC,SLO) (RPI)

Raber, Nellie M. INDEX OF WILLS, FAIRFIELD COUNTY 1803-1855, KNOX COUNTY 1808-1855, AND TUSCARAWAS COUNTY OHIO (BOOKS 1-9, 1809-1894). (Lakewood OH: author, 1955) 77p (LDS)

RAGERSVILLE, AUBURN TOWNSHIP, OHIO, 1830-1980, THE SESQUICENTENNIAL STORY OF A COMMUNITY. (Sugarcreek OH: Ragersville Hist.Soc., 1980) 253p (LDS)

REMINISCENCES OF DOVER, 1879.

Rhodes, Edwin S. FIRST CENTENNIAL HISTORY AND ATLAS OF TUSCARAWAS COUNTY OHIO. (New Philadelphia OH: Tuscarawas Centennial Assoc., 1908)(Reprint,Strasburg OH: Gordon Print., 1973) 236p (DAR,LDS,OGS,SLO)(RPI)

Rodabaugh, James H. SCHOENBRUNN AND THE MORAVIAN MISSIONS IN OHIO. (Columbus OH: Ohio Hist.Soc., 1961, 3rd ed.) 36p (LDS)

Rudy, Ethel M. A SURNAME INDEX TO PORTRAIT AND BIOGRAPHICAL RECORD OF TUSCARAWAS COUNTY OHIO PUBLISHED 1895 BY C.OWEN & CO., CHICAGO. (Alamogordo NM: Trading Post Gen.Pubs., 1984) 16p (LDS,LC,SLO)

Sesquicentennial History Committee. RAGERSVILLE, AUBURN TOWNSHIP, OHIO, 1830-1980, THE SESQUICENTENNIAL STORY OF A COMMUNITY. 1980. (SLO)

Smith, Clifford N. FEDERAL LAND SERIES: A CALENDAR OF ARCHIVAL MATERIAL ON THE LAND PATENTS ISSUED BY THE U.S.GOVERNMENT, VOL.2: FEDERAL BOUNTY LAND WARRANTS OF THE AMERICAN REVOLUTION. (Chicago: American Library Assn., 1972) 416p

Tuscarawas Co Chapter OGS. 1830 CENSUS INDEX, TUSCARAWAS COUNTY OHIO. (New Philadelphia OH: the society, 1987) 14p (LDS)

Tuscarawas Co Chapter OGS. EVANS CREEK LUTHERAN CHURCH RECORDS OF BUCKS TWP., TUSCARAWAS CO.OH. (New Philadelphia OH: the society, 1975)(SLO)

Tuscarawas Co Chapter OGS. HISTORICAL ATLAS OF TUSCARAWAS COUNTY OHIO 1875-1908, COMBINED. (New Philadelphia OH: the society, nd) (SLO)

Tuscarawas Co Chapter OGS. HISTORY OF TUSCARAWAS COUNTY OHIO. 1988 (in progress) (New Philadelphia OH: the society, 1988?)

Tuscarawas Co Chapter OGS. INDEX FOR 1875-1908 COMBINATION ATLAS MAP OF TUSCARAWAS COUNTY OHIO. (New Philadelphia OH: the society, 1980) 65p (OGS,LDS)

Tuscarawas Co Chapter OGS. INDEX, WILL & INTESTATE OF TUSCARAWAS CO OHIO 1809-1850 & WILL INDEX VOL 1-12, 1809-1902. (New Philadelphia OH: the society, 1981) 17p,19p (OGS)

Tuscarawas Co Chapter OGS. SALEM EVANS CREEK LUTHERAN CHURCH, BUCKS TOWNSHIP, TUSCARAWAS COUNTY OHIO. (New Philadelphia OH: the society, 1975) 60p (LDS)

Tuscarawas Co Chapter OGS. TUSCARAWAS COUNTY OHIO MARRIAGES 1808-1844, VOLUME I. (New Philadelphia OH: the society, 1979) 124p (OGS,LDS)

Tuscarawas Co Chapter OGS. TUSCARAWAS COUNTY OHIO MARRIAGES 1845-1863, VOLUME II. (New Philadelphia OH: the society, 1981) 164p (OGS,LDS)

Tuscarawas Co Chapter OGS. TUSCARAWAS COUNTY CEMETERIES, VOL.I, AUBURN, BUCKS, FRANKLIN, WAYNE & SUGARCREEK TWPS. (New Philadelphia OH: the society, 1981) 260p (OGS,SLO)

Tuscarawas Co Chapter OGS. TUSCARAWAS COUNTY CEMETERIES, VOL.II, DOVER, DOVER TOWNSHIP. (New Philadelphia OH: the society, 1983) 320p (OGS)

Tuscarawas Co Chapter OGS. TUSCARAWAS COUNTY CEMETERIES, VOL.III, YORK, JEFFERSON, SALEM, CLAY & WARWICK TWPS. (New Philadelphia OH: the society, nd) (SLO)

Tuscarawas Co Chapter OGS. TUSCARAWAS COUNTY CEMETERIES, VOL.IV, FAIR FIELD, LAWRENCE, SANDY, UNION & WARREN TWPS. (New Philadelphia OH: the society, nd)(OGS)

Tuscarawas Co Chapter OGS. TUSCARAWAS COUNTY CEMETERIES, VOL.V, MILL TWP. (New Philadelphia OH: the society, 1987) 318p (OGS)

Tuscarawas Co Chapter OGS. TUSCARAWAS COUNTY CEMETERIES, VOL.VI, OXFORD, PERRY, RUSH & WASHINGTON TWPS. (New Philadelphia OH: the society, 1987) 228p (OGS)

Tuscarawas Co Chapter OGS. TUSCARAWAS COUNTY CONNECTIONS. (New Philadelphia OH: the society, 1982) 366p (OGS,LDS,DAR,SLO)

Tuscarawas Co Chapter OGS. VETERANS' GRAVE REGISTRATIONS, TUSCARAWAS COUNTY OHIO. (New Philadelphia OH: the society, 1987)

Tuscarawas Co Retired Teachers Assn. HISTORY OF EARLY TUSCARAWAS COUNTY SCHOOLS. (New Philadelphia OH: Buckeye Joint Voc.School, 1978) 247p (LDS)

TUSCARAWAS COUNTY MARRIAGES, STARTING 1808. (SLO-mic)

U.S.FEDERAL CENSUS OF AUBURN TOWNSHIP, TUSCARAWAS COUNTY OHIO - 1880. (Sugarcreek OH: Ragersville Hist.Soc., nd) 29p

Weinland, Joseph E. SCHOENBRUNN: THE FIRST TOWN IN OHIO - A MORAVIAN MISSION TO THE INDIANS. (Dover OH: Seibert Printing Co., c1930) 36p (OHS,LDS)

ZOAR: AN OHIO EXPERIMENT IN COMMUNALISM. (Columbus: Ohio Hist.Soc., 1960) 74p (LDS)

# UNION COUNTY

| | |
|---|---|
| CREATED: | 1820 FROM DELAWARE, FRANKLIN, LOGAN & MADISON |
| COUNTY SEAT: | MARYSVILLE 43040 |
| COURT HOUSE: | COURT & 5TH, MARYSVILLE 43040 |
| LIBRARY: | 231 S. COURT ST., MARYSVILLE 43040 |
| HISTORICAL SOCIETY: | 246 W. 6TH ST., MARYSVILLE 43040 |
| GENEALOGICAL SOCIETY: | UNION COUNTY CHAPTER OGS, |
| | PO BOX 438, MARYSVILLE 43040 |
| | publication: UNION ECHOES |
| HEALTH DEPARTMENT: | 621 PLUM ST., MARYSVILLE 43040 |
| | (separate office for Marysville city) |
| ARCHIVAL DISTRICT: | OHIO HISTORICAL SOCIETY, COLUMBUS |
| LAND SURVEYS: | VIRGINIA MILITARY DISTRICT |
| BOUNDED BY: | EAST: DELAWARE CO. |
| | NORTH: HARDIN & MARION CO. |
| | WEST: CHAMPAIGN & LOGAN CO. |
| | SOUTH: FRANKLIN & MADISON CO. |
| TOWNSHIPS: | Allen, Claiborne, Darby, Dover, Jackson, Jerome, Leesburg, Liberty, Millcreek, Paris, Taylor, Union, Washington, York. |

## COURT RECORDS: (LDS MICROFILM)
Auditor:
    Bounty & commutation record, 1865-1866.
    Land sale, 1820-1843.
    Tax duplicates, 1820-1838.
Childrens' Home:
    Admittance & indenture records, 1884-1907.
Clerk of Courts:
    Common Pleas journal, 1820-1855.
    Common Pleas record, 1820-1853.
    Supreme & District Court record, 1820-1878.
Commissioners:
    Journal, 1820-1900.
    Index to journal, 1820-1900.
    Turnpike directors' records, 1874-1888.
Probate Court:
    Account records, vD-W, 1876-1901.
    Administration records, v1-3, 1820-1852.
    Administration dockets, v1-2, 1870-1907.
    Birth records, v1-4, 1867-1909.
    Birth registration & correction, v1-4, 1941-1969.
    Death records, v1-3, 1867-1903.
    Executors bonds & letters, vB-E, 1861-1903.
    Guardian bonds & letters, 1855-1894.
    Guardian bonds & appointments, v5, 1895-1906.
    Marriage records, v1-G, 1820-1904.
    Marriage index, 1820-1859.
    Naturalization records, 1860-1906.
    Probate journals, v1-22, 1852-1901.
    Settlement records, 1851-1875.
    Will records, vA-H, 1852-1903.

Recorder:
  Grantor & grantee index, 1811-1954.
  Deed records, 1819-1925.
  Mortgage index, 1851-1901.
  Soldier discharge records, v1-2, 1861-1899.
Miscellaneous:
  Marysville, First Presby.Church, records, 1829-1898.
  Milford Center, Upper Liberty Presby.Church, records, 1821-1850.

## OHIO HISTORICAL SOCIETY: (MICROFILM)
Auditor:
  Bounty & commutation record, 1865-1866.
  Land sale, 1820-1843.
Childrens' Home:
  Admittance records, 1884-1907.
Clerk of Courts:
  Common Pleas journal, 1820-1855.
  Common Pleas record, 1820-1853.
  Supreme & District Court record, 1820-1878.
Commissioners:
  Journal, 1820-1900.
  Index to journal, 1820-1900.
  Turnpike directors' records, 1874-1888.
Miscellaneous:
  Marriage records, 1820-1865, by DAR.
  Death records, Champaign & Union Cos., by DAR.

## CENSUS RECORDS  (OHS,SLO,OGS,LDS)
1820-1880, 1900-1910; 1890 VETERANS; 1880,1900 SOUNDEX; 1910 MIRACODE

## AGRICULTURAL CENSUS SCHEDULES  (OHS,SLO-mic)
1850,1870

## PRODUCTS OF INDUSTRY CENSUS SCHEDULE  (OHS,SLO-mic)
1850,1860,1870,1880

## MORTALITY CENSUS SCHEDULES (OHS,SLO-mic)
1850,1860

## NEWSPAPERS: [GUIDE TO OHIO NEWSPAPERS, 1793-1973]
Marysville, Milford Center, Plain City, Richwood.

## TAX RECORDS (OHS & LDS)
1820-1838.

## MANUSCRIPTS:
Diary of Harry Dague, Raymond OH, farmer & merchant, 1884-1903. (OHS)
Dun family papers, 1802-1936. (OHS)

## GENEALOGICAL PERIODICAL ARTICLES
Bell, Carol Willsey. OHIO GENEALOGICAL PERIODICAL INDEX: A COUNTY GUIDE (Youngstown,
  OH: author, 6th ed., 1987)

**PUBLISHED SOURCES:**

1883 BEER'S HISTORY OF UNION COUNTY OHIO, VOL.I & II. (Reprint, Evansville IN: Unigraphic, 1980) 1236p (OGS)

Ancestrails of Northern Union County Ohio. GLEANINGS FROM THE RICHWOOD GAZETTE, VOL.I, 1872-1876. (Richwood OH: author, 1982) 132p. (OGS,SLO)

Bouic, Margaret M. GENEALOGICAL INDEX OF DELAWARE, UNION & MORROW COUNTIES OHIO. (Marysville OH: author, nd) (SLO,OHS,OGS,DAR,LDS)

Bouic, Margaret M. NEWSPAPER AND CEMETERY RECORDS, MARYSVILLE, OHIO. 1981? 51,37,9p (DAR)

Bouic, Margaret M. NOTES ON MARYSVILLE TRIBUNE APRIL 3, 1850 TO SEPTEMBER 5, 1860. (SLO)

Bouic, Margaret M. UNION COUNTY OHIO COMMON PLEAS COURT RECORDS, 1820-1850. (SLO)

Bouic, Margaret M. UNION COUNTY CEMETERY RECORDS. (SLO)

Burnham, Maria D. MISCELLANEOUS DEATHS OCCURRING IN UNION AND CHAMPAIGN COUNTIES OHIO FROM 1870s TO 1930s. n.d. (OHS,SLO,LDS)

Crist, A.C. HISTORY OF MARION PRESBYTERY: ITS CHURCHES, ELDERS, MINISTERS, MISSION-ARY SOCIETIES, ETC. 1908. 352p (DAR)

Curry, William L. HISTORY OF JEROME TOWNSHIP, JEROME, UNION COUNTY OHIO. 1913. 203p. (OGS,SLO,DAR,LDS)

Curry William L. HISTORY OF UNION COUNTY: ITS PEOPLE, INDUSTRIES AND INSTITUTIONS. (Indianapolis: B.F.Bowen & Co., 1914) 1113p (DAR,OHS,LDS)

Curry, William L. WAR HISTORY OF UNION COUNTY. 1883. 128p (OHS,SLO,DAR)

Daughters of the American Revolution. CEMETERY INSCRIPTIONS, MISCELLANEOUS VOLUME I, OHIO. (SLO)

Daughters of the American Revolution. MARRIAGE RECORDS, UNION COUNTY OHIO, 1820-1865. (SLO,DAR,LDS)

Daughters of the American Revolution. MILITARY RECORDS AND HISTORICAL NOTES OF AN-CESTORS OF THE REVOLUTIONARY WAR, LEGENDS OF THE EARLY UNION COUNTY SET-TLERS, AND CHAPTER HISTORY. 1941? 63p (DAR,SLO)

Daughters of the American Revolution. MISCELLANEOUS OHIO CEMETERIES. (LDS,SLO,DAR)

DROFLIM-MILFORD HIGH SCHOOL YEARBOOK 1932. (Milford OH: Milford High School, 1932) 84p. (OGS)

Durant, Pliny A. THE HISTORY OF UNION COUNTY, OHIO: CONTAINING A HISTORY OF THE COUNTY; ITS TOWNSHIPS, TOWNS, MILITARY RECORDS. (Chicago: W.H. Beers, 1883)(Reprint, Marysville OH: Union Co Chapter OGS, 1980) 1236p (OGS,OHS,LC,SLO,DAR,LDS)(RPI)

Hardesty, H.H. MILITARY HISTORY OF OHIO - UNION COUNTY EDITION. 1886/87. (OHS)

HISTORY OF SOME OHIO CHURCHES [INCLUDES FIRST PRESBYTERIAN CHURCH, MARYS-VILLE]. 1916-1929, 4v (DAR)

Hixson, W.W. PLAT BOOK OF UNION COUNTY. (Rockford IL: author, nd) (OHS)

Kennedy, Willella S. MARYSVILLE, OHIO, 1819-1969. (SLO)

Kennedy, Willella S. OUR HERITAGE; BEING LITTLE STORIES OF UNION COUNTY. (Marysville OH: Journal Tribune, 1963) 118p. (OHS,LC)

Marysville Map Co. UNION COUNTY OHIO. 1908. (SLO)

Matusoff, Karen. CENTRAL OHIO LOCAL GOVERNMENT RECORDS AT THE OHIO HISTORICAL SOCIETY. (Columbus: Ohio Hist Soc., 1978) 38p. (OGS)

MEMORIAL RECORD OF THE COUNTIES OF DELAWARE, UNION AND MORROW. (Chicago: Lewis Pub Co., 1895) 501p. (LDS,SLO,OHS,OGS,DAR)(RPI)

MILITARY HISTORY OF OHIO [UNION COUNTY]. 1886-1887. (OHS)

Mowry, A.W. NEW HISTORICAL ATLAS OF UNION COUNTY OHIO. (Philadelphia: Harrison, Sutton & Hare, 1877). (OGS,OHS,SLO) (RPI)

Robb, Lena. ADULT INHABITANTS OF MARYSVILLE, UNION COUNTY OHIO, 1910. (SLO)

Robinson, Dorothy J. LOWER LIBERTY PRESBYTERIAN CHURCH, 1821-1930. 1982. 69p (SLO)

Robinson, Mrs. James L. SESSIONAL RECORDS OF YORK CHURCH [PRESBYTERIAN, UNION CO]. (Plain City OH: author, nd) 14p (OGS,SLO)

Smith, Clifford N. FEDERAL LAND SERIES: A CALENDAR OF ARCHIVAL MATERIAL ON THE LAND PATENTS ISSUED BY THE U.S.GOVERNMENT, VOL.4, PT 1: GRANTS IN THE VIRGINIA MILITARY DISTRICT OF OHIO. (Chicago: Amer.Libr.Assn., 1982) 395p

Smith, Clifford N. FEDERAL LAND SERIES: A CALENDAR OF ARCHIVAL MATERIAL ON THE LAND PATENTS ISSUED BY THE U.S.GOVERNMENT, VOL.4, PT 2: GRANTS IN THE VIRGINIA MILITARY DISTRICT OF OHIO. (Chicago: Amer.Libr.Assn., 1986) 306p

Union Co Chapter OGS. BIBLE RECORDS, MUSEUM OF UNION COUNTY HISTORICAL SOCIETY, MARYSVILLE, OHIO. 1981. (SLO)

Union Co Chapter OGS. DARBY-JEROME TOWNSHIPS, CEMETERY RECORDS, UNION COUNTY OHIO. (Marysville OH: the society, 1982) 158p (OGS,OHS,LDS,SLO)

Union Co Chapter OGS. DOVER - JACKSON - LEESBURG - MILLCREEK TOWNSHIPS, UNION COUNTY OHIO CEMETERY RECORDS. (Marysville OH: the society, 1986) 134p (OGS,OHS)

Union Co Chapter OGS. FAMILY HERITAGE - UNION COUNTY OHIO. 1985. (Marysville OH: the society, 1985) 205p (OGS)

Union Co Chapter OGS. INDEX OF UNION COUNTY OHIO ATLAS 1877 [MOWRY]. (Marysville OH: the society, 1987?) 44p (OGS,OHS)

Union Co Chapter OGS. LIBERTY - PARIS - TAYLOR - WASHINGTON TOWNSHIPS, UNION COUNTY OHIO CEMETERY RECORDS. (Marysville OH: the society, 1986) 164p (OGS,OHS)

Union Co Chapter OGS. MARYSVILLE: OAKDALE CEMETERY RECORDS, VOLS. I & II. (Marysville OH: the society, 1984) 418p (OGS,OHS)

Union Co Chapter OGS. MARYSVILLE, UNION COUNTY OHIO PRESBYTERIAN CHURCH MEMBERSHIP ROLL 1829-1929. (SLO)

Union Co Chapter OGS. PRESBYTERIAN CHURCH MEMBERSHIP ROLL, 1829-1929. MARYSVILLE, UNION COUNTY OHIO. (Plain City OH: the society, 1981) 30p (OGS)

Union Co Chapter OGS. UNION - ALLEN TOWNSHIPS CEMETERIES. (Marysville OH: the society, nd) 1v (OGS,SLO)

Union Co Chapter OGS. YORK TOWNSHIP CEMETERY RECORDS, UNION COUNTY OHIO. (Marysville OH: the society, 1982) 135p (OGS,LDS,SLO)

Wagner, Charles W. CEMETERY RECORDS OF UNION COUNTY OHIO. (SLO)

WORLD'S WAR NEWS OF OHIO (ESPECIALLY OF) UNION COUNTY, 1918-1919. (OHS)

Young, Irene A. MILFORD CENTER, OHIO SESQUICENTENNIAL,1816-1866-1966.(SLO)

# VAN WERT COUNTY

| | |
|---|---|
| CREATED: | 1820 FROM DARKE COUNTY |
| COUNTY SEAT: | VAN WERT 45891 |
| COURT HOUSE: | MAIN ST., VAN WERT 45891 |
| LIBRARY: | 215 W. MAIN ST., VAN WERT 45891 |
| HISTORICAL SOCIETY: | PO BOX 20, VAN WERT 45891 |
| GENEALOGICAL SOCIETY: | VAN WERT COUNTY CHAPTER OGS, |
| | PO BOX 485, VAN WERT 45891 |
| | publication: VAN WERT CONNECTION |
| HEALTH DEPARTMENT: | 140 FOX RD., VAN WERT 45891 |
| | (separate offices for Van Wert city & Delphos) |
| ARCHIVAL DISTRICT: | BOWLING GREEN STATE UNIVERSITY, BOWLING GREEN |
| | (see Biggs' Guide to records) |
| LAND SURVEYS: | CONGRESS LANDS, E & S OF 1ST PRIN.MERIDIAN |
| BOUNDED BY: | EAST:    ALLEN & PUTNAM CO. |
| | NORTH:  PAULDING CO. |
| | WEST:    ADAMS & ALLEN CO., INDIANA |
| | SOUTH:  AUGLAIZE & MERCER CO. |
| TOWNSHIPS: | Harrison, Hoaglin, Jackson, Jennings, Liberty, Pleasant, Ridge, Tully, Union, Washington, Willshire, York. |

## COURT RECORDS: (LDS MICROFILM)
Auditor:
> Tax duplicates, 1833.
> Deeds & lots sold for taxes, 1829-1883.
> Enumeration of soldiers & sailors.

Clerk of Courts:
> Chancery record, v1-2, 1839-1855.
> Common Pleas appearance docket, 1838-1856.
> Common Pleas journal, 1837-1847.
> Complete record, criminal, v1, 1838-1852.
> Complete record, v1-43, 1839-1892.
> District Court record, 1842-1884.
> Divorce record, v1-4, 1902-1925.
> Judgment index, v1-5, 1838-1912.
> Journal, vA-X, 1837-1907.
> Juvenile division, Mothers' pension docket & record, 1915-1936.
> Supreme Court record, 1843-1875.

Commissioners:
> Indigent soldiers burial record, 1886-1926.
> Admission to county hospitals, 1920-1932.

Coroner:
> Records of inquest, 1880-1938.

Probate Court:
> Marriages, 1840-1951.
> Birth records, 1867-1908.
> Death records, 1867-1908.
> Guardians docket, 1873-1896.
> Naturalizaton records, 1852-1905.
> Will records, v1-10, 1840-1911.
> Administrators docket, v2-5, 1862-1903.
> Probate journal, v1-16, 1852-1910.
> Complete record, v1-18, 1856-1910.
> General index to estates, 1839-1933.

Recorder:
> Deeds, 1838-1886.
> Index to deeds, n.d.
> Soldiers discharge, 1865-1953.
> Original entry record, section 16, 1824-1864.

Sheriff:
> Jail register, 1874-1912.

## OHIO HISTORICAL SOCIETY: (MICROFILM)
Clerk of Courts:
> Common Pleas appearance docket, 1838-1856.
> Common Pleas journal, 1837-1847.

Probate Court:
> Marriages, 1840-1863,1891-1899.
> Guardians docket, 1873-1896.

Recorder:
> Deeds, 1838-1886.
> Index to deeds, n.d.
> Soldiers discharge, 1865-1953.

Sheriff:
> Jail register, 1874-1912.

Miscellaneous:
   Marriage records, 1850-1865, by DAR.

**CENSUS RECORDS (OHS,SLO,OGS,LDS)**
1830-1880, 1900-1910; 1890 VETERANS; 1880,1900 SOUNDEX; 1910 MIRACODE

**AGRICULTURAL CENSUS SCHEDULES (OHS,SLO-mic)**
1850,1870

**PRODUCTS OF INDUSTRY CENSUS SCHEDULE (OHS,SLO-mic)**
1850,1860,1870,1880

**MORTALITY CENSUS SCHEDULES (OHS,SLO-mic)**
1850,1860

**NEWSPAPERS: [GUIDE TO OHIO NEWSPAPERS, 1793-1973]**
Convoy, Middlebury, Van Wert, Willshire.

**TAX RECORDS (OHS & LDS)**
none listed; see parent counties.

**GENEALOGICAL PERIODICAL ARTICLES**
Bell, Carol Willsey. OHIO GENEALOGICAL PERIODICAL INDEX: A COUNTY GUIDE (Youngstown,
   OH: author, 6th ed., 1987)

**PUBLISHED SOURCES:**
Amstutz, Jim & K.McMillen, ed. VAN WERT COUNTY SESQUICENTENNIAL 1821-1971. 1971. 72p
   (OGS)
Bassett, Lois. MARRIAGE BOOK II, VAN WERT CO. OHIO 1852-1864. (Venedocia OH: author, 1987)
   26p (OGS)
Bassett, Lois, ed. VAN WERT GENEALOGICAL QUARTERLY. V1-4, 1984-1987.(LDS)
Bassett, Lois. WILL BOOK II, VAN WERT COUNTY, OHIO - ABSTRACTS, WILLS PROBATED 1873-
   1882. (Venedocia OH: author, 1988?) 16p
Biggs, Deb. GUIDE TO LOCAL GOVERNMENT RECORDS AT THE CENTER FOR ARCHIVAL COL-
   LECTIONS. (Bowling Green OH: Bowling Green State Univ, 1981) 104p (OGS)
Christian, Donna K. GUIDE TO NEWSPAPER HOLDINGS AT THE CENTER FOR ARCHIVAL COL-
   LECTIONS. (Bowling Green OH: Bowling Green State Univ, 1980) 64p (OGS)
Daughters of the American Revolution. DATA OF THE VAN WERT COUNTY, OHIO, MARRIAGE
   RECORD: BOOK I. 1948. 64p (DAR)
Gilliland, Thaddeus S. HISTORY OF VAN WERT COUNTY OHIO AND REPRESENTATIVE CITIZENS.
   (Chicago: Richmond & Arnold, 1906) 803p.(DAR,OHS,SLO,LC,LDS) (RPI)
Griffing, B.N. AN ATLAS OF VAN WERT COUNTY, OHIO. (Philadelphia: Griffing, Gordon & Co.,
   1886) 67p (DAR,SLO)
Hinshaw, William Wade. ENCYCLOPEDIA OF AMERICAN QUAKER GENEALOGY, VOL.V, OHIO.
   (Baltimore: Genealogical Pub.Co., 1973) (SLO,OHS,LDS)
HISTORY OF VAN WERT COUNTY OHIO 1981. ( Van Wert Co Hist Soc., 1981) 440p (OGS,LC,LDS,SLO)
HISTORY OF VAN WERT AND MERCER COUNTIES OHIO. (Wapakoneta OH: R.Sutton & Co.,1882)
   481p. (DAR,SLO,LC) (RPI)
Knapp, Horace S. HISTORY OF THE MAUMEE VALLEY. (Toledo OH: author,1872) 685p.
   (DAR,OHS,SLO)
Levinson, Marilyn. GUIDE TO NEWSPAPER HOLDINGS AT THE CENTER FOR ARCHIVAL COL-
   LECTIONS. 2nd Edition. (Bowling Green OH: Bowling Green State Univ., 1987)
Marbaugh, Elodee. 1850 CENSUS OF VAN WERT COUNTY OHIO. (Willshire OH: author, nd) 120p
   (OGS)

Marbaugh, Elodee. VAN WERT COUNTY OHIO MARRIAGE BOOK NO.1 1840-1855. (Willshire OH: author, 1982?) 68p (OGS,LDS)

Mollenkopf, Mrs. J.W. INDEX, MARRIAGE RECORD BOOK I, VAN WERT COUNTY OHIO. [1840-1855] (np: author, 1961) 67p (OGS,SLO,LDS)

Monroe, Beryl P. VAN WERT COUNTY RECORDS [newspaper items] (SLO)

PORTRAIT AND BIOGRAPHICAL RECORD OF ALLEN AND VAN WERT COUNTIES, OHIO (Chicago: A.W.Bowen & Co., 1896) 909p (OHS,SLO,DAR,LDS)

PORTRAIT AND BIOGRAPHICAL RECORD OF MERCER AND VAN WERT COUNTIES, OHIO. (Chicago: A.W.Bowen & Co., 1896)(Reprint, Evansville IN: Unigraphic, 1971) 909p (DAR,LDS)

Prill, Helen. A GUIDE TO HISTORICAL AND GENEALOGICAL SOURCES OF VAN WERT COUNTY OHIO. (Van Wert OH: author, 1982) 50p. (OGS,LDS,SLO)

Prill, Helen. INDEX TO HISTORY OF VAN WERT COUNTY OHIO AND REPRESENTATIVE CITIZENS BY T.S.GILLILAND 1906. (Van Wert OH: author, 1984) 186p (OGS)

RECORD OF MERCER AND VAN WERT COUNTIES OHIO. 1896. 909p. (SLO)

Slocum, Charles. HISTORY OF THE MAUMEE RIVER BASIN. 1905. 638p. (SLO)

Swank, Rev. John E. HISTORY OF TRINITY EVANGELICAL LUTHERAN CHURCH, CONVOY OHIO 1854-1979, INCLUDING THE HISTORIES OF BETHLEHEM, MT.ZION AND OTHER AREA LUTHERAN CHURCHES. (Convoy OH: author, 1979) 102p (OGS)

Van Wert Co Chapter OGS. VAN WERT COUNTY OHIO CEMETERY INSCRIPTIONS, VOL.I. - TULLY TOWNSHIP. (Convoy OH: the society,1982) 156p (OGS,LDS)

Van Wert Co Chapter OGS. VAN WERT COUNTY OHIO CEMETERY INSCRIPTIONS, VOL.II - UNION & HOAGLIN TOWNSHIPS. (Convoy OH: the society, 1983) 121p (OGS,LDS,SLO)

Van Wert Co Chapter OGS. VAN WERT COUNTY OHIO CEMETERY INSCRIPTIONS, VOL.III - WOODLAND CEMETERY, PLEASANT TOWNSHIP. (Convoy OH: the society, 1986) 303p (OGS,LDS)

VAN WERT COUNTY, OHIO, PLAT BOOK AND FARM DIRECTORY. 1977. (OGS)

Winter, Nevin O. HISTORY OF NORTHWEST OHIO. (Chicago: Lewis Pub.Co., 1917) 3v. (SLO,OHS)

# VINTON COUNTY

| | |
|---|---|
| CREATED: | 1850 FROM ATHENS, GALLIA, HOCKING, JACKSON & ROSS COUNTIES |
| COUNTY SEAT: | McARTHUR 45651 |
| COURT HOUSE: | MAIN ST., McARTHUR 45651 |
| LIBRARY: | 122 W. MAIN ST., McARTHUR 45651 |
| HISTORICAL SOCIETY: | PO BOX 474, McARTHUR 45651 |
| GENEALOGICAL SOCIETY: | (CHAPTER OF OGS FORMING) |
| HEALTH DEPARTMENT: | ST.RT.93 NORTH, PO BOX 458, McARTHUR 45651 |
| ARCHIVAL DISTRICT: | OHIO UNIVERSITY, ATHENS (see published Guide to records) |
| LAND SURVEYS: | CONGRESS LANDS, OHIO RIVER SURVEY (SOUTH) OHIO COMPANY |
| BOUNDED BY: | EAST: ATHENS & MEIGS CO. NORTH: HOCKING CO. WEST: ROSS CO. SOUTH: GALLIA & JACKSON CO. |
| TOWNSHIPS: | Brown, Clinton, Eagle, Elk, Harrison, Jackson, Knox, Madison, Richland, Swan, Vinton, Wilkesville. |

**COURT RECORDS: (LDS MICROFILM)**
Auditor:
    Enumeration of school-aged youth, 1850-1863.
Commissioners:
    Journal, 1850-1904.

Index to journal, 1850-1908.
Probate Court:
  Birth records, v1-4, 1867-1951.
  Birth registration & correction, 1941-1962.
  Death records, 1867-1952.
  Marriages, v1-8, 1850-1914.
  General index to files.
  Naturalizations, 1877-1926.
  Probate journal, v1-4, 1852-1880.
  Wills, 1853-1876.
Recorder:
  Deed records, v1-17, 1850-1876; index v1-2 covers v1-31.
Miscellaneous:
  New Plymouth, Presbyterian Church, records, 1829-1907.

## OHIO HISTORICAL SOCIETY: (MICROFILM)
Auditor:
  Enumeration of school-aged youth, 1850-1863.
Commissioners:
  Journal, 1850-1904.
  Index to journal, 1850-1908.
Miscellaneous:
  Marriage records, 1850-1865, by DAR.
  Cemetery records of Hocking & Vinton Cos., by DAR.

## CENSUS RECORDS  (OHS,SLO,OGS,LDS)
1850-1880, 1900-1910; 1890 VETERANS; 1880,1900 SOUNDEX; 1910 MIRACODE

## AGRICULTURAL CENSUS SCHEDULES  (OHS,SLO-mic)
1850,1870

## PRODUCTS OF INDUSTRY CENSUS SCHEDULE  (OHS,SLO-mic)
1850,1860,1870,1880

## MORTALITY CENSUS SCHEDULES (OHS,SLO-mic)
1850,1860

## NEWSPAPERS: [GUIDE TO OHIO NEWSPAPERS, 1793-1973]
McArthur.

## TAX RECORDS (OHS & LDS)
none listed; see parent counties.

## GENEALOGICAL PERIODICAL ARTICLES
Bell, Carol Willsey. OHIO GENEALOGICAL PERIODICAL INDEX: A COUNTY GUIDE (Youngstown, OH: author, 6th ed., 1987)

## PUBLISHED SOURCES:
Adams, Marilyn. INDEX TO CIVIL WAR VETERANS & WIDOWS IN SOUTHERN OHIO, 1890 FEDERAL CENSUS (Columbus: Franklin Co Chapter OGS,1986) 84p
Arledge, Tacy. 1880 VINTON CO. OHIO CENSUS INDEX (New Holland, OH: au thor, 1983). 43p (OGS,OHS)
Benson, Myron C. THE WAY IT WAS: HISTORY OF THE HARRISON TOWNSHIP, VINTON COUN-TY, PUBLIC SCHOOL SYSTEM. 198? 85p (LDS)

Biggs, Louise O. A BRIEF HISTORY OF VINTON COUNTY OHIO. (Columbus OH: Heer Printing, 1950) 184p. (OGS,SLO,DAR)

Clark, Marie T. OHIO LANDS: CHILLICOTHE LAND OFFICE, 1800-1829. (Chillicothe: author, 1984) 144p (OGS,SLO,OHS)

Daughters of the American Revolution. CEMETERY RECORDS OF HOCKING AND VINTON CO., OHIO. 1953. 34p (DAR,LDS)

Daughters of the American Revolution. MARRIAGE RECORDS VINTON COUNTY OHIO. (SLO,LDS)

Daughters of the American Revolution. MISCELLANEOUS CEMETERY RECORDS OF ALLEN...VINTON COUNTIES OHIO. (SLO)

Daughters of the American Revolution. VINTON COUNTY. 1936? 69,46p (DAR)

Hardesty, H.H. MILITARY HISTORY OF OHIO - VINTON COUNTY EDITION. 1886/87. (OHS)

Harris, Charles H. THE HARRIS STORY. 1957. 329p (SLO)

HISTORIES OF ATHENS, GALLIA, MEIGS AND VINTON COUNTIES, OHIO: NEWSPAPER CLIPPINGS FROM THE DYE COLLECTION. (SLO,LDS)

HISTORY OF HOCKING VALLEY, OHIO (Chicago: Interstate Pub Co., 1883) 1392p (DAR,SLO,OHS,LDS)

Hixon, Frances. VINTON COUNTY MARRIAGES, 1850-1870. (OHS)

Hixon, Frances W. WILKESVILLE TOWNSHIP, VINTON COUNTY OHIO CEMETERY INSCRIPTIONS. 1982. 36,69p (LDS,SLO)

Hoy, Loisene. PIONEERS OF THE RACCOON VALLEY AND SURROUNDING AREAS, NO.1 & 2. (SLO)

Lake, D.J. ATLAS OF VINTON COUNTY, OHIO. (Philadelphia: Titus,Simmons & Titus, 1876) 43p (LDS,OGS,SLO)(RPI)

Ohio University. GUIDE TO LOCAL GOVERNMENT RECORDS AT OHIO UNIVERSITY. (Athens: OU Library, 1986) 61p.

Ogan, J.Miles. VINTON COUNTY OHIO (MAP) 1958. (LDS)

Ogan, Lew. HISTORY OF VINTON COUNTY, WONDERLAND OF OHIO. (McArthur OH: au thor, 1954) 314p. (LDS,SLO)

Short, Joan. INDEX TO HISTORY OF VINTON COUNTY OHIO. 14p (LDS)

Taylor, Charles. EARLY HISTORY AND WAR RECORD OF WILKESVILLE AND SALEM. 1974. (SLO)

Taylor, Charles B. STORY OF THE PRESBYTERIAN CHURCH AT WILKESVILLE OHIO. (SLO)

TOMBSTONE INSCRIPTIONS, VOLS. I & II. (SLO)

Whiteman, Jane. SURNAME INDEX TO 1883 INTERSTATE PUB. HISTORY OF HOCKING VALLEY OHIO (Tulsa OK: author, 1980) 28p (LDS)

Willard, Eugene. A STANDARD HISTORY OF THE HANGING ROCK IRON REGION OF OHIO. (Chicago: Lewis Pub.Co.,1916) 2v. (SLO,DAR,LDS)

# WARREN COUNTY

| | |
|---|---|
| CREATED: | 1803 FROM HAMILTON COUNTY |
| COUNTY SEAT: | LEBANON 45036 |
| COURT HOUSE: | 300 E.SILVER ST., LEBANON 45036 |
| LIBRARY: | 101 S. BROADWAY, LEBANON 45036 |
| HISTORICAL SOCIETY: | 105 S. BROADWAY, LEBANON 45036 |
| GENEALOGICAL SOCIETY: | WARREN COUNTY CHAPTER OGS, |
| | 300 E.SILVER ST., LEBANON 45036 |
| | publication: HEIR LINES |
| HEALTH DEPARTMENT: | 416 SOUTH EAST ST., LEBANON 45036 |
| | (separate offices for Lebanon city, Franklin, Mason & Loveland) |
| ARCHIVAL DISTRICT: | UNIVERSITY OF CINCINNATI, CINCINNATI |
| LAND SURVEYS: | VIRGINIA MILITARY DISTRICT |
| | CONGRESS LANDS, BETWEEN THE MIAMI RIVER SURVEY |
| | SYMMES PURCHASE |
| BOUNDED BY: | EAST:   CLINTON CO. |

|                | NORTH: | GREENE & MONTGOMERY CO. |
|                | WEST:  | BUTLER CO.              |
|                | SOUTH: | CLERMONT & HAMILTON CO. |

TOWNSHIPS:   Clear Creek, Deerfield, Franklin, Hamilton, Harlan, Massie, Salem, Turtle Creek, Union, Washington, Wayne.

## COURT RECORDS: (LDS MICROFILM)

Auditor:
  Tax duplicates, 1816-1838.
Childrens' Home:
  Record of inmates, v1, 1874-1952.
  Trustees minutes, 1874-1926.
Clerk of Courts:
  Chancery record, v1-15, 1824-1851.
  Civil docket, 1803-1852.
  Civil minutes journal, 1803-1812, 1811-1852.
  Civil record, 1808-1851.
  Common Pleas general index, 1803-1870.
  Common Pleas special sessions, 1803-1814,1830-1851.
  Supreme Court general index, 1805-1875.
  Supreme Court chancery record, v1-3, 1831-1851.
  Supreme Court minutes, v2-3, 1817-1851.
  Supreme Court record, v1-6, 1804-1845.
  Supreme Court issue docket, 1803-1851.
Commissioners:
  Journal, 1869-1901.
  Index to journals, 1803-1901.
Probate Court:
  Administrators bonds & letters, 1865-1881.
  Birth records, 1867-1908.
  Birth records registration & correction, 1941-1964.
  Death records, 1867-1908.
  Marriage affidavits, v1-Y, 1854-1869.
  Marriage records, v1-10, 1867-1924.
  Marriage licenses issued, 1803-1854.
  General index to marriage licenses, n.d.
  Guardians bonds, v1-4, 1860-1890.
  Executors bonds, v1-2, 1865-1881.
  Bonds & letters, 1803-1865.
  Probate minute books, v1-10, 1851-1882.
  General index to estates, v1-3, 1803-1970.
  Probate records, v10-28, 1844-1886.
  Will records, v1-23Z, 1804-1889.
  Will index, v1 1804-1895.
  Final record, v6-7, 1881-1886.
  Naturalization records, v1-2, 1856-1906.
Recorder:
  Apprenticeship & indenture records, 1824-1867.
  Grantor & grantee index to deeds, 1799-1880.
  Deeds, v1-92, 1795-1910.
Treasurer:
  Commutation receipts, 1864.
Miscellaneous:
  Providence Baptist Church, records, 1820-1846.
  Beech Grove Monthly Meeting, 1888-1963.

Cane Creek Monthly Meeting, records, 1790-1836.
Clear Creek Monthly Meeting, records, 1808-1942.
Fall Creek Monthly Meeting, records, 1792-1953.
Harveysburg Monthly Meeting, records, 1832-1952.
Hopewell Monthly Meeting, records, 1795-1911.
Miami Monthly Meeting (Hicksite), records, 1803-1954.
Miami Monthly Meeting, records, 1768-1960.
Miami Quarterly Meeting, minutes, 1808-1947.
Ridgeville, Presby.Church, records, 1875-1880.
Springborough Monthly Meeting, records, 1824-1875.
Springborough Monthly Meeting (Hicksite) records, 1816-1885.
Turtle Creek Monthly Meeting, records, 1908-1914.
Women's Foreign Missionary Society (Friends) members, 1912-1921.
United Society of Believers, church records, 1801-1911.
Carlisle, New Jersey Presby.Church, records, 1837-1901.
James Ebrite Daily School records, 1866-1886.
Shakers in Union Village, Warren Co., Ohio, 1837-1884,1902-1911.

**OHIO HISTORICAL SOCIETY: (MICROFILM)**
Childrens' Home:
Record of inmates, v1, 1874-1952.
Trustees minutes, 1874-1926.
Clerk of Courts:
Chancery record, v1-15, 1824-1851.
Civil docket, 1803-1852.
Civil minutes journal, 1811-1852.
Civil record, 1808-1851.
Common Pleas general index, 1803-1870.
Supreme Court general index, 1805-1875.
Supreme Court chancery record, v1-3, 1831-1851.
Supreme Court minutes, v2-3, 1817-1851.
Supreme Court record, v1-6, 1804-1845.
Supreme Court issue docket, 1803-1851.
Commissioners:
Journal, 1869-1901.
Index to journals, 1803-1901.
Recorder:
Apprenticeship & indenture records, 1824-1867.
Treasurer:
Commutation receipts, 1864.
Miscellaneous:
Bible, family & cemetery records, v1-5, by DAR.
Church & marriage records, 1803-1814, by DAR.
Tombstone inscriptions, by DAR.

**CENSUS RECORDS (OHS,SLO,OGS,LDS)**
1820-1880, 1900-1910; 1890 VETERANS; 1880,1900 SOUNDEX; 1910 MIRACODE

**AGRICULTURAL CENSUS SCHEDULES (OHS,SLO-mic)**
1850,1870

**PRODUCTS OF INDUSTRY CENSUS SCHEDULE (OHS,SLO-mic)**
1850,1860,1870,1880

MORTALITY CENSUS SCHEDULES (OHS,SLO-mic)
1850,1860

NEWSPAPERS: [GUIDE TO OHIO NEWSPAPERS, 1793-1973]
Franklin, Lebanon, Mason, Waynesville.

TAX RECORDS (OHS & LDS)
1806-1807,1809-1814,1816-1838.

GENEALOGICAL PERIODICAL ARTICLES
Bell, Carol Willsey. OHIO GENEALOGICAL PERIODICAL INDEX: A COUNTY GUIDE (Youngstown, OH: author, 6th ed., 1987)

PUBLISHED SOURCES:
Bell, Carol W. (Flavell) WARREN COUNTY OHIO AREA KEY. (Kiowa CO: Area Keys, 1977) 104p (SLO)
Berry, Ellen T. & David A. EARLY OHIO SETTLERS: PURCHASERS OF LAND IN SOUTHWESTERN OHIO, 1800-1840. (Baltimore: Genealogical Pub.Co., 1986) 372p (OGS,SLO,OHS)
Bone, Frank A. ATLAS OF WARREN COUNTY OHIO. 1891. (SLO)
Brenner, Robert. MAINEVILLE OHIO HISTORY: 100 YEARS AS AN INCORPORATED TOWN, 1850-1950. (Cincinnati: John S.Swift Co., 1950) 216p (DAR,LDS)
Brien, Lindsay M. A GENEALOGICAL INDEX OF PIONEERS IN THE MIAMI VALLEY OHIO: MIAMI, MONTGOMERY, PREBLE AND WARREN COUNTIES OHIO. (Dayton: Colonial Dames of America, 1970) 196p (LDS,DAR)
Brien, Lindsay M. INDEX TO MIAMI VALLEY RECORDS, MIAMI COUNTY CEMETERY RECORDS, V.5. (SLO)
Brien, Lindsay M. MIAMI COUNTY CEMETERY RECORDS. (np: author, nd) 177p (LDS)
Brien, Lindsay M. MIAMI VALLEY WILL ABSTRACTS FROM THE COUNTIES OF MIAMI, MONTGOMERY, WARREN AND PREBLE IN THE STATE OF OHIO. (SLO,DAR)
Brien, Lindsay M. MIAMI VALLEY RECORDS, VOL.VI, QUAKER RECORDS. (Dayton OH: Miami Valley Gen Soc, 1986) 121p (OGS)
Brien, Lindsay M. MIAMI VALLEY RECORDS, 5v (SLO,LDS)
Brien, Lindsay M. OUR FOREFATHERS ... GENEALOGY OF MIAMI VALLEY FAMILIES. 1r mic. (SLO)
Bucklew, William H. HISTORICAL COLLECTIONS II - WARSAW AND THE WALHONDING VALLEY - WARREN, OHIO, SESQUICENTENNIAL 1834-1984. (Warsaw OH: Warren Sesquicentennial Comm., 1984) 280p (OGS)
Craig, Robert D. WARREN COUNTY OHIO RECORDS. c1963. 28p. (LDS,SLO)
Daughters of the American Revolution. MARRIAGE RECORDS OF WARREN COUNTY. (SLO)
Daughters of the American Revolution. BIBLE, FAMILY & CEMETERY RECORDS OF WARREN COUNTY, OHIO [titles vary]. 24v. (SLO,DAR,LDS) [NOTE: this extensive collection is more fully described in MASTER INDEX OHIO SOCIETY DAUGHTERS OF THE AMERICAN REVOLUTION GENEALOGICAL AND HISTORICAL RECORDS VOLUME I, 1985]
Daughters of the American Revolution. MARRIAGES OF YESTERYEAR: MARRIAGES (EARLY) OF WARREN COUNTY OHIO 1803-1814 AS PUBLISHED BY THE WESTERN STAR, 1940. (DAR,LDS)
Daughters of the American Revolution. MARRIAGE PERMISSION SLIPS, WARREN COUNTY OHIO, 1803-1850. (Newport KY: the society, 1979) 63p. (SLO,DAR)
Eldridge, Mabel. THE HISTORY OF FRANKLIN IN THE GREAT MIAMI VALLEY. (Franklin OH: Franklin Area Hist.Soc., 1982) 360p (LDS,SLO)
Everts, L.H. COMBINATION ATLAS MAP OF WARREN COUNTY OHIO. 1875. 84p (LDS,DAR,SLO) (RPI)
Floyd, Marjorie D. EVERY NAME INDEX TO MIAMI VALLEY OHIO PIONEERS BY LINDSAY M. BRIEN. (Dayton OH: author, 1980) 38p (LDS)
Foley, Harriet E. CARLISLE, THE JERSEY SETTLEMENT IN OHIO, 1800-1980. 1980. 189p (SLO)
Gilmour, A.G. WARREN COUNTY, ILLUSTRATED. (Lebanon OH: Gilmour Studio, 190?) 1v (LDS)

Hassett, Mary F. HISTORICAL SOUVENIR OF FRANKLIN OHIO, 1796-1913. 1913. 136p (LDS)

Heiss, Willard. WARREN COUNTY OHIO MARRIAGE RECORDS, 1803-1834. (Indianapolis: author, 1977) 163p.

Heiss, Willard. WARREN COUNTY OHIO MARRIAGE RECORDS, 1834-1854. (Indianapolis: author, 1977) 163p.

Hinshaw, William Wade. ENCYCLOPEDIA OF AMERICAN QUAKER GENEALOGY, VOL.V, OHIO. (Baltimore: Genealogical Pub.Co., 1973) (SLO,OHS,LDS)

HISTORY OF WARREN COUNTY OHIO. (Chicago, W.H.Beers & Co.,1882) (Reprint, Lebanon OH: Warren Co Chapter OGS, 1982) 1070p (OGS,LDS,SLO,DAR)(RPI)

INDEX TO TESTAMENTARY MATTERS PROBATE COURT [WARREN CO OH] (Cincinnati OH: Cardinal Research, nd) np (GH)

McHenry, Chris. SYMMES PURCHASE RECORDS, 1787-1800. [BUTLER,HAMILTON & WARREN CO] (Lawrenceburg IN: author, 1979) 106p (OGS,LDS)

McKay, Will S. THE CENTENNIAL ATLAS AND HISTORY OF WARREN COUNTY, OHIO. (Lebanon OH: Centennial Atlas Assn., 1903) 114p (LC,OGS,SLO,LDS,SLO)

MEMOIRS OF THE MIAMI VALLEY OHIO. (Chicago: Robert O.Law Co.,1919) 3v (OHS,SLO)

Phillips, Hazel S. THE GOLDEN LAMB. (Oxford OH: Oxford Press, 1958) 68p (LDS)

Phillips, Hazel S. THE LEBANON OHIO PRESBYTERIAN CHURCH. (LDS)

Phillips, Hazel S. TRADITIONAL ARCHITECTURE, WARREN COUNTY OHIO. (Oxford OH: author, 1969) 129p (DAR)

Porter, Thomas J. HISTORY OF THE PRESBYTERIAN CHURCH OF OXFORD, 1818-1825 1900. (Oxford OH: author, 1902) 212p (LDS)

PROCEEDINGS CENTENNIAL ANNIVERSARY MIAMI MONTHLY MEETING, WAYNESVILLE, OHIO, 10TH MONTH, 16-17, 1903. (Waynesville OH: Miami Gazette, 19??) 174p (LDS)

Ridlen, Colleen C. WARREN COUNTY OHIO MARRIAGES, 1803-1812. (Indianapolis IN: The Researchers, 198?) 23p

SESQUICENTENNIAL--MONROE OHIO, 1817-1967. (Monroe OH: History Committee, 1967) 53p (LDS)

Smith, Clifford N. FEDERAL LAND SERIES: A CALENDAR OF ARCHIVAL MATERIAL ON THE LAND PATENTS ISSUED BY THE U.S.GOVERNMENT, VOL.4, PT 1: GRANTS IN THE VIRGINIA MILITARY DISTRICT OF OHIO. (Chicago: American Library Assn., 1982) 395p

Smith, Clifford N. FEDERAL LAND SERIES: A CALENDAR OF ARCHIVAL MATERIAL ON THE LAND PATENTS ISSUED BY THE U.S.GOVERNMENT, VOL.4, PT 2: GRANTS IN THE VIRGINIA MILITARY DISTRICT OF OHIO. (Chicago: American Library Assn., 1986) 306p

Smith, William E. HISTORY OF SOUTHWESTERN OHIO, THE MIAMI VALLEYS. 1964. 3v. (SLO)

Springman, Rose Marie. AROUND MASON OHIO: A STORY. (Mason OH: Mason Hist Soc., c1982) 270p (OGS,LDS)

Townsley, Gardner H. HISTORIC LEBANON: BEGINNING WITH BEEDLE'S STATION IN 1795. 1940. 48p (DAR,LDS)

Warren County Chapter OGS. WARREN COUNTY CEMETERY RECORDS, VOL.1-3. (Lebanon OH: the society, 1984-85) (LDS)

Warren County Historical Society. DEERFIELD TOWNSHIP CEMETERY RECORDS, ROSE HILL, MASON, WARREN COUNTY, OHIO, 1800-1970. (DAR,LDS)

Warren County Historical Society. WAYNE TOWNSHIP CEMETERY RECORDS, MIAMI CEMETERY, WAYNESVILLE, 1867-1906. (DAR,LDS)

WARREN COUNTY OHIO RECORDS OF APPRENTICESHIP AND INDENTURE 1824-1832 & 1864-1867. (Bowie Md: Heritage Books, 1987) 51p (OGS)

WARREN COUNTY CEMETERY RECORDS, FRIENDS MARRIAGES, BIBLE RECORDS. 1r mic (SLO)

WARREN COUNTY OHIO MARRIAGES, 1803-1854. 1r mic. (SLO)

WARREN COUNTY OHIO MARRIAGE RECORDS 1867-1872 (Cincinnati OH: Cardinal Research, nd) np (GH)

WARREN COUNTY OHIO MARRIAGE RECORDS 1861-1867 (Cincinnati OH: Cardinal Research, nd) np (GH)

WARREN COUNTY OHIO MARRIAGE RECORDS 1872-1876 (Cincinnati OH: Cardinal Research, nd) np (GH)

WARREN COUNTY OHIO MARRIAGE RECORDS 1854-1861 (Cincinnati OH: Cardinal Research, nd) np (GH)
WARREN COUNTY PROBATE INDEX, G-Z, 1851-1900. (OGS)

# WASHINGTON COUNTY

CREATED: 1788, AN ORIGINAL COUNTY
COUNTY SEAT: MARIETTA 45750
COURT HOUSE: 205 PUTNAM ST., MARIETTA 45750
LIBRARY: 615 FIFTH ST., MARIETTA 45750
HISTORICAL SOCIETY: WASHINGTON COUNTY HISTORICAL SOCIETY,
401 AURORA ST., MARIETTA 45750
publication: TALLOW LIGHT
GENEALOGICAL SOCIETY: WASHINGTON COUNTY CHAPTER OGS,
PO BOX 2174, MARIETTA 45750
publication: WASHINGTON
HEALTH DEPARTMENT: 342 MUSKINGUM DR., MARIETTA 45750
(separate office for Marietta city)
ARCHIVAL DISTRICT: OHIO UNIVERSITY, ATHENS
(see published Guide to records)
LAND SURVEYS: OHIO COMPANY
CONGRESS LANDS, SEVEN RANGES
CONGRESS LANDS, OHIO RIVER SURVEY (SOUTH)
DONATION TRACT
BOUNDED BY: EAST: PLEASANTS & TYLER CO., W.VA.
NORTH: MONROE & NOBLE CO.
WEST: ATHENS & MORGAN CO.
SOUTH: PLEASANTS & WOOD CO., W.VA.
TOWNSHIPS: Adams, Aurelius, Barlow, Belpre, Decatur, Dunham, Fairfield,
Fearing, Grandview, Independence, Lawrence, Liberty, Ludlow,
Marietta, Muskingum, Newport, Palmer, Salem, Warren, Waterford,
Watertown, Wesley.

**COURT RECORDS: (LDS MICROFILM)**
Auditor:
Civil War rosters, v1860-1870.
Lands sold for taxes, 1823-1865.
Transfers, 1820-1824,1848-1892.
Tax assessors' report, 1846.
Tax duplicates, 1800,1816-1838; 1801-1850.
Clerk of Courts:
Common Pleas record, 1825-1853.
Common Pleas appearance docket, 1818,1831-1835,1840-1841.
Common Pleas canvass books, 1897-1899.
Quarter Sessions record, c1800-1802.
Common Pleas, docket book of action, 1790-1814,1805.
Common Pleas enumeration, 1803.
Common Pleas journal, v1-10, 1808-1848.
Complete record, civil, 1795-1825.
Court dockets, 1852-1881.
Execution docket, 1804-1879.
Common Pleas final record, v1-10, 1804-1822.
Quadrennial enumeration, 1887-1911.
Poll books & tally sheets, 1802-1908.

Supreme Court docket & journal, 1808-09,1818-1819,1821-1824,1835-1841.
Supreme Court appearance docket 1818-1841.
Justice docket 1841-1844.
Commissioners:
    Journal, 1797-1862,1840-1902.
County Home:
    Directors' minutes, 1865-1914.
    Infirmary register, 1836-1920.
Probate Court:
    Birth records, 1867-1914.
    Death records, 1867-1908.
    General index to admr., exr, grdn, 1852-1949.
    Administrators, executors docket, 1852-1897.
    Guardians docket, 1861-1906.
    Admr., exr., grdn. bonds & letters, 1803-1888.
    Guardians bonds & letters, 1865-1889.
    General docket, 1876-1892.
    Executors bonds & letters, 1867-1888.
    Administrators record, 1867-1889.
    Naturalization records, 1859-1905.
    Marriage records, v1-19, 1789-1918.
    Index to marriage records, v1-3, 1803-1865.
    Probate journal, vA-N, 1852-1886.
    Probate record, vA-9, 1789-1855.
    Record of wills, v1-5, 1853-1889.
Recorder:
    Grantor & grantee index, 1788-1900.
    Deed records, 1788-1881.
    Deceased soldiers & sailors, 1861-1865.
    Military discharges, 1861-1914.
Sheriff:
    Jail register, 1868-1927.
Surveyor:
    Record of surveys, v1-12, 1805-1873.
    Index to surveys, 1827-1873.
Miscellaneous:
    Thomas M. McFarland papers, Belpre, 1821-1867.
    Census 1800,1803,1810; death notices, 1811-1830, etc.
    Manuscript census of Washington Co., 1830 (Campus Martius Museum)
    Township history by Hathaway, 1888.
    List of French lawsuits on file in Campus Martius Museum, 1793-1802.
    Poll book, Belpre Township, 1806.
    The 100th anniversary of Mrs. Nancy Frost.
    Dudley Davis, Pioneer, & Davis records.
    Diaries of Benjamin Dana, 1794-1795.
    Misc. items from Campus Martius Museum.
    Rufus Putnam list of nonresident land owners, 1811.
    Marietta Silver Greys, 1861.
    Ohio National Guard, discharges, Co B, 46th Regt., 1866.
    Warren, teachers daily register, 1852-1853.
    Barlow, Presbyterian Church, records, 1852-1877.
    Beverly, Cumberland Presby.Church, records, 1885-1896.
    Fearing Twp., Presbyterian church sessional records, 1810-1855.
    Harmer, Congregational Church, records, 1840-1888.
    First Religious Society, Marietta, 1864.

New Matamoras Presby.Church, records, 1850-1898.
Waterford Baptist Church, records, 1818-1904.
Belpre Town clerk, proceedings, 1800-1870.
Waterford Township Assessor, list of taxable property, 1841-1842.
Bank of Marietta, bank records, 1807-1861.
Peter McLaren papers, 1859-1890.
Ebenezer Sproat papers, 1792-1806.
John Russell papers, 1791-1832,1883,1886.
Camp Marietta papers, 1862-1869.
Muskingum Township Farmer's Club, records, 1874-1956.

## OHIO HISTORICAL SOCIETY: (MICROFILM)
Auditor:
  Civil War rosters, v1860-1870.
Clerk of Courts:
  Common Pleas record, 1825-1853.
  Common Pleas appearance docket, 1818,1831-1835,1840-1841.
  Common Pleas canvass books, 1897-1899.
  Quarter Sessions record, c1800-1802.
  Common Pleas, docket book of action, 1790-1814,1805.
  Common Pleas enumeration, 1803.
  Complete record, civil, 1795-1825.
  Quadrennial enumeration, 1887-1911.
  Poll books & tally sheets, 1802-1908.
  Supreme Court docket & journal, 1808-09,1818-1819,1821-1824,1835-1841.
Commissioners:
  Journal, 1797-1862,1840-1902.
County Home:
  Directors' minutes, 1865-1914.
  Infirmary register, 1836-1920.
Recorder:
  Deceased soldiers & sailors, 1861-1865.
  Military discharges, 1861-1914.
Sheriff:
  Jail register, 1868-1927.
Miscellaneous:
  Marriage records, 1789-1864, by DAR.
  Will records, c1790-c1860, by DAR.
  Bible, death & marriages,Davis family, & school records,1880-1897.
  Family records, by DAR.

## CENSUS RECORDS  (OHS,SLO,OGS,LDS)
1800, 1810, 1820-1880, 1900-1910; 1890 VETERANS; 1880,1900 SOUNDEX;
1910 MIRACODE.

## AGRICULTURAL CENSUS SCHEDULES  (OHS,SLO-mic)
1850,1870,1880

## PRODUCTS OF INDUSTRY CENSUS SCHEDULE  (OHS,SLO-mic)
1850,1860,1870,1880

## MORTALITY CENSUS SCHEDULES (OHS,SLO-mic)
1850,1860

**NEWSPAPERS: [GUIDE TO OHIO NEWSPAPERS, 1793-1973]**
Belpre, Lowell, Lower Salem, Marietta.

**TAX RECORDS (OHS & LDS)**
1800,1808-1814,1817-1838.

**GENEALOGICAL PERIODICAL ARTICLES**
Bell, Carol Willsey. OHIO GENEALOGICAL PERIODICAL INDEX: A COUNTY GUIDE (Youngstown
OH: author, 6th ed., 1987)

**PUBLISHED SOURCES:**
1810 CENSUS OF WASHINGTON COUNTY OHIO. 14,10p (LDS)
Alderman, Mrs.L. CENTENNIAL SOUVENIR OF MARIETTA OHIO. 1887. 101p. (SLO)
Andrews, Israel W. WASHINGTON COUNTY AND THE EARLY SETTLEMENT OF OHIO.
(Cincinnati: P.G.Thomson, 1877)(Reprint, Marietta OH: Washington Co.Hist.Soc., 1976) 83p
(DAR,LC,LDS,SLO)(RPI)
Andrews, Martin. HISTORY OF MARIETTA AND WASHINGTON COUNTY OHIO. (Chicago:
Biographical Pub.Co., 1902) 2v. (DAR,LC,LDS,SLO)(RPI)
Austin, L.G. ILLUSTRATED HISTORICAL AND BUSINESS REVIEW OF WASHINGTON COUNTY
OHIO FOR THE YEAR 1891. (Coshocton OH: Union Pub.Co., 1891) 283p (LDS)
Bailey, Kenneth P. THE OHIO COMPANY OF VIRGINIA AND THE WESTWARD MOVEMENT, 1748-
1792. (Glendale CA: Arthur H.Clark Co., 1939)
Barker, Joseph. RECOLLECTIONS OF THE FIRST SETTLEMENT OF OHIO. (Marietta OH: Marietta
College, 1958)
Beach, Arthur G. A PIONEER COLLEGE: THE STORY OF MARIETTA. (Chicago: John F. Cuneo Co.,
1935) 325p (LDS)
Bennett, W.P. MARIETTA IN THE FORTIES: AND HER EVOLUTION IN HUMAN AFFAIRS. (Mariet-
ta OH: no pub., 1905) 21p (LDS)
Berry, Ellen T. & David. EARLY OHIO SETTLERS: PURCHASERS OF LAND IN SOUTHEASTERN
OHIO, 1800-1840. (Baltimore: Genealogical Pub.Co., 1984) 129p (OHS,SLO,OGS,DAR)
Biedel, Helen C. A DIGEST OF THE SCHOOL RECORD BOOKS OF WILLIAM BIEDEL: WATER-
TOWN, WASHINGTON COUNTY OHIO, FOR THE YEARS 1880-1897. 1957. 12p (LDS,SLO)
Biedel, Helen C. DAVIS RECORDS: WASHINGTON COUNTY OHIO - EARLY GATEWAY TO THE
WEST. (SLO)
Biedel, Helen C. NOTES AND INDEX TAKEN FROM THE MINUTES OF CATS CREEK (LATER,
LOWELL CHURCH) ADAMS TOWNSHIP, WASHINGTON COUNTY OHIO, MAY 12, 1832-OC-
TOBER 14, 1871, BAPTIST DENOMINATION. 1964. 26p (LDS)
Biedel, Mrs. Herbert W. A DIGEST OF THE SCHOOL RECORD BOOKS OF WILLIAM BIEDEL, WATER-
TOWN, 1880-1897. (SLO)
BIRTHPLACE OF THE NORTHWEST TERRITORY. (Marietta OH: Marietta Northwest Territory
Celebration Commission, 1938) 64p (LDS,DAR)
Campus Martius Museum. CEMETERY RECORDS OF WASHINGTON AND MONROE COUNTIES
OHIO. nd. 250p. (SLO)
Cayton, Robert F. THE CITY OF MARIETTA, OHIO: 1788-1987, A BIBLIOGRAPHY. (Marietta OH:
Marietta College Library, 1988)
CENSUS OF WASHINGTON COUNTY OHIO, 1810. 1946? 50p (DAR,OGS)
CENTENNIAL SOUVENIR OF MARIETTA OHIO: SETTLED APRIL SEVENTH, 1788: CELEBRATION,
APRIL SEVENTH, 1888. (Marietta OH: E.H.Alderman & Sons, 1887) 101p (LDS)
CENTURY REVIEW OF MARIETTA OHIO: EARLY HISTORY, NATURAL ADVANTAGES, SCHOOLS,
CHURCHES, SECRET AND SOCIAL SOCIETIES. (Marietta OH: Marietta Board of Trade, 1900)
132p (LDS)
Clines, Charles E. SOME REMINESCENCES (sic) OF MARIETTA IN THE YEARS OF THE 50'S AND
60'S. (LDS)
Cochran, Wes. 1850 CENSUS OF WASHINGTON COUNTY OHIO. (Parkersburg WV: author, 1985)
371p (OGS,LDS)

Conner, Mrs. Robert M. MOUND CEMETERY AT MARIETTA OHIO.

Conner & Masters. PIONEER CEMETERIES OF SOUTHEASTERN OHIO 1801-1980. [Mound Cem., Marietta] (Cambridge OH: Guernsey Co Chapter OGS, 1981) 49p (LDS,DAR,SLO)

Cottle, Delmer L. & Elizabeth. INDEX TO WALL MAP OF WASHINGTON COUNTY, OHIO, 1845. 1972. (SLO)

Cottle, Delmer L. & Elizabeth. INDEX TO WASHINGTON COUNTY OHIO TAX MAP BY WILLIAM LOREY & PUBLISHED BY EDWIN P. GARDNER, 1858. 1971. (SLO)

Cotton, Willia D. SKETCH OF MOUND CEMETERY, MARIETTA OHIO. (Marietta OH: Marietta Register Print., 1906) 45p (SLO,LDS)

Craig, Robert D. WASHINGTON COUNTY OHIO MARRIAGES, 1789-1822. (Cincinnati: author, 1963) 35p (LDS,DAR)

Daughters of the American Revolution. BIBLE AND CEMETERY RECORDS OF WASHINGTON COUNTY OHIO. (SLO)

Daughters of the American Revolution. BARTLETT METHODIST CHURCH CIRCUIT RECORDS. (SLO,DAR)

Daughters of the American Revolution. BIBLE & FAMILY RECORDS. (SLO,DAR)

Daughters of the American Revolution. BIBLE RECORDS. (SLO,DAR)

Daughters of the American Revolution. BIBLE RECORDS FROM THE CAMPUS MARTIUS MUSEUM COLLECTION OF BIBLES. 2v. (SLO)

Daughters of the American Revolution. DAYBOOK OF LUCINDA NOFFSINGER PATTERSON. 1973. 52p (DAR)

Daughters of the American Revolution. FAMILY BIBLE RECORDS. (SLO,DAR)

Daughters of the American Revolution. FAMILY RECORDS. (SLO,DAR)

Daughters of the American Revolution. INDEX AND DEATH NOTICES FOUND IN EARLY NEWSPAPERS PUBLISHED IN MARIETTA OHIO. (LDS)

Daughters of the American Revolution. MARRIAGE RECORDS, 1789-1864. 2v. (SLO,LDS,DAR)

Daughters of the American Revolution. MOUND AND HARMAR CEMETERY TOMBSTONE INSCRIPTIONS AND INTERMENT RECORDS. (LDS)

Daughters of the American Revolution. NAMES OF PERSONS MENTIONED IN THE EARLY RECORDS IN THE PROBATE COURT, MARIETTA, WASHINGTON COUNTY, OHIO OF VOLUMES I,II,III,IV,V. (LDS)

Daughters of the American Revolution. REVOLUTIONARY SOLDIERS BURIED IN WASHINGTON COUNTY OHIO: CONTAINING MILITARY RECORDS AND SHORT HISTORY OF LIVES. 1923. 83p (DAR,LDS)

Daughters of the American Revolution. WASHINGTON COUNTY DEATH RECORDS 1811-1865; TAKEN FROM NEWSPAPERS PUBLISHED IN MARIETTA OHIO. 1938. 73p (DAR)

Delafield, John. A BRIEF TOPOGRAPHICAL DESCRIPTION OF THE COUNTY OF WASHINGTON, IN THE STATE OF OHIO. (New York: J.M.Elliot, 1834) 39p (LC)

Dennis, James L. WASHINGTON'S DARKER BROTHER, ONE HUNDRED YEARS OF BLACK HISTORY IN WASHINGTON COUNTY OHIO, 1788-1888. (Parkersburg WV: author, 1986) 76p (LDS,SLO,LC)

Devol, Jerry B. WOLCOTT FAMILY CEMETERY, WATERTOWN TWP., OHIO. (LDS)

Dickinson, Cornelius. A CENTURY OF CHURCH LIFE: A HISTORY OF THE FIRST CONGREGATIONAL CHURCH OF MARIETTA OHIO. (np: E.R.Aldermann & Sons, 1896) 226p (LDS,DAR)

Dickinson, Cornelius. A HISTORY OF BELPRE, WASHINGTON COUNTY OHIO. (Parkersburg WV: Globe Print., 1920) 243p. (SLO,LDS,DAR)

Doak, Mrs. John. A LIST OF THE MINISTERS OF THE GOSPEL IN WASHINGTON COUNTY. 6p (LDS)

Doak, Mrs. John. WASHINGTON COUNTY, OHIO EARLY MARRIAGE RECORDS, 1789-1803. 25p (LDS)

Emerson, William D. WASHINGTON COUNTY, OHIO. (Cincinnati: Klauprech & Menzel's, 1845)(Reprint, Marietta OH: Washington Co.Hist.Soc., 1976) 34p (LDS,LC)

Gard, Nellie A. COPY OF WASHINGTON COUNTY OHIO DURHAM TOWNSHIP SCHOOL BOARD CLERK'S RECORD BOOK, 1855 TO 1896. (LDS)

Graham, Bernice & E.Cottle. ABSTRACT OF PROBATE RECORDS, WASHINGTON COUNTY OHIO, WILLS, ESTATES, GUARDIANSHIPS, 1789-1855. 1982. (SLO)

Graham, Bernice & E.Cottle. WASHINGTON COUNTY OHIO MARRIAGES, 1789-1840. (Marietta OH: Washington Co.Hist.Soc.,1976) 187p (LDS,SLO,DAR)

Green, Karen M. PIONEER OHIO NEWSPAPERS, 1802-1818: GENEALOGICAL & HISTORICAL ABSTRACTS. (Galveston TX: Frontier Press, 1988) 362p (OGS)

Hawley, Owen P. INDEX TO "A PIONEER COLLEGE" BY ARTHUR BEACH. (Marietta OH: The Sign of Aladdin's Lamp, 1966) 48p (LDS)

Hildreth, Samuel P. BIOGRAPHICAL AND HISTORICAL MEMOIRS OF THE EARLY PIONEER SETTLERS OF OHIO. (Cincinnati: H.W.Derby, 1852) 539p. (LDS,SLO)

Hinshaw, William Wade. ENCYCLOPEDIA OF AMERICAN QUAKER GENEALOGY, VOL.IV, OHIO. (Baltimore: Genealogical Pub.Co., 1973) 1424p (SLO,OHS,LDS)

Historical Records Survey. INVENTORY OF THE COUNTY ARCHIVES OF OHIO, NO.84, WASHINGTON COUNTY (MARIETTA) (Columbus OH: author, 1938) 330p (DAR,LDS,OHS)

HISTORY OF WASHINGTON COUNTY OHIO. (Cleveland: H.Z.Williams Bros., 1881)(Reprint, Knightstown IN: Bookmark, 1976)(Reprint, Marietta OH: Washington Co Chapter OGS, 1989) 739p. (OHS,SLO,LDS,DAR) (RPI)

Hulbert, Archer B. THE RECORDS OF THE ORIGINAL PROCEEDINGS OF THE OHIO COMPANY. (Marietta OH: Marietta Historical Commission, 1917)

INDEX TO VOL.2 (1795-1803) OF THE COMPLETE RECORD SERIES OF CIVIL CASES, COURT OF COMMON PLEAS, WASHINGTON COUNTY, NORTHWEST TERRITORY (OHIO). 1984. (SLO)

Jackson, Ronald V. & G.Teeples. EARLY OHIO CENSUS RECORDS. [1800,1803,1810, WASHINGTON CO] (Salt Lake City UT: author, 1974) 64p (OGS)

James, Alfred P. THE OHIO COMPANY, ITS INNER HISTORY. (Pittsburgh: University of Pittsburgh Press, 1959)

Jordan, J.L. WASHINGTON COUNTY CHILDRENS HOME SOUVENIR, 1867-1917. 32p (LDS)

Jordan, Wayne. THE PEOPLE OF OHIO'S FIRST COUNTY. (Columbus OH: no pub, 1940) 10p (LC)

Kempfer, Lester L. THE SALEM LIGHT GUARD. [WASHINGTON COUNTY'S CO.G, 36TH REGT. OVI 1861-1865). (Chicago: author, 1973) 126p

Lake, D.J. ATLAS OF WASHINGTON COUNTY, OHIO. (Philadelphia: Titus, Simmons & Titus, 1875)(Reprint, Knightstown IN: Mayhill Pub., 1972)(Reprint, Kokomo IN: Selby Pub., 1985) 96p (DAR,LC,LDS,OGS,SLO) (RPI)

Lewis, Thomas W. SOUTHEASTERN OHIO AND THE MUSKINGUM VALLEY, 1788-1928: COVERING ATHENS, BELMONT, COSHOCTON, GUERNSEY, LICKING, MEIGS, MONROE, MORGAN, MUSKINGUM, NOBLE, PERRY AND WASHINGTON COUNTIES. (Chicago: S.J.Clarke Co.,1928) 3v. (SLO,DAR,OHS)

Loring, George B. NINETY-FIFTH ANNIVERSARY OF THE SETTLEMENT OF OHIO AT MARIETTA. 1883. 76p. (SLO)

McDonnell, F.M. THE BOOK OF MARIETTA: BEING A CONDENSED, ACCURATE AND RELIABLE RECORD OF THE IMPORTANT EVENTS... (Marietta OH: author, 1906) 156p (LDS)

McKitrick, Arthur. CEMETERY INSCRIPTIONS FROM WASHINGTON COUNTY OHIO. 1973. 4v (LDS,SLO)

Marietta College. THE CENTENNIAL CELEBRATION, 1835-1935. (Marietta OH: the college, 1935) 174p (LDS)

MARIETTA DILY NEWS ABSTRACTED MAY 5 TO JUNE 2, 1883. 1982. (SLO)

MARIETTA OHIO 1776-1976. (SLO)

Martin, Eleanor. BIBLE, FAMILY, CHURCH AND CEMETERY RECORDS, WASHINGTON COUNTY. (LDS)

Martin, Eleanor. RECORDS OF BARTLETT METHODIST CHURCH CIRCUIT, ALSO FAMILY BIBLE RECORDS. (LDS)

Maxwell, Fay. WASHINGTON COUNTY OHIO MARRIAGE INDEX: MALES AND FEMALES, MARRIAGES, 1797-1803, NORTHWEST TERRITORY & MARRIAGES, 1803-1822, WASHINGTON COUNTY OHIO. (SLO,LDS)

Maxwell, Fay. INDEX FOR WASHINGTON COUNTY, NORTHWEST TERRITORY,OHIO 1800 CENSUS AND INDEX FOR WASHINGTON COUNTY MARRIAGES, 1791-1803, ALSO REVOLUTIONARY

SOLDIERS BURIED IN WASHINGTON COUNTY AND BIRTH AND DEATH DATA ON MANY EARLY SETTLERS. (SLO,LDS)

Miller, Louis E. MARIETTA OHIO HISTORIES. (LDS)

Newton, Charles H. VOLUNTEERS OF WASHINGTON CO., OHIO WAR OF THE REBELLION, 1861-1865. (Marietta OH: author, 1913) (LDS)

Ohio University. GUIDE TO LOCAL GOVERNMENT RECORDS AT OHIO UNIVERSITY. (Athens: OU Library, 1986) 61p.

Owen, Elizabeth T. FORT FRYE ON THE MUSKINGUM: BEVERLY, OHIO. 1932.

Percival, Eleanor H. DUCK CREEK ACRES. (Columbus OH: author, 1952)

Pioneer Assn. THE NINETY FIFTH ANNIVERSARY OF THE SETTLEMENT OF OHIO, AT MARIETTA. (Marietta OH: author, 1883) 76p (LDS,LC)

Pioneer Committee. NINETY-EIGHTH ANNIVERSARY OF THE SETTLEMENT OF OHIO AT MARIETTA AND THE NORTHWEST TERRITORY. (Marietta OH: author, 1887). 26p. (SLO)

Plumb, Charles S. THE HISTORY OF AMERICAN UNION LODGE NO.1, FREE AND ACCEPTED MASONS OF OHIO, 1776 TO 1933. (Marietta OH: the lodge, 1934) 463p (LDS)

Potts, Genevieve M. ABSTRACTS OF WILLS AND ADMINISTRATION OF ESTATES, 1788-1850. (SLO)

Potts, Genevieve M. WILLS OF WASHINGTON COUNTY OHIO. 2v. (SLO,LDS,DAR)

Potts, Genevieve M. ST.MARY'S ROMAN CATHOLIC CHURCH, MARIETTA, OHIO. 1943. 79,11p (DAR)

Preston, Laura C. HISTORY AND SOME NECDOTES OF THE SETTLEMENT OF NEWBURY, WASHINGTON COUNTY OHIO. (Marietta OH: Marietta Journal Print.,1909) 24p. (SLO,LDS) (RPI)

Pruden, M.M. PRUDEN'S COMBINED BUSINESS DIRECTORY AND GAZETTEER: EMBRACING...MARIETTA...FOR THE YEARS 1899-1900. (Charleston WV: Pruden Pub.Co., 1900) 353p (LDS)

Riley, Nancy. FIRST CONGREGATIONAL CHURCH, MARIETTA, OHIO, "THE CHURCH OF THE PIONEERS,", 1796-1826. (Waterford OH: author, 1987) 182p (OGS)

Riley, Nancy. RECORDS OF THE CONGREGATIONAL CHURCH IN HARMAR, OHIO, ORGANIZED JAN.1, 1840. (Waterford OH: author, 1987) 123p (OGS)

Roe, Frederick B. ATLAS OF THE CITY OF MARIETTA, WASHINGTON COUNTY OHIO, AND VICINITY. (Chicago: Geo.F.Cram, 1902) 38p (LDS,SLO)

Rothbone, O.L. TOWN CLERK'S RECORD BOOK OF DUNHAM TOWNSHIP TRUSTEE'S MEETINGS, 1855-1902. (SLO)

Roush, Herbert L. UNKNOWN SETTLEMENT. A HISTORICAL NARRATIVE OF LITTLE HOCKING, WASHINGTON COUNTY OHIO, 1789-1984. (Parsons WV: McClain Print.Co., 1983) 334p (LDS,SLO)

Row, Frederick B. ATLAS OF THE CITY OF MARIETTA, WASHINGTON COUNTY OHIO. 1902. (SLO) (RPI)

Sams, Catherine. CORNER CEMETERY INSCRIPTIONS, BELPRE TOWNSHIP. (Little Hocking OH: author, n.d.) 12p

Sams, Catherine. DECATUR PRESBYTERIAN CHURCH CEMETERY INSCRIPTIONS. (Little Hocking OH: author, n.d.) 19p

Schneider, Norris F. BLENNERHASSETT ISLAND AND THE BURR CONSPIRACY. 1965. 36p. (SLO)

Schneider, Norris F. HISTORY OF LOWELL AND ADAMS TOWNSHIPS, WASHINGTON COUNTY OHIO. (Lowell OH: Midwest Book, 1946). 27p. (SLO,LDS)

Schneider, Norris F. THE MUSKINGUM RIVER: A HISTORY AND GUIDE. (Columbus OH: Ohio Hist.Soc., 1968) 48p (LDS)

Slaughter, Raymond D. INDEX 1880 CENSUS, WASHINGTON COUNTY, OHIO. 1984. (SLO)

Slaughter, Raymond D. INDEX 1900 CENSUS OF WASHINGTON COUNTY OHIO. (SLO)

Sloan, Helen H. PIONEER CEMETERIES OF WASHINGTON COUNTY OHIO, 1789-1940. (LDS,SLO)

Sloan, Mrs. C.R. FAMILY BIBLE RECORDS, WASHINGTON COUNTY OHIO. (SLO,DAR,LDS)

Stone, Benjamin F. FROM RUTLAND TO MARIETTA: LEAVES FROM THE AUTOBIOGRAPHY OF BENJAMIN FRANKLIN STONE. (LDS)

Summers, Thomas J. HISTORY OF MARIETTA. (Marietta OH: Leader Pub.Co., 1903) 328p (LDS,DAR,SLO)

Titus, . PLAT BOOK OF WASHINGTON CO OHIO. 1875.

Wallcut, Thomas. JOURNAL OF THOMAS WALLCUT, IN 1790: WITH NOTES BY GEORGE DEXTER. (Cambridge MA: University Press, J.Wilson & Son, 1879) 42p (LDS)

Washington Co Chapter OGS. FIVE GENERATIONS IN WASHINGTON CO., OH. (Marietta OH: the society, 1988?) 95p (OGS)

Washington Co Chapter OGS. ROCKLAND CEMETERY INSCRIPTIONS, 1822-1984. (Marietta OH: the society, 1988?) 180p (OGS)

Washington Co Chapter OGS. TOMBSTONE INSCRIPTIONS, ROCKLAND CEMETERY, BELPRE TOWNSHIP, WASHINGTON CO OHIO 1822-1984. (Little Hocking OH: the society, 1985) 244p (OGS,OHS,LDS)

Washington Co Chapter OGS. WATERFORD CEMETERY INSCRIPTIONS. (Marietta OH: the society, 1988) 41p (OGS)

Washington Co Chapter OGS. WATERTOWN CEMETERY READINGS. (Little Hocking OH: the society, 1986) 79p (OGS,SLO)

Washington Co Historical Society. INDEX TO HISTORY OF MARIETTA AND WASHINGTON COUNTY OHIO BY MARTIN R.ANDREWS. (Marietta OH: the society, 1976) 181p (DAR)

Washington Co Historical Society. WASHINGTON COUNTY OHIO TO 1980: A COLLECTION OF TOPICAL & FAMILY SKETCHES. (Marietta OH: the society, 1980) 403p (LC,DAR,SLO)

Washington County Public Library. A BIBLIOGRAPHY OF MATERIAL PERTAINING TO STATE AND LOCAL HISTORY AND GENEALOGY. PART 1. (Marietta OH: the library, 1972) 41p

WASHINGTON COUNTY NORTHWEST TERRITORY COURT OF COMMON PLEAS INDEX 1795-1803. (Bowie MD: Heritage Books, nd) 64p (OGS)

Waters, Wilson. THE HISTORY OF SAINT LUKE'S CHURCH, MARIETTA, OHIO. (Marietta OH: J.Muller & Son, 1884) 280p (LDS,DAR)

Whiteman, Jane. SURNAME INDEX TO HISTORY OF THE UPPER OHIO VALLEY, Brant & Fuller, 1891) 49p (OGS)

WIGGINS & WEAVER'S OHIO RIVER DIRECTORY FOR 1871-1872: EMBRACING...MARIETTA. (Cleveland: authors, 1872) 419p (LDS)

Yon, Paul D. GUIDE TO OHIO COUNTY AND MUNICIPAL GOVERNMENT RECORDS FOR URBAN RESEARCH. (Columbus: Ohio Hist Soc., 1973) 216p.(OHS)

Young, Roger O. WASHINGTON COUNTY OHIO IMMIGRATION AND NATURALIZATION ABSTRACTS, 1808-1840. (LDS,SLO,OHS)

# WAYNE COUNTY

| | |
|---|---|
| CREATED: | 1808 FROM COLUMBIANA COUNTY |
| COUNTY SEAT: | WOOSTER 44691 |
| COURT HOUSE: | PUBLIC SQUARE, WOOSTER 44691 |
| LIBRARY: | 304 N. MARKET ST., WOOSTER 44691 |
| HISTORICAL SOCIETY: | 546 E. BOWMAN ST., WOOSTER 44691 |
| GENEALOGICAL SOCIETY: | WAYNE COUNTY CHAPTER OGS, |
| | 546 E. BOWMAN ST., WOOSTER 44691 |
| HEALTH DEPARTMENT: | 203 S. WALNUT ST., WOOSTER 44691 |
| | (separate offices for Wooster city, Orrville, Rittman & Norton) |
| ARCHIVAL DISTRICT: | UNIVERSITY OF AKRON, AKRON, OHIO |
| | (see Folck's Guide to records) |
| LAND SURVEYS: | CONGRESS LANDS, OHIO RIVER SURVEY (NORTH) |
| BOUNDED BY: | EAST: STARK & SUMMIT CO. |
| | NORTH: MEDINA CO. |
| | WEST: ASHLAND CO. |
| | SOUTH: HOLMES CO. |
| TOWNSHIPS: | Baughman, Canaan, Chester, Chippewa, Clinton, Congress, East Union, Franklin, Green, Milton, Paint, Plain, Salt Creek, Sugar Creek, Wayne, Wooster. |

## COURT RECORDS: (LDS MICROFILM)
Auditor:
Tax records, 1816-1838.
Clerk of Courts:
Appearance dockets, v1-17, 1812-1852.
Supreme Court record, v1-3, 1813-1852.
Common Pleas general index, v1, 1817-1874.
Common Pleas journal, v1-18, 1818-1852.
Chancery record, 1817-1849.
Probate Court:
Birth records, v1-4, 1867-1908.
Birth registration & corrections, 1941-1966.
Death records, v1-2, 1867-1908.
Marriage license index, v4, 1843-1861.
Marriage records, v1-23, 1813-1934.
Executors & administrators bonds, v1-2, 1849-1870.
Executors bonds, v3, 1870-1880.
Administrators bonds, v4, 1880-1889.
Guardians bonds, v1-4, 1849-1896.
Appraisement & sales, v3-7, 1831-1844.
Civil dockets, vA-7, 1837-1888.
General index to court cases, 1808-1950.
Probate journal, v1-33, 1852-1898.
Will records, vA-18, 1817-1911.
Naturalization records, 1861-1903.
Recorder:
Deed index, c1813-1914.
Deed records, v1-162, 1813-1910.
Treasurer:
Religious incorporations & ministers licenses, 1819-1856.
Miscellaneous:
Chippewa Township Presbyterian Church, records, 1827-1879.
Dalton, Presbyterian Church, records, 1816-1895.
Dalton, Presby.Church, Woman's home & missionary records, 1880-1893.
Fredericksburg, Cumberland Presby.Church, minutes, 1879-1898.
Fredericksburg, Presby.Church, records, 1851-1872.
Jackson, Presbyterian Church, minutes, 1827-1875.
Kidron, Sonnenberg Mennonite Church, records, 1822-1940.
Orrville, Presbyterian Church, records, 1865-1896.
Salt Creek Assoc.Presby.Church, treasurer's records, 1834-1865.
Wooster, First Presby.Church, records, 1833-1899.
Wooster, First Reformed Church, pastor's register, 1883-1888.
Wooster, Wayne Presby.Church, records, 1872-1888.
Wooster, Westminster Presby.Church, records, 1874-1892.

## OHIO HISTORICAL SOCIETY: (MICROFILM)
Clerk of Courts:
Appearance dockets, v1-17, 1812-1852.
Supreme Court record, v1-3, 1813-1852.
Common Pleas general index, v1, 1817-1874.
Common Pleas journal, v1-18, 1818-1852.
Chancery record, 1817-1849.
Miscellaneous:
Marriages, 1812-1864, by DAR.
Bible records, by DAR.

Cemetery records, males, by DAR.
Index to 1820 census, by DAR.

**CENSUS RECORDS (OHS,SLO,OGS,LDS)**
1820-1880, 1900-1910; 1890 VETERANS; 1880,1900 SOUNDEX; 1910 MIRACODE

**AGRICULTURAL CENSUS SCHEDULES (OHS,SLO-mic)**
1850,1870,1880

**PRODUCTS OF INDUSTRY CENSUS SCHEDULE (OHS,SLO-mic)**
1850,1860,1870,1880

**MORTALITY CENSUS SCHEDULES (OHS,SLO-mic)**
1850,1860

**NEWSPAPERS: [GUIDE TO OHIO NEWSPAPERS, 1793-1973]**
Creston, Dalton, Kidron, Orrville, Rittman, Shreve, West Salem, Wooster.

**TAX RECORDS (OHS & LDS)**
1814,1816-1838.

**GENEALOGICAL PERIODICAL ARTICLES**
Bell, Carol Willsey. OHIO GENEALOGICAL PERIODICAL INDEX: A COUNTY GUIDE (Youngstown
    OH: author, 6th ed., 1987)

**PUBLISHED SOURCES:**
Baker, Charles B. HISTORY OF THE NEGRO IN WOOSTER, OHIO. (SLO)
BAKER'S MAP OF WAYNE COUNTY OHIO, 1856. (Apple Creek OH: Wayne Co Chapter OGS, 1987)
    36p (OGS)
Beachy, Leroy. CEMETERY DIRECTORY OF THE AMISH COMMUNITY IN EASTERN HOLMES AND
    ADJOINING COUNTIES IN OHIO. 1975. 200p (LDS)
CALDWELL'S ATLAS OF WAYNE COUNTY, OHIO, 1873 & 1897, reprint. (OGS)
Caldwell, Joseph A. CALDWELL'S ATLAS OF WAYNE COUNTY OHIO. (Mt.Vernon OH: Atlas
    Pub.Co.,1897) 143p (LC,SLO)
Caldwell, John A. CALDWELL'S ATLAS OF WAYNE COUNTY, OHIO, AND THE CITY OF WOOSTER.
    (Sunbury OH: author, 1873) 113p (LDS,OGS,SLO)(RPI)
CEMETERY INSCRIPTIONS, OVERTON CEMETERY, CHESTER TOWNSHIP, WAYNE COUNTY
    OHIO. 1982. 13p. (OGS)
COMMEMORATIVE BIOGRAPHICAL RECORD OF THE COUNTIES OF WAYNE AND HOLMES.
    (Chicago: J.H.Beers & Co.,1889) 2v (LDS,DAR,SLO)(RPI)
COMMEMORATIVE BIOGRAPHICAL RECORD OF WAYNE COUNTY OHIO. (Chicago: J.H. Beers
    & Co.,1889) 608p (LC,SLO,LDS)(RPI)
Daughters of the American Revolution. AUTHENTIC RECORD OF THE SOLDIERS OF THE
    AMERICAN REVOLUTION WHO ARE BURIED IN WAYNE COUNTY, OHIO. (SLO)
Daughters of the American Revolution. BIBLE RECORDS, WAYNE COUNTY OHIO. (SLO,LDS)
Daughters of the American Revolution. CEMETERY RECORDS, SMITHVILLE OHIO. (SLO)
Daughters of the American Revolution. CEMETERIES OF CONGRESS TOWNSHIP, WAYNE COUN-
    TY, OHIO, 1810-1973. (SLO)
Daughters of the American Revolution. EARLY RECORDS OF THE HOLY TRINITY LUTHERAN
    CHURCH, CANTON, OHIO AND EMMANUEL'S UNITED CHURCH OF CHRIST, DOYLES-
    TOWN (WAYNE COUNTY) OHIO. (SLO)
Daughters of the American Revolution. EMMANUEL CHURCH, DOYLESTOWN, OHIO, 1817-1936.
    (SLO)
Daughters of the American Revolution. INDEX TO THE 1820 POPULATION SCHEDULE OF WAYNE
    COUNTY OHIO. (SLO,DAR,LDS)

Daughters of the American Revolution. LIST OF MALES BURIED IN WAYNE COUNTY OHIO WHOSE AGES MAKE THEM ELIGIBLE FOR THE REVOLUTIONARY WAR, WAR OF 1812, AND THE MEXICAN WAR. (SLO)

Daughters of the American Revolution. MARRIAGE RECORDS OF WAYNE COUNTY OHIO, 1812-1867. 6v. (SLO,DAR,LDS)

Daughters of the American Revolution. OHIO CEMETERY AND CHURCH RECORDS. (SLO)

Daughters of the American Revolution. SOME CEMETERY RECORDS OF CUYAHOGA, FULTON, MEDINA, LORAIN & WAYNE COUNTIES. 1938. 175p (DAR,LDS)

Daughters of the American Revolution. TOMBSTONE RECORDINGS CEMETERIES OF CONGRESS TWP., WAYNE COUNTY, OHIO: 1810-1973. 1973? 149p (DAR)

Daughters of the American Revolution. UNPUBLISHED RECORDS RELATING TO FAMILIES OF MEMBERS OF THE WOOSTER-WAYNE CHAPTER, NSDAR. 1972. 98p (DAR)

Douglass, Benjamin. HISTORY OF WAYNE COUNTY OHIO: FROM THE DAYS OF THE PIONEERS AND FIRST SETTLERS TO THE PRESENT TIME. (Indianapolis: Robert Douglass, 1878) 868p (LC,DAR,SLO,LDS) (RPI)

Douglass, Benjamin. HISTORY OF THE LAWYERS OF WAYNE COUNTY OHIO FROM 1812-1900. (Wooster OH: Clapper Printing, 1900) 307p (SLO,LDS)

Duff, William A. HISTORY OF NORTH CENTRAL OHIO: EMBRACING RICHLAND, ASHLAND, WAYNE, MEDINA, LORAIN, HURON, AND KNOX COUNTIES. (Topeka: Historical Pub.Co., 19831) 3v (DAR,OHS)

Falstaff, Jake. COME BACK TO WAYNE COUNTY OHIO. (Boston MA: Houghton Mifflin Co., 1942) 244p

Folck, Linda. LOCAL GOVERNMENT RECORDS IN THE AMERICAN HISTORY RESEARCH CENTER AT THE UNIVERSITY OF AKRON. (Akron: U of Akron, 1982) 40p. (OGS)

Frey, Russell W. THE HISTORY AND LEGENDS OF ROGUES HOLLOW. (Rittman OH: Rittman Press, 1958) 100p (LC)

Harter, Mrs. Bert. GERMAN REFORMED & LUTHERAN CHURCH RECORDS, BAPTISMS, DEATHS FROM WAYNE, STARK, MEDINA & SUMMIT COUNTIES, TRANSLATED FROM THE GERMAN. (Doylestown OH: author, 1962)

Harter, Mary. EARLY RECORDS OF HOLY TRINITY LUTHERAN CHURCH, CANTON, OHIO, AND EMANUEL'S UNITED CHURCH OF CHRIST, DOYLESTOWN, OHIO. (DAR,LDS)

HIGH CHURCH: 150TH ANNIVERSARY, EMANUEL UNITED CHURCH OF CHRIST, DOYLESTOWN, OHIO, 1817-1867.(LDS)

HISTORICAL SKETCHES OF KIDRON, OHIO. (np: Harvey Gardner, 1936) 63p (DAR)

HISTORY OF WAYNE COUNTY OHIO. (Indianapolis: B.F.Bowen, 1910) 2v. (DAR,LDS)(RPI)

Kauffman, Vera. HISTORY OF SHREVE, OHIO: CLINTON TOWNSHIP, WAYNE CO., 1853-1953. (np: author, 1953) 103p (DAR)

Lawrence, Carl. BRIEF HISTORICAL MEMENTO OF DALTON, OHIO. (Dalton OH: author, 1940) 62p (DAR)

Lehman, James O. SONNENBERG, A HAVEN AND A HERITAGE: A SESQUINCENTENNIAL HISTORY OF THE SWISS MENNONITE COMMUNITY OF SOUTHEASTERN WAYNE COUNTY. (Kidron OH: Kidron Community Council, 1969) 384p (LDS)

Lutz, John J. THE OLD TUSCARAWAS CIRCUIT AND INTRODUCTION OF METHODISM INTO WAYNE COUNTY, OHIO. 1955. 24p (DAR)

McCorkle, Elyzabeth S. INDEX TO THE 1820 CENSUS OF WAYNE COUNTY OHIO. (SLO)

MINUTES OF THE CENTENNIAL MEETING OF THE WOOSTER BAPTIST ASSOCIATION: BAPTIST CHURCH, MASSILLON, OHIO. 1939. 28p (DAR)

Notestein, Lucy L. WOOSTER OF THE MIDDLE WEST. (New Haven CT: Yale Univ.Press, 1937) 333p (LDS)

Phillips, C.A. WAYNE COUNTY OHIO EARLY CENSUSES AND TAX LISTS. (Wooster OH: Wayne Co.Hist.Soc., 197?) 73p (SLO,LDS)

Powell, Esther W. ST.MICHAEL'S EVANGELICAL LUTHERAN CHURCH HISTORY, 1830-1930. (Akron OH: author, 1967) 80p (DAR,SLO,LDS)

Raber, Nellie M. MARRIAGES WAYNE COUNTY OHIO, 1812-1864. (LDS)

Rigor, Joseph E. THE DOYLE FAMILIES [AND THE] HISTORY OF DOYLESTOWN, PENNA., DOYLES-TOWN, OHIO & DOYLESTOWN, WISC. (Buchanan MI: author, 1979) 98p (LDS)

Rutt, Harvey S. HISTORY OF CHESTER TOWNSHIP, WAYNE COUNTY, OHIO: AND THE GENEAL-OGY OF THE SHAUM AND HOLDEMAN FAMILIES. (Smithville OH: author, 1930) 155p (LDS)

Smith, Richard G. CENSUS OF 1880 OF WAYNE COUNTY OHIO. (Evansville IN: Unigraphic, 1979) 323p (OGS,SLO)

Smith, Richard G. INDEX TO WILLS AND ESTATES II, WAYNE COUNTY OHIO, 1852-1900. (Wooster OH: Wayne Co.Hist.Soc., 1987) 220p (OGS)

Smith, Richard G. SEVENTY-FIVE YEARS OF WAYNE COUNTY OHIO MARRIAGES 1813-1888. (Wooster: Wayne Co Hist Soc, 1979) 147p (OGS,LDS,SLO)

Smith, Richard G. WAYNE COUNTY TAX LIST 1826. (Wooster: Wayne Co Hist Soc, 1981) 74p (OGS,LDS,SLO)

Smith, Richard G. WAYNE COUNTY WILLS, ESTATES AND GUARDIANSHIPS, 1812-1852. (Wooster: Wayne Co.Hist.Soc., 1981) 143p (OGS,LDS,SLO)

Smith, Richard G. FEDERAL CENSUS OF 1820, WAYNE COUNTY OHIO. (Apple Creek OH: author, 1981) 71p. (OGS,LDS)

Sterling, Mrs.V.O. HISTORY OF FREDERICKSBURG OHIO. 1951. 134p. (SLO)

Wayne Co Chapter OGS. 1856 MAP OF WAYNE COUNTY. (Wooster OH: the society, 1988?) (OGS)

Wayne Co Chapter OGS. DOUGLAS HISTORY OF WAYNE COUNTY. (Wooster OH: the society, nd) (OGS)

Wayne Co Chapter OGS. REPRINT OF BAKER'S MAP OF WAYNE COUNTY, 1856. (Wooster OH: Wayne Co.Hist.Soc., 1987) 36p (OGS)

Wayne Co.Hist.Soc. HISTORIC HERITAGE OF WAYNE COUNTY, OHIO, BEING A DIRECTORY OF 256 HISTORICAL HOUSES AND BUILDINGS. 1976. (SLO)

Wayne Co.Hist.Soc. WAYNE COUNTY OHIO BURIAL RECORDS. (Wooster OH: the society, 1975) 737p (OGS,SLO,LDS)

Wayne Co.Hist.Soc. WAYNE COUNTY OHIO ABSTRACTS OF NATURALIZATION RECORDS 1812-1903. (Wooster: the society, 1985) 142p (OGS,SLO)

# WILLIAMS COUNTY

| | |
|---|---|
| CREATED: | 1820 FROM DARKE COUNTY |
| COUNTY SEAT: | BRYAN 43506 |
| COURT HOUSE: | MAIN & HIGH ST., BRYAN 43506 |
| LIBRARY: | 107 E. HIGH ST., BRYAN 43506 |
| HISTORICAL SOCIETY: | 433 SNYDER ST., MONTPELIER 43543 |
| GENEALOGICAL SOCIETY: | WILLIAMS COUNTY CHAPTER OGS, PO BOX 293, BRYAN 43506 publication: OHIO'S LAST FRONTIER |
| HEALTH DEPARTMENT: | 310 N.LINCOLN AVE., MONTPELIER 43543 (separate office for Bryan city) |
| ARCHIVAL DISTRICT: | BOWLING GREEN STATE UNIVERSITY, BOWLING GREEN (see Biggs' Guide to records) |
| LAND SURVEYS: | CONGRESS LANDS, E & N OF 1ST PRIN.MERIDIAN MICHIGAN SURVEY |
| BOUNDED BY: | EAST: FULTON & HENRY CO. NORTH: HILLSDALE CO., MICHIGAN WEST: DE KALB & STEUBEN CO., INDIANA SOUTH: DEFIANCE CO. |
| TOWNSHIPS: | Brady, Bridgewater, Center, Florence, Jefferson, Madison, Mill Creek, Northwest, Pulaski, Springfield, St. Joseph, Superior. |

## COURT RECORDS: (LDS MICROFILM)
Auditor:
 Tax duplicates, 1837-1850.
Clerk of Courts:
 Appearance dockets, 1852-1857.
 Common Pleas journal, v1-4, 1824-1857.
 Chancery record, v1-2, 1841-1856.
 Common Pleas general index, v1-2, 1824-1878.
 Supreme Court complete record, 1833-1849, 1855-1860.
Commissioners:
 Infirmary records, 1874-1955.
County Home:
 Register, 1874-1955.
Probate Court:
 Birth & death records, 1867-1941.
 Marriage records, 1824-1918.
 General index, 1825-1972.
 Administration docket, 1853-1893.
 Administrators bonds, 1845-1852, 1858-1873.
 Guardians bonds & letters, 1857-1873.
 Executors bonds & letters, 1858-1886.
 Admin., exr., grdn. accounts, 1856-1887.
 Real estate record, 1852-1864,1872-1886.
 Inventory & sale bills, 1856-1888.
 Probate journal, v1-10, 1852-1890.
 Civil docket, v1-2, 1859-1887.
 Naturalizations, 1836-1839, 1842, 1860-1929.
 Will records, v1-9, 1827-1911.
Recorder:
 General index to deeds, 1824-1964.
 Deed records, v1-55, 1830-1886.
 Soldiers discharges, v1-3, 1865-1946.
 Record of veterans' graves, 1859-1972.
Miscellaneous:
 Bryan, First Presby.Church, records, 1872-1946.
 Bryan, Trinity Episcopal Church, records, 1870-1982.
 Bryan, Trinity Lutheran Church, records, 1862-1961.

## OHIO HISTORICAL SOCIETY: (MICROFILM)
Clerk of Courts:
 Appearance dockets, 1852-1857.
 Common Pleas journal, v1-4, 1824-1857.
 Chancery record, v1-2, 1841-1856.
 Common Pleas general index, v1-2, 1824-1878.
 Supreme Court complete record, 1833-1849, 1855-1860.
County Home:
 Register, 1874-1955.
Probate Court:
 Civil docket, v1-2, 1859-1887.
 Naturalizations, 1836-1839, 1842, 1860-1929.
Recorder:
 Deeds, v49-55, 1881-1886.

**CENSUS RECORDS (OHS,SLO,OGS,LDS)**
1830-1880, 1900-1910; 1890 VETERANS; 1880,1900 SOUNDEX; 1910 MIRACODE

**AGRICULTURAL CENSUS SCHEDULES (OHS,SLO-mic)**
1850,1870,1880

**PRODUCTS OF INDUSTRY CENSUS SCHEDULE (OHS,SLO-mic)**
1850,1860,1870,1880

**MORTALITY CENSUS SCHEDULES (OHS,SLO-mic)**
1850,1860

**NEWSPAPERS: [GUIDE TO OHIO NEWSPAPERS, 1793-1973]**
Bryan, Edgerton, Edon, Montpelier, Pioneer, West Jefferson, West Unity.

**TAX RECORDS (OHS & LDS)**
1827-1838.

**GENEALOGICAL PERIODICAL ARTICLES**
Bell, Carol Willsey. OHIO GENEALOGICAL PERIODICAL INDEX: A COUNTY GUIDE (Youngstown OH: author, 6th ed., 1987)

**PUBLISHED SOURCES:**
Biggs, Deb. GUIDE TO LOCAL GOVERNMENT RECORDS AT THE CENTER FOR ARCHIVAL COL-LECTIONS. (Bowling Green OH: Bowling Green State Univ, 1981) 104p (OGS)
Bowersox, Charles A. STANDARD HISTORY OF WILLIAMS COUNTY OHIO. (Chicago: Lewis Pub.Co.,1920) 2v. (DAR,LDS,SLO)(RPI)
Christian, Donna K. GUIDE TO NEWSPAPER HOLDINGS AT THE CENTER FOR ARCHIVAL COL-LECTIONS. (Bowling Green OH: Bowling Green State Univ, 1980) 64p (OGS)
Clegg, Michael, ed. DEFIANCE, FULTON, HENRY, PAULDING, PUTNAM, WILLIAMS & WOOD COUNTIES OHIO NEWSPAPER OBITUARY ABSTRACTS, 1838-1870 (OHIO NEWSPAPER SERIES VOL.5) (Ft.Wayne IN: author, 1987) 75p (OGS)
COMBINED ATLASES OF WILLIAMS COUNTY OHIO, 1874,1894 AND PLAT BOOK OF 1904. (Reprint, Evansville IN: Unigraphic, 1976) (DAR,LDS,SLO)
COMMEMORATIVE BIOGRAPHICAL RECORD OF NORTHWESTERN OHIO INCLUDING THE COUNTIES OF DEFIANCE, HENRY, WILLIAMS & FULTON. (Chicago: J.H.Beers & Co., 1899) 616p (LDS,DAR,OGS,SLO)(RPI)
Goodspeed, Weston A. THE COUNTY OF WILLIAMS, HISTORICAL AND BIOGRAPHICAL. (Chicago: F.A.Battey, 1882) 820p. (LDS,SLO,DAR) (RPI)
ILLUSTRATED HISTORICAL ATLAS OF WILLIAMS COUNTY OHIO. 1874. (RPI)
Knapp, Horace S. HISTORY OF THE MAUMEE VALLEY. 1872. 667p. (SLO)
Levinson, Marilyn. GUIDE TO NEWSPAPER HOLDINGS AT THE CENTER FOR ARCHIVAL COL-LECTIONS. 2nd Edition. (Bowling Green OH: Bowling Green State Univ., 1987)
Lupien, David L. OUR GARDEN OF EDON. (Edon OH: American Legion, 1984) 95p (SLO,LDS)
Shinn, William H. THE COUNTY OF WILLIAMS. (Madison WI: Northwestern Hist.Assoc.,1905) 611p (DAR,LDS,SLO) (RPI)
Slocum, Charles. HISTORY OF THE MAUMEE RIVER BASIN. 1905. 638p. (SLO)
Whetro, Jacquelyn Y. MONTPELIER, OHIO, 1845-1976. (Montpelier OH: Bicentennial Committee, 1976) 64p (DAR,SLO,LDS)
Williams Co Chapter OGS. 1870 JEFFERSON TOWNSHIP, WILLIAMS COUNTY OHIO CENSUS INDEX. (Bryan OH: the society, 1987)
Williams Co Chapter OGS. INDEX TO 1920 BOWERSOX HISTORY OF WILLIAMS COUNTY, VOLUME II. (Bryan OH: the society, 1987)
Williams Co Chapter OGS. WILLIAMS COUNTY RECORDS GUIDE. 1982. (SLO)

Williams Co Chapter OGS. SURNAME INDEX [OF MEMBERS]. (Bryan OH: the society, 1982) 50p. (OGS,SLO)

Williams Co Chapter OGS. WILLIAMS COUNTY OHIO MARRIAGE RECORDS - VOLUMES I,II,III. (Bryan OH: the society, 1984) 121p (OGS,LDS,SLO)

WILLIAMS COUNTY OHIO 1820-1975 (Portage MI: Clann Cearr Ltd., nd) np

Williams Co.Hist.Soc. WILLIAMS COUNTY, OHIO: A COLLECTION OF HISTORICAL SKETCHES AND FAMILY HISTORIES COMPILED BY MEMBERS AND FRIENDS OF THE WILLIAMS COUNTY HISTORICAL SOCIETY, 1978-1980. (Montpelier OH: the society, 1978-1980) 2v (LDS,SLO)

Winter, Nevin O. HISTORY OF NORTHWESTERN OHIO. (Chicago: Lewis Pub Co, 1917) 3v (SLO,OHS)

Works Project Program. BRYAN AND WILLIAMS COUNTY OHIO. (Gallipolis OH: Downtain Printing, c1941) 117p. (LDS,SLO)

# WOOD COUNTY

CREATED:                    1820 FROM LOGAN COUNTY
COUNTY SEAT:                BOWLING GREEN 43402
COURT HOUSE:                1 COURTHOUSE SQUARE, BOWLING GREEN 43402
LIBRARY:                    251 N. MAIN ST., BOWLING GREEN 43402
HISTORICAL SOCIETY:         13660 COUNTY HOME RD., BOWLING GREEN 43402
GENEALOGICAL SOCIETY:       WOOD COUNTY CHAPTER OGS,
                            PO BOX 722, BOWLING GREEN 43402
                            publication: NEWSLETTER
HEALTH DEPARTMENT:          541 W.WOOSTER ST., BOWLING GREEN 43402
                            (separate offices for Bowling Green city, Perrysburg, Rossford,
                            Northwood & Fostoria)
ARCHIVAL DISTRICT:          BOWLING GREEN STATE UNIVERSITY, BOWLING GREEN
                            (see Biggs' Guide to records)
LAND SURVEYS:               CONGRESS LANDS, E & N OF 1ST PRIN.MERIDIAN
                            TWELVE MILE SQUARE RESERVE, 1805
BOUNDED BY:                 EAST:      OTTAWA, SANDUSKY & SENECA CO.
                            NORTH:     LUCAS CO.
                            WEST:      HENRY CO.
                            SOUTH:     HANCOCK CO.
TOWNSHIPS:                  Bloom, Center, Freedom, Grand Rapids, Henry, Jackson, Lake,
                            Liberty, Middleton, Milton, Montgomery, Perry, Perrysburg, Plain,
                            Portage, Ross, Troy, Washington, Webster, Weston.

## COURT RECORDS: (LDS MICROFILM)
Assessor:
    Quadrennial enumerations, 1842,1855,1857,1859-60,1895,1899.
Auditor:
    Tax records, 1822-1838.
    Tax duplicates, 1827-1843.
Blind relief commission:
    Records of the commission, 1908-1913.
Board of Education:
    School register, 1863-1877.
Board of Elections:
    Poll books and tally sheets, 1821-1873.
Clerk of Courts:
    Common Pleas chancery record, v1-3, 1823-1856.
    Supreme Court record, v1, 1825-1838.
    Supreme Court final record, v2-3, 1838-1859.
    Supreme Court final record index, 1838-1859.

Supreme & District Courts complete journal, v2, 1841-1876.
Appearance dockets, v2-24, 1826-1899.
Commissioners:
Infirmary records, 1868-1915.
Probate Court:
Index to files, v1-3, 1820-1960.
Birth & death records, 1894-1908.
Marriage records, 1820-1929.
Birth records, 1867-1909.
Registration of birth records, 1941-1965.
Death records, 1867-1908.
General index, executors & administrators, 1820-nd.
Administration record, 1820-1866.
Administration docket, vA-B,1-2, 1821-1885.
Probate journal, v1-18, 1852-1896.
Final record, vA-M, 1852-1894.
Guardians' docket, v1-2, 1852-1888.
Will record, v11-18, 1899-1910.
Naturalization records, 1859-1906.
Recorder:
General index to deeds, v1-6, 1820-1912.
Deed records, 1821-1902.
Mortgage records, 1838-1881.
Soldiers' discharge & index, 1865-1937.
Soldiers' Relief Commission:
Soldiers' relief record, 1887-1921.
Burial of indigent soldiers, 1897-1941.
Miscellaneous:
Bloomdale, Trinity United Methodist Church, records, 1881-1967.
Bowling Green, First Presby.Church, records, 1832-1974.
Pemberville, First United Presby.Church, records, 1878-1982.
Pemberville, St.Paul's Evan.-Luth. Church, records, 1881-1925.
Pemberville, Salem Evan.-Luth.Church records, 1848-1983.
Pemberville, Bethlehem Lutheran Church, records, 1800-1945.
Perrysburg, First Presby.Church, records, 1849-1885.
Emanuels Gemeinde Evangelical Lutheran Church, Stuttgart, Ark.
    (contains St.Jacobs Lutheran in Montgomery Tp., 1844-1879)
Northwest Ohio Genealogical Society Cemetery inscriptions.

## OHIO HISTORICAL SOCIETY: (MICROFILM)
Clerk of Courts:
Common Pleas chancery record, v1-3, 1823-1856.
Supreme Court record, v1, 1825-1838.
Supreme Court final record, v2-3, 1838-1859.
Supreme Court final record index, 1838-1859.
Supreme & District Courts complete journal, v2, 1841-1876.
Probate Court:
Administration docket, vA-B,1-2, 1821-1885.
Guardians' docket, v1, 1852-1885.
Will record, v11-18, 1899-1910.
Recorder:
Soldiers' discharge & index, 1865-1937.
Miscellaneous:
Marriage records, 1820-1865 & Scotch Ridge Cemetery, by DAR.

CENSUS RECORDS  (OHS,SLO,OGS,LDS)
1830-1880, 1900-1910; 1890 VETERANS; 1880,1900 SOUNDEX; 1910 MIRACODE

AGRICULTURAL CENSUS SCHEDULES  (OHS,SLO-mic)
1850,1870,1880

PRODUCTS OF INDUSTRY CENSUS SCHEDULE  (OHS,SLO-mic)
1850,1860,1870,1880

MORTALITY CENSUS SCHEDULES (OHS,SLO-mic)
1850,1860

NEWSPAPERS: [GUIDE TO OHIO NEWSPAPERS, 1793-1973]
Bloomdale, Bowling Green, Bradner, Custar, Grand Rapids, No.Baltimore, Pemberville, Perrysburg,
Prairie Depot, Rising Sun, Rossford, Tontogany, Wayne, Weston.

TAX RECORDS (OHS & LDS)
1822-1838.

GENEALOGICAL PERIODICAL ARTICLES
Bell, Carol Willsey. OHIO GENEALOGICAL PERIODICAL INDEX: A COUNTY GUIDE (Youngstown
    OH: author, 6th ed., 1987)

PUBLISHED SOURCES:
Andreas & Baskin. AN ILLUSTRATED ATLAS OF LUCAS COUNTY AND PORTION OF WOOD
    COUNTY, OHIO. 1875. (OGS,SLO)(RPI)
Angel, James L. WOOD COUNTY HISTORICAL CHURCH RECORDS SURVEY. (Bowling Green OH:
    B.G. State Univ, 1979) 56p. (OGS,OHS,LDS)
Bell, Carol W. (Flavell). WOOD COUNTY OHIO GENEALOGICAL GUIDE: GUIDE TO GENEALOGI-
    CAL SOURCE MATERIAL. (Youngstown OH: author, 1978) 75p (LDS)
Biggs, Deb. GUIDE TO LOCAL GOVERNMENT RECORDS AT THE CENTER FOR ARCHIVAL COL-
    LECTIONS. (Bowling Green OH: B.G.State Univ, 1981) 104p (OGS)
Christian, Donna K. GUIDE TO NEWSPAPER HOLDINGS AT THE CENTER FOR ARCHIVAL COL-
    LECTIONS. (Bowling Green OH: B.G.State Univ, 1980) 64p (OGS)
Clegg, Michael, ed. DEFIANCE, FULTON, HENRY, PAULDING, PUTNAM, WILLIAMS & WOOD
    COUNTIES OHIO NEWSPAPER OBITUARY ABSTRACTS, 1838-1870 (OHIO NEWSPAPER SERIES
    VOL.5) (Ft.Wayne IN: author, 1987) 75p (OGS)
Cochran, Fred. THE 100TH ANNIVERSARY HISTORY OF THE SCOTCH RIDGE PRESBYTERIAN
    CHURCH, 1869-1969. (DAR,LDS)
COMMEMORATIVE HISTORICAL AND BIOGRAPHICAL RECORD OF WOOD COUNTY OHIO.
    (Chicago: J.Beers, 1897) 2v. (SLO,LDS,DAR) (RPI)
Cox, Helen B. FORT MEIGS CEMETERY: LOCATED WOOD COUNTY OHIO, NEAR PERRYSBURG.
    (LDS)
Danford, Ardath. THE PERRYSBURG STORY, 1816-1966. 117p. (SLO)
Daughters of the American Revolution. MARRIAGES OF WOOD COUNTY OHIO, 1820-1865.
    (SLO,LDS,DAR)
Daughters of the American Revolution. SCOTCH RIDGE CEMETERY, WOOD COUNTY OHIO.
    (SLO,LDS)
Emerine, Andrew. FOSTORIA HIGHLIGHTS: OF SOME OF THE OCCURRENCES IN FOSTORIA
    DURING THE PAST 120 YEARS. (Fostoria OH: First National Bank, 1954) 32p (LDS)
Evers, Charles W. MANY INCIDENTS AND REMINISCENSES OF THE EARLY HISTORY OF WOOD
    COUNTY OHIO. (Bowling Green OH: The Democrat, 1910) 264p (LDS,DAR)
GRAND RAPIDS OHIO: A SOUVENIR OF THE PAST AND PRESENT, JULY 1897. (np: Huffman,
    1897) 49p (LDS)
Griffing, B.N. ATLAS OF WOOD COUNTY OHIO. 1886. (SLO)

Hardesty, H.H. HISTORICAL ATLAS OF THE WORLD ILLUSTRATED. (Chicago: author, 1875) 89p (LDS)

HISTORICAL ATLAS OF WOOD COUNTY OHIO. 1912. (OGS)

Jones, Paul W. PRESBYTERIANS IN BOWLING GREEN OHIO 1855-1980. (Bowling Green OH: First Presbyterian Church, 1980) 30p (OGS,LDS)

Knapp, Horace S. HISTORY OF THE MAUMEE VALLEY. (Toledo OH: author, 1872) 685p. (DAR,OHS,SLO)

Levinson, Marilyn. GUIDE TO NEWSPAPER HOLDINGS AT THE CENTER FOR ARCHIVAL COLLECTIONS. 2nd Edition. (Bowling Green OH: Bowling Green State Univ., 1987)

Morris, Edward, ed. THE NORTH BALITMORE (OHIO) STORY 1876-1976. (npl: Centennial Book Committee, 1976) np. (OGS)

Murray, Melvin L. HISTORY OF THE METHODIST CHURCH IN FOSTORIA OHIO, 1833-1900: THE RETURN OF RISDON. (Fostoria OH: Gray Printing, 1968) 39p (LDS)

Nelson, Larry L. MEN OF PATRIOTISM, COURAGE & ENTERPRISE: FORT MEIGS IN THE WAR OF 1812. (Canton OH: Daring Books, 1985) 156p (LDS)

Northwest Library District. GENEALOGICAL RESOURCES GUIDE. (Bowling Green OH: author, 1983) 86p. (OGS)

OUR HERITAGE: ST.JOHN'S LUTHERAN CHURCH, STONY RIDGE, OHIO, 1869-1979. 16p (OGS)

PORTRAIT AND BIOGRAPHICAL RECORD OF CITY OF TOLEDO AND LUCAS AND WOOD COUNTIES. (Chicago: Chapman Bros., 1895) 523p (DAR,LDS,SLO)

Slocum, Charles. HISTORY OF THE MAUMEE RIVER BASIN. 1905. 638p. (SLO)

Stevens, Marilyn. THE VILLAGE [GRAND RAPIDS OHIO]. 1961. 58p. (SLO)

STORY OF HASKINS, OHIO, 1869-1969. 1969? 39p (LDS)

Van Tassel, Charles S. A GENEALOGIST'S WORKBOOK FOR THE FIRST ONE HUNDRED YEARS OF BOWLING GREEN OHIO 1833-1933. 1933. (Bowling Green OH: Wood Co Chapter OGS, 1983) 201p (OGS,LDS)

Van Tassel, Charles S. HISTORICAL HIGHLIGHTS OF WOOD COUNTY. (np: Sentinel-Tribune, nd) 15p (LDS)

Van Tassel, Charles S. MEN OF WOOD COUNTY AND FAMILIAR FACES OF OHIO. (Bowling Green OH: author, 1896?) 183,89p (DAR,SLO)

Winter, Nevin O. HISTORY OF NORTHWESTERN OHIO. (Chicago: Lewis Pub Co., 1917) 3v. (SLO,OHS)

Wood Co Chapter OGS. AN INDEX TO THE 1880 U.S.CENSUS OF WOOD COUNTY, OHIO (Bowling Green OH: the society, 1983) 106p (OGS,LDS)

Wood Co Chapter OGS. AN INDEX TO THE 1870 U.S.CENSUS OF WOOD COUNTY, OHIO (Bowling Green OH: the society, 1985) 66p (OGS,LDS)

Wood Co Chapter OGS. AN INDEX TO WOOD CO.OHIO WILLS, ESTATES & GUARDIANSHIPS 1851-1900. (Bowling Green OH: the society, 1986) 61p (OGS)

Wood Co Chapter OGS. CEMETERIES IN LIBERTY TOWNSHIP, WOOD COUNTY OHIO. (Bowling Green OH: the society, 1983) 130p (OGS,LDS)

Wood Co Chapter OGS. CEMETERIES IN PORTAGE TOWNSHIP, WOOD COUNTY OHIO. (Bowling Green OH: the society, 1985) 149p (OGS,LDS)

Wood Co Chapter OGS. OAK GROVE CEMETERY IN BOWLING GREEN (CENTER TWP) WOOD COUNTY OHIO. PARTS I & II. (Bowling Green OH: the society, 1985) 276p (OGS,LDS)

Wood Co Chapter OGS. UNION HILL CEMETERY, PLAIN TOWNSHIP, WOOD COUNTY OHIO. (Bowling Green OH: the society, 1984) 176p (OGS,LDS)

Wood Co Chapter OGS. WOOD COUNTY OHIO CHAPTER - OUR BEGINNINGS 1977. (Bowling Green OH: the society, 1985) 119p (OGS)

Wood Co. Hist.Soc. WOOD COUNTY OHIO ATLASES, 1875-1912. (Bowling Green OH: the society, 1982) 1v (LDS)

# WYANDOT COUNTY

CREATED:                        1845 FROM HANCOCK COUNTY

COUNTY SEAT:                UPPER SANDUSKY 43351
COURT HOUSE:               SANDUSKY & WYANDOT AVE., UPPER SANDUSKY 43351
LIBRARY:                   224 W. JOHNSON ST., UPPER SANDUSKY 43351
HISTORICAL SOCIETY:        130 S. SEVENTH ST., UPPER SANDUSKY 43351
GENEALOGICAL SOCIETY:      WYANDOT COUNTY CHAPTER OGS,
                               PO BOX 414, UPPER SANDUSKY 43351
                               publication: WYANDOT TRACERS
HEALTH DEPARTMENT:         127A S.SANDUSKY AVE., UPPER SANDUSKY 43351
                               (separate office for Upper Sandusky city)
ARCHIVAL DISTRICT:         BOWLING GREEN STATE UNIVERSITY, BOWLING GREEN
                               (see Biggs' Guide to records)
LAND SURVEYS:              CONGRESS LANDS, E & S OF 1ST PRIN.MERIDIAN
BOUNDED BY:                EAST:    CRAWFORD CO.
                           NORTH:   SENECA CO.
                           WEST:    HANCOCK & HARDIN CO.
                           SOUTH:   MARION CO.
TOWNSHIPS:                 Antrim, Crane, Crawford, Eden, Jackson, Marseilles, Mifflin, Pitt,
                           Richland, Ridge, Salem, Sycamore, Tymochtee.

## COURT RECORDS: (LDS MICROFILM)
Clerk of Courts:
    Common Pleas complete record, v1-50, 1845-1907.
    General index, 1845-1886.
    Judgment index, v1-4, 1845-1919.
Probate Court:
    Birth & death records, 1867-1908.
    Birth records, v1-10, 1880-1940.
    Marriage records, v1-10, 1845-1919.
    General index of marriages, 1845-1951.
    Marriage license applications, v1, 1845-1858.
    Final record, v1-7, 1852-1889.
    General index to files, 1845-1952.
    General index to estates, v1-3, 1845-1906.
    Administration docket, 1845-1866, 1880-1903.
    Probate docket, 1862-1871.
    Guardian docket, 1879-1920.
    Civil docket, vA-E, 1866-1906.
    Will record, v1-7, 1845-1911.
    Guardians bonds & letters, 1860-1895.
    Administrators bonds & letters, 1860-1895.
    Executors bonds & letters, 1860-1895.
    Probate record, v1-6, 1852-1887.
    Probate journal, v1-16, 1852-1914.
    Inventory, v1-8, 1845-1888.
    Complete record, v7-14, 1887-1914.
    Naturalization records, 1860-1905.
Recorder:
    Deed records, 1826-1886.
    General index to deeds, 1826-1946.
    Mortgage record, 1845-1888.
    General index to mortgages, 1845-1888.
    Miscellaneous record, v1, 1879-1937.
    Soldiers discharge records, 1862-1924.
Miscellaneous:
    Upper Sandusky, First Universalist Church, records, 1870-1912.

**OHIO HISTORICAL SOCIETY: (MICROFILM)**
Probate Court:
Final record, v1-7, 1852-1889.
Will record, v6, 1901-1906.
Miscellaneous:
Marriage records, 1845-1865, by DAR.
Index to grantor deeds, 1826-1870, by DAR.
Cemetery records, by DAR.

**CENSUS RECORDS (OHS,SLO,OGS,LDS)**
1850-1880, 1900-1910; 1890 VETERANS; 1880,1900 SOUNDEX; 1910 MIRACODE

**AGRICULTURAL CENSUS SCHEDULES (OHS,SLO-mic)**
1850,1870,1880

**PRODUCTS OF INDUSTRY CENSUS SCHEDULE (OHS,SLO-mic)**
1870,1880

**MORTALITY CENSUS SCHEDULES (OHS,SLO-mic)**
1850,1860

**NEWSPAPERS: [GUIDE TO OHIO NEWSPAPERS, 1793-1973]**
Carey, Nevada, Sycamore, Upper Sandusky.

**TAX RECORDS (OHS & LDS)**
none listed; see parent counties.

**GENEALOGICAL PERIODICAL ARTICLES**
Bell, Carol Willsey. OHIO GENEALOGICAL PERIODICAL INDEX: A COUNTY GUIDE (Youngstown
OH: author, 6th ed., 1987)

**PUBLISHED SOURCES:**
Baughman, A.J., ed. PAST AND PRESENT OF WYANDOT COUNTY, OHIO: A RECORD OF SETTLE-
MENT, ORGANIZATION, PROGRESS AND ACHIEVEMENT. (Chicago: S.J. Clarke, 1913) 2v
(LDS,DAR)
Biggs, Deb. GUIDE TO LOCAL GOVERNMENT RECORDS AT THE CENTER FOR ARCHIVAL COL-
LECTIONS. (Bowling Green OH: Bowling Green State Univ, 1981) 104p (OGS)
BIOGRAPHICAL MEMOIRS OF WYANDOT COUNTY OHIO. (Logansport IN: B.F.Bowen, 1902) 686p
(SLO,LDS) (RPI)
Christian, Donna K. GUIDE TO NEWSPAPER HOLDINGS AT THE CENTER FOR ARCHIVAL COL-
LECTIONS. (Bowling Green OH: Bowling Green State Univ, 1980) 64p (OGS)
Daughters of the American Revolution. MARRIAGE RECORDS OF WYANDOT COUNTY OHIO, 1845-
1865. (SLO,LDS,DAR)
Daughters of the American Revolution. WYANDOT COUNTY OHIO CEMETERY BURIAL RECORDS,
VOL.I-6. (Upper Sandusky OH: author, 1982) 1023p. (LDS,OGS,SLO,DAR)
Hardesty, H.H. MILITARY HISTORY OF OHIO - WYANDOT COUNTY EDITION. 1886/87. (OHS)
Hare, A.J. ATLAS OF WYANDOT COUNTY, OHIO. 1879. (OGS,SLO,LDS)(RPI)
HISTORY OF WYANDOT COUNTY OHIO. (Chicago: Leggett, Conaway & Co., 1884) 1065p.
(DAR,SLO,LDS) (RPI)
Knapp, Horace S. HISTORY OF THE MAUMEE VALLEY. (Toledo OH: author, 1872) 685p.
(DAR,OHS,SLO)
Levinson, Marilyn. GUIDE TO NEWSPAPER HOLDINGS AT THE CENTER FOR ARCHIVAL COL-
LECTIONS. 2nd Edition. (Bowling Green OH: Bowling Green State Univ., 1987)

Marsh, Thelma R. LEST WE FORGET: A BRIEF SKETCH OF WYANDOT COUNTY'S HISTORY. (Upper Sandusky OH: author, 1967) 54p (LDS)

PLAT BOOK AND HISTORY OF WYANDOT COUNTY OHIO, 1937. (np: Wyandot Agriculture Society, 1937) 110p (LDS)

Prentice, Anna L. CEMETERY BOOK OF WYANDOT COUNTY OHIO. (Upper Sandusky OH: author, c1892) (OGS)

Saltsman, Harriet A. GRANTOR INDEX TO DEEDS AND RECORDS OF WYANDOT COUNTY, UPPER SANDUSKY, OHIO, 1826-1870. (SLO,LDS)

Slocum, Charles. HISTORY OF THE MAUMEE RIVER BASIN. 1905. 638p. (SLO)

Watts, Arethusa. MOSTLY GHOSTS, STAGECOACH INNS - HOTELS, COVERED BRIDGES, TOWNS, IN WYANDOT COUNTY OHIO. (Upper Sandusky OH: Wyandot Co Chapter OGS, 1986) 99p (OGS,SLO)

Winter, Nevin O. HISTORY OF NORTHWESTERN OHIO. (Chicago: Lewis Pub Co., 1917) 3v. (SLO,OHS)

Wyandot Co Chapter OGS. OHIO'S RANK AND FILE IN THE WAR OF THE REBELLION. (Upper Sandusky OH: the society, 1988) (OGS)

Wyandot Co Chapter OGS. WYANDOT COUNTY OHIO FAMILY BIBLE RECORDS. (Upper Sandusky OH: the society, 1987) np.

Wyandot Co Chapter OGS. WYANDOT COUNTY DIRECTORY - 1877. (Reprint, Upper Sandusky OH: the society, 1987)

Wyandot Co Chapter OGS. WYANDOT COUNTY OHIO NATURALIZATION RECORDS, 1842-1929. (Upper Sandusky OH: the society, 1986) 46p (OGS,LDS,SLO)

Wyandot Co Chapter OGS. 1870 FEDERAL CENSUS OF WYANDOT COUNTY. (Upper Sandusky OH: the society, 1988) (OGS)

Wyandot Co Chapter OGS. 1880 WYANDOT COUNTY OHIO FEDERAL CENSUS INDEX. (Upper Sandusky OH: the society, 1987) 69p (OGS)